The Interpretation of
I Corinthians

R. C. H. LENSKI

Augsburg Fortress
Minneapolis

THE INTERPRETATION OF I CORINTHIANS
Commentary on the New Testament series

First paperback edition 2008

Copyright ©1946, 2008 Augsburg Fortress. All rights reserved. Except for brief quotations in critical articles or reviews, no part of this book may be reproduced in any manner without prior written permission from the publisher. Visit http://www.augsburgfortress.org/copyrights/contact.asp or write to Permissions, Augsburg Fortress, Box 1209, Minneapolis, MN 55440.

Richard C. H. Lenski's commentaries on the New Testament were published in the 1940s after the author's death. This volume was copyrighted in 1937 by the Lutheran Book Concern, published in 1946 by the Wartburg Press, and assigned in 1961 to the Augsburg Publishing House.

ISBN 978-0-8066-8079-8

The paper used in this publication meets the minimum requirements of American National Standard for Information Sciences—Permanence of Paper for Printed Library Materials, ANSI Z329.48-1984.

Manufactured in the U.S.A.

First Epistle
To the Corinthians

DEDICATED TO
THE CLASS OF 1928
of the
THEOLOGICAL SEMINARY
CAPITAL UNIVERSITY
Columbus, Ohio

Edwin Ackerman, B. S.
George Bubolz, A. B.
Orrin Consear, A. B.; B. D.
Herbert Dornbrock, A. B.
Edward Fendt, A. B.; B. D.
William Fritz, A. B.
Millard Glessner
Edward Goedeking, A. B.
Elmer Kastner, A. B.
Paul Lautenschlager, A. B.
Jesse Lippoldt
Laurence Miller, A. B.
Henry Oestreich, A. B.
Carl Pohlman, A. B.
John Richardson, A. B.
Lewis Schaaf†
Paul Schnizler, A. B.
Harold Schulz, A. B.
Harley Sipe, A. B.; B. D.
Theodore Stellhorn, A. B.
George Strobel
Walter Wiggert, A. B.
Harold Yochum, A. B.; M. A.; B. D.
Henry Young, A. B.; B. D.
Elmer Zimmerman, A. B.

Who read First Corinthians with me in 1927-1928 with such enthusiasm as to inspire the task of interpreting eventually the entire New Testament. I finished the whole New Testament by completing *The Interpretation of Revelation* on January 12, 1934.

ABBREVIATIONS

R. = A Grammar of the Greek New Testament in the Light of Historical Research, by A. T. Robertson, 4th ed.

B.-D. = Friedrich Blass' Grammatik des neutestamentlichen Griechisch, vierte, voellig neugearbeitete Auflage, besorgt von Albert Debrunner.

C.-K. = Biblisch-theologisches Woerterbuch der Neutestamentlichen Graezitaet von D. D. Hermann Cremer, zehnte, etc., Auflage, herausgegeben von D. Dr. Julius Koegel.

T. = Synonyms of the New Testament, by Richard Chevenix Trench, D. D.

C. Tr. = Concordia Triglotta. The Symbolical Books of the Ev. Lutheran Church, German-Latin-English. St. Louis, Mo., Concordia Publishing House.

NOTE. The translation is intended only as an aid in understanding the Greek.

INTRODUCTION

The observation is certainly correct that First and Second Corinthians are in the full sense of the word "letters" and not pieces of literature that were intended for publication, and not "epistles," learned compositions set down in letter form by a literary man. This observation establishes the genuineness of these writings in a peculiar way so that all attempts to prove that they were not written by the Apostle Paul are profitless efforts. No man, save the great apostle, could have composed these two "letters."

The fact that these compositions have the character of "letters" causes some peculiar difficulties to the present-day interpreter. Only the original recipients of these letters could catch every intimation contained in Paul's words. We of today meet one difficulty after another in our attempts at projecting ourselves back into the situation as it existed in Corinth. We find ourselves facing insuperable difficulties when reconstructing the complex situations that Paul would clear up with his instructions and his admonitions. Yet such a task will always be highly attractive and profitable. It bids us enter the throbbing life of one of the most important of the apostolic congregations and at the same time enables us to come into closest touch with the soul of the great apostle who forms and shapes that life with the divine power of the gospel.

An appreciation of the fact that these two writings are "letters" will have another wholesome effect. It will save the interpreter from the recent attempts to cut up these letters and to make three or four or even more of the two, or from rearranging certain portions so as to have them accord with the interpreter's idea as to how Paul should have written to these Christians at Corinth. None of us can hope to know the Corinthians as Paul, who founded the church in their midst, knew them. The danger we must guard against is that we may fail to follow the mind of Paul as it meets the needs that existed at Corinth. It would be quite fatal to follow our own imagination and, instead of penetrating into the heart of the letters themselves, to find in them ideas of our own that never entered the apostle's mind.

The outstanding fact that these are "letters" that were written to the Corinthians by Paul has, however, been made to yield too much. These are not ordinary letters such as we write today. Although they have the character of real letters, their contents are eternal verities. They are authenticated with a divine seal. They speak a truth that is eternal and cannot change. These "letters" are throughout grounded on divine facts that no change of time affects.

Both the range of these facts and the penetrating perception with which they are presented in order to direct the minds and the hearts of the Corinthians far transcend all that even our great men have been able to achieve in their most pretentious writings. Even the keenest modern mind must run until it is out of breath in order to follow Paul as he walks on through these mere "letters," and then, despite all such exertion, it will be left far behind. Paul always sees all the facts, he never loses one of them in the course of his presentation, and he sees the true significance of each fact and the true relation of those that belong together. As a grand sample of this kind study the paragraph 15:20-28. He has many others of the same kind. The modern interpreter should be content to let Paul carry him in his arms as he walks along through these "letters"; only then can we hope to keep up with him as children do with a father.

Moreover, these divine facts and verities receive perfect expression, although these writings are only "letters." Every word is the proper word, every number and every tense are true to the thought. We may put every term and every thought under a microscope and we shall find never a flaw. Where, except in the New Testament, have "letters" such as these appeared? Think of the many commentaries that have been written about these "letters," commentaries that scrutinize every single word, phrase, and thought. Yet the last commentary is not yet within sight. And all this tremendous effort which is spent to elucidate what are simply known as "letters" has not yet exhausted their contents nor brought to full light the perfection of their expression.

So often the masterly qualities of the mind that composed these "letters" are overlooked by the interpreter. No philosopher and no orator ever wrote like the tentmaker who dictated these simple "letters." Therefore one should not fault Paul for the inaptness of his argument, criticize him for mixing his figures, chide him for contradicting himself. These are "letters," yet they are literature. Passage after passage, when it is considered merely as a composition, stands out with imperishable power and unfading beauty. Who has ever written about love like this man whose heart was full of love? The interpreter who fails to perceive this mastery cannot do justice to Paul.

Paul writes about spiritual truth in these "letters" —absolutely the highest subject with which the human mind and heart can occupy themselves. He is in full possession of this truth and pours it out in all its richness and its power wherever it is needed. Centuries have tested this truth and have found it pure gold. We live spiritually by this wealth today; so will all believers who succeed us. In all these writings there is not a single error, contradiction, or inadequacy. The foes of our faith have scanned every sentence with a hostile eye in order to find some flaw in thought or in word. No other letters were ever so minutely examined as Paul's are. The service these foes have rendered us should be fully appreciated. The result of their efforts is negative in *toto*. The truth Paul enunciated in these "letters" shines as brightly today as it did on the day on which he wrote.

Only one explanation is adequate to account for all this. No man could write as this man wrote by means of his own natural powers or by means only of his own regenerated powers. The evidential reason of this fact is that no man has ever been able to do so. The one explanation for the ability of Paul and of his fellow apostles is divine inspiration. The hand of the Holy Spirit is evident in all that he wrote. I Cor. 3:13. The only disproof of Paul's inspiration that would be worth consideration would be the composition of some "letters" that are equal to this and are written by a man who is not inspired. The Holy Spirit guided Paul's mind and thought so that the result bears the divine stamp. I Cor. 14:37, 38. This written result is the real evidence of inspiration. It covers in indissoluble union Paul's thought and his word. This is what the church terms Verbal Inspiration — and there is none other as a point of fact. There is not one wrong or faulty word. This is Paul's mind indeed; Paul's thoughts indeed; Paul's words indeed; yet all of them are under the divine mind and will. This alone is the adequate explanation for the "letters" that lie before us. And this explanation is a fact and not a theory and still less a hypothesis. You actually touch this fact every time you read a section from Paul's writings.

* * *

In 146 B. C. the Roman general Mummius crushed the aspirations of Greece toward independence by the complete destruction of Corinth. For a hundred years the site of the city lay waste. Julius Caesar sent a colony of veterans and descendants of freedmen to rebuild the city, and in due time a new Corinth arose from the old ruins, that vied in prosperity with the more ancient city.

Corinth is situated on the so-called Isthmus, a strip of land that connects the lower peninsula of Greece with the mainland; hence the term "isthmus" is now used with reference to any strip of land between two seas. The city was situated on a tableland 200 feet above the sea; and behind it on the south rose a towering rock about 2,000 feet high, called the Acrocorinthus and having a summit that was extensive enough to permit the building of a town upon it. It was grander than the Acropolis of Athens or even than Gibraltar. Corinth had two harbors, Cenchreæ on the eastern sea and Lechæum on the western. Aristides called the city "a palace of Neptune," others spoke of it as "the city of the two seas," "the eye of Greece," "the capital and grace of Greece."

The situation of Corinth determined its character to a great extent. It was a city that was admirably adapted for shipping and for trade. This fact invited a mixed population. Paul wrote Romans while he was in Corinth, and the list of Latin names found at the end of that letter agrees with the historical statement that Corinth was a Roman colony. Jews naturally found a place in Corinth, and their number was increased when the edict of Claudius expelled the Jews from Rome. Among the arrivals from Rome, due to this edict, were the tentmaker Aquila and his wife Priscilla.

The descriptions of Corinth found in ancient writings state that there were many temples in this city, several of which were devoted to Egyptian deities. The fact that Egyptian deities were worshiped in this Greek city is accounted for by the extensive trade carried on with Alexandria. It was, therefore, not strange that Apollos should go to Corinth, for he had studied in the schools of Alexandria. This trade brought much wealth to Corinth; nevertheless, a large number of slaves and of poor people were found here besides the wealthy. The congregation founded by Paul was composed chiefly of converts from the lower classes.

Corinth was a wicked city even as larger cities in the empire went at this period. The very term "Corinthian" meant a profligate, and the verb "to Corinthianize" meant to have intercourse with prostitutes. The temple of Venus in the old city boasted that a thousand female slaves were kept there who were free to strangers. Venus worship was a mark of the new city likewise although we have no account of the females connected with the new temple. *Non cuivis homini contingit adire Corinthum* (Horace) became a proverb which was translated also into Greek. Money was freely spent for sinful pleasures. Paul wrote his description of pagan vice, Rom. 1:18-32, in Corinth. One of the chief attractions was the Isthmian games, the custody of which was restored to the new city. Greeks and Romans flocked to these contests, and the mobs came in crowds; but the effect of these spectacles was degrading.

Corinth was never famous for its philosophers; the name of not one outstanding Corinthian philosopher is known to us. Its boast was trade and the arts. Corinthian brass became famous, and Corinthian capitals and pillars are still known in architecture. While philosophic and speculative ideas were undoubtedly current in Corinth, we should go wrong if we thought that the members of this congregation were swayed by philosophic considerations because Corinth was located in Greece. Thus, for instance, today many claim to have γνῶσις (they call it "science") who are not scientists or philosophers. Likewise, today many deny the resurrection on the basis of reasoning only without a trace of speculative philosophy. The puffed up people whom Paul scores in Corinth, and the few doubters there who made free with the resurrection were no better than many superficial scientists and philosophers of modern times.

* * *

Paul came to Corinth for the first time on his second missionary journey toward the close of the year 51. What we know about his successful labors during the 18 months of his stay is recorded by Luke in Acts 18:1-7. Paul left Corinth in the year 53. He wrote First Corinthians in Ephesus during the spring of the year 57. This letter is in good part Paul's reply to a letter just sent him by the Corinthians through the three messengers mentioned in 16:15-18. Prior to this time Paul had written a letter to the Corinthians, the only knowledge of which we have from his own reference to a statement in that letter (5:9). How and why this letter was lost no one knows. It is proper to assume that oral news reached Paul from Corinth at various times during the interval between 53 and 57, likewise that news from him reached the Corinthians.

Shortly before Paul wrote First Corinthians he dispatched Timothy to Corinth, sending him by the land route through the other congregations that lay along this route, Acts 19:22; I Cor. 4:17; 16:10. Paul expected Timothy to arrive in Corinth after First Corinthians had reached the congregation, and he requested that he be returned without undue delay to Paul at Ephesus. Timothy thus knew nothing about First Corinthians until he had come to Corinth and had found the congregation in possession of the letter. Beyond these few facts we know nothing about Timothy's visit to Corinth.

Paul left Ephesus, as he had promised in 16:8, shortly after Pentecost in the year 57. Before leaving he dispatched Titus directly to Corinth by the sea route while Paul himself took the longer land route over which he had sent Timothy before Easter. Titus was to go directly to Corinth and then to return by land to Troas in order to bring a report to Paul. This program was not carried out entirely as planned. Titus was delayed, and Paul became anxious and went on from Troas and met Titus in Macedonia. Titus brought excellent news from Corinth. After receiving a full report from Titus, Paul wrote Second Corinthians in Macedonia, probably in Philippi, and sent Titus back to Corinth with this letter. The introduction to Second Corinthians shows that Timothy was with Paul on this journey, but this is all we know. Paul must have found important work to be done in the different congregations along his route, and this important work caused him to change his original plan which contemplated going directly by sea to Corinth, stopping there a short time, then hastening to Macedonia, and then returning to Corinth. Instead of following this original plan he first attended to the work in these other congregations and then came to Corinth. He arrived there in the late fall of 57.

A brief visit of Paul's to Corinth is indicated in II Cor. 2:1; 12:14; 13:1, 2. This visit probably occurred before Paul wrote First Corinthians or between the writing of First and Second Corinthians. Paul reached Corinth for the third time according to his program outlined in I Cor. 16:3, etc., and remained there over winter, for three months, Acts 20:2, etc. He then left for Jerusalem on the journey which Luke describes at length, Acts 20:3, etc.

* * *

Introduction 15

The widest field for conjecture is opened up by some of the data here presented. One group of suppositions centers about Timothy's visit to Corinth. Did he reach Corinth, as Paul contemplated, *after* Paul's letter had been delivered? Some think that he arrived at and departed from Corinth *before* the letter was delivered and that this fact explains Paul's silence regarding this visit of Timothy's to Corinth. Others suppose that Timothy never got to Corinth and that this failure explains the absence of further information. Still others think that Timothy came to Corinth and found Paul's letter there; and then they surmise that some disturbances arose in Corinth, which Timothy failed to quell and as a result of which he hastened back to Paul at Ephesus with a gloomy report. Thereupon Paul sent a better man, Titus, just before Paul himself left for Corinth by land.

Another group of conjectures centers on the lost letter and its contents. Not satisfied with Paul's brief remark in I Cor. 5:9, efforts are made to find the rest of this letter in the two canonical letters; this is done by means of a documentary hypothesis.

A third group of conjectures deals with the brief, painful visit to Corinth which Paul made. The imagination is allowed to play on the phrase ἐν λύπῃ occurring in II Cor. 2:1. This view has its variations but usually runs in this fashion: Timothy arrives in Ephesus with very bad news from Corinth regarding the reception of First Corinthians; Paul hurries to Corinth by sea; he appears there as a sick man, is indignant and harsh, and suffers a thorough defeat at the hands of opponents; he does not remain long but hurries back to Ephesus and soon leaves again for Corinth after Pentecost. Even the time between Easter and Pentecost would be too brief to allow for this view.

The history of interpretation shows that down to recent times the various questions that naturally arise from the silence of Luke in Acts and from that of Paul in his two letters were either left as they are, unanswered, or received simple and innocuous explanations. In later times "the parties" in Corinth (1:21) began to cause some agitation among the critics, and a number of explanations were offered. This trend still persists. Soon it was, however, overshadowed by a volume of effort to illumine all the silences of Luke and of Paul by means of hypotheses until now practically all of the possibilities of conjecture in this field are exhausted.

The more radical minds began to cut up the text of Paul's canonical letters, first, in order to recover one or more lost letters, secondly, to reconstruct and to revamp the canonical letters themselves. These operations ran their course until they denied the authorship of Paul's canonical letters. These letters were regarded as a conglomerate that was formed in the second century; Second Corinthians appeared only as a pseudo-composition that was compiled by somebody from reminiscences. To the Hollanders belongs the credit for running the entire hypothetical scheme into the ground. We no longer have any letters to interpret.

This hypercritical spirit bore other fruit. In a large number of places the obvious sense of Paul's words is questioned and contradicted. The question of sources is raised. Where did Paul get this, and where did he get that? Both pagan and Jewish apocalyptic literature is scanned with painful effort and the assurance is given that here lie the sources for many of Paul's teachings and for many of the terms he employs. He is credited only with using some of this source material "in his own way." Where pagan and Jewish sources furnish no clear trace they are, nevertheless, assumed as a reality—we are at present only waiting for the uncovering of these sources.

We decline to furnish the names of these critics and to list their findings. For our purpose they are arid territory. It is love's labor lost to refute their contentions. Only in certain instances wrong conceptions that might secure lodgement are exposed and refuted. Paul's logic, his rhetoric, and his psychology are also elucidated and vindicated.

So many commentators overburden their introductions by restating their exegetical findings in lengthy detail and by adding a good deal of material from other sources. We can dispense with this cumbersome method. The very best references to grammar are inserted wherever they seem helpful. The translation aims only at making clear the sense of the original.

Philipp Bachmann has the correct idea regarding the interpreter's aim. He should discard the enormous ballast of false opinions and ephemeral notions and not lose himself in hopeless efforts to clear up little historical details. He should seek as the palm of his effort to penetrate with heart and mind into the "demonstration of the Spirit and of power" (I Cor. 2:4) which is presented in Paul's letters for the spiritual upbuilding of the Corinthian congregation in the faith of our Lord Jesus Christ.

CHAPTER I

The Greeting, 1:1-3

The greeting follows the regular form that is used by Paul in all his letters. First, the writer's name in the nominative; secondly, the persons to whom he writes in the dative; thirdly, the words of greeting again in the nominative. Thus in this letter: "Paul ... and Sosthenes ——— to the church, etc., ——— grace and peace." Each of the three parts of the greeting, as is frequently done by Paul, receives an amplification. In Paul's letters these amplifications invariably reflect the thought and the feeling that are in his heart as he sets out to write. The greeting thus foreshadows the contents and the character of the letter.

1) Paul, called as an apostle of Jesus Christ through the will of God, and Sosthenes, the brother.

In this instance the addition to the writer's name is compact and weighty. Paul stresses his peculiar nearness to Jesus Christ as being one sent by him and at the same time points to the divine authority behind his words, an authority his readers are to acknowledge and to obey. All the instructions and the admonitions of this letter rest on this solid basis. They are all so important because they come from a called apostle of Jesus Christ. An "apostle" is one who is commissioned and sent and thus an individual who represents his sender. The title is itself highly significant. While the term is at times used in a wider sense so as to include also the immediate assistants of the apostle like Barnabas, Timothy, and others, this is evidently not the case when the word is employed in the introduction to a weighty letter. Only the Twelve and Paul are "apostles" in the strict sense of the term.

The addition κλητός, "called," a verbal that is used much like a past participle in the passive, brings to view the idea that is latent in the term "apostle," namely that this ambassador of Christ became such by an immediate call from Christ himself. Paul is thinking of the scene on the road to Damascus. The genitive "of Jesus Christ" therefore also denotes more than mere possession (an apostle who belongs to Jesus Christ); it includes origin and agency (an apostle whom Jesus Christ called and sent). Yet there is no reason to assume that in this connection Paul contrasts himself with others who falsely claimed apostleship and were not called and sent by Jesus Christ. Paul is merely putting himself in the correct light for his Corinthian readers in order that they may properly receive what he writes to them.

The addition "through God's will" enhances what has just been said. Paul's call on the road to Damascus was mediated (διά) by a volition (θέλημα) formed on God's part. In another connection Paul shows how far back this will of God goes, namely to his very birth. Paul's call was not produced by a set of fortuitous circumstances. Not accidentally or in a temporal and a passing manner was Paul called. Nor did he grow into the call by a kind of evolution or spiritual development on his part. As far as Paul was concerned, he was developing in the very opposite direction, had, in fact, already reached the state of the most violent antagonism to Christ. What turned him about and changed his entire character and his life was "God's will."

This is, however, not an arbitrary or absolute volitional act that worked irresistibly upon Paul so that he was forced to become a believer and an apostle. The Scriptures know of no divine volitional acts of this kind. Paul himself says: "I was not disobedient unto the heavenly vision," Acts 26:19, and implies that he might have disobeyed and set his will against that of God. The volition of God through which he became an apostle emanated from the good and gracious will of God, the saving will of his love which employs the law and the gospel and by these gracious means lifts men from death to life, from enmity to devotion and service. In this way Paul was "called through God's will" and received his high commission as "an apostle of Jesus Christ." The full weight of this divine commission ever rested on Paul's soul, and in writing to the Corinthians he bids them, too, to recognize this commission and all that it implies for them.

Paul associates another with himself in writing this letter: "and Sosthenes, the brother." In First and in Second Thessalonians Paul combines two others with himself and in Galatians an undetermined number of persons. Sosthenes is thus not designated as being merely the amanuensis of Paul. The apostle dictated most or all of his letters. Who received his dictation in the present instance is a matter of conjecture. It may have been Sosthenes, it may have been some other efficient scribe. The association of Sosthenes with Paul in the composition and the sending of this letter means much more, namely that Sosthenes and Paul had talked over the contents of this letter and had fully agreed on all that is here transmitted. In other words, Sosthenes subscribes to all that Paul has to say.

Many suppose that this Sosthenes is the individual mentioned in Acts 18:17 and is thus a character who was well known to the Corinthians and one who was conversant with the situation in Corinth. It is also supposed that he was a half-Christian when he was compelled to act as a spokesman before the proconsul Gallio and for this reason bungled his job. Then the Jews beat him severely before Gallio's tribunal (the lictors of Gallio performed the deed) and thereby aided in making him completely a Christian. The flaw in this story is the fact that the Sosthenes mentioned in Acts was so rabid that, when Gallio ordered the Jews to leave, he persisted in remaining until the lictors put speed into him with their rods.

Moreover, in this letter Paul does not write to the Corinthians *"your* brother," does not intimate that any connection whatever exists between Sosthenes and the Corinthians. The Jewish Sosthenes mentioned in Acts is not ·the Christian "brother" of Paul's letter. We know nothing about him beyond this mention of "the brother" in this letter. His name is not intended to add authority to Paul's letter. The authority back of it is vested in the apostle. In associating himself with this brother Paul conveys the idea that the voice of apostolic authority here unites with the voice of brotherly solicitude and that each is represented in a person who is known to the Corinthians.

2) The recipients of the letter are, first of all, designated collectively as a body and then described as to their Christian character and their associates. **To the church of God which is at Corinth, having been sanctified in Christ Jesus, called as saints, together with all that call on the name of our Lord Jesus Christ in every place, theirs and ours.**

The term ἐκκλησία, "church," designates the local congregation in Corinth. The word signifies "assembly," it is derived from ἐκ and καλεῖν and designates an assembly that gathers in answer to a call issued for that purpose. This may, of course, mean any kind of gathering, civic, social, etc. When the Christian *ecclesia* is to be indicated, a modifier is always added to differentiate it and to mark its Christian character. Here it is the church "of God," the assembly which belongs to God in a peculiar way. It is best to take the genitive in the broadest sense since God is the originator, lord, living power, protector, comforter, and ruler of the church. Everything about this *ecclesia* is according. Thus we see how Paul regards the Corinthians when he now writes to them; and he evidently desires, we may say even calls upon them, to regard themselves in the same way when this letter is read to them.

The note thus struck is amplified by the addition: "having been sanctified in Christ Jesus." Now, however, Paul uses the plural whereas with the term *ecclesia* he employed the singular. So often Paul loves to dwell on the two or more sides of a concept or an idea. The perfect participle ἡγιασμένοι tells of a past act and its present and continuing result. The Corinthians, once made holy by the grace of God in Christ Jesus, by faith continue in this holiness. This term, οἱ ἡγιασμένοι, is a standard designation for true Christians in the New Testament; it is like οἱ πιστεύοντες, "they that believe," οἱ κλητοί, "they that are called," etc. The idea expressed in ἁγιάζειν is separation from everything profane and worldly and devotion to God in Christ Jesus. Theologically this is called "sanctification in the wider sense," for it includes conversion, faith, justification, and the life in good works—all that has made and still makes us the Christians that we are. This is to be distinguished from "sanctification in the narrow sense," namely the life in good works, which constitutes the fruit of faith and justification.

The phrase "in Christ Jesus" is to be understood as meaning "in union and communion with Christ Jesus" or "in connection with him." Our entire Christian life became such and is such only in vital connection with Christ Jesus. The moment this little preposition ἐν is cancelled we cease to be ἡγιασμένοι in any sense. A fruitful study could be made of this pregnant phrase which recurs again and again in Paul's letters in all manner of connections; the studies that have been made are not satisfactory.

Paul calls the Corinthians "they that are sanctified" in spite of the fact that he has much fault to find with them. Those who overstrain the term to mean "total sanctification," or, if not that, a pietistic, puritanic, or other type of self-chosen "holiness," are here corrected by Paul. He likewise corrects those who go to the other extreme and think that holiness remains where grave faults are allowed to continue and become permanent in a congregation. Observe how Paul rings the changes on the Savior's name. "Christ Jesus," which names his person and his work in one breath, is the one source of our Christian being.

Paul now adds appositionally: "called as saints." He thus makes a double combination. Like Paul, the Corinthians are also "called" — he in his office "called as an apostle"; they in their church membership "called as saints." The other connection is by way of ἅγιοι, "saints," which takes up and emphasizes ἡγιασμένοι, "they that are sanctified." That is what makes them saints or "holy persons." In this they have a like experience with Paul. He was made what he is by God's call; they likewise.

In the epistles κλητός and κλητοί always signify called effectively, the call being both extended and accepted. In the Gospels the term is used as denoting only the call extended so that "the called" are merely the *invitati*, Matt. 22:14. The verbal with its passive idea points to God as the agent who effectively called the Corinthians by both extending the call and enabling them to accept it by his grace. It is not strange that Paul uses ἡγιασμένοι combined with ἅγιοι in addressing this letter to the Corinthians, for the entire burden of it is instruction and admonition to be more fully just what these two terms convey.

Thus far Paul has fixed attention only on Corinth, "the church which is at Corinth," the assembly of saints which gathers in that city. It is characteristic of the apostle that he does not stop with this idea. Although all he has to say applies to this city and to its Christian congregation, Paul sees these people and wants them to see and to feel themselves a part of a vaster whole. So he adds: "together with all that call on the name of our Lord Jesus Christ in every place, theirs and ours." While the Corinthians are grouped as one congregation in Corinth they are joined with (σύν, associative) many others, namely all those in every place who call upon the Lord's name.

The others thus named are, of course, not another and more extensive group to whom this letter is also addressed. Paul is not writing a world encyclical. They are fellow Christians of the Corinthians; and whenever the Corinthians think of themselves they are to remember the entire spiritual body of which they are a part. Here there is the true antidote for individualism and sectionalism. We are not to be Christians just by ourselves but members together with all the saints of God.

When Paul describes the Corinthians he states what God has made of them, "they that are sanctified, that are called saints," the passive idea is found in both expressions. When Paul describes the fellow Christians of the Corinthians he does the reverse: he states what these Christians themselves do, namely "call on the name of the Lord." The one description we may call objective, the other subjective. To call on the Lord's name is at the same time the simplest and the most sufficient way of designating in others than ourselves what not only makes but also shows them to be Christians. For calling on the Lord's name is a confessional act, one that men generally are able to perceive. We know that this act can be truly performed only "in connection with the Holy Ghost," I Cor. 12:3; and it certainly "saves," for it goes together with a believing heart, Rom. 10:9,10.

But why did Paul vary the designations for the Corinthians and for those other Christians? When we are bidden to look at ourselves we can be asked to look into our own hearts (holiness); but when we are bidden to look at others we cannot and really dare not judge their hearts, we must attend to the confession which they make in calling on the Lord. An unacceptable distinction is made at this point when this *Anrufung Christi* or calling on the Lord is regarded as only a *relative Anbetung* or a relative worship of Christ, an adoration "beneath" that accorded God. This is done in support of subordinationism, the doctrine that Christ is God in a secondary or lower sense. Exegetically there is no ground here or anywhere else in the Scriptures for such a lowering of Christ, the true Son of God. The very contrary is true. To call on the Lord Jesus Christ means the same as to call on God, i. e., to worship him as God.

Paul loves the full, sonorous designation "our Lord Jesus Christ." In the possessive "our" he, of course, includes himself. "Jesus Christ" combines the incarnate person and his mediatorial work. "Our Lord" acknowledges this person as our heavenly Savior, Master, and King, to whom we belong with body and with soul. "To call on him" means to praise, bless, thank, worship him, and to ask of him all that we need for body and for soul.

Paul writes: to call on "the name." The "name" always designates the person so that there is no difference whether we call on the person or on his name. Yet the two are not identical, and we may note the peculiar manner in which the Scriptures speak so pointedly of the Name. For instance, we are to be baptized "in the name" of the Father, etc. This "name" signifies the revelation of the person. It is more than our names, which are usually only labels although even we are known by our names, those given to us as babes and those acquired by our character, work, etc. We know God, Christ, etc., by their name or revelation, for in their cases the name brings them into connection with us so that we truly know, trust, love and revere them.

There is much discussion regarding the final genitive αὐτῶν καὶ (or τε καὶ) ἡμῶν, "theirs and ours." Suffice it to say that "theirs" refers to "they that call on the name," etc., and "ours" refers to the two writers of the letter. The Corinthians are to think of themselves as being joined together with all those who confess the Lord "in every place" over the entire world wherever they may be, and all these places may be divided into two, "theirs and ours." The effect of the last genitive is that Paul and Sosthenes are placed among those that call on the Lord's name, the "place" or residence of these two being Ephesus where the letter is being written.

3) The greeting itself is like that found in other letters of Paul's, such as Romans, Galatians, and Ephesians: **Grace to you and peace from God, our Father, and the Lord Jesus Christ.** The grammarians supply the optative of wish εἴη or some other verb form, but we prefer to regard the nominatives as being exclamatory and thus needing no verb form even in thought.

In these greetings the term χάρις or grace takes the place of the secular χαίρειν, "that ye rejoice," and denotes the undeserved *favor Dei* as it is in God's heart together with all the gifts of that favor, especially such as pertain to the persons involved. Thus "grace to you" means: May God and the Lord give you an abundance of his undeserved gifts!

"And εἰρήνη" is the Hebrew *shalom*, the German *Heil*, and denotes the condition that results when God is our friend, and all is well with us. The objective condition of "peace" is always the fundamental thing which, of course, also has accompanying it the subjective feeling of peace, namely rest, satisfaction, and happiness in the heart. The condition is constant and essential, the feeling may or may not always be present. The condition is to be our fixed possession, and this fact will assure us that, when the feeling fluctuates and at times sinks very low, it will revive to greater strength. The order of these two, grace and peace, remains constant, grace is always first, peace always second. This is due to the fact that grace is the source of peace. Without grace there is and can be no peace; but when grace is ours, peace must of necessity follow.

In order to characterize the exalted value of these gifts Paul adds the modifiers: "from God, our Father," etc. The preposition ἀπό conveys the idea that the blessings indicated are to flow down to us from above. The thought of origin is also included. By using the preposition ἀπό, "from," only once the two objects governed by it, "God, our Father," and "the Lord Jesus Christ," are regarded as a unit and are thus placed on a level of equality. This is so self-evident that no scholar in the Greek will deny it. Yet subordinationism and those who in other ways modify or cancel the Godhead of Christ lower the position of Christ that is here expressed by Paul's phrase. This is done by calling attention to the two names "our Father" and "Lord" and by finding a difference of being in these names so that Christ's deity is lowered or lost.

To be sure, not only the two persons here mentioned but all three persons of the Godhead have different names. The entire Scripture tells us that. How this fact involves a subordination of one person to the other is not apparent. The fact that one person is called our Father and the other our Lord Jesus Christ does not lower the second. It merely shows that in the Holy Trinity all three persons were not fathers, all three were not incarnate, etc., but that each bears a distinct relation to us and our salvation which is unaffected by the identity of their essence.

The names which Paul uses here and elsewhere apply to the revelation the persons have vouchsafed to us in connection with the divine work of salvation. The first person is "our Father" because we are his children in Christ Jesus; and the second person is "the Lord" or "our Lord" because he has redeemed, purchased, and won us so that we are his own and live under him in his kingdom and serve him in everlasting righteousness, innocence, and blessedness (Luther). As long as this one preposition coordinates our Father and our Lord and makes them one fountain of saving grace and peace, no ingenuity of men will be able to sever them and introduce a subordination.

The Introduction, 1:4-9

4) Paul loves to begin his letters to congregations with a statement of his gratitude for their spiritual well-being. This is an entirely natural way of beginning a letter and resembles many of our letters to friends when we hear that they are doing well. The introduction to the present letter is certainly marked with praise. But the passives show that this is praise for what God has wrought and not for anything the *Corinthians* have done. This fact is quite significant for an understanding of the body of the letter, which has much to criticize in regard to the Corinthians.

Yet Paul is not writing in an ironical manner when he uses these passive verbs. Such irony would be foolish and ethically wrong. Nor is Paul thinking of only a part of the congregation when he writes this praise, passive though the verbs be (those "of Paul" or those "of Christ" or the two combined), for the letter is addressed to the church as a whole. What Paul writes by way of praise is true of the Corinthians in general, and while he thus points to that which is delightful among them, it is understood from the very beginning that he will have fault to find in other respects.

So the apostle begins: **I thank my God always concerning you on the basis of the grace of God which was given you in Christ Jesus,** etc.

A little personal touch is added by inserting "my" before "God," although some MSS. omit this pronoun. Paul is speaking about his prayer life when he writes: "I thank my God." He ever bore his congregations on his heart and constantly prayed for them. He does not merely ask God to bestow grace and gifts upon them to supply their spiritual needs, he always remembers with a grateful heart the many gifts God has already granted to his people. Even when there is much to ask for them, these needs do not dim Paul's eyes to the shining gifts God has already granted. This thankfulness on Paul's part is an example for us all. God loves to add new blessings when past blessings are received and cherished with true gratitude.

Paul's prayers rest on (ἐπί with the dative) the grace which God has vouchsafed to the Corinthians in connection with (ἐν as in v. 2) Christ Jesus. "Grace" is itself the highest and most comprehensive of God's undeserved gifts and here embraces all that God has so freely bestowed on the Corinthians. Yet Paul marks this gift expressly as a gift by adding the aorist participle δοθείσῃ, "which was given." The tense of the participle emphasizes the past fact of God's giving and at the same time summarizes all God's giving. The great Giver is "God," and the sphere of his giving is the blessed circle drawn by the phrase "in Christ Jesus." All the divine gifts of grace which enrich the Corinthians and all the grace itself from which they flow are connected from beginning to end with "Christ Jesus," i. e., with his person and his work.

5) While "grace," as here used, is all-comprehensive and includes all of God's gifts to the

Corinthians, Paul is thinking of this grace as being something specific and concrete, hence he now specifies: **that in everything ye are enriched in him, in all utterance and all knowledge.** The passive of the preceding participle "was given" is continued in the case of the verb "were enriched." A second time Paul thus draws attention to what *God* has done for the Corinthians: by the gift of his grace he "made them rich." The verb πλουτίζεσθαι instead of the more frequent περισσεύειν, "to abound," is more select. It suggests that formerly the Corinthians were poor spiritually, yea utterly destitute, but that this has now been wondrously changed — they have come into great spiritual wealth. It is certainly true that the Corinthians possess, without any merit or worthiness on their part, tremendous spiritual riches.

The idea of greatness is enhanced by the phrase "in everything." God had withheld nothing from them. And all that he had given them was, of course, ἐν αὐτῷ, in connection with Christ. For the third time we meet this significant phrase in these first lines. While the aorist is historical and again sums up the entire enrichment in one punctiliar idea, Paul does not intend to refer only to his own past work in founding the congregation. Nor can he by the use of this aorist mean that the Corinthians were so enriched at one time, but that they had now lost a good part of this enrichment through faults of their own, the faults Paul is about to discuss. The aorist merely sums up all their wealth from the beginning to the present time. The question of faults and losses is not touched as yet. It is enough that God has been so good to the Corinthians.

They have been made rich by God "in everything." What this means is now stated: "in all utterance and in all knowledge." The word λόγος means more than "utterance" or speaking; it includes the thought as well as its expression by means of the sounds of language. The comprehensive phrase "in all utterance" cannot be restricted to some specific type of utterance such as the speaking in tongues, which Paul intends to discuss in this letter. The phrase must here refer to any and every form of expressing the saving truth of Christ, namely practical and theoretical, devotional and apologetic, pastoral instruction and admonition and public preaching and teaching. This, of course, includes the knowledge that is necessary for such utterance whenever teaching is engaged in. However, the addition "in all knowledge" does not intend to express this self-evident plea, for then "knowledge" should be mentioned first and "utterance" second. The "knowledge" here added to "utterance" is the result of the latter. Where all the forms of teaching and of admonition abound, there, as a natural result, all the forms of knowledge will spread in the congregation and thus likewise abound. Such, then, was the wealth with which the Corinthians were enriched when Paul wrote this letter. Paul and Apollos and other notable men had taught the Corinthians, and this work had been done among them with very rich results.

6) The next clause indicates the deeper effect produced in the hearts of the Corinthians: **even as the testimony of Christ was confirmed in you.** "In you" means in your hearts by an increase of faith. Instead of writing "the gospel," Paul says "the testimony of Christ" was confirmed in you. This is not the testimony which others brought to the Corinthians "concerning Christ" as R. 500 supposes (objective genitive), but the testimony which Christ himself made while he was here on earth (subject genitive) as we see from I Tim. 6:13: Jesus τοῦ μαρτυρήσαντος ἐπὶ Ποντίου Πιλάτου, and from many other references to Christ's testimony. The verb is again passive: "was confirmed," made solid and strong in your hearts, the

passive pointing to God as the agent and thus strengthening the effect of the previous passives. To confirm Christ's testimony in you means to plant it solidly in your hearts by faith. Giving is the broadest of the three verbs; making rich is more specific; confirming narrows the idea down still more and refers it to the very hearts of the Corinthians.

7) The next clause: **so that you come behind in no gift,** with its present infinitive, points out the result of all of this past activity of God's as it is found in the present condition of the Corinthians. As Paul sees them now, they "come behind" in no gift. We may say that they come behind no other of the various churches. God has done no less for them and in them than he has accomplished in others. Or, leaving out the comparison with other congregations, the Corinthians fall short, as far as God's activity in their case is concerned, in no respect. Since Paul is here speaking in general terms, "in no gift" cannot refer to the special charismatic gifts of the early church but must point to the general gracious gifts of God with which true believers are always duly endowed, the spiritual blessings of Christianity in general.

We may ask how Paul determines when a congregation does not fall behind or come short. The added participial clause contains the answer: **waiting for the revelation of our Lord Jesus Christ.** A congregation does not come behind or fall short when it is waiting for the Lord's revelation. The present participle does not include patient waiting, quiet holding out, but refers rather to an expecting something which one does not as yet have but to which one is looking forward. In the case of the Corinthians the object of their waiting is "the revelation of our Lord Jesus Christ," which, of course, refers to the last great day. This is, indeed, a "revelation" because the Lord will then reveal himself fully by visibly appearing to the universe in all his glory. Whoever is equipped to look forward aright to that glorious revelation does not "come behind in any gracious gift."

8) The two present tenses "ye do not come behind" and "waiting for" point to the present state of the Corinthians. Yet "the revelation" of Christ lies in the future. In order to bridge this interval Paul adds the relative clause concerning Christ and then in v. 9 the new sentence concerning God. Concerning Christ, whose glorious revelation the Corinthians await at the last day, Paul writes: **who shall confirm you until the end as not to be accused in the day of our Lord Jesus Christ.** Observe these solemn repetitions of the sacred name "our Lord Jesus Christ." They echo through this introduction.

The future tense "shall confirm you" has the force of a divine promise. But as throughout this introductory paragraph Paul thanks God for what *God* has done for the Corinthians, so in this relative clause it is *Christ* and his work that are stressed. *He* will confirm the Corinthians. The phrase "until the end," as its position indicates, modifies the verb "shall confirm" you. And "end" is here not the end of life but the final end marked by the day of the Lord.

The verbal ἀνεγκλήτους, "as not to be accused," is forensic so that no indictment can be lodged before a judge. This shows the character of "the day" of the Lord. In that day he shall be revealed as the Judge of the whole world. And now his "confirming" becomes clear. He confirms us by keeping us true in the faith so that we have daily forgiveness of sins and are kept from deadly errors and sins by which faith would be destroyed and we should fall into the condemnation of the devil.

9) Paul doubles this assurance and promise: **Faithful is God, through whom ye were called into the fellowship of his Son Jesus Christ, our Lord.**

The adjective πιστός is placed emphatically forward and means trustworthy, reliable. The preceding context shows in what respect this is true, namely in respect to all that he does for our final salvation. If we were left to depend on ourselves we should surely be lost; but we can trust God completely. The work he has begun in us he will most certainly also complete. For this reason Paul reaches back with the relative clause: "through whom ye were called," to the very beginning of God's work upon the Corinthians. This last verb, too, is in the passive. Yet Paul writes διά, "through" whom, and not ὑπό, "by" whom. The passive verb itself contains the idea that God is the agent in our effective call, the *causa principalis* of that call (ὑπό). When Paul writes διά he adds the idea that God is also the supreme medium through whom the call is extended to us. It is a matter of how one desires to present God when speaking about the call. This God is "faithful" and worthy of our trust, not only in regard to what he will from now on do for our salvation, but also because his faithfulness reaches back to the very first moment of our saving contact with him. God, who began the blessed work in the Corinthians, cannot at any time thereafter become indifferent or show neglect.

The phrase "into the fellowship," etc., embraces the entire communion with Christ, including the consummation at the last day. In this life our communion with Christ is mediated on his part by Word and sacrament, in and through which he comes to us, in and by which he makes his abode with us and dwells in us. There is no fellowship of Christ with us apart from his Word and sacrament. On our part this communion with Christ is mediated by faith. Love, devotion, worship, and all works by which we serve him are never independent but spring forth as the fruits of faith. Take away faith, and the communion ceases forthwith. It is as pure and intense as our faith is pure and intense. Everything else indicates only the character and the degree of our faith.

When he closes the introductory paragraph Paul again uses the sacred name, but this time he adds the designation "his Son." The claim that Paul never calls Jesus the Son of God is here refuted by the clearest language. Likewise the abstract claim that Jesus is not truly God. "His Son" appears without a modifying adjective or phrase for the sufficient reason that Jesus is God's Son in no modified sense. Instead of placing him on a lower level than that occupied by the Father (subordinationism) or making him a being that was created somewhere in eternity by the Father (Arianism) or reducing him to a mere human being who received divine glory from the Father (rationalism, etc.), Paul's designation places our Lord on an equality with the Father. The nature of "his Son" cannot differ from that of the Father. Every other instance in which Jesus is called God's Son in the Scriptures, in which his oneness with the Father is asserted together with his eternal pre-existence, helps to make plain what "his Son" signifies in the present connection. Paul, of course, adds "his Son" at the end of this paragraph in order to establish all that he writes about Jesus as our Lord. For Jesus cannot be our Lord and together with the Father our one fountain of grace unless he is, indeed, God's own Son, equal with the Father and one with him in essence.

A silent significance illuminates the entire paragraph. Paul does not praise the Corinthians as such for their faith or for their love and their works. He only thanks God for God's grace, gift, confirmation, etc. The passive verbs have a silent purpose. For Paul concludes with God's and God's Son's confirmation in view of the final judgment. The Corinthians are to feel that they still need confirmation in various respects. When Paul visits the congregations he has founded he does this in order to confirm them. He is God's humble instrument in this vital and necessary work. This letter intends to serve the same blessed purpose. The Corinthians are to be quite sure as to how they shall appear at the last great day. On God they can rely, but how about themselves? This is, indeed, a masterly introduction to the letter that now follows.

The First Part of the Letter

The Preachers of the Corinthians, 1:10-4:21

I. The Party Contentions, 1:10-17.

II. The Foolishness of Preaching the Cross of Christ, 1:18-31.

III. The Preachers of the Wisdom of the Cross, chapter 2.

IV. The Preachers as God's Co-workers, 3:1-9.

V. God's Building, 3:10-23.

VI. God's Tried and Faithful Stewards, chapter 4.

I. The Party Contentions, 1:10-17

10) In his other letters Paul first offers doctrine and secondly admonition. In this letter he at once writes: "I admonish you." The "confirmation" promised to the Corinthians in v. 8 is thus to be realized at once. While this letter is thus to be built up of admonition, this admonition is often combined with doctrinal statements and explanations of the greatest value. Paul begins: **Now I admonish you,**

brethren, through the name of the Lord Jesus Christ, that you all speak the same thing, and that there be no factions among you, but that you be perfected in the same mind and in the same judgment.

Paul uses the common transitional δέ, "now," and also the loving address "brethren" with its friendly appeal to the heart. There were many troubles and faults among the Corinthians, and yet these do not sever the fraternal tie that binds them to Paul. While this is true and should not be minimized, a deduction such as the following would be contrary to Paul's intention: that congregations may settle down permanently into evil conditions like those which existed in Corinth without impairing their fraternal relations with Paul and with those who are true as he was. For this entire letter is directed at one thing only, namely to remove the faults and the evils that had begun to show themselves in Corinth. Only because Paul intends to and most sincerely hopes to accomplish this purpose does he write to these "brethren." His tone is gentle and matches the fraternal address. The English versions which translate "I beseech" may mislead, for παρακαλῶ does not mean "I beg" but rather "I call upon you," "I summon," "I admonish you." This word is tactful and brotherly, and yet Paul is not forgetting that he writes as an apostle of Jesus Christ, v. 1. The authority he would exercise is the same whether it speaks softly or finds itself compelled to speak sternly.

Paul mediates (διά) his summons "through the name of our Lord Jesus Christ." Once more we hear the full, solemn designation of the Savior, which always brings to mind all of his saving power and grace. And now again (v. 2) the ὄνομα or "name" is joined with this designation, which directs our attention to the revelation by which Christ makes himself known to us, and by which we know him. In all that Paul intends to write in his admonition he will use Christ's name or revelation to enlighten and to move. There is no saving or no cleansing power apart from this "name." After verbs of urging or commanding the subfinal ἵνα, "that," may be used, R. 1046, which introduces the substance of the admonition or the command.

Here it is: "that you all speak the same thing." The subject as well as the object of the verb are emphatic by their position. In a broad way Paul states in this brief summary the theme of the entire first part of his letter: *That All May Speak The Same Thing.* They are all to be a unit in what they think and say as Christians, for λέγω always involves the thought that is put into words and never indicates merely the sounds of the lips or the form of expression.

A negative formulation is at once added, and this by coordination, καί: "and that there be no factions among you," divisions or parties that disrupt the unity that ought to be. When Paul writes "you all" he does not imply that some of the Corinthians are not speaking as they ought. So he also writes: "that there be," and not: "that there may no longer be" (μηκέτι ᾖ, or μὴ γένηται), leaving unsaid whether the "factions" are already actual or only impending. We catch a glimpse of Paul's heart. He is not swift to put the worst construction upon questionable conditions, to surmise evil, or to exaggerate. In this respect we shall always find him to be the same.

Paul's carefulness appears also in the third and positive statement which he attaches with the slightly adversative δέ: "but that you be perfected," etc. Instead of the present subjunctive καταρτίζησθε, which would imply an actual torn condition that is to be remedied, he writes ἦτε κατηρτισμένοι and uses the perfect participle as a predicate after ἦτε: "that you may be (or may go on being) such as have been perfectly fitted out" (from ἄρτιος). Paul thus omits the implication that the Corinthians are actually divided at this time.

Such an implication is sometimes read into Paul's words, and a correspondingly dark picture is painted of the conditions existing in Corinth; yet such a dismal picture is not in accord with the facts. The Corinthians are to be Christians who have been perfected, adjusted, and well furnished "in the same mind and in the same judgment." The two phrases elucidate Paul's statement in which he calls on the Corinthians to speak the same thing. When they are properly equipped they will not differ among themselves in regard to spiritual understanding or in regard to spiritual judgment. Back of our speaking is the mind or the understanding by which we grasp a subject; and, having grasped it, we form our judgment and our conclusions; and these we put into speech.

Both νοῦς, "mind," and γνώμη, "judgment," are neutral terms and may deal with secular or spiritual matters; here, of course, the latter are meant. Paul desires that the same mind and the same judgment be found in all of the Corinthians and not divergent or contradictory conclusions. Yet mere harmony and agreement is not Paul's ideal but a unity of right understanding and of judgment. This is the thought that underlies his words. The apostle is not thinking in a special way about doctrinal unity as he does in Eph. 4:3, etc., although this, too, is included. He has in mind the various questions that have arisen in Corinth and the contradictory answers the Corinthians have given to these questions. The situations that had developed were not properly understood by some, and hence their judgments, too, had been warped. As a result some spoke in favor of a thing, others against it; or there was even a variety of opinions.

Similar clashes occur in our congregations today. Paul would not have us believe that differences of this kind are immaterial as long as no doctrine is directly involved. If they are allowed to continue, the result must eventually be σχίσματα, factions and rents in the congregation, which are not only disturbing but also destructive in their effect.

11) With all plainness of speech Paul now states to what he refers and addresses his readers even more tenderly than he did before: **For it has been signified to me concerning you, my brethren, by Chloe's people that there are contentions among you.**

The aorist ἐδηλώθη merely states the fact that Paul has obtained this information, yet, placed forward as it is, this verb has the emphasis: due information has reached Paul. "By Chloe's people," literally, "by those that belong to Chloe," remains indefinite for us since we know nothing about this lady nor about the people who belong to her, whether these were relatives of hers or possibly slaves. Was she one of the well-known members of the congregation at Corinth whose people had occasion to visit Paul at Ephesus? Or did she herself reside in Ephesus, and had some of her people been at Corinth? The Corinthians need no further explanation.

Paul names the source of his information. He is not entertaining idle rumors which do so much damage in the church before their evil buzzing can be finally quieted. Nor is Paul secretive. The Corinthians need not ask: "Who told him?" Paul is quite open. The Corinthians themselves had sent a letter to Paul, which he had just received, in which they asked him about a number of things that troubled them, but they had said nothing in their letter about the ἔριδες or "contentions" that Chloe's people reported to him. We do not know why the Corinthians said nothing on this subject. We note only that Paul does not reprove them for this omission. Perhaps they did not realize the danger that threatened them through these bickerings.

We may ask whether it was ethically proper for those of Chloe to tell Paul what they knew about the conditions existing in Corinth. The question answers itself, for Paul accepted and acted on the information he thus received. Observe, too, that τῶν is plural. A number of witnesses attested the facts to the apostle. This is not a case of "talking behind people's backs." *Aus Liebe zur Besserung etwas an gehoerigem Ort anzeigen ist keine Suende wider das achte Gebot, nur huete man sich, dass ueber die Wahrheit nichts hinzugesetzt werde.* Hedinger. Another caution is in place: "Beware lest ill-will or secret malice prompt you to report." Paul's information is to the effect that ἔριδες or "contentions," *Zaenkereien*, quarrelings, prevail among the Corinthians.

12) Paul at once specifies: **Now this I mean, that each one of you says, I am of Paul; and I of Apollos; and I of Cephas; and I of Christ.**

Only as a matter of history would there be any value in discussing the many varying opinions that have been held in regard to these Corinthian parties. Suffice it to say that Paul enumerates four different parties. Yet the case is overstated when these parties are called σχίσματα, splits or divisions. That stage had not yet been reached. The term ἔριδες implies only that the members who used these various slogans wrangled with each other. Of course, if this wrangling were to continue, actual schisms and divisions would eventually result. The genitive used with εἰμί denotes attachment: "I belong to Paul," etc. Paul and Apollos had labored in Corinth, Peter had not, and, of course, Christ had not.

The first three slogans implied that those who used them boasted of the excellency, the special gifts, and the grand results attained on the part of the man whose name they vauntingly proclaimed. Some had been converted by Paul, others by Apollos who followed Paul, and still others by Peter. The latter members had come to Corinth after Paul had left and in all probability were Jewish Christians from Palestine who extoled Peter as the foremost of the Twelve. Apollos, learned and eloquent and at the same time very successful, could easily have gained a contentious personal following after he left this field of his labors. Since he was the founder of the congregation Paul certainly stood high in the estimation of the original members. The wrong and the dangerous feature attendant upon the estimation in which these men were held was not the fact that these great teachers had their devoted personal admirers, who praised their excellencies and their achievements in the church, but the fact that these friends should exalt these teachers to an unwarranted degree, pit the one against the other, and misuse their good names for the purpose of forming parties and wrong distinctions in the congregation.

Some of the members in Corinth sensed the wrong nature of this proceeding and thus came to make their shibboleth: "I of Christ." This was in a manner correct. As Paul continues writing, we observe that he discusses only three of these contentions, for the most part only two, the one centering about himself and the one centering about Apollos. The party of Peter was in all likelihood small. Paul says no more regarding the Christ party. Only in 3:21 we read: "Let no one glory in men"; then in v. 23: "You are Christ's"; compare 1:31: "He that glorieth, let him glory in the Lord." All this indicates that Paul in a way sided with the Christ party. He can, however, not say this outright. It will not do to place Christ into competition with man as the head of a party over against other parties. The fault of the Christ party is the fact that it allows itself to become only a party and thus is also drawn into the party wranglings.

13) In a highly effective manner Paul at once explodes the folly of this entire party matter. He reduces the contentions of the Corinthians to absurdities. That is the true "understanding" and "judgment" concerning them. **Is Christ divided? was Paul crucified for you? or were you baptized in the name of Paul?**

We regard the first sentence as a question and not as an exclamation although the Greek has no interrogative particle. Such a particle is not always needed. To make the first sentence exclamatory and the other two interrogative would be too odd. "Has Christ been divided?" does not, of course, intend to ask whether he has been cut up into parts so that we have him in so many separate parts (this is the force of the perfect tense). This dividing refers to different kinds of Christ: a Paul Christ, an Apollos Christ, a Peter Christ, and beside these just a plain, unmarked Christ. The very idea is absurd to Christians. Christ is one, absolutely and always one. Why, then, these silly wranglings?

There is, however, another possibility. When some say: "I belong to Paul," while others say: "I belong to Christ," the former speak against the latter as though Paul, too, were a kind of Christ or in some way an equivalent of Christ. Hence the question: "You certainly do not intend to say, what your words strangely seem to imply, that Paul was crucified for you?" The particle $\mu\acute{\eta}$, like the Latin *num*, implies a negative answer. Crucifixion is mentioned as the outstanding redemptive act of Christ. The very idea that Paul might thus be crucified for the Corinthians is absurd. This question is put only with regard to Paul although it could with equal right have been put with regard to Apollos and with regard to Peter. Paul is not flattered by these Corinthians who claim this attachment to him. The reverse is true. So Paul mentions only his own party and their absurd action and lets the readers supply the questions regarding the other two preachers.

"Paul," "Apollos," "Peter," and "Christ" are *names*, and the Corinthians used them as labels in their party contentions. Thinking of that, Paul asks: "Or, certainly, you were not baptized 'in Paul's name' or with a Paul baptism?" Only One was crucified for our redemption, and so there are also not different baptisms, a Pauline, an Apollos, and a Petrine baptism, but only one, the Christ baptism. Any other notion is absurd. And yet this very absurdity is contained in the shibboleths of the Corinthians. Here Paul again castigates only his own party and allows his readers to supply what is necessary for the rest. When he asks these questions Paul finds no fault with the fourth party, the one that names itself after Christ. This does not, of course, mean that they were wholly faultless, for in a way, when they lower Christ to the level of a party head and thus place him in competition with other party heads, this party, too, is in the wrong.

Strange to say, men still invent Christs to suit their own religious whims. Instead of the Christ that was, and is, and ever shall be, the same yesterday, and today, and forever, they create a changeable and a variously colored Christ. All of them are distortions of the genuine and only Christ, some of them have a Christ in only the Oriental garments. He is to them no longer virgin-born, nor risen from the dead, nor equal in essence with the Father, etc.

The phrase "in the name of Paul" intends to allude to the great commission: baptizing "in the name" of the Father, etc. In regard to the term "name" see v. 2 and 10. To baptize in the name, etc., does not mean to baptize by the authority of, etc. The preposition $εἰς$ is static and has the idea of sphere: "in," not that of direction: "into" (as even the R. V. still translates).

In the Koine, the Greek of this period, εἰς has already invaded the territory of the static verbs and the verbs of being so that we find even εἶναι εἰς. See R. 591, etc., on the entire subject. "In the name" = in union or in connection with the revelation, etc. There is such a "name" of Christ in connection with which we are baptized, but no such "name" of Paul, which makes it absurd even to think of being baptized "in the name of Paul."

14) Paul is grateful to God for the fact that, while he labored in Corinth, he was providentially led so that he personally baptized only a few among the first converts in the Corinthian congregation. **I thank God that I baptized none of you save Crispus and Gaius.** He can write "none of you" because this states the rule of his procedure; he then adds the few exceptions. These were so few in number that they could never constitute a party on the ground of their baptism through the agency of Paul. Crispus is the late ruler of the Jewish synagogue, one of the very first converts to be gained in Corinth, Acts 18:8, who was baptized by Paul. Gaius we know as Paul's host on his later visit to Corinth when Paul there wrote the letter to the Romans, Rom. 16:23.

15) The negative purpose clause: **lest anyone should say that you were baptized in my name,** depends on the previous ὅτι clause: "that I baptized none of you," etc., and not on the main verb: "I thank God." If Paul had baptized many in those early days of his labor in Corinth, and if all these now gave Paul's name to a party that had been formed by them, those of the other parties or any slanderous person among them might say that those people who constituted Paul's party had been baptized in Paul's name.

To understand what Paul refers to we should not think of a substitution of the name of Paul for that of the Trinity in the formula of baptism, for that is not the idea to be conveyed. To be baptized in Paul's name is an expression that is parallel to the one that was well known, namely to be baptized in Christ's name or in Jesus' name. "Christ" and "Jesus" are not found in the baptismal formula, so also Paul's name need not be in order to make it a baptism in his name. Although it is administered in the name of the Triune God, baptism is said to be, a baptism in Jesus' name because he is the saving Mediator (note above "crucified"); and thus the sacrament is distinguished from the various Jewish washings and lustrations that were connected with the old ceremonial law. Baptism in Paul's name, while, of course, using the Trinitarian formula for the act, would mean to place the mediatorial saving power in Paul's person. The outrageous idea which Paul combats throughout is that men or any man should in any way be substituted for Christ in the church, whether by loving attachment or by vituperative hostility ("lest anyone should say"). We may today be glad to say that we were baptized (confirmed or married) by some beloved and revered pastor, but let no one go beyond that and attribute any special efficacy to that pastor's acts.

16) Some are surprised that Paul should add: **Now I baptized also the household of Stephanas; besides I do not know whether I baptized anyone else.** Stephanas was an important person who together with his family had done much for the Corinthians. At this very time he was in Ephesus with Paul, I Cor. 16:15. The question is asked: "How could the baptism of so important a family come to Paul's mind as a kind of afterthought?" The answer lies in 16:15. Stephanas was "the first fruits of Achaia" (note: not of Corinth), and while he was now a member of the congregation in Corinth he had been baptized in Athens where he was the first person in all Achaia (Greece) to be converted. When Paul runs over in his mind the

persons whom he had baptized in Corinth he naturally did not at once remember this family whom he baptized before he even reached Corinth.

There is likewise surprise that Paul should confess: "Besides I do not know whether I baptized anyone else." A considerable time had elapsed since Paul had left Corinth, and he had been very busy in other places. Here, as elsewhere, we see that God does not proceed in a mechanical fashion in Inspiration, but that he uses the minds of the chosen writers with such powers as they have. In this instance God does not consider it necessary to stimulate Paul's memory itself or to give it other aid so as to recall the entire list of people whom he had baptized while he was in Corinth. He may or he may not have baptized a few more. The point to be noted is this, and that alone is stressed, that Paul never baptized a sufficient number to constitute a party of any kind in the Corinthian congregation, and he is glad of that fact.

17) This may, however, cause surprise. Should Paul, like our pastors, not be happy to have brought as many families as possible into the church by means of baptism? Paul explains at once (γάρ): **For Christ sent me not to baptize but to preach the gospel.** This explanation is perhaps even more surprising than the question of surprise which it answers. It was a habit of Paul's, we may say, to pursue a thought to its real end, and to do so at once or eventually. This is the case here. The Lord's commission reads: "Disciple by baptizing," μαθητεύσατε βαπτίζοντες, Matt. 28:19, and, thinking superficially, one might conclude that the apostles were to go on baptizing as many people as possible, but this is not the case. The duty of the apostles (the chosen men whom the Lord sent, ἀπέστειλε) was to go from place to place and to spread the gospel (note εὐαγγελίζεσθαι) as far as possible. Thus the work assigned to them is really preaching and

teaching. The work of administering baptism when the preaching and the teaching had produced conversion was a matter that any assistant of an apostle could easily attend to, for it certainly required no immediate apostolic call.

So also the elders or pastors whom the apostles appointed in the newly founded congregations went on indefinitely, baptizing the new converts that were won after the apostles had left. Nothing derogatory is thus implied in regard to the sacrament itself or to its vital importance, it is merely the slight task of administering the sacrament of which Paul speaks. The chief apostolic work, that for which men of no lesser standing than apostles were required, Paul declares is εὐαγγελίζεσθαι, spreading the gospel itself in the wide world.

With the word εὐαγγελίζεσθαι Paul reaches the great truth which he intends to elaborate more fully in this letter, this matter of preaching the gospel and judging rightly those who do this preaching. The point at issue in Corinth is therefore at once added: to preach the gospel **not in word-wisdom in order that the cross of Christ may not be made empty.**

Much has been written about the "wisdom" which Paul begins to discuss. This σοφία is beyond question a vital term in this first part of Paul's letter. At this early stage of our study we need to note only that this is "the wisdom of the wise," v. 19, and that it goes together with "the prudence of the prudent"; it is "the wisdom of the world," v. 20, and is opposed by another wisdom, "the wisdom of God," and by Christ himself as the embodiment of "God-wisdom." More details will be furnished by the paragraphs that follow, but already here we have enough information to determine what the σοφία which Paul repudiates signifies.

It cannot signify merely the philosophic *form* of preaching the gospel as though this is forbidden to Paul; also, as distinguished from this form, it is quite self-evident that Paul would not preach the *substance* of the worldly wisdom of his time. We need not sharply divide substance from form. It should be rather self-evident that, where the substance is to be found, there the natural and the proper form to express that substance ought also to appear; and where the substance is absent, the form that accompanies it ought also to disappear; and if it is appropriated by another substance, the form will be unnatural, a mere mask that honest men will discard. The genitive λόγου also does not mean "form," for in verse 18 Paul uses λόγος with reference to the cross of Christ.

This distinction between form and substance overlooks the preposition ἐν: Paul dare not preach ἐν σοφίᾳ λόγου, "in word-wisdom." The preposition denotes sphere. Paul's preaching of the gospel must remain entirely outside of the sphere here indicated. The inside of this forbidden sphere is σοφία λόγου, both nouns are without the article so that they are practically a compound term, *Wortweisheit*, "word-wisdom." The chief term is, of course, "wisdom"; this is to be taken in the sense indicated in the two verses following. The minor term is "word" in its natural sense of "statement," the expression of thought by means of language. "Word" is here practically equivalent to "doctrine," save that the doctrine is also spoken. Paul is to keep his entire gospel preaching away from the sphere, the inside of which consists of the world's "wisdom-statement" or "wisdom-doctrine."

The translation of our versions is rather misleading: "wisdom of words." The Greek does not have the plural, and Paul does not have in mind a wisdom that consists of "words" or offers only "words." Moreover, we should not overlook the fact that the whole matter of preaching the gospel, εὐαγγελίζεσθαι, also deals with λόγος, "statement" or "doctrine," for in the very next verse we meet "the word (λόγος) of the cross," and again in 2:4 Paul has "my word (λόγος) and my proclamation (κήρυγμα)," both terms denoting the substance he proclaims.

We have a parallel in the Judaizers we meet in Galatia. They preached the gospel in connection with the law, they mingled the two and thereby nullified the gospel. They made of Christ a law-Christ, a Christ that does not, of course, exist. Something similar occurred in Corinth where Greek philosophic notions prevailed. The danger was present that some would admire and desire to have preached to them, not the gospel that Christ proclaimed, but a wisdom-gospel, a philosophy-gospel, a gospel that was fitted to the proud Greek learning of the day.

A similar situation exists today with regard to our current, so-called "science." Preachers who accept the hypotheses and the speculations of this "science" without question try to put the gospel or what they make of the gospel into what they consider a necessary and fitting connection with (ἐν) this "science," especially with "evolution" and its supposed but spurious facts and deductions. The resulting mixture is not the gospel. Paul's οὐ, "not," is highly peremptory even by its position at the head of the phrase: "not in word-wisdom." It completely bars out this kind of procedure. The gospel is in no way to be accommodated to any modern scientific or other wisdom. The plea of modernists that certain Scriptural "categories of thought" are worn out and must now be replaced by modern categories is a species of deception that does away with eternal, unchanging verities under the claim that they are only temporary modes of thought.

What this mode of procedure results in, and what Christ's purpose is in forbidding it, Paul states with brevity and with force: "in order that the cross of Christ may not be made empty." The combination of human wisdom with the gospel makes the gospel itself of none effect, κενός, "empty," without inner reality or substance. The gospel would not only lose some quality or some part of itself; it would evaporate entirely and leave only a hollow show of gospel terms and phrases. Instead of saying that the gospel would be made void and empty, Paul writes "the cross of Christ," because this is the very heart of the gospel. If the cross is cancelled or lost, the entire gospel is gone. On the cross Christ died for our sins, and this is in brief what "the cross" signifies: atonement for sin and guilt, reconciliation with God, forgiveness and peace blood-bought. Everything else contained in the gospel radiates from this vital center. If this center is blotted out, all the rays emanating from it are dissipated in everlasting night.

II. The Foolishness of Preaching the Cross of Christ, 1:18-31

18) The new paragraph begins with an explanatory γάρ and connects with what Paul has just said about emptying out the cross of Christ. To nullify the cross is to nullify the gospel, no matter how this may be done. Preachers and hearers who are guilty of this nullification may, of course, still use the term "cross of Christ" and may make it mean this or that according to their own wisdom, but the substance will be gone, only the shell of the cross will be left. "For" explains the matter by stating the nature of the cross: **For the word of the cross is to them that are perishing foolishness, yet unto us who are being saved it is the power of God.**

The first sentence points out where the trouble lies. Paul writes the λόγος of the cross, which is the same term that was used in the preceding verse. This "word" of the cross is the "statement" or "doctrine" by which the cross of Christ is set before our hearts so that we may believe and accept it in trust. We at once see that "word" cannot refer to mere form as distinct from substance. This "word" contains, offers, and bestows all that is included in the cross, in Christ's sacrificial and atoning death.

Yet when certain people hear this blessed "word" of the cross they look at it only with the eyes of their human wisdom and thus deem it to be only μωρία, "foolishness." They see no sense in it. Some try to put sense into it: they add their own σοφία to this σταυρός, their "wisdom" to this "cross." After it is thus embellished, but in reality nullified, they are pleased with the gospel (as they still call it) and with the cross. Alas, these are the ἀπολλύμενοι, those in process of going to perdition. This present participle is qualitative or descriptive. It does not, however, convey the idea that they are from eternity fated to go to perdition; it merely describes these people as they are when they hear about the cross and think it all foolishness. Some of them may later on still be won for the cross although Paul intimates nothing on that point. It is altogether evident that they are on the road to perdition for the reason that the one means able to save them, "the word of the cross," sounds like "silliness" to them. Nor will they gain anything by altering either the cross or the word of the cross, the gospel. Such an alteration would, in fact, utterly deprive them of all help.

In the two antithetical statements which Paul makes regarding the word of the cross he says nothing about the wonderful power of this word to enlighten the heart so that this word eventually appears as what it really is, not foolishness, but the efficacious wisdom of God. He is content to set down the two contrasting statements. His one object is to show the utter folly of trying to improve the word of the cross by casting it into the word of human wisdom in order to get rid of its apparent "foolishness" for a certain class of people. The Corinthians must know how great this folly is so that they, who now have and believe the word of the cross, may not after all suffer shipwreck in faith and also be classed with those that are perishing.

The μέν is followed by δέ, which indicates the balance between the two statements. This same "word of the cross" (note it well) "to them that are being saved, (namely) to us, is the power of God." This cannot seemingly be true, but it is nonetheless. Again we have a present participle which is qualitative and descriptive and conveys the idea that these persons are in a saved condition and continue therein. Paul adds ἡμῖν, "to us," and merges himself with the Corinthians and assumes that all of them as a unit cling to the cross by faith. Of course, only by "the word of the cross," i. e., by the saving power of both that word and that cross are they σωζόμενοι, such as are being saved. But this very fact shows that for them the cross is, actually is, δύναμις Θεοῦ, *Gotteskraft*, a power of God that demonstrates itself as such by saving.

When he is thus contrasting the two ideas why does Paul not say that the word of the cross is "God's wisdom"? Because "power" is the only proper correlative to "being saved." Power — nothing less — is required to save. Yet this δύναμις or "power" should not be regarded as omnipotent power, the almightiness which called the world into being by its fiat. This power cannot rescue sinners; if it could, the cross on Calvary would never have been needed. The power Paul has in mind is God's grace which alone reaches sinners.

"Those that are being saved" is the proper opposite to "those that are perishing." So in this group of opposites "God's power" is the term that correctly matches "foolishness." That which is "foolishness" is always powerless and cannot save those who are perishing; and what we deem to be "foolishness," even though it be most wonderful power, we throw aside and thus prevent it from saving us. Yet the direct contrast which Paul draws in regard to the word of the cross is only a preliminary explanation which shows that the judgment in regard to this word depends on two directly opposite kinds of people. More is to follow. Yet even now it is clear that the Corinthians and we could do ourselves no greater harm than to let those who despise and spurn the gospel alter that gospel and make it something that pleases them.

19) Before proceeding Paul substantiates what he has just said by a Scripture quotation, citing Isa. 29:14: **For it is written:**

**I will destroy the wisdom of the wise,
And the prudence of the prudent will I reject.**

The perfect tense γέγραπται = has been written and now stands so. These perfects, which are used so often, imply that the written Word stands for all time, for every age, with all that the Word contains, Rom. 15:4. The two lines quoted from Isaiah are Hebrew poetry in the form of a *parallelismus membrorum*. In this instance the parallelism is coordinate: the second line restates the thought of the first line in other words. The beauty of the poetry thus lies in the thought itself as much as in the form of expression. In the days of King Hezekiah, God declares in regard to the political cunning and the secret, tricky plans of this king's advisers, by which they hoped to escape the Assyrian danger, that he would deal wondrously with his people by at last saving it by his own great deeds so that the wisdom of the wise would perish and be forced to hide itself. The LXX makes God the subject of the two declarations. Paul is content to follow this translation. But instead of the Hebrew "shall be hid," LXX, "I will hide," Paul writes, "I will reject." When Paul translates independently into Greek he gives the sense rather than the words, for a rejected thing is cast aside, disappears, and is thus hidden.

The quotation is very much to the point with its statement in regard to the wisdom of the wise, etc. This "wisdom" of Hezekiah's advisers was exactly like that which was trying to magnify itself in Corinth. It emanated, not from God, but from godless thinking. The "prudence" of their tricky scheming failed to take into account God's promise and his power and was thus fit only to be cast aside and to be utterly forgotten. Paul would have his readers conclude from this quotation that what God did with this kind of wisdom in the days of old he does with all wisdom of this kind: he will destroy it and bring it to nought.

20) In a triumphant tone Paul now declares that God's threat in regard to this spurious wisdom was actually carried out. **Where is the wise? where is the scribe? where is the disputer of this age? did not God make foolish the wisdom of this world?**

All of these questions are uttered in one breath as it were and are really but one question. Paul is no longer quoting but is merely alluding to Isa. 19:12 and 33:18, much as all of us do when we refer to our A. V. If we are well read in it, some of its expressions rise to our lips almost automatically. In Isa. 19:12 the prophet asks concerning Pharaoh's supposedly wise counselors: "Where are thy wise men?" The very question implies that they have been made fools. When he recalls the prophet's question Paul uses the singular σοφός, but this means "any wise one," no matter which one; and thus Paul, too, implies that all of them have turned out to be fools.

In Isa. 33:18 the prophet describes the peace which shall follow after the terrors of the Assyrian danger are past. Men will then ask in astonishment, "What has become of the scribe, γραμματεύς, who was to tabulate the tribute that had been forced from the Jews?" They will also ask what has become of the man who was to weigh the money, and of the man who was to count the towers of the walls which the Assyrians had planned to capture: "Where are all of them!" Isaiah says, "All of them will be gone." Out of the number of these significant questions Paul selects only the one concerning "the scribe" and, like Isaiah, asks, "Where is the scribe?" i. e., anyone that is a γραμματεύς. To these two questions which allude to Isaiah's words of old Paul adds a question of his own, one that he regards as necessary in this connection, for which, however, the Old Testament furnishes no reference or no suggestion: "Where is the disputer of this age?"

While σοφός is a general expression and may designate any man that is governed by worldly wisdom, the term exactly describes the people in Corinth who were captivated by their bit of philosophy. The Greeks surely loved their σοφία, "wisdom," and extended themselves to become σοφοί. The two other terms bear even a more precise reference. For γραμματεύς is the regular Jewish term for "scribe," one who is learned in the Jewis law; and συζητητής is the regular Hellenic term for a "disputant" in the Greek philosophic schools and in their general discussions and debates. They sought to become expert in philosophical learning and in dialectical skill. The genitive "of this age" or "of this world age" is to be construed only with "disputer" and not with all three terms, for "the disputer of this age" is an expression that was coined by Paul himself while the other two terms were borrowed from Isaiah.

The term αἰών denotes an era, but one that is marked by what occurs in it and is thus stamped with a peculiar character. The Scriptures distinguish "this world age" from "the age to come." The former denotes the world era in which we now live, which is marked by sin in all its manifestations; the latter denotes the blessed eternity that shall follow this present era. In a sense it is, of course, true that the wise, the scribe, and the disputer belong to this world age, for the three operate only with worldly, transient, spurious wisdom. In fact, they never get beyond this wisdom. It is the gospel alone which connects us with the era to come, and this gospel is the truth which all the wise of this world reject as long as they remain only worldly wise. Summing up, we may say: σοφός = one who is versed in a subject, here in philosophic ideas; γραμματεύς = one who is versed in literature; συζητητής = one who is versed in the art of discussion. All three of these abilities may, of course, be possessed by one person, for the Jewish scribes were also fond of disputing and of arguing, as were the Greek sophists.

Since the second reference to Isaiah introduces also the Jewish idea of σοφία, Paul's three questions cover the entire domain of mere human or worldly wisdom, no matter by whom or in what manner it is traversed. If the Corinthians sought some of this "wisdom" in the heralds of the gospel, whether in the Jewish form of legalistic teaching after the manner of a "scribe" or in the Hellenistic form after the manner of a Greek "disputer" or dialectician, they were surely wrong.

This is made self-evident by the next question which implies an affirmative answer: "Did not God make foolish the wisdom of the world?" He most certainly did. All that the wise, the scribe, and the disputer have to offer is here summarized in the phrase "the wisdom of the world," the genitive of possession also characterizing this "wisdom" as belonging to the world (the world = men). The expression also reveals what this wisdom really is. All of this world wisdom God turned into silliness, and the aorist ἐμώρανεν states the historic fact. Paul would, of course, not say that God wrought a change in this wisdom and made something else out of it, namely silliness; he merely showed what this wisdom really is, namely nothing but silliness. Men merely thought it wisdom; when God touched it, its true character of folly became evident.

21) When and how did God do this? We must have full proof for what Paul asserts as a fact. He furnishes that proof and introduces it with the logical γάρ, "for." **For since in the wisdom of God the world through its wisdom knew not God, God made it his good pleasure through the foolishness of preaching to save the believing.**

The world of men failed completely in regard to the one and supreme thing it needed: it did not know God. The aorist οὐκ ἔγνω states the whole tragic fact as a fact. Ἔγνω does not refer to mere intellectual knowledge but to the genuine realization which grips, holds, and dominates the entire person. Men never attained to this real knowledge of God; they did not know him. When he speaks to them in the gospel even today, they laugh; they do not think that it is God speaking. See John 8:19 regarding the Jews with reference to this point; even though they talked about God and boasted about him they did not know him.

In the New Testament ἐπειδή is not temporal but causal: "since." Here it introduces the reason that God employed such a thing as "foolishness" when he was dealing with the world in order to produce such a mighty result as salvation. The phrase "in the wisdom of God" is strongly emphatic by reason of its position. The article as well as the genitive mark this as a particular, specific wisdom, namely God's own wonderful wisdom. This genitive "of God" shows, on the one hand, whose thoughts of wisdom are contained in this wisdom and, on the other hand, what character this wisdom thus possesses.

The preposition ἐν marks a sphere: God placed men, the whole world of men, into this sphere which was entirely filled with his wisdom, and yet despite all this they did not know him. Here is a grand universe of wisdom spread out before the eyes and the hearts of men and surrounding them on every side: all the wonderful, incomprehensible thoughts of God in the whole round of nature, the works of his creation and his providence, the whole course of history, the wondrous constitution of man himself, a *cosmos in parvo*, and, in the case of the Jews, even the Old Testament revelation in addition. All this substance of divine wisdom lay before the world of men (ὁ κόσμος) and normally should have had the effect that they should know the true God who was thus gloriously revealed, Acts 14: 15-17. But the very opposite resulted, Acts 17:23, etc.

Why? Because men applied their own foolish, worldly wisdom to this wondrous sphere of divine wisdom. They employed the wrong medium (διά). The world operated (and still does so) "through its wisdom," the substance of its own thinking and reasoning. Even the Jews read the Old Testament, not in its own light, but in the light of their own notions and their own desires and thus failed utterly to see the God of grace. As Jesus told them, God was not their Father, they did not know him; if they had known him they would unquestionably have recognized his Son, John 8:19, etc.

The world's wisdom always goes off into its own proud, self-sufficient, self-glorifying paths and thus blinds itself to God's wisdom which is spread out around it. The astronomer gazes at the miracle of the stars for years and then tells us with an air of finality that he has found no God. The natural scientist announces that the brutes are his ancestors and declares that all life has evolved from a tiny cell that was found in the primordeal slime. Pantheism proclaims: "God is all, and all is God." So the catalog of human achievement lengthens and proclaims what "the world" "through its wisdom" (using it as a medium) has done and still does "in the wisdom of God" (in this vast sphere of most wondrous wisdom).

This is true even of the church. When the wisdom of revelation as it is found in the Scriptures is read through the medium of our own preconceived notions ("through its wisdom"), the true knowledge of God and of salvation or of some blessed divine doctrine is perverted ("did not know"). Not even intellectually did the world know God, to say nothing about having attained to spiritual and saving knowledge. The result of the world's "wisdom" shows it to be altogether μωρία, "foolishness." Paul's proof is incontrovertible. But by stating this proof for the fact he asserted Paul also shows *why* God then proceeded as he did (ἐμώρανεν, made foolish the world's wisdom).

We now learn also *how* God proceeded when he made foolish the world's wisdom. He did so in a most astounding way. He did it by the silliness of preaching. Paul writes, "It was God's good pleasure" to proceed in this matter as he did, εὐδόκησεν, he "pleased" to do so (we also have the noun εὐδοκία, God's "good pleasure"). The verb as well as the noun signify 1) God's free determination; 2) a determination that is good and gracious toward those concerned. Nothing compels God, he is moved to act by his own heart and will. And again, when his good pleasure acts it always blesses; it is never God's εὐδοκία to destroy or to damn. God's good pleasure is the expression of his saving love and grace. In determining his gracious plans God, of course, took into account the condition of the world as Paul here describes it. Whereas the world failed because it used the false medium of its own wisdom ("through its wisdom"), God chose the very opposite kind of a medium; instead of "wisdom" he actually took "foolishness," silliness, the last thing anyone would expect him to take, "the foolishness of preaching."

Be sure to note the correspondence of the two διά phrases, and that in each instance the preposition introduces a medium. By employing foolishness where the world used wisdom God really made a joke of the world and of its lofty wisdom. This is, however, the blessed irony of divine love. For whereas the world failed utterly with its tremendous show of wisdom, God succeeded without the least trouble with this tiny medium that looks so useless and even so childish.

"Preaching," κήρυγμα, is not the act of making a proclamation but the contents of what is proclaimed. The verb κηρύσσειν = to announce as a herald, κῆρυξ, and is one of the standard terms for preaching. To announce as the Savior of the world one who died the vile death of a criminal on the cross seems, indeed, to be the acme of foolishness. To expect that this announcement will do what all the world with its mighty effort of wisdom failed to do, namely actually to lift man up again into communion with God, only intensifies the impression of utter foolishness. In all the world such a scheme was never heard of.

But we should note carefully that in this proceeding God breaks completely with the σοφία or wisdom of the world. Not even in one slight point does he accommodate himself to this wisdom. He runs directly counter to it. That shows the great mistake we make when we try to make Christ palatable to our age (as we call it), try to accomodate the gospel to men and to their wisdom and their ways of thinking, try to make the κήρυγμα or proclamation reasonable to them. The gospel is not even an argument, a piece of reasoning that is gauged to convince men; it is only an announcement. And the astounding thing about this announcement is the fact that it meets men's hearts square on, in a direct clash, that it aims to reverse them completely, to set them going in the very opposite direction. It intends to convert, to turn them completely around; nothing less. God does not even use a special degree of γνῶσις (compare ἔγνω) or "knowledge" so that only people who are educated to the necessary philosophic degree may be reached. In fact, this "foolishness" that God chose differs even from the "wisdom" he revealed in nature, etc., before men's eyes. Search the world of nature as we will, it does not even put us on the track of the gospel.

And yet this "foolishness" succeeds: σῶσαι, the aorist infinitive states what is actual, it actually saves, rescues, delivers; it accomplishes the very thing the perishing world needs, the mighty thing which it could and did not attain with all its wisdom. Of what benefit is all the wisdom of this world or, for that matter, all else that men have in this world if it fails to bring them salvation? But note well: "to save the believing." The divine κήρυγμα and πίστις are correlatives. The proclamation calls for faith and is received only by faith. The verb "to believe" as well as the noun, which in the Greek is derived from the same root (πιστεύειν and πίστις), denote the confidence and trust of the heart which rely on the gospel proclamation and on its contents. The present participle characterizes the persons: such as believe and go on believing or trusting the glad news. God revenged himself upon the wise world by using foolishness to bring about its salvation — but what a blessed revenge!

Both "the foolishness of preaching" and "believing" lie in a sphere that is entirely different from that in which "the wisdom of this world," the wisdom of "the wise, the scribe, and the disputer" operate, namely in the higher domain of spiritual contact which is wrought by God through the gospel of Christ. Again we should not imagine that God first tried the one way, σοφία and γνῶσις, and when that failed, used another, μωρία and πίστις, by which he then finally succeeded. While the foolishness of preaching was established for all nations during the New Testament era it also marked the entire Old Testament era back to the days of Adam. Faith is the door to salvation from the very beginning.

22) A second "since" introduces a parallel to the previous sentence, but a parallel that is elaborated in fuller detail. We have had the general term κόσμος, "world," we now have an explication of that term, "Jews and Greeks." **Since both Jews ask for signs and Greeks seek after wisdom, we, etc.**

The two καί, "both . . . and," combine Jews and Greeks into one great class and place them over against "we." They differ from each other, but their difference does not change their relation to the gospel. "Jews" are a prominent part of this general class, namely the great majority of their nation that persisted in unbelief; "Greeks" constitute another prominent part, and they are here named as the chief representatives of the Gentile or non-Jewish world. Paul does not add "barbarians," for the mention of the two most prominent classes is adequate in this connection. No articles are used, hence "Jews" as a class and "Greeks" as a class are referred to.

Whereas Paul previously uses the general term "the wisdom of the world" he now specifies the two grand types in which this world wisdom appears: the Jews "ask for signs" — this has come to be their characteristic; while Greeks "seek after wisdom" — this is their distinguishing mark. The Jews ask or require (αἰτοῦσι) signs because they had the Old Testament. That Testament promised great signs in connection with the Messiah, and when Jesus came, they felt that they had the right to require them. Now Jesus met the Old Testament promises most completely and wrought the very signs foretold by God in great abundance. He more than accredited himself and thus pleads with the Jews: "Believe the works," John 14:11. But instead of following the Old Testament the Jews applied their own wisdom to its promises and thus expected a Messiah who was equipped, not with signs of grace and mercy, but with signs "from heaven," juggling the clouds or making the moon and the stars play hide and seek.

The Greeks were of a different type. Having no Bible, they were left to their own thoughts and their own reasonings. They accordingly sought ($ζητοῦσι$), tried to attain, "wisdom," something in the way of a rational explanation of the universe and of their own being. They demanded principles, chains of reasoning, systems of philosophy which began with some fixed point and reached out as far as possible from that. They found, too, what they were seeking after. But what they found was like shifting sand, for one system abrogated another, and they finally ended in a skepticism like that of Pilate who exclaimed: "What is truth?"

Both of these types of world wisdom still persist but now in modernized form. Some want the church to heal all social and even all physical evils. They demand an imposing, outward ecclesiastical organization that will sweep the world before it. They look for a millennium and the outward triumph of the gospel over all the world. Signs, signs, big tangible, overpowering results! Others bank on their reason; they assume that their intellect is able to penetrate into everything. So they follow philosophy in its latest forms, "science" with its claims and hypotheses, other kinds of modern learning, and refuse to take seriously anything else.

All these fail, and in the very nature of the case must fail.

23) Whereas previously Paul says that "it was God's good pleasure" he now writes ἡμεῖς, "we," the preachers of the gospel through whom God sends out his proclamation. Since both Jews and Greeks are on the wrong track, **we preach Christ crucified, to Jews a deathtrap, to Gentiles foolishness.**

Paul defines succinctly what he means by "the foolishness of preaching." What is this "foolishness"? "Christ crucified." Christ, the One whom God anointed as our Redeemer, died on the cross and won salvation for the world. The perfect participle ἐσταυρωμένον states that, once crucified, Christ now stands before us continuously as such. The fact of his crucifixion has become something permanent and enduring from the very moment when that fact occurred. This crucified Christ is both the sum of the gospel and the center from which every part of the gospel radiates, and in which all of its parts meet. This Christ "we preach," κηρύσσομεν, the proper verb for κήρυγμα, "we proclaim" as God's heralds, shout him out to the ears of the world. The present tense means that this is our one, constant business.

The amplification is extended by two datives which are marked by the particles of correspondence μέν and δέ. The translation: "to Jews a stumbling block," is incorrect and one that misses the main point. One may stumble, even fall and rise again, but the word used here refers to something that is fatal and deadly. A σκάνδαλον (later form of σκαδάληθρον) is the stick of a trap to which the bait is fixed and by which the trap is sprung, metaphorically an offense, but always one that is fatal in its effects. The figure is that of a deathtrap which kills the victim. What acts thus for the Jews and makes them reject Christ is the fact of his having been crucified. From this fact, of course, result many other things such as the complete abrogation of circumcision and of the ceremonial law, the absence of the signs they expected, etc. But this offense ceases entirely the moment the false wisdom that lies at the root of it is given up and recognized as spurious.

Now the second dative: "to Gentiles foolishness." The word "Gentiles" is a wider term which embraces all non-Jews and thus makes plain what Paul means by Greeks who, because of their culture and their learning, were the upper class and thus the chief representatives of all Gentiles. In their wisdom these Gentiles scoff at the very idea that Christ's blood should expiate the world's guilt. "Anything but that!" they reply. The whole story of Christ is so much silliness to them. The old "blood theology" still has these opponents who consider it μωρία.

24) The two depressing datives are followed by a third which sounds a tone of joy and triumph: **but to the called, Jews as well as Greeks, Christ, God's power and God's wisdom.**

The two terms "deathtrap" and "foolishness" are not to be regarded subjectively, a trap and a foolishness *in the opinion* of Jews and of Gentiles, but objectively as expressing *God's intention;* for he intended them to be nothing less than an actual trap and actual foolishness to this worldly wisdom. Christ was that and is that today, and God wants it so. This gives us the clue to the third dative: "to the called, Jews as well as Greeks." This third class is composed of both Jews and Greeks, ethnologically considered, and becomes one class by being freed from its former false worldly wisdom. These people are now "the called" (see v. 2), and the verbal states that God called them (by the gospel) and that this call proved effective in them by separating them from "the world." The called are the saved mentioned in v. 18 and the believing mentioned in v. 21.

In σωζόμενοι, those that are being saved, the reference is to the divine agent who saves and to the supreme blessing which he bestows, namely salvation. In κλητοί, the called, there is the same reference to the agent and another to the effective means employed, namely the call (gospel). While these two terms show what has happened *to* us, πιστεύοντες shows what has occurred *in* us: we ourselves believe, but in response to the proclamation which came to us and called forth faith in our hearts. Hodge repeats Calvin's teaching: "There is a twofold call of the gospel; the one external by the Word; and the other internal by the Spirit." Paul teaches that there is one and only one call, namely that contained in ἡ μωρία τοῦ κηρύγματος, "the foolishness of preaching," the Word, the gospel. This call is identical for all men. Paul tells us here that some reject this call and that others are won by it. The Word and the Spirit are never separated; where the Word is, there is the Spirit, and where the Spirit is, there is the Word. The κλητοί of our passage received no other call than did the Jews and the Greeks who resisted its gracious power.

Again, not merely subjectively *in the opinion* of the called, but objectively *in fact*, the Christ whom we preach is both "God's power" and "God's wisdom," who is proved as such by the successful call of the κλητοί. In their own experience they have found Christ to be that. In both expressions "God" is emphatic: *God's* wisdom. What "the called" find Christ to be matches in a way what the foolish Jews and Greeks require and seek. The Jews require signs; but these could be wrought only by God's power. Yet the most stupendous signs wrought by omnipotence in the skies could not save a single Jew; but this power of God, the power of his grace in Christ Jesus, did save both Jews and Greeks. The Greeks seek wisdom, speculative, earthly wisdom. Yet all the philosophies and all the sciences of these two millenniums have never saved a single Gentile. This the wisdom of God alone has done, actually and wondrously saved both Jews and Greeks. "God's wisdom" is in a sense "foolishness"; unregenerate reason always thinks so. But the fact that this "foolishness" does actually save proves, not by a system of philosophic reasoning that is intended for the intellect, but by actual fact and reality as exhibited in "the called" that are saved, that this "foolishness" is "God's wisdom."

The idea of "power" is new in this paragraph, yet it is involved in the term "to save," v. 21, for only power can do that; and it is implied in the demand for "signs," for only power can work them. Power and wisdom conjoin in the description of "Christ" as the content of the saving proclamation of the gospel. Power and wisdom are inseparable attributes in God. Both are needed for accomplishing our salvation. So Christ is both in one, God's power, God's wisdom. Only divine wisdom could plan to make Christ crucified known in the world by means of the gospel, and only divine power, the power of grace, could execute this plan of wisdom and actually do this saving by it. The emphatic genitives "God's" characterize this power and this wisdom as being infinitely above everything that is merely human, above all that human minds could possibly conceive. Yet the caution should be added never to confuse *this* power of God with his omnipotence, for we are saved by the power of grace, love, mercy, attributes that are altogether distinct from omnipotence.

25) That Christ is God's power and God's wisdom is seen from a subjective fact, that experienced by the called who are actually and in fact saved through Christ. Paul does not rest with that thought. He adds the objective proof, for even apart from the called it is true and a mighty fact which the Corin-

thians and all of us should keep before our eyes that God's power and his wisdom are supreme. Why is it that the called have the experience they do? **Because the foolishness of God is wiser than men, and the weakness of God is stronger than men.**

It is difficult to render the exact meaning of the Greek into English, for instead of the abstract term μωρία, our English "foolishness," which Paul has been using thus far he now writes τὸ μωρὸν τοῦ Θεοῦ, which we can reproduce only in an awkward way: "the thing that is foolish on God's part." The context shows that Paul has in mind, not merely the general quality of foolishness, but beyond that also the foolish thing itself with which God operates, which is Christ crucified. We see that this neuter τὸ μωρόν continues to match the idea of σοφία or wisdom. To match the other idea, that of δύναμις or power, Paul again uses the neuter τὸ ἀσθενὲς τοῦ Θεοῦ, "the thing that is weak on God's part," instead of the abstract ἀσθένεια, "God's weakness." Again, as the context shows, Christ crucified is referred to. Compare II Cor. 13:4: "He was crucified through weakness, yet he liveth through the power of God"; to which Paul adds: "For we also are weak in him, but we shall live with him through the power of God toward you." By using these two neuters Paul avoids ascribing the abstract qualities of foolishness and of weakness to God as though they were two of his actual attributes, for as attributes both of them are contradictory to God's very being.

God indeed uses a foolish and a weak thing in giving salvation to a world that loves to see wisdom and power in its own false fashion, but this foolish thing on God's part "is wiser than men," and this weak thing on his part "is stronger than men." Only the two facts are stated, and they are to impress us as facts. Yet they imply so much with regard to God that our minds cannot grasp it all. God moved only a little finger, as

First Corinthians 1:25, 26

it were, in confounding the proud notions of wisdom and of power which the world entertained. What might have happened if he had called on all the resources of his infinite wisdom and power? He made only a slight move, as it were, one that appears so inadequate, but behold its actual tremendous effect! For it is surely a foolish and a weak thing to let God's own Son die miserably on the cross; it did not only appear so to men although it did that, too, in the highest degree. And yet this foolish and this weak thing outranks and absolutely outdoes all the wisdom and all the power of men, not only the wisdom and the power they actually possess, but also all that they conceive in their minds. If men were asked how God should proceed to save the world they would certainly not say by sending his Son to the cross. Yet this is what God did, and, behold, this act saves! So wise is this foolish thing, so powerful this weak thing. The adjective ἰσχυρότερον has in it ἰσχύς, *Staerkebesitz*, inherent strength, irrespective of whether it is put forth or not. It is thus distinguished from κράτος, strength that is put forth. This fits well the idea of Christ crucified as here presented, for inherent in his cross but not outwardly displayed at all is this strength of God that exceeds all that men know.

26) We may begin a new paragraph with v. 26 as also the address "brethren" would lead us to do. Yet the line of thought begun in v. 18 continues, and the connective γάρ shows that the subject is to be further elucidated. This also explains why Paul ends v. 25 with a duality, power and wisdom, and does not bring the two down to a unit. For it is his custom — an evidence of his great mastery in thinking through the great realities of God — first to expand a truth in two, three, or more lines as may be required and then to focus these lines into their one true, unified center where they come to rest. In no secular writer

has the author ever found anything to compare with the mastery found in Paul.

So Paul begins with γάρ as if he would say: What I have just told you about this wisdom of God's μωρόν and this strength of God's ἀσθενές you can actually see in your own selves. **For look at your calling, brethren, that there are not many wise after the flesh, not many powerful, not many wellborn.** The Corinthians need only look at their own κλῆσις, the call of grace that came to them through the gospel and by its power of grace made them what they now are, namely κλητοί. Let them glance over the list of members in Corinth. The verb is imperative: "look at," not indicative: "you see," for the former fits the connection exactly.

What Paul wants the Corinthians to see is the plain fact that is open to all eyes that care to take note of it, "that there are not many wise," etc. This ὅτι clause is epexegetical to τὴν κλῆσιν ὑμῶν, and we need supply only "are," εἰσί. The great majority of the membership of the Corinthian congregation consisted of plain people although there were among them some men of intellectual and even political and social standing. There were slaves who stood very low in the social scale, freedmen or former slaves who were now set free who enjoyed a somewhat higher standing, and also men like Stephanas, Crispus, Sosthenes, and Erastus, the city treasurer (Rom. 16:23). "Not many wise," etc., means, of course, that there were at least some in the Corinthian congregation who belonged to the higher classes. Paul does not need to say that they dropped all carnal pride in regard to their outward standing when they yielded to "the call." But the fact is outstanding: God does not choose worldly greatness, he rejects it. His principle runs counter to that of the "world" most directly and emphatically. Where men have this type of worldly greatness, all pride in it is removed from their hearts when grace humbles them at the foot of the cross.

We now see why Paul left the duality in v. 25 and did not reduce it to a unity; he intends to expand and to broaden it before he finally reduces it to a unit. So he now enlarges it by the use of three terms: the wise, the powerful, and the wellborn. The first of these terms must have a modifier, "after the flesh," to indicate what sort of "wise," σοφοί, Paul has in mind. For the Scriptures, too, make us "wise unto salvation through faith which is in Christ Jesus," II Tim. 2:15. "Wise after the flesh" means wise after the norm or judgment of the flesh (κατά is frequently so used); and "flesh" marks the sinful and depraved character of the "world." When anyone is thus wise after his own fleshly and worldly conceit and is drawn and won by God's gracious call, his foolish conceit disappears through the humility of faith.

The other two terms are clear without a modifying phrase. The δύνατοι are those who are able and thus "mighty" to do far more than others. They may wield authority in one way or in another, be men who command respect by what they do and are capable of doing. The first two terms follow the two categories which Paul has thus far used, the third adds another, "the wellborn," or noble, the aristocracy of birth, "blue blood." Grace reaches even this high class and wins notable converts from it. In Corinth there were some converts from the so-called "best families."

27) When Paul now states whom God did choose by means of his gracious call he expands this idea still more. He names four groups and then climaxes these four with a comprehensive and astonishing final group which also embraces these four. This is typical of Paul. He first expands widely and then concentrates all into a vital feature. **On the contrary, God chose the foolish things of the world**

in order that he might put to shame the men that are wise; and God chose the weak things of the world in order that he might put to shame the things that are strong; etc.

These two groups are known to us from preceding statements, yet we note important new features regarding them in Paul's restatement. When Paul repeats he loves to add; compare the two statements of Jesus to Nicodemus, John 3:3, 5; also Mark 10:23, 24. In the category of "wisdom" Paul has thus far used the abstract term μωρία or "foolishness" to indicate the opposite of "wisdom" and the neuter singular τὸ μωρόν or "the foolish thing." He now adds the neuter plural τὰ μωρά or "the foolish things" in order to make the present statement entirely general so as to include not only persons as such but likewise some feature in or about them and, in fact, anything whatsoever that bears a character of this kind. The genitive τοῦ κόσμου, the foolish things "of the world," is added and is twice repeated in order to designate these things as being foolish in the evaluation of the world.

Not accidentally did God select the foolish things but purposely. He intended to heap shame on the σοφοί of the world. We should note that this term is masculine: the people or the men who are wise. Our versions are a little indefinite on this point. Note that in the next statement the corresponding term is not masculine but neuter. The world's "wise men" are covered with honor, they bear high titles and university degrees, they have great fame and are looked upon as final authorities. Their professional pride is often according. With God, however, they have no standing whatever, they are completely cast out. They must be because all the σοφία of these worldly σοφοί is spurious and opposed to God.

When God chose the foolish things of the world his purpose was to heap shame on these men. The verb κataισχύνειν may mean to fill with the feeling of shame, *beschaemen*, or to bring to shame and disgrace, *in Schande bringen;* here the latter meaning is in place. This divine purpose is already fulfilled, for its date coincides with God's elective act which has occurred in the past. In the presence of God shame is already their lot. Here in the world they still strut in high honor, but this strutting is all a hollow show, about to burst like a bubble the moment the election of God is revealed at the last day.

The next statement is nearly an exact parallel. This refers to the category of power. God chose "the weak things of the world," the neuter plural is exactly like the one found in the previous statement. So also is the purpose clause: "in order to put to shame the things that are strong" (with inherent strength, compare v. 25). There is a change in the neuter plural: "strong things" whereas the previous statement has "wise men." This expression does not, of course, intend to exempt the strong men, for this neuter plural embraces the entire category, whoever and whatever is strong in the eyes of the world. God intends to disgrace all of it by his choice. He did so when he made his choice and shall do so when the effect of it shall be fully revealed. God was constrained to proceed in this manner because all the strong things in the κόσμος (world) of men are only strong shams, with no reality of strength in their make-up, and full of hostility against God. The whole world lieth in wickedness.

28) The third statement takes up the new category that is added in v. 26, "the wellborn": **and the base things of the world,** τὰ ἀγενῆ, the very opposite of οἱ εὐγενεῖς, and again we note the neuter plural of the entire category (persons and things in the widest sense). "The base things" are the baseborn things or more exactly the things that have nothing whatever in their birth or origin to distinguish

them, the commonest of the common. These God chose. This is an astounding fact when we think of the claims, honors, and pride of the people who deem themselves "wellborn." Paul is not pedantic, and he does not add: "in order to put to shame the things that are wellborn." There is no need to say it, we already know it.

So he at once adds: **and the things that are accounted as nothing,** as οὐδέν. Even the genitive "of the world" is dropped since, having read thus far, we have it in mind. The perfect participle = the things that were at one time set down as being nothing at all by the world and continue to be thus rated as nil. We are on the way to an anticlimax and certainly have descended very far. We laugh at things foolish; we scorn or pity the weak; we despise things base and common; and we utterly disregard things rated as nothing. The translation of our versions: "things that are despised," is not exact enough and may mislead. For the third and last time Paul repeats **God chose** and thus drives home this astounding fact. Each time the Greek reads: ἐξελέξατο ὁ Θεός. It is almost like a refrain, the subject and the predicate are reversed and each is thus made emphatic by its position. Moreover, both are emphatic in the Greek because of their position after the objects; and this occurs three times in succession. The composition as composition is masterly.

One might well be excused if he should suppose that when Paul reaches "the things accounted as nothing" he has come to the end of the anticlimax. Yet there is one last and still lower step that Paul does not fail to see: **and the things that are not,** that do not even exist. While this is the lowest step in the series, beyond which even the mind cannot go, it is at the same time more. Paul himself indicates that by not repeating: "God chose." It is, of course, again God and his choice which take these things that are minus even an existence; there is no need to say it as far as that is concerned.

But when we are told that God chose for himself things that do not even exist, this last group in reality includes the four groups previously mentioned. A new light thus flashes back upon those four other groups. In foolish things true wisdom does not exist; in weak things true strength does not exist; in baseborn things true (divine) origin does not exist; in things that are counted as nothing true value does not exist. Nil runs through all four of them, something that does not exist. While this nil is one that the judgment of the world affixes to these four groups which it casts aside, the judgment of God in regard to these groups is by no means the reverse as if he has keener eyes than the world and sees wisdom, strength, good birth, and good value in these things and therefore chooses them. Quite the contrary; God, too, sees the nothingness in them.

When this is perceived, we shall see that Paul did not assemble five groups and range them in succession. He and we use only four to form a complete line. The fifth specification, "things that do not exist," is not coordinate with the preceding four. Non-existence could be paired only with one other, namely existence. Now all these four are in reality hollow with non-existence, but in each of the four this is a non-existence of something specific, of wisdom, strength, etc. These types of non-existence end with the fourth group. What Paul now adds is non-existence itself. The nil in the four is a *nil privativum*; the nil Paul states at the end is the *nil negativum*: non-existence itself. In this masterly way the four cords that dangle apart from each other are tied into a final knot. Did God choose lack of this and lack of that? Why, he chose very lack itself!

The negative μή in τὰ μὴ ὄντα is altogether regular with a participle, and nothing subjective should be read into it. The question as to whether actual non-existence is referred to or only an existence that amounts to nothing is often answered in favor of the latter. But the fourth group means this, namely "things reckoned as nothing." Besides, this raises the question as to in whose opinion "things non-existing" amount to nothing. It cannot be in God's opinion because in three previous groups Paul writes "of the world"; yet it also cannot be in the world's opinion because the world cannot possibly have an opinion regarding what does not exist. "The things that are not" simply are not apart from the opinion of anyone. Yet, although they are non-existent, God already sees, knows, and even chose them. Do you ask what they are? The new life God's grace creates in our hearts, our faith and our good works, our glory to be when we reach heaven. These God chose for himself before any of them were.

Three times Paul writes ἐξελέξατο ὁ Θεός with the resulting emphasis. The middle voice = God chose for himself; and the aorist, by a definite past act. This is really an eternal act although no modifier to that effect is added. It antedates the "call" in time, for on it the call rests and from it the call springs. The fact that God chose at all, and that he chose as he did, is due solely to himself. Yet this elective act is neither blind nor arbitrary, for he chose according to certain fixed and definite principles which are here revealed to us. God elected the foolish, the weak, and the despised things of the world, not because in men of this class there is anything meritorious and deserving above others. He chose also some who are wise, great, noble, etc., not, indeed, as such, but as men whom he is able to make lowly and humble like the others he chose. There can be no merit in foolishness and lack of culture, in weakness and lack of strength, in baseness of birth, in complete good-for-nothingness, and, to sum it all up, in utter non-existence. How could there be?

First Corinthians 1:28, 29 79

Yet God can work only where there is nothing. God can enter only where the place is not already filled. Only where God can first sweep out what is "of the world" can he bring in what is "of the kingdom of heaven."

We again have a purpose clause: **in order that he might bring to nought the things that are.** For this reason God chose "the things that are not." The two purpose clauses found in v. 27 that Paul writes out, as well as the two others he might have written out in the first half of v. 28, merge in this final purpose clause which deals with all the things the world has. "The things that are," τὰ ὄντα, embrace everything men see, know, admire, handle, everything they count as valuable and real. These things actually exist, such as worldly wisdom, power, good birth, etc., and are thus the opposites of the things that do not exist, such as no wisdom, no power, no nobility, no money, etc. Yet, while these things exist, they are all merely transient. They are a vain show and nothing more. Therefore it is a true, right, and most beneficial purpose that God expose them in their vanity and non-value lest men go on relying upon them to their everlasting disappointment and loss. In the previous purpose clauses the verb employed is "put to shame"; here it is more intense: "to bring to nought," to put completely out of commission, to abolish. The aorist intensifies the completeness: "actually abolish." This purpose is fufilled throughout the ages and will reach its ultimate fulfillment at the last day when the last of the things of the world that are will be swept out of existence forever.

29) A final purpose clause concludes all that Paul says regarding God's choosing: **that no flesh should glory in the presence of God.** We may call this the grand ultimate purpose. For this reason, it seems, Paul uses the rarer conjunction ὅπως (always

with μή when it is negative) and makes this ultimate purpose stand out from the previous minor purposes that are introduced by ἵνα. The Greek idiom joins the negative to the verb: "not glory," whereas the English joins it to the subject: "no flesh." Back of this ultimate purpose there lie two thoughts: first, that all flesh is everlastingly trying to glory in God's presence, and that God stops it on this account; secondly, that no flesh really has anything in which to glory, it only thinks it has, it only deceives and cheats itself, and that therefore for very truth's sake and in order to undeceive men themselves God must stop this glorying. All have come short of the glory of God. Their only hope is to realize their utter emptiness. Then God will fill them with his own blessed and saving realities. "Flesh" means man in his fallen state, and the context allows us to include all that pertains to man in this state. "In the presence of God" reads as if the hour of judgment is referred to when man faces God, any hour when that happens.

30) In v. 26 Paul asks the Corinthians to look at themselves and at the character of their membership. In v. 27-29 the divine principle back of this kind of membership is described. In v. 30 Paul returns to the Corinthians and rounds out the thought begun in v. 26. **Now of him are you in Christ Jesus, who was made wisdom to us from God and righteousness and sanctification and redemption.**

The main emphasis is on ἐξ αὐτοῦ, "of him," and δέ is merely transitional (not "but"). The fact that the Corinthians are now what they are is due wholly to God; ἐκ denotes the originating cause, *das ursaechliche Ausgehen*. Eph. 2:8: "not of yourselves, it is the gift of God." "Of him" overthrows all the wisdom, power, etc., of the world at one blow. If any of the Corinthians are admiring these spurious values they must now feel ashamed. They can import nothing that is admirable or valuable from the world. God alone is the source and the cause of all that they really are in Christ Jesus.

Paul writes ὑμεῖς, "you," which gives this word some emphasis, but he does not place it first in the sentence and make it contrast with the wise, great, etc., in the world. The silent contrast is between what the Corinthians now are (ὑμεῖς ἐστέ) and what they once were. They are now "in Christ Jesus," in saving union with him (he is named according to his person and his work). To be "in Christ" is a phrase that is constantly used by Paul; hence we construe: "you are in Christ." We do not associate the phrase with the whole sentence: "of him are you" (and this) "in Christ." "In Christ" = in union and communion with him. This union is mediated objectively by the Word, subjectively by faith. So every believer of the Word is "in Christ," in vital, blessed connection with him.

And now there follows the wonderful description of what it really means to be "in Christ," a description that is intended to contrast tremendously with the poor things of which the world boasts so proudly and, secondly, with the original emptiness and poverty of those whom God has chosen. Grammatically this description is a relative clause joined to "Christ Jesus": "who," etc. The aorist passive ἐγενήθη "became," "was made," has the force and the meaning of the middle ἐγένετο; the Koine coined many such passive forms and loved to use them. The sense is, of course, not passive. The tense is historical. No stress at all rests on ἡμῖν, "us." Paul now joyfully includes himself and, in fact, all his fellow Christians. That means that we should not refer "became" to the moment when the Corinthians were joined to Christ, i. e., when he subjectively became theirs by faith; but to the moment when Christ wrought out our redemption on the cross, then for the Corinthians, for Paul, and for all of us he "became" objectively what Paul now states. And the phrase "from God," like "of him" (God), once more stresses the divine source over against anything that comes from "the world." The preposition ἀπό has the thought of transition from God to us.

Are the Corinthians desiring "wisdom," actual wisdom? In Christ they have the very highest and the most blessed wisdom that comes to them from God himself. This σοφία consists of all the gracious, heavenly, and efficacious thoughts of God that are embodied in Christ Jesus, which enlighten our souls, to which *sophia* there is none comparable. Paul might have stopped with this statement regarding Christ's being made wisdom for us but he expands the idea by adding four infinite treasures that lie in Christ and are ours and once more uses four to indicate completeness.

We do not translate τε καί "both . . . and": "both righteousness and holiness," to which pair there would be added: "and redemption." These three would then, as an epexegesis, define "wisdom." But this epexegesis would give "wisdom" a sudden new sense that would be contrary to the one this term has thus far had. The little τε intends to connect σοφία and δικαιοσύνη, and the two καί add the other two nouns. We note, however, that the idea of δύναμις or power, which was hitherto joined with σοφία or wisdom, is now omitted, for none of the three terms added to wisdom contains the special idea of power. When he is displaying what Christ is to us who are joined to him Paul reaches out into those glorious treasures about which the world knows nothing. We are blessed in Christ far beyond anything the world attempts. And δικαιοσύνη is the first of the three additions to wisdom. This is the *justitia imputata*, that quality which is ours when God's verdict acquits the believer for Christ's sake. Where has the world anything to compare with that? This term is always forensic. There is a judge, a court with its bar of justice, one who stands at that bar, and a verdict pronounced by the judge, in this case a verdict of acquittal. Read Rom. 3:21-30, and see the word in C.-K.

Next is ἁγιασμός, "sanctification" in the narrow sense, since it is subsequent to righteousness in the present connection (compare v. 2) and here indicates a life of good works. Christ dwells in us, and our thoughts, words, and deeds show it. The world knows of no such inner transforming power. The very idea of "holiness" is foreign to its mind, for the essence of holiness is separation from the world and devotion unto God.

Finally ἀπολύτρωσις, which, because of its position after the preceding terms, cannot signify the original "redemption" wrought by Christ on the cross but must refer to our own final "redemption" from sin and death through Christ and our translation into glory. The world has nothing to compare with this. All men are redeemed or ransomed because Christ paid the λύτρον or price of his sacrificial blood for all of them. But only those who benefit by this redemption eventually enter heaven. They are thus the redeemed in a narrow sense. The others spurn Christ's "redemption," these appropriate it by faith and reach its consummation by their transfer into glory.

Nothing less than this entire blessedness of our state of salvation is made ours in Christ Jesus. It embraces earth and heaven, time and eternity. What is contained in the aorist infinitive σῶσαι used in v. 21 is here unfolded. The fact that it can be only ἐξ αὐτοῦ, "of him," (God), is surely self-evident.

31) Paul now gathers all that he has said into a single focus in the way he usually loves to do when he comes to the end of a matter. He uses a purpose clause and parallels it with the one found in v. 29. There he writes in the negative: "that no flesh should glory in God's presence." Here he writes the cor-

responding positive: **that, even as it is written: He that glorieth, let him glory in the Lord!**

The final unit of thought into which Paul thus ties everything together and brings all to its resting point is our glorying: Let us glory, not in ourselves, but in the Lord! Paul abbreviates Jer. 9:23, 24: "Let not the wise man glory in his wisdom, neither let the mighty man glory in his might" (note the correlation of "wisdom" and of "power" which Paul himself has used); let not the rich man glory in his riches: but let him that glorieth glory in this, that he understandeth and knoweth me, that I am the Lord which exercise lovingkindness, judgment, and righteousness in the earth: for in these things I delight, saith the Lord." Paul retains the impressive imperative "let him glory" of the original Hebrew, although he writes a purpose clause. We may supply the subjunctive ᾖ after ἵνα: "in order that it may be even as it is written," etc., which makes the clause regular; or we may call this an anacoluthon (broken construction), one that is purposely employed by Paul. The latter view is entirely acceptable when we remember that Paul does purposely make use of an anacoluthon as a mode of expressing his thought. Paul is usually excused for employing such language on the ground that his thoughts so crowd in upon his mind that he at times breaks the construction of his sentences, but such an excuse is superficial because it fails to perceive that the anacoluthon is exactly what Paul chooses to express the desired thought. In regard to the formula of quotation, γέγραπται, perfect tense, see v. 19. We are, indeed, to glory, but in something that is far different from the glory of the world.

Does "in the Lord" refer to God or to Christ? The former is urged because "of him" in v. 30 and "in the presence of God" in v. 29 both refer to God; yet the reason for this interpretation may be the quiet support of subordinationism. On the other hand, it is urged that Christ is referred to by "the Lord" because of the emphatic phrase "in Christ Jesus" found in v. 30, and because in that verse all our spiritual blessings are connected with Christ. The question may be decided when the original of Jeremiah is consulted, for this speaks of *Yahweh*. To glory in the Lord means to stop all boasting and all reliance on ourselves and on anything in ourselves or produced by ourselves and with a trustful, joyful, thankful heart to sing the praises of him from whom all our spiritual blessings flow.

Summing up what Paul writes, we may say that it is the gravest and the most dangerous error to promulgate the gospel by means of the wisdom of the world, whether that be the wisdom of our present or of any previous age. For thus at least a part of the glory is withdrawn from Christ and transferred to this false wisdom. The real issue at stake in the Corinthian "wranglings" about men is clearly brought out. With all the energy at his command Paul determines to stop these disputes. All praise and all glory of men must cease, and the praise and the glory of God alone must prevail in Corinth and in the entire church.

CHAPTER II

III. The Preachers of the Wisdom of the Cross, Chapter 2

In order to draw the Corinthians still farther away from their "wranglings" (ἔριδες, 1:11) and their glorification of men or glorying in men Paul reminds them of the manner of his preaching among them when he founded their congregation. At the same time he reminds them of the result he intended to attain and did actually attain by this preaching.

1) Καί in κἀγώ attaches the new section to the previous one as it also tends in the same direction. After dwelling on the principles involved in the Corinthian contentions about men Paul now reminds the Corinthians of the contents of his preaching and of the way in which he preached when he first worked among them. **And I, having come to you, brethren, came not with excellency of statement or of wisdom, proclaiming to you the testimony of God.**

He, indeed, brought them this blessed testimony but he made no attempt to modify it so that in such a new garb it might appeal to them. The addition of the aorist participle ἐλθών to the aorist verb ἦλθον: I "having come . . . came" is not intended as an intensification of the idea of Paul's coming, for which there is no call here. In fact, the coming is subordinate to the main thought of proclaiming the testimony, and Paul might have written: "Having come, I did not proclaim," etc. By inserting "I came" and then proceeding with "not . . . proclaiming" Paul is more precise and says not merely that some time after his coming, but at once, simultaneous with his coming, he preached as he did.

It is pointless to dispute whether the κατά phrase is to be construed with "came" or with "proclaiming," for this present participle combines with the main verb to form one idea: "I came proclaiming." The next phrase adds the norm which Paul repudiated when he was making his proclamation to the Corinthians: "not with excellency of statement or of wisdom." These are not partitive genitives as though Paul used only a moderate and not an excessive amount of this excellency. The genitives are epexegetical or qualitative: Paul did not at all preach with an excellency that consists in λόγος or in σοφία. Any use of these means would have exalted them above the gospel, and the Corinthians might have been attracted by these means and not by the gospel.

Both λόγος and σοφία are entirely general here, they are without the article or other modifiers. They are also two separate concepts as the "or" indicates and are not combined as they were in 1:17, "wisdom of statement." Λόγος, as used by Paul, is equivalent to the German *Rede* so that "excellency of statement" = eloquent and persuasive oration after the fashion of the Greek orators. Such a presentation the wisdom of the world has to offer but never the gospel. The term σοφία is, of course, worldly wisdom and philosophy.

The dative "to you" is merely incidental and lacks all emphasis. Hence there is not a contrast as though Paul avoided these means only in the case of the Corinthians although he had employed them elsewhere. The following supposition is also contradicted, namely that at Athens, where Paul had been just before he came to Corinth, he had tried this "excellency" when speaking to the philosophers and had accomplished little through its use so that he now resolved to return to his old way of preaching. Also at Athens Paul preached as he had always done, and he did not fail there; quite the contrary. Paul's words imply rather that when he came to Corinth — and he probably had the same experience when he came to Athens — he felt a certain temptation, when speaking to these Greeks, to employ a manner of preaching that might have made a strong appeal to them, namely fine dialectical oration or striking speculative thought; but nothing of the kind was ever uttered by him.

The readings differ as to the object of "proclaiming." We much prefer: proclaiming "the testimony of God" instead of "the mystery" (see R. V. and margin). The genitive "of God" may be subjective: God did the testifying; it is scarcely objective: the testimony that deals with God, which is too general an expression to indicate the gospel. One may regard this as a genitive of origin: the testimony God has imposed on his witnesses. Then, too, "testimony" becomes significant, for every testimony given unto us must be repeated simply as it is. It dare not be altered or embellished with strange oratory or wisdom of our own.

2) Paul continues and explains (γάρ) what he did not do: **For I decided not to know anything among you save Jesus Christ, and him crucified.** Yet when he is thus explaining what he decided to cast aside Paul also mentions the positive means which he determined to use. Paul intimates that he knew well enough what would probably please and easily captivate the Corinthians, being what they were. He made his decision, ἔκρινα, to use nothing whatever of this sort. He remained true to his Lord and to himself. Did he risk failure or meager results? He did not allow that to sway him.

The plea that our age demands certain modifications of the gospel captivates many today, and they do not decide as Paul did. Of course, they intend to lose nothing of the gospel but only to aid it in finding more ready and widespread acceptance among men. But such good intentions on our part reflect on the Lord's intentions, who originally made the gospel what it is. His intentions always work out to the glory of his name, ours, even when they deviate only slightly from his, dim the glory of his name — may even darken that glory.

We may construe οὐ with ἔκρινα: "I did not decide to know a thing among you save," etc.; or with εἰδέναι: "I decided not to know," etc. There is little difference in force. In was Paul's decision to know only Christ crucified. Yet εἰδέναι, "to know," indicates that even in his own mind and not merely in his presentation Paul decided to know only Christ. This he decided in spite of the fact that the crucified Christ must of necessity be unpalatable to both Greeks and Jews in Corinth. The emphasis is on the participle ἐσταυρομένον; the cross always offends. The perfect participle states the past fact of the crucifixion and then the enduring effect of that fact: Christ, once crucified, is such forever. It is important to note that "Christ and him the one crucified" is in no way restrictive as though Paul presented only a portion of the gospel in Corinth and omitted other portions. Nor does Paul say: "I decided to use only the center of the gospel and to leave out the rest." "Jesus Christ as the one crucified" is the perfect summary of the entire gospel; whatever is not comprised in this summary is not gospel, not gospel in any sense.

Paul offers no excuse for preachers who desire to eliminate certain teachings of the gospel on the plea that they can thus reach and attract more people than if they insisted also on these teachings. Paul intends to omit, even in his own mind, any addition to the gospel, any admixture, any sugar-coating of it by human, worldly wisdom. He states the same truth in Gal. 3:1: "before whose eyes Jesus Christ was openly set forth crucified." "Crucified" means blood, death, sacrifice, atonement, substitution, reconciliation as the Scriptures show in full detail. The cross is reduced to a merely human level when, through human statement and wisdom, it is made to mean only martyrdom for one's convictions or is regarded as a mere symbol of love.

3) Paul once more draws attention to his own person: **And I in weakness and in fear and in much trembling got face to face with you.** The context does not suggest that Paul intends to contrast himself with other preachers who may feel more cheerful than he. This second "I" offers only additional information regarding the first "I." Verses 1 and 2 show that Paul discarded λόγος and σοφία and came only with the cross. Now we learn that even beyond that there was no personal impressiveness about Paul when he began his work in Corinth. The three phrases are placed before the verb for the sake of emphasis. The aorist ἐγενόμην πρὸς ὑμᾶς does not mean: "I was with you," which would take in the entire time of Paul's stay in Corinth; or: "I came to you," which Paul has already said in v. 1 with the correct verb ἦλθον. This is the German: *Ich geriet bei euch,* and πρός is reciprocal (Paul facing the Corinthians, and they him). Acts 18:9-11 sheds the only light we have on the condition into which Paul got when he arrived in Corinth to begin his work there. From this passage we learn that God cheered Paul by means of a vision at night, from which fact it is fair to conclude that he needed to be cheered. The surmise that Paul was thoroughly discouraged by failure in Athens, whence he had just come, does not rest on facts.

"Weakness" may well refer to poor physical condition or sickness. We should rid ourselves of the idea that Paul was always in robust health and was always physically fit. Those who would make him an epileptic have yet to prove their supposition. A man who was afflicted with this disease cannot use his brain as Paul constantly used his when he was composing his letters. The aorist reports a weakness that occurred only at this one time. A man who labored as intensely as Paul did, who traveled under the hardship of those days and endured in mind and in body what Paul bore, may well report that at one very inconvenient time, just when he began work in an important place and wished he were quite fit, he found himself "in (bodily) weakness."

While Paul merely parallels the three phrases, the latter two, "in fear and in much trembling," naturally go together as referring to his mental condition, which was a reaction to the physical. Fear and trembling refer, of course, not to concern for his own person, but for the work and its success in Corinth. The phrase πρὸς ὑμᾶς suggests Paul's facing the Corinthians in his poor condition; Robertson calls πρός the face-to-face preposition. Run down as he was, he was a poor figure to come πρός, face to face with people who admired oratory and philosophic presentation. Paul feared and trembled that his condition might work a prejudice against the blessed message he had to bring.

4) Paul succeeded in spite of his poor condition for the very reason that he threw aside mere human aids and relied on the divine. God once more showed that he had chosen for himself "the things that are accounted nothing," yea, "the things that are not." **And my statement and my preaching (were) not in persuasive words of wisdom but in demonstration of the Spirit and power, that your faith should not be in the wisdom of men but in the power of God.**

These are the highly significant facts which Paul bids the Corinthians remember. Paul uses two terms to describe the message he brought to Corinth: "my statement and my preaching," both of which include the substance and the form of its presentation. The repetition is for the sake of emphasis, and λόγος is broader than κήρυγμα which means any "statement" Paul made of the gospel plus the public "proclamation" he made in the synagogue. No verb is needed in the Greek. The thing that he spoke (λόγος), the thing that he announced as a herald (κήρυγμα) was devoid of "persuasive words of wisdom." The entire sphere (ἐν) indicates what Paul avoided. He used no philosophic terms, categories of thought, or reasonings that were calculated to captivate his hearers and to persuade their minds to assent.

Paul remained in an entirely different sphere (ἐν), "in the demonstration of the Spirit and power." The noun ἀπόδειξις is found nowhere else in the New Testament and denotes proof or demonstration of some proposition or of some claim or fact. The genitives can scarcely be subjective: proof offered by the Spirit and power; they are objective: proof demonstrating that the Spirit and power are present. Πνεύματος καὶ δυνάμεως are closely combined as forming a kind of unit, the latter is even without the article. There is no spiritual power — and none other is here referred to — apart from the Holy Spirit. And both are always connected with the λόγος and the κήρυγμα of the gospel. At no time and in no true presentation and for no hearer are the gospel λόγος and κήρυγμα ever minus the Holy Spirit and the saving power of his grace. The Corinthians thus experienced the *testimonium Spiritus sancti*. Some, indeed, resisted, but a goodly number were brought to faith and to a new life. It goes without saying that no "persuasive words" in the employment of human "wisdom" (the genitive is subjective) could have produced such a result.

5) While the purpose clause that now follows refers to v. 4, it really includes all that is stated in v. 1-4.

First Corinthians 2:5

To think that Paul expresses merely his own purpose is only a small part of the truth. Back of Paul's is God's purpose. It is he who wants our faith grounded on the true foundation: not "wisdom of men" but "power of God." Instead of connecting the negative particle μή with ἵνα, "lest," Paul connects it with the verb μὴ ᾖ, "may not be." The effect of this construction is to make the statement regarding human wisdom more weighty and independent: "may not be in the sphere of men's wisdom," to which for the sake of completeness there is added: "but in the sphere of God's power." This manner of stating the thought reflects the trouble found in Corinth where so many are inclined to rank the human too highly. "To be in," εἶναι ἐν, may, of course, refer to locality, but Paul constantly uses it with reference to a vital inner union and communion, the essence of which is faith, "may be in," i. e., in union with.

The plural "men's" wisdom deserves notice as a variant for "the wisdom of the world," 1:20. This plural denotes many men, and not only many as found in one generation but in successive generations. Their "wisdom" is not constant by any means, it changes completely from age to age. What a sorry thing when any man's confidence and trust (πίστις) in religious things is joined only (ἐν) to "men's wisdom" which changes ceaselessly because each new generation finds all manner of unreality, untruth, and falseness in the wisdom of the generations that have preceded. Such a "faith" would be disastrous. To found it on something that can never change because it is not the product of changing "men," ἄνθρωποι, "human beings," but of "God," that is safe, and that alone. Paul might write in God's "wisdom" but writes in God's "power," for the wisdom of God is not like that of men, only an intellectual product. Every thought of God is reality and thus power, a power that always and everywhere and to all eternity asserts itself and triumphs. Paul writes "power" but in the sense of 1:24: Christ crucified, "the power of God." This power of changeless grace is to be the basis of our faith. In order to realize this divine purpose (ἵνα) Paul preached as he did in Corinth and throughout his work. And this purpose was achieved in Corinth.

6) Paul has thus far exposed the vacuity of human wisdom. The stress is on this negative feature. Christ crucified appears to the world as foolishness. Yet this foolishness actually saves (σῶσαι, aorist, 1:21); this is a result which no human wisdom can bring to pass. Only incidentally, when he is exposing human wisdom, does Paul mention the fact that the foolishness of the cross is wisdom (1:24, 30). Now Paul develops the thought that the gospel is in reality the only genuine wisdom. Do the Corinthians want wisdom? Well, here it is, the one supreme wisdom in the whole universe!

Wisdom, now, we are speaking among those perfected, yet not the wisdom of this world age, nor of the rulers of this world age who are coming to nought.

"Wisdom" is placed emphatically forward, it is the theme of this grand paragraph. The particle δέ is both continuative and adversative. Whereas Paul has just written two ἐγώ he now writes λαλοῦμεν, "we are speaking," but he does not employ ἡμεῖς; and this unemphatic "we" runs through this section. It is not a majestic plural, for no writer uses such a plural immediately after he has employed two emphatic "I." Paul is using a true plural which includes all those who preach the gospel properly without, however, referring to any who may be preaching it faultily. And he uses λαλεῖν (not λέγειν) because the former means only to speak or give utterance. The real preachers of the gospel are only a voice through which God conveys the gospel to men. What this "wisdom" is to which they lend voice will now become clear.

There is much discussion in regard to ἐν τοῖς τελείοις, "among the perfected," although this phrase intends simply to designate the auditors among whom this speaking is done, namely those who have apprehended Christ. The view that οἱ τέλειοι designates the more mature Christians as distinguished from the νήπιοι or babes mentioned in 3:1, has the implication that Paul speaks something else to these babes, something that is not "God's wisdom." What could that be? The effort is also made to distinguish between that which is preached to the babes, namely only the elementary parts of the gospel, and that which is preached to the τέλειοι, namely the "wisdom" of the deeper mysteries of Christianity. But this view that "wisdom" includes only the difficult things in the gospel is contrary to all that Paul has already said in regard to this "wisdom" when he calls Christ crucified "the wisdom of God," 1:24. All attempts to name the deeper things which constitute this "wisdom" for the more advanced Christians offer matter that is foreign to Paul's words and thought. The simple fact remains that the entire gospel in all its parts is σοφία, including every part that anyone may label elementary.

The τέλειος is one who has reached the τέλος or goal. The context invariably determines the goal referred to and the sense in which the term is employed. The present context speaks of only two classes of people: such as accept the gospel in faith and such as spurn the gospel and prefer their own wisdom. No reference has been made to undeveloped Christians. The fact that Paul speaks of such in the next chapter does not give a special meaning to τέλειος as it is employed in this chapter. The τέλειοι are those who have reached Christ crucified as the goal. We have no good English equivalent for this Greek word. "The perfect" is rather misleading; "those perfected" is perhaps as well as we can do although also this translation is inadequate.

We now see why Paul uses the present tense λαλοῦμεν, "we go on speaking" wisdom. Whereas v. 1 and 3 employ historical aorists when referring to the past, to the time when Paul first preached in Corinth, this present tense mentions what Paul and his helpers do as a regular thing when they speak among believers who have come to apprehend Christ. All of their preaching is really "wisdom," true wisdom and nothing less. No contrast is implied as though they speak something else among unbelievers. Since the stress of the entire sentence is on "wisdom," there is no contrast in the τέλειοι except the natural one, that these will appreciate what Paul and others thus preach as "wisdom" while, of course, the rest, because of their unbelief, will not admit that the cross is "wisdom"; they call it folly.

Paul at once and in a strong way differentiates this divine wisdom from the other kind: "yet not the wisdom of this world age," the genitive characterizes the quality. On "world age" see 1:20. This αἰών or "age" (era) must end. Then what about its "wisdom"? Nor can a stream ever rise higher than its source. More specifically and referring to the reppresentatives of this transient wisdom, Paul qualifies it as belonging to "the rulers of this world age," those who are foremost and leaders of others because of their learning, their power, or their birth, 1:20, 26. The fact that Paul includes political rulers and their spurious religious wisdom we shall see in a moment when we consider v. 8. "Already in this world one card castle of human wisdom after another tumbles down, and finally the sentence of destruction that is uttered against all worldly things will be executed in the judgment to come." Besser. This thought is expressed in the qualitative genitive τῶν καταργουμένων (see 1:28), "who are coming to nought," really, "abolishing themselves" however proudly they now strut about. Every word and every act of theirs are only another step forward on this road. Its end is indicated in καταργήσῃ, 15:24, "when he shall have abolished." People "who are abolishing themselves" have a poor "wisdom" to offer, one that would induce others also to abolish themselves.

7) No; this is not the kind of wisdom Paul and his helpers offer to believers; "on the contrary," ἀλλά, it is the very opposite. The negative description is now supplemented by the positive: **on the contrary, we are speaking God's wisdom in mystery, the one that has been hidden, which God did foreordain before the world ages unto our glory.**

Paul repeats: "we are speaking God's wisdom" and now adds the qualitative genitive "God's" in order to distinguish this wisdom from the spurious "wisdom of this world age." In this genitive "God's" which we call qualitative there lies much more, namely origin and contents as well as nature. Two types of wisdom compete for men's souls. Paul and his colaborers offer the divine. Which do the Corinthian believers want?

There is no difficulty "in mystery" which modifies "wisdom." R. 589 construes it with the verb: "we speak in the form of mystery," but we question that ἐν ever means "in the form of." But apart from that, if something is "in the form of," it is "wisdom." Wisdom may have a form; the verb "we are speaking" can have no form. Entire phrases, especially those with ἐν, very frequently modify nouns or even pronouns. In the present instance the ἐν phrase is rather remotely removed from the verb. Luther translates: *Wir reden von der heimlichen Weisheit Gottes,* which is substantially correct although it converts the phrase into an adjective. No article is found with "mystery," hence the quality of the noun is stressed: this wisdom is connected with mystery. The article would point to some special mystery, one that is known in this case; none such exists in this instance.

The fact that this is a wisdom that is connected with mystery is at once explained, first by adding a participle with the article attributively and then by adding two relative clauses. "That hath been hidden," τὴν ἀποκεκρυμμένην, is passive with God as the agent, and the tense is perfect: God hid this wisdom and it still bears this character; and for this reason it is certainly connected with mystery. This mystery goes back to eternity, to a time prior to the ages or eons which constitute the course of time for the world. Then God προώρισεν, fixed and ordained in advance, this σοφία. This is the verb that is regularly employed to designate God's act of foreordaining or predestinating. Before man was formed, before the first phosphor light of his little wisdom began to glow, God's wisdom was complete, God's decision was fixed as to the object and as to the result of that wisdom.

This aorist προώρισεν, which takes us back into eternity, recalls the thrice repeated ἐξελέξατο, also aorist, found in 1:27, 28. While neither of these terms is here connected with persons, the very election and predestination of the gospel principles and contents involves also persons, in particular the elect. Paul indicates as much with the phrase "for our glory." This δόξα is the final goal to which God determined to bring us, that blessed state in which we shall see the Lord of glory as he is and shall be made like unto him. What, pray, is all human wisdom compared with this wisdom of God's grace, which reaches from eternity to eternity, which is full of divine, spiritual power to lift us sinners from sin, corruption, and death to everlasting glory?

8) No wonder Paul can add a second relative clause to describe this wisdom: **which not one of the rulers of this world age has known, for if they had known it they would not have crucified the Lord of glory.** Not only is it not theirs to begin with, originating, as it did, far higher and far earlier than theirs and sweeping on its sublime course far above their puny thoughts; but not one of them, rulers though they are in this world age, even "hath known" it, hath realized it in the past or at any time since and thus made it his own intellectually and spiritually when it was brought to him by God. The verb γινώσκειν is used with reference to the true apprehension and actual realization.

A striking and a convincing proof is at once added with γάρ: "for if they had known," etc. This is a regular conditional sentence that expresses a past unreality: εἰ with an aorist in the protasis and an aorist with ἄν in the apodosis: if they had known (but they did not know) they would not have crucified (but they did crucify). The crucifixion of Christ is the final demonstration of the fact that the world's highest representatives did not and do not know God's wisdom. The Jewish and the Roman political leaders are here referred to, but in Christ's time the former were also the ecclesiastical rulers. They even had the Old Testament revelation to give them knowledge. Yet they did not know. All their guilty and fatal ignorance comes to the surface in the crucifixion of Christ, John 18:38; Luke 23:34; Acts 3:17; 13:17. The Jewish and the Gentile authorities of Christ's day are typical in this respect. "World is world; wherever the world lets out its real self in its leaders, there Christ is killed, in Jerusalem and in Rome, everywhere, always." Besser.

Note the tremendous contrast between "crucify" and "the Lord of glory." The one represents the deepest disgrace, the other the highest exaltation and majesty. The person is here designated according to his divine nature (Lord of glory) while the thing predicated of him belongs to his human nature (crucified). Theologically speaking, we here have the *Communicatio Idiomatum* (the Communication of Attributes), and this is an instance that belongs to the first group, the *genus idiomaticum*. To this group belong all the Bible statements which predicate of the person of Christ, no matter how it is designated (with a divine, a human, or a merely personal or official name), either human or divine attributes, acts, etc. (or both combined). Zwingli disposes of these Bible statements by inventing a special figure for them, his *allœosis*, a mere verbal change. Since such a figure of speech is unknown to rhetoric, others seek to improve on Zwingli by calling this synecdoche: the whole placed for the part; in the present instance the whole person whereas only his humanity is meant. This is no better. In either case we should have only mere words that do *not* mean what they really say.

Luther: "Zwingli calls that an *allœosis* when something is said of the divinity of Christ which really belongs to the humanity, or vice versa. As Luke 24:26: 'Ought not Christ to have suffered these things, and to enter into his glory?' Here Zwingli juggles, asserting that the word Christ is understood of the human nature. Beware, beware, I say, of the *allœosis!* For it is a devil's mask, for at last it manufactures such a Christ after whom I certainly would not be a Christian; namely, that henceforth Christ should be no more and do no more with his sufferings and life than any other mere saint. For if I believe this that only the human nature has suffered for me, then Christ is to me a poor Savior, then he himself needs a Savior. In a word, it is unspeakable what the devil seeks with the *allœosis*. . . . . If the old weather witch, Dame Reason, the grandmother of the *allœosis*, would say,

'Yea, divinity cannot suffer or die'; you shall reply, 'That is true'; yet, because in Christ divinity and humanity are one person, Scripture, on account of this personal union, ascribes also to divinity everything that happens to the humanity, and vice versa. And it is so in reality; for you must certainly answer this, that the person (meaning Christ) suffers and dies. Now the person is true God; therefore it is rightly said: 'The Son of God suffers.' For although the one part (to speak thus), namely the divinity, does not suffer, yet the person, which is God, suffers in the other part, namely in his humanity; for in truth God's Son has been crucified for us, that is, the person which is God. For the person, the person, I say was crucified according to the humanity." *C. Tr.* 1027, etc., *F. C.* VIII, 39.

"The Lord of glory" is the Son of God who possesses all the divine attributes, the sum of which the Scriptures call his δόξα or "glory," for they all shine with heavenly splendor. By his incarnation this Lord of glory assumed our human nature. He also entered a state of lowliness, "he humbled himself, becoming obedient even unto death, yea, the death of the cross," Phil. 2:8. He suffered crucifixion in his human nature; yet it was *he* that suffered this. His person is one, forever undivided.

9) The wisdom which Paul and others are now speaking, this wisdom which is connected with mystery, of which the world rulers had no inkling as is evidenced by their putting Christ to the cross, Paul now states by means of a quotation: **but as it has been written:**

What eye saw not, and ear heard not,
And into the heart of man entered not,
Whatever God made ready for them that
    love him.

This is the wisdom which Paul and the other apostles speak, and it is plain that it is combined with mystery. As regards the construction, καθώς depends on λαλοῦμεν: "we speak as it has been written." The quotation is the remote object of λαλοῦμεν: "we speak . . . what eye saw not," etc. And ἀλλά is parallel to the ἀλλά occurring in v. 7, both adversatives contrast the divine mystery wisdom with that of the world and with the blindness of the world rulers. The effort to make v. 9 the object of the ἐκάλυψεν occurring in v. 10: "what eye saw not, etc. . . . to us did God reveal," etc., breaks down at several points. For if we construe: "as it is written . . . God did reveal," the quotation would have to state that God made this revelation, and yet the quotation which Paul uses states nothing of the kind. Moreover, ἀλλά, "on the contrary," refers to something negative that precedes and introduces the opposite of that negative; and the quotation does exactly that. In the same way καθώς points backward and not forward.

Since the days of Clement of Rome who lived forty years after Paul wrote this letter to the Corinthians the source of Paul's quotation has been in dispute. As far as some known or some unknown apocryphal source is concerned, the fact is now established that no New Testament writer ever quotes from apocryphal sources, and the formula: "even as it has been written," always introduces inspired canonical utterances. It would be strange to find that Paul makes an exception in this instance. We know, too, that Paul often quotes freely and also combines Old Testament sayings. His reason is always evident: he wishes to stress certain expressions that are found in the passages which he quotes; these he conserves while the rest, about which he is unconcerned, is formulated to fit the general connection in which he writes. We ourselves exercise the same liberty.

First Corinthians 2:9

Bearing these facts in mind, we shall have no difficulty in this case. Paul uses Isa. 64:4 and Isa. 65:17 for the second line. When he uses expressions from these two passages Paul's evident object is to show the mystery character of the wisdom which he and others are preaching. The expressions he thus desires are especially three: the one regarding the eye that does not see, the one regarding the ear that does not hear, and the one regarding the heart that does not even conceive the thought. This psychological arrangement and progression: eye, ear, heart, is Paul's own. Since he found no single Old Testament passage that contained these three, he combines two such passages freely and thus secures the three. The object which is thus not perceived by eye, ear, and heart Paul restates from Isa. 64:4 by using the prophet's thought quite exactly.

No heathen people ever conceived a God who would actually take care of those who placed their reliance on him. The idea that this God of Israel could be such a God never entered their minds. Delitzsch translates: "From ancient time on no one has heard, has perceived, no eye has seen a God except thee, who acts for him that waits on him." Then he comments: "No ear, no eye, has ever come to perceive the existence of a God who acts like Jehovah, i. e., effectually takes the part of those who rest their hope on him." August Pieper in his excellent *Jesaias II* translates and comments in the same way: "The enemies believe in no intervention of the gods or of one god in behalf of a definite nation. From of old they have never heard of such a thing or actually seen it, no eye has ever beheld the like. Therefore they are not afraid but are quite assured in their violation of Israel that they have nothing of this kind to fear from the God also of this people although the prophets and teachers of Israel speak of it. But the Lord is, indeed, an actual exception among the gods. He is, in fact, a God who interferes for those who wait on him."

From Isa. 65:17, Paul desires only the expression: "come upon the heart," A. V. margin, which he renders into Greek: "entered not into the heart of man," and preserves as much as possible the Hebrew idiom which uses "heart." The object that is not perceived by eye, ear, and heart is: "what he hath prepared for him that waiteth for him," A. V., or more literally: God, "who acts for him that waits on him." Paul restates this but gives the same sense and thus changes the final dative. The LXX has the plural: "for them that await mercy." Paul retains this plural when he writes: "for them that love him." But, as in other places in his letters when divine benefits are mentioned, the recipients of these benefits are designated as those that love God. Rom. 8:28: "To them that love God all things work together for good."

The quotation, in the formulation which Paul employs, finds such favor that from early days onward we meet it in all manner of connections. It is often used with reference to heaven and with reference to the blessedness that awaits us in the life to come. This use is legitimate, indeed, although it narrows the sense originally intended by Paul. All that God offers us in the gospel, all that he has prepared for us, and all he does for us in Christ Jesus, not only the glory of the joy in heaven, is contained in the wisdom that Paul and his helpers preach to us to make us wise unto salvation. All of it not even the foremost among men, apart from God, ever perceived or conceived; it was all "hidden in mystery." God alone revealed it in the gospel and now reveals it to us by means of the gospel.

The "heart" is conceived as the organ of thought and as such is paralleled with the senses, "eye and ear." "To come upon ($\epsilon\pi\iota$) the heart" is idiomatic for our "entering the heart," conceiving in the mind. Some prefer the reading ἁ instead of ὅσα in the third line; "things which," instead of "as many as," taking their number together. The aorist ἡτοίμασεν is probably historical. We may refer it back to eternity and then think of the one eternal act of making ready; or, regarding the aorist as constative, we may think of the preparation made during the entire Old Testament time. If we wish to specify what things God thus made ready we shall not go amiss if we mention pardon, sonship, peace, etc., and finally everlasting glory in Christ Jesus.

10) But to us God made revelation through the Spirit, for the Spirit searches all things, even the deep things of God.

The emphatic ἡμῖν, "to us," does not refer to Christians in general but resumes the silent "we" of the two λαλοῦμεν, "we speak," occurring in v. 6 and 7, namely the apostles who are commissioned to speak this wisdom and to make it known. As God originally hid this wisdom in mystery, v. 7, so in due time he and he alone revealed it. In the Greek: "God made revelation" or "revealed" needs no object, the reader at once understands what was thus revealed. After stating to whom God made this wondrous revelation Paul states the medium which God employed: "through the Spirit," the third person of the Godhead. Both the Revelator and the Medium are thus far above anything that transmits human wisdom. Paul here sets aside the view of a religious evolution among the Jews which at last resulted in Christianity. God discarded absolutely all human religious wisdom and in his "revelation" set up something that was entirely new and transcendently superior.

The statement that this revelation was made "through the Spirit" takes us into the profundities of the Godhead itself and assigns a reason for it: "for the Spirit searcheth all things," etc. There is, of course, no thought here of setting the Spirit over against the other two persons of the Godhead as if he alone searches all things. All we know is what Paul states here: the Spirit, who is one in essence with the Father and the Son, exercises this divine function. It is best not to attempt to follow this thought any farther. All we can add is that in the economy of grace it is the Spirit's office to convey God's revelation to us.

The verb "to search" that is used with reference to the Spirit cannot mean, as it does in our case, a process of investigation such as going from one thing to another, putting two and two together, and thus making one discovery after another. The tense is the timeless present. In one timeless act the Spirit sounds the absolute depth of "all things," πάντα (not merely τὰ πάντα, all that God created and that now exists) in heaven and in earth, millions of them being beyond the human mind. They include "even the deep things of God," his essence and his attributes as well as his thoughts, his purposes, his plans, his providences in regard to us, etc. Rom. 11:33. And in these "deep things" we may well include the cross of Christ which involves the Holy Trinity itself, the incarnation, the union of the two natures in Christ, etc. Although we know something about these things through the Spirit's revelation, their inner profundities are still "in mystery" to our minds.

11) To aid us at least a little in our efforts to apprehend what is too high for our finite minds Paul introduces an analogy. **For who knows of men in general the things of some particular man save the spirit of that particular man that is in him? Even so the things of God no one has known save the Spirit of God.**

The inner feelings, the motives, the thoughts, and the volitions of any individual man (τοῦ ἀνθρώπου, note the individualizing article) only the spirit of the individual man (again τοῦ ἀνθρώπου) knows. Who else can know them even though he belong to men in general (ἀνθρώπων, partitive genitive)? They are hidden from him, they belong to another whom he sees only from the outside, into whose spirit he cannot penetrate. When the Scriptures distinguish the πνεῦμα from the ψυχή of man, the πνεῦμα or "spirit" is the real seat of the ego, the latter only the soul life which animates his body. In this sense Paul says that only "the spirit," the real ego of that particular man, knows the real things that center in himself. This is true also with respect to God.

The analogy is adequate only in regard to the one point stressed, for there is an obvious difference between man's spirit and the Spirit of God. Man's πνεῦμα is "in him," ἐν αὐτῷ, was put there when God created man and breathed his breath into man and made him a spirit ego. No counterpart to this exists in God, the essence of whose Spirit is identical (ὁμοούσιος) with that of the Father and of the Son. We cannot extend Paul's analogy beyond the one point indicated lest we mislead ourselves in regard to God. As man's spirit alone knows what is in himself, thus (οὕτω) God's Spirit alone knows what is in God, i. e., "the things of God," all of them, those that are utterly unsearchable to us and those that are included in his love, grace, purposes, and plans for us, with which latter Paul is here concerned. The perfect ἔγνωκεν = has known from eternity and thus ever knows and uses this human tense with reference to a timeless divine act. Thus in some tiny fashion Paul explains (γάρ) to us why the Spirit is God's divine medium for revelation to us. Human wisdom needs no such explanation of the medium of its transmission.

12) Having thus made plain the great Revelator and the infinite profundity of his knowledge, Paul con-

tinues with the revelatory act mentioned in v. 10: "To us he made revelation." Once more we have the emphatic pronoun ἡμεῖς, "we," which continues through v. 13. **Now we received, not the spirit of the world, but the spirit which is from God in order that we might know the things graciously granted us by God.**

How do "we," the apostles, get the divine wisdom which we proclaim to God's people? Objectively, of course, by means of a revelation which God makes to us. But more must be said. How is this revelation lodged in us subjectively so that we may possess it subjectively and thus become channels for its transmission? The apostles do not receive the Spirit's revelation like phonographic records which know nothing of that which is impressed upon them. Paul has quite significantly referred to the spirit of each man and has stated how that spirit knows what pertains to that man. Regarding this subjective side Paul tells his readers: "We received not the spirit of the world but the spirit which is from God," etc.

The term πνεῦμα signifies animus, that which constitutes the specific character of a man, i. e., of the ego that is in him. The world's spirit is thus that which animates the world, lends its distinctive character to the world. It is what makes the world "world." Because of this its spirit the world ever loves its spurious wisdom. We see this spirit fully illustrated in the world's leaders who crucified Christ. This "spirit of the world" is not the faculty of reason created in man although this "spirit" frightfully abuses also this faculty just as it abuses τὰ μέλη, the members of the body, and all other possessions. This "spirit" is "received"; men get it from the world by birth and by every kind of contact. Its characteristic mark is the fact that it is "of the world," τοῦ κόσμου, qualitative genitive. As long as a man has this "spirit" he is unfit to receive the Spirit's revelation, v. 14, he despises the wisdom of God.

The apostles received the very opposite kind of "spirit" or animus: "the spirit that is from God." Our versions are careful to print "spirit" without a capital letter. And Paul is careful not to write "the spirit of God" although he writes "the spirit of the world," but "the spirit from God," τὸ πνεῦμα τὸ ἐκ τοῦ Θεοῦ, the one that is derived from God, ἐκ denoting source. This is the spirit of true faith and trust toward God, the spirit of humility and love, the opposite of the spirit of "the rulers of this world age," v. 6. How the apostles "received" this new spirit Paul is not concerned to state, he registers only the fact with a decided historical aorist. The Corinthians know the life's history of Paul and of the Twelve. Thus subjectively God prepared the apostles to become recipients of his revelation so that they might transmit it. God could use only men of this type, humble though they were; he could employ absolutely none of the world rulers, powerful and great though they seemed to be.

From God the apostles received this subjective preparation "in order that they might know the things graciously granted them by God." These are the things that comprise "the wisdom" of which Paul is speaking, the things which eye saw not, etc. The agent who "graciously granted" and gave these things to the apostles is indicated in the regular way: "God" and ὑπό with the genitive. The apostles were to "know" these things. This is the subjective side of the objective divine act of revelation. The apostles are to possess these blessed things personally for themselves although God's main purpose is that, by themselves apprehending these things, the apostles might convey them to others.

The context indicates that Paul is speaking about the gospel, for the transmission of which to men generally the apostles (ἡμεῖς) were the divinely chosen human instruments. When "we" is referred to believers in general, and when χαρισθέντα is thus taken to refer to the effects of the gospel in our hearts, as well as when this participle is restricted to the future blessings of the saints in heaven, the thread of Paul's instruction is broken.

13) This is evidenced also by the following. In v. 6 and 7 Paul asserts: "We speak wisdom... we speak God's wisdom." He then adds important explanations as to how the apostles get this wisdom objectively by revelation and subjectively by reception into their minds and hearts. Now Paul concludes with the same λαλοῦμεν, "we speak," and once more shows what he and his fellow apostles speak and adds a statement in regard to the character of the very words they employ when they are thus speaking. **Which things also we speak, not in words taught of man's wisdom, but in those taught of the Spirit, combining with spiritual words spiritual things.**

The relative ἅ resumes "the things graciously granted by God," the entire sum of the divinely granted wisdom, all that God revealed to the apostles in the gospel. For the third time Paul says "we speak," λαλοῦμεν, these things: we are engaged in carrying out our apostolic command to teach these things to all nations and to the church that has begun to receive them. Paul is doing this very thing when he is now writing to the Corinthians. In fact, the apostles still teach us to this very day through their written word.

The very "words" which the apostles employ in their divinely commissioned speaking are now described, first by means of a negative and secondly by means of a positive statement. "Not in words taught by man's wisdom" declares that not even in regard to the "words" is God's wisdom dependent on the world's wisdom. Not even the λόγοι of the latter are exalted enough to serve for uttering the former. The philosophers, the dialecticians, and the rhetoricians of the world created and employed many concepts or "thought words" (λόγοι) to express their worldly reasoning, but the apostles did not adopt them for their utterance of the divine wisdom. They could not, for these terms and expressions would not be adequate for what the apostles had to convey. The genitive taught "by human wisdom" really expresses an ablative idea, R. 504, and this suggests the great teachers of those days and the disciples who adopted their reasoning.

Here is Paul's answer to the modern commentators who make efforts to trace many of the terms and expressions found in Paul's letters to ancient apocalyptic or to Hellenistic philosophical sources. Their results are negligible. No gospel thought wears a dress of pagan or pseudo-Jewish terms. The non-Christian world of today also has learned teachers who wield a great influence. Because they are animated by "the spirit of the world," v. 12, their *logoi* are valueless for God's wisdom. It is wasted effort to shape the wisdom of the gospel so that it will fit these foreign forms of thought and language. One cannot, for instance, rewrite Genesis 1 and 2 in the language of the evolutionary hypothesis. The modernists of today regard the Scriptures as wisdom of the world and then, because the Scriptures are old, proceed to do with them as they do with the old philosophies of the world: they discard such "categories of thought" (as they call them) as are no longer modern in their opinion, such as our age, they say, has outgrown.

"On the contrary," Paul writes, "we speak in words taught by the Spirit." The very words which the apostles speak are taught them by the Spirit. He is their teacher even as to the "words." This is proof positive for Verbal Inspiration which is taught throughout the Scriptures and is actually and factually apparent in the Scriptures. The Spirit is the teacher of the *logoi* in regard to all that the apostles spoke and hence also in regard to all of the gospel which they wrote, for the two are identical.

This view has been called "the mechanical theory of Inspiration," which degrades the sacred penmen into mere automatons and machines; it is also called "the dictation theory." The diversity of style manifested by the individual writers of the sacred books has been adduced to overthrow Verbal Inspiration. But Paul is here stating a fact. To call it a "theory" is incorrect. A fact cannot be overthrown, a theory is easily upset. Paul says: We (apostles) were taught the words by the Spirit (ablative, R. 576). The Spirit is the greatest teacher in the universe. His teaching of the *logoi* of inspired apostolic utterance is no more mechanical than his teaching of the contents of these words, for the two invariably go together, and we today teach truth only by means of words that are fit to convey that truth, and in no other way. The Spirit's teaching, the most perfect in the world, is the very highest type of spiritual operation. The very fact that the Spirit used each writer with his fund of words and his personal style when recording the gospel shows that everything mechanical was removed from this teaching of the Spirit. If he had compelled all of the writers to use the same fund of words and the same style, we might harbor the suspicion that he proceeded mechanically, and only then, and even then we might be mistaken. Amid all the variety that resulted from the dynamic use which the divine Master Teacher made of the different writers the one astounding fact stands out: not a single writer utters a false note, uses one.

false word or phrase, or contradicts with a single statement expressed in his style what another holy writer expresses in a different style. If this it not Verbal Inspiration — and there is no other — then what, pray, shall it be called?

There is a beautiful paronomasia in Πνεύματος and πνευματικοῖς πνευματικά. The adverb πνευματικῶς instead of the dative has insufficient attestation although Luther so translates: *und richten geistliche Sachen geistlich.* Grammatically and exegetically πνευματικοῖς can refer only to λόγοις and to ἐν διδακτικοῖς (sc. λόγοις) Πνεύματος. The neuter plural πνευματικά likewise refers to the neuter plural relative ἅ at the beginning of v. 13. The *things* which the apostles speak are "spiritual things," πνευματικά, and they speak them in connection with "spiritual *words*," πνευματικοῖς (sc. λόγοις).

The participle συγκρίνοντες = *zusammensichten,* to combine with discrimination, to separate from other matter and to combine anew, or simply to combine. In a terse way Paul thus sums up what he has said at greater length: as a result of using words taught them by the Spirit himself and not those gained from other sources he and his fellow apostles combine only spiritual *words* with the spiritual *things* they preach. Both the spiritual things and the spiritual words that convey them emanate equally from the Spirit, and the apostles combine the two accordingly. This is Paul's definition of Verbal Inspiration. Note that λόγοι, *Worte,* is the proper term in this connection and not ῥήματα, *Woerter.* We also heed Besser's admonition not to treat spiritual things in words of human wisdom as though they ever needed such foreign dress. The rags of our own wisdom would only desecrate the divine truth which God clothes in royal apparel.

Our English versions regard both πνευματικοῖς and πνευματικά as neuter: "comparing spiritual things with spiritual" (sc. things). Why Paul should make such a statement is an unanswered question. After emphasizing, as he does, the *logoi* or "words" which he and his fellow apostles use, how can he then, when he should clinch what he says about the *logoi*, suddenly veer off in another direction? The English marginal translation is no better: "interpreting spiritual things to spiritual men." Nothing is said about "men" in the context. If Paul refers to "men" in a context where only "words" have been considered he should insert the word "men." Moreover, this rendering gives the participle the highly unusual sense of "interpreting" which is found only in the LXX of Gen. 40:8. The American committee of the R. V. offers the correct translation: "combining spiritual words with spiritual things."

14) After speaking of the character of the divine wisdom and of its inspired transmission in words taught by the Spirit alone Paul presents the reception which this wisdom experienced among men. **Now a natural (carnal) man does not receive the things of the Spirit of God, for foolishness are they to him, and he is unable to understand them because they are spiritually judged.**

In the word ψυχικός we have a vivid illustration of the manner in which even the words of God's wisdom are derived from the Spirit. Paul takes the word which the later Greek literature "constantly employed in praise of the noblest part of man" and reduces it to its proper level. Paul no longer regards ψυχικός as a word of honor but, together with σαρκικός, uses it to designate man as a being who is under the dominion of sin. Both of these terms are opposites of πνευματικός, "spiritual." The word ψυχικός refers to a person who has only the ψυχὴ ζῶσα and not the πνεῦμα of divine regeneration, one, therefore, who has only the natural powers of the ψυχή and is moved and controlled only by them. Since these are altogether corrupt because of sin, every activity of his soul and his mind will be darkened accordingly. The word σαρκικός (κατὰ σάρκα ὤν, fleshly) refers to one who obeys the promptings of his bodily nature. We have no adjective in English that is derived from "soul" which corresponds to the Greek ψυχικός from ψυχή. Hence the translation "natural man" or "unspiritual" or "carnal," one might say "psychial," but this is too learned.

This type of man "does not receive the things of the Spirit of God," which Paul has described, when they are offered to him in preaching and in teaching. He does not "accept" them into his heart for what they are, precious divine truth. To a natural man they sound like μωρία (1:21), silliness, something insipid, tasteless, absurd. In his pride he may call them "fables" that are fit only for children. They clash with his own perverted ideas and desires, condemn them, and work to root them out. Hence his opposition.

The case is even worse. Paul denies not only the fact: "does not receive"; he denies also the ability: "cannot understand." "To receive" is in a way "to understand"; yet "to understand" indicates how "to receive" is meant. For this verb γνῶναι indicates more than intellectual apprehension, it means actual realization. This verb corresponds to "the wisdom" which Paul is describing, the substance of which consists of "the things of the Spirit of God," the entire gospel with all that it offers, its objective gifts and treasures like the saving deeds of God and its subjective blessings like life and salvation. The ψυχικός lacks the faculty and the organ for this knowing and this receiving. He has nothing beyond the organ of purely human condition, and this does not reach into the spiritual realm. Just as a blind man cannot see the sun, so this man cannot see the radiance of the Sun of righteousness; just as a deaf man cannot hear the sweetest music, so this man cannot appreciate the sweet tones of the gospel. Only he that is of God heareth God's Word, John 8:47. Luther on Ps. 90 (*F. C.* II, 20-21) : In his natural state "man is like a pillar of salt, like Lot's wife, yea, like a log and a stone, like a lifeless statue which uses neither eyes nor mouth, neither sense nor heart. For man neither sees nor perceives the terrible and fierce wrath of God on account of sin and death but ever continues in his security, even knowingly and willingly, and thereby falls into a thousand dangers and finally into eternal death and damnation... until he is enlightened, converted, and regenerated by the Holy Ghost, for which indeed no stone or block, but man alone, was created." *C. Tr.* 889. There is no synergism of any kind. It is wholly God's work of grace which opens the blind ears, the carnal heart, by his Spirit and his Word.

The natural man cannot know the things of the Spirit "because they are spiritually judged." A "psychial" man cannot exercise a spiritual function. The two exclude each other. In the same general sense as "receive" and "know" Paul now writes "judge." Yet ἀνακρίνεται is a juridic term. It is used with reference to a judge who examines a prisoner in advance of his trial. The things of the Spirit are judicially and properly examined and probed only πνευματικῶς, "in a spiritual way." Being of the Spirit and in their nature spiritual, how can they be probed so as to determine their real import and value in any other than a spiritual way? And who except a spiritual man can do this? An ass and a sow want thistles. What do they care for the odor of roses and of lilies?

15) In v. 14 Paul explains the rejection of the divine wisdom. His statement is naturally of a negative character. In v. 15 he sets forth the reception of this wisdom, and his statement is naturally positive. How necessary it is that the Corinthians

understand both! Paul confines himself to his subject, which is not the doctrine of conversion, how the natural man becomes a spiritual man, but the real character of the gospel wisdom, a wisdom that is so lofty that a natural man cannot reach it but only he who is spiritual. So Paul writes: **But the spiritual man judgeth all things, yet he himself is judged by no one.** "The spiritual man" is the very opposite of "a natural man." He can do what Paul states here, for he is a new creature by having received "the spirit that is from God," v. 12. He has the spiritual organ and thus the ability to do what Paul says. The verb ἀνακρίνειν is retained (ἀνά, to follow up a series of points, plus κρίνειν in order to distinguish and to arrive at the true value): to investigate or probe judicially, to judge.

Yet πάντα, thus to judge "all things," comes as a surprise, for it goes far beyond the wisdom of the gospel. A moment's thought, however, shows us that the natural man does not probe and judge aright even the common things of this life, to say nothing about the gospel; does not see their true nature, purpose, relation, etc. He magnifies these things out of all proportion and hence devotes himself to them exclusively and thus misuses them. But the spiritual man has the true standard whereby to measure even these earthly things. He may sometimes be slothful in this respect and let the wisdom of this world deceive him as the Corinthians are in danger of doing, and he therefore needs the admonition: "Be renewed in the spirit of your mind," Eph. 4:23.

The particles μέν and δέ place two things in juxtaposition. The first causes surprise, but the second does so still more: "yet he himself is judged by no one." The spiritual man is able to judge (investigate and value aright) the natural man, but not vice versa. When the natural man, nevertheless, tries it he only makes a fool of himself. What does he know about spiritual things, to say nothing about a spiritual man? What organ has he or what criterion for judging one who is spiritual? He is bound to call the spiritual man a fool and never realizes that the folly is all on the other side. He cannot see our wealth nor his own emptiness while we can see both. It all sounds strange at first, and yet it is quite true and simple. It will do the Corinthians good to ponder this.

16) Paul establishes what he thus says in regard to the spiritual man, namely that he is judged by no one. **For who did understand the Lord's mind so that he shall instruct him? But we have Christ's mind.**

Paul appropriates Isa. 40:13 just as he does in Rom. 11:34. The prophet's words express just what Paul desires to say at this point, and so he simply adopts the prophet's words as his own. The proof which Paul offers is a syllogism, the conclusion of which Paul need not state in so many words, for we can easily draw it. Major premise: Of course, no one knows the Lord's mind and instructs him — this is admitted as self-evident. Minor premise: We have Christ's mind — he revealed it to us, and so this, too, must be admitted. Ergo, the self-evident conclusion: No one can instruct, know, probe, judge us, in a word, evaluate aright what we are and have. *Id est*, no fool of this world. God, of course, can; Christ and all who have his mind can, but no one else can.

What folly is it then for those who have not even the ability to accept the things of God's Spirit, who deem them to be foolishness, to sit in judgment on these things and on the people who possess them and glory in them! Do they, perhaps, intend to instruct the Lord? Will they attempt this impossible, presumptuous, blasphemous thing? Isaiah spoke about *Yahweh*, and what the prophet said Paul refers to Christ as the last sentence shows. Christ is God, and God's wisdom, in which no one can instruct Christ, has its origin in the Trinity.

The relative ὅς has the consecutive idea, R. 724, hence we translate: "so that he shall"; and not: "that he may," A. V., which is final. The R. V.'s translation is indefinite. "To know the Lord's mind" is to know its contents, its thoughts, its plans, and its purposes, i. e., the wisdom of the gospel. No natural man who has only his worldly mind ever knew the divine mind. To have "Christ's mind" is to possess its contents by way of a gracious gift (χαρισθέντα ἡμῖν, v. 12).

The emphasis is on ἡμεῖς and on ἔχομεν: *We* are they who *have* his mind. One who is great enough through his own ability to know the Lord's mind might, perhaps, presume to instruct the Lord — note the crushing irony in the suggestion. We, to whom the Lord graciously revealed his mind, are only too thankful to receive this blessed wisdom, and no presumptuous thought, such as improving on that wisdom, will ever enter our minds. This emphatic "we" again refers to the apostles as we have seen throughout this section. To the Corinthians, Paul brought the mind of Christ and made them share in the divine gospel wisdom. Will they now fall back into their former state and with worldly wisdom tell the Lord how to improve his mind and to make the gospel wisdom what they think it ought to be? Paul's thrust is sharp indeed, but the Corinthians need it. We, too.

Blessed are the apostles who first received the mind of Christ, and blessed are all who received the same mind from and through their inspired words. As we walk thus in the light of God's wisdom, having our minds and our spirits renewed, we are surely a puzzle to the world. But let its criticism and its mockery never disturb us; let us rather test ourselves constantly so that we may never deviate from the mind of Christ.

CHAPTER III

IV. God's Co-Workers, 3:1-9

Paul begins with the "wranglings" (ἔριδες) found in Corinth, 1:10, and points out their absurdity in a preliminary way. Then he adds the paragraphs concerning the character of the gospel as foolishness and as wisdom and concerning its reception by the apostles through revelation and inspiration. On the basis thus laid Paul now proceeds to settle completely with the Corinthian wranglings.

1) As he did in the first paragraph of chapter 2, Paul again reaches back to the time when he first worked in Corinth, but he does so only briefly in oder to compare the present state of the Corinthians with their beginnings in the faith, a comparison that must fill them with shame, for they still act like babes, babes who have not grown up. This is bound to hurt their pride, but Paul intends that it should. He calls them "brethren"—shall we say baby-brethren? **And I, brethren, was not able to speak to you as to spiritual but only as to fleshy people, only as to babes in Christ.**

The historical aorist takes us back into the past when the Corinthians were beginners in the faith, and the aorist infinitive sums up the speaking and the preaching of Paul at that time. The pronoun "I" is emphatic, for the apostle was their preacher at that time. The Corinthians were beginners in those early days and as such could not then be treated as πνευματικοί, real spiritually minded people, but only as σάρκινοι, people still fleshy in their way of thinking and acting and not able, like a truly spiritual man, to judge aright all things, 2:15. Paul does not fault the Corinthians for this early condition of theirs, for he adds the apposition "as babes in Christ." We must all be "babes" at first in the natural course of our spiritual development. There is something tender in the term, and it implies maternal solicitude on Paul's part and motherly care in helping these babes to grow up and to become strong and mature spiritually. Thank God that the Corinthians were converted by Paul's preaching and were united to Christ in faith and thus began their Christian career!

While νήπιοι, "babes," removes all blame, it still suggests an unsatisfactory condition of immaturity that ought soon to pass away. This suggestion is even stronger in the word σάρκινοι, "fleshy." Paul does not use ψυχικοί (2:14) to describe this early state of the Corinthians, for this term denotes people who are totally devoid of the Spirit, who therefore cannot be "in Christ." The term σάρκινος = σὰρξ ὤν and names the substance of which one is composed, "fleshy." A person of this kind may be "in Christ" as Paul here states regarding the Corinthians when they were still beginners in the faith, yet such a one ought to change from this condition as soon as possible. To have too much flesh is to have too little of the spirit or the new life in Christ. Unless the flesh is greatly reduced and the spirit increased, the latter will soon be smothered and killed. While the spirit is at first naturally weak like a babe it must soon grow strong in order to maintain itself, and the stronger it grows, the better.

2) Paul tells the Corinthians: "When you were still quite fleshy and babes in Christ as to the spirit, mere ABC scholars in the faith, I had to treat you as such in order to make you grow, and I did so." **Milk I gave you to drink, not meat, for not yet were you able.**

Milk is for babes, they cannot digest solid food. This is a case of zeugma, R. 1201, for the verb "I gave you to drink" is proper only with "milk" and not with "meat," solid food. Paul does not intend to say that these two figurative terms are to designate two groups of gospel doctrines, milk doctrines and meat doctrines. It is an erroneous deduction that preachers ought to withhold certain doctrines from beginners in the faith because these are too hard for their spiritual stomachs to digest. Some carry this idea so far that they think that certain doctrines are fit only for preachers and for theologians and not at all for ordinary church members. The doctrines of predestination and conversion have been treated in this manner.

But all that Christ and Paul say about these and about other doctrines they address to all the members of the church. Paul always preached "all the counsel of God," Acts 20:27. Paul does not distinguish between two sets of doctrines but between two modes of presenting all doctrines. In fact, like Christ, he used more than two modes, for in every case he took into consideration the spiritual development of his hearers. See how Jesus uses one mode in Matt. 18:22 and then a far simpler one in the attached parable. He proceeds thus in many instances and condescends to reveal the most marvelous things of the gospel "unto babes," Matt. 11:25.

After saying in v. 1: "I was not able," Paul now adds in explanation: "for you were not yet able." Paul's inability was not due to lack or inefficiency in himself but to the spiritually undeveloped condition of the Corinthians. When saying "not yet" Paul implies that the Corinthians would advance beyond the beginner's stage in due time. Also that he would gladly have offered the Corinthians solid food had they been ready to receive this form of food.

Paul speaks about the early days of the Corinthians with the two aorists. With the present tense he now suddenly turns and strikes home with a severe rebuke regarding their present condition: **nay, not even now are ye able.** During all this time the Corinthians had been proud of their ability. Had Paul not preached mightily in their midst, and was he not followed by the great Apollos? Did Paul not acknowledge the great spiritual wealth God had given them (1:5)? How can Paul, then, now say a thing so severe as this? Paul knows how the Corinthians will wince under this lash, but he is far from administering it as he does and then trying to soften the hurt. Instead of following such a procedure he at once proves conclusively that the Corinthians are actually still fleshy and babes, far behind the state they should have attained. Although boasting of being able during all this time, they are still unable. At one time they were naturally immature without special blame; now their immaturity is a different matter. Regarding ἀλλά as being confirmatory and continuative see R. 1185, etc.: "yea." "Now" is cumulative: this inability persists contrary to nature and to expectation.

3) Paul's proof for the unnatural inability of the Corinthians is as direct as is his startling charge: **for you are yet fleshly, for whereas among you there is jealousy and wrangling, are you not fleshly and are you not walking after the manner of men?**

Paul repeats the charge "you are yet fleshly" and then proves it. He makes a fine distinction when he now calls the Corinthians σαρκικοί. At one time, in their early days, they were σάρκινοι, still largely made up of flesh because their spiritual part was still in the infant stage. They could then not help it, they were "fleshy" in heart, mind, and life and yet giving promise that they would soon outgrow that stage. But something has interfered with their development, Paul finds that they are now σαρκικοί (κατὰ σάρκα ὤν), "fleshly," people who ought to obey the true spiritual norm and yet by a choice of their own obey the norm of the flesh. The difference between the two terms is: "fleshy," and you cannot help it; "fleshly," and you can but do not help it. "Fleshy," you carry a bad load but will soon be rid of most of it; "fleshly," you follow a bad norm and refuse to get rid of it. Paul approves of neither condition but cannot especially blame them for the former whereas he must decidedly blame them for the latter. Our versions erase the difference by using one word, "carnal," as a translation of both Greek terms.

But is this carge of still being fleshly in thought and in act true in regard to the Corinthians? Paul makes them answer for themselves. He asks two questions, the answers to which are implied as being self-evident because the facts they point out are undeniable. "For whereas there is among you jealousy and wrangling, are you not fleshly," etc.? The Corinthians cannot deny it. By ζῆλος, "jealousy" or "envy," Paul refers to the vice of the heart which loves to lower another and to exalt self. Its natural product is ἔρις, "wrangling" or "strife," 1:11, compare Gal. 5:20. Is it not a fact, Paul asks, since you Corinthians have these vices in your midst, that you are still fleshly? And Paul explains just what he means by fleshly by adding to his question: "and are you not walking after the manner of men?" With κατὰ ἄνθρωπον he indicates the norm of this their wrong conduct, the norm which animates man as a mere man and as such is far from God and contrary to the norm he requires us to obey. Men who are "spiritual" (2:15) follow a different norm, one that leads to love and to peace.

4) A second question, which contains a second γάρ, proves that envy and strife do, indeed, exist among the Corinthians. **For, whenever one says: I am of Paul, and another, I am of Apollos, are you not mere men?** Does this not show that you are just

common, unregenerate men like those in the world, you who act so much like them? "Are you not (mere) men?" explains the previous question in regard to walking "after the manner of men."

The Corinthians may have expected a different kind of proof, for they may not have considered their contentions such a serious matter. For when they wrote to Paul they never mentioned a word on this subject. Paul's words must, therefore, have struck them rather forcefully. Really serious faults in the church quite frequently make little or no impression on the members while lesser failings stir them up. The Pharisees were meticulously concerned about tithing mint and cummin and left undone the weightier matters of the law, judgment, mercy, and faith, Matt. 23:23. Envy and strife are always deplorable. Spirituality does not thrive in such an atmosphere. To seek honor for men, and to seek honor from men whereas Christ should be all in all, is courting deadly danger. To put men into rivalry with Christ and to glorify men at the cost of Christ, whether this be done consciously or unconsciously, is to assail Christ himself. If we only always had a Paul to step in with the full corrective gospel power!

We see that Paul repeats the slogans of only two of the four Corinthian parties. Perhaps these were the most prominent or the worst although this is a surmise. The other two are, of course, not innocent. See the discussion of 1:12.

5) In 1:11, 12 Paul states the fact of the wrong existing in Corinth. He repeats this in a fuller and more telling way in 3:1-4. Then in 1:13, etc., Paul corrects the wrong. He does the same in 3:5, etc., but his correction now probes to the very bottom. As he did in chapter one, he begins with questions and then with οὖν connects these questions with the proof for the Corinthians' wrong which he has just

offered. **What, then, is Apollos? and what is Paul? Ministers through whom you believed, and each as the Lord gave to him.**

The Corinthians are making party heads of these men and each party glorifies its man to the detriment of Christ and the gospel. Now what (not "who," A. V.) are these men? And Paul again names them. The Corinthians ought to know, and this knowledge should have prevented them from elevating men as they did. These men are only the Lord's διάκονοι, both equally only his servants. Paul does not say δοῦλοι, for this term stresses the feature that the servant's will is subservient to the Master in all things. When Paul calls himself and Apollos διάκονοι, "ministers," he has in mind the beneficial service they rendered the Corinthians. Then he at once states the chief feature of that service: "through whom you believed." The aorist may be ingressive: "came to believe"; it may also be constative, summing up the entire activity of believing on the part of the Corinthians.

For such benefit received the Corinthians may well hold Paul and Apollos in grateful remembrance. But Paul is also concerned to have them remember that the real source of their blessings is the Lord. "Through whom" characterizes Paul and Apollos as being no more than *causae instrumentales* in the Lord's hands. The Lord alone is the *causa efficiens* in working and in preserving faith. Paul modestly places Apollos on a par with himself when he states what service they rendered the Corinthians. Although Paul alone founded the congregation he seeks no special honor for himself above that accorded to others.

Because Paul and Apollos are only the Lord's ministers, therefore also any difference in the service which these two rendered the Corinthians is due to the Lord. So Paul adds: "yea (καί, cumulative) to each as the Lord gave." It was he who portioned out to Paul and to Apollos what each did in Corinth. Most assuredly then, all credit and all glory for what was thus achieved in Corinth belongs to no man but to the Lord. Both men did strenuous work in Corinth, yet Paul considers all of this work as a gift to him and to Apollos, a gift that called for their joint gratitude.

There were, of course, differences between these two men and between the measure of their work and their success, but this, too, was due to the Lord and to his giving. In this simple and true way Paul draws the eyes of the Corinthians away from men, including himself, and fixes their gaze on God. His own pure heart, which is free from all envy and jealousy, reaches out to the hearts of the Corinthians in order to impart the same purity to them. Away with all invidious comparisons! What each of us is able to do in the church is an undeserved gift from the Lord's hands. Bend the knee and give him thanks!

6) How did the Lord employ Paul and Apollos in Corinth? **I planted, Apollos watered, but God caused the growing.** The Lord graciously granted to Paul the work of originally planting the Corinthian field while to Apollos he graciously granted the work of watering what had been planted. These activities on the part of these two men are, of course, not mutually exclusive, but it is not necessary to stress that fact in this connection. In these very terse statements, which are even without connectives, it is sufficient to touch upon only the major feature of each man's work. To plant, to water — these activities belong together. One is as necessary as the other.

One must know the Orient in order to understand how vital for constant growth watering is in areas where no rain falls during the entire summer. The planting done at Corinth was not intended to produce a quick, transient crop that is grown in the damp winter season; it was rather like the planting of trees and of vines that need the water courses (Ps. 1:3) the year 'round. So in Paul's imagery planting and watering are complementary. Each man did what the circumstances made necessary and natural.

But God's activity belongs in an entirely different class: he, and he alone, did what neither of these men or any man could do, he "caused the growing." A man can place the seed into the ground or set out young plants in the soil, a man can keep that soil moist in one way or in another, but what man is able to cause the growing? If God does not cause it, it will never be caused. This fact the Corinthians should have considered, and their party wranglings would have been an impossibility.

In v. 5 Paul says that the Lord (Christ) assigned each minister his work, here he says that God made things grow. Both are divine acts, evidence that Christ and God are of equal power and of equal majesty. The change of tenses is important. The two aorists: "I planted," "he watered," point into the past — the men did their little work and are gone. So it is still: each performs his little instrumental task and leaves. When he is describing God's activity Paul writes the imperfect ηὔξανεν which refers to an act begun in the past but going on and on indefinitely, for the tense is open and sets no terminus. Paul and Apollos have left Corinth, God is still there and causing the growing. Why quarrel about men when the Corinthians should unite in praising God?

7) **So, then, neither the one planting is anything, nor the one watering, but only the one causing the growth, God.** This is the only correct conclusion. Men are nothing, and God is not only something (τι) but, as the contrast implies, he is everything. "God" is placed emphatically at the end. The three present participles are qualitative and describe

the persons with reference to the action in which they engage.

8) Paul carries this comparison of men with God, namely of men as God's ministers compared with God as their Lord, to its very climax. **Now the one planting and the one watering are one, and each according to his own labor shall receive his own wages.** Δέ is continuative, "now." Whatever differences may appear between him who plants and him who waters disappear the moment we look from men to God. These men fuse together and form ἕν, "one thing," one unit. The very idea of separating them and pitting one against the other vanishes into thin air. This tiny word ἕν is the final refutation of the dangerous differences which the Corinthians are making their party slogans.

There are, of course, differences between the Lord's ministers. Does he not send one to plant and another to water? This, too, is his business. But even greater differences appear, particularly in the κόπος, the hard and tiring labor which each performs. Some throw their whole heart into their labor, some have much harder tasks to perform, greater burdens to bear, some are called to labor longer than others. Hence another difference appears: they shall receive different wages. Well, then, is this at least not some justification for the Corinthians when they made efforts to establish differences between their ministers? The very opposite is true. For the "wages" which each worker shall receive as his own are not the concern of men but the supreme concern of God. What a mistake the Corinthians are guilty of when they usurp this function of God's, when one wretched party tries to exalt one man against another, and a second party exalts the other man! If the Corinthians will only follow Paul's example and look to God, all such dangerous proceedings on their part will stop. Each minister shall receive his "wages" of grace at the hand of his gracious and generous Master. Matt. 19:27-29.

"His own wages" makes plain that there will be a difference; this is the one indicated in the parable of the Talents and in that of the Pounds. And the norm or rule which the Lord will apply in apportioning these different wages is expressed in the phrase "according to his own labor." "His own wages" and "according to his own labor" have the two emphatic positions in the sentence. The two parables mentioned show that in all cases the wonderful wages will so exceed the labor of each servant that each will be utterly astonished at the reward which he receives from his magnanimous Lord. In comparison with such wages the little glory which some misguided party in Corinth would bestow becomes a farce.

9) The fact that this apportionment of wages is a matter that belongs wholly to God the double statement with γάρ establishes. **For God's co-workers are we; God's husbandry, God's building, are you.**

The emphasis rests on the three possessives: "God's ... God's ... God's." Two of these declare that even the Corinthians are God's. His are the laborers, his the field with its planting, his the building. Paul does not write co-laborers, for God works but never labors; so he writes "co-workers." The preposition σύν found in the noun connects God's ministers with him and not these ministers with each other save as they are all equally joined with him. "We," of course, refers only to Paul, to Apollos, and to men in the ministry (διάκονοι), and we cannot extend it so as to apply it to Christians generally. The Christian ministry is still a distinct office. Behold the honor which Paul here bestows upon this office! Full of labor though it be, it makes us co-workers with God.

Yet this truth involves much more: all that these workers plant, water, and build is likewise God's, and

God's alone. The Corinthians are a vineyard that is planted and tilled by God's workers and belong to God. There is no σύν in this statement, nor in the one that says that the Corinthians are God's building. This marks the difference. Paul tells the Corinthians: We ministers belong to God as his fellow workers, you, the congregation, belong to him only as his field and his building. The holy office is something more than ordinary membership in the congregation. The Corinthians acted as if these ministers were theirs, to be measured and weighed at pleasure, to be exalted or to be lowered, to be rewarded with praise or to be chastised with criticism. Paul takes these ministers out of their hands, they are God's, doing his work under his special call and commission.

While he thus pronounces these ministers to be God's he at the same time states that the Corinthians, too, are God's, but they are such as the fruit and result of this joint work of God and of his ministers. This truth lies in the two designations γεώργιον, the land with its planting, and οἰκοδομή, the building. There can be no vineyard or other planted field unless someone first works and plants it; nor can there be a building great or small unless someone first erects it. In a subordinate way Paul could say: You Corinthians are our field, our building. But this would be stating only a small part of the truth. The ministers are only God's humble instruments and no more. The real Worker back of them is God himself, and so the entire result is his, supremely his. A double motive must, then, deter the Corinthians from their party cries and contentions: 1) they are misusing God's ministers who because of their very office belong to God; 2) they are thereby untrue to themselves who as the very product of this ministry also belong to God.

A second figure is introduced at the end of this verse by the term "God's building," which forms a link of transition to the next paragraph, in which this new figure and its rich features are to be elaborated.

V. God's Building, 10-23

If the Corinthians will cease to be fleshly and will look upon their true ministers as God's own ministers, if they will realize that God himself will reward each one rightly, they will never tolerate party strife, and they will even rightly view themselves as a product of God's ministry and thus as God's congregation. But back of this party strife in Corinth lies the unholy desire to introduce human wisdom and thus to corrupt the very gospel itself. No minister has as yet stressed this human wisdom in Corinth, at least Paul does not intimate such a state of affairs. But where this pseudo-wisdom is admired by a congregation, there is danger that ministers will be sought who will cater to this dangerous appetite. Instead of building with imperishable truth some may build with perishable material or even forsake the true foundation altogether. This is the danger to be guarded against. "Let each man take heed how he is building." The congregation is to be God's own temple, and woe to him who builds so as to make it anything else! Let no man be mislead by this false wisdom and fall into God's condemnation. Such is the trend of this section, which is dominated by the figure of a building which is advanced to that of a temple, v. 10-17. The section closes with admonition and assurance, v. 18-23.

10) Paul begins with the work that was done in Corinth when the congregation was founded and was built up in the true faith. Now, however, no prominence is given to the persons who did this work. While Paul himself laid the foundation he alludes to himself only incidentally when he mentions this part of the work and uses no emphatic ἐγώ, and when he is speaking about the continuance of the work he mentions only

the fact that it was done by "another," ἄλλος, whoever this may be, and mentions no name or names. Somebody had to begin the work; it was Paul who did it although God could just as well have sent someone else. Likewise, somebody had to go on with the work; it was, we know, especially Apollos who did this although God could have found somebody else. It is the character of the work that Paul wants the Corinthians to note and not the persons whom God employed.

According to the grace of God given to me as a wise architect I laid a foundation, and another builds thereon. Paul disclaims any special credit for starting the work at Corinth. The fact that he was enabled to do so was due entirely to God, was in harmony with his undeserved favor toward Paul, and was in the nature of a pure gift granted to him. In this way Paul regards his own labor in Corinth. He sees only God's "grace" and gift (the aorist participle to express the single past act of bestowal) for which he is truly grateful. That is what he wants the Corinthians to see likewise. The Paul party in Corinth will collapse the moment this is done, and all other parties will likewise disappear.

God's grace and gift consisted in the fact that "as a wise architect I laid a foundation." Paul's meaning is plain: he first placed Christ and the true gospel into the hearts of the Corinthians. Of course, nobody builds without a foundation. The wisdom of Paul consisted, not in laying a foundation, but in laying the right one in the right way. The little word "wise" intends to recall all that Paul said in chapter two regarding the gospel as the true, divine wisdom. While he calls himself a "wise architect" he is not thinking of some wonderful quality of his own mind and intellect but of the true gospel wisdom made his by revelation (2:10). The pride and the satisfaction expressed in the adjective "wise" are pure and holy, for they rest altogether on the consciousness of possessing God's revealed wisdom. We meet this adjective again in 4:4 and in other utterances of Paul's. He knew what he had and with what he worked, and he did not merely assert that what he had was the real wisdom as is the case with many ἄσοφοι who boast of having the genuine gospel merely to justify themselves. Thus also Paul was sure of his great reward, Acts 20:27; II Tim. 4:6-8.

When Paul adds "and another builds thereon" he is giving utterance to a statement that lies in the very nature of the case. A foundation is laid but once, after that the erection of the building itself proceeds. The verb used here really means: another "does the upbuilding." This figure illustrates the entire work of increasing the outward number and the inward faith of the congregation. When Paul writes ἄλλος, "another," this word is to be taken in a general sense like our "somebody else." For this reason he employs an aorist to describe his own work which is past and a present durative tense to indicate the work of building which goes on indefinitely and is going on even now as Paul writes these lines.

That also shows the pertinence of the admonition: **And let each take heed how he builds thereon!** When he calls himself a "wise architect" Paul renders a verdict on his past work of laying the foundation. That was rightly done and is entirely finished. But the building operation is still in full progress and is in the hands of somebody else. It will go on even after Paul is dead. Even now Paul has reason to fear that some of this present work is not being done aright. Hence this admonition and the instruction regarding wise and regarding unwise building.

11) When Paul demands that every man who is engaged in the work of building in Corinth test his work most carefully, he by no means exempts

himself and the work he did in laying the foundation in Corinth. Such an exemption would place him in a class by himself and thus lend support to the Paul party in Corinth, the very consummation Paul would avoid. No; Paul's work, like that of all his successors, must be tested just as theirs is, for they, all of them, are the Lord's διάκονοι. For this reason Paul states the explanation (γάρ): **For, as regards foundation, no one can lay another beside that lying already, which is Jesus Christ.** This is the test to which Paul submits his own work in Corinth. All true building of the church, whether it includes starting a congregation or only continuing one already started, must be in perfect harmony with the one divine foundation which, once laid by God, now lies forever.

When Paul writes that he "laid a foundation" in Corinth he means only that he began the work in that place. Laying a foundation in this sense is in contrast with the erecting of the superstructure. And both expressions used in v. 10 apply to one locality only, which is in this instance Corinth. A vaster thing is meant by the one and only foundation that Paul says is "lying," κείμενον, a present tense, lying permanently and forever. Paul says nothing about him who laid this foundation or how it was laid. There is no need for these details. The Corinthians must bear in mind especially that no second foundation like unto this can ever be laid by anyone. They shall also note what this foundation is, namely "Jesus Christ." When this is understood, all the work of the Lord's διάκονοι, whether it consist of starting a congregation or of later building it up, can be adequately tested, and it can be determined whether such work is really genuine or not.

What had Paul done in Corinth when he there "laid a foundation"? "As a wise architect" he established the hearts of the Corinthians on the one and only foundation, Jesus Christ. All that Paul taught, preached, and practiced in Corinth was done to this end and to this end alone. All of the Corinthians must needs testify to this effect. Paul, therefore, makes no empty claim when he terms himself a wise architect, he states a fact. What Paul had thus begun, others continued, but their work is now called "building" work. And this is to be tested by the same standard. If it establishes the hearts of the Corinthians more and more on the one and only foundation Jesus Christ, if all teaching, all preaching, and all practice serve this end alone, then this work, too, is that of wise architects, true successors of Paul. But recent developments among the Corinthians raise a doubt on this score. For that reason Paul writes these paragraphs, the doubt must be removed.

Our versions translate as though Paul had written: ἄλλον γὰρ θεμέλιον, "other foundation" no one can lay; whereas Paul writes: θεμέλιον γὰρ ἄλλον, "as regards foundation, another no one can lay." The emphasis is on the first word, θεμέλιον, which is either an accusative absolute or an adverbial accusative. When it comes to foundation, Paul says, there *is* only one, and no one can lay a second. We may translate παρά other "than" that (already) lying; or another "beside" that (already) lying. It is a question whether ἄλλον is comparative or not. Paul intimates that someone may, indeed, try to lay a new and a different foundation, that he may even think that he has done so and persuade others to think so also, but the very idea is an impossible absurdity. To forsake this one and only foundation in any way is fatal.

In this connection "Jesus Christ" is inclusive and not exclusive, not even partitive. His entire person and all his work are the foundation that lies fixed and solid forever. He is not merely the center to which something else may be added; he is both center and circumference. His name does not represent only a few doctrines such as one or another age may deem "vital," but includes all the teachings of Scripture, whether you and I deem them vital or not. This foundation, which is Jesus Christ, is objective, "lying" as such before all of us. All other alleged foundations are subjective, i. e., imaginary; they are like the sand referred to in Christ's conclusion of the Sermon on the Mount.

12) Paul now tells us what he has in mind when he utters his warning that we must take heed how we build. Yes, there are differences among the architects or builders, not the foolish and the wrong differences which the Corinthians think they see, but actual and grave differences such as they ought to see lest in Corinth they build in a wrong way or even wreck the temple of God. Paul considers three classes of builders: 1) those who are truly wise (v. 10); 2) those who are unwise and introduce wrong material although they do not leave the foundation; 3) those who are fools and destroy God's temple. The eventual fate of these three classes Paul also indicates. This presentation leaves the question untouched as to what a congregation ought to do with a διάκονος or "minister" who uses faulty material in building or starts to wreck God's temple. There is no reason to enter upon this question in the case of the Corinthians since all their διάκονοι had been faithful men. The Scriptures answer this question in other connections.

Now (δέ, continuative) **if anyone builds on the foundation gold, silver, costly stones, wood, hay, stubble, each one's work shall be made manifest.**

The indefinite "anyone" does not intend to say that one individual builder uses all of these different materials for the structure he erects but, as the distributive "each one's," ἑκάστου, shows, that one builder uses one kind of these materials, another builder a different material. In decidedly different ways, then, the architects may build on the "foundation, Jesus Christ."

The materials used may range all the way from gold to stubble. Paul marks six gradations without using an "or" to indicate a division of the six, yet the fact that he intends to enumerate two groups is perfectly plain because of the great inherent difference in value between the materials named in the two groups. In the one group we have gold, silver, and costly stones, than which there is no more valuable material; in the other we have pieces of wood, hay, and stubble, than which there is no cheaper material. It will not do, then, unduly to stress the manner of building by laying all the emphasis on πῶς, "how," in v. 10 and at the same time assume that all six materials may be used equally in building on the "foundation" just so the manner be right. Such an interpretation loses sight of the test by fire to which each man's structure must eventually submit, v. 13. Moreover, if the manner of building is the chief consideration and the material used only an incidental feature, why does Paul mention all these different materials in such a marked way, and why does he say nothing at all about differences regarding the manner of building? As far as manner is concerned, that exhibits itself in the material which the builder chooses and deems fit for the superstructure to be erected on this grand foundation which is Christ.

Some builders use only precious material; but there is a difference even in their choice, namely between gold, silver, and costly stones. Silver is less valuable than gold, and lovely marble less valuable than silver. Yet these three are evidently intended to represent material that harmonizes as it should with the great and precious foundation. Likewise, hay is even poorer than ξύλα, pieces of wood picked up here and there,

First Corinthians 3:12 139

and stubble is altogether unfit. Who would think of placing material of this type on such a glorious foundation? When Paul descends to stubble, the matter becomes wholly ridiculous in its impossibility. All this is plain when one considers the figurative terms placed side by side. But more must be said.

While Nero built a Golden House in Rome, this was not constructed entirely of gold. We know of no silver house that man ever built. Fine marble structures and wooden houses or huts are frequent, even grass-covered huts are found among savages, but not even a hut was ever built out of stubble. Paul, therefore, does not intend to list actual building materials such as men use. For in this connection "gold" does not mean that some gold was used for ornament only, but that the structure was built of gold throughout; no man ever used this metal to such an extent. And at the other extreme "stubble" does not mean that some stubble was used and worked into clay brick for instance, (Exod. 5:12), but that the structure was made of stubble throughout; no man ever attempted to use such material for constructing even the meanest hut. We fail to understand Paul's figures aright when we take them as a reference to materials which men actually use. "If one builds gold . . . stubble" assumes that one does this, but such an assumption is contrary to what men actually do in ordinary life.

We here have an instance in which the common human actualities are disregarded and only the spiritual are thought of. Jesus employs similar illustrations. No man ever did or would do what Jesus says the owner of the vineyard did in the parable of the Wicked Husbandmen: send one set of servants after another to such murderous men and at last send even his son. As a story of human events it is impossible. What of it? just so it pictures what Jesus desires. In the same way Paul writes about a man who builds an entire structure out of gold and again one entirely out of stubble.

But what does this figurative language mean? Two interpretations are offered. The one lets these six materials denote *persons* for the reason that the foundation is the person Jesus Christ and because the church consists of persons. But this interpretation contains a flaw. We may, indeed, conceive of a minister who receives into his congregation a crowd that is made up of all sorts of people that only nominally profess Christianity. Such a thing is done often enough at present. Such congregational material might be termed wood, hay, and stubble. But we cannot conceive that, when these persons perish in the judgment fire, the man who accepted these persons and of them built up his congregation should himself in the end escape, "he himself shall be saved," v. 15. If these materials denote persons, then the builder who uses persons who are fit to be termed wood, hay, and stubble must himself also perish with this combustible material.

The other interpretation lets these six materials denote *doctrines* or rather the substance of the teaching employed by the ministers of the church. Thus gold, silver, and costly stones are the teaching of the "wisdom" of the gospel which is full of the everlasting ἀλήθεια or truth; wood, hay, and stubble are teachings and church practices that are devoid of this wisdom and this truth. A similar illustration uses, not, indeed, the building, but the foundation, in one case the rock of Christ's words or teachings, in the other sand or the disregard of Christ's teachings.

The view that the building erected on the foundation Jesus Christ is not a doctrinal structure but one that is composed of the souls of men is unsatisfactory. The teachings here referred to are not systems of doctrine that are set down in books but kinds of teaching that are put into men's minds and hearts, which therefore produce certain results in their lives. We need think only of Corinth where some were inclined to use the wood, hay, and stubble of human wisdom as the choicest kind of teaching with which to fill the hearts of the people. Paul still calls them brethren, but this kind of teaching filled Paul with alarm for all who received it in any way. We ourselves find pastors and people who admire such wood, hay, and stubble in teaching and in church practice (which is itself the strongest kind of teaching since actions speak louder than words) as though it were gold, silver, and costly stones. Because of ignorance some misapprehend what the Scriptures teach, or they have been taught incorrectly. That is so much wood that will never stand the judgment fire. Some go farther. They justify what the Scriptures condemn and teach men accordingly. This is hay, or, worse still, wretched stubble, outrageous stuff to connect with Jesus Christ. The fire will devour it in a flash.

Two things must be remembered about this correct interpretation: 1) that the foundation is not abandoned when wood, hay, and stubble are built into the church; 2) that such building is by no means without the gravest danger, both for those who are builders and for those who are being built. For it is but a step from using the wrong material, mistaking wood, hay, and stubble for gold, silver, and valuable stone, or thinking them equal to these, to changing to a wrong foundation, losing the true Christ, and accepting one who is self-made in order the better to match the admired wood, hay, and stubble.

13) The protasis: "if one builds," followed by the future in the apodosis: "shall be made manifest," is a condition of reality. While the building process goes on, much deception remains, also much self-deception in regard to the true character of the materials that are used. Not even the gold is always recognized

as what it is, to say nothing of the lesser silver, or still lesser costly stone. But "each one's work shall be made (or become) manifest" in the end so that all deception or even doubt shall disappear.

The statement with γάρ explains this: **for the day shall declare it because it is revealed in fire; and each one's work, of what sort it is, the fire itself shall test.**

"The day," ἡ ἡμέρα with the definite article and no further modifier, means the great final day of judgment that is so often named in the Scriptures. The object of δηλώσει, "shall declare" or make plain, is ἑκάστου τὸ ἔργον, "each one's work," which naturally becomes the implied subject of ἀποκαλύπτεται, "is revealed." It is not the day that is revealed, the day merely "comes," ἔρχεται, as the Scriptures say. Each man's "work" is what he actually built up on the foundation. How the day of judgment shall make that plain, as well as why this day does it as no previous day has done, the clause with ὅτι states. Each builder's work "is revealed" as just what it is. The agent implied in the verb is God. This revelation is intended for the whole world of men and of angels, the builder himself being, of course, included. Here men may deceive themselves and others but they shall not be so successful in the final apocalypse.

"In fire" is figurative for "in judgment," namely the absolutely righteous judgment of God. The point of comparison in "fire" is not its light but its consuming power. The materials mentioned prepare for this figure, for three are incombustible, and three are combustible. The consuming power of this divine fire appears in other Scripture utterances, II Thess. 1:8; Heb. 12:29; Deut. 4:24; Mal. 3:2. Fire separates precious metal from dross and destroys sham and falseness and leaves truth and reality. Paul uses three verbs to indicate what the final day with its judgment upon every builder's work shall bring: make plain — be revealed — test or test out. The making plain shall be brought about by a testing out, δοκιμάζειν. A thing is tested or proved to determine whether it is genuine. So also a person may be tested as to whether he is fit for an office or whether he is what he ought to be, C.-K. Here the medium, "the fire itself," indicates the method that is used in the last great test.

14) If anyone's work shall abide which he built up, he shall receive wages. Paul retains the idea of "wages" mentioned in v. 8 and says that they shall be awarded for work that proves to be genuine and carefully defines this work by means of the relative clause "which he built up." Such a clause does not appear in the next verse which records the fate of the spurious work. The aorist is in place, for the work is completed when it comes to the final test. The condition is again one of reality which agrees with Paul's objective presentation in v. 12 and again in v. 15. In regard to the genuine work Paul writes that it "shall abide" in the sense that it shall remain undamaged by the fire of testing; thus he keeps the figure and also the reality back of the figure. To think of a fire that is so intense as to melt gold and silver and to spall or burst marble and other costly stones is to overdo Paul's figure. The fact that the "wages" mentioned are entirely a gift of grace need not be stated after a phrase like that found at the beginning of v. 10. Yet these wages are duly promised to all faithful teachers and preachers of the gospel; Rev. 4:4; 11:18; I Cor. 9:17; II John 8; Dan. 12:3. They consist in higher degrees of glory and in the delightful eternal contemplation of the work these builders have wrought by the Lord's grace.

15) The absence of a connective heightens the contrast between the two parallel statements. **If anyone's work shall be burned up, he shall suffer loss though he himself shall be saved, yet so as through**

fire. The impossibility of letting τὸ ἔργον refer to the persons gathered into the church is obvious. The verb κατακαίω, to burn up completely, to be consumed, the opposite of μένειν, to abide, excludes the very idea, for in no sense can persons burn up. "The work" is the ignorant, mistaken, non-genuine teaching, all of it being sticks of wood (ξύλα, plural), or only hay, or, still worse, stubble. This burns up because there is no divine reality in it. The figure does not, however, change so that fire and burning up now denote God's wrath. Paul still speaks of the divine judgment, and this burning up denotes the complete rejection of the work of the unwise builders, their teaching and all that they thought they had accomplished in men's hearts through it.

For the builder the result is: "he shall suffer loss." All to which he devoted his life shall be suddenly swept away. He shall stand bare where he might have had so much. Hence there is, of course, no thought of wages for him, and this is the great loss. Many great "works" shall thus go down in ashes in the judgment and be absolutely disowned by the Lord. Many proud builders who were acclaimed by men while they lived and were honored with great tributes when they were buried shall hang their heads when all their work becomes nothing in the fire test. But many a humble preacher, of whom nobody made much in life, shall shine at that day because he wrought gold, silver, and precious stones.

Though it strikes us as strange, Paul nevertheless writes regarding the unwise builder: "he himself shall be saved." This is due to the fact that, despite his wretchedly faulty work, despite even the very stubble of his teaching, he remained on the great "foundation Jesus Christ." It is a manifestation of wondrous grace on God's part that such a foolish builder should be allowed to escape although he is stripped of the glory of the faithful. "Yet as through fire" indicates the narrow escape. He is like a man who flees from a burning building, is badly frightened, and saves nothing but his life. Even here "fire" means divine judgment. The picture seems to be somewhat on this order: this builder stands in the house of his work, and when the judgment-fire strikes and devours it, he rushes out. Who wants to spend all his life in the ministry and then end in such a way?

Two things are now, however, clear. The teaching of wood, hay, and stubble cannot signify heretical doctrines such as subvert the very foundation of faith in Christ. They are perhaps vacuous teachings that do not deserve the name of doctrines at all, human notions added to the gospel. They are actually sectarian doctrines that are false and dangerous enough and yet do not destroy the cross as such. Paul says throughout that the unwise builder builds something, wrong though it is, on the foundation. In the second place, although Paul avoids all mention of the hearers of this kind of teaching, the only fair conclusion we can draw in regard to them is that, like their teacher, they, too, escape as through fire.

While Paul himself contrasts only two builders, one whose work shall remain, and one whose work shall be burned up, additional possibilities are at least suggested. One may build a structure that is made entirely of gold and not use silver at all; another may use only silver, still another only costly stones. Or, one may build with some gold, etc., and yet foolishly add some wood, etc., and thus lose some of his wages. Let us all strive with all our might to use as much gold as possible!

Paul's word regarding fire is used by the Catholics as proof for their doctrine of purgatory. But this fire is restricted to the last day; it is not a fire of purgation but of final judgment; it is intended for the builders and only by a deduction for certain unwise Christians.

16) The third possibility follows. The first two Paul treats altogether objectively by refraining from all direct personal reference. The third he states subjectively by even asking the Corinthians a direct question in regard to themselves. The first possibility is that a teacher builds upon the foundation in a true way (gold, etc.); the second that a teacher builds on it in a false way (wood, etc.). The third is, however, not building at all (the idea of this figure has been exhausted) but the opposite of building, φθείρειν, destroying and wrecking. Let us note in this connection that the line between using wrong material in building and the terrible work of destroying the divine structure is quite faint and easily crossed with fatal results.

In presenting the final possibility Paul advances the idea with which he began when he spoke of the "foundation" and of the building which the builders erect thereon. He did not immediately state what this structure is. With an effective asyndeton and a question which is directed to the Corinthians he now does this. **Do you not know that you are God's sanctuary, and that the Spirit of God dwells in you?** The question as such and its point in regard to the "sanctuary" intend to startle. The form of the question takes for granted that the Corinthians do know what Paul asks. The force of the question is to have the Corinthians vividly recall what they know because of its great importance in the present connection.

No article is needed with ναός, for only one such sanctuary now exists even as only one existed in Israel. We must distinguish this ναός, the structure containing the Holy Place and the Holy of Holies, from the ἱερόν which included all the courts and all the structures on the Temple hill. Even in the Old Testament the people who used the Temple of God were themselves considered the real temple of God. When Paul calls the Corinthians God's sanctuary he does not mean that each congregation is a separate temple-sanctuary so that there are many such sanctuaries. On the contrary, God's people are one spiritual temple or sanctuary, and wherever God's people are, there that sanctuary is found.

With an explicative καί Paul at once explains how he comes to call the Corinthians "God's sanctuary," which is a term that certainly places them on a very high level: "and the Spirit of God dwelleth in you." The basic and self-evident proposition is this: where God dwells, there is his sanctuary. He is, indeed, everywhere by virtue of his omnipresence but he does not "dwell," οἰκεῖ, everywhere. As one adopts an οἶκος as his home, so God dwells with and in his people. This is the specific gracious presence that is always mediated by Word and Sacrament, for which the Scriptures employ the most beautiful imagery, which is summarized by the church in the term *unio mystica*. God's indwelling separates, sanctifies, sets apart for himself all who are thus honored and blessed.

It is true that the *unio mystica* is personal for each believer, and yet Paul's phrase "in you" includes the entire congregation as a unit. The divine indwelling unites into one all who are thus blessed; it does not separate except from the world, it joins together. The divine indwelling is ascribed to all three persons of the Godhead, John 14:17, 23, for the *opera ad extra sunt indivisa*. When this act is ascribed, as is done in this case, to the Spirit, we may recall that his office and his function are to sanctify us unto God.

17) The erection of gold, etc., and of wood, etc., on the foundation Jesus Christ includes all the teaching of the builders, that by which they begin to gather people together to form a congregation like Paul's lay-

ing the foundation in Corinth, v. 10, and that of building up such a congregation outwardly and inwardly. These teachers are, therefore, properly pictured as architects or builders, and their work as erecting some kind of structure on the great foundation. When Paul now proceeds to speak about destroying God's sanctuary he can no longer use the figure of builders who erect something, for to destroy and to wreck are the very opposite of building up. This damnable work is also restricted to the actual sanctuary of God that true builders have already erected. For this reason Paul first focuses the attention of the Corinthians upon themselves as being the sanctuary of God built up by his own work and by that of other true builders. And then with a sudden turn he focuses the eyes of the Corinthians on this nefarious work of tearing down what has been built up in Corinth with such great labor.

If anyone destroys the sanctuary of God, him shall God destroy, for the sanctuary of God is holy, since of such kind are you. The structure of the conditional sentence is chiastic in the Greek, which brings the two verbs sharply together and lends them great emphasis. We are unable to duplicate this in English. The sense of the two verbs $\phi\theta\epsilon\iota\rho\epsilon\iota$ and $\phi\theta\epsilon\rho\epsilon\hat{\iota}$ is therefore identical. We cannot translate as the A. V. does: "If any man *defile*, etc., him shall God *destroy*." We translate: "If anyone *destroys*, him shall God *destroy*."

Paul does not say how he conceives this destroying. We shall not go far wrong when we say that, if the Corinthians themselves are God's sanctuary because of the indwelling of the Spirit, he destroys this sanctuary, be he teacher or layman, who by lies and deceptions drives the Spirit out of the hearts of the Corinthians and fills them with the spirit of the world. The man who does this nefarious work cannot possibly have the Spirit in his own heart. On this fearful work compare Matt. 18:6, 7. Yet Paul is not intimating that in Corinth anyone has advanced to this third stage, that of wrecking the faith and the godly life of the Lord's people, but he issues a grave warning nevertheless. The future tense "shall destroy," like the futures occurring in all the previous statements in v. 13-15, refers to the last day although it does not, of course, exclude any preliminary judgments which God may deem it necessary to inflict.

The severity of this final judgment, namely destruction in hell, is justified by the addition "for the sanctuary of God is holy," separated from the world and entirely set apart for him. This is the worst among human crimes, *nefas*, a monstrous deed. What Paul writes about it is general and in this sense objective although v. 16 already lends a subjective touch. Paul intensifies this touch into a direct application to the Corinthians when he adds the relative clause with οἵτινες. But this relative is unusual. Does οἵτινες mean simply οἵ? Even then the remarkable attraction in number from the singular antecedent ναός (ἅγιος) to the plural predicate ὑμεῖς would remain and call for an explanation. Moreover, the one relative cannot be substituted for the other. R. 960 says: "There is an argument in οἵτινες." We cannot translate in the easy fashion: "which (sanctuary) ye are," as our versions do. This loses even the decided emphasis on "you." We must render: "since of such kind are you." The indefinite relative οἵτινες is causal and includes "since," which makes plain what Robertson means by saying it contains an argument.

Paul's statement really involves a syllogism. Major premise: Whoever destroys the sanctuary of God, God will destroy him, for his sanctuary is holy. Minor premise: You Corinthians are holy and God's sanctuary. Conclusion, implied: Whoever destroys you,

150   Interpretation of First Corinthians

God will destroy him. The verb φθείρειν may mean either "destroy" or "corrupt" as the context determines. We have no English verb that has this double sense. The German renders it well: *Wer den Tempel verdirbt, verderben wird den Gott,* which even retains the chiasm of the Greek wording.

18) The last clause in v. 17 prepares the way for the admonitions which now follow. They contain the practical deductions which the Corinthians should carry into effect. Paul might have used the connective οὖν, "therefore." **Let no one deceive himself. If anyone thinks he is wise among you in this world age, let him become a fool in order that he may become wise.**

Paul intends this not only for the teachers in Corinth but for all the Corinthians, for "no one" and "anyone" obtain their range from "you" in v. 17; and μηδείς is regular because μή is the negative with imperatives, R. 1170. The danger to be found in Corinth is that some, many, possibly even all may deceive themselves with respect to the entire subject which Paul is discussing, that of wisdom, of teachers, and of the kind of work which they do. By using the singular "no one," etc., Paul appeals to each individual personally; compare the same singular in v. 21.

Without a connective Paul states what he means by this self-deception and at the same time points out how to escape its snare: "If anyone thinks (δοκεῖ, *sibi videtur, sich etwas darauf einbildet,* has the conceit) he is wise among you." This is the great danger: one may have the conceit that he is truly wise when he in reality is the very opposite. The phrase "in this world age" does not modify "wise" as though Paul describes this person as thinking himself "wise in this world age." He thinks he is spiritually wise among the Corinthians. It is Paul who appends the phrase "in this world age" to the entire sentence: in this world age

First Corinthians 3:18 151

a man may flatter himself that he has the true wisdom whereas all that he possesses is what he has obtained from this world age. He is surely badly deceived, for his wisdom is altogether imaginary.

To this man Paul says: "let him become a fool," μωρός as far as this deceptive world wisdom is concerned. Let him discard this wisdom, have himself called "a fool" by the adherents of this wisdom, yea, appear as "a fool" to himself for doing so "in order that he may become wise" in the true sense of the word through the everlasting wisdom of Jesus Christ, which is far above anything connected with this transient world age. In this admonition Paul presents the very heart of all that he has discussed thus far. This practical deduction each of the Corinthians is to make for his own person and his own life. In this connection it is quite immaterial whether he considers himself wise in the world's wisdom or wise in adhering to some teacher whom he foolishly rates as wise in regard to this wisdom.

But the real danger that lurks in this conceit of deeming oneself wise is not so much in being filled (subjectively) with a false idea concerning oneself but in the fact (objectively) that this worldly wisdom detracts from Christ and thus destroys that on which all salvation and all true wisdom depend, namely the cross of Christ, 1:17. Hence also the way in which to escape the dangers of this conceit is not by trying to supplement the world's wisdom by adding some of the wisdom of Christ to it, or vice versa, but only in utterly casting aside the spurious wisdom, in no longer holding to any of it, and thus in actually becoming a fool.

And yet such a one will not, after all, be a fool, for by the way indicated one will achieve the inner attitude for really appropriating Christ and will actually attain (γένηται σοφός, the aorist indicating actuality) the true wisdom. Note the sharp oxymoron between μωρός and σοφός and the masterly exactness with which every word is placed. In this statement of Paul's there is, of course, no repudiation of the genuine results of science in any department as far as these pertain to our earthly life, but there is a complete repudiation of any and of all hypotheses, theories, and speculations, scientific, philosophic, or popular, which lord it over Christ and the Scriptures.

19) In a simple but highly effective way γάρ proves that Paul's injunction is correct: **For the wisdom of this world is foolishness with God.** And this finding is in turn substantiated by the Scriptures which tell us how God treats those who are worldly wise: **For it has been written** (see 1:19): **He taketh the wise in their craftiness,** Job 5:13, to which a second proof is added with the words "and again" (it is written). Instead of following the translation of the LXX: "Who captures wise men in (their) understanding" Paul translates the Hebrew with more exactness: *Er, der die Weisen in ihrer Verschmitztheit erhascht.*

A πανοῦργος is capable of anything in an evil sense, hence the abstract noun = "craftiness." To be taken in craftiness as when a crafty scoundrel or criminal is arrested, is to be exposed and then, of course, to be punished accordingly. It is crafty reasoning by which the "wise" put their sham wisdom across and rob men's souls of Christ and of true wisdom altogether or in part. The fact that God catches them in the very act and exposes all their craftiness is factual evidence that his wisdom completely outranks theirs, and nothing is more convincing than a fact.

20) Paul adds Ps. 94:11: **The Lord knows the reasonings of the wise, that they are useless.** Both the Hebrew and the LXX have "of men" while Paul has the interpretative translation "of the wise." The Lord "knows" means that he recognizes their reason-

ings as just what they are. These διαλογισμοί of the worldly wise are the thoughts at which they arrive, *ihre Ueberlegungen*. What the Lord sees is that all their carefully thought-out conclusions are μάταιοι, ineffectual. They do not reach the goal and in this sense are "useless"; κενοί would be "hollow" like an empty nut, without substance. The ineffectiveness of these wise men is illustrated by the schemes, plots, and tricky questions of the Lord's enemies, by which they tried to entangle him. Jesus always saw completely through their cunning and frustrated their designs with a word or two. So again God's wisdom exposes the wise men as fools. His wisdom and his judgment alone prevail. Let the Corinthians keep that in mind and not deceive themselves by admiring worldly wisdom, whether it is found in their own minds or in the teachers who may offer their "reasonings" to the church.

21, 22) What is the proper conclusion to be drawn from all this? **Wherefore let no one glory in men.** This sums up all nicely for the Corinthians and does so in just the form they need. At the beginning of a new sentence ὥστε is only an inferential conjunction, R. 949, and not hypotactic. The admonition given in v. 18: "Let no one deceive himself," and this one found in v. 21: "Let no one glory in men," are a pair. This self-deception consists in glorying in men; and any glorying in men is self-deception. To glory in men, καυχᾶσθαι, means to boast about them, their qualities, teachings, and wisdom in any measure or degree apart from Christ and the wisdom of the gospel. The Corinthians were on the way to that type of glorying.

Yet the reason which Paul appends for his injunction is surprising: **For all things are yours,** (and then he lists in v. 22) **whether Paul, or Apollos, or Cephas, or the world, or life, or death, or things present, or things to come,** and then again, and now wonderfully effective: **all yours.** Does it seem at first glance as though the statement that Paul, Apollos, and Cephas belong to the Corinthians justifies the existence of different parties in Corinth? That view will be dropped when the mind catches the force of Paul's statement, which adds much more to these men than the Corinthians have ever considered. They are divided into wrangling parties, each vaunting itself in regard to only one man, and thus in the most foolish way each party makes itself wretchedly poor when the Lord who is infinitely generous bestows upon them all these men with all the precious gospel for which they stand and so much more in addition that the Corinthians cannot grasp it all. Why literally "all things" are theirs! And they should fall down on their knees and worship the Lord who makes them so gloriously rich. Philosophers, too, love the proposition: *Omnia sapientis esse;* but what an inferior idea they have of "all things" and of "the wise man" who thinks they are his!

Paul would, of course, at once say what he means by "all things." And since his mind is divinely inspired, he reaches out beyond the immediate range of the thought which he has been elaborating. Yet the new wealth which he suddenly enumerates to the Corinthians is not something that is heterogeneous to the wisdom that has been his great theme. He neither digresses nor runs off on a tangent. This divine σοφία whose praises he sings actually reaches out to all that he now mentions and includes nothing less.

There is first the group of the three significant men whom the blind party spirit in Corinth pitted against each other, Paul, Apollos, and Cephas. Christ is omitted in a marked way, for Christ cannot and dare not be mentioned as occupying the same level with men. Nor dare he be named as one in a list of men, although such a list might include the greatest of men. How foolish to pit these men against each other when all three of them, including all that divine grace had bestowed upon each of them, belonged equally to the Corinthians! Yet they did not, indeed, belong to them in order that they might boast about them but rather in order that they might accept them with humble thanks.

Next to the three men which form one group is placed the second: the world, life, and death. No article is needed with κόσμος, for there is only one "world," which here does not mean "the unbelieving world" but the ordered universe which God himself has created and into which he has placed us. In a sense in which the pagan σοφοί with their unspiritual and merely carnal minds never understood it this wonderful cosmos belongs to the Christians in Corinth. Nor does Paul mean merely that the world is only ideally theirs, and that the reality of its possession lies in the eon to come. Through the wisdom of Christ we see the universe as it actually is, namely God's creation; we find his power, wisdom, and beneficence in all its creatures; we receive a thousand earthly blessings in this world from the hand of God, as many as our lives can hold; upheld by his grace, we serve him in this world and faithfully work for his glory. Thus the world is ours. And no worldly sophist can say the same.

"Life and death" might appear as a pair like "things present and things to come," but they belong in the same group with the cosmos. For this is ζωή, the divine life principle, the spiritual life in Christ Jesus which is born of the living Word in regeneration. "Life" in this sense cannot be paired with "death" as its counterpart, for temporal death is only the transfer of our ζωή from this earthly cosmos to the abode of God, heaven. The wise of this world know nothing of this "life" in Christ, they concern themselves only with the life of their earthly existence, the ψυχή which animates their bodies. Yet the spiritual life comes to us in this world as it came to Paul in

Damascus. Who can utter all the blessedness that this life includes? Thanks be to God that it is ours! And with it also "death," the release from all sin, temptation, evil with which we wrestle now because the cosmos, great and wonderful though it is, has been invaded by Satan. The Christian falls asleep in Jesus, and so "death is ours" as a blessed end.

The last two constitute a pair, ἀνεστῶτα, the things that have already set in and are now here, and μέλλοντα, the things that are about to be. A third cannot be added, for there is nothing beyond "the things to come," otherwise Paul would have added it. "Present things" are all those that surround us here in time as long as we live (ἀνεστῶτα, perfect tense, but the perfect forms of this verb are always used in the sense of the present), all the objects, situations, events, and experiences that we meet. The best commentary is furnished by Paul himself in Rom. 8:28, 32.

Present things are ours because they bring us good. "It is as if this multitude of servants surrounded us and on bended knees held out their precious offerings to us. Some of these servants like pain, injury, sickness, grief, and death may at first have a strange look to us who do not know our own royalty sufficiently. It is God who commissions them all and makes each one bring us some blessing so that as kings unto God we shall lack nothing." *Kings and Priests*, by the author, page 26. The term μέλλοντα refers to the αἰὼν μέλλων, the heavenly eon about to come, and denotes all that shall be ours in eternal life. Both terms are terms of time and yet as neuter plurals denote that which fills these concepts of time. No tongue can tell what the things that are about to come will be.

"All yours!" Paul writes. The thought overwhelms one with blessedness. Paul's eyes are clear, they see and glory in all this wealth. The Corinthians should also see it and glory with him. Then all their bickerings will die out and be swept away like a fog.

These lines cannot be considered abstractly, without personal reference to the Corinthians, because both at the beginning and at the end Paul writes all are "yours." The view of pagan Greeks and Latins that the wise man (philosophically wise) *rules* all things should not be found in Paul's words, for "are yours" denotes possession and not domination. The universe, for instance, is ours, but we do not rule it. Paul's conception of the cosmos differs *in toto* from that of the philosophers; read Rom. 8:38. The beauty and the rhythm of this wonderful passage from Paul's pen have been made visible even to the eye. If curved lines are drawn to enclose these lines, we have the tracing of a lovely vase:

) All things are yours (

(Whether Paul, or Apollos, or Cephas)
(Whether world, or life, or death)

) Whether present, or coming (

(All yours)

(And you Christ's, and Christ God's.)

The first line has one unit. The second and the third lines each have three units. The fourth line has two units. The fifth line has one unit. The base line, the bottom of the vase, has a pair of units. These two verses are a part of the basis of Luther's famous essay *Von der Freiheit eines Christenmenschen.*

23) Christ is significantly not named along with Paul, Apollos, and Cephas. He now receives his place. But not in the form: "Christ is yours," as though he can in any way be ranked with these other possessions. No; the reverse is true. Although the Corinthians have all these possessions, they are themselves a possession: **And you are Christ's.** This genitive "Christ's" shows plainly that the previous genitive "yours" includes no thought of ruling, which is clinched by the final statement: "and Christ is God's," which cannot express rule. Wonderfully blessed are we with all our spiritual and all our earthly possessions, yet exceeding all these possessions is the blessing that envelops them all, that we ourselves are Christ's possession. Here is the true slogan which abolishes all others: ὑμεῖς Χριστοῦ. "You" means all of the Corinthians as one body. This wipes out the "I" in the old slogans, one individual over against the others, which was also the fault of the so-called Christ party.

When God is reached, the cumulation attains its climax. **And Christ is God's** is at times used in support of subordinationism, and even when it is not so used this statement seems to make Christ lower than God. The answer is, however, not that the term "Christ" points only to the human nature (which is not accurate), of which it may, indeed, be said that God is above it. "Christ" denotes office, "The Anointed One," anointed to be prophet, high priest, and king for us, he is incarnate, indeed, yet both God and man. And Θεός is the Triune God. This makes plain that Paul's statement does not deal with the inner relation of the first and second persons of the Godhead. So also εἶναι τινος always denotes possession and not rank and subordination. In all that pertains to his redemptive office and his work Christ belongs to God, for God sent him, anointed him, glorified him, and thus Christ is God's.

"Are yours" involves, first of all, the objective reality which is the basic feature of this possession. For all things are ours only by a gracious granting on the part of God. We are likewise Christ's by his gracious election (1:27, 28) and adoption. And again Christ is God's only because of God's great mission. Secondly, "are yours" involves a subjective acceptance and appropriation. We must take and use "all things" as the Grantor intends so that we remain wholly Christ's and in no way disturb our relation to him. If this relation is disturbed or broken, all things are no longer ours as God intends. This extends even to God. For we are to leave Christ as he truly is, namely God's, and thus are we to be his and not to turn Christ into something else by notions of our own, viz., making him a party head and his holy name a party slogan. Thus Paul gently corrects the Christ party in Corinth by implication.

Sound, true, and blessed will remain all taking on our part from Christian teachers and all other taking from God, all joy in Christian teachers and all other joy that God grants us, when all this becomes an expression of our belonging in Christ to God. Ph. Bachmann.

CHAPTER IV

VI. God's Faithful Stewards, chapter 4

Since all of the Corinthian teachers are ministers of God (3:5), and since also the Corinthian congregation is God's, the rating of these ministers belongs to God. The Corinthians dare not, therefore, set up human standards of their own that are derived from some worldly wisdom of theirs, whereby to rate these ministers. They must do as Paul does: abide by God's judging.

Paul, Apollos, and Peter were faithful. The distinctions which the Corinthians made between them were based on other points, unwarranted points. This fact explains why Paul does not discuss the question regarding unfaithful teachers who preach and teach false doctrine. All that needs to be said on this point is stated in 3:16, 17. In 4:5 Paul writes: "and then each one shall have his praise from God," and says nothing about blame. So he here deals only with the faithful. In other connections Paul tells us that we ourselves are, indeed, to judge preachers and teachers, and if they bring false doctrine, we are to withdraw from them and separate ourselves. Rom. 16:17.

1) Thus let a man consider us as Christ's attendants and stewards of God's mysteries.

The οὕτω is not correlative to ὡς: "so . . . as," and we do not translate as our versions do: "*so* account of us *as*," etc. With verbs of judging (here λογίζεσθαι) we naturally have predicate objects (here "attendants and stewards"), and we have ὡς ("consider us as," etc.) or may not have it ("consider us attendants," etc.). "So" is not needed to magnify "as." Moreover, this οὕτω introduces the sentence with a strong accentuation, which cannot be the case if it is to be regarded as a correlative of the very slight ὡς. Finally, the two emphatic genitives "of Christ" and "God's" in a marked way point back to the same strong genitives occurring in 3:23. Therefore οὕτω = "thus," as just stated in 3:23. Just as and in the manner as, οὕτω, the Corinthians belong to Christ, and Christ to God, the apostles on their part (ἡμᾶς with emphasis) "as," ὡς, attendants and stewards belong to both Christ and God.

In 3:5, "ministers through whom you believed," stresses the relation of the apostles to the Corinthians, here Paul points out their relation to God. It is characteristic of Paul to complete a thought thus. "Us," which is fully stated in the Greek and placed before the verb, is emphatic while ἄνθρωπος, which is minus the article, is very similar to the indefinite *man* in German. The verb means "consider," but this is a considering that is due, not to mere feeling, liking, or casual impression, but to a careful estimation of the reality. The Corinthians are not considering what their teachers actually are, for they are advancing them as heads of parties, which they are not.

They are to consider them as "Christ's attendants," for that is what they really are. While etymologically ὑπηρέτης = *Ruderknecht*, underrower in a galley, this specific meaning had become lost, and to the Greeks the term meant only an attendant or helper who assists a higher master. In this case Christ is that master. Every apostle and every minister and pastor is only an underling, a helper, or an attendant of Christ. His sole function is to take orders and at once and without question to execute them. His will is only that of his Master.

More people than just the Corinthians should remember that truth. Too many attendants deal with the Lord's orders as they themselves please, they pervert them so as to suit themselves and their congregations; and too many congregations themselves issue orders to the attendants as if the latter were their attendants and not the Lord's.

In order to emphasize the significance of this position of the ministers Paul adds a second designation: "stewards." An οἰκονόμος is often a slave to whom his master and owner entrusts property which he is to administer. In this instance God is the master. Compare the slaves or δοῦλοι mentioned in the two parables Matthew 25:14 and Luke 19:13; Joseph in Gen. 39:4; the *oikonomos* in Luke 16:1, who, however, does not appear as a *doulos*. No special difference is intended by making the attendants belong to Christ and the stewards to God, and this differentiation does not indicate a subordination of Christ to God, for these attendants and stewards are the same persons, and their ownership by Christ and by God indicates equality. In the case of the stewards a special genitive is needed, for they must administer property in order to be classed as stewards. The genitive "God's mysteries" names the property, namely God's gifts for our salvation as embodied in the gospel. These are mysteries, for man's wisdom knows nothing about them.

In both terms "attendants" and "stewards," the prominent idea is that of complete subordination to a master, and in the latter also that of special accountability. A helper merely takes his orders and at once carries them out without question. A steward also takes his orders and carries them out in due process, and then returns and renders his account. He works, as it were, by himself, in the absence of his lord, who trusts him to this extent. But he is always and fully accountable. He dare not deviate in the slightest from his orders, nor try to improve upon those orders with wisdom of his own in order to please others.

Again, more people than just the Corinthians should remember that truth. Too many stewards change their orders to please themselves and their congregations; and too many congregations act as though they owned these stewards and as though they are accountable only to them. Because the day of reckoning has not yet come, all concerned feel secure; but this security is a false security.

Since he is entrusted with valuable properties, a steward naturally ranks higher than a mere attendant, although both are slaves. This steward who is set over the mysteries of God possesses a corresponding dignity with which men may not interfere, and, having received his trust from God, even God thereby honors him as the incumbent of this office. Thus "attendant" points to lowliness, and "steward" to dignity, and both combined indicate how the Corinthians are to regard their ministers. Yet both men are slaves, are owned by their Lord who uses them as he wills, to whom all their labor and all results of their labor belong, and who, after their services have been rendered, owes them neither wages nor reward.

2) Our answer to the textual question involved in the first words of this verse is to adopt the reading that is best attested: ὧδε λοιπὸν ζητεῖται ἐν τοῖς οἰκονόμοις, ἵνα πιστός τις εὑρεθῇ. **In this case, then, it is required in the stewards that one be found trustworthy.**

The adverb ὧδε means "here," namely "in this case" of the slaves just mentioned. We may regard λοιπόν as a mere particle that is equivalent to "then"; or we may make it stronger, equivalent to the German *uebrigens*. It then points to the one remaining consideration to be mentioned in this connection. Paul has, however, used two designations in v. 1, "attendants and stewards"; now he intends to disregard "attendants" and to consider the higher term "stewards" in the sequel. For this reason he adds the epexegetical phrase "in the stewards" and uses the article of previous reference: the stewards just referred to in v. 1. We may paraphrase Paul's thought: You Corinthians are to consider us apostles and ministers as attendants and stewards of the Lord. Very well, yet, especially as far as these stewards are concerned, you must note the general rule which naturally applies also to them as stewards. And then Paul states that rule: the thing sought in such stewards is "that one be found trustworthy or reliable." In his characteristic manner Paul combines the plural "in these stewards" with the singular "that one be found faithful," any one of them. The singular suggests that each one of them should ask himself: "Am I a reliable steward?"

The subfinal ἵνα clause is the subject of ζητεῖται, "it is required," it is sought. One may, of course, say that also an attendant ought to be found faithful. But this type of servant works under the eye of his master. The steward is placed over some estate at a distance from his master's presence and makes periodic reports. Hence the aorist εὑρεθῇ, which is suitable only to a situation of this kind. "Trustworthy" means: so that his master may completely rely on him. The word is to be viewed wholly from the master's standpoint: "trustworthy" in the judgment and according to the verdict of the master. Our heavenly Master makes no mistake in judging the trustworthiness of the ministers to whom he has entrusted the gospel and the church.

In this connection we decline to wrestle with a supposed discrepancy, namely that Paul seems to speak only regarding the divine stewards and again seems to state only a general principle that is applicable to any and to all stewards, human or divine. Paul does not suspend us between these alternatives. Nor need we strike out the phrase "in the stewards" and thus reduce Paul's statement to the general principle indicated. Paul combines the general principle with the specific application in the case of the stewards regarding whom he speaks.

The verb ζητεῖν is used with reference to judicial inquiry in regard to a certain point, here the point of faithfulness. Thus it corresponds well with the verb ἀνακρίνειν, which is used in much the same way although it generally has the broader meaning of a general judicial inquiry. Other things, too, may be sought in a steward: ability, experience, and the like, but faithfulness is the indispensable qualification.

3) With an emphatic ἐμοί Paul now specifies by directing attention to himself, but only as an example of the entire class indicated in "stewards" and most certainly not as an exception to the rule mentioned in v. 2. **Now to me it is a very small matter that I be subjected to judicial examination by you or by any human court; yea, I do not judicially examine even mine own self.**

Since Christ and God alone are Paul's masters, these alone have the authority to examine and to judge him. The phrase εἰς ἐλάχιστον takes the place of a predicate nominative; it resembles the Hebrew with l^e although it is more in accord with the older Greek idiom, R. 458. The superlative ἐλάχιστον is elative, "a very small matter," R. 670. This phrase conveys only the idea that an inquiry into Paul's conduct on the part of the Corinthians is a small matter to him subjectively: *mich beruehrt es sehr wenig*, to me it is a small item. Objectively it would, of course, be a graver matter. Only when men follow the example of the Corinthians and act as though they are a minister's sole judge can we say with Paul that their judgment is a small matter to us, and we can do this because we consider only the judgment of Christ. Only when a congregation exercises its proper right and truly applies the Lord's Word to a pastor's teaching and to his conduct must he not only submit to the investigation but also regard it as a matter of utmost gravity.

The subfinal ἵνα clause is also the subject of the sentence: "that I be subjected, etc., is a small matter," etc. The verb ἀνακρίνειν, which is used thrice in succession, means "to institute a juridical inquiry " and the passive means "to be subjected to such an inquiry." Thus Annas attempted to examine Christ although he lacked the authority to do so, and Christ refused to submit to his probing, John 18:9, etc. Pilate also examined Christ, and the Lord submitted to his examination, John 18:33. The procedure implied in ἀνακρίνειν always precedes the activity indicated by κρίνειν, rendering the verdict which may be either guilty or not guilty (compare Pilate's verdict).

After stating that an investigation which the Corinthians may choose to inaugurate matters little to Paul he at once extends the thought; whether he be tried by the Corinthians "or by any human court," concerns him little. The noun ἡμέρα is here used in a technical sense and has the force of *Gerichtstag*, it is like our day in court. The emphasis is on "human" court in contrast with an investigation by the divine court; and every such human court is implied, for no article is used. Being the Lord's steward, Paul is amenable only to his Lord. He goes even a step farther: "yea, I do not judicially examine even mine own self." The ἀλλά is not adversative but copulative, R. 1186: "yea." We should rather expect to find the emphasis placed on the subject by means of a weighty "I" or "I myself," instead of this it is placed on the object: "even mine own self" I do not submit to such an inquiry.

A fine point is involved. Of course, if Paul were to investigate himself he, too, would be only a human court and not his own real and final judge. That he

First Corinthians 4:4 167

would not usurp such a position even when judging himself goes without saying. What Paul intends to say reaches beyond this self-evident thought and declares that, as regarding himself, he finds no occasion or reason for subjecting himself to an introspective judicial inquiry. The reason is stated in v. 4.

4) **For I am conscious of nothing against myself; yet hereby I am not justified; but he that judicially examines me is the Lord.**

Judicial examinations are usually not held unless some evidence of guilt appears. Why, then, as γάο explains, should Paul place *himself* under such an inquiry? Paul declares that in regard to his apostolic administration of the mysteries of God he is conscious of no dereliction. While he refers particularly to his faithfulness in the office of preaching, teaching, and administering the gospel entrusted to him, this necessarily involves his general conduct as a Christian. Paul lived pure in heart and life. He was not sinless, but he conducted himself in such a way that his conscience, guided by the light of the Word and the Spirit, could not find cause for rebuking him. In 3:10 Paul calls himself "a wise architect." He repeats that thought here from a different viewpoint. And he does so with due Christian pride and assurance, without a false note of any kind.

We see this clearly when we note that Paul at once adds: "but hereby I am not justified," acquitted and pronounced innocent and guiltless. The passive δεδικαίωμαι implies that Christ is the one proper judge to whom Paul is answerable. Paul turns from an investigation that is instituted by and a verdict that is rendered by the Corinthians or by any other human court to the divine judge and the divine court, for he adds: "but he that judicially examines me is the Lord."

This turn in Paul's thought should not be overlooked. There is a vast difference between the action of a human court and that of the divine court as far as the Lord's ministers and, we may add, as far as any believer is concerned. To them human courts, investigations, and findings are but "a very small matter," in reality altogether nothing, when such courts are influenced by wrong notions such as the poor wisdom of the Corinthians. But the Lord's court is an entirely different matter to them.

The verb δικαιοῦν is always forensic: "to *pronounce* a verdict of acquittal," and hence it never means "to *make* just" (examine C.-K. at length in regard to this term). Note also the tense and its implication: "I have not been justified," namely by a verdict rendered in the past, a verdict that now continues to stand to my credit.

When Paul says that, although knowing nothing against himself, he is not already acquitted by the Lord he does not mean that he is still in uncertainty in regard to his final acquittal by the Lord or that he does not trust his own conscience regarding this acquittal, since conscience may, indeed, err. What he means is that the final verdict which the Lord will pronounce is still a matter of the future.

Nor is Paul speaking about his δικαίωσις or acquittal at the moment when faith was kindled in his heart, for of this acquittal he and every Christian is so sure that, as long as faith continues, each must declare with all divine assurance: δεδικαίωμαι, "I have been and am acquitted!" He is speaking about the final divine acquittal at the last day which, coming after all his apostolic work is done, shall render the Lord's public sentence upon it before the whole world of men and of angels. This verdict, Paul writes, is still outstanding. It will be rendered by the real judge in the case: "he that judicially examines me is the Lord." The adversative δέ contrasts this judge with the Corinthians, with any human court, and even with Paul himself.

The substantivized present participle ὁ ἀνακρίνων characterizes the Lord as the judge to whom the function of making judicial inquiry into Paul's conduct of his office rightly belongs, to whom Paul therefore also submits. The tense of the participle says nothing as to the time when this judge acts in this capacity. At the right time and in the right way this judge makes his investigations.

This statement of Paul's does not intend to indicate that all ministers are to be given a free hand to do what they think is right until the Lord at last judges them. What Paul says is that men must not usurp the Lord's judgment seat and judge the Lord's ministers according to their own wisdom. Paul does not for one moment judge himself in this way. Yet the Corinthians were judging their ministers in this manner. Men do it to this day. Even ministers judge themselves in this way. Paul certainly examined and judged himself, for he writes: "I am conscious of nothing against myself." He cannot say this unless he has examined himself most carefully. Paul has the Lord's own Word, that very Word which will judge Paul at the last day, John 12:48. After examining himself according to that Word Paul finds no dereliction in himself. This is not strange since Paul conducts his entire ministry with an eye only to abiding true to that Word.

Paul is far from appealing only to his own consciousness and to his own conscience in contrast with the judgments which the Corinthians were pronouncing concerning him. Conscience may be asleep, ignorant, misled in some way. The man who appeals only to his conscience when he is confronted by the Word and swears that he is "just as conscientious as you are" is only putting his own conscience upon the judgment seat of the Lord and of his Word. At Worms Luther made his appeal: "My conscience is bound in the Word of God!" So our consciences, too, must be bound by the Word, by every part of it; not by some man's interpretation or twisting of the Word, not by some manipulations of the Word which I myself may contrive, but by the Word as it really is, as it "goeth forth out of my mouth," Isa. 55:11. Such conduct retains the Lord in the seat of the supreme judge. If we do that we can smile at the human courts that try to pre-empt the Lord's throne.

But even this appeal to a conscience so bound is proper only when one is dealing with men. No true minister would think of making it when he is dealing with the Lord, for he and his Word are one. Like Paul, he acknowledges: "Hereby I am not yet acquitted." This does not, however, imply that his acquittal is thereby still in doubt. Such an acknowledgment is merely a confession that my own consciousness of complete faithfulness to the Word is not yet my acquittal. It is my blessed assurance that I shall most surely be acquitted at that day. The acquittal itself is granted and can be granted only by the Lord: "then shall each one have praise from God," v. 5.

5) With ὥστε, "therefore," "consequently," Paul draws the practical conclusion from what has been said, and he does this in the form of an admonition to the Corinthians. **Therefore judge nothing before the time, until the Lord come, who also will light up the hidden things of the darkness and make manifest the counsels of the hearts; and then each shall have his due praise from God.**

The ἀνακρίνειν to which Paul has referred naturally issues in a κρίνειν, the pronouncement of a verdict that is either favorable or unfavorable. When the apostle forbids the latter, the former is also thereby forbidden, for it would be pointless to subject a minister to an

First Corinthians 4:5   171

investigation that would not lead to a decision. The kind of judging which Paul forbids in regard to himself and to any teacher in the church is that indicated in v. 4, which assumes that the teachers are subject to the congregation as constituting the final authority. Only when a teacher teaches and practices contrary to the Word has the congregation the right both ἀνακρίνειν and κρίνειν, and then such an investigation and such a judging in no wise usurp Christ's authority but only vindicate the authority of Christ's Word against a man who is violating that Word. Nothing of this kind had, however, occurred in Corinth, hence Paul does not discuss this angle of the subject.

By πρὸ καιροῦ τι, "something out of season" or "untimely," Paul indicates the kind of judging in which the Corinthians were indulging. Against this Paul warns. The entire thought is this: As far as I am concerned, any investigation you may institute matters very little; I certainly perform no such investigation of myself since Christ is my investigator; consequently I urge you not to judge anything about me untimely. If we may infer what lies back of them from Paul's words, it would be this: the Paul faction lauded Paul over against Apollos and against Peter while the Apollos and the Peter factions found all manner of fault with Paul. Paul's admonition is directed against both proceedings. While he personally paid no attention to this kind of praise or blame, the worst feature about it was that the Corinthians were acting in a way that was highly derogatory to Christ who gives his differing gifts and opportunities to his "stewards," who knows what is in their minds and hearts as they do their work, and who will apportion their rewards to them in due time.

Every verdict rendered before this time is both illegal and invalid; it could emanate only from some foolish person who is not a properly constituted judge although he pretends to be such a one. "Before the time" is defined by "until the Lord come," which is a brief statement but one that certainly points to the real "day" when the Lord will officiate as the judge of all. And his judgment will be not only one that is legal but also one that is truly competent, for he will do what none of the Corinthians and what no human court can possibly do: "who also will light up the hidden things of darkness." When it is used with a relative καί = "also" and ushers in a point that is pertinent to what has just been said.

Paul has been using only *voces mediae*, neutral terms: ἀνακρίνειν and κρίνειν. He has also referred only to himself in order to exemplify the object of investigation and the pronouncing of a verdict. Now he goes a step farther. For "the hidden things of darkness" refers to the Corinthians and their secret motives for judging him as well as to himself and to his own motives. The genitive "of the darkness" is usually understood to refer only to a darkness which hides something from human eyes. Yet in the New Testament "the darkness" constantly signifies the evil power which as such must shun the light (φῶς, compare φωτίσει). It has that meaning here. Christ will illumine with light not only "the hidden things" not seen by our eyes at present but also "the hidden things of the darkness," the wrong things that now seek the cover of the evil darkness. And such evil things may be found not only in the teachers whom the Corinthians judge but also in their own hearts when they practice this untimely and uncalled for judging. "For we must all appear before the judgment seat of Christ," II Cor. 5:10. Paul does not say that the Corinthians are included in this darkness, but such a deduction lies on the surface.

A second specification regarding what the Lord will do by his absolutely competent judgment is added:

"and will make manifest the counsels of the hearts." "Counsels" is again a neutral term, for these counsels may be either good or evil in their nature. They will be made manifest, namely as what they are. This is the effect of φωτίζειν, pouring light upon them. The Greek conception of "heart" is not like that of the English. To the latter it is chiefly the seat of the feelings, but to the former it is the central organ of the entire conscious personality which determines its thinking, feeling, and willing, especially the latter. We may translate: *die Willensregungen des Herzens*. This does not, however, refer only to the tendencies and the stirrings that fail to eventuate into volitions but also to the inclinations and the motives that lie at the secret roots of our volitions whether we ourselves are fully conscious of them or not.

Paul uses the plural "of the hearts" although he has spoken directly only of himself ("me" at the end of v. 4). He, of course, refers to himself only as an example of an entire class. This plural is a hint also to all of the Corinthians and is aimed also at their motives both when elevating and when faulting Paul (Apollos, Peter). In these two clauses we thus have a description of the Lord's ἀνακρίνειν. It is certainly competent in a way that is utterly impossible to a human court.

While the double relative clause gently includes the Corinthians, Paul's chief interest lies in the Lord's "stewards." He therefore closes this paragraph with the assurance: "and then each shall have his due praise from God," or: "his due praise shall come to each," etc. He speaks only about praise, for the teachers particularly concerned are himself, Apollos, and Peter, and in no way does Paul anywhere cast blame or even the suspicion of it on these other men. As to others who may be unfaithful and those who may receive no reward at all enough is said in 3:12-17.

The article, ὁ ἔπαινος, indicates the praise or divine commendation that is due to each "steward," compare Luke 19:17-19. This will differ; but even he who receives the least will be overwhelmed by its greatness. "From God" reads as though Paul implies that this is a gift of grace from God's hand. Both Christ and God are named as judge in the Scriptures, but Θεός is to be understood in the sense of the Triune God. Let the Corinthians, then, by party wranglings not try to exalt one man and to detract from another. That is sorry business, does grave injustice and harm, and interferes with the Lord.

6) Both the address "brethren" and the character of the following show that a new paragraph is introduced, one that is closely connected with the foregoing. Paul has thus far restrained his feelings and has written quite calmly and rather objectively; now the floodgates of his emotion are thrown open. **Now these things, brethren, I have in a figure transferred to myself and Apollos for your sakes in order that in our persons you might learn this thing of not going beyond what has been written,** (namely) **that you may not be puffing yourselves up, one man in favor of the one against the other.**

Paul has been writing about himself and about Apollos, but this has been done by a kind of transfer, Paul and Apollos do not need any of the things Paul has written, the persons who need all of this are the Corinthians. The verb μετασχηματίζω means to alter the σχῆμα or form. Paul and Apollos are in perfect accord and well understand their holy office; the trouble lies entirely on the side of the Corinthians who pit the one against the other and understand aright the office of neither. For this reason Paul thus far wrote about himself and Apollos δι' ὑμᾶς, "on account of you," the Corinthians.

Paul's purpose in using this transfer is: "that in our persons you might learn" a certain thing. The emphasis is on ἐν ἡμῖν, "in us," "in our persons," using Paul and Apollos as examples (ἐν with persons = "in the case of"). Paul associates himself with Apollos because both are persons from whom the Corinthians might well learn how to act. The aorist μάθητε means: actually learn. What Paul intended the Corinthians to learn is marked by τό, and this article substantivizes μὴ ὑπὲρ ἃ γέγραπται, "not beyond what has been written" (on the tense compare 1:19). An ellipsis occurs after μή. This is a common idiom in the Greek and one which must be completed when the thought is rendered into English: "not (to go or to think) beyond what has been written."

Some think that Paul is merely quoting a proverb or at least a well-known saying; but such a proverb or such a saying has never been found. And to what writing would a proverb or a saying refer by the phrase "beyond what has been written"? This could not be the Scriptures; it would have to be some other writing — which leaves us completely at sea. Now the next clause gives us some information in regard to the substance of "what has been written," beyond which the Corinthians must not go. It is the admonition that they should be duly humble and not be puffed up when contending about persons. We know, too, that Paul constantly uses γέγραπται, "it has been written," when he refers to the Old Testament writings. Yet we see that he here quotes no special Old Testament statement but refers only in general to "what has been written" and merely indicates what this is in the next clause. Hence we conclude that Paul is phrasing this admonition in his own words when he urges the Corinthians not to go beyond what all of them know is written in the Old Testament Scriptures, which urges us in so many ways not to be proud or contentious.

The thing that is written, which Paul wants the Corinthians to observe in their conduct, is this that no one should puff himself up "in favor of one person as against another person," proudly boasting that Paul in his favorite and never Apollos or Peter; and vice versa, either Apollos or Peter. This is exactly what the Corinthians were doing with their party slogans. Paul now rebukes the Corinthians directly, without further resort to a transfer that would soften his words. The New Testament has several instances where ἵνα with the indicative present is employed, and this is one of them, R. 984; and in this instance ἵνα is subfinal, for it states what is written and is to be observed by the Corinthians, which fact may explain the use of the indicative with this ἵνα.

The present tense φυσιοῦσθε points to a course of conduct which the Corinthians are to avoid: they are never at any time to act in this manner. The very idea of puffing oneself up has a ludicrous touch — that is what a frog does when he croaks. Paul often combines the plural with the singular; here that *you Corinthians* refrain from puffing yourselves up, *one man* talking in favor of one person and against the other person. What applies to all is to be observed by each one. In the Greek the two phrases are emphatic by position, one by being placed before, the other after the verb.

7) Three pointed questions now puncture the bubble of Corinthian pride. This is done in order to bring these foolish people down to the level of a proper Christian humility. The connective γάρ points to the reasons that the Corinthians should not puff themselves up; γάρ is to be referred to all the questions. The reason lies in the self-evident answers implied in the questions. **Who maketh thee to differ?** means: differ so that thou hast an advantage over others. "Who in the world gave thee a preference

over others? Nobody! Thou dost only imagine such preference." The full implication is: "Who, by his authoritative acknowledgment, gave thee the right to consider thyself superior to others so that they must look up to thee and admire thee?" By the use of the second person singular "thou" Paul retains both the second person and the singular which he had employed in the last clause of v. 6.

The question is, of course, not general as though any kind of an advantage were referred to, and it is not to be answered in this general way. It rests on the concrete idea of puffing oneself up by boasting of following one great teacher in contrast with others who are esteemed as being inferior. Who gave thee this advantage? Thou gavest it to thyself. Thou dost foolishly invent it so as to be able to throw out thy chest and to boast. The Corinthians would prefer to have better apostles than other Christians had — how they would then boast! If they were living today they would demand no less than an archbishop. Now nobody gives thee a preference like that; you Corinthians are all alike and on the same level with all other Christians. Just as Paul and Apollos are not boasting, the one claiming that he is better and higher than the other, so the Corinthians should not imagine that they had an advantage when some of them followed Paul and others followed Apollos.

The first question deals with an imaginary possession, the second with an actual possession which one may misuse for puffing himself up. **And what hast thou that thou didst not receive?** The context again yields the sense. What hast thou of saving knowledge and of wisdom, of repentance, of faith, of love, and of Christian virtue, that was not given thee and that thou didst not merely receive? Thus they had also been given the teachers, Paul, Apollos, and others, through whom all this grace was conveyed to them, to all of them equally.

The aorist "didst receive," points to the fact. Simply by receiving it each one of the Corinthians obtained what he now has. The moment he looks at his actual possessions in this true light as an unmerited gift that was dropped into his lap by a gracious hand above he will kiss that hand and never think of boasting. If God used a Paul, an Apollos, a Peter, that, too, is a part of his grace and gift and reason enough for thanks and not for puffed-up pride.

Hence Paul adds the third question which really expands the second. **Now if thou didst also receive it, why dost thou glory as if thou didst not receive it?**

The καί does not have the concessive force of "although" thou didst receive it; it is only a strengthening of the verb: if thou "also" didst receive it and obtain it only in this way. The Corinthians ought to praise and to thank God in proper humility instead of boasting as though what they have is due, not to a gracious gift from God, but to some superiority in themselves. It is surely reprehensible to receive something and then to act as though one had not received it. And it is more reprehensible to boast and to glory. Paul does not need to specify that all that the Corinthians actually had, whether it was much or little, they had as separate individuals received from the Lord alone. The agency which the Lord had used in making them the recipients of his gifts, especially Paul and Apollos, is quietly taken for granted. This agency will strike them with terrific force in a moment.

8) The three questions asked in v. 7 are short and have the intention of puncturing their bubble of pride and the further intention of bringing the Corinthians down to the level of true Christian humility. But they needed still more. **Already you are filled full; already you grew rich; without us you**

reigned; and would, indeed, that you reigned in order that we, too, might get to reign with your help!

This is irony and sarcasm (R. 1148 and 1198, etc.), but the Corinthians fully deserved it; it is a bitter medicine but one that is good for healing their disease of unwarranted pride. Luther comments: "Paul mocks them, for he means the opposite of what he says." One must understand the Greek in order to catch fully the scathing force of Paul's rebuke. It has become popular today to decry irony and sarcasm as being unbecoming to preachers and to Christian writers. The use of these weapons is deemed an evidence of the flesh and not of the spirit. Yet Paul beyond question employs them here, which means that they, indeed, have their proper place in spite of the delicate souls who would rule them out.

The first three parallel statements have no connectives. They are heaped up in a swift climax. The asyndeton adds life and movement and is frequently found in impassioned discourses, R. 428. The two ἤδη, "already," lend a peculiar force to the first two statements so that we might translate: "Think of it, already you are filled full!" "Think of it, already you have grown rich!" These prideful Corinthians, Paul implies, act as though they are already in the great kingdom to come instead of realizing that they are still in this poor, miserable world. Full satiety, riches, and honor are three blessings promised in the coming eon to the hungry, the poor, and the despised, compare the Beatitudes of the Sermon on the Mount. The Corinthians boasted, each with his own party, as if they were already at this goal. Paul's crushing irony is intensified when he presently describes himself and his fellow apostles as being the actual outcasts of the world. See how far these pupils have left their poor teachers behind — of course, in their own imagination! Behold what their "wisdom" has done for them!

Why, you are already filled full, κεκορεσμένοι, from κορέννυμι, "to satiate." Who can feed you more? Changing the figure: You have already grown rich. Who can offer you more? And then the climax by means of a third figure: You have already attained royalty and have come to reign as kings. Who can offer you a crown? The perfect participle marks a present condition, and the two verbs in the aorist are ingressive and indicate the entrance upon a condition. A new turn appears in the third statement; instead of repeating "already" Paul introduces the significant phrase "without us," the poor apostles. Paul writes as though he marvelled at their ability: All of this you have achieved without us! In some way you secured a better wisdom than we have to offer, one that has carried you up so wonderfully high! There is a special sting in this emphatic phrase "all without us." Silly people to act as though they had left Paul, Apollos, and Peter far behind, the very men from whom they had obtained everything they really had!

Paul is sarcastically describing their φυσιοῦσθαι κατὰ ἑτέρου, "puffing themselves up against another." He is bitterly castigating their foolish illusions. Christ and the gospel wisdom do appease our hunger and our thirst, do make us spiritually rich (1:5), do make us kings and priests unto God and Christ, but not in the manner which the Corinthians exhibited, so that we become puffed up with fleshly pride and spend our time in boastful wrangling. Christ and the gospel will also eventually lead us to the fullness, riches, and royal glory of heaven, but only silly Christians act as though they had already attained that height.

A quick turn is made with καί. The Corinthians are staging such a pitiful sham; would that they had the reality: "and would, indeed, that you reigned!"

And now, after this sigh, the sting contained in the phrase "without us" is made to penetrate still deeper, for Paul adds with a climax of irony: "in order that we, too, might get to reign with your help," have just an humble little place by your side! Now, poor apostles that we are, we have no opportunity to procure anything so ennobling by efforts that we know how to put forth. "Otherwise children have part in the position of their fathers, and disciples are not above their teachers; here, however, no other way remains for the teachers if they, too, would already be in a glorious state than to wish, to be allowed to have part in what the disciples have attained for themselves or imagine they have attained." Ph. Bachmann. "Thus the roles have been exchanged: he, the apostle, their 'father,' must from his lowliness see to what dizzy heights they have attained." J. Weiss. Note that ὄφελον, which γε strengthens, is used like a particle, in this case with the indicative, an aorist because the wish relates to the past while an imperfect would relate to the present although in both cases the wish is unfulfilled, R. 923, 841, 1004, 1148, etc. The abutting of the two pronouns ἡμεῖς ὑμῖν makes the two clash; and σύν with the verb together with the subject "we," "we with your help," is the opposite of the previous phrase "without us."

The conviction that Paul should not and could not employ irony in his writings leads to the attempt to understand this passage accordingly. The futility of this attempt is seen in the climax of Paul's words, where he speaks of the royal reign. In order to eliminate the irony at this point the two verbs ἐβασιλεύσατε must be understood in different senses: the first referring to reigning in this life, the second to reigning in the life to come. If Paul intended to make this difference he would himself have indicated it by adding the necessary modifiers to bring about this effect.

Lacking such an indication on his part, we are compelled to take both verbs in the same sense. In the second place, the order of the pronouns, first "we, too," and then "with your help," would have to be reversed, for in the heavenly kingdom the Corinthians could reign only with the apostles, and not the apostles with the Corinthians. So the irony remains.

9) Moreover, the irony continues as δωκῶ γάρ indicate. This γάρ cites the reason for Paul's wish: For in my opinion the condition of the apostles is such that to be privileged to rule by your help would seem very desirable to them. This humble δωκῶ, "it seems to me," which states only as Paul's opinion what is in truth an astounding fact, namely the pitiful condition of the apostles, cuts into the rash pride of the Corinthians the more. For if the Corinthians were what they imagine themselves to be, how high and mighty ought the apostles not to be ranked and be entitled also to rank themselves? Well, this is Paul's opinion of the apostles. **For, it seems to me, God set forth us, the apostles, as the lowest, as men sentenced to die, since we were made a theatrical spectacle for the world, both to angels and to men.**

Paul does not need to draw on his fancy when he is saying this about himself and about his associates. What he states is the cold and deliberate fact although the Corinthians seem to forget it. They are also oblivious of the truth that certain serious implications concerning themselves are contained in that fact. Here, too, the quality of Paul's irony begins to become plain. In flows out from a burning heart, one that is itself deeply hurt, and it wounds others with stinging facts, not in order to revenge itself upon them, but in order to save them from falseness by the full energy of the truth.

The first stress is on "God," for it is he who did this astounding thing with the apostles; the Corinthians did something quite different in regard to themselves. The main stress is, however, on the implied comparison between the apostles and the Corinthians. "Is the lofty height on which you think you stand a height that is divinely real? Us, it seems to me, God has treated differently." Us, the apostles, who may well expect and be expected to stand as first and as highest, "sitting on twelve thrones," Matt. 19:28, God set forth to be the last in the sense of "lowest." The verb states the fact that, having made us the lowest of all, he showed this publicly. "Us, the apostles," and "lowest" are placed together in striking contrast. And Paul at once states in what sense the apostles were last and lowest: "as men sentenced to die," as criminals condemned, like Christ, to capital punishment. If we should ask what people constitute the dregs of society we should think first of criminals under the shadow of the gallows. Can a more terrific contrast be imagined between the self-exalted Corinthians and these apostles regarding whom the world thought that they were not fit to live?

The ὅτι clause at once proves that the apostles were set forth as men who were fit only to die the death of criminals: "since we were made (or have become) a theatrical spectacle for the world," θέατρον, a public exhibition, when we were led to execution so that the world might gaze upon us. Paul refers to flogging, stoning, other violent abuse, including killing; the latter especially when we remember that the Roman world made public exhibitions of the executions which took place in the amphitheaters.

The term "world" is explained by the double apposition "both angels and men." These are the spectators. The angels are most likely mentioned first because they are higher and are able to see more of the apostolic suffering, much that is hidden from men. Regarding the angels we, too, know that they are deeply interested in the elect whom they are sent to serve (Heb. 1:14). Besides, the angels are interested in the course of the gospel on earth. "Men" are hostile and coldly indifferent.

10) Now come the bitter antitheses: We—You —what a difference! **We, fools for Christ's sake; but you, smart in connection with Christ. We, weak; but you, strong. You, refulgent, but we, disgraced.**

The Greek has no copulas, and the English translation is weakened when they are inserted. Each contrast is like a blow. "We, fools for Christ's sake" because for his sake and for that of the gospel we cast aside all human wisdom and as a consequence are rated as ignoramuses and know-nothings. "But you, smart in connection with Christ," φρόνιμοι *klug*, sagacious, prudent, here with a questionable touch; "wise" in our versions is too good a word. O yes, they still maintain connection with Christ, but as smart people who know how to use even Christ for their advantage, *gescheute, aufgeklaerte Christen*, Meyer.

Paul could not write a second διὰ Χριστόν, "for Christ's sake." The contrast in the phrases is emphatic: "for Christ's sake" and "in connection with Christ." The Corinthians are not ready to forego and to lose all for him in order to gain all in him. They seek to cling to him with one hand and to the world and its wisdom with the other hand. Smart people, indeed! In this instance the phrase ἐν Χριστῷ has a decidedly qualified meaning, which is quite different from the sense in which Paul otherwise regularly employs it, namely to express a wholehearted union and communion with Christ. The translation offered by our versions: "wise in Christ" tends to mislead.

"We, weak," but scarcely in a physical sense but rather in the sense of the unimpressive, negligible because we scorn to use the cheap means which impress men and win their admiration and their applause but are content for our success to rely only on the hidden power of the gospel. "But you, strong," full of strength and wholly able, *Kraftmenschen*, competent to make a powerful impression by wielding the mighty wisdom to which the world always yields.

The sudden inversion, "you" first and "we" last, is due to Paul's intention to continue his writing in v. 11 by giving additional information in regard to the "us." The inversion is by way of transition to the following. "You, refulgent," ἔνδοξοι, enveloped in glory, already crowned, as it were, with a halo about your heads, men stooping before you and humbly accepting your every word. This describes their reigning as kings, v. 8. "But we, disgraced," left utterly without honor among men, deprived of even common human respect, men who can be spoken of and treated with the lowest contempt. Human wisdom exalts before the world, divine wisdom is served with contempt by the world.

Paul in no way vindicates himself. This is quite remarkable, for in other connections he asserts that he is nevertheless an apostle, that God is nevertheless with him and upholds and honors him. No heroic note is sounded in the midst of these sad, minor chords. This tends to produce a far greater effect. Besides, a higher note would mislead the Corinthians. If after all that he has said Paul would now claim to be high, great, and honored in God's sight, the Corinthians could easily misuse such a claim. They might in the first place discount all that he writes concerning being so low, and they might secondly after all justify their own pride by persuading themselves that their pride, too, was after the pattern given them by Paul.

11) The terms Paul employed thus far were quite general and were drawn from the broad categories of wisdom, power, and honor. He now proceeds to fill these categories with specific particulars

by setting down a catalog of cold facts. **Even to this present hour we both hunger and thirst and are naked and are cuffed and are homeless, and we labor, working with our own hands.**

The Corinthians are "already" in a grandiose state, but in contrast with that "already" the apostles are in a deplorable state "even to this present hour." We apostles, Paul would say, have not as yet come as far as you Corinthians; you are "already" on the height, we poor apostles are still "to this present moment" down in the depths.

The wording itself does not indicate whether the six statements are to be divided into three groups of two each or into two groups of three each. The latter is in all likelihood preferable, for then the statements would better accord with the third group of three members listed in v. 12. We thus have a total of nine statements, three groups of three members each.

Because of their extensive and continued travel, so often only on foot, over wide, uninhabited stretches and much arid territory the apostles often go hungry and thirsty, and their shoes and their clothing are worn out. The Taurus passes were crossed repeatedly. In II Cor. 11:26 Paul mentions his journeyings, perils in rivers, perils of robbers, perils in the wilderness, perils in the sea, hunger, thirst, cold, and nakedness. Lack of sufficient clothing, especially during inclement weather, is thus mentioned repeatedly. The linguistic point, whether to read γυμνητεύειν or γυμνιτεύειν, belongs to the textual critics.

"We are cuffed" or buffeted means struck with the fists on the body or the face as slaves and criminals were frequently abused by brutal men. This was the height of indignity. The term can scarcely apply to official scourgings, it refers rather to uncalled-for, vulgar, physical abuse, Acts 14:19, etc. "We are homeless," ἀστατοῦμεν (to be ἄστατος), without a fixed abode, shifting about constantly. This term implies even more: as they traveled from place to place after having broken with their Jewish past and connections and yet not having become Gentile, the apostles found no welcome in any of the new places to which they came. We may recall the Jewish hostility experienced in Corinth itself.

The addition: "We labor, working with our own hands," is used as an indication of dishonor. The adjective ἰδίαις is stronger than the possessive pronoun "our own" hands; as it does generally throughout the New Testament so it here, too, conveys the idea that the apostles are compelled to earn their own living by means of their own hard manual labor. In other connections Paul speaks of this feature of his life, not as a mark of shame, but as indicating a means of personal independence. Here the note of irony still continues, for Paul speaks from the viewpoint of the puffed-up Corinthians. Nor should we overlook the bitterness conveyed in all of the specifications here laid before the Corinthians. Why should Paul endure all these arduous privations for the sake of such unworthy and such thankless people as the Corinthians?

12) There is a change of tone in the final group of statements, each consisting of a participle and a verb. **Being reviled, we bless; being persecuted, we hold out; being defamed, we speak kindly.** The thought expressed is, however, not the idea that Paul and his fellow apostles do not allow these sufferings to affect them, but rather that they rise superior to them through nobleness of mind. Paul still follows the note struck in ἀτιμία, comparing the low condition of the apostles with the lofty idea which the Corinthians have of themselves. So little do the apostles resemble the proud Corinthians that they do not meet reviling by hurling back into the throat of their enemies their own wicked allegations but rather by replying with

the Christian meekness ordered by the Lord, Luke 6:28: "Bless them that curse you."

"Being persecuted" can so early in Paul's career scarcely refer to any of the official pagan persecutions, for these came at a later period, it rather has in mind the Jewish outbreaks of violence against the apostles because they were regarded as traitors to the law, Gal. 5:11; 6:12. "Being persecuted, we hold out," ἀνεχόμεθα, "hold up" under the infliction with quiet patience by simply suffering what men impose without complaining, defending, or retaliating. This noble course frequently encourages the persecutors to continue their wicked actions against men who seem helpless and defenseless and who fail to strike back. But even then: ἀνεχόμεθα.

13) The reading δυσφημούμενοι has less textual support than the far commoner βλασφημούμενοι. The exceptional character of the former, which Paul uses only here, argues strongly for its genuineness. But what is meant by παρακαλοῦμεν? It cannot be regarded as indicating an action of love, for the entire context does not deal with this theme but with that of abject lowliness. The sense cannot, then, be: we entreat God for our slanderers; or: *wir reden troestlich;* or: *geben bittende Worte,* "intreat" (our versions), beg our vilifiers to desist. The verb must here mean *beguetigen.* "Being defamed," we are not angry, make no retort in kind, resort to no violent measures in counteroffense such as people use who are concerned solely about their own honor; we simply "go on speaking kindly." Paul is throughout laying emphasis upon the voluntary humility that displays itself in this way, a humility which the world considers cowardly or even despicable. Indeed, the apostles seem far beneath the Corinthians in every way.

All verbs and all participles found in v. 11, 12 are in the present tense, which indicates customary and usual action such as marks a definite course of conduct. This tense is open, i. e., the conduct indicated goes on indefinitely and extends even into the future. The three circumstantial participles used in v. 13 express the minor action, while the finite verbs express the major actions. The important feature is the fact that under the circumstances indicated the apostles "bless, hold out, speak kindly." Paul uses many word patterns which form an interesting study. In v. 13 the first and the third verb end in -οῦμεν and thus even rhyme; see similar arrangements in Rom. 12:8; I Cor. 13:8, and elsewhere.

Only when v. 12 is not taken as a reference to heroic actions on the part of the apostles but to despised lowliness does the concluding statement of v. 13 properly follow. **Like the rubbish heap of the world did we become, the offscouring of all men, until this moment.**

All of the preceding present tenses describe the general and continued state of the apostles; now the positive aorist states the fact of their deepest degradation. It has actually come to the point where no other comparison adequately describes the condition of the apostles; they had become a heap of rubbish, the very offscouring of humanity. The arrangement of the words is remarkably impressive. "Until this moment" is strikingly placed at the end and reverts to the phrase used at the beginning of the entire catalog in v. 11: "even to this present hour." These two phrases are the staples between which the chain swings. The two figurative terms "rubbish heap" and "offscouring" have the emphatic positions, the one before the verb, the other after it, without a connective. While the aorist tense of the verb registers a fact it does so without emphasis. Thus Paul brings description of the apostles to a dramatic close.

The term "rubbish heap," περικαθάρματα (plural), from καθαίρω, to clean or to remove by cleaning, denotes the mass of sweepings and litter that is gathered together when one cleans up "all around" (περί), R. 618. The second term, περίψημα (singular), means "offscouring," that which is removed by scouring a filthy object, ψάω. The two genitives are placed chiastically, the one after its noun, the other before it. Both are subjective, but, like δικαιοσύνη Θεοῦ in Rom. 1:17, of the estimating subject, "righteousness in the eyes of God"; thus "a heap of rubbish in the eyes of the world," and "offscouring in the eyes of all men."

Luther translates: *ein Fluch der Welt und ein Fegopfer aller Leute.* He has the second term define the first. The term κάθαρμα (and perhaps also περικάθαρμα, although this is not certain) was used in a ritual sense with reference to one who gave himself as a sacrifice in order to remove from the community some stain for which the gods were visiting some plague or some other calamity upon the city or the country. Only a man who was so wretched as to have no more use for his life could be obtained for this purpose. He would feast for a year on white bread, figs, and cheese until the day for the sacrifice arrived and would then be offered up. This is the idea back of Luther's translation *Fluch* or curse. Whether the second term περίψημα also had such a ritual meaning cannot be ascertained; Luther assumed that it had.

But Paul scarcely had such a thought in mind in this connection. He was certainly not feasting for a time in order to die when that happy time should be past. Christ gave his life in vicarious sacrifice for the world and not Paul and the apostles. While περικάθαρμα is extensively used in the sense of "wretch" and a good-for-nothing fellow, this meaning is altogether general. Paul uses the plural in the case of the first figurative term and the singular in the case of the second; if he had sacrifices in mind, both terms would necessarily be plural. Finally, the two genitives cannot mean that the world and all men offer the apostles as sacrifices in order to ward off some calamity from themselves; yet if the figure of sacrifices is retained, these genitives could have no other meaning.

Our versions make πάντων neuter: "of all things," but it is synonymous with "of the world" and thus must mean "of all men," masculine. It is characteristic of Paul's style to use a singular and then to resume the thought with a plural that has the same general sense, or vice versa. In this very sentence we have two pairs of plurals and singulars that are arranged chiastically: like the rubbish heaps (plural) of the world (singular), the offscouring (singular) of all men (plural). Paul has reached the limit; beyond these debasing terms even he cannot go.

These are the stern and the shameful realities regarding the apostles, and they are content to be treated in this manner. What an object lesson for the Corinthians, "that in us you might learn not to go beyond what has been written," 4:6!

14) Coming to the closing paragraph of the first part of his letter, Paul makes no application of what he has written but leaves that task to the Corinthians themselves. He at once states why he writes with such deep feeling, namely to warn them (v. 14) as their father (v. 15, 16) who has sent them a messenger, (v. 17) and who plans to come to them in person. As we understand the character of Paul the assumption is unwarranted that in v. 6-13 Paul works himself up to a high pitch of feeling and then, having cooled off and perhaps waiting until the next day, writes v. 14, etc., in a calmer mood. Some also state that in this new paragraph Paul seeks to make amends for the cutting expressions which he has used in the one that precedes. A good answer to such an assumption would be that,

when we write hastily and say too much, we tear up what we have written and write more carefully. The fact is, however, that Paul never lets his feelings run away with him, and when he writes with deep emotion and even employs irony he exercises perfect control of himself in every word and follows only the loftiest spiritual purpose.

Thus he continues: **Not as shaming you am I writing these things, on the contrary, as admonishing my beloved children.** The present tense "I am writing" makes the impression that Paul simply continues writing without an interval of time between the paragraphs. The two present participles repeat this idea. Both are circumstantial and state facts, and, as is often the case with regard to participles, carry the main idea that is to be conveyed. It is self-evident that Paul is writing; the main point of his writing is the fact that he is not shaming but admonishing so that he could have simply said: "I am not shaming you but admonishing my beloved children." For this reason οὐ is used with the first participle instead of μή, which makes the negation clear-cut as is proper in stating a fact, R. 1137. This οὐ has even a literary touch; Paul has used about a dozen participles with οὐ. The position of the two participles, one at the beginning, the other at the very end, likewise indicates that Paul is stating facts. Paul thus tells the Corinthians what he is doing when he writes as he actually does and not merely what he intends to do when he writes. The Corinthians are not to put their interpretation upon Paul's words and impute this or that wrong intention to them but are to accept as fact what Paul is stating with his words.

This answers the view that the participles express purpose or aim, for only future participles are regularly thus employed, R. 877, and present participles only rarely, and then never with the negative οὐ. Yet, even if a purpose could be found in these participles so as to have them read: "not in order to shame you but in order to admonish you," this would not in the least be an admission on Paul's part that he at first did intend to shame the Corinthians and that he is now sorry for this intention and seeks to make at least rhetorical amends by now saying that his intention is to admonish his beloved children. The Corinthians may, indeed, feel ashamed under the lash of Paul's irony; they certainly have reason to feel thus. Paul is, however, engaged in something that is far more important than merely making them ashamed, he is offering them Christian admonition. Shame touches only the feelings, admonition reaches the heart.

The verb νουθετεῖν means to appeal to the mind (νοῦς plus τίθημι), hence in this sense "to admonish," or in the present instance "to warn." The companion term is παιδεύειν, to discipline a child. Compare the corresponding nouns found in Eph. 6:4 on this distinction. Superficially regarded, Paul's ironical expressions might sound like disciplinary castigation; understood in the proper way, they are full of appeals to the mind, full of meaning to reach the heart with earnest warning. Moreover, this is parental warning which is addressed to the Corinthians "as my beloved children." Here and in the following verse Paul explicitly denies that his sharp words emanate from an "unfatherly" spirit and are lacking "love" as is sometimes asserted.

15) Paul even stresses the point of his paternal relation to the Corinthians. **For though you have ten thousand slave guardians in Christ, yet not even many fathers; for I alone begot you in Christ Jesus through the gospel.** This is the fact that Paul never for a moment forgets. Because the Corinthians are his own children, he is free to speak to them with sharp and stinging words; if they were strangers, his words might be resented.

A παιδαγωγός is a slave who has charge of the son of a wealthy family, leads him to school, and sees to it that the son conducts himself properly; hence not "instructor" (A. V.), or "tutor" (R. V.), but "slave guardian." Paul refers to these guardians only incidentally and negatively as not being fathers in order to make prominent his own special relation to the Corinthians. We thus have no right to stress unduly the fact that these guardians were slaves, nor should we lay stress on whatever dislike the boys may have had for the guardians that attended them. Paul speaks of these guardians as being a blessing and compares it with the greater blessing of having a father.

Although the Corinthians have ten thousand slave guardians, they yet have not even many fathers. Paul speaks with an hyperbole both in the use of the extravagant number "ten thousand" and in the far lesser number "many" (instead of "several"). Like the rest of the hyperboles found in the Scriptures, this one, too, does not mislead but only enhances the effect of the thought that whatever many guardians one may have he certainly can have only *one* father. Of course, "in Christ" or "in connection with Christ" is added, for Paul is speaking only of spiritual relationships; and while the phrase appears only as a modifier of "guardians" it must be supplied also with "fathers."

No invidious comparison with Apollos or another of the Corinthian teachers is here made; the great number "ten thousand" completely excludes that possibility. So also does ἐὰν ἔχητε, "though you may have," which includes all the teachers who in future years may serve the Corinthian church. Paul speaks as he did in 3:6, where he distinguishes the one who plants from the one who waters; and as he did in 3:10, where he speaks of himself as having laid the foundation and of others who build on that foundation. Moreover,

Paul delights in associating himself with his fellow workers by means of the pronoun "we," 3:8, 9.

"For I alone begot you" explains Paul's exceptional relation to the Corinthians. Because this "I" is written out in the Greek it is emphatic, and it is made still more so by its juxtaposition with "you": ἐγὼ ὑμᾶς, and by its strong contrast with the idea of "many fathers"; hence we translate "I alone." Paul carefully qualifies this strong statement concerning himself: "in Christ Jesus" he begot the Corinthians. This emphatic phrase is, however, not intended to designate this begetting as being spiritual, the opposite of mere natural begetting. The contrast implied is not one between a spiritual and a fleshly begetting but between the presence and the absence of Christ, ἐν, "in union," not apart from Christ. This phrase describes the blessed nature of this begetting. It implies that apart from Christ, Paul could have begotten nothing. Because Paul "begot" the Corinthians, therefore his is the peculiar and the specific relation of being a spiritual father to the Corinthians, and in the nature of the case they can have but one such father.

Paul is not thinking specifically of conversion. "I alone begot" is not equivalent to "I converted"; for others who succeeded Paul also converted many. "I begot" is a new figure for the "I laid a foundation" used in 3:10. He was responsible for the very first conversions, and this fact makes him the "father" and the Corinthians "my beloved children."

The one medium through which Paul attained this was the gospel. The phrase "through the gospel" is so important because there are some who tend to ascribe such begetting to spiritual contact with strong Christian personalities. Not the greatness of Paul's spirituality started the Corinthian congregation but the strong and efficacious power of the gospel of which Paul was the humble bearer, 2:1-5. Therefore to consider the mention of the gospel rather superfluous in this connection and only an indelicate way of indicating what kind of begetting is meant, is wide of the mark. Nor is the figure destroyed or weakened by the addition of the phrase "through the gospel," it is interpreted.

Here we have one of those numerous cases in the Scriptures in which a metaphor and its literal interpretation are woven together like threads of gold and of silver as when David says: "The Lord (literal) is my shepherd (metaphor)"; or Jesus himself: "I (literal) am the vine (figure); ye (literal) are the branches (figure)." Trench calls this Biblical allegory. Only when we remember passages such as I Pet. 1:23-25 can we see the effectiveness of Paul's word: "I begot you through the gospel."

16) Paul very properly continues with οὖν, "therefore," for children should normally be like their father. We say normally, for the idea of possible vicious fathers is foreign to the context. **I admonish you therefore, be imitators of me,** compare 11:1. The little enclitic μου has no accent whatever, and none can be supplied for it from any source. This means that Paul is not contrasting himself with the slave guardians mentioned in v. 15 or with anyone else and telling the Corinthians: "Imitate *me* and not the others." The emphasis is on "imitators" and on the verb "be and continue to be" (present tense and thus durative); the implied contrast is failure to be what Paul thus enjoins. Compare Gal. 4:12; Phil. 3:17; II Thess. 3:9 in regard to this admonition.

One might be inclined to think that Paul urges the Corinthians to pattern after his humble spirit and his lowliness of mind in accord with the picture he paints of the apostles in v. 11-13. Yet he adds no modifiers to his admonition but leaves it quite broad and general. In what respect the Corinthians are to pattern after Paul he indicates in v. 17, where he tells them that Timothy was sent to them to remind them of "my ways," "even as I teach everywhere in every church." Paul's gospel teaching is the pattern which the Corinthians are to reproduce in their midst.

17) For this reason I sent to you Timothy who is my child beloved and faithful in the Lord, who shall remind you of my ways in Christ, even as I continue to teach everywhere in every church.

The doctrine produces the conduct; the objective gives birth to the subjective. Paul's beloved children in Corinth will be and will continue to be like the father who founded their congregation if they abide by his original teaching. *Gerade deshalb* (for this very reason) Paul sent Timothy to Corinth with certain instructions. According to 16:10 Timothy went on his mission before Paul began to write this letter and was to arrive in Corinth after this letter had been delivered to Corinth. Thus Paul informs the Corinthians in regard to his coming. It seems that Paul had received both the information which Chloe's people brought regarding the Corinthian factions (1:11) and also the letter which the Corinthians themselves had sent him *after* Timothy had left Ephesus.

The instructions which he gave Timothy were general and not specific, he had told him simply to remind the Corinthians of the truths which Paul taught constantly and everywhere so that they, too, might adhere to them more closely. After Timothy had left Ephesus, all this new and disturbing information in regard to the Corinthians reached Paul, and he hastens to write this letter, calculating that it will reach Corinth before Timothy arrives there. The bearer of the letter would go by sea; Timothy was traveling far more slowly by land.

The first relative clause: "who is my child beloved and faithful in the Lord," merely describes Timothy in an affectionate way. "My child," like the similar term used in v. 14, is taken to mean that Paul had converted Timothy although Acts 14:6 does not mention his conversion, and in Acts 16:1 Luke refers to him as already being a Christian. He helped Paul and Silvanus found the Corinthian congregation, II Cor. 1:19. Paul vouches for his trustworthiness in the Lord and desires that the Corinthians receive him with all confidence.

While the first clause and its present tense are merely explanatory, the second and its future tense, like the Attic usage of this tense, convey purpose: "who shall remind you," etc., R. 960, 989. The verb ἀναμιμνήσκειν regularly governs two accusatives. What does Paul mean with "my ways"? Do they signify Paul's conduct and manner of life so that the Corinthians were to remember Paul's actions and to copy them? Such a view would disregard the question as to whether Paul's ways were really the right ways, were actually in accord with the true norm of right. Paul would never take the answer to this question for granted.

The Old Testament constantly uses the Hebrew equivalent for αἱ ὁδοί in the objective sense: the ways that God has marked out in his Word. These divinely prescribed ways Paul had made his own, and he calls them "mine" only in this sense. Note the use of the singular in Acts 9:2; I Cor. 12:31; II Pet. 2:2, "the way of truth"; and the plural in Rev. 15:3, "righteous and true are thy ways." The modifier "in Christ" is emphatic and important. These ways are Paul's teachings and his church practice in union with Christ, and not one of them ever wanders away from Christ.

"Even as" does not describe the manner in which Timothy is to do this reminding in Corinth, for the point of this clause is the substance of Timothy's reminding. This clause is a somewhat loose apposition to "my ways": "even as I teach," etc.; or we may supply "my ways": "even as I teach these ways everywhere in every church." The verb is durative: "as I go on teaching," for Paul does not go to one congregation and teach and practice there in one way and then to another place to teach and to practice differently. He does not make his ministry in one locality give the lie to that in another place.

This is the trouble with some ministers today. No; already in this verse Paul after a manner enunciates the principle that was later to become famous: *quod apud omnes et ubique*. In no way does he ever violate the catholicity of the church. There is a silent reproof in this final clause. Paul teaches one and the same truth always and everywhere, his doctrine and his church practice never varied. But the Corinthians needed Paul's messenger to remind them of this teaching. They were wavering, perhaps already actually deviating from "the ways" which they, like the rest, had been taught. A sad commentary on their supposed progress.

18) Paul's mission of Timothy as also the letter he is now writing are only stopgaps; he intends to go to Corinth in person. So Paul adds a continuative δέ and writes regarding his own coming. **Now some are puffed up as though I were not coming to you.** The aorist "did become puffed up" intends to state the fact and shows that Paul is fully informed about this inflated talk of "some." Who they are the Corinthians, of course, know, for they have heard their talk; we can only surmise that they were some of the members who boasted about their "wisdom." Their wish may have been father to their thought, for they would rather that Paul might not come.

Since δέ is placed far back in the sentence between the participle and its subject, μοῦ πρὸς ὑμᾶς is brought together: "I to you." These persons say: "Paul is not coming to *us*." They mean: "*He* knows better than to come to *us*." The present ἐρχομένου is due to the fact that the Greek retains the original tense when the change to indirect discourse is made, for these persons said: "Paul is not coming." Paul states this as their opinion: "as though," ὡς. It was no innocent opinion, for those who voiced it puffed themselves up (a reminder of v. 6) when they were doing so and made themselves appear important and pretended that Paul had not the courage to face them. Paul refers to what these puffed-up people say, because, having sent Timothy to Corinth, he does not wish this action of his to be misunderstood as though he himself is afraid to come. Whether others had made the contrary assertion that Paul would certainly come, Paul does not intimate.

19) These people are sadly mistaken. Paul is not a coward as far as facing opposition in Corinth or elsewhere is concerned. **But I will come shortly to you if the Lord will; and I will know, not the word of them that are puffed up, but the power.**

Since the verb is placed so emphatically forward, we may even translate: "I will indeed come!" How "shortly" 16:8 states, namely at the time of the following Pentecost (the Jewish festival). Thus he actually gives the date. Paul intends to start in a few weeks. Yet he adds "if the Lord will" (a condition of expectancy with the aorist of a definite volition on the Lord's part), not as though there were a doubt as to Paul's plan regarding his coming, but because he submitted to his great master Christ in all his movements.

Nor does Paul leave an uncertainty regarding the object of his coming. He is coming to face these very people who are now so blatant, to take their exact measure. "I will know," γνώσομαι, really know, what is in them. The perfect participle has its natural sense which implies a present condition: have been and thus are now still puffed up. He will pay no attention to what they may say in their pride, but will find out τὴν δύναμιν, what genuine power is behind what they say. We immediately learn why he makes this sharp distinction.

20) **For not in connection with (mere) word is the kingdom of God, on the contrary, in connection with power.** We should note the expression: οὐκ ἐν . . . (ἐστί), ἀλλ᾿ ἐν κτλ., which means neither "consists in," "rests on," nor "is conditioned by"; for ἐν denotes the accompanying circumstance, which in this case happens to be also a mark of recognition. Wherever the kingdom of God reaches down among men it is accompanied, not merely by words (like the science and the wisdom of men), but by power from on high, the power of divine grace, and by that power we may also "know" and recognize it. For this reason Paul intends to look for this "power" among these proud people ("some") in Corinth when he arrives among them.

In these two phrases ἐν has much the same force as the ἐν in v. 21, ἐν ῥάβδῳ, except that it here also gives a mark of recognition. The preposition is not Hebraistic. The negative οὐ denies the phrase "in connection with word," over against which ἀλλά places the positive opposite "in connection with power." The danger confronting "some" in Corinth is the fact that Paul will find in them none of this power of the kingdom; he will meet only words, assertions, empty display, sham power. For we must add that the power of the kingdom, by which it is also always easily recognized, produces true faith, true confession, true love, and a galaxy of true Christian virtues. As far as the charismatic gifts are concerned, these belong to the minor effects and evidences.

With "the kingdom of God" Paul reverts to v. 8: "you reigned," ἐβασιλεύσατε, where he referred to the imagination of the proud Corinthians who thought that in them already in this life the glory of the kingdom is displaying itself by means of their great wisdom, etc. Paul asserts that "the kingdom of God" exists and reaches down into the earth and manifests itself in power. This divine kingdom must, however, not be conceived after the analogy of earthly kingdoms. These are to be found where the people are, for the people constitute these earthly kingdoms apart from the earthly king; for when he dies or abdicates, the kingdom still continues to exist. But the kingdom of God does not in this manner consist of the communion of saints or of the church. God's kingdom exists where God is to be found, with all the power of his grace in Christ Jesus, and there alone. To be sure, true believers will also be found there, but only because God produces them with the power of his grace. We enter this kingdom only because God's saving power transforms us in a wonderful way and makes us partakers of his kingdom.

When Paul, therefore, says that he will know "the power" of these puffed-up Corinthians he does not refer to a power of their own but to this divine gospel power of God. He would know whether they truly possess this. Paul knows about no power that *we* have "for furthering the kingdom of God." This modern, pietistic way of thinking and speaking about the kingdom is foreign to him, for no man can further or build God's kingdom. God alone sends, furthers, and consummates his kingdom. Or we may say, this kingdom builds itself through its own inherent power.

21) Paul is coming to Corinth? How do the Corinthians want him to come? **What do you want? Shall I come to you with a rod or with love and a spirit of mildness?** They may have their choice. Paul is ready to come in either way. Regarding τί with

only two alternatives see R. 737. The two prepositions ἐν indicate accompanying circumstance and are similar to v. 20: "provided with a rod," etc., R. 589. "Rod" is figurative for severe chastisement as a father may chastise "children," v. 14. The subjunctive ἔλθω is employed because of the rhetorical question: "Shall I come?" R. 928, bottom; 930, second paragraph. The tense is due to the nature of the act. The future indicative could also have been used.

The alternatives which Paul places before the Corinthians are "the rod" and "love and a spirit of mildness." Do they want severity or loving mildness? The latter is possible only in the event that they repent. But is it right ever to use the rod of severity? Paul certainly implies that it is. In fact, this phrase, "coming with a rod," intends to meet every challenge that "some" in Corinth may have in mind to offer Paul. The degree of severity with which Paul may strike depends, of course, on the kind and the degree of the opposition to the truth which he may meet. If this opposition proves incorrigible, he will use the rod even to the extent of expulsion from the congregation. Thus "rod" is intended as a warning.

More frequently a question is asked in regard to "love." If Paul came with a rod, would he come without ἀγάπη? This question, however, confuses the thought. Paul is not writing about love in general which extends to all men, even to the wicked, but about his paternal love which is restricted to "my beloved children," v. 14, who as such children accept the admonition of their father. This father love cannot be bestowed upon those who repudiate their father, who persist in their evil cause, who must thus be expelled from the family in Christ. God loves all men, also the wicked; but God loves his children in a specific way, namely as his children, and because of this love he bestows all the fatherly gifts upon them, which he cannot bestow upon the wicked in the very nature of the case.

Does πνεῦμα πραΰτητος signify the Holy Spirit? Then Paul would write at least "mildness of *the* Spirit." Since "love" is a quality that is found in Paul's heart, this "spirit" must also be such a quality, and the genitive "of mildness" is qualitative and equal to but stronger than "a mild spirit." Moreover, in Scripture analogy the Holy Spirit is never a person with whom we operate. Finally, it is quite impossible to parallel the Holy Spirit with a rod or stick.

Paul has reached the end of the first great part of his letter. We see that he constantly operates with the realities, the actual facts, and not only with a few of them but with all of them. These facts he pits against the shams, the pretenses, and the pride that rests upon them. He expects the facts to win. If they do not, so much the worse for those who spurn them. We note Paul speaking with calm objectivity, fully conscious of the great realities he is presenting. Again we see Paul moved with deep feeling, showing a great heart that is quivering with sorrow and with pain, yet his emotions are ever under perfect control. The power and the effect of his words are beyond question, in fact, they still continue. God's Spirit still speaks through these immortal words.

CHAPTER V

The Second Part of the Letter

Moral Delinquencies in the Congregation, chapters 5 and 6

I. The Case of Open Incest, chapter 5

1) Without a preamble Paul proceeds *medias in res* and succinctly states the flagrant case that demoralized the Corinthian congregation. **In general one hears among you of fornication, and of such fornication as does not occur among the Gentiles, namely that one has his father's wife.** Much effort is spent to determine what ὅλως means in the present connection. The R. V. strangely translates "actually," which is out of the question. The translation "everywhere" cannot be substantiated from any other source and seems to have been chosen only because the evil report regarding Corinth is supposed to have been circulated far and wide. All efforts to connect ὅλως with something in the preceding chapter have failed; hence its meaning cannot be determined from this investigation. The search for rare and exceptional uses of this adverb, especially in the papyri and the ostraca, is interesting but rather unpromising. Luther, whom the A. V. follows, is on the right track when he abides by the ordinary meaning of ὅλως and translates: *Es geht ein gemein Geschrei* (converting the adverb into an adjective although *Geschrei* is too strong), "It is reported commonly." But both of these translations labor under the impression that Paul is speaking concerning a report that has gone out from Corinth and has become *gemein* or "common" in other Christian churches.

There is also confusion regarding the rest of the sentence. The subject of ἀκούεται is undoubtedly the noun πορνεία, and this means that the phrase "among you" modifies the verb; thus literally: "In general fornication is heard among you," or more smoothly: "Among you one hears of fornication." The matter is talked about in your midst; your members hear about it from one another; the thing is no longer a secret, unknown to you. Luther and our versions translate: It is reported "that there is fornication among you," as though ἐν ὑμῖν πορνεία should be taken together as constituting a subject clause. R. 803 also lends support to this rendering by regarding the passive verb as impersonal: "it is reported," which then calls for the clause: "that there is," etc.

Here we have an instance where the preconception as to what the writer is thought to say has affected even the grammar. Traces of this preconception are evident even when the sentence is properly construed as far as the subject is concerned. It seems to be a foregone conclusion that this hearing in regard to fornication does not take place among the members in Corinth (ἐν ὑμῖν) but abroad in other churches. If the clause is not arranged so as to read: "that there is fornication among you," then the equivalent of such a clause is secured by attaching the phrase "among you" to "fornication" as indicating where the fornication occurs. But in the Greek the phrase would then have to follow "fornication."

The plea that fornication cannot be heard has no validity, for crimes are constantly heard in the obvious sense that reports concerning them reach our ears. What Paul writes is that the Corinthians hear reports of fornication in their own midst, even about the terrible case he now specifies, and yet remain puffed up as before, do not as much as mourn, to say nothing of taking strenuous action.

The explicative καί specifies by naming the flagrant case with which Paul confronts the Corinthians. Paul states it succinctly: "that a man has his father's wife." It was such a case "as does not occur even among the Gentiles" or pagans, to say nothing about Jews and Christians. Even Roman law forbade unions of this kind; they are naturally abhorrent. One does not need Christianity to repudiate them. Although some monstrous cases are known to have occurred in the old pagan world, this fact does not overthrow the rule that among the Gentiles a case such as this one which had occurred at Corinth is unheard of. Lev. 18:8 and Deut. 22:30 record the pertinent Jewish law. "So that," ὥστε, is equal to ὡς. While ἔχειν γυναῖκα might include marriage, we assume no marriage in this case since Roman law prohibited such unions. Hence this union did not have even the semblance of regularity. The article used with "father" is equal to the possessive "his father."

Paul refrains from mentioning the man's name. We may say that he does this because the case is not as yet closed, for in other cases where men are actually expelled Paul does name them. The fact that the father was dead cannot be assumed because of II Cor. 7:12. Such an assumption would make the case a little less horrible, yet would not eliminate its worst feature. Nothing further is said about the woman in question. In order not to make the case appear worse than is necessary, we infer that she was the man's stepmother. Likewise, the absence of further reference to the woman is best taken to indicate that she was still a pagan. Finally, we assume that this case developed after the man had been received into membership in the Corinthian congregation and not before. What induced him to perpetrate such a deed as this, and why the congregation ever allowed this relation to continue after the act became known, is not revealed to us. Were the members at Corinth so taken up with their factional wrangling that their eyes were closed even to this kind of moral turpitude? Or did this man occupy such a prominent place in the congregation that the members did not venture to challenge his crime?

2) We may assume that the former was the case, for Paul continues: **And you are still puffed up and did not rather mourn in order that he who did this deed might be removed from your midst.** This verse may be regarded as a question although the Greek has no particle to indicate that it is such. "You," placed forward, is emphatic: "*You*, still puffed up as you are," allow this to pass without concern? Instead of boasting about themselves they should "rather" (μᾶλλον) do a far more appropriate thing, be filled with sorrow. For this matter concerned not only the sinner involved, it concerned all of them.

Paul first mentions the feeling which this outrageous occurrence should have evoked in the hearts of the Corinthians, and this is not anger and indignation but grief and deepest sorrow: "and you did not rather mourn." This indicates the motive that ought to underlie proper Christian disciplinary action: grief over the devil's success, sorrow for our congregation because it suffers such disgrace, mourning for the soul of the sinner who has been overwhelmed with sin and guilt.

The next clause, however, mentions the action that should emanate from this sorrow, namely the disciplinary removal of the sinner: he should have been expelled from the congregation. Sometimes a congregation merely deplores open moral defections in its midst and, like Eli of old, contents itself with that. Such conduct means that the feeling of sorrow is still too shallow. The congregation thus remains partaker of the sin and guilt. The Corinthians lacked even this sorrow. No wonder they did not proceed "in order that he who did this deed might be removed from your midst," ἀρθῇ, from αἴρω, aorist subjunctive passive. The present infinitive ἔχειν describes the man's action as continuing, ὁ ποιήσας, an aorist points to the act as being done and thus as a fact; τὸ ἔργον is often used with reference to an evil deed.

3) The Corinthians have taken no action; Paul takes action at once and informs the Corinthians regarding what he has done and what, as far as he is concerned, stands (this is the force of the perfect κέκρικα). **For I, absent in body though present in spirit, have already passed judgment as present on the man who did thus perpetrate this thing: In the name of our Lord Jesus, you and my spirit duly assembled together, by the power of our Lord Jesus to deliver such a man over to Satan for the destruction of the flesh in order that the spirit may be saved in the day of the Lord Jesus.**

"For" intends to explain that, although the Corinthians did not even mourn when this case began to be reported in their midst, Paul has done more. "I," written out, is emphatic, and μέν, although without a corresponding δέ, implies that others are to join Paul in the action he describes.

But Paul is in Ephesus, and the Corinthians are far away in Corinth. This situation is taken care of by the participles: "absent in body though present in spirit." The separation is only physical, "as to the body"; Paul is, nevertheless, present in Corinth, namely "as to the spirit" (datives of relation). We need not puzzle our heads about this type of presence, for we still say: "I am with you in spirit," when in some important matter mind and heart are united with distant friends.

The perfect κέκρικα conveys the idea that Paul judged the case and that this judgment stands; the force of the tense is intensified by the adverb "already." Paul intends to say that the case is so clear in every respect that he finds no reason to hesitate regarding the verdict — that is settled. Succinctly he again states the case which justifies this quick verdict: I have already passed judgment "on the man who thus perpetrated this thing." "Thus" and "this thing" indicate the gravity of both the manner and the crime: "in this abominable way" this man perpetrated "this abominable deed." The substantivized participle τὸν κατεργασάμενον is a stronger expression than the preceding ὁ ποιήσας, for it indicates that the finished deed was done in a shameless way and is equivalent to our "perpetrator." The man did the thing although every law of God and of man most emphatically prohibits such a crime and terms it incest.

Thus Paul's immediate verdict is fully justified. No just judge could act otherwise. Yet Paul carefully adds: I have passed this judgment "as present" with you. We shall see in a moment why this addition is so important. The translation: "I have already resolved," is unacceptable because the direct object follows immediately: "the man who thus perpetrated this thing." This accusative is the direct object of κέκρικα because of its position and cannot be the object of the remote infinitive παραδοῦναι, which has its own object: "such a man."

4) Paul then records the actual verdict in due legal form and uses the infinitive of indirect discourse. Regarding its form and its length Bengel remarks: *graviter suspensa manet et vibrat oratio.* The substance of the verdict is simple: "to deliver such a man over to Satan" (direct discourse: "I deliver over," etc.). Yet all the additions and the modifications attached to this verdict are of the utmost importance.

First, the set formula: "In the name of our Lord Jesus." The solemn announcement of the verdict begins with this phrase in order to mark the manner of the grave action that is taken. Sometimes this simple formula without additions or modifiers is employed:

"In the name of our Lord Jesus Christ. Amen." The statement of the legal action then follows. We thus decline to regard this solemn formula as a mere modifier of the following genitive absolute as though Paul intends to say no more than that he and the Corinthians are assembled in the Lord's name. The very nature of this grave formula is such that it cannot belong merely to some subsidiary act that also needs to be mentioned when a full statement of the verdict is made but must belong to the supreme act itself which constitutes the verdict.

In phrases of this kind ὄνομα is often regarded as an expression of authority or of representation so that "in the name" equals: "by the authority of our Lord," etc., or: "as representing our Lord," etc. But ἐν means "in union with," and ὄνομα is that by which the Lord makes himself known and by which he is known to us, namely his revelation. Thus the phrase means: "in union or in accord with the revelation of our Lord Jesus." In all vital actions of the church such as the one here recorded the essential point is that these actions accord fully with the revelation which Christ has made to us in his Word.

A second formula follows, which is legal in its nature and thus necessary to the verdict here placed on record by Paul. It reads like the preamble to a resolution or a decision when it is set down in proper form: "We being duly assembled," etc. Paul cannot, however, say "we" in this case because he is in Ephesus and is present in that assumed assembly in Corinth only "in spirit." So he writes "you and my spirit duly assembled together." We should not consider κέκρικα, "I have passed judgment," apart from this association of Paul's spirit with the Corinthians in a duly called assembly. Twice before he has emphasized this point of his presence in Corinth in connection with the rendering of this verdict: first, "I, absent in body yet present in spirit"; secondly, "passed judgment as present."

Why this emphasis on his presence in Corinth for this judgment? Why can he not say right here in Ephesus: "I here and now give this verdict"? Why is his presence in a duly called meeting of the congregation so essential? Because not even an apostle can of himself and by himself excommunicate a person from a Christian congregation. The attempt to do such a thing is papal arrogance. No pastor can expel a member no matter what the member has done. Expulsion is an act that can be performed only in a duly called meeting of the congregation. If a wrong-minded congregation refuses to expel where it ought to, the person involved remains a member to the disgrace of the congregation. The pastor should use all proper efforts, as Paul does here, to persuade the congregation to take action. If it refuses, the pastor, who is Christ's slave-steward (4:1) and directly responsible to him for the mysteries of God entrusted to his hands, has the right to withhold from the unexpelled sinner the Lord's Supper, etc., in order to safeguard his own conscience and his office so that he may not become a δοῦλος or slave of men.

When Paul writes regarding his presence in spirit in the duly assembled meeting of the Corinthians, we see that he does not, after all, mean that it is he alone who expels by virtue of his supreme apostolic power. For then he would neither need to be present, nor would the Corinthians need to hold a duly called meeting in the matter. If Paul were physically present with the congregation he would as an apostle and as the founder of this church naturally lead and direct the congregation in its action, would preside at the meeting, and would formulate properly and then announce publicly the verdict arrived at even as he does now "already" in his letter.

Yet in reality Paul's presence, either in the body or in the spirit, is not an essential feature of this or of any other action of the congregation so that his absence, or the absence of a pastor, or of a representative of the clergy, would make proper action impossible. Paul rebukes the congregation for not having acted at once, without him, and for having delayed so long. This is the only reason he enters into the case at all, i. e., now urging and leading the congregation to do its duty. They in and of themselves have the full right and the power to act. Ordinarily a congregation has a pastor when an expulsion impends, but the presence of a pastor is not in itself an essential feature of the action as if without a pastor the congregation were either not complete or not competent. Note the use of συνάγεσθαι to indicate a meeting that is duly brought together. Only in this instance does Paul use this verb; elsewhere, five times, he writes συνέρχεσθαι, which merely states the coming together.

The proper preambles have been formulated, and now the verdict they usher in follows. This begins with the phrase "by the power of our Lord Jesus." The very meaning of the preposition σύν, "with the help of," settles the question as to whether this phrase depends on the preceding genitive absolute or on the following infinitive "to deliver over." People are not assembled "with the help of a power" or "together with a power," but they do act "with the help of" and "together with a power." R. 624. The Corinthians are enabled to take such drastic action against one of their members because they have the power of their Lord. This is, of course, his gospel power which has two divine functions, one to admit to union with God (contrition and faith), the other to debar from this union (impenitence, unbelief, hardening), Mark 16:16; John 20:22, 23. Luther: "I believe that when the called ministers of Christ by his divine command deal with us, particularly when they exclude the manifest and impenitent sinners from the Christian congregation and again absolve those who repent of their sins and are willing to amend — that this is as valid and certain, also in heaven, as if Christ, our dear Lord, had dealt with us himself."

Deissmann, *Light from the Ancient East*, 304, etc., finds "the unobtrusive little word σύν" a technical term that is used in pagan magical and cursing formulas. He gives one example: "I will bind her . . . in fellowship with Hecate, who is below the earth, and the Erinyes." But while σὺν θ' Ἑκάτ(η)ι may mean "in fellowship with Hecate," Paul does not write "in fellowship with *the power* of the Lord," which is something quite different. There is no need to add other examples of σύν used with εἶναι, for no such combination is found in Paul's words. Deissmann overlooks κέκρικα, a legal term, and συναχθέντων ὑμῶν, a legally called assembly, in fact, the legal formulation of Paul's verdict, something that is far removed from magic and magical curses. The fact that Satan is mentioned in Paul's verdict is not a reason for concluding that this is not a verdict but a form of some magical curse.

5) To deliver over to Satan means negatively to expel from Christ's kingdom and positively to relegate to Satan's kingdom. Yet let us remember that this is a court action, a judical verdict. By his crime and his impenitence the man placed himself into Satan's power. He merely deceived himself and others by thinking that he was still a Christian because he was being wrongfully allowed to continue his outward connection with the church. This wrongful outward connection now ceases. After this verdict has been rendered, he and all the Corinthians know the fact that the man is under Satan and not under Christ.

A misleading thought is advanced when it is stated that there is a difference between what is called expulsion from a congregation and deliverance unto Satan. Nor can it be supposed that only an apostle could deliver unto Satan while the congregation might expel in its own right, ἀρθῇ, v. 2. As to the latter claim compare v. 13, where Paul uses ἐξάρατε as denoting the very action inaugurated by the apostle here in v. 3-5. In the case of all impenitent sinners to expel is identical with handing over to Satan, for if a man no longer belongs to Christ, then he *eo ipso* belongs to Satan. *Tertium non datur.* Only when the question is one of doctrine is there a possibility that he who holds some false doctrine and will not abjure it may still have enough of the gospel in his heart to keep him in faith. Yet because of his obdurate holding to false doctrine the congregation must disown him although it thereby makes no special pronouncement as to his possible faith. The congregation must keep itself clean. Such a separation is similar to a separation from errorists and erring churches in general, Rom. 16:17.

Deissmann concludes that παραδοῦναι is also a technical pagan term that is taken from the ritual of cursing and is here adopted by Paul but adduces as proof only a Greek papyrus of the fourth century A. D.: "Daemon of the dead . . . I deliver unto thee N. N. in order that . . ." He tells us that such curses were written on tablets and reached their address by being buried in the ground, and that in their formulas of expulsion Christians substituted Satan for the pagan demons. But this is again specious. Paul's pronouncement is that of a court. When a court decrees: "We nand thee over," παραδοῦναι, this means "into custody of a jailor." It just so happens that the same verb παραδίδωμι is employed in both instances. In this case Satan is the equivalent of the jailor. Just because Satan is mentioned here we are not justified in advancing the idea of cursing and of demons who carry out curses.

"Such a man" is the necessary object of the infinitive "to deliver over." The individual in question has been already described as to his crime and as to his guilt, v. 1-3. Now Paul says that he is "such," a man of this type and this character. This designation virtually establishes the general principle that every man of such a character should be dealt with in a similar manner. This is the correct attitude to assume in all cases of Christian discipline.

In cases of expulsion the congregation is, first of all, concerned about itself. For its own sake it must rid itself of flagrant sinners, v. 13. If no adequate measures are taken, the congregation itself becomes partaker of the sinners' guilt. But, in the second place, the congregation is also concerned about the sinners. If there is even a remote possibility that they can yet be saved, the attempt to save them must be made. This truth lies in εἰς which indicates the proximate purpose and in ἵνα which introduces the ultimate purpose. The truth of the matter is not that, when a moral delinquent is expelled, the congregation thereby intends to send him to perdition. Deissmann, whom R. 628 follows, should not find here a parallel with the pagan ritual of cursing. Such curses intend to send to perdition; Christian expulsion is a last resort that intends to save, ἵνα σωθῇ.

"For the destruction of the flesh." The word σάρξ is not identical with the body, σῶμα, and this statement does not refer to bodily suffering including also bodily death. How can the ultimate purpose of saving the sinner be attained when he is brought to death? And who is to kill this sinner? Satan? In his *Introduction to the New Testament* Zahn writes as though the Corinthians were to perform the execution. Yet no congregation has the right to kill, and no executioner is listed among the church officers. In Second Corinthians Zahn has Paul reverse himself: after the congregation disobeyed to the extent of not *killing* the man, Paul, too, now does not want him *killed*.

When "flesh" is identified with "body" although it be termed the physical seat of sin, unwarranted interpretations are given also to πνεῦμα and the saving of the spirit of the sinner, for the Scriptures know nothing of the final salvation of a sinner's spirit apart from his body. Either both are saved, or neither is saved. In this very letter Paul teaches the glorious resurrection of the body of every sinner that is saved. In view of this fact these interpreters introduce the salvation also of the body of the dead sinner. Moreover, the silent assumption that Satan is to work the destruction of the body reacts on the final clause so that the agent implied in the passive verb "may be saved" of necessity also becomes Satan.

The words σάρξ and πνεῦμα are to be understood in the ethical sense. This Corinthian sinner had allowed the flesh to triumph over the spirit or new principle that had been implanted in his heart by the gospel. Expulsion is the last possible means for undoing this work of sin. By publicly turning the man away from Christ and over to Satan the "flesh" which Satan had caused to triumph in him receives opportunity to develop unchecked. All barriers, even the outward shams, are now down. He is free to give full sway to his fleshly lusts. But by their very excess these have a tendency to defeat themselves, for the works of the flesh produce bitterness and gall as their fruits. The prodigal, separated from his father, came down to the level of swine. That helped eventually to save him, not as a *causa efficiens*, but as a contributing factor in God's hands. Some sinners must taste the dregs before they realize what their sin really is. For this reason Paul mentions no agent in connection with the "destruction." By running to its own extreme the "flesh" defeats itself.

In this way the ultimate purpose may, after all, be achieved: "that the spirit may be saved in the day of the Lord Jesus." Thus it was, indeed, achieved in the prodigal and also in this Corinthian sinner, in him even more speedily. Instead of calling this clause regarding the sinner's final salvation *eine ueberraschende Wendung* (a surprising turn) in Paul's verdict, we shall thus become aware of the fact that it is altogether proper and not at all surprising. Whatever surprise there may be lies in the fact that by formally delivering a man over to Satan the actual "destruction of the flesh" could result.

We know, of course, that a σώζειν cannot take place without the proper divine means of grace. Although Paul does not allude to them as little as Jesus does in the parable of the Prodigal, these means are necessarily included. This, in its way, pertains also to the destruction of the flesh. When the prodigal sat among the swine, the recollection of his father and of the abundance in his father's house revived in his mind. That is what as the efficient cause drew him to contrition and repentance so that he was saved. The expelled sinner takes with him the memory of Christ, of the gospel, of the church, etc. When his flesh has brought him low, this memory may yet succeed in saving him. The πνεῦμα, the spiritual life, which was crushed by the σάρξ may be rekindled and "saved." Nor is there need to talk about the σῶμα or body in this connection since the spirit is never saved without the body.

Paul adds: "in the day of our Lord Jesus," and thus for the third time mentions this sacred name in his verdict. This is the great day on which the Lord, our Judge, shall appear before the whole world of angels and of men and shall render just judgment to all. Then he shall confirm publicly every true gospel judgment of his church and shall publicly accept also every sinner who has been saved through the gospel discipline which he has committed to his church. The forensic idea thus dominates the entire verdict.

6) Considering what Paul is compelled to demand in the matter of this case of incest he rightly adds: **Your reason for glory is not good,** καλόν, "excellent" in the moral sense. Indeed, how could people who allowed such moral obliquity to remain in their midst still think they had reason to boast? The term καύχημα denotes the thing in which one glories and makes his boast as distinct from καύχησις, the act by which one glories. "Not good" is a litotes and means "bad," κακόν. Yet our versions and prominent commentators translate as though Paul has written the latter term: "It is bad in the face of your delinquency in this case to boast; you ought to be ashamed." One cannot, however, refrain from asking why Paul does not write καύχησις if this is what he means. Moreover, the act of boasting is bad only when there is something amiss about the reason for boasting. So it appears that Paul writes καύχημα because this is what he has in mind. The Corinthians may speak of wisdom, great spiritual charismata, etc., this case of open immorality is evidence that their reason for boasting is anything but good.

Yet someone may object: This is only one case, and we dare not generalize on the basis of one case. Paul answers in a telling way: **Do you not know that a little leaven leavens the entire lump?** His reprimand is by no means a matter of generalizing and drawing an unwarranted conclusion from a single case. Paul may be using a proverb or a common saying that was well known to the Corinthians. But aside from the source of his expression the fact itself is self-evident to the Corinthians, they certainly know that it takes only a bit of leaven to leaven an entire mass of dough. The entire congregation is necessarily involved in the case which Paul brings to their attention. Not, indeed, in the sense that one evil man makes the whole congregation evil, but in the sense that by allowing one vicious case in their midst the entire membership becomes involved in the guilt of this one case. Yeast or leaven is used figuratively in the New Testament in both a good sense (Jesus in the parable, Matt. 13:33) and an evil sense (Jesus regarding the teaching of the Pharisees, Matt. 16:6-12; Paul a second time in Gal. 5:9). The point of the saying lies in the contrast between "little" leaven and the "entire" lump.

7) This evil leaven must be removed. **Clean out the old leaven in order that you may be a new lump even as you are unleavened.** This injunction, however, means far more than the removal of the one flagrant case or of this and of other bad cases. For the leaven that operated to such a vicious conclusion in this one case and was contaminating the entire congregation is really "the old leaven" (note the article), that specific leaven that is "old" because it is left over from the old life they once lived apart from Christ. Paul traces the Corinthian disinclination to take action against this one vicious case to its real source, the old worldly and fleshly disposition that was carried over in their hearts from their former life. The aorist: "Clean it out!" is peremptory and denotes a most thorough cleaning as also ἐκ indicates.

The figure of cleaning out the old leaven is taken from the Jewish custom of removing all leaven and anything leavened from the house in preparation for the Jewish Passover Feast. Its force is thus at once perceived. In the purpose clause: "in order that you may be a new lump," we should note the adjective νέος which means "new" in the sense that the thing did not exist before while καινός means "new" in the sense that a thing differs from what is old. Both terms are used with reference to our new Christian nature in Eph. 4:23, 24. Here Paul says that the Corinthians are not merely to be a lump that is "new" in so far as they differed from what they once were, but "new" in a sense in which they had not before been. They are to be a lump of dough that is just freshly mixed, to which nothing in the way of yeast has been added. Their Christian character and life are to be like an entirely fresh start. He might also have used the other word: new and no longer old, and this, too, would have been pertinent; but he prefers the word νέος because it is stronger.

"Even as you are unleavened," however, wards off a possible misunderstanding as though Paul is now calling upon the Corinthians for the first time to emerge from the old life and to make a new start. No; what Paul bids them do is "in accord with the fact that they are already unleavened." Paul acknowledges them as brethren throughout, hence as ἄζυμοι ὄντες. "To be unleavened" is the Christian's essential characteristic, for he is reborn, a new creature, etc. In fact, Paul could not have told the Corinthians to clean out the old leaven if they had still been an unconverted people because spiritual powers are needed for this purging. So Paul now reminds the Corinthians of what they really are as Christians, namely ἄζυμοι, "unleavened." It would be altogether abnormal for such people to allow an old leaven again to work among them; καθώς, "even as," "according," often points to a norm. There is no stress on ἐστέ as its position shows, and we should not translate: "according as you *are* unleavened."

By calling the Corinthians "unleavened" Paul appeals to a subjective motive, namely to the real character of the Corinthians as Christians. But there is more, namely the greatest possible objective motive or reason for this cleansing that Paul enjoins. Thus "also" adds, and "for" names the reason. **For also our Passover was sacrificed, Christ.** The pronoun has no emphasis, otherwise the Greek would at least place it before "the Passover." The stress is on "the Passover," namely on Christ and on the fact that this was sacrificed (θύειν, to slay, to offer, to send up in smoke). The figure begun with leaven is thus extended into allegory. According to the ancient Jewish rite a lamb was slain, and that slain lamb was made (for each family or for a similar group) the Passover. In a similar way Christ was slain to be our Passover Lamb. The connection of this lamb with Paul's admonition is implied yet is evident and clear: the Passover Lamb slain, and the Passover Feast thus begun, and yet the old leaven not cleaned out of the house — what a contradiction! If such a thing would be frightful in the case of the Jews who slew and ate only lambs which were merely types, how much worse is it for us Christians who have our divine Lamb, the antitype, slain once for the deliverance of the world!

We need not trouble in the present connection to distinguish between the lambs that were slain at the first Passover in Egypt and those that were slain year by year in grateful commemoration of that ancient deliverance. Paul lays the stress on ἐτύθη, on the fact of the sacrificial slaying, not on the eating of the flesh of the lambs. Paul thus recalls to the Corinthians the deliverance wrought for them by Christ's blood, and in the pronoun "our" he includes himself. What was done in Egypt and what was done year by year since that time are thus combined.

8) **And so let us celebrate, not with old leaven, neither with leaven of badness and wickedness, but with unleavened bread of sincerity and truth.** After the Lamb had been slain, the Passover celebration should proceed: "Let up keep festival." The connective ὥστε is paratactic, not hypotactic, R. 999. The subjunctive ἑορτάζωμεν is independent of ὥστε, for it would be the subjunctive even if the connective were omitted. This subjunctive is hortative, R. 931. We translate:

"And so let us keep the feast." The festival or feast we are to celebrate (ἑορτή) embraces the entire Christian life — an attractive figure, indeed. All the modifiers, too, retain the figure.

These are first negative and then positive. "Not with old leaven" points backward to v. 7 and the cleaning out of the old leaven of the worldly and the fleshly spirit. "With the old leaven" is general and includes any and all leaven that is old and belongs to the worldly spirit. Hence the more specific addition "nor with leaven of badness and wickedness." These genitives are appositional or definitive, R. 498. This leaven consists of badness and wickedness. The genitives thus interpret the figure of "leaven." The two genitives denote one idea since they are synonyms: κακία, "badness," when something is altogether inferior and not what it should be ("malice" in our versions is incorrect); πονηρία is active evil or "wickedness"; *Schlechtigkeit und Boshaftigkeit*. Both appertain to the case of the man whom the Corinthians should have expelled as well as to their evil way of taking no action whatever in this case.

The positive side is likewise expressed by two genitives: "but with the unleavened bread of sincerity and truth." As the opposite of ζύμη Paul uses the neuter plural ἄζυμα, *matzoth*, *Ungesaeuertes*, thin sheets of bread that are baked without yeast (but not τὰ ἄζυμα, which designates the festival itself). The genitives are again appositional and interpretative and again present one idea. The word εἰλικρίνεια means purity and sincerity, without the admixture of a foreign substance. In this connection the foreign substance would be the evil leaven which adulterates the pure motives and actions of the Corinthians. The synonymous term is ἀλήθεια, "truth," which is here regarded as a moral quality, the inner desire for divine reality which tolerates and accepts no shams. These are the cakes of pure, unleavened bread on which the Corinthians are to feast all their life long in one continuous celebration. The combined genitives thus apply to the special case of the man and to the way in which the Corinthians should deal with him and to the character and the conduct of the Corinthians in general.

These last three verses are full of the imagery of the Jewish Easter festival, the Passover. Paul's marked use of this imagery at this time has led to the generally accepted conclusion that he wrote this letter shortly before the Jewish Passover season, so that his mind was naturally filled with this imagery. With this dating of his letter corresponds his plan to start on the journey to Corinth at the coming of the Jewish Pentecost festival. But it would be unsafe to conclude either that the old Jewish festivals were still celebrated in the newly formed Christian congregations, or that corresponding Christian festivals were already celebrated at this early date.

9) In this connection, that of the incestuous man, Paul corrects a perversion of the admonition he had sent the Corinthians in a letter of a previous date. **I wrote you in my letter not to associate with fornicators.** The phrase "in my (the) letter" is quite decisive, R. 757. We have a parallel in II Cor. 7:8, where Paul refers to this present letter with the identical phrase. It is quite impossible that this phrase should refer to the letter which Paul is now engaged in writing and thus to regard ἔγραψα as the so-called epistolary aorist, because the Corinthians could not twist and misunderstand a sentence of this letter before the letter came into their hands. Nor can we assume that Paul is afraid that they might misunderstand after they had received this letter and that he is, therefore, warding off such a possible misunderstanding in advance. For in the portion of the present letter thus far completed we nowhere find the warning "not to as-

sociate with fornicators," nor anything that can be construed as an equivalent. This makes inevitable the conclusion that one of Paul's letters to the Corinthians has been lost to us. How it came to be lost we do not know. Yet we have no reason to assume that the New Testament canon is incomplete, or that the doctrine of Inspiration is in any way affected. God's providence did not consider it necessary to preserve this lost letter to us, and that suffices. Moreover, there is evidence that Paul wrote still other letters that are not embodied in the New Testament canon, Col. 4:16.

"Not to associate with fornicators" is the infinitive of indirect discourse used for the original imperative: "Be not associating with," etc., the present tense marking a course of conduct, R. 1047 and 1170. The verb is the reciprocal middle: "not to mingle yourselves with fornicators," R. 811: σύν + ἀνά + μίγνυσθαι = mix yourselves — up — with.

10) From the explanation which Paul gives of the admonition which he had sent the Corinthians we see how the Corinthians evaded the force of that admonition. When Paul wrote them not to associate with fornicators, they took that to refer to any and to all fornicators anywhere and everywhere and thought all were to be avoided in the same manner. By driving Paul's injunction to the extreme they converted it into an impossible requirement and thus disregarded it entirely. So they paid no attention to fornicators even in their own midst, among them being the perpetrator of this vicious case of incest. The Corinthians perhaps touched on their view of Paul's command in the letter they sent to him. At any rate, Paul corrects this foolish evasion.

Not entirely with the fornicators of this world, or with the covetous and extortioners, or with idolaters; since then you are obliged to depart out of the world.

This is the negative side of Paul's elucidation of the admonition he had written to the Corinthians, the positive side follows in v. 11. "I wrote you to keep aloof from fornicators, that is, not entirely from the fornicators of this world," such an extravagant idea is far from my mind. Verse 10 is not a continuation of the quotation from Paul's previous letter but an explanation which Paul now gives. Thus οὐ πάντως, "not entirely," belong together, and οὐ is used (not μή) because only one word is negatived, the adverb "entirely."

"Not entirely with the fornicators of this world" is the elucidating apposition which Paul now adds to the previous briefer dative "with fornicators" (v. 10), which the Corinthians were pleased to misunderstand. This simple apposition intends to say: "I evidently meant: not entirely from all the fornicators you may come in contact with in the world." While Paul quietly explains, the simplicity of his explanation reflects on the good sense of the Corinthians who should have understood Paul in the first place.

"Not entirely," etc., is careful and exact. It intends to say that even in the case of such outside fornicators some contacts are to be avoided, we may say those of an intimate, personal nature while, of course, certain other contacts are unavoidable, we may say those of a business nature. We cannot supply: "I wrote" after the negative and read: "Not did I write, entirely with the fornicators of this world." While it is true that Paul did not add these specifications in his first letter, no reader or hearer can be expected to make the pause thus required after "not" and in his mind supply "I wrote." He will automatically combine "not" and "entirely" and read "not entirely."

By adding to "fornicators" the other classes of open sinners: "or with the covetous and extortioners, or with idolaters," Paul lifts the matter above a reference to only one kind of sinners and indicates that a principle is involved which is applicable to all open and flagrant sinners. "Not entirely" applies to all of them. The fornicators are one class, the covetous and extortioners another class, and the idolaters a third. Paul is, of course, not concerned about cataloging all the flagrant sinners in the world. He mentions three classes as being sufficient for his purpose, namely that his command concerning fornicators rests on a general principle.

A πλεονέκτης is one who seeks to get more than belongs to him, a greedy, avaricious person, and here one whose greediness appears in his crooked actions so that the congregation is able to see it clearly. A ἅρπαξ is of the same type and thus is paired with the covetous man; he does not stop at even violent measures to rob others. The first two classes sin against the second table of the law, the third class is even worse in that it sins against the first table. While he is posing as a member of a Christian congregation the idolater still runs after gods that are no gods.

What is involved in "not entirely" is explained by a deduction: "since then you are obliged to depart out of the world." The protasis must be supplied, and ἐπεί with the imperfect presents only the apodosis, a nonfulfilled present, R. 965 and 1014. Regarding the imperfect consult R. 887. It was ridiculous on the part of the Corinthians to read Paul's command in the former letter so as to involve an absurd and impossible conclusion; but it was even worse on the basis of it to exempt themselves from disciplining the flagrant fornicator in their midst. The ἄρα indicates it is a conclusion that is evident in the premise, it is the German *allerdings*.

11) The negative explanation of Paul's command is supplemented by the positive. The former pertains to the open sinners in the world, the latter

to the open sinners in the church. **Now, however, I wrote you not to associate, if one who is called a brother be a fornicator, or covetous, or an idolater, or a reviler, or a drunkard, or an extortioner, with such a man not even to eat.**

Because the aorist ἔγραψα is identical with the aorist found in v. 9, and both refer to Paul's lost letter, therefore "now, however," is not temporal but logical. The translation of the R. V. is therefore unacceptable: "But now I write"; the translation of the A. V. is better: "I have written," although this may mean: in the present letter, which would not be correct. Paul repeats the prohibition "not to associate" from the quotation used in v. 9 and thus places it before his positive explanation as he placed it before the negative. The original prohibition of his first letter stands and is even emphasized in this letter. He does not need again to quote in full: "not to associate with fornicators," because in v. 10 he has already advanced to the principle involved. As far as open sinners in the world are concerned, the principle "not to associate" applies "not entirely" but, as already stated, only in part; but as far as open sinners in the church are concerned, it does apply "entirely."

Hence he states positively: Keep aloof altogether, "if one who is called a brother be" an open sinner. And now Paul adds to the previous list: "be a fornicator, or covetous," etc., and names a full list of six in order to make his meaning entirely plain. He cannot say merely "if one be a brother," for men of this type, although they outwardly belong to the congregation, are not really "brethren." He must add: one "who is called a brother," who has the ὄνομα or name of "brother" but is lacking what this name implies. Here the principle is to be applied "entirely": no association of any kind with such a man. To the types of open sinners previously named Paul adds λοίδορος, "a reviler" or "railer," one who is incorrigibly given to the vice of abusing the character of other people; and μέθυσος, "a drunkard."

The condition of expectancy ἐὰν ᾖ intimates that the church may expect cases of this kind. It is needless to say that this expectation has been amply fulfilled in the entire history of the church. Even open sinners who offend against the first table of the law are found such as idolaters, and this word is not to be understood only in the sense of Eph. 5:5: "a covetous man, which is an idolater," but also in the sense that men who bow before Christ's altar are determined at the same time to bow before non-Christian altars. Estius comments on the old days in Corinth: "Either from the heart, or led by fear, or by the will to please, or by some other reason, he mingles with the rites of unbelievers in order either to worship an idol by a mere outward act or to eat of idol sacrifices." In his *Kirchengeschichte* Hauck reports that in Germany Columba saw baptized and unbaptized people at a beer offering to Wotan. And Gregory of Tours: "The report comes to us that many Christians run both to the churches, and — which is terrible to say — do not remain away from the rituals of demons."

All these devotees of sin against God and against man are summed up in "such a man": "with such a man not even to eat," II John 10. Even common social fellowship is to cease. "Not to associate with" = "not even to eat with," i. e., in the real sense to avoid "entirely." And μηδέ, *nicht einmal*, not even, indicates a climax. "Not even to eat with such a man" has no reference to the ancient Agape, for here the expression is absolute, without a single modifier.

As far as men of the world are concerned, men who never professed Christianity and who live in some glaring sin, Paul does not say: "Associate with them in every way"; but: "Associate with them only in certain restricted ways." This means that we may associate with them in such ways (business and the like) that do not make us partakers of their sin and guilt, lead to the impression that we condone their sins and evil ways, or subject us to contamination in any way. But those who profess the faith and then again fall into open sin against either the first or the second table of the law are in an entirely different class. It is not their vice or their idolatry that put them into this separate class but their turning traitor to the faith — they have become renegades. "For if, after they have escaped the defilements of the world through the knowledge of the Lord and Savior Jesus Christ, they are again entangled therein and overcome, the last state is become worse with them than the first. For it were better for them not to have known the way of righteousness than, after knowing it, to turn back from the holy commandment delivered unto them. It has happened unto them according to the true proverb, The dog turning to his own vomit again, and the sow that had washed to wallowing in the mire," II Pet. 2:20-22. To treat them in a familiar way would make the impression also upon their minds that having become such dogs and sows is not so terrible after all. Yet the ultimate reason for this seeming harshness must not be lost sight of, 5:5. From the action and the bearing of the congregation toward him the expelled man is to realize the gravity of his sin and his precarious spiritual condition so that, if possible, where all other means have failed, this realization may yet have a saving effect.

12) Two striking facts validate what Paul has just said, hence he writes γάρ. **For what have I to do with judging those without? Do not you judge those within whereas those without God judges?** These facts are undeniable. By putting them into the form of questions the truth they contain will strike with

fuller force. The difference between the sinners that are "of the world," v. 10, and those "that are called brethren," v. 11, is strongly emphasized by stating their respective relation to the church; the former are "those without," the latter "those within," the adverbs are substantivized by the Greek article. "To judge" is a *vox media*, i. e., to bring them before a Christian judgment bar and to pronounce a favorable or an unfavorable verdict upon them. And τί μοι (ἐστί) = "what business is this of mine?" namely κρίνειν, an infinitive subject, R. 944. The evident answer is: "It is none of my business."

The second question emphasizes the first and makes it clearer. When Paul speaks of himself (singular) in the first question he does so only in order to exemplify. Therefore he now adds "you" (plural), the Corinthians. "Do not you judge those within whereas those without God judges?" That is, indeed, the true state of affairs. "Those within" are all those who profess the name of Christ with us and call themselves our brethren. We ourselves belong to those within. And all of us are judged by our brethren, namely as to whether we really belong within or not, whether we really are the brethren we profess to be.

In his question Paul merely states the fact that we do thus judge each other; yet this fact implies our right to judge thus. The evidence on which we judge is that of lip and life, word or profession and actual conduct. Christians never have the right to judge a member's heart. *Herzensrichterei* is interference with God's prerogative. If either the profession of the lips or the evident conduct of the life violates the faith, and if all efforts of the church which has applied the law and the gospel have failed, the sinner must be judged as no longer belonging within. Thus to judge those within, to determine who rightly belongs within and who does not, is our only business. It is ours in the nature of the case since no true congregation could be organized or could continue to exist without this judging.

13) The situation is entirely different regarding those without. We certainly do not need to judge those that are without, for they do not even attempt to come in. God will attend to them, and it is our business to leave them in God's hands. When Paul says in 6:2 "that the saints shall judge the world" he by no means forgets that he has just written that we have no business to judge those without. He is here speaking of disciplinary judging. The world or those without are not subject to the discipline of the church and to judging connected with discipline. It is God alone who disciplines the world with judgments. But the world as well as the church are subject to the Word and to every pronouncement of that Word. Thus we who have that Word do judge also the world whenever we utter any of the pronouncements or the verdicts of the Word.

Having made clear these decisive facts concerning those subject to and those not subject to our discipline, Paul in a rather brusque and peremptory way returns to the case with which he began in 5:1. **Remove the wicked man from yourselves!** In Deut. 17:7 and 24:7 nearly identical words are used: καὶ ἐξαρεῖς τὸν πονηρὸν ἐξ ὑμῶν αὐτῶν, so that one is inclined to think that, while Paul does not quote, he at least appropriates this ancient injunction. The verb ἐξάρατε is the same verb as ἀρθῇ in v. 2, but is strengthened by ἐκ. The aorist imperative is sharp: no if or and — act! "The wicked man" names him according to the generally wicked character of his sin and thus again touches the great principle involved in the case and thereby fitly concludes Paul's instruction on the matter.

CHAPTER VI

II. Litigation before Pagan Courts, 6:1-11

After concluding his exhortations in connection with the case of incest Paul continues with the matter of litigations before pagan courts and then deals with fornication in general in 6:12-20. This order has been thought strange since the case of incest and the subject of fornication would seem to belong together. Some of the explanations offered for Paul's arrangement of materials seem fanciful. One thing is certain, we have no call to reconstruct Paul's letter; it is our task to understand what he has written and to learn why he wrote as he did. In this instance the arrangement of the subjects is entirely simple. First comes the one definite case of incest; secondly come the recurrent cases of litigation which are also definite. These special cases receive priority. Then follows the general subject of fornication. This arrangement is entirely natural.

The line of thought in our section is as follows:

1) Litigation before pagan courts is unworthy of a Christian congregation.

2) Difficulties between brethren should be adjusted within the congregation.

3) The very occurrence of such difficulties disgraces a congregation.

4) All such ἀδικία should have disappeared when the Corinthians became Christians.

The entire subject is handled in a masterly way, with telling rhetorical skill, and with a mighty array of thought and fact.

1) Without the use of a connective Paul at once confronts the Corinthians with the deplorable facts.

Dare any of you, having a matter against another, go to law before the unrighteous and not before the saints?

"Dare" does not express the boldness of the act involved but the lack of shame thus shown. "Any of you" is indefinite. It does not refer to some particular case but to any case of this nature that occurs at any time. Actual cases of this kind must have occurred in Corinth. Paul, however, deals only with this wrong as such. He takes the Corinthians severely to task in order once and for all to stop this wrong way of settling disputes and to inaugurate the right way, yes, to prevent disputes from arising. He calls for no disciplinary action on the part of the congregation regarding these litigations. For the cure of certain evils strong admonition and full instruction are enough. In graver cases the stronger medicine of actual discipline must be added. When Paul writes about one "having a matter against another" he means one member against another, but πρός denotes reciprocity, for each of the two has something against the other. One sets up his claim, and the other sets up a counterclaim with the result that the aggravating matter remains unsettled. Then they rush to the pagan law courts. If the matter in question were entirely one-sided, Paul would have used κατά.

The verb κρίνεσθαι is middle, to go to law in one's own behalf, R. 811. A sharp oxymoron is evident in κρίνεσθαι and ἐπὶ τῶν ἀδίκων, seeking justice before the unjust (judges) instead of before the saints or fellow church members. The two plurals "the unrighteous" and "the saints" are generic, the former referring to all non-Christians, the latter to all Christians, although in a given case of actual litigation only certain individuals of either class would function as judges. In the trial of Jesus before the Jewish and the pagan tribunals and in Paul's own trials before pagan authorities Paul's phrase "before the unrighteous" finds abundant corroboration.

In the legal practice of today all manner of injustice still prevails. Yet Paul has the deeper view that the whole world is "unrighteous," and its law courts are only part and product of this world while the Christian Church is not only "righteous" but "holy," and all judges and courts of the church are, therefore, of the same character. If attention be drawn to the fact that even the most august church courts have been glaringly unjust in their verdicts, the rejoinder is that the world's spirit of injustice dominated these church courts so that, while they operated with a show of sanctity, they were really subject to the secular spirit.

There is a natural difference between the two tribunals which Paul contrasts. The pagan judges operate with legal power and machinery in a regular order of law or trial; when Christian brethren are asked to decide disputes they have no legal and police power and no legal machinery but serve voluntarily, operate with arbitration and the Christian sense of fairness, and rely on moral power for their results. But for all ordinary disputes between Christians, if these *must* be carried that far, the submission of the case to tried and trusted brethren should certainly be preferred. The trouble in Corinth lay, not only with the litigants who would run to pagan courts, but with the entire congregation which interposed no check upon such actions. Hence Paul first addresses the litigants and then turns to the church as such.

2) Does such a litigant think that his Christian brethren are not competent to judge justly such cases as had come up between members in Corinth? Paul intimates that such can scarcely be their serious opinion. **Or do you not know that the saints shall judge the world? Well, if with you sitting as a court**

the world is judged, are you unworthy of the lowest tribunals? The argument is from the major to the minor. Those who are worthy of sitting as judges in a supreme court are certainly not unworthy of functioning in a tiny local court. Surely, the Corinthians know that much. Or is Paul mistaken as to their knowledge regarding this self-evident point?

One of the fundamental teachings of Christianity is that the saints shall judge the world. Dan. 7:22; Ps. 49:14; Matt. 19:28; Rev. 2:26; 3:21; 20:4. But it is one thing to know a truth and quite another to be alive to it and to act upon it when the time comes. We judge the world now. Paul does it when he calls the world "unrighteous." Whoever has the Word of God and rightly uses that Word thereby judges the world, and judges it truly. And in the final judgment at the last day the saints shall be Christ's associate judges. This is a part of their royal rule as crowned kings. The Corinthians thought themselves "wise men"; well, here they have a place where they may use some real "wisdom." We may note that this judging is not identical with that which is repudiated in 5:12: "What have I to do with judging those outside?" As far as disciplinary judging is concerned, the church deals only with "those inside," see the remarks on 5:12.

The force of καί is stronger than that of the mere copulative conjunction "and," it is more like our "well," for in chainlike manner it begins to repeat the previous statement: "Well, if with you sitting as a court the world is judged," etc., but now the passive and the present tense are used. The phrase ἐν ὑμῖν is an instance of the forensic ἐν, *coram*, "with you sitting as judges," R. 587. The condition is one of reality; without question the saints do judge the world.

What a tremendous act — to judge the world! What lofty dignity for those to whom such judgment is committed! Paul always hurls the full power of fact against wrong thought and wrong action; he overwhelms and never merely moves a little. And now some foolish church member in Corinth presumes to think that the saints who judge the world are "unworthy" to adjudicate in some trivial affair between himself and a brother? The very idea is ridiculous. And he must rush off to some pagan judge who stoops before idol shrines to have his case tried. This multiplies the absurdity. The R. V.'s "the smallest matters" is a mistranslation, for κριτήρια ἐλάχιστα (elative superlative, R. 670) are not the most insignificant cases that might be tried but the lowest type of tribunals such as justice of the peace courts; and the genitive is not the genitive of price (Blass in R. 504) but is equal to the ablative, R. 516: "are you unworthy of sitting as the lowest kind of court?"

3) The case can be stated still more effectively. In the world which is subject to our judging the angels rank highest. So Paul adds: **Do you not know that we shall judge angels? to say nothing of common life affairs.** This argument is again *a majori ad minus* with the minor concentrated in μήτι γε βιωτικά. This minor is not a part of the question (our versions) but an assertion: "to say nothing," etc. And μήτι γε is elliptic, *vollends aber*, B.-D. 427, 3. It is used only here by Paul but is frequently found in the classics: "not at all (to mention that we shall judge) common life affairs." The contrast is tremendous: "angels" on the one hand and βιωτικά on the other, things connected with βίος, *vita quam vivimus*, the course of our physical existence as distinguished from *vita qua vivimus*, the life principle itself which animates us.

The Corinthians are not to make this deduction; Paul himself states it. In v. 2 the contrast is between the Corinthians as world judges and as judges of petty courts; in v. 3 the contrast is between the cases judged, between angels and common affairs, and this contrast is intensified, for angels are the mightiest persons, and these affairs are the trifling things about mine and thine, about what you said and what I said, etc. Regarding the judging of angels compare Isa. 24:21; II Pet. 2:4, and Jude 6. Many passages speak about the connection between the angels and us, Heb. 2:14; I Pet. 1:12; Eph. 2:20, etc., 3:10; Rom. 8:38. The Word by which the saints judge extends also to the angels. Osiander writes: "Just as we find a law of mediation in the ministration of grace from man to man although the Lord remains supreme, so we find the same law of mediation in the final ministration of justice, the believers judge the world including the angels, yet the Lord is always supreme. In what this judging consists, in promulgating or confirming the verdict or in otherwise assisting, we must leave until the great act takes place."

4) By repeating βιωτικά Paul again links the thought together like a chain. Coming to the little tribunals that deal with the everyday affairs of life, do the Corinthians really intend to choose judges for these courts that have no standing whatever in the church? **If, then, you have courts for common life matters, do you seat as judges such men as are accounted nothing in the judgment of the church?**

To regard this sentence as a question is more effective than to regard it as a declaration. In v. 2 the condition is necessarily one of reality, εἰ κρίνεται, for the world is, indeed, judged by us, and Paul intends to imply just that. In v. 4 ἐὰν ἔχητε is properly a condition of expectancy, for Paul thinks of the cases about common earthly affairs that may arise from time to time. Here again κριτήρια, which is now modified by βιωτικά, denotes courts or tribunals, namely such as deal with these common matters. The object of the verb may be placed before the conjunction as it is here placed before ἐάν. "If, then, you have courts for common life matters," Paul asks, is this what you do, "seat as judges such men as are accounted nothing in the judgment of the church?" That is, indeed, what the Corinthians were doing. By taking their cases to the pagan judges the Corinthians "seat" them, namely make them sit on the judge's bench to try their cases.

Paul has already called these judges "the unrighteous." Now he specifies by stating who it is that renders this verdict upon them, who says that they are unrighteous. But he now uses a stronger negative term than "unrighteous," namely "men accounted as nothing" (οὐδέν). This is the verdict of the church, ἐν τῇ ἐκκλησίᾳ, again the forensic ἐν, *coram*: "in the judgment of the church" or "before her judgment bar." This verdict of the church is even made emphatic by τούτους, which here, as often, follows a participial description to stress the description: "such men" or "men of this kind," namely mere heathen judges, them you make your arbiters? Paul himself appeared before pagan judges, but they were not of his choosing, he was compelled to appear before them, and we know what justice he received.

By saying that these pagan judges are accounted as nothing at the bar of the church Paul corroborates what he says about the saints judging the world, v. 2. Yet he does not assail their legal standing in the state, or preach rebellion and lawlessness, or offer disrespect to the judiciary of the state, Rom. 13:1-7. The judgment bar of the church deals with spiritual findings and not with secular matters. Spiritually considered every pagan or unbeliever is "nothing," and this includes every official pagan personage. Yet every case that occurs among Christians, even the smallest dispute, turns essentially on points that are spiritual in their nature and thus are far above not only the common law of the state but also far removed from the mind and the apprehension of a pagan judge. In fact, even if a judge should be a Christian, his duties as a secular judge debar him from applying Christian, spiritual principles to his official judicial actions. And yet the Corinthians run to such judges and such courts.

The context does not favor making the verb imperative as some interpreters do: "Seat as your judges, when you have disputes, members of your own, those who are counted as nothing, least esteemed and least capable in the estimation of the church." Thus the A. V.: "set them to judges who are least esteemed in the church." It would be the height of folly on Paul's part to send such a command to the Corinthians. Such an order would shake their confidence in him completely and induce them to resort to the state courts more than ever. The church has always done the very opposite in her practice. She has always chosen the most capable and most experienced men in her midst to settle disputes. This interpretation would give καθίζετε the meaning "establish a court," but there is no necessity to understand this word in such an unusual sense. And then "men who are accounted as nothing," is taken to refer only to "the simple members" of the church, those who are looked down upon by the proud, whereas the term is the equivalent of "the unrighteous," namely pagan judges mentioned in v. 1.

5) In 4:14 Paul writes that he does not intend to shame the Corinthians but to admonish them. Here he expressly tells them: **I say** (this) **to move you to shame,** πρός expresses intention. The Corinthians had forgotten the spiritual pride which they should have as Christians. They ought to be ashamed to run off to pagan courts. Yes, there are certain things which we ought to be ashamed to do; but if we do them, the moment we see what we have really done, shame should fill us.

Here there is evidence of Paul's pastoral wisdom in dealing with his people. Not a few faults disgrace our members, for which disciplinary action would not be the proper remedy; the true and effective remedy is to set those faults into the right light, to show how they disgrace the profession and the lofty character of a Christian, and thus to win our members to truer, higher, more Christlike ideals.

In this effective manner Paul concludes the first point of his discussion on litigations.

The second point tells the Corinthians that disputes in their midst should be settled by themselves. **So, then, is it possible that among you there is not even a single wise man who shall be able to adjudicate between his brother** (and another), **but brother goes to law with brother, and that before unbelievers?**

"So, then," sums up the situation as Paul has just described it, *sic igitur*, running off to pagan courts as you do. Ἔνι = ἔνεστι, it is an old Greek idiom, R. 313, from ἐνί (the strengthened ἐν) with the accent moved forward: "is it possible?" Also οὐδείς ἐστιν ὅς is idiomatic, R. 726: "is there no one who?" There is a sting in the term "wise man": Among all of you Corinthians is there not even a single "wise man"? This sting is intensified when it is remembered that this wise man would have but a slight task to perform, one that required only a modicum of wisdom. And yet the Corinthians cannot achieve so much although all of them boast so loudly about their wisdom. The fact that a discreet and wise man would be chosen to act as an arbitrator Paul assumes without further remark; he certainly does not expect them to choose a man who is inferior as the faulty translation of v. 4 in the A. V. suggests.

In the relative clause: "who shall be able to adjudicate between his brother (and another)" ἀνὰ μέσον is only a compound preposition governing the genitive, a kind of prepositional circumlocution which is found four times in the New Testament. It has the meaning "between." There is a difficulty in the use of the singular τοῦ ἀδελφοῦ αὐτοῦ, literally, "between his brother," for which no satisfactory explanation has been offered. If we had the plural "between his brethren" or a collective noun, all would be clear. We should not charge Paul with slovenliness of style. Such a statement only dodges the difficulty. To change the meaning of the preposition "between" into *gegenueber* (over against) is only *eine Verlegenheitsauskunft* (a convenient evasion) and not a solution. Paul knew that this singular with αὐτοῦ was proper, the Corinthians also knew it, we do not — at least not as yet. The sense is fortunately plain: to decide between one brother and another.

Paul is very careful to write διακρῖναι, "to adjudicate between" or "to decide between," and not κρῖναι, "to judge." For when a Christian brother or several Christian brethren act in a case of dispute between their brethren they do not function as legal judges in a secular court but render a Christian decision which involves much more. Their chief difficulty will also usually be with the complainant who comes with charges against a brother and demands "his rights," or insists on admissions on the part of his brother, or demands that the brother be expelled. This may, in a way, help to explain the Greek singular "his brother." The future "who shall be able" is a regular future which refers to any case that may come up.

6) Both features are reprehensible, going to law at all and especially taking their matters before unbelievers. "And that" calls attention to the worst feature. The verb "goes to law" is the same as that used in v. 1. The pagan courts and their judges are now called ἄπιστοι, "unbelievers," men who are devoid of "faith," which latter really makes the Christian

what he is. To these judges the whole world of faith in which the Christian lives, moves, and has his being is *terra incognita*. Yet every dispute among Christians involves faith in one way or in another, some fault that is hurtful to faith, some virtue that ought to grace faith. And these are the real things about which Christians ought to be concerned in any dispute apart from the mere question of injury which they may or may not have suffered, or the mere justice which they may or may not be able to secure. Yet in these vital matters that touch our faith "unbelievers" cannot function as judges; the very law of secular courts debars them from that.

What a sad spectacle to see one Christian brother going to law with another Christian brother before unbelievers! Are they unconcerned about the real matters of faith that are involved in their dispute? Is their entire concern only about secular law and justice? Do they care nothing about their hearts? Is the Christian wisdom of their own faithful brethren in the church, which might, indeed, do something for their faith, nothing at all to them? Even when they obtain full justice, is that all they want? Yet even that is not always obtained in secular courts. Jesus did not obtain it from pagan Pilate, nor Paul from the pagan governors of Palestine. And, worst of all, the Corinthian congregation stands by and lets these foolish litigations before unbelievers go on without even a word of protest. Where is this wisdom of theirs of which they are so proud? Are these some of its fruits?

This is Paul's second point in regard to the litigations at Corinth, and it certainly strikes home.

7) The third point is this: the very fact that the Corinthians have difficulties that are pressed to the point of requiring adjudication is a reflection on their Christian character. **Already, then, in general it is a loss for you that you have lawsuits with each**

other. It is not necessary to adduce the aggravating circumstances regarding the kind of judges you choose, "already" the fact that you have all these disputes with each other is "in general" a decided loss. The οὖν is, perhaps, not genuine but an insertion by a copyist from v. 4; in both places μὲν οὖν = *demnach* or *also*, "then" or "accordingly" and connects with what precedes. Both "already" and "in general" intend to generalize so that the argument is now *a minori ad majus*. In v. 2, 3 Paul argues: If you judge the world, even angels, you can certainly act as judges in petty courts and regarding petty matters (argument from the major to the minor, in fact, from the greatest to the least). Now he argues: You ought to settle your own disputes and, what is far more important, you ought to be above having disputes, for the greatest loss lies in having them at all (argument from the lesser to the greater). For if the Corinthians have no disputes at all and thus exclude the greater loss, they themselves will not even need to settle them and thereby suffer a lesser loss than by running off to pagan courts.

The idea suggested by ἥττημα, a rare word, is that of defeat and loss; it is the opposite of νικᾶν, to conquer, to win. "Defeat" in the R. V. is not strong enough, and "fault" in the A. V. points in the wrong direction. "Loss" is what the Corinthians thus suffer "in general," a great loss in honor and in dignity for one thing and an equally great loss in Christian fellowship and love. Matters ought never to arrive at the point where it is necessary to have κρίματα, litigations, no matter who adjudicates them, namely "incriminations," one member being constrained to bring serious charges against another. Long before they reach that stage such things should be settled quietly, otherwise the loss is very great.

But how can the occurrence of disputes be prevented? In an exceedingly simple way which even makes their beginnings impossible. **Why not rather let yourselves be wronged? Why not rather let yourselves be defrauded?** Both verbs are probably middle voice and have the permissive sense which is closely allied to the causative and approaches the passive, R. 808: "let yourselves," etc.

This is exactly what Christians so often forget. When a fancied or a real wrong has been done them, they think they must demand and secure redress. They at least feel that the brother who supposedly wronged them or who actually did them wrong must be humbled and made to ask their pardon. Or to take a more specific case, this is also true when one is defrauded or thinks he is. Simply to suffer the wrong, the injustice, or the injury does not occur to many Christians. The least they do is to set up a loud complaint and then continue complaining and ill will. To forgive at once and to forget so thoroughly as to make no complaint at any time, is an unknown ethical practice even to brethren who think they are σοφοί, well read in the Scriptures and rather advanced Christians. Of course, when Paul asks the Corinthians why they do not rather suffer wrong he in no way excuses those who actually do wrong, nor encourages them to continue their wrongdoing. What obligation they have is plain; it needs no elucidation here.

8) Instead of following the right course when they are wronged or defrauded the Corinthians do the very opposite: **Nay, you yourselves do wrong and defraud, and this to brethren**, either by wronging and defrauding them or by retaliating for mistreatment received from them. The present tenses of this verse imply a course of conduct. The Corinthians not only refuse to suffer wrong and injustice and thus to avoid most of the great loss to which Paul draws their attention, they go on doing wrong and inflicting injury, and that to the brethren to whom they owe a special

obligation as brethren and thus increase their loss to the greatest proportion. No wonder, then, that the Corinthians had all sorts of litigations in their midst.

The third point in Paul's discussion reveals the disgraceful condition existing among the Corinthians, a condition that should never have made progress.

9) All such ἀδικία should have disappeared when the Corinthians became Christians. Paul warns them that it is wholly foreign to the kingdom of God. **Or do you not know that unrighteous people shall not inherit God's kingdom? Be not deceived: neither fornicators, nor idolaters, nor adulterers, nor voluptuaries, nor pederasts, nor thieves, nor covetous, nor drunkards, nor revilers, nor extortioners, shall inherit God's kingdom.**

The two "why" occurring in v. 7 are the logical hinges on which there swings the question: "Or do you not know?" etc. Paul's thought is: "I cannot understand why you do not rather let yourselves be wronged, etc., unless it be that you do not know that the unrighteous shall not inherit," etc. Paul's question implies that the Corinthians certainly do know, and that they cannot deny that they know, for what he has said about the unrighteous belongs to the very elements of Christianity. Since ἄδικοι, as well as the entire list of sinners following, has no article, the quality is stressed: "unrighteous people," they who are such. Compare the "unrighteous" judges mentioned in v. 1. Let the Corinthians beware! None that are unrighteous in God's sight inherit his kingdom. "Unrighteous" and "God's" are juxtaposed in the Greek in order to intensify the contrast.

While "God's kingdom" does not need the articles since only one such kingdom exists, and since the genitive also makes this kingdom definite, the emphatic way in which it is named *God's* kingdom shows how opposite in character it is to all that is unrighteous.

Paul refers to the kingdom of glory. God's kingdom is found already in this life and exists wherever the power of God's grace operates in men's hearts and makes them truly righteous; compare 4:20. But when Paul speaks about inheriting the kingdom he necessarily refers to the kingdom that is still above us, which is filled with heavenly blessedness. Paul might have said that the unrighteous cannot enter into or remain in the kingdom as it exists here on earth, but it is characteristic of his thinking and his writing that in many connections he includes the whole sweep of time and of eternity, of this world and of the world to come; compare, for instance, v. 2, 3, our judging the world, even angels.

"Shall inherit" should not be reduced to mean only "shall participate in." The view that no process of inheritance is indicated is refuted by Rom. 8:16, 17: "if children, then heirs." In order that we may inherit, God first makes us his children who naturally inherit because of their birth and his sons who inherit legally because of their legal standing. Again, God has made his will and testament in his promises which are duly sealed and attested in his Word, and in this will he names us as the heirs. We do more than merely to participate in the kingdom. The latter may be done without ownership as when a slave participates in the shelter, the food, etc., of a grand mansion, John 8:35; but only a son abides in the house forever, for he owns it. So we "shall inherit" and own. The "unrighteous" are not named as heirs in the will.

"Be not deceived," Paul writes because regarding this very point people constantly deceive themselves although it is so self-evident and so elementary, yes, the simplest catechism truth. Thousands who are living today are ἄδικοι, "unrighteous," and yet expect to reach heaven at last. The negative μή shows that the verb is imperative, R. 947.

Now Paul repeats 5:10, 11 and adds an entire list of the unrighteous so that the Corinthians shall surely know what he means. He uses ten designations, for ten symbolizes completeness. This list of ten classes is not exhaustive but *representative*. Paul writes objectively, yet any one of the members in Corinth who needed a warning can apply what he says to himself. As far as the arrangement of the list is concerned, Paul seems to heap up all of these classes of sinners in one great mass. Seven οὔτε are followed by three οὐ, apparently only for the sake of variation.

Efforts to detect a reason for the order of the designations result in finding no order. The fact is that Paul intends to follow no definite order in presenting this list. Just as the number ten symbolizes completeness, so this motley array which is devoid of order pictures the mixture of sinners as they actually occur in the world: a fornicator sits beside an idolater, a thief beside a drunkard, any of these sinners beside any others. They are all of one kind, all headed for hell; why should an apostle trouble even to group them — let the devil do that if he cares. Deissmann, *Light from the Ancient East*, 320, etc., reports some interesting parallels from popular pagan sources.

In a papyrus of *circa* 245 B. C. Deissmann found the word μαλακός, which he translates "the effeminate." This word is used in a secondary (obscene) sense and is an allusion to the foul practices by which musicians eked out their earnings. The term is not an equivalent of *mollis*, one who submits himself to a pederast. There is no reason that this vice should be indicated twice by naming its passive and its active perpetrators. It denotes a voluptuary.

The ἀρσενοκοίτης is a pederast, *cinaedus*, "abusers of themselves with men," our versions. Regarding ἅρπαξ Deissmann tells us that this was current as a loan word in Latin comedy and was used in the sense of swindler.

Paul himself distinguishes it from λῃστής, "robber," or "brigand," II Cor. 11:26. He himself had suffered at the hands of such hold-up men.

10) At the beginning of the sentence "God's" precedes "kingdom" evidently in order to juxtapose the "unrighteous" and "God's" so as to form a clashing contrast; here at the end of the sentence the genitive follows in ordinary fashion. Yet Paul repeats: "shall not inherit God's kingdom" as if he would hammer this elementary truth into the consciousness of the Corinthians. Gross immoralities are one of the outstanding marks of the kingdom of this world. They begin with all forms of idolatry, false religion and irreligion, and include especially, as Paul's list shows, sexual vices, sins against property, and sins of the tongue. While the requirements for inheriting God's kingdom go much farther than the avoidance of such open sins, the presence of any one of them in a man is evidence that he is debarred from heaven, and this plain negative fact Paul re-emphasizes.

11) In closing this section regarding litigations Paul reminds the Corinthians of the blessed state they entered when they left the company of all the evil men he has named. This loving reminder is to confirm them in their new state in order that they may not become apostates. **And such some of you were; but you had yourselves washed, but you were sanctified, but you were justified in the name of our Lord Jesus Christ and in the Spirit of our God.**

The predicate of the masculine plural τινές is the neuter plural ταῦτα, which is quite proper in the Greek, but this neuter plural has a derogatory sense: *solches Gelichter*, such rubbish, or trash. "Some," Paul writes and keeps to the facts, only some, not all, for there were not a few persons among Jews and pagans who hated these vices and lived respectably, the Jews did not practice idolatry; and some of these were among

250   *Interpretation of First Corinthians*

the number that had been brought to Christ — sinners all but not stooping to the grossest forms of sin. The predicate ἦτε is significant because of its tense: "you were" — once but now no longer.

The limitation that only some were once gross sinners ends with this statement. The three adversative statements include all of the Corinthians. The three ἀλλά, "but," are not only highly rhetorical but make each verb stand out independently. Each of these three statements is therefore complete in itself. Each covers the same ground as the others, but each does it in its own way. To be baptized is to be sanctified, and vice versa. And this is true of each act in relation to either of the other two. Paul most impressively describes what happened to the Corinthians when they were brought to Christ.

All three verbs are aorists and not perfects. It has been said that there are sermons in tenses, and there is a sermon in these. Perfects would mean that the activity expressed by these three verbs as definite past acts still continues into the present as an unchanged condition, and that it remains unchanged. The three aorists state only what occurred in the past (historical aorists) and stop there. These aorists thus leave open the question as to whether the present still fully agrees with what took place so blessedly in the past. Yes, there is a sermon in these tenses.

While all three verbs are aorists, only the last two are passives, and the first is most significantly a middle. This middle ἀπελούσασθε does not mean: "you were washed" (passive), R. V.; nor: "you are washed" (perfect), A. V.; nor: "you washed yourselves" (ordinary reflexive middle) R. V. margin and R. 807; but: "you let yourselves be washed" (causative or permissive middle), R. 809, "you had yourselves washed," as we translate. Paul is, of course, speaking about baptism, but when he uses ἀπολούειν he at once names the effect of baptism, the spiritual washing away of all sin and guilt, the cleansing by pardon and justification. This causative or permissive middle, which is exactly like the same middle ἐβαπτίσαντο used in 10:2, adds what the passive would omit, namely that with their own hearts the Corinthians themselves desired and accepted this washing and cleansing. In their case baptism was not a mere outward, formal, or only symbolical act. And what they desired they obtained: they were cleansed of sin and guilt.

The two passives that follow: "but you were sanctified, but you were justified," are different as far as their voice is concerned. Considered by themselves, both state only what God, the agent behind these passives, did and no more. And yet the force of this first middle in this series of three acts affects also the two passives. This does not mean that the passives are changed and now receive a middle tinge; they remain what they are. But the Corinthians could not also be sanctified and justified by God (passive) if they had not in their own hearts desired and accepted the true cleansing of baptism. The moment they accepted that in true faith they were also at that moment sanctified and justified. Thus, not only in tenses but also in voices there are real sermons.

"You were sanctified," separated from sin unto God, and were thus made holy. "That he (Christ) might sanctify it (the church), having cleansed it by the washing of water with the Word," Eph. 5:26. This is total sanctification, the removal of all sin and guilt; it makes us ἅγιοι, "saints," and ἡγιασμένοι, "people sanctified," two of the standard terms employed in the New Testament to designate Christians. This sanctification is not total in the sense that we shall not and cannot sin, are perfect in this respect, need no more forgiveness of sins, need no longer pray the Fifth Petition of the Lord's Prayer. I John 1:8. But this sanctification drives out sin more and more, we grow in grace, II Pet. 3:18, and by daily contrition and faith continue constantly and totally cleansed, I John 1:9.

Paul might have stopped after mentioning the verb in the middle voice or after the first verb in the passive. Paul adds another passive; so important is all that occurred when the Corinthians were made Christians: "you were justified." The word δικαιοῦν and its passive δικαιωθῆναι always have a forensic force: "ye were declared just" by God, the Judge, by a verdict pronounced from his judgment seat. See C.-K. regarding this vital term and regarding its derivatives. God justifies the sinner for Christ's sake the instant that God brings that sinner to contrition and faith: "My son, thy sins are forgiven thee!"

In these three verbs there lies much more than the verbs themselves express, namely this that these Corinthians, who were once thus washed, made holy, and declared righteous in God's sight, ought to remain so and be so still. It would be monstrous if by open pollution they should now revert to their former state, to what they once "were," and again become ἄδικοι, "unrighteous."

The two ἐν phrases are to be construed with all three of the verbs. And this connection with all three of the verbs is pertinent in every respect and vital and not intended merely to create the impression that divine persons and divine powers were active in these three acts. It is also useless to puzzle our heads about the meaning of ἐν and about the fact that it is once connected with the "name" and again with the "Spirit": "in the name of our Lord Jesus Christ and in the Spirit of our God." In both instances "in" has its natural meaning: "in union with," "in connection with." There is no instrumental idea in the preposition since neither this name nor the Spirit can serve as an instrument nor are ever thus described in the Scriptures. Nor does "in the name" express a subjective condition and "in the Spirit" the objective condition that are connected with the three verbs.

"The name of our Lord Jesus Christ" is his revelation, which is presented in the Word and reveals him in his person and his work (Jesus Christ) and in his saving relation to us (Lord). This revelation is the comprehensive means of grace for our salvation in connection with (ἐν) which alone the three acts named can take place. "The Spirit of our God" is the divine person through whose agency alone the three acts are possible. He brings the revelation of Christ to us by the Word and thus implants Christ into our hearts by faith. Only in connection with (ἐν) his agency can the three acts named take place. Both "the name" and "the Spirit" are objective, but ἐν is like the link or tie which connects us with these two objectives; where this "in" ("in union with") is actualized, there faith is implanted, and thus this "in" brings us cleansing, holiness, justification.

We note incidentally that the entire Trinity is named in connection with the three great saving acts. With the solemn mention of the holy names this section of the letter comes to a fitting close.

III. The Sanctity of the Body, 6:12-20

Regarding the connection of this third section with the two sections preceding see the introductory remarks on section two. Again Paul starts *medias in res*.

12) **All things are lawful for me but not all benefit. All things are lawful for me, but I will not be dominated by anything.**

This statement resembles a principle or rule of life. And now Paul begins to discuss it. The Corinthians formulated this principle thus: "All things are lawful to me" or "are permitted to me," and by repeating it on all sorts of occasions made it a shield for many questionable and even wrong actions. The principle itself they had received from Paul, but instead of understanding and using it aright they made it cover doubtful and evil actions and thus misused it. Paul, it seems, had learned about this misuse from private sources just as he had found out about the case of incest and the litigations.

The matter is so important in many respects that Paul feels he must clear up the misunderstanding and stop the abuse. We need not credit even the more educated of the Corinthians with a philosophic effort to penetrate Paul's principle of Christian liberty, for we have no hint to that effect. So also Paul's way of setting the Corinthians right is governed entirely by practical considerations. It is rather usual when Christians are released from the fetters of legalism by throwing open to them the beautiful gates of Christian liberty that they tend to turn this liberty into license. The correction, however, lies not in again erecting some form of legalism like the Pharisaic οὐκ ἔξεστι, "it is not lawful, not allowed," and in abrogating πάντα μοι ἔξεστι, "all things are lawful, are allowed for me," but in clearly defining and explaining just what this Christian principle contains.

In the first place, "all things" cannot be understood in the absolute sense, for this would vitiate the entire principle and make it pernicious. What God forbids is never allowed; what God commands, no man is allowed to set aside. Wrong is wrong and is outside of the domain of liberty; right is right and is also outside of this domain. "All things" is by the very context restricted to the so-called adiaphora, to the things that are not specifically commanded or forbidden by God. These are left to the Christian's own judgment and thus lie in the domain of Christian liberty.

When Paul writes "for me" and "I" he merely exemplifies in his own person what is true of any and of every Christian. In fact, this pointed repetition: "All things are lawful — all things are lawful for me!" sounds like a quotation from the lips of some of the Corinthians. And they, in turn, when they uttered this slogan were quoting no less an authority than Paul himself; he had taught them this very principle.

Not for a moment does Paul now retract this principle nor say, "This is not so." He opens no new or no old gate to the legalism toward which so many, and some very earnest, Christians are inclined even to this very day. That would be a mistake that would be at least as serious as the one the Corinthians were making by abusing the principle. The way out lies in an entirely different direction. Paul, first of all, points to what may be called the self-evident minor limitation contained in the principle itself: "All things are lawful for me, but not all benefit." "Yes," Paul would say, "all things are, indeed, lawful for me — I fully agree with you — but that is only the half of it; you must add the other half: not all things bring benefit, not all things further and aid us even in our earthly life, to say nothing about our spiritual life and our Christian profession."

In the clause "not all things benefit" Paul omits "me" — "benefit me," for the range of benefit includes not only me and my person but also all others who are affected by what I do or refrain from doing. This is, then, the right way, the only sensible way in which to apply the principle that all things are lawful for me. It is pure folly to insist on *the formal right* expressed by the principle and to ignore *the actual advantages or disadvantages* that will result in any given case. When in a given case no advantage accrues or actual harm results for myself or for others, insisting on mere formal liberty only defeats its own end.

We may add that the right to do a thing or to use a thing naturally also involves the right not to do or to use that thing. And the exercise of this double right is in its very nature governed, first of all, by the consideration of the resulting advantage or the disadvantage, whichever it may be. To illustrate from common life: I have the formal right to eat a certain food; but if that particular food should make me ill, οὐ συμφέρει, I should be a fool to eat it just because I have the formal right to do so. Yet no one would dare to set up a law that would bind my conscience before God and forbid the eating of that food.

This is, however, only the minor side of the matter, the graver side follows. Again the principle stands: "All things are lawful for me"; there is no question about that. But in its very nature this principle involves a fundamental limitation if we may call it so: "but I will not be dominated by anything." Now the contrast is between *things* and *persons,* "anything" and "I." Decisive between the two is the ἐξουσία, authority, power, domination. "Yes," Paul would say, "it is perfectly correct that in the case of all of the adiaphora I may use any or all of them as being lawful for me, but in doing so I will not allow myself to be dominated by even as much as one of them." The genitive τινὸς is neuter since it refers to πάντα. Here lies the greatest danger of foolishly applying the principle of liberty, viz., that all things are lawful for me. One might himself suffer more or less harm or do some harm to others; that would be bad enough. But to become a helpless slave of some "thing" would be deplorable in the extreme.

When Christians plead Christian liberty to justify some action of theirs they usually imagine that they can remain the masters. Paul does not elaborate this side of the subject and show how easy it is to deceive oneself in this respect. He simply enunciates only the natural limitation that is contained in "all things are lawful for me." *"I"* will not be dominated by a *thing* is to be echoed by every one of the Corinthians. The future tense: "I will not be dominated," means more than: "for myself I am resolved not to be dominated," for while resolutions may be good enough they often fail of realization. The tense denotes fact, and οὐ negatives the entire sentence: this will not occur to Paul, it is excluded. Note the paronomasia: ἔξεστι and ἐξουσιασθήσομαι, the latter being both a select verb and a rare form of the verb (passive) and being chosen for the basic idea of ἐξουσία.

If the Corinthians understand the great principle of Christian liberty, all danger of not living up to it vanishes of its own accord.

13) After clearing up the principle itself Paul proceeds to apply it to the Corinthians. He does this, first of all, objectively, without personal reference, after that, with personal reference, but even then only as a matter of instruction. As a background we may picture to ourselves the temptations that continue to beset the members of the Corinthian congregation and try to besmirch them. And in connection with such temptations we may visualize the efforts to whitewash sins from the new Christian standpoint by catching up and misapplying the doctrine of Christian liberty: "All things are lawful."

Thus the Corinthians seem to place on the same level the appetite for food and the appetite of sex and apply equally to both: "All things are lawful." They failed to see the great difference. Now as to the appetite for food, this is the situation: **Foods for the belly, and the belly for foods; but God shall abolish both it and them.**

Here we have a clear case to which the principle as defined by Paul applies. The food we eat is βρῶμα, the act of eating is βρῶσις. Anything that comes under the heading of βρώματα is for the stomach, intended for it by God; and the reverse is true, the stomach is intended for all that is food. The food must, of course, profit us both as to selection and to quantity. And again, we must maintain our ἐξουσία and not become slaves of our appetite as drunkards or gluttons do. And this relation between food and the organ for its digestion continues during this life. God, who made both, will eventually put both out of commission, καταργήσει. In the Parousia no digesting and no organ for that purpose are needed to keep the body alive. Regarding the change of our bodily organs compare Matt. 22:30; I Cor. 15:44, 51. This is the real reason that foods belong to the adiaphora. "Foods and the belly . . . are transient things . . .; therefore they are adiaphora." Melanchthon. *Quae destruentur per se liberum habent usum.* Bengel.

Now it seems that some of the Corinthians tried to parallel with the stomach and food the sexual organs and their use: these organs for any and all use, and any and all use for these organs—"all is allowed," for at the Parousia these organs, too, and their use "God will put out of commission, will abolish." But such reasoning is specious and wholly fallacious. Paul exposes this in a simple way. As he pointed to the facts in regard to the stomach and food, so he points to the facts in this case. **But the body is not for fornication but for the Lord, and the Lord for the body; and God both raised the Lord and will raise up us through his power.**

These are the facts. This statement regarding the body and the Lord is composed exactly like the one regarding foods and the stomach with only the necessary qualifications inserted. Paul writes "the body" and not, as in the previous statement, only one organ of the body. For in this case the fact is that the entire body is involved in the matter of sex and we may add the entire mental constitution. With this initial vital difference corresponds the divine intention concerning the body: "the body for the Lord," and therefore here, too, the reverse: "the Lord for the body."

Now foods and the belly are on the same level, that of "the lower story," as someone has aptly said; they are physical, for this life only. The facts in the case of the body and the Lord are different, for the Lord is on the supreme level of heaven and glory. Between foods and the belly the line is horizontal; but between the body and the Lord the line is perpendicular. Every attempt to make it horizontal is wrong, violates the facts. One cannot and dare not say: "the body for fornication"; this would be a lie. To utter it and to act on it breaks and destroys the relation between the Christian's body and his Lord. The line is not horizontal or, still worse, downward, for "the body is not for fornication"; on the contrary, the line is straight upward, "the body for the Lord."

In this instance, then, the principle that "all things are allowed" cannot be applied. God himself regulates the sex relation. He limits it to two distinct spheres, the one that is stamped with his approval, the other with his severe disapproval; both are thus entirely removed from the territory of the adiaphora. God instituted marriage in Paradise, hence "a man shall cleave unto his wife, and they shall be one flesh." God forbade fornication in the Decalog: "Thou shalt not!" "The body is not for fornication." Marriage does not destroy the spiritual relation of the body to Christ and of Christ to the body; fornication does destroy that relation or makes it impossible in the first place. These are the facts. The four datives may be called ethical: foods for the body to nourish it, and the belly for foods to receive the nourishment; the body for Christ to obey and to honor him, and Christ for the body to bless and to save it.

14) All of this becomes clearer when the Parousia is considered. In both cases, that of the stomach and that of the body, Paul looks at all the facts. He does not do as mere mundane philosophers, in particular the everyday kind do: consider only a few transient physical facts. What God eventually does in the one case, and what he eventually does in the other case, this decides. In the one case "he will abolish," καταργήσει; in the other "he will raise up," ἐξεγερεῖ, and thus conserve forever. Regarding the assertion that Paul intends to indicate no difference between the verb ἤγειρε used with reference to Christ, "raised," and ἐξεγερεῖ used with reference to us, "will raise up," the reverse is true. Christ's body never saw corruption, our bodies are subject to corruption and thus rot in the grave and turn to dust, I Cor. 15:50-54. The preposition ἐκ thus suggests the grave and its decay "from" or "out of" which God will raise our bodies.

Paul does not say merely that God will raise up our bodies. This would not suffice because the body is not alone, it bears a gracious and a heavenly relation to "the Lord." Hence he writes: "and God both raised the Lord and will raise up us," καί . . . καί, "both . . . and." He did the one, he will do the other. But the two acts are not mere parallels, they constitute a unit. We (including our bodies) who belong to the Lord by grace share the resurrection with him. In the case of both acts of resurrection Paul names the persons: God raised "the Lord," will raise up "us." The two acts are thus alike: we shall be raised up as he was raised. His soul was united with its body, and thus the Lord was raised; our souls shall be united with their bodies, and thus we shall be raised up.

It does not seem as though Paul uses the pronoun ἡμᾶς, "us," only instead of "the bodies" or "our bodies," but, as he does in the case of the Lord, in order to intimate that in this raising up our bodies shall again be joined with our souls. Paul often reaches out to cover all sides of a subject. The assumption that by using the pronoun "us" Paul corrects himself regarding the importance of the body because our present body shall not be raised up at all but a new and entirely different body, is unwarranted. The denial of the identity of the resurrection body with our present body leads those who voice this denial to attribute such an assumption even to the inspired writer.

Paul's statement is rounded out by the phrase: "through his power." We may content ourselves with attaching it to only the one verb "he shall raise up us," although Eph. 1:19, 20 shows that it was the same power that raised up Christ. "His power" is God's omnipotence. The resurrection of the body is a divine miracle — nothing less. Human reason cannot fathom it.

15) In v. 13, 14 Paul furnishes the factual *proof* that fornication is not an adiaphoron like the eating of food but is wholly contrary to Christ, to whom our bodies belong, as God shall also raise them up. In v. 15, 16 Paul adds to the proof a statement regarding the *abominableness* of fornication. The latter rests on the former, but by combining it with the former Paul brings the enormity of this sin fully to the consciousness of the Corinthians. The presentation continues in its simple and lucid manner by just using the facts so that their force overwhelms.

Do you not know that your bodies are members of Christ? Shall I remove the members of Christ and make them a harlot's members? God forbid.

Paul first appeals to the basic fact that our bodies are members of Christ. "Do you not know?" implies that the Corinthians do know, and that the fact pointed out in the question is undisputed by them. Compare Rom. 12:1, 6, 12-14. What is really involved in the statement that "the body is for the Lord, and the Lord for the body" is now combined in the unit thought that our bodies are "members of Christ." Just as we ourselves possess our own members and use them as our own for our own purpose, so my entire body and your entire body are members of Christ to be used by him alone for his own purposes. What is a fact regarding our entire person, body, mind, and spirit, is evidently also a fact when the body is considered by itself. For we all belong to Christ, not partly but in entirety.

This fact, however, involves a self-evident conclusion, οὖν: "Shall I remove the members of Christ and make them a harlot's members?" The abominableness of the very suggestion is repudiated by: μὴ γένοιτο, an aorist optative of wish (one of the few optatives still found in the Koine which is used often by Paul), literally: "Let it not be!" and in our idiom: "God forbid!" "Perish the thought!" The action expressed by the aorist participle ἄρας (αἴρειν) precedes that indicated by ποιήσω, literally: "having removed . . . shall I make?" One must first sever these members from Christ to whom they belong, for only thus could they be made to belong to the harlot. Paul asks: "Do you Corinthians want me to do a thing like that?" and again uses himself as an example for all. And ἄρας conveys much more than the far commoner λαβών, namely *das verwegene Sichvergreifen an den Gliedern Christi*, Meyer. The contrast pivots on the genitives "of Christ" and "of a harlot," hence we have the chiastic arrangement: the members *of Christ . . . a harlot's* members.

16) "Or do you not know," etc. = "Or if this repudiation (God forbid!) of the statement of the case I have made (robbing Christ of his members and making them a harlot's members) still seems doubtful to you (which I can hardly believe), do you not know," etc.? Paul is fully aware of the place where the doubt may lie for some or at what point

some may try to raise a doubt. They would not question the statement that their bodies are "the members of Christ," for that would mean to repudiate their own Christianity, but they might deny that by an act of fornication their bodies would assuredly become the members of a harlot. That, they would say, is surely overstraining the result of contact with a whore. Therefore Paul writes another "do you not know." **Or do you not know that he who joins himself to a harlot is one body with her? for, The two, says he, shall be one flesh.**

Whereas before the act there are two separate and distinct bodies, the fornicative act makes one single body of the two. No question can be raised regarding this point. It is also vital in Paul's array of facts. This is true whether men know it or not, acknowledge it or not, are ready to reckon with it or not, either in Corinth or elsewhere. The unimpeachable proof is therefore at once added with γάρ; it is the Scriptures themselves.

The participle ὁ κολλώμενος is middle (not passive, our versions) and characterizes the person: "he who joins himself" to the harlot by means of the sexual act of committing fornication. One such act bestows this character just as one theft makes a thief, one killing a murderer. The Greek article used with "harlot" indicates the one concerned. The simple φησίν needs no subject in the Greek. It is used in the New Testament to introduce passages that are so well known that neither God nor the Scripture need to be indicated as being the subject, it is like the German *heisst es*.

The fact that by an act of fornication the two sinners become "one body" is established by the quotation of Gen. 2:24: "The two shall be one flesh." "Flesh," σάρξ, *basar*, denotes merely the substance of which the "body" is composed and needs no further explanation. Incidentally, too, "flesh," which applies to all of the body, excludes the evasion that in the sexual act only a small part of the body, namely the sexual organs, are involved. In Genesis the statement refers to the legitimate sexual union that is consummated in marriage, yet here, too, the oneness of flesh is due to the sexual union and to that alone and not to the legitimacy of the union. Paul is entirely correct when he uses this passage to prove the oneness of flesh in an illegitimate sexual union. The act of sexual union with a harlot makes the two "one body," which means "one flesh." The stress is not on the noun "flesh" but on the two numerals "one."

The Hebrew lacks "the two," yet Jesus has it in Matt. 19:5, Paul again in Eph. 5:31, the Rabbis also introduce it. Instead of stating that "the two" was later inserted into the text in the interest of monogamy we should acknowledge that "the two" is exactly what the original Hebrew means when it says: "They shall be one flesh," the man and his wife. Regarding the predicate εἰς σάρκα μίαν instead of a nominative, note the Hebrew l^e and see R. 481; in German: *werden zu einem Fleisch*.

17) With δέ Paul introduces the directly opposite union and merely states the fact as such without again asking: "Do you not know this fact?" **But he that joins himself to the Lord is one spirit with him.** This parallels the other statement exactly: "He that joins himself to a harlot is one body with her." The two opposites clash in every word. What is meant by "the body for the Lord, and the Lord for the body" in v. 13 is now defined by "he that joins himself to the Lord." The body as such could, of course, never belong to the Lord, it is always the person as such that belongs to him and thus the body: "he who joins *himself*" (middle, not passive as in our versions). This belonging of our body to the Lord and of the Lord to our body is on the part of him who so belongs, not a passive, but

an active relation, one of the great activities of our faith and our love. This activity marks the character of that person, he is ὁ κολλώμενος. Yet we must say that, while in the opposite case a single act of fornication is enough to bestow the evil character, here the very nature of faith and of love is durative and the spiritual character is bestowed accordingly.

The body for the Lord, and the Lord for the body, means that we join ourselves to the Lord in faith and in love and remain thus joined to him. But this means still more, for he who thus joins himself to the Lord "is one spirit with him." This is the opposite of the result that is obtained when one joins himself to a harlot. These two can become only one body and one flesh, can consummate only a physical union, and one that lies on the very lowest material plane, is wholly unspiritual, utterly carnal and base. What the harlot is in her vice and degradation he becomes who joins himself to her. Of his own volition he descends to her in her filthiness.

What a difference when one joins himself to the Lord! He becomes one spirit with the Lord. For while our union with Christ involves also our bodies as a part of our person it is really a union of the spirit and only as such includes our bodies. Christ and the Christian become "one spirit," he in us, and we in him in a wondrous mystical union. This is the very highest plane that by what is highest in our being, namely the spirit, lifts us into a union that is completely spiritual, blessed, and heavenly. This is the *unio mystica* which is so abundantly attested in the Scriptures. With no absorption of our spirit into Christ, with no mingling or fusion of the two, with no loss of the identity of either, our spirit is joined to Christ's so that one thought, one desire, one will animate and control both, namely his thought, desire, and will. This mystical union is adumbrated in the marital union of husband

and wife, Eph. 5:28-33, yet only adumbrated, for no human relation is capable of doing more.

The great practical summation of this entire array and this comparison of facts is self-evident: **Flee fornication!** The asyndeton makes the conclusion the stronger. *Severitas cum fastidio.* Bengel. Some sins we must necessarily face, fight, and thus conquer. From others we recoil with a shock, their baseness and their stench repel us, we flee. Fornication is and should be one of these. Paul writes φεύγετε for another reason. He recognizes the danger that lies in our sinful flesh. So he admonishes: flee lest a spark ignite the tinder and fire the passion and the lust, and you be scorched in the flames, Prov. 7:6-27.

Here we have an instance when Paul uses the gospel and not the law for inculcating a moral requirement. He might with a stern and a threatening finger have pointed to the Decalog with its commandment: "Thou shalt not commit adultery!" and thus have been done with fornication. That method has its proper place, especially where men's ears are dull toward gospel appeals. A more favorable light is cast on the moral situation obtaining among the Corinthians from Paul's use of the gospel method in their case. Not only were the ears of these people still open to the appeal based on gospel facts, we must also conclude that those of the Corinthians who misused the dictum concerning adiaphora and full Christian liberty still intended to cling to Christ and not in the least to fall away from him. Only in the case of such people can Paul use patient explanation and the reminders: "Do you not know?" He first clears up the principle concerning adiaphora and secondly sets the pertinent gospel facts before them so that all of them can see for themselves what these facts signify, how they *prove* that fornication is utterly against Christ, and how they reveal that fornication is utterly *abominable* when it is compared with their relation to Christ.

18) If Paul were preaching law he might stop with the command to flee fornication although even in the sense of law this negative involves its corresponding positive. He is preaching gospel: "Flee fornication!" since your bodies are members of Christ. Just because this is gospel Paul must go on and add the great gospel positive: "Glorify God, therefore, in your body!" v. 20. Because all of this is indeed gospel, a second evident reason intervenes that prompts Paul to advance beyond the call to flee fornication. He cannot stop with the gospel fact that we are "one spirit with Christ," for this mystic union pertains not only to our spirit but also to our body which now becomes the "sanctuary" (ναός) of the Holy Spirit so that in this sense, too, we are no longer our own, having been bought with a price. Thus Paul reaches the cross of Christ, the very heart of the gospel, and there he may bring his appeal to a close. Those who know this price, the cross and its atoning blood, will be ready to "glorify God in their body."

How simple it is now in this gospel light to show the enormity of a sin like fornication! Without a connective Paul begins the final step. **Every sinful act that a man may do is outside of his body, but he that commits fornication sins against his own body.**

Paul again states undeniable facts in comparing sinful acts in general with that of fornication in particular. Also this is only a necessary preliminary statement that paves the way for the following. It really states the major premise of a syllogism: Fornication, as does no other sin, violates the body. The minor premise will follow: The Christian's body is the Spirit's sanctuary. And then the conclusion of this syllogism is plain: Fornication, as does no other sin, desecrates the very sanctuary of God. This conclusion runs downward — the sanctuary is desecrated. It must be completely reversed. Major: Fornication, as does no other sin, desecrates the body. Minor: Now our body is the Spirit's sanctuary. Ergo: We not only flee fornication but glorify God in our body.

Sexual sins bear a vicious character all their own. They are peculiarly unsavory and hence entail shame and disgrace in a peculiar manner. They rot the body, fill the mind with rottenness, and rapidly eliminate the sinner from this life. One of these markedly peculiar features Paul cites in this connection: this ἁμάρτημα, result of sinning, is not like other sinful acts and results, "outside of the body," but "the fornicator (characterizing participle, substantivized) sins against his own body." Paul is speaking of the result of sinful deeds, hence he writes ἁμάρτημα and not ἁμαρτία and even adds: "which a man may do or perpetrate." We have no reason whatever for restricting the sins which Paul may have in mind to those listed by him in v. 9,10. We err also when we question or challenge Paul's statement regarding the exceptional character of fornication by referring to a sin like suicide or others that damage the body like drunkenness, gluttony, addiction to drugs, etc. Paul is far more profound: no sinful act *desecrates* the body like fornication and sexual abuse. In this sense fornication has a deadly eminence. A sanctuary is desecrated by befouling it *within*; so this sin desecrates the sanctuary of the body. All other sins besmirch the sanctuary on the *outside* only.

19) "Does this fact seem new and strange, perhaps questionable, to you Corinthians? Then do you not know?"—and Paul states why the statement just made by him is true. "Or do you not know?" has the same force as it had in v. 16. The Corinthians do know what Paul is about to state, but, as in the case of so many things that we indeed know, we fail to apply them to our lives. We let them lie unused in the lumber room of our intellects. Regarding our body it is the great fact that was already touched upon in v. 13, etc., but is now stated fully: **Or do you not know that your body is a sanctuary of the Holy Spirit in you, whom you have from God?** We now see fully what Paul meant when he wrote a moment ago: "The body for the Lord, and the Lord for the body."

Our humble, earthly body is nothing less than "a sanctuary of the Spirit," and Paul writes "Holy Spirit," for because of its very name "a sanctuary" is holy. He uses ναός, the inner sanctuary itself, not ἱερόν, which may mean only the outer temple courts. The genitive "of the Holy Spirit" denotes possession but not in the sense that one may merely own a building without dwelling in it, for Paul adds two modifiers. First the phrase "in you," which is placed attributively after the Greek article. Only as being "within us," dwelling in us, does the Holy Spirit own our body as his sanctuary. Paul writes "in you" and not "in your bodies" and thus abides by the fact. For the Spirit dwells in us as persons and makes us "one spirit with the Lord," v. 17, and in this profound way takes possession also of our body so that this body actually becomes his sanctuary.

In the second place Paul adds the relative clause: "whom you have from God," οὗ for ὅ by attraction to the genitive antecedent. We are the Spirit's, and he is ours, a blessed mutuality but one that is "from God," a most gracious gift to us. The moment we hold this fact beside the other that fornication desecrates our body as does no other sinful act, the true character of this vicious sin becomes clear to us.

20) The blessed fact that we are the Spirit's sanctuary has two sides: one that he is ours, the other that we are his. The latter lies in the genitive:

your body a sanctuary "of the Holy Spirit." But Paul restates it in so many words, and first in negative form: **You are not your own,** you do not belong to your own selves. As the Spirit's sanctuary we belong wholly to him, and that certainly includes also our body, so that this body itself can be called his sanctuary. To this is added the positive: **for you were bought with a price.** The positive is linked to the negative by making it the proof (γάρ) for the negative. Effect and cause are thus combined: our having been bought (cause) results in our no longer being our own (effect).

The aorist "were bought" is historical and reports the fact: God bought us when on Calvary he paid the blood of his own Son as the price, Acts 20:28. God, indeed, bought all men with this price, even those who deny the Lord, II Pet. 2:1; yet what is thus true of all men in a general way is true of Christians in a particular way, for they have actually come into God's possession, are "a people for God's own possession," I Pet. 2:9, R. V., the price paid for them is not in vain.

The genitive of price, τιμῆs, needs no modifiers; the brevity has more weight, for, as it does so often, it suggests the idea of a great price. In 7:23 this same fact that we were bought with a great price is used in a different connection, namely that we are slaves of God and must not again become the slaves of men. In the present connection the great fact of our purchase establishes that we, including our body, no longer belong to our own selves, no longer dare desecrate our body with fornication, but must ever glorify God in our body.

Paul adds the capstone to the positive part of his presentation. **By all means, then, glorify God in your body!** We might expect Paul to close by saying to the Corinthians: "By all means, then, sanctify your body as a sanctuary of God!" But, as he does in so many instances, Paul, like Jesus, passes over what, after all, would be only an intermediate thought and not the real climax and at once reaches the climax that alone properly ends the discussion. The thought cannot be carried higher than this admonition to glorify God in our body. To be sure, that includes also the sanctification of our body. But "God" and not "our body" is the ultimate consideration.

The aorist "glorify" is urgent because of its tense. This tense implies that the glorification thus urged must be attained. The present imperative would not only be milder in its urgency, it would also imply a gradual process and thus leave open the question of full glorification. To glorify God in our body means so to use our earthly body that men may actually see that also these our bodies belong to God. We refuse to use them for sinful acts, we reserve them wholly for obedience to God.

The urgency expressed by the aorist tense is increased by the postpositive particle δή, for which we have no English equivalent. It is really climacteric and points to what is now at last entirely clear, R. 1149. We attempt to reproduce its force by the cumbersome turn "by all means, then."

Fornication is an all too common sin, and much has been said, preached, and written about its vicious character. Yet who can point to a treatment that in any way compares with this one paragraph dictated by St. Paul's inspired lips? Principle and facts are combined, and these facts reach to the profoundest depth and to the most sacred height and are yet presented with a simplicity and a lucidity that are unique. While we appropriate the substance, let us not fail to appreciate also the manner and the form in which it is stated.

CHAPTER VII

The Third Part of the Letter

Questions regarding Marriage, Chapter 7

Paul deals with this entire subject in a practical manner and bases his discussion on the situation existing in Corinth at this time. In fact, in their letter the Corinthians had asked Paul a number of questions in regard to these matters, and in this chapter he gives his reply. We may divide the chapter according to the various paragraphs and make sections accordingly or more summarily into only two or three sections as is indicated in the following.

I. In General regarding Marrying or Remaining Unmarried, 1-7

1) Paul begins with a transitional δέ and places a caption at the head of this part of his letter, namely the phrase: **Now concerning the things you wrote.** This is the first caption of this kind and indicates a formal reply to specific inquiries. We shall meet others as we read on, 7:25; 8:1; etc., all of them are alike, phrases introduced with περί. They help us materially in understanding why Paul writes on certain subjects. We need to supply nothing with each of these περί phrases, for each is intended only as a heading.

This first phrase is indefinite, for it fails to name the subject concerning which the Corinthians had made inquiry; the others that follow are definite, each states the subject. Yet we have no difficulty in determining the reference of this first caption; a glance at Paul's reply shows that the Corinthians had written to him regarding questions relating to marriage. One point they had mentioned in particular, namely that regarding maidens, 7:25. Paul's letter thus deals with two sizable groups of subjects: such as he himself introduces on the basis of positive information he had concerning the Corinthians; and such as the Corinthians themselves present to him in order that he may send them necessary instruction.

In beginning his extended reply to the questions about marriage Paul first of all lays down a general thesis, a proposition which forms the basis for all that he has to say on the points involved. **It is excellent for a man not to touch a woman; yet on account of fornications let each have his own wife, and each have her own husband.** This is the entire matter in a nutshell.

The first proposition in Paul's thesis is that it is καλόν, morally excellent, for a man not to touch a woman, i. e., to remain celibate, unmarried. "To touch a woman" is euphemistic for the sexual contact and intercourse in marriage. Verbs of touch are followed by the genitive. Confusion results when this part of Paul's thesis is taken abstractly, when it is regarded as being addressed to all Christendom and is to apply for all ages of the church. Paul writes for the Corinthians and for their specific circumstances at the time. We have Paul's own commentary on this καλόν. In v. 28 he writes: "I would spare you," in v. 35: "for your profit"; in v. 38: "shall do better"; and in v. 40: "happier." All these expressions refer to the Christians in Corinth, to their situation at that time, in particular to the difficulties and the dangers they had to face. Paul in no way contradicts Gen. 2:18: "And the Lord God said, It is *not good* that the man should be alone." In Eden God spoke for the human race. Paul writes to Corinth, to the Christians only, and such as were living in the worst pagan surroundings.

Paul does not call the unmarried state καλόν, "excellent," in contrast to marriage as being κακόν, "base"; for he himself at once commands marriage. To remain unmarried and to marry are each "excellent," each in its own way. Regarding the unmarried state Paul says that it is καλόν, "excellent," in opposition to an idea that this state is perhaps οὐ καλόν, "not excellent," or κακόν, actually "base." He intends to say to the Corinthians that something is to be said in favor of remaining unmarried. Under what circumstances and in what respect this is true he will elucidate later. Paul's "excellent" cannot be used in support of the papal order to priests, "forbidding to marry," I Tim. 4:3; nor in support of celibacy as being a higher degree of holiness.

2) The second half of Paul's thesis is a general command to marry: "each" (man) and "each" (woman), "let each have" (wife, husband). The two accusatives "his own wife" and "her own husband" clearly point to monogamy and accord with the original divine institution of marriage, Matt. 19:3-9. The varied modifiers ἑαυτοῦ and ἴδιον are used only for the sake of style, for both have the same meaning. But Paul is here writing, not on the institution of marriage as such, but in answer to specific inquiries from the Corinthian congregation regarding its own members.

This explains why Paul adds "on account of fornications," and why he places the phrase in the emphatic position. The Greek article as well as the plural of the noun refer to the acts of fornication that would result if marriage were prohibited or should cease. The accusation brought against Paul that he thus places marriage on a very low level as though it were only the lesser of two evils, is unwarranted. For in Eph. 5:22, 23 the same Paul writes about the high and holy aspects of marriage as no man has ever done. But some forget that this apostle is a thoroughly practical man who knows also the weakness of human nature, especially when it is in the midst of countless seductions to sin. From this viewpoint he writes "on account of fornications," and even the efforts of Rome to establish only the limited clerical and monastic celibacy more than justify Paul's phrase.

3) After the basic thesis has been properly set down, Paul first elaborates the second half of it and then turns to the first half. **To the wife let the husband render her due and likewise also the wife to the husband.** The nominatives and the datives are arranged chiastically. The normal situation in this sinful world is that each man have his own wife, and each woman have her own husband (γυνή is used in the sense of "woman" and in the sense of "wife" as the context determines). This normal situation includes just what Paul here writes, the normal sexual intercourse between man and wife which was contemplated in the original institution of marriage and was not changed by the principles and the spirit of Christianity. Husband and wife are to render to each other τὴν ὀφειλήν, the specific obligation involved in the marital union, the *debitum tori* (*des Ehebettes*, the marriage bed). "Likewise" as well as the parallel thought in the statement place both on an equality regarding this "due." So also the verb ἀποδίδωμι, because of the force of ἀπό, means to give what one owes or is under obligation to render. It is evident that Paul excludes all false asceticism, for this nullifies the essential nature of marriage.

How much may we read between the lines which Paul here writes? Does Paul ward off a false asceticism which was found in Corinth? Did some members advocate total sexual abstinence in the married state? As we read on, especially v. 5, 6, this seems a fair deduction. Thus the phenomenon that extremes so often meet would again be illustrated in Corinth: on the one hand a lax libertinism and a license that had to be severely curbed, and on the other hand a false and a dangerous asceticism that had to be rooted out lest the vilest sins creep in under its pious cloak.

4) The imperatives used in the two preceding verses are now followed by two plain indicatives which state two facts. Although Paul writes no "for" or other connective, these two facts are the reasons for the preceding injunction that husband and wife must render their marital obligation to each other. **The wife does not have the authority over her own body but the husband; and likewise also the husband does not have the authority over his own body, but the wife.**

Paul is at pains to word the two statements exactly alike and even writes out the two verbs whereas in v. 3 he allows the second verb to be supplied by the reader. In other connections Paul upholds the headship of the husband and requires the submission of the wife. But in regard to their sexual relation both are on the same level, both have equally lost their ἐξουσία, authority or right over their body, both have transferred that authority equally to the other. The wife's body is, indeed, her own, but her husband has the authority over it in regard to the obligations just mentioned; and the same thing is true in regard to the husband. Bengel notes the *elegans paradoxon* in both statements between "her (his) own" and "has no authority."

All false, individualistic independence on the part of either wife or husband is barred out. Why this must be barred out the significant phrase in v. 2 has already made plain, "because of fornications." In v. 3 the arrangement is chiastic, in v. 4 it is parallel. Yet in v. 3 "the husband" is followed by "the wife" while in v. 4 "the wife" is followed by "the husband," which

First Corinthians 7:5

produces another chiasm. These arrangements are intentional and help to convey the complete equality of husband and wife in regard to their sexual relations with each other. We may mention them in either order, either first, either second; what Paul says is true.

5) Again no connective is needed, for the deduction is plain: **Do not deprive one another,** i. e., in regard to sexual obligation. This must stand as the rule and the normal conduct in marriage. What v. 3 expressed in positive form is now repeated in negative form; what v. 3 states for each separately is now combined; what v. 3 states objectively in the third person singular is now expressed subjectively by the second person plural. We see Paul's mastery of thought and of expression in employing all these variations and combinations in just the right manner. He weaves a perfect pattern.

Now comes the one exception: **except as may be by agreement for a term that you have leisure for prayer and again be together in order that Satan may not tempt you on account of your incontinence.** The exception may occur when husband and wife mutually agree to refrain from sexual intercourse for a certain short term (πρὸς καιρόν) and for a religious purpose. Paul is speaking generally, hence he makes no reference to sickness, to separation due to travel, etc. He speaks only about voluntary abstinence while husband and wife are living together. To εἰ μή τι, which is our English "except," the addition of ἄν lends the touch of expectancy: "it may be," such instances may and probably will occur, B.-D. 376. No verb is needed, R. 1025. "By agreement" is really "due to agreement," ἐκ, *aus Uebereinkunft.*

The first ἵνα clause has occasioned much discussion because it ushers in two verbs, the second of which does not indicate purpose. This ἵνα is subfinal, which means that it does not state the purpose of the temporary continence but the contents of the mutual agreement. The agreement is: "that we have leisure for prayer and again be together" when the time agreed upon expires. Paul states this in the second person: "that you have," etc. The phrase ἐπὶ τὸ αὐτό is idiomatic and may be used with εἶναι (here ἦτε), "be together" again sexually as before. In this agreement husband and wife are again on the same level. To make such an agreement or not to make it lies in the sphere of Christian liberty.

Much interest has been aroused by the first part of the agreement, the arrangement to provide leisure for prayer. Although Paul uses the article τῇ προσευχῇ, no one has discovered fixed seasons for special devotions like our Lenten season or Holy Week in the apostolic church. All we have is this intimation on Paul's part, which makes the impression that agreements such as this were not unusual among the Corinthians. Paul also gives them his full approval.

It seems as though Paul is referring to private devotions, when some family sets apart a week or more for this purpose. The sexual abstinence would then resemble the practice of fasting which obtained in the first period of the history of the Christian Church. It would be carried out in order to keep under the body, to master and fully to control its appetites, as an aid to strengthening the spiritual life. In Paul's mind, of course, no trace of work-righteousness taints this voluntary practice as though either the devotions or the abstinence are meritorious before God. Nor does Paul's approval of such agreements between husband and wife support the suggestion that cohabitation in marriage is, after all, a kind of impurity that leaves a stain or taint upon married people. Regarding that point Heb. 13:4 is decisive: "Marriage is honorable in all, and the bed undefiled."

The second ἵνα is plainly final and refers to the resumption of sexual intercourse, "lest Satan tempt you on account of your incontinence." Paul would permit and advise only temporary abstinence with a religious background and is very frank in stating the reason, "on account of your incontinence." This may not flatter our human nature but it certainly fortifies by honestly naming the weak point. The verb and the noun are placed so that both receive the full emphasis. The noun ἀκρασία (= ἀκράτεια), "incontinence," negates κράτος and should be distinguished from ἀκρασία (in which the second α is short), "a bad mixture." Satan is here pictured as being constantly on the watch to bring Christ's followers to fall. It must be our purpose to thwart his nefarious attempts.

6) Paul's next sentence has been variously understood: **Now this I say by way of concession, not by way of command.** The term ἐπιταγή is an order or a command that is issued by a proper authority. As the opposite of this συγγνώμη can mean only "favor" or "concession." But what is τοῦτο, "this," that Paul states not as a command which requires unquestioned obedience but as a favor or concession that may be used or left unused? One answer given is that τοῦτο refers to the resumption of the sexual relation in marriage after a season of devotions; that Paul does not command this resumption but only concedes it; that Paul's principles and his ideals would really require that the married should abstain permanently by mutual consent. But this assumption contradicts all the imperatives used in v. 2-5, all of which are even durative (iterative) and therefore in the present tense, and it also perverts Paul's ideal.

Another view is that the antecedent of τοῦτο is to be sought as far back as v. 2; that Paul now informs the Corinthians that these imperatives used in v. 2 (and v. 5) are not intended as such but are only concessions to our weak human nature; that Paul's real ideal is the celibate state and no sexual intercourse whatever. This assumption uses another route but arrives at the same goal. But why should anyone, least of all Paul, give commands and even repeat these commands with durative imperatives and then in the end say that he does not intend them as commands? Nor is the celibate state Paul's ideal.

The simple fact is that τοῦτο regularly refers to something that has just been said, and here a glance at the preceding sentence shows that its antecedent is all that follows εἰ μή τι ἄν. "This" = what I have just said about such agreements which you may make to abstain and to devote yourselves to prayer for a time and then to come together again in order to ward off temptation. Observe that this antecedent is preceded by an imperative: "Do not deprive one another." Someone might think that he ought therefore to read an imperative sense also into the exception which Paul adds, "except as may be by agreement," etc. Such an imperative sense does not, of course, lie in these words, and Paul now says that he does not have in mind such a sense. He cannot and he does not order such a temporal sexual withholding by any "command," he makes mention of it only by way of a "concession," one that is connected with his commands (the imperatives used in v. 2 and 5), which stand as such and must remain. And "concession" or "favor" is the correct term, for when a general obligation is laid down by specific commands, exceptions are properly called concessions.

7) Paul now states most clearly what his ideal is. **Yet I would that all men were even also as I myself; nevertheless each has his own charismatic gift due to God, one thus, another thus.**

This ideal is, therefore, not at all the cessation of marriage, or the abolition of the sexual side of marriage, or the celibate state for all. For none of these is a "charismatic gift due to God," and all of these contradict God's institution of marriage and its divinely ordered sexual relation. Paul's ideal is the ἐγκράτεια, entire self-mastery as to the sexual life and freedom from temptation in this regard. This explains why he favors the concession of temporary abstinence as explained above. This self-control and self-mastery is the charismatic gift which Paul had from God.

God grants many charismatic gifts to his church, but he distributes them, "dividing to each one severally even as he will," I Cor. 12:11. None of these gifts is intended for all Christians. Paul used this charismatic gift of his in the interest of his life's work as an apostle who traveled far and wide and for this reason rejoiced that he had complete sexual self-mastery as a gift from God and could thus remain without a wife and a family. Yet, as far as Paul's right is concerned, he states emphatically: "Have we no right to lead about a wife that is a believer even as the rest of the apostles, and the brethren of the Lord, and Cephas?" I Cor. 9:5. If Paul had felt the need he, too, could have married. The other apostles did, Peter included, and by so doing they, in their way, maintained Paul's ideal just as Paul maintained it by not marrying.

This charismatic gift of sexual self-control is valuable also in the married state, for it frees from all temptation (last clause of v. 5). The fact that in this state such control does not mean avoidance of all legitimate sex contact v. 3 places beyond question. Nor is this ideal of self-control something that is exceptional in Paul's case, perhaps the result of his life as a bachelor, for Jesus himself speaks about the same matter and in the same way in Matt. 19:10-12: "All men cannot receive this saying, save they to whom it is given. ... He that is able to receive it, let him receive it." It is not for worldly people but for believers only, and they are to exercise this virtue and this gift.

282   *Interpretation of First Corinthians*

Each one has his own charismatic gift, "one thus, another thus," one in one manner, another in a different manner. Yet this does not mean that a strong inclination toward marriage is one of God's charismatic gifts for the simple reason that no grace and no special gift of grace is needed for that, the constitution of our nature suffices entirely. What Paul means is that one Christian has a special gift from God in one direction, another in an entirely different direction. Grace works in all manner of directions as Paul shows *in extenso* in I Cor. 12:8, etc.

Note that θέλω δέ is used to express an unfulfilled wish: "I wish, but, of course, it is out of the question." To obtain this thought we usually translate: "I would," etc. There is no abruptness in the present tense, R. 923. The fact that Paul expresses this wish while by means of his actual distribution of charismatic gifts God acts differently, involves no disagreement or clash. Many other gifts besides sexual self-control are so fruitful and so lovely in themselves that we might well wish them for all Christians, yea, all men, and yet we know in regard to our wish, as Paul knew regarding his wish, that it must remain unfulfilled. With predicates ὡς is common and καί is not redundant but lends a gentle touch of its own. In ἐμαυτόν we have one of the few indirect reflexives found in the New Testament, R. 688.

In this paragraph the refined reticence and the delicacy of expression in discussing so intimate a subject deserve our attention. Certain things had to be said and to be understood, and Paul says them in the right way. The purity of his mind is reflected in every word and expression. This is the model for preaching and Christian discussion. Legal codes like those of the Old Testament and our modern laws require much plainer language for their purpose.

II. *Special Groups and the Question regarding Marriage, 8-24*

8) Verses 8-24 belong together because they deal with special groups in the congregation at Corinth.

The Unmarried and the Widows, 8, 9. — Paul himself names this group and then gives his brief counsel. The connective δέ is not intended to emphasize λέγω as now applying something that has already been mentioned above, for "I say" has its own emphasis. Δέ is only transitional in the usual manner. The practical principles on the subject of marriage have been laid down; Paul now applies these principles to the different groups in the congregation. **Now I say to the unmarried and to widows: It is excellent for them if they remain even as I.**

The term "unmarried" really includes all individuals mentioned in this first group, yet καί adds "widows." This conjunction is often used thus to single out a part from a whole in order to give it special attention. Widows might, indeed, have special reasons for thinking their state a sad one and thus for desiring to have it changed. To all the unmarried, in particular also to the widows, Paul writes: "Excellent for them if they remain even as I." This is the same καλόν as the one found in v. 1. Instead of imagining or permitting anyone to tell them that something is κακόν or amiss about their state so that they ought to do everything possible to change it, Paul assures them that their state, too, is καλόν, "excellent" with a moral excellence of its own. If they then choose to remain in this state, all is well and good.

Note the conditional clause: "if they remain or shall remain"; the decision rests entirely with them. There is no inkling of a command: "Remain even as

I!" No moral pressure even: "You ought to remain even as I!" The condition is the common one used to express expectancy, which means that Paul assumes that some will remain unmarried. That is all: if they so decide, who can find fault? But in this connection "even as I" is not identical with "even also as I myself" in v. 7. In v. 7 this personal reference points to the charismatic gift of self-control; in v. 8 it points only to remaining unmarried.

9) But a natural reason may urge toward marriage, and that very decidedly. **Yet if they have not continency, let them marry; for it is better to marry than to burn.** The condition with ἐάν occurring in v. 8 expects some to remain unmarried; the condition with εἰ in v. 8 merely takes up the actual cases for whom remaining unmarried is not advisable. The plural used in v. 9, "if they have not," etc., is indicative only of the rule that applies to the cases specified, those who lack the charismatic gift of complete sexual self-control. And here Paul uses the decisive aorist imperative: "Let them marry!" Brief and to the point. Whoever lacks the gift of ἐγκράτεια (Paul uses the corresponding verb) in which Paul rejoiced, needs marriage — let him or her enter marriage! The negative particle used with an entire εἰ clause is μή; here οὐ negates only the verb: "have not continency." Paul is discussing no sentimental, economical, social, or even providential features connected with marriage or nonmarriage. He is counselling consciences on how to avoid sin.

This explains the reason (γάρ) which Paul assigns: "It is better to marry than to burn." The moral point decides, and "better" is meant in this sense. Paul is again succinct and to the point; there is no need to say another word. The difference in the tenses is important: "to marry" is an aorist to express a single definite act; "to burn" is a present to indicate a recurrent condition. The latter is middle, "to burn in oneself" with the strong fire of sexual desire, which, deprived of marriage, may result in criminal satisfaction or may in secret devastate the inner spiritual life. But the alternatives offered are not two evils, the lesser of which should be chosen, but a good on the one hand and an evil on the other, "for marriage is honorable in all." Paul states the facts unblushingly: one either has or has not the gift. If he has he *may* remain unmarried although he, too, may marry. Nor does Paul say that it would be "better" for him to remain unmarried; all he says is that, if he elects not to marry, his unmarried state, like Paul's, is "excellent." But if one lacks the gift, only one course is in order, he must marry, for moral danger is too deadly.

The Married Christians, 10, 11. — 10) "Now to the married," with its transitional δέ, takes up another group, those who have entered marriage and are now in this state. However, a glance at v. 12, etc., shows that in v. 10, 11 Paul is speaking about couples in which both husband and wife are Christians, for in v. 12 he deals with mixed marriages. **Now to the married I give command, not I myself but the Lord, that a wife be not separated from a husband (but even if she be separated, let her remain unmarried or else let her be reconciled to her husband), and that a husband send not away a wife.**

To this group in which both husbands and wives are Christians Paul does not write λέγω, "I say or state," as he did in v. 8, but παραγγέλω, "I command," "I issue orders." Yet it is in reality not Paul but the Lord himself who issues this order, for the order here stated is the one issued by Jesus himself in Matt. 5:32; 19:6, and when Paul says, "I give command" (present tense), he means that the order of Jesus has continuous, permanent force. In this instance Paul can use a word that was spoken by Jesus himself in regard to the permanency of marriage, a word that has validity for all time. There are some other questions about marriage, on which Jesus had no occasion to speak while he was here on earth. When Paul himself answers some of these questions he does so as the Lord's apostle through whom the Lord now speaks. No matter how the divine command comes to us, whether from the Lord's own lips or from the pen of the Lord's apostle, the command has equal binding power.

Paul states in words of his own the Lord's order to all Christian couples and uses two accusatives with infinitives: γυναῖκα ἀπὸ ἀνδρὸς μὴ χωρισθῆναι . . . καὶ ἄνδρα γυναῖκα μὴ ἀφιέναι: "that a wife be not separated from a husband . . . and that a husband send not away a wife." The sense of the double command is that neither a Christian wife nor a Christian husband should disrupt and thus destroy the marriage in which they are joined. While the wording is different, μὴ χωρισθῆναι to indicate the activity of a wife, and μὴ ἀφιέναι to state the action of a husband, the substance of the commands is the same, for in v. 13 and 15 the verbs are reversed. The Greek offers a choice of verbs. Jesus used ἀπολύειν in Matt. 5:32; ἀποτέμνειν, ἐκβάλλειν, and ἀποπέμπειν could also be employed according to the connotation that might be desired.

We may note that Paul is not dealing with a case in which a Christian wife or a husband commits fornication and thereby disrupts the marriage tie; Jesus, too, disregards this in Matthew 5 as needing no comment since it *eo ipso* destroys the marriage. It is likewise important to note that, like Jesus, Paul is not speaking of divorce in the sense of a court action such as we connect with the word "divorce." Marriage between Christians is to be permanent, and neither spouse is to dissolve it. The wife is not to permit anything to separate her from her husband, the husband is not to send away his wife, whether in addition either of them goes also to a secular court and has the disruption made legally permanent or not.

The question as to why the wife is mentioned first is usually answered by saying that cases in which the wife would act are more numerous. This is questionable. In v. 12 and 13 Paul has the order reversed. In Matt. 5:32; 19:5, etc., Jesus mentions only the husband who dismisses his wife because this was a common practice among the Jews since they supposed that it was authorized in Deut. 24:1. When Mark (10:12) writes for Gentile Christians he adds also the wife's action. It would seem that the wife is mentioned first because Paul thinks of her as leaving of her own accord, by *her* act dissolving the marriage; thus the husband is mentioned in the second place, he by his act sends away his wife from their home. This also explains the verbs used: χωρισθῆναι regarding the wife's action, a passive: she is separated from her husband by something, she leaves him; ἀφιέναι regarding the husband: he sends her away, makes her leave him and their home. The order is proper: she leaves — he makes her leave. The A. V. is right in translating ἀφιέναι "put (send) away"; the R. V. is wrong: "leave not his wife," for he makes *her* leave, he sends *her* away.

In regard to this double prohibition we should note its effect upon Jewish Christians in Corinth. As former Jews they would remember that the husband thought he could send away his wife for even the slightest reason by merely giving her a letter of divorcement, we may say her walking papers. The Lord himself forbade such a procedure. How even the disciples felt about the Lord's dictum we may gather from Matt. 19:10.

The Roman state law and custom, of which the Gentile Christian would think, granted either party the right to take the initiative in dissolving a marriage.

In addition it made distinctions between the marriages themselves. Marriages between slaves had no legal standing (and thus permanence) whatever. There were not a few slaves (7:21) in the congregation at Corinth. Marriage between a freedman (one released from slavery) and a slave had a low legal standing. In general, during this period of Roman history the permanency of marriage unions was exceedingly uncertain. The effect of the Lord's command on the complete permanency of Christian marriage may thus be estimated.

Yet Paul refers to the Lord's command, not as one that is now for the first time being made known to the Corinthians, but as one that is well known to them; he only reminds the Corinthians of its force and calls their attention to the fact that it applies to wives as well as to husbands.

11) The sentence introduced by ἐάν is plainly a parenthesis since it is inserted between the two coordinate infinitive clauses, the one regarding the wife, the other regarding the husband. The sentence considers only the case of the wife: "but even if she be separated, let her remain unmarried or else let her be reconciled to her husband." There can be no question that this applies also to a Christian husband who is forced to leave his wife. Since he employs ἐὰν δὲ καί, the condition of expectancy, Paul expects cases such as this to occur. When we apply the words also to a husband we must retain the same verb, ἐὰν χωρισθῇ, the one that is here used with reference to the wife, and not change to the verb that is found in the following infinitive clause, namely ἀφιέναι.

Paul uses only the passive "be separated" and does not intimate what may force a wife (or a husband) into such a separation from a Christian spouse. To assume, as has been done, that the reason was of a religious nature, that such a separation was brought about in order to avoid all sexual contact so as to secure greater devotion to the Lord, is unwarranted. To think of adultery on the part of the spouse from whom separation is made is equally out of the question, for this would disrupt or destroy the marriage. Therefore also Paul does not speak of this, least of all in this parenthesis which, like the entire sentence, deals with marriage partners both of whom are Christians. All that can be said is that various reasons may bring about a separation and cause a wife (or a husband) to leave.

Does Paul say that the Lord commands that the two shall live together nevertheless? No; there is nothing in Paul's word to this effect. What Paul says is this: "let her (him) be reconciled to her husband (to his wife)." The manner in which Paul writes indicates that he makes this a part of the Lord's own command. We have no word of the Lord that states this directly; so we take it that Paul deduces this from what the Lord says regarding marriage in Matthew 5 and elsewhere.

When we compare all that the Lord said regarding marriage we see what is meant by the command: "let her (him) remain unmarried or else," etc. Marriages were so often disrupted in order that the dissatisfied spouse might marry another; note Matt. 19:9, "and shall marry another." For this reason so many of the Jews got rid of their wives — they wanted some other woman. We have thousands of similar cases today. This is forbidden Christians: "let her (him) remain unmarried." Otherwise, "let her (him) be reconciled." What this involves for her (him) who disrupts the marriage in order to marry another person is obvious — such a person forfeits her (his) Christian character and membership. For such a person but one other possibility remains, reconciliation with the deserted spouse. The conclusion is often drawn that, although the two are separated as indicated (and we may add, perhaps even legally divorced), they are, nevertheless, still married in the sight of the Lord and thus also in the sight of the church. Paul could easily have said that in just a few words; he did not do so although he is reminding the Corinthians of the Lord's own command regarding marriage.

What Paul writes still leaves a number of questions unanswered for us who are living under different circumstances. The best we can do is to absorb fully what the Lord and his apostle say and then to answer such additional questions in the light of their words and in their spirit. As far as Paul is concerned, he intended to visit Corinth and would thus answer all further questions in person.

Husbands and Wives in Mixed Marriages, 12-16.

12, 13) A third class in Corinth needs information on this subject. This includes "the rest," namely husbands and wives in mixed marriages. **Now to the rest say I myself, not the Lord: If some brother has a wife unbelieving, and she consents to dwell with him, let him not send her away. And a wife whoever has a husband unbelieving, and he consents to dwell with her, let her not send away her husband.**

The cases that came to the attention of Jesus were those of Jews, in which husband and wife belonged to the Jewish faith. Jesus, therefore, had no occasion to pronounce on the sort of cases that Paul had to treat among the Corinthians. Hence Paul cannot appeal to a λόγιον or statement of Jesus when he is instructing the Corinthians regarding these. He must himself speak (λέγω) regarding this type, but he does so as an apostle who has divine apostolic authority. Thus, as he writes, divine Inspiration applies to what he now records as his own apostolic statement just as fully as it did to what he records in v. 10, 11 in restating the Lord's *logion* in its application to the Corinthians.

What he writes is so clear as to need little further comment. Both sides, that of a husband and that of a wife in a mixed marriage, are formulated with equal fulness, and both almost exactly alike. Even the two verbs: "let him (her) not send her (him) away," are identical. From this we gather that, when Paul varied the verbs in v. 11, he intended to express no material difference. The two demonstrative pronouns, καὶ αὐτή and καὶ οὗτος, which are used instead of relative pronouns or instead of accusative participles after ἄπιστον (namely συνευδοκοῦντα), lend a formal tone to Paul's pronouncement. They have the effect of legal phraseology.

Paul mentions the consent of only the unbelieving persons, that of the believing parties is taken for granted. A possibility of dissent would lie only with the unbeliever. In both of the instances considered "unbelieving" includes Jew as well as pagan; either might insist on separation and divorce. The two conditional clauses with εἰ contemplate the two cases as real and as actually occurring. "To dwell with him (her)" is literally "to house with him (her)" and means to continue the marriage relation. Mixed marriages are certainly not ideal; yet they are as truly marriages as other marriages are. Paul also does not forbid them as, of course, he also does not advise them. He takes them as they are and delivers his instructions accordingly.

14) Instead of seeking ethical reasons for disrupting such a marriage, a proper view of this type of marriage discloses the ethical reason for leaving it intact. **For the unbelieving husband is sanctified in his wife, and the unbelieving wife is sanctified in the brother, else evidently your children are unclean, but now they are holy.**

There are other reasons that this kind of marriage should certainly be continued once it has been entered into. Paul seeks to remove all doubt that a believer might have as if by continuing in such a marriage he (or she) might become contaminated in some way. Paul declares the opposite as being true. Instead of the believer's being made unholy by this marital union, the unbeliever is made holy. This is true equally for an unbelieving wife and for an unbelieving husband. By placing the verbs forward in the Greek this fact is made emphatic in the case of both: *"Sanctified is* the the unbelieving husband, and *sanctified is* the unbelieving wife" — nothing less. The two perfect tenses point to a present, continuing condition.

Since Paul writes plainly: "the unbelieving husband" and "the unbelieving wife," he excludes all thought of personal spiritual sanctification. As far as their persons are concerned, all unbelievers are unsanctified. He uses the passive "have been sanctified" and then two ἐν phrases: "in connection with his wife," "in connection with the brother," which R. 587 explains as a case of ἐν with persons: "in the person of" the believing spouse. A certain sanctity is conferred (passive) upon the unbelieving spouse, unbelieving though this spouse is, when by the marriage tie he is joined to a believing spouse, who is one of God's saints. The unbelieving spouse is party to a Christian marriage. Through the believing spouse the blessings of a sanctified marriage are bestowed upon the unbelieving spouse and thus more is given (passive) to him than his unbelief deserves. Thus Melanchthon also comments on our passage that "the use of marriage is permitted and holy on account of faith in Christ just as it is permitted to use meat, etc." *C. Tr.* 371, 31. Marriage should be sanctified by faith on the part of both parties, but one believing spouse alone already brings that sanctification to the marriage. It is, therefore, a blessed thing for an unbelieving person to be married to a true and faithful believing spouse.

This is established by pointing to the effect of such a marriage on the children born to it: "else evidently your children are unclean, but now they are holy." Paul uses the strong protasis of reality, ἐπεὶ ἄρα ἐστι, R. 1026, ἄρα indicating what is evident. The children are "holy" from the moment of their birth in the same sense as the unbelieving father or the mother has holiness conferred upon him or her, i. e., by being born in Christian wedlock, which is in this case made so by one of the parents. This is what should comfort a Christian father or a mother who are living in a mixed marriage.

Foreign to Paul's thought is the idea that a sort of holiness is conferred upon the unbeliever by the marital sexual relation with a believer. Likewise the thought that by means of such a marriage the unbeliever enters into a sacred relation with the Christian congregation, for the pronoun "your" (children) cannot refer to the congregation but refers only to the parents of the children. Paul intimates nothing in regard to the baptism of such children. The conclusion that infant baptism could not have yet been practiced in these early days is unwarranted. The holiness which Paul here predicates regarding children has nothing to do with this sacrament and the regeneration wrought by the Spirit, John 3:5. It is exactly like that bestowed upon the unbelieving parent. In regard to the baptism of such children born in mixed marriages the only proper conclusion is that the believing parent would bring the children to this sacrament so that, being born in a holy wedlock, they may also be sanctified by the new birth in Christ.

15) But the unbelieving spouse may positively refuse to continue in marital union with a believer. Cases such as this occur frequently in foreign mission fields to this day. What then? **But if the husband,**

the unbelieving one, keeps himself separate, let him keep himself separate! The brother or the sister has not been placed in bondage in such circumstances, but God has called us in peace.

In v. 11 Paul uses the passives χωρισθῆναι and χωρισθῇ. One might regard χωρίζεται and χωριζέσθω as passives; but they are intended to be middle because the unbelieving husband separates himself. He simply leaves his believing wife. Whether he also proceeds to procure a legal divorce makes no difference in the case whatever. What disrupts and destroys the marriage is the fact that he keeps himself separated. Paul uses a condition of reality and thus thinks of an actual case. The two verbs are durative: "If he keeps himself separate, let him keep himself separate." In the expression ὁ ἀνὴρ ὁ ἄπιστος the addition of the adjective by means of a second article emphasizes the adjective: "the husband, the unbelieving one" (R. 776), and thus makes evident that it is his unbelief which causes him to abandon his believing wife and thus ends his marriage with her.

Paul writes succinctly: χωριζέσθω, "let him keep himself separate!" Short and done with. What can, indeed, be done when an unbeliever takes such action? The marriage is ended; let it remain thus. While Paul writes ὁ ἀνὴρ ὁ ἄπιστος, we see that he has in mind both cases, an unbelieving husband deserting his believing wife, an unbelieving wife deserting her believing husband. What is now the status of such a believing spouse? "The brother or the sister has not been placed in bondage ἐν τοῖς τοιούτοις, in such circumstances." The verb is placed emphatically forward and is itself strong: "not has been enslaved the brother or the sister."

The perfect tense states more than the present used in our versions. The perfect reaches back to the day when the unbelieving spouse entered upon the desertion and states that from that moment onward the believing spouse has not been held bound. From that day onward the fetters of the marriage tie have been broken and remain so, now and indefinitely. The deserting spouse broke them. No law binds the believing spouse. Let us add that no odium on the part of Christians has a right to bind such a believing, deserted spouse. It goes without saying that a believing spouse will by Christian kindness and persuasion do all that can be done to prevent a rupture. But when these fail, Paul's verdict is: "Thou art free!"

Desertion is exactly like adultery in its effect. Both disrupt the marriage tie. For that matter, the case is the same as when in olden times a wife was forced out of the home by her husband. The essence of marriage is union. When this is disrupted, the union which God intended to be a permanent one is destroyed, sinfully destroyed. There is only this difference in the case of adultery, the innocent spouse may forgive and continue the marriage, or may accept the dire result, the sundering of the marriage. In the case of desertion the former is not possible; the deserted spouse can no longer continue a marriage, for none exists. To speak, as is generally done, of "two causes for divorce" is a mistake. In the first place, neither Jesus nor Paul discusses what we term "divorce," namely legal court action; both speak about what destroys a marriage. In the second place, just as a man may be murdered in various ways, the one frightful thing being that he is murdered, so no matter how a marriage is destroyed, the terrible thing is its destruction.

It is a separate matter as to what the innocent spouse does by way of obtaining the civil court action regarding his or her status in civil law in regard to property rights and the like. Court action may be most necessary after a marriage is wrecked but it should not be considered the all-important thing, nor should it be confused with what has actually destroyed the marriage. In the case of desertion, when a spouse runs away, a special question arises: "Will the one who has deserted perhaps change his (her) mind and return?" Both the church and the courts have rightly set time limits as to how long the innocent party should wait until a formal pronouncement is made to the effect that the desertion is, indeed, permanent. While setting such a time limit is a human matter, ecclesiastical or legally secular, it harmonizes with Paul's decision.

When Paul adds: "but God has called us in peace," he refers to peace with our fellow men. The perfect tense "has called" points to the enduring state of the Christians as people who are now living under God's gracious and effective gospel call, a call that is connected with "peace," which is not merely the opposite of strife but includes the idea of well-being. The implication is that a deserting spouse shall not destroy this "peace." Paul at once adds a plain explanation that is intended to protect this peace against the false legalistic ideas of Christians who are inclined to go to extremes.

16) This explanation (γάρ) is directed against the one point that might be urged by a deserted Christian's conscience against peacefully accepting such desertion, namely the thought of thus losing all opportunity of saving the unbelieving spouse. **For how knowest thou, O wife, whether thou shalt save thy husband? or how knowest thou, O husband, whether thou shalt save thy wife?**

The vocatives make the questions highly personal and thus the more effective. If here or there a spouse grieved over such a supposed lost opportunity, Paul brushes such grief aside. A Christian wife will, indeed, try to win an unbelieving husband, I Pet. 3:1: "That, even if any obey not the Word, they may without the Word be gained by the behavior of their wives."

A Christian husband will do the same. But what opportunity can be found when a spouse is so adverse as eventually to separate himself or herself entirely? Thus the two questions answer themselves: "How knowest thou?" τί, adverbial accusative: "in what respect." The wife and the husband will have to answer: "I have no way of knowing." And Paul's implied reply is: "Then dismiss the matter." After all, the business of saving a soul belongs to God; he alone determines the human instruments as well as all other providential aids which he will employ. Let not even a spouse assume too readily that she or he is the God-chosen instrument.

These questions have been understood in the exactly opposite sense. Such a sense may be obtained by making v. 15 a parenthesis and thus connecting v. 16 with v. 14: the unbelieving spouse is sanctified by the believing spouse, for she will save her husband, or he his wife. This may also be done by connecting v. 16 with the phrase "in peace" in v. 15: the Christian, being called in peace, will convert the non-Christian spouse to this same peace. Both combinations are artificial, and both rest on a preconception, namely that the believing spouse will save the unbelieving — the very thing which Paul questions, the very thing which often did not happen, unbelieving spouses even going so far as to desert the believing for the very reason that they believed. There is no need to make v. 15 a parenthesis; no casual reader could surmise that this is Paul's intention. To attach v. 16 to a subordinate clause in v. 15 is unsatisfactory, since it fits the chief thought exactly: the Christian spouse is not bound. Nor does εἰ mean *ob nicht*, "whether not," in the New Testament, εἰ = "whether."

Excursus on the Ethical Principle Involved, 17-24.

17) This excursus is typically Pauline, for it shows that what Paul posits for the specific case of marriage

relations is really a general Christian principle and as such applicable to many other relations, some of which are introduced as illustrations. This breadth of vision is found throughout Paul's writing. He never stops at the halfway mark, he always makes us see the whole. Thus his writings always give the reader the fullest satisfaction. Too much wrong theology and wrong church practice has resulted from failure to go far enough in apprehending what the Scriptures say.

Also the manner of presenting the principle is full of beauty. The principle itself is restated thrice, and the two illustrations used are couched in the effective form of questions and answers. At times, when these features of style are discussed, too much it attributed to pagan Greek influences. At other times Jewish apocryphal and apocalyptic sources are postulated as the source of Paul's terms, expressions, and so-called "theories." All honor to historical interpretation which reads Paul through the eyes and the ears of his own day, but Paul is not a borrower but is original throughout.

Only as the Lord apportioned to each, as God has called each, thus let him walk. And thus I ordain in all the churches.

This is the first statement of the principle that underlies all the preceding injunctions and instructions in regard to marital relations although it, of course, also says much more. The sense of εἰ μή (*ausser*, B.-D. 448, 8) is "only" or "except," but it is not to be construed with the verb "let him walk," R. 1025. In ἐμέρισεν (the aorist, which is better attested than the perfect) there lies the noun μέρος, the special portion, here in the sense of task, assigned by the Lord to each Christian in his personal situation in life, whether single, married, or deserted by a spouse; and the aorist merely points to the divine act which made the apportionment. The Greek places the emphasis on "each" and on "the

Lord": *he* in his right as the Lord gives to *each* under his gracious jurisdiction a special assignment in keeping with the course of his providence.

The parallel clause adds the divine κλῆσις in which each Christian is found by virtue of the Lord's grace. The perfect tense κέκληκεν is in order because it implies the present standing of the Christian as one of "the called." Our portion in life is thus to be viewed in connection with our saving call, our providentially allotted task in union with our position as one of Christ's own.

Accepting both our portion in life and our saving call as coming from God and from the Lord, "thus," in this manner, "let each walk" or go on in his life. The portions allotted to different persons vary greatly, the call is one and the same, but both are from above. Let us rest content with that.

Thus Paul ordains in all the churches, namely as an apostle with the authority divinely entrusted to him. This statement is necessary in order that the Corinthians may understand that what Paul writes to them on the practical subjects mentioned above is not something that was newly devised for the Corinthians alone but something that was applied by Paul in all the churches. The principle is universal for Christians. The verb "I ordain" is strong because of the preposition and because of the middle voice.

18) Now the first illustration which is couched in simple questions and answers and thus has a dramatic touch but is taken from a feature of life that is entirely removed from questions regarding marriage. **Was someone called who has been circumcised? Let him not become uncircumcised! Has someone been called in uncircumcision? Let him not be circumcised!**

The two questions and the two answers are close parallels, but the formulation has a good deal of linguistic variation: an attributive participle, "who has been circumcised" matched by a phrase, "in uncircumcision"; first the indefinite "someone" before the verb, then the indefinite after the verb; first an aorist, "was called," then the perfect, "has been called"; first the aorist imperative, "let him not become uncircumcised," then the present imperative, "let him not be circumcised" (let him not engage in having that done).

The reasons formulated in the minds of those concerned for desiring the change are not indicated. If they were of a religious nature, we should expect some reference to this fact. But a Jewish Christian might have a variety of reasons that might prompt him to desire to hide his origin from Gentile Christians and from pagans. A Gentile Christian might likewise imagine it to be to his advantage to appear as if he, too, had originally belonged to the chosen nation. Paul tells both: Remain as you were originally called when you became Christians. In both cases he combines the person's "portion" with his saving "call," once with the aorist which simply marks the fact of his call, secondly with the perfect which adds the state that is due to this call. The removal of circumcision was often secured by a surgical operation which allowed the foreskin again to project, hence Paul's expression μὴ ἐπισπάσθω, *ne sibi attrahit, sc. praeputium*, which uses the Jewish technical term. Jews who followed the Greek mode of living and built a gymnasium at Jerusalem "hid the circumcision of their genitals, that even when they were naked they might appear to be Greeks," Josephus, *Ant.* 12, 5, 1.

19) As far as circumcision and uncircumcision are concerned, the matter is decidedly simple. **Circumcision is nothing, and uncircumcision is nothing; but the guarding of God's behests.** Being "nothing," why should a Christian treat them as being something? In spite of Paul's own words we are told that Paul

after all treats the matter, not as an adiaphoron, but as a matter of religious consequence, for how could he otherwise object to making the indicated changes? The answer is obvious: "Just because these are adiaphora and amount to nothing, make no change. Why dissemble your origin when you who were once a Jew or you who were once a pagan are now by God's grace and call a Christian?" Paul's principle thus applies even in these slight matters.

"But the guarding of God's behests" is something, i. e., something vital. Disregard the providential portion allotted to you in life and concentrate on this one vital point. "The guarding," with its article in the Greek, is definite: that which is your business in your Christian profession; while "God's behests," without the article, is qualitative: these being such, i. e., nothing less than behests of God.

The term τήρησις means more than "keeping," holding or observing; it means "guarding" like a guard who is posted to watch and to protect against violation or removal. Guarding includes more than our own personal observance of God's behests, it includes watchfulness on our part so that others, too, may not take away these behests or violate their requirements. The ἐντολαί are really "behests," not in a legal sense as "commandments" or laws like those of Moses, but in the gospel sense, the requirements of faith, love, etc., which were given to us as friends of Jesus, John 15:14, see also v. 10-12. These "behests" are beyond question our real concern as followers and friends of Christ.

20) Paul states the principle once more, but with variations by combining emphasis and explanation. **Each in the call wherewith he was called, in that let him remain.** The two parallel clauses found in v. 17 are now reduced to a unit: "the call wherewith he was called," or, in one word, "the call." The minor idea of portions in our earthly life is merged in the

major blessing of the call. We should not regard κλῆσις in the sense of a man's profession, position, or life work, for this is the standard apostolic term for the effective gospel call which makes a man a true Christian. This sense of the term is heavily emphasized when Paul heaps up the cognates, a noun, a relative, a verb, and in addition to all this a demonstrative: "in the call — by which (call) — he was called — in that (call)" let him remain, continue to remain as the present imperative implies. Three similar verb forms are found in the next two verses.

The dative ᾗ is an attraction to the case of its antecedent from the cognate accusative ἥν which belongs to the passive verb, R. 716. By combining into one the different portions meted out to us with the great thought of God's effective call of grace Paul obtains a variety of "calls." All are identical in the vital respect, namely as the one call of grace that has come to each of us; yet they all vary and differ in the minor points as one Christian has this portion, another that portion in life from God. Compare 1:26.

21) Here, for instance, is one such "call": **Wast thou called, thou a slave? Do not worry about it! But if thou art also able to become free, use it the rather.**

So this is one call with which a person may be called: a slave may be called by the grace of God and by that call, slave though he is, be made a Christian. There were not a few slaves in the Corinthian congregation. "A slave" is predicate to the subject of the verb. Paul tells such a slave: "Do not worry about it!" or: "Let it not trouble thee!" The Greek is idiomatic. As the reason for this injunction Paul will presently state the blessedness of this kind of a call. "Also," καί, adds the ability to become free to the having been called as a slave. Paul is thinking of an actual case in which a slave is able to secure his freedom, for the condition is one of reality. Then, Paul says, take the freedom and use it rather than the slavery. The comparative "rather" implies alternatives, one of which is to receive the preference, the one indicated by the context.

Some think that Paul has in mind the exactly opposite. Having written: "Stay in your position in life!" this must in the present case mean: Once a slave, always a slave! Yet in v. 15 by forsaking a believer an unbelieving spouse changes the status of the believer completely from a married estate to a single estate, for Paul writes: "he (she) has not been placed in bondage," οὐ δεδούλωται. Does Paul cancel this οὐ, "not," in the case of the slave and demand for him δεδούλωται: forever a δοῦλος, a slave? Incredible! All that Paul says is that while a Christian is a slave he is not to worry about his status; if it changes to one of freedom, so much the better.

Slaves were legally freed in various ways, sometimes even without their consent as by a master's death and testament. This automatically set the slave free. Slaves were also freed by a master's generosity or as gratitude in reward for notable service. One method was to deposit the slave's savings in the temple of some god, who was thus supposed "to buy the slave for freedom," Deissmann, *Light from the Ancient East*, 333. Thus we find many freedmen, former slaves set free, and among them men of great importance. Can we suppose that Paul's ethics demanded that such freedom should be rejected? Moreover, all Christianity shows no ethical principle which forbids a slave to accept or legitimately to secure his freedom.

The interpretation centers on the imperative χρῆσαι and the dative to be supplied. Some supply τῇ δουλείᾳ, but the apodosis: "use it the rather," follows from the protasis: "if thou art also able to become free." From this protasis the dative object of the main verb "use" is to be drawn. "Use it," we may say, means "use liberty," τῇ ἐλευθερίᾳ. Linguistically more exact would be, "use this that thou didst become free," ἐλεύθερος γενέσθαι, exactly as the protasis has it. Luther is right: *brauche des viel lieber*. The R. V. translates ἀλλά with the climacteric "yea," yet the simple adversative "but" is satisfactory. The argument that freedom was often not good for a slave is not cogent, for in more cases slavery was certainly not good for the slave. The view that Paul intends to forbid only the purchase and not the gift of freedom, is unsatisfactory. Finally, if the preference indicated by μᾶλλον were that for slavery instead of freedom, it would be so abnormal as to require the strongest kind of reason, but Paul's words do not supply such a reason.

It is quite true that Christianity is not revolutionary, and that it tolerated slavery until general Christian influence made it intolerable. But it is not true that the ethics of Christianity ever forbade a man to improve his social or his economic condition by rightful means. The one principle to be applied here is "the guarding of God's behests." Where Christianity is a new force, the danger may arise that men degrade it so that it becomes a disruptive ferment to upset law, order, customs, etc., in anomistic, even revolutionary ways. Against all such tendencies the Scriptures stand adamant.

22) Paul cannot add the parallel case of a free man becoming a slave, except abstractly, since no such case existed in Corinth. Paul deals with facts and not with hypothetic abstractions as pagan philosophers do. So he proceeds at once to illumine both the injunction to a slave not to be worried because he is a slave, whatever disabilities this entails, and the injunction to use freedom when a slave is able to attain it or is already a freedman. This is the force of γάρ. **For he who was called in the Lord as**

a slave is the Lord's freedman; likewise the free man who was called is a slave of Christ.

We may put it abstractly: slavery in Christ is true freedom; freedom in Christ is true slavery. The delicate shading in the two subjects is erased by our versions which translate both subjects alike. The first subject is "he who was called," to which there is added predicatively "as a slave," which hints that he was such only when he was called and hence may change his status later on. The second subject is "the free man," one who is free whether he was born free or set free, to which there is added predicatively "who was called," which hints at nothing more, for he will remain a free man. To be sure, both calls are "in the Lord," in connection with him and his grace. And "Lord" is the proper term, for through the call both this slave and this free man bow to Christ as Lord.

The two predicates are exactly alike save for the genitives. A slave who is called by that call becomes "a freedman of the Lord," ἀπελεύθερος, dismissed to freedom by the Lord, by a gracious act of manumission, to the spiritual freedom of a child of God. While "the free man," ὁ ἐλεύθερος, who has this status among men, by the call becomes "a slave of Christ," now belongs to Christ as his spiritual Master. In "freedman (ἀπελεύθερος) of the Lord" the genitive is that of the agent, he releases unto freedom; in "a slave of Christ" the genitive is that of possession, he belongs to Christ. Thus also Paul uses "Christ" in the latter connection. The cases of the two men are thus in a strange manner "likewise" or similar. In both we see slavery, and in both freedom. In the first bodily slavery and the spiritual freedom or release from sin, guilt, bondage of sin, death, and all evil; in the second, bodily freedom and the spiritual bondage which binds to heavenly obedience, service, good works, a slavery that is as sweet as any freedom that can be imagined. The terms "free man" and "slave" appear like opposites, and they are that in earthly and merely human relations, but in the blessed call of the Lord they flow together and become one, each expressing only one side of the same blessed relation.

23) This convergence is now focused in the unit idea of "price." Paul loves such unification in his concluding statements. They gather the extended elaboration into one point, where it is left to rest. **You were bought with a price; be not slaves of men.** The great fact of our purchase is stated in 6:20, in a different connection. "You were bought with a price" is one of those deep and mighty statements, written by Inspiration, which reach through the entire Christian life and down to its very bottom. Beautiful like a diamond when it is viewed in different gold settings, it is no less glorious when it is held up and looked at by itself.

You were bought with a price whether you are slaves or free men; in this respect you are all alike. The aorist "were bought" refers to the price of Christ's blood and death that was paid for us all on the cross. The gracious and efficacious "call" turns Christ's property over to him. Those who spurn the call in unbelief were also bought with the same price but rob Christ of his property, II Pet. 2:1. Because of its very brevity the genitive of price, τιμῆς, denotes a great price.

Having been bought thus, "be not slaves of men," not an aorist but a present imperative. "Become not" in the R. V. is misleading, for it sounds too much like an aorist. The aorist would denote entire cessation of the relation to Christ, total reversion to the slavery of men. The present denotes that Christians may revert to the old bondage by various foolish thoughts and actions. Instead of rejoicing in full freedom these Christians would still continue to carry some of the fetters.

They would be "slaves of men" by letting the worldly ideas of men still rule them in one or in the other respect, in the way in which they regard human slavery and human freedom, circumcision and uncircumcision, marriage, the single state, or any other part of the Christian life as we must live it in this imperfect world.

24) In conclusion Paul once more and for the third time restates the ethical thesis which he has elaborated in detail. **Let each wherein he was called, brethren, therein remain with God.** Let that principle govern as a principle of Christ and of the new life, as one of the precious gospel behests we are to guard, not as an iron-bound law. From the second person plural used in v. 23 Paul turns to the third person singular and touches "each" personally. He inserts the affectionate address "brethren," for the great apostle himself is one of this blessed company whom Christ owns. As "brethren" the Corinthians will gladly heed what their "brother" tells them.

Yet in every restatement which Paul makes we may look for a new touch. In regard to our call v. 24 is only an abbreviation of v. 20, but the final phrase is new: let him remain "with God." The Greek conceives this as being "beside God," παρά with the dative, resting and remaining at God's side in peace and contentment. This our "call" does for us, namely places us in such a delightful position beside God. Called to his side, safe and happy there, let us disregard and never lay undue stress on our condition, station, or outward form of life. Let us not keep looking downward to these things that may be more or less hard, disagreeable, and subject to change although they need not be changed; let us look upward to God, for our one obligation is to remain (durative present imperative μενέτω) "with God."

III. *Regarding Maidens, 25-38*

When he answers the questions regarding maidens Paul takes a comprehensive view, hence we have the preliminary elaborations in v. 25-35 and then the brief answer in v. 36-38.

In order to understand this section of Paul's letter we should have regard to the intimations that Paul's view of the unmarried state had lost favor among the Corinthians after Paul's departure from their midst. His teaching was being criticized in various ways. One phase of the information desired from him is further instruction in regard to maidens. Had the Lord, perhaps, left some word in regard to them? We see why Paul is obliged to answer at some length and also why he fortifies his answer in different directions. First, against the assumption that the unmarried state is inferior to the married state and that it involves a certain loss. Some of those living in Corinth evidently think so. Secondly, against a false asceticism which considers the sex features of marriage wrong and contends especially that unions with unbelievers should not be allowed. Thirdly, a libertinistic tendency over against which as well as over against other tendencies the binding force of marriage must be emphasized. Finally also a narrow legalism that is ready to inflict a yoke on the conscience in regard to the natural relations of life.

It is not an easy task for Paul to straighten out this snarl of opinions, tendencies, and cross tendencies. None of the questions that arose in Corinth regarding these subjects was simple, and each plays into the other. For this reason Paul puts up barriers, now on this, now on that side, and then states the true principle which is the key to the solution of the problem. After this he illumines that principle by introducing illustrations from other sources. One way in which to learn to appreciate the reply which Paul gave is to face this complicated situation in Corinth yourself and to write out what *you* think ought to be the reply and then to compare it with Paul's reply. There is no need to say more.

The Preliminary Considerations, 25-35. — 25) Here we meet the second περί phrase (see v. 1) by which Paul takes up a point in the letter sent him by the Corinthians. The fact that they should ask whether the Lord himself had, perhaps, left any directions in regard to Christian maidens does not necessarily imply a meager knowledge on the part of the Corinthians regarding what Jesus had taught. It may just as well imply that in Corinth certain persons insisted on some "command" that came directly from the Lord himself and then claimed that there was none and so drew false conclusions from that fact.

Now Paul is far removed from resorting to evasion or to equivocation. When the Lord settles a question, Paul says so, v. 10, 11; when the Lord has no pronouncement, Paul again says so, v. 12 and our present verse. But parallel to the personally spoken *logia* of the Lord is the apostolic authority bestowed by the Lord, and although this was mediated through the apostles it is just as binding as the Lord's own *logia*. This authority Paul asserts in v. 12, compare Luke 10:16. In addition, questions may and do arise to which neither a *logion* of the Lord nor an authoritative dictum of an apostle furnish a direct answer. For the direct answer depends on the accompanying circumstances, and thus according to the circumstances, the answer may in one case be "yea," in another may be "nay." Our only guide is the general gospel principle that applies to the individual case. This is true regarding the παρθένοι.

Who are the παρθένοι? Various opinions are expressed. One such idea is that they are bachelors and maidens who have voluntarily vowed to remain celibate. They are even called *Amtsjungfrauen,* virgins who were officially recognized as such by the congregation, we might call them monks and nuns who have not as yet withdrawn to monasteries. Another idea advanced is that these were couples, bachelors and maidens who were betrothed to each other, but not in order eventually to marry, but rather always to remain celibate. It has even been claimed that they lived together so that the maiden might have male protection, and the bachelor might enjoy the company and the housekeeping of the maiden.

All of these and similar ideas are read into the text without the shadow of support. They are moral monstrosities that are impossible in the church except as morbid excrescencies. Not until the third century do we hear of *sorores,* devoted virgins, who lived together with ascetics and clerics and even shared their beds in order to demonstrate their strength of will and their ability to retain chastity, a practice which, of course, only too often ended in the very reverse. The church strongly opposed these unions at the time, and they disappeared. Later on they were revived when the socalled Joseph marriages, or angel marriages of Roman Catholicism, originated. Meusel, *Kirchliches Handlexikon,* article *Subintroductae.* Yet no one ever thought of appealing to this paragraph of Paul's letter in justification of all these morbid practices and during the controversies they enkindled. Nowhere has Paul the least hint that vows were taken, and nowhere is there a trace of official recognition.

The Greek term παρθένος signifies maiden or virgin, and Paul uses the feminine article and thereby excludes all reference to a bachelor. This term is only rarely used to designate an unmarried man; in the New Testament it is found in Rev. 14:4 and in a sense which the context makes plain. While these "maidens" thus belong to the general class of the unmarried already considered by Paul in v. 8, 9, they, nevertheless, constitute a distinct class, and one that, as we shall see, required an extensive and particular treatment.

Now concerning the maidens I have not a command of the Lord, but I give my judgment as one who has had mercy conferred upon him by the Lord so that I am trustworthy.

Paul has no command which was left by the Lord concerning Christian maidens that touches the question as to whether their fathers should or should not give them in marriage. Paul also has no divine revelation from Christ which he can with apostolic authority present as such. The latter he does not say with so many words but implies when he offers only his "judgment." This is not a mere personal opinion that is due to personal likes or dislikes or anything else that produces only personal preferences; it is the weighty "judgment" (γνώμη) and advice of one who is in every way qualified to render it. The expression: "I give (render) my judgment," does not mean to offer a resolution which the congregation at Corinth is to vote upon, for such a sense would require a different verb, C.-K. 249.

Paul does not say that he offers this judgment of his as an apostle, for he would thereby appeal only to his authority. He re-enforces his judgment as being one that is worthy of acceptance on the part of the Corinthians by mentioning his apostolic qualification for rendering such a judgment "as one who has had mercy conferred upon him by the Lord so that I am trustworthy." "As" has the causal idea "because," etc., R. 1128, 1140. The perfect participle implies that the mercy that was once conferred upon Paul is still his. This is the mercy that chose him, a pitiful persecutor of the church, and made him one of the Lord's apostles.

Paul's humility is evidenced by this description of himself. Those Corinthians who demanded no less than a command from the Lord himself perhaps did so in an arrogant tone; Paul meets them with a tone of humbleness. The emphasis is, however, on the result of this divine mercy: "so that I am trustworthy," 4:2. The infinitive εἶναι is not intended to indicate purpose merely but expresses an actual fact.

While Paul is humble when he recalls the mercy he received from the Lord, humble even before the Corinthians, he yet asserts his reliability and his trustworthiness, for this the Lord wrought in him by his mercy. The term πιστός cannot mean merely "a believer" like others, including the Corinthians themselves, for believers often make mistakes. Paul offers his judgment to the Corinthians as an apostle of whom by his mercy the Lord made a trustworthy steward who should administer the affairs of his church. As such he now speaks and expects the Corinthians to receive his judgment accordingly.

26) Paul begins to state his judgment. **I hold, therefore, that this is excellent because of the present distress—that it is excellent for a person so to be.** "I suppose" in the A. V. is too weak; "I think" in the R. V. is not strong enough. When one is rendering a judgment, νομίζω means: "I hold" or "I consider." The construction is merely pleonastic; the emphatic τοῦτο is resumed and expanded by the epexegetical ὅτι clause, R. 1205, thus doubling καλόν and emphasizing this significant term: excellent — quite excellent.

First of all, then, Paul applies to the maidens the principle already stated in v. 8 as being valid for all the unmarried. Do some individuals in Corinth perhaps think that it is bad for a girl not to be married? No; it is quite excellent for her, too, to be as she is. Paul uses ἄνθρωπος much as we use "person": it is excellent for any person to remain single, it is no less, then, for a maiden. The two verbs ὑπάρχειν and εἶναι are used only to obtain variation although the former is somewhat stronger; both mean "to be."

And now Paul explains why he regards this to be excellent, namely "because of the present distress." There is no need to let the participle mean only the "impending" distress, for the perfect of this verb is always used in the durative present sense. By this "distress" Paul refers to the painful and terrible experience which the confession of Christ may at any time bring upon a believer. Paul had many such experiences, and the Corinthians may well recall what the hostile Jews tried to do to Paul in the very city of Corinth. The days of the extensive pagan persecutions were drawing nigh. A girl that married and reared a family might thus be doubly and trebly overwhelmed, for her beloved husband might become involved, or she with him — and what about the children? History records many agonizing cases. Paul thus very properly writes that, in the face of the situation prevailing at that time, "a person" may well prefer to remain alone, untrammeled by tender family ties. No wife and no children needed to rend their hearts when Paul went on his journeys and often faced death itself.

27) But Paul must be on his guard against all possible misunderstanding. If it is better, as he says, for a man to remain alone, some individuals in Corinth may stress this to the extreme and seek release from existing marriages. **Art thou bound to a wife? Do not seek release. Art thou released from a wife? Do not seek a wife.**

The two perfect tenses employed in the two questions, literally: "hast thou been bound" and "hast thou been released," refer to present conditions as the result of a past act. Didst thou marry at one time, and art thou thus married now? Wast thou in some way released from the marriage tie at some past time, and art thou still thus released? The questions are direct, personal, and thus stronger than mere conditional clauses would be. Paul addresses men, for he speaks about being bound to a wife or being released from a wife. Yet this is true in the case of women as well as in the case of men. In fact, both the questions and the answers include the women as well as the men, nor could the men possibly be treated as exceptions.

The moment Paul says with reference to unmarried girls that in his judgment it is excellent for them to remain unmarried because the present distress makes it excellent for any person to be single, he must face the questions: "How, then, about people who are already married? Ought not their marriage to be dissolved?" The answer to these questions is negative and must be so for the reason stated previously in v. 10: the Lord forbids such dissolution. Whatever distress may come, married people must bear it as best they can. The term λύσις is general: any form of "release" that would "loose" or dissolve the existing marriage.

But if a person is not as yet married, Paul's advice applies not to seek marriage because of the present distress. This applies to the whole category of the unmarried, to maidens, of course, for Paul has them in mind especially, but also to unmarried men, to widowers, and to widows. Being bound to a wife and its opposite being released from a wife refer to actual marriage, to its presence or to its absence as the case may be. The effort in these expressions to find the particular "betrothals" which the church of a later age had to oppose is a misunderstanding of Paul's simple words.

28) But more must be said, decidedly more. Paul's judgment and his advice in regard to remaining unmarried "because of the present distress" lie altogether in the domain of expediency and dare not

be transferred to the domain of moral right or wrong. Paul is stating what is *best* and most expedient under given circumstances and not what is *right* or what is *sin* under these circumstances. Therefore he is compelled to add: **Nevertheless, even if thou shalt marry thou didst not sin; and if the maiden shall marry she did not sin. Yet such shall have tribulation for the flesh, and I am sparing you.**

"If thou shalt marry" is addressed to a man although it, of course, involves also some unmarried woman to whom he is to be married. Because, however, the question at issue is one concerning unmarried girls, Paul singles out such an individual in particular: "and if the maiden shall marry." He twice uses the condition that expresses expectancy. For reasons already stated in v. 9 marriages of all types will necessarily take place, and Paul himself writes: "Let them marry!" In the first protasis some texts have γήμῃς, others γαμήσῃς, which is only a later form of the aorist. The aorist is used in both conditional clauses because the rite is a single act, but the subjunctive refers to the future: if thou "shalt marry"; if she "shall marry." Yet both of the apodoses have aorist indicatives which refer to the past: "thou didst not sin," "she did not sin." This is matter of viewpoint: a future act is considered from the standpoint of its completion and is then spoken of as if it were already done, R. 1020, 1022.

Viewing these coming marriages in this manner, Paul declares in regard to all of them, including in particular that of a maiden: there was no sin in forming these marriages. The whole matter of marrying in spite of the present distress or of not marrying because of the present distress has nothing to do with committing or with avoiding sin. No one must entertain such an idea or draw conclusions from such an idea. Paul seems to fear something of the sort because the Corinthians perhaps wanted to know whether the Lord had left a command regarding the marrying of maidens. Let it be understood then, Paul says, that it is no more a sin for a maiden to marry than for any other person.

But, of course, those who do marry during these evil times must expect tribulation. "Such shall have tribulation for the flesh" — Paul states this as a fact and refers not merely to the tribulation that is ordinarily incident to the married state, regarding which the marriage liturgy remarks: "Days of adversity will also come"; but "tribulation" (literally "pressure") that is due to wicked agitation against the gospel and is increased because of tender ties. The dative "for the flesh" depends on "tribulation" because the Greek term is derived from a verb that governs the dative, R. 526. "Flesh" refers only to our human nature as such and thus includes both mind and body. When it comes, this infliction will be hard to bear. Paul knows it: "I for my part (emphatic) am sparing you," namely by counselling you as I do, by trying to make your life easier for you and not harder. Paul reveals his ethical motive here.

29) Back of all these considerations regarding the question of marriage and non-marriage there lies the attitude of the true Christian toward all the transient temporalities of this earthly life. What Paul says regarding all these questions relating to marriage will be rightly apprehended only when we, too, know what this Christian attitude ought to be, and when we learn to share it with Paul. **But this I say, brethren, the period has been shortened. Henceforth let even those that have wives be as not having them, and those that weep as not weeping, and those that rejoice as not rejoicing, and those that buy as not possessing, and those that use the world as not over-using it; for the form of this world is passing away.**

The preamble: "But this I say, brethren," impresses the following statements upon the hearts and the minds of Paul's Corinthian readers. Unless they understand these well they will not penetrate into the inwardness of Paul's advice and instruction regarding marriage.

First he can announce a divine grace, viz., "the period has been shortened," καιρός, this "season" or "period" of the world age which precedes the final coming of Christ. Jesus himself says: "And except those days had been shortened, no flesh would have been saved; but for the elects' sake those days shall be shortened," Matt. 24:22. The verb συνστέλλω means "to draw together" and thus to shrink or to shorten. God graciously compressed the season that is marked by tribulation so that it may not become so extended that his saints cannot bear it.

Here we again meet the thesis that Paul was entirely certain that the Parousia would occur during his lifetime, and that the shortening of which he speaks implies a reduction to a few years at the longest. The fact is quite otherwise. Even as we now, so Paul at his time had to be ready for the Lord's return at any time. We, therefore, see him reckoning with the imminence and with the delay of Christ's return and speaking of it now in one, now in the other way. For the hour (period) and the day (date) were not revealed to him as they are not revealed to us. He knew what we also know, namely that the Lord's return shall be unexpected, and no more.

The sentence introduced by ἵνα is not a purpose clause. Nor is this ἵνα subfinal, it is an elliptical substitute for the imperative that expresses what is commanded without the use of a verb that denotes a command, B.-D. 387, 3; R. 994: "Henceforth let even those that have wives be," etc. We may consider τὸ λοιπόν an adverbial accusative or a nominative absolute, R. 487, but it certainly belongs to the ἵνα sentence and is placed before ἵνα only for the sake of emphasis: "as for the rest," or "henceforth." The first καί = "even" and singles out those who have wives while the other καί are ordinary connectives.

Now there follow five lovely exemplifications of the Christian's freedom from this transient world. The life and the heart are in the world, the hands and the heart do their part in the world, yet they are not brought into captivity by the world, 6:12. The number five is the half of ten and thus permits us to add other illustrations. These exemplifications are by no means a heterogeneous collection; all of them fit into the connection beautifully; they are like the examples cited in v. 18 and 20. First, "those that have wives," which omits the mention of the opposite class since they are naturally exempted from this command — having no wives, they will live as having none.

30) Then "those that weep," for there will be tears in the married state, perhaps bitter tears if persecution lifts its hand. Paul can happily add: "those that rejoice," for the picture is not entirely a dark one, nor is Paul a pessimist who paints only in somber colors — God will provide also joys and rejoicings. Then "those that buy," for Christians need food, shelter, and clothing, and families require many things for their households. Paul is no theorist; all the practical features of life are near his thinking.

31) Finally, "those that use the world" (but Paul does not write "this world," worldly pleasures and vices) since Christians are placed into the midst of the world and are not to escape from the world, 5:10. The last four groups include all Christians although the activities mentioned apply in their own way to those who are married. The verb χράομαι is here followed by the accusative instead of the usual dative, "in response to the general accusative tendency," R. 476. And καταχράομαι does not mean "not to use" nor "to misuse"

or "to abuse" as our versions translate, for such translations mar the symmetry of the entire series, but "to overuse," to use to excess.

One does not understand how Paul's beautiful picture of the true Christian in the midst of the world can create the impression that Paul "is here trying to salve his conscience" for having been too strict when he dissuaded Christians from entering marriage, and that he is practically retracting a large part of what he said.

Paul's ethics have also been questioned. It has been said that he contradicts what he says elsewhere, and that he does not at all offer a Christian ideal for today but hampers all progress, crushes out all feeling, turns Christians into callous ascetics, etc. Luther is held up as a man who progressed far beyond Paul in love to wife, children, etc. Paul, indeed, orders husbands to love their wives, Eph. 5:25; and bids us weep with those that weep, Rom. 12:15. Yet in the present famous passage he mars none of these fine ethical precepts. Only when Paul's negatives are sundered from their corresponding positives and thus overstrained can any man read a coldness, callousness, and unethical indifference into them and charge Paul with overstatement.

What does Paul really say? Marriage, tears, joys, purchases, the whole world of earthly things — we Christians may have all of them, use all of them, experience all of them — how? for what they are, as belonging to the σχῆμα or form of this present world. What Paul says is true: as soon as we go beyond this limit and permit any or all of these to interfere with our spiritual life and our relation to the life to come, a false ἐξουσία (6:12b) or power reaches into our lives and begins to ruin them. Compare Luke 12:18-20.

As for Luther, he actually is the best example of a man who followed Paul's program, for he used everything that Paul mentions yet did so that all things were made subservient to true and higher ends. For this reason he even married rather than remain single. As far as progress in our modern age is concerned, so much of it is used — as Paul, to be sure, would not dream of using it — for the self-glorification of men; not to glorify the Lord but to deny him his glory.

"For the form of this world is passing away." That is the key (γάρ, explanation or reason); it is also a commentary on the shortening of the time, v. 29. It "is passing away," παράγει, constantly slipping by, even at this moment — nothing about it is stable. Paul does not say "the world" is passing away; or even "this world"; he specifies more closely: "the form of this world," its σχῆμα or fashion. The entire expression, in particular the verb παράγει, seems to be borrowed from the ancient theatrical language: the role of the old σχῆμα is being played out, and a new σχῆμα is about to step onto the boards.

We at once see that marriage, weeping, etc., are only a part of this form and fashion of the world which is ever moving on and away, is transient, for a day, "life's little day." Why try to cling to them, to make of them more than they are, to value them above their real worth? The decisive passage of Scripture regarding the question as to whether this present world will be annihilated or will be transformed is Rom. 8:19-23, which declares for the latter. Not the world as such but its form is passing away and will at last pass away completely.

32) After having shown what this present time or season requires of all of us, in particular of those who have wives, Paul turns to what our own spiritual interest should be. **Now I desire that you be free from cares** — "you," all of you Corinthians. Verses 32-35 pivot on the term μεριμνᾶν, "to have care or cares" in the sense of devoting special attention and effort to

some person or some thing. Paul's desire is that the Corinthians may be ἀμέριμνοι, free from cares; and in a moment we shall see that he means free from cares of a certain kind, such as interfere with the supreme purpose to which we should all devote ourselves. Under the caption of cares Paul sketches the two classes, the unmarried and the married, and in this setting presents a part of his judgment in regard to maidens.

33) **The unmarried man has cares about the things of the Lord, how he may please the Lord; but the married man has cares about the things of the world, how he may please his wife, and he is divided. But the unmarried woman and the maiden has cares about the things of the Lord, to be holy both in the body and in the spirit; while the married woman has cares about the things of this world, how she may please her husband.**

In v. 33, 34 we meet an important textual question which must be decided before an interpretation can be begun. The Greek text of Westcott and Hort is used here. This is not the same as the text that is used for the translation given in the margin of the R. V., the Greek for which is found in A. Souter, note (n).

First the unmarried man; then the married man. Next the unmarried woman and the maiden; then the married woman. What about the cares that devolve upon each? The unmarried man has only one set of real cares, namely those "about the things of the Lord," which is explained by the indirect question: "how he may please the Lord," the aorist ἀρέσῃ, succeed in actually pleasing him. In all his thinking and his doing he has really only the Lord to consider and no other person.

Quite otherwise is the case of the married man, the one who entered marriage as the substantivized aorist participle describes him. He has cares about the things of the world that are necessary for his family life; and again the indirect question helps to make the matter clear: "how he may please his wife," succeed in pleasing her, for he and she are one flesh. In addition to the question how he may succeed in pleasing the Lord, for him the second question arises (which will not be denied its answer) how he may at the same time please her. Hence "he is divided" in the matter of cares, some call him in one direction, some in the other direction. The perfect tense indicates that he was hitherto so divided and is so now. What being thus divided means we see from the case of Martha: "Thou art anxious (literally, divided) and troubled about many things," trying to do a number of things at the same time, Luke 10:41.

34) When he is speaking about the women Paul combines the unmarried woman (γυνή may be either "woman" or "wife" as the context requires) and the maiden. Like the unmarried man, each of these has only one set of cares. Paul uses a singular verb with the double subjects, which is quite usual when each subject is considered by itself. Instead of repeating the indirect question which he used in connection with the men Paul varies his style by using a subfinal ἵνα clause that is appositional to "the things of the Lord." The sole care of each of these women is "to be holy both in the body and in the spirit." We now see what pleasing the Lord means: his pleasure is that we be holy in our entire person. This is, of course, holiness in the Scriptural and not in the monkish sense of the term. Both body and spirit are named because this holiness affects both sides of our nature, the material as well as the immaterial. Our souls and our bodily members are holy when we separate them from sin and devote them wholly unto the Lord, do his will and his alone.

In regard to the married woman, the one who entered marriage (again the substantivized aorist participle), her case is exactly like that of the married man: she has her set of cares "about the things of the world" in her family life, "how she may please her husband." Paul does not need to add "and she is divided," for his readers can supply this without effort.

Paul describes a condition which our daily experience makes evident to us all. One great difference between the unmarried and the married state is brought to our attention: the former is dominated by only one set of cares, the other by two. The present tenses of all the verbs state so many facts. We blur the point which Paul makes when we argue that single persons also have earthly cares; or when we try to compare individual cases: on the one hand, a childless couple with a few cares, on the other, a widower or a widow with a cluster of little ones and many distressing cares. The same is true in regard to pleasing the Lord and living holy in body and in spirit.

We need not inform Paul regarding young widows who incline to wax wanton, I Tim.. 5:11; and he himself immortalized that lovely couple Aquila and Priscilla, with whom he made his home in Corinth and perhaps in Ephesus. Paul does not intend to lose himself in a labyrinth of cases. As Christians we all have one supreme set of cares, how to please the Lord. Whoever enters upon marriage assumes another great set of cares, how to please the wife or the husband. This simple fact is true to this very day. The implication is not that these two sets of cares may or will clash. They are two, that is enough. They are distinct, and thus they divide. If Paul had sinful things in mind he would have written "the things of *this* world."

35) Paul now tells the Corinthians why he writes these things. **Now this I say for the advantage of our own selves, not in order to cast a noose upon you, on the contrary, as an aid to seemliness and devotion to the Lord without distraction.**

The entire question is not one of sinning or of avoiding sin but of spiritual advantage. The adjective σύμφορον is substantivized by the addition of the article (τὸ συμφέρον would be the neuter participle used as a noun, R. 1109) and is here construed with the second person plural reflexive: "for the advantage of your own selves," R. 687, 689. Paul's words are dictated solely by a concern for the spiritual interest of the Corinthians, to further them in the Christian life as much as possible.

This point is amplified by a negative and by a positive addition. Paul's purpose (ἵνα) is not to cast a noose upon the Corinthians; he is not like a hunter who ropes a wild animal in order to render it helpless. Paul is not throwing a noose of legal commandments about the necks of the Corinthians in order to force their consciences into helpless surrender. In fact, he is not using the law at all but the very opposite, the liberty of the gospel which enables us always freely to choose what most enhances our spiritual advantage.

"On the contrary," the strong adversative ἀλλά; Paul aims at something that is totally different. The preposition πρός denotes purpose like ἵνα and repeats the same preposition found in the main clause: "I say this *for* the advantage of our own selves . . . *for* the seemliness and devotion" which you owe to the Lord. For the sake of smoothness we translate this second πρός "as an aid to" seemliness, etc. Paul uses two substantivized adjectives (instead of abstract nouns) in order to express his positive purpose and thus matches the substantivized adjective that was used in the first phrase with πρός. First the minor purpose: "as an aid to seemliness," to propriety as far as the outer conduct that is visible to the eyes of men is concerned. The word does not mean "chastity" as such but indicates the proper decorum in word and in deed which is expected of all whether they are married or unmarried.

Each has his cares and must attend to them in the way that is proper to a true Christian.

But this minor purpose is combined with the major purpose so that the two form a unit, for the two adjectives have but one Greek article. "Seemliness and devotion" naturally go together in the case of a Christian; both spring from one inner source. The adjective εὐπάρεδρον is interesting: εὐ = well; παρά = beside; ἕδρα (ἕζομαι) = seat or sitting: sitting well beside a task, faithful attendance upon a person or a thing, devotion to. Paul's chief purpose is to promote among the Corinthians the fullest devotion to the Lord on the part of each individual, and this explains what Paul means by cares for the things of the Lord, how to please him.

The thought is enhanced by the addition of the adverb ἀπερισπάστως, "undistractedly," "without distraction," which recalls Martha's action: περιεσπᾶτο, she was distracted about much serving of food and of drink; for this she received the Lord's rebuke, Luke 10:40. Paul thus wants us to be like Mary who chose the good part, the one thing needful, which the Lord would not allow Martha to take from her, namely complete devotion to the Lord and his Word. Here, too, we see what Paul means by being "divided" in our cares. Martha was thus divided (μεριμνᾷς, Luke 10:41), anxious about many things, mere temporalities, and was yet trying to please the Lord. She failed because she was thus divided. The same danger confronts us, too, when the things of the world, which we think we must attend to, draw us in one direction, and the things of the Lord draw us in the other direction. Mary clung to the one thing needful, to that with a single mind, and she succeeded.

The Answer in regard to Maidens, 36-38.

36) Paul has taken care of all the different angles which the question raised by the Corinthians may present to them. Now he comes to the direct answer

itself. When we are considering this answer we must remember the control which a father had over the marriage of his daughter in ancient times, remnants of which exist today in the custom that the aspiring son-in-law asks the father for the hand of his daughter, and that at the wedding the father gives the daughter away. **Now if one holds that he is acting unseemly toward his maiden daughter in case she be past the flower of her age, and if it ought to be this way, let him proceed to do what he is minded; he does not sin; let them marry.**

This is a case when the father ought to give his daughter in marriage, or a guardian his ward. The verb νομίζει is used as it was in v. 26: if he "holds" or has the conviction. Paul thinks of an actual case, hence he writes the condition of reality. This is a case in which the father comes to the conclusion that he is acting toward his daughter in an unseemly way, ἀσχημονεῖν (the opposite of τὸ εὔσχημον "seemliness" in v. 35). The unseemliness lies, not in the fact that he is compelling his daughter to become an old maid, but in the fact that his refusal to consent to have his daughter married would subject her to the danger of seduction.

Hence we have the clause: "if she be past the flower of her age," ὑπέρακμος, beyond the ἀκμή, peak, bloom, zenith, etc.; here the word refers to full sexual maturity. Before she reached this stage the father did not need to harbor misgivings. Now, however, if he continues to deny her a proper marriage he himself feels that he is not acting properly in regard to her.

Therefore Paul adds: "and if it ought to be this way." First the father's own subjective conviction, secondly the objective condition of his daughter, her sexual maturity euphemistically expressed; we may say: "if it cannot be otherwise" than that she ought to marry. This clause introduced by καί depends on εἰ as the indicative ὀφείλει shows and not on ἐάν, which would require the subjunctive. The adverb οὕτως belongs to ὀφείλει γίνεσθαι, which should be read together as one concept, and ὀφείλει is impersonal: "it ought to be thus" as her sexual maturity indicates. The girl desires to marry, in fact, she ought to marry, and her father realizes that he would be acting improperly by forbidding her to marry.

Then "let him proceed to do what he is minded," have her married. The translation "what he pleases" is indefinite and misleading as though Paul means that he may still refuse consent to her marriage. The present middle imperative ποιείτω = "let him proceed to do in his own interest" what he is minded. "He does not sin," for the whole question concerning maidens does not turn on sin or no sin. "Let them marry," namely the young people concerned, the subject of the plural verb is derived from the context, R. 1204. Even if Paul had written the singular "let her marry," a second person would be involved.

37) The case may, however, be quite the opposite (δέ). **But he who stands steadfast in his heart, subject to no necessity, but has power regarding his own will and has made this his decision in his own heart, to keep his own maiden daughter, he shall do excellently.** Four factors determine this father's course, and Paul formulates them according to their nature and their weight. The first is the father's own firm resolution: he does not want his daughter to marry because of the consideration which Paul has presented. The implication is that, in spite of all that Paul has said about the preference for the unmarried state at this time, some other father might resolve to have his daughter marry or might leave the matter entirely to her. The first stand of this father, however, to keep the daughter at home is one which he makes "in his heart," of his own accord, following Paul's

advice. Ἔστηκεν (this perfect is always used with the force of a present) ἑδραῖος = "stands steadfast."

Two closely related points follow, the first is expressed by a participle: "subject to no necessity," literally, "having no necessity" such as the other father faces. This daughter has no especial sexual urge to marry, and her father has no special obligation toward her due to this circumstance. Paul could now continue with another participle but reverts to the relative ὅς and uses a finite verb: "but (who) has power regarding his own will," i. e., is able to decide the matter entirely according to his own will. This construction makes parallel the first and the third factor, the father's firm stand and the freedom to follow his own will. The latter shows that the father is not arbitrary or simply stubborn. Yet the second and the third factors are also linked together in both form (ἔχων and ἔχει) and substance, for the freedom of the father in regard to his own will is due to the absence of necessity on the daughter's side which might compel him. The other father may also desire to have his daughter remain single but is obligated to decide differently.

Paul is not yet through but adds the fourth factor, the father's final decision: "and (who) has made this his decision in his own heart," namely, "to guard his own maiden daughter." We might think that the first factor is sufficient, the father's firm stand in his own heart, at least with the addition of the other two factors, freedom from necessity and thus unhampered ability to decide. But Paul requires one additional thing, the rendering of a formal decision, κέκρικεν, the perfect tense to indicate a decision that, once rendered, stands. All of this creates the impression that Paul considers the matter as solemn and serious, to be finally settled only when the necessary requirements are properly met. The demonstrative "this" is followed by the appositional infinitive: "this . . . to keep his own maiden daughter," i. e., to take care of her in his own home as a maiden all her days.

The objection that the daughter's will is left entirely out of consideration is not in accord with the fact. For in each case the father considers the physical make-up of his daughter, and that means her desires and wishes as well. Thus the fact is that what eventually influences the father to decide one way or another is not simply his own will but the daughter under his care.

Paul commends the second father's ultimate decision: "he shall do excellently," καλῶς, which recalls καλόν in v. 1, 8, 26; "excellently," not in a superior moral way, but most advantageously for the Christian profession during most trying times. The future tense intimates that the outcome will prove the fact. Some texts have the present tense "he does excellently."

38) Paul repeats this more extensive reply to the question of the Corinthians in briefer form. **So then, both he who gives his own maiden daughter in marriage does excellently, and he who does not give her in marriage shall do more excellently.**

The comparison pivots on the two adverbs "excellently" and "more excellently," both are to be considered in the light of the preceding elucidation. Each course has its own advantage, yet the second exceeds the first. The excellence is one of degree only. The circumstances decide. But not according to law or legalistic points but only according to the gospel and true gospel principles and considerations.

The interpretation herewith presented stood unchallenged for centuries until during recent years a few modern interpreters produced an innovation. Compare the remarks on v. 25. Aside from the moral impossibilities advocated by this new interpretation as well as the unchallenged historical data which make this interpretation unsatisfactory, Paul's language does

330   *Interpretation of First Corinthians*

not yield the sense found in it. The father mentioned in v. 36 and 37 is ignored, and the spiritual bridegroom takes his place, who is "betrothed" to the maiden in question (although Paul knows nothing of such "betrothals"), namely spiritually with a vow on the part of both that they will remain celibate (although Paul knows nothing about these vows). In v. 36 this bridegroom finds that he cannot carry out his vow because of his own sexual urge, and rather than to have him bring disgrace upon his bride Paul is thought to say that the couple should break their vows and marry. Paul then says this bridegroom "does not sin." And it seems to escape the notice of these modern interpreters that the ancient "betrothals" were in reality marriages. The other bridegroom has better sexual control over himself (nothing is said about his bride), is able to keep his vow, and so guards his bride throughout life and keeps her a virgin.

Do they live together? Then what about the "seemliness" Paul seeks to further in v. 35? Will people say nothing about a couple of this kind that lives together? Can we imagine that a man like Paul has nothing to say to these spiritual bridegrooms and their brides except that the one does "excellently" and the other "more excellently"? But in v. 38 the participle of γαμίζειν is used twice. This verb invariably means "to give in marriage" and never "to marry." Yet this new theory holds that the verb has this latter meaning, for the bridegroom marries, he does not give in marriage, which is the action of the father. Since all research fails to find the meaning this theory should have for its support, the true meaning is accepted with this result: the spiritual bridegroom gives his bride in marriage to another man in order to save his own celibacy! We are, of course, to believe that he has such a right, that the bride consents, and that the other man stands waiting, and that Paul approves such conduct with the verdict: "Excellent!" More may be said, but let this suffice.

Appendix on Remarriage, 39, 40. — 39) To complete the subject, so many aspects of which Paul has covered, he adds a word on widows and their remarriage. **A wife is bound for as long a time as her husband lives; but if her husband be fallen asleep, she is free to be married to whomsoever she desires, only in the Lord.**

The perfect δέδεται (probably gnomic, R. 897) means that, once bound by the marriage tie, a Christian wife remains thus bound as long as her husband lives, which is self-evident from v. 10. Desertions on the part of unbelieving husbands have been treated in v. 15. But a Christian husband may die, "be fallen asleep," the passive is used in the middle sense, an aorist expresses the single act of dying, the condition is one of expectancy, ἐάν with the subjunctive. Then the widow is free to be married again. Paul states this in so many words. The antecedent of ᾧ would also be in the dative, R. 720, yet see also 716. Paul mentions widows in v. 8 but does not there say that they may marry again. He now weaves in this loose thread, for he never likes to let one of them hang. Widows may certainly marry again.

"Only in the Lord" would be beyond question if the Christian widow be married to a Christian husband. Paul seems to have that in mind in this "judgment" (v. 25) which he is delivering to the Corinthians. Yet many take "in the Lord" in a wider sense, namely, "in a Christian way" or "in the fear of the Lord," asking his blessing. For there are cases in which a marriage with a non-Christian may be justified.

40) **Yet more blessed she if she remain as she is** (οὕτως, "thus"), **according to my own judgment. And I, too, for my part think I have God's Spirit.**

Regarding the substance of this γνώμη or "judgment" see v. 8 and 26. This judgment is one that was well considered on Paul's part, it is no mere opinion or notion. Paul is wholly controlled by spiritual considerations in his findings. Μακαριωτέρα is more than "happier" (our versions), for this does not refer to the ordinary human contentment found in marriage. "More blessed" is the meaning, spiritually richer. Yet the comparative is important, for it denotes only degree and does not deny this blessedness to the widow who marries.

Ἐγώ is emphatic, "I on my part"; δέ is copulative, "and"; καί in κἀγώ is "too." Thus: "And I, too, on my part." Paul writes δοκῶ: *minus dicit, plus intelligit*. This is one of Paul's effective understatements, cf. 4:9, into which we should not put too little. All that Paul writes in answer to the questions relating to marriage which the Corinthians had addressed to him emanates from "God's Spirit" and the principles of the gospel. Legalists will desire a different type of answer, one that is composed of laws and legal regulations. Paul's is the gospel way: Above all things hold fast to the Lord; prefer everything that will aid you in this and discard whatever will not.

CHAPTER VIII

The Fourth Part of the Letter

Food Offered to Idols, 8:1-11:1

We may divide this part into four sections:
I. Love for the Weak, chapter 8.
II. Paul, an Illustration of Love, chapter 9.
III. Old Testament Examples and the Lord's Supper in Warning, 10:1-22.
IV. Conduct in Detail, 10:23-11:1.

The phrase **Concerning Offerings to Idols,** which begins this part of Paul's letter, stands out as a caption even more decidedly than the similar headings found in 7:1, 25, for it is scarcely in any way connected with the first sentence. This part, then, deals with *Food Offered to Idols.* Paul answers the inquiries submitted to him through the letter from Corinth.

Questions regarding these meats were certainly in order. The pagan temple rituals, many state occasions, festivals of various kinds of societies, the lives of families and of individuals, all involved sacrifices to the gods and the participation of larger or smaller circles in the feasts connected with these rituals. The desire to participate in such feasts as well as the obligations of family connections or of friendship raised the question as to how far a Christian might go in this regard.

A part of the animal was burned on the pagan altar, the rest was prepared for the feast that followed. Meat that was not consumed at the feast would be taken home and eaten there, and a Christian who was invited to dine with a pagan family might have such meat set before him. Meat that was left over from idol feasts also found its way into the butcher shops and was sold there like ordinary meat. Yet the claim that all butchering had a ritualistic feature goes too far. This is true only with reference to far earlier times. Only the term ἱερεῖα survived from these earlier times, but it came to mean only animals to be butchered. Imported meat, game, and in Corinth especially fish, were naturally unconnected with heathen gods and their altars. During the ordinary butchering of animals for the regular sale of meat the butcher did, perhaps, cast a few hairs that were taken from the animal's brow into the flames, but perhaps he neglected even this. The term εἰδωλόθυτον, "idol offering," is the Christian designation, the pagan term would be ἱερόθυτον, "sacred offering."

I. Love for the Weak, chapter 8

1) Paul begins: **We know that we all have knowledge. Knowledge puffs up, but love builds up.** The Corinthians, it seems, had made a statement in their letter to Paul to the effect that they were all duly informed in regard to idols and idol meats. Paul replies that that is correct, "we," both you and I, know that we have knowledge, in fact, we "all" know it. The content of this knowledge he will mention presently although the caption already intimates that it is knowledge about idol meats. We should not, however, miss the peculiar stress which he places on this knowing and this knowledge: "We *know* that we all have *knowledge*." One can be too conscious of his knowledge. Thus knowledge itself may mislead. It is good in itself, but one must know how to use it, with what to combine it, or he will still go wrong. The Corinthians, it seems,

sought to solve their difficulties by means of their knowledge alone. Here Paul begins his correction.

"Knowledge puffs up, but love builds up." Without question, ignorance is a great handicap. The church cannot praise ignorance or make ignorance a principle of its work and reduce either its doctrine or its practice to the level of the ignorant. We must, therefore, have knowledge and must dispense it in order to dispel ignorance everywhere. Yet knowledge alone or knowledge unduly stressed proves dangerous. It tends to puff up, to make a man proud when he is comparing himself with others. This is true with regard even to Christian men. In the case of our present-day scientists we see knowledge and what passes for knowledge rise to the height of arrogance.

Something else is needed in addition to knowledge, something that will enable us to employ our knowledge aright, namely love, love to God (v. 3), which naturally includes love to our fellow Christians, the power that impels us to serve the true interest of our brethren. This love "builds up" or "edifies." Instead of fostering pride in our own hearts and puffing us up, love considers others, aids them in strengthening their spiritual life and in protecting it from danger. The article with γνῶσις merely refers back to this term which is found in the preceding sentence while the article with ἀγάπη is only the article which a Greek abstract noun may or may not have.

2) The statements regarding knowledge and regarding love are now advanced to greater clearness. **If one thinks he knows anything, not yet does he know as he ought to know; but if one loves God, he is known by God.** While this may suffice as an ordinary translation it fails to bring out the force of the tenses used in the original. "If one thinks he has come to know and thus still knows (perfect tense) anything, not yet did he actually get to know (aorist)

as he ought actually to know (aorist); but if he continues to love (present, durative) God, he has come to be known and is thus still known (perfect) by God."

Paul has in mind two actual, contrasting cases, hence he uses two conditions of reality and thus describes what he means in a concrete way. He would say: Look at these two concrete examples. One is that of a man who came to know something in the past and is sure that he still knows it. Consider this matter of idols and of idol meats; he may have learned and thus still know the facts about both. If, however, he stopped with this he never really came to know when he acquired his knowledge about these matters in the past in the way (καθώς) he really ought to know these matters. His lack does not lie in the facts or in the amount of his acquired knowledge — these may be quite complete; one cannot charge him with ignorance. His lack lies in the manner of his knowing, and this is a serious lack, indeed.

3) Now consider the other concrete case. Here is a man who is filled with continual love to God, the love (ἀγάπη, ἀγαπᾶν) of true understanding and true purpose toward God (not mere affection for God). We might expect Paul to say: Here is a man who loves his brethren with the love of true understanding and Christian purpose, he knows in the right way as one ought really to know. But this would be stopping at the halfway station. For the love of the brethren must always be the outflow of love to God. Hence Paul at once reaches out to our love to God.

This man, Paul says, has been and thus is still known by God. Here Paul again leaps over the intermediate point that this man knows in the right manner, which is true enough as far as it goes but does not go far enough by half. So Paul reaches out to the ultimate point: this man has been and thus is known of God. Here, then, is the γνῶσις that really counts, one that is not mere knowledge, however correct and extensive, but one that is united with and permeated by love to God, the love of true understanding and true purpose. In regard to the questions at issue among the Corinthians, Paul would say: "What is the use of mere knowledge in trying to solve these perplexing questions about idol meats? Mere knowledge gets you nowhere with your brethren or with God. Only a knowledge that is permeated with love, love that rises to God, will make him acknowledge us and our knowledge as his own. With such a γνῶσις we can solve these questions about meats offered to idols."

Here we meet the use of γινώσκειν in the sense that is frequently found in the New Testament (for instance Matt. 7:23; John 10:14): *noscere cum affectu et effectu*, a knowing which acknowledges the person known, knowing as one's own with the affection of love and with the effect of blessing. What is the value of our knowing, even our knowledge of God in contrast with idols, if in the end God does not know us as his own?

4) After the explanation regarding knowledge the resumptive οὖν takes up the original question in regard to idols and idol meats. The question itself is first restated and made more specific: **Concerning the Eating of Idol Offerings,** this περί phrase is again in the nature of a caption as in v. 1. May a Christian *eat* such meat or may he not? The knowledge regarding this matter with which the Corinthians seem to have been satisfied is now clearly and fully formulated. **We know that there is no idol in the world, and that there is no God save one. For even if there are so-called gods, whether in heaven, whether on earth, even as there are gods many and lords many, nevertheless for us there is one God the Father, of whom are all things and we for him, and one Lord Jesus Christ, through whom are all things and we**

through him. "We know," Paul writes as if to say: "There is no difference of opinion between us in regard to these simple facts. They belong to the elements of Christian knowledge."

We translate: "There is no idol in the world," just as we translate: "There is no God save one"; for οὐδέν is not the predicate: "an idol is nothing," A. V., but modifies εἴδωλον just as οὐδείς modifies Θεός. The world, of course, contains many images that are called "idols" such as those of Jupiter, Mercury, Apollo, Venus, etc., but nowhere do beings exist that correspond to these images; such reputed beings are simply non-existent. What kind of beings are in fact connected with these images and idols Paul tells us later, namely demons. Here he deals only with the "knowledge" voiced by the Corinthians. "No God save one (God)" constitutes the exception, and εἷς is the numeral. The oneness of God is numerical in the mathematical sense.

5) This point of knowledge regarding the non-existence of idol beings and the existence of the one true God, which is shared by Paul and by the Corinthians, is so important that Paul amplifies it with an explanation (γάρ). "Even if there are so-called gods" grants the supposition for the sake of argument although "even if" regards the supposition as in reality not being true and in the face of it holds to the opposite that only one God exists, R. 1026. Note that εἰσί is placed forward because it has emphasis: "even if there *are*," etc. The heathen have beings that are called gods by them. "Very well," Paul says, "let us grant for the moment that they *are* gods and let us include all of them, 'whether in heaven,' their major gods, Jupiter and his company, 'whether on earth,' their minor gods such as dwell in forests, streams, fountains, etc."

The concession of actual existence is made by the "even if" clause, which is naturally one of reality. The next clause: "even as there are gods many and lords many," justifies the concession, for it is a fact that the heathen world is full of such gods and such lords. The εἰσί is again placed emphatically forward: "even as there *are*," etc. The heathen deified their emperors, for instance, and these actually existed. On the title Κύριος as used with reference to both gods and emperors Deissmann, *Light from the Ancient East*, 353-361, sheds much interesting light, and Paul, no doubt, adds this title because it was universally recognized in the pagan world. Many Christians chose death in preference to calling the emperor *Kyrios* when such a confession was demanded of them by a heathen tribunal.

Note the repetition of the word "many": "gods many and lords many"; all of the heathen hold polytheistic beliefs, they have a vast multitude of gods, and their very number marks their vast inferiority to the true divine Being who is One, and only One. "Suppose they *are* actual beings," Paul says, "this whole host of gods and deified lords, what of it?" We need not seek in the Old Testament or elsewhere for actual beings who bore the titles "gods" and "lords" such as angels or governmental personages in order to justify Paul's words, for he is speaking only about heathen divinities and divine lords.

6) "It makes no difference," Paul says, "how we may rate them even if we allow that such beings do exist, 'for us' they are wholly out of the question, 'for us' only One exists who is 'God.'" This emphatic dative "for us" is not subjective and thus parallel to λεγόμενοι, "called" gods by men. Paul is not saying, "Heathen people think and say so while we think and say otherwise." "Except one" in v. 4 is objective fact

and not subjective opinion. God has revealed himself to us; therefore and therefore alone "for us there is one God," and before this one God the entire polytheistic host disappears whether it be regarded as actual or only as fabled.

The addition to Θεός sounds like a solemn, formal, liturgical confession: "the Father, of whom are all things and we for him," etc. The Father is the first person of the Godhead, he is called Father in relation to the Son, in relation to all creatures as being their Creator, and in relation to us as being his children in Christ Jesus. Because he is the Creator and is called so *per eminentiam* in the Scriptures, Paul writes: "of whom are all things," ἐξ οὗ denoting ultimate source, and τὰ πάντα, *das All*, the universe, all that actually exists, that is called into being by his word. "And we" includes the believing Corinthians and Paul and thus all believers. Paul mentions "we" particularly because of our special relation to the Father: "we for him" with our entire being directed toward him in faith, love, worship, etc.

While Paul might have stopped with the mention of the Father he continues, "And one Lord Jesus Christ, through whom are all things and we through him." He does this mainly for one reason, viz., because he has above said "lords many." While the title Κύριος is bestowed upon the Godhead as such and upon the Father as the first person, it is also and eminently, as here, bestowed upon the Son. Already this shows that the Son is true God, unabridged and not subordinate to the Father. His personal and his official name is "Jesus Christ," not only because this is precious to all Christians, but also to designate him as the incarnate Son and our Redeemer. His deity is plainly marked by the significant phrase "through whom are all things," the same τὰ πάντα as before. His pre-existence is indicated in the phrase "through whom are all things," and the prepositions ἐκ and διά mark the respective activities of the Father and of the Son in the work of creation.

A vast amount of learning and research is marshalled in an effort to connect Paul's statement with the ideas of the Jew Philo and of others who philosophize about a personal or an impersonal intermediary in the creative act of the Father. But John's word stands: "The Word was God . . . All things were made by (διά, through) him; and without him was not anything made that hath been made," John 1:1-3. All philosophizing that deviates from this fact is *eo ipso* inadequate. See the author's Interpretation of John's Gospel.

The addition "and we through him" is a parallel to the preceding "and we for him." Hence it does not say that we, too, were created through the Lord, but that we were in the ethical sense re-created through the Lord as believers. He is the *causa medians* in our regeneration and spiritual life. Moreover, "through him" is constant: as long as we are what we are, it is through him. "One God and one Lord excludes all pagan notions about gods as such for the Christian consciousness." Meyer.

7) After evaluating the knowledge as such and then stating its contents Paul proceeds to the application. **Nevertheless, not in all is this knowledge, but some, due to the custom hitherto in connection with the idol, eat as an idol offering, and their conscience, being weak, is defiled.**

There is not a contradiction between v. 1: "we all have knowledge," and the statement found in this verse: "not in all is this knowledge" (the Greek article refers to the knowledge already mentioned). For Paul at once explains in regard to what point the knowledge of some is insufficient: "due to the custom hitherto" (dative of cause, R. 532), when they were still Gentiles and attended idol feasts. They cannot, now that they are Christians, rid themselves of the old feeling regarding the idol that is honored by such a feast. The genitive "of the idol" merely connects the custom with the idol: "the custom connected with the idol."

So these Christians, too, know well enough that idols have no real existence, and that only one God truly exists, v. 4; but what is true with reference to knowledge in so many cases applies also to them: this knowledge alone does not suffice them. The old custom or habit of thinking regarding the idol still has its effect, not, indeed, as though they still think that the idol is a real being, but that they eat "as an idol offering." In other words, due to their habit of former times, their Christian knowledge regarding idols does not rid them of the consciousness that what they thus eat is sacrificial idol meat. They still feel that eating such meat in some way connects a person with the idol, unreal though that idol is to whom that meat has been sacrificed. This is their weak point.

The result is that their conscience, being still weak, is defiled whenever they partake of such meat. A weak conscience is one that is not fully clear as to whether an act is right or wrong. Here the act of eating this kind of meat is in itself not wrong, but the conscience has the feeling that it may be wrong, or that it is wrong. And just telling itself that it is not wrong does not help. This is the *conscientia consequens,* a bad or an uncertain conscience after performing an act that seems at least questionable; for Paul is speaking about Christians who actually eat and then have a bad conscience regarding their eating. A defilement or stain is the result for this weak conscience. This is always a dangerous effect. A man simply *must* follow his conscience unless he is willing to commit moral suicide. But when his conscience wavers because of weakness, when he is not certain whether he has done right, fearful lest, after all, he has done wrong, the condition of such a soul is pitiful. The verb μολύνειν is used in the Scriptures with reference to staining oneself with anything idolatrous or sexual, the two being closely joined.

8) A transitional δέ ushers in Paul's own exposition of the matter, which has a double purpose in mind: first, to assist those who have a weak conscience and eat idol meat only with compunction; secondly, to correct those who have a strong conscience and eat without compunction and are proud of doing so. **Now food will not affect our standing with God. Neither, in case we shall refuse to eat, are we the worse; nor, in case we shall consent to eat, are we the better.**

Food has no power to determine our relation to God in one way or in another. The emphasis rests on "food" and on "with God"; the former is too small, and the latter too great to produce such an effect. The verb is neutral: "will not affect our standing," literally, "will not place us beside God," i. e., beside him in a favorable position or in an unfavorable position. The translation offered by our versions loses this neutral force and substitutes the favorable idea: "will not commend us to God"; while that offered by other translators substitutes the unfavorable idea: "will not bring us into judgment with God."

The fact that the verb is neutral is made clear by the two specifications: neither the refusal nor the consent to eat makes a difference with God. The two conditional clauses contemplate cases that may occur at any time. The two aorist verbs μὴ φάγωμεν and φάγωμεν denote definite acts, "shall not eat" and "shall eat," which we translate "shall refuse to eat" and "shall consent to eat." In the apodoses the tenses are present and thus durative. Refusal to eat does not imply that we are falling behind or are losing something in our relation to God: "neither are we the worse." Consent to eat does not mean that we are abounding or are gaining something in regard to our standing with God: "nor are we the better." Not eating leaves us with no deficit that we should deplore, ὑστερούμεθα, and eating gives us no balance to our credit to which we may point with pride, περισσευόμεθα.

These facts (note the present tenses) have an implied application to the weak consciences and intend to overcome this weakness. On the other hand, these facts apply frankly to those who think themselves strong in comparison with the weak and imagine that their eating without a hesitation of conscience gives them an advantage over the others in respect to God. This notion, Paul says, is a mistake.

9) The decisive point lies, not in the food and in its refusal or its consumption, but in something else. **But see to it lest by any means this power of yours become a stumbling block for the weak.** This question regarding eating or not eating idol meats turns, not on "knowledge" alone that applies only to him who eats or does not eat, but chiefly on the consideration for others, namely the weak, and the effect that our eating or our not eating may have upon them. Not our "knowledge" but our "love" for the weak must govern our action. A πρόσκομμα is something that lies in a path, against which an unwary foot may strike and cause a person to stumble or to fall; metaphorically, anything that may cause a person to sin and to suffer injury to his soul.

10) Paul illustrates this truth by an example (γάρ). **For if one shall see thee who hast knowledge reclining in an idol's temple, will not the conscience of him who is weak be bolstered up to eat idol offerings?** Paul is merely supposing a case that is likely to occur (the condition of expectancy) and is not speaking about a case that did actually occur. A man

accepts an invitation to a certain celebration that is held in an εἰδωλεῖον, idol temple or temple court. He is an individual who is proud of having the proper "knowledge" and hence feels perfectly free to attend, knowing that he will not be contaminated. Because the temple is a public place, anyone may see who is present at the feast. Now one of the weak brethren sees his Christian brother dining at the idol celebration, κατακείμενον, "reclining" on a couch after the Oriental fashion of eating. What will be the natural result?

He who has the weak conscience will be bolstered up also to eat of idol meats, τὰ εἰδωλόθυτα in general which does not specify when or where he may eat such meat; and εἰς τό with the infinitive indicates conceived or actual result, R. 1072: "so that he eats," etc. The first man incurs no danger by his eating; but the other, whose conscience is weak, may fall into the gravest danger when he tries to imitate the example he has seen.

The verb οἰκοδομηθήσεται is striking: "will his conscience not be edified?" This has an ironical sound. The verb "build up," "edify," which is always used in a good sense in the New Testament, is here used quite otherwise. It seems that the strong and the boastful members of the Corinthian congregation justified their inconsiderate action toward their weaker brethren by saying that they wished "to build up" these brethren and make them strong. Paul asks: "Is this the way in which you would build them up?" *Ruinosa aedificatio*, Calvin. *Egregrie aedificabitur!* Meyer. A demolition calling itself edification. The verb never means "to embolden" as our versions translate it; we venture to use "bolster up" which retains somewhat the idea of the original.

Many other words were formed after the manner of εἰδωλεῖον or εἰδώλιον: Ἀπολλώνιον, the temple of Apollo, Ποσιδώνιον, Ἀμμωνιεῖον, Ἀνουβιεῖον, Ἑρμεῖον, Ἰσιεῖον, etc. A papyrus has this invitation: Ἐρωτᾷ σε Χαιρήμων δειπνῆσαι εἰς κλείνην (= κλίνην, table-couch) τοῦ κυρίου Σαράπιδος ἐν τῷ Σαραπείῳ αὔριον ἥτις ἐστιν ιε (= 15th day of the month) ἀπὸ ὥρας θ (= 9th hour). Note κύριος as a title for the god. Heathen temples had large halls or platforms and kitchens for such feasts; those feasts were sometimes celebrated in the open air. Another invitation reads: "To Paulina a δεῖπνον and εὐνή (Beilager) τ. Ἀνουβέως is promised in the temple."

11) There is no need to answer the question asked in v. 10. Better than a formal answer is the terrific blow which Paul drives home. **For the weak perishes in connection with this knowledge of thine, the brother for whose sake Christ died.** Wonderful "knowledge of thine" which does not see what it is really doing! Yes, he will be built up — call it that if you will; you build him up, and under your brotherly care — "he perishes," spiritually, perhaps eternally.

A tragic apposition says still more: "the brother for whose sake Christ died." Two mighty obligations converge: the one toward the brother, and the other toward Christ. Your knowledge is so great that you do not love your brother enough to abstain from an idol feast in order to save his soul. Your knowledge is so great that you do not see the price which Christ paid by his death to save your brother's soul. The fact of brotherhood should be enough to impel you to reflect with tenderness and concern upon anything that may drive a weak brother to destruction. Regard for Christ should keep you from at least helping to rob him of the soul for which he paid so great a price. "For whose sake" includes the entire purpose of Christ's atoning death. Christ died to save your brother — to this extent Christ loved him; by your selfish knowledge and proud power you help to destroy your brother — that is the extent to which *you* love him.

12) After pointing to the result which this action has upon the weak brother Paul points out the result it has upon the selfish actors themselves. From the dramatic second person singular he now changes to the broader second person plural. He often varies the number. After having individualized he now generalizes. **And thus, by sinning against the brethren and by wounding their conscience when weak, you sin against Christ.**

After Paul persecuted the Christians, Jesus asked him: "Why persecutest thou *me?*" Acts 9:4. A sin against the brethren is so serious because it is a sin against Christ. The two present participles "by sinning" and "by wounding" point to a course of action, namely partaking of idol meats as occasion offers. The verb τύπτειν means "to strike a blow" and thus "to wound." The present participle "when weak" describes the helpless condition of the conscience which is unable to endure the blow.

To sin against the brethren is serious enough, but when this sin also strikes Christ, the sinners may well become alarmed, for their folly now reacts upon themselves. To what degree they sin against Christ, and what the result will be for them, Paul leaves unsaid. Disquieting silence!

13) From the second person singular Paul changed to the second person plural and now changes to the first person singular: concentrating, spreading, and concentrating again, and all is full of dramatic life. Paul exemplifies by referring to himself. **Wherefore, if food entrap my brother, I will in no wise eat flesh to eternity in order that I may not entrap my brother.**

The condition deals with a reality and is strong accordingly. Although Paul uses himself as an example he enunciates a principle that is far broader in its application than to idol offerings; he adduces a statement that covers all βρῶμα or food and all "flesh" (κρέα is found only twice and only this neuter plural formation from κρέας in the New Testament, R. 268) or meat food of any kind; in fact, this is a principle that applies to a large number of similar matters. Only twice in the New Testament we meet the inferential conjunction διόπερ, "on account of this," "wherefore," R. 1154, which Paul uses here to draw the final conclusion.

The figure suggested by σκανδαλίζω is that of the crooked stick in a trap to which the bait is affixed and by which the trap is sprung; but the word is used metaphorically, "to give offense," it is like our derivative "to scandalize," i. e., to outrage. Yet the offense is always fatal; the trigger springs the trap and thus kills the victim. A stumbling block causes only a painful fall. We imitate the Greek by rendering "to entrap." The A. V.'s translation is incorrect: "if meat make my brother to offend."

Rather than to give such fatal offense to a brother, Paul says, "I will in no wise eat flesh to eternity," οὐ μή, "not at all," the strongest form of negation that is construed with the indicative and here with the volitive subjunctive. The aorist is constative and summarizes all eating. The phrase εἰς τὸν αἰῶνα, "for the eon" = "to eternity" and is idiomatic. The repetition in the final clause: "in order that I may not entrap my brother," emphasizes the two points that are vital to the principle that is here voiced: first that of the brother, secondly that of entrapping him, which is properly expressed by the aorist of accomplished result (σκανδαλίσω) while the present indicative is proper in the conditional clause of reality (σκανδαλίζει). Note also the shift in accent that is made prominent in the Greek: "entrap *my brother*" and then "*my brother entrap.*" Paul is, above all, determined not to harm a brother, to harm by fatally catching him in a trap.

We who are strong in knowledge must be equally strong in love. Knowledge alone is nothing, knowledge combined with love is everything. We must protect the weak until they, too, become strong. Negatively, we must not offend their conscience; positively, we must bear with them and instruct them. With reference to the entire subject compare also Rom. 14:2, 3, 13-23.

CHAPTER IX

Paul an Illustration of Love, chapter 9

The principle of self-denying love which Paul has just applied to the practice of eating idol meats is so important that he elaborates it by using himself as an example. Although he is an apostle and as such possesses the highest liberty he in various ways accommodates his conduct to the people whom he serves. He thus concludes this new section with the admonition that the Corinthians follow the same principle in their conduct. Only in a few instances does Paul weave in apologetic features that concern himself. We heartily agree with Meyer's judgment that this is *eine tieftreffende und schlagende Eroerterung* (a deeply probing and effective discussion).

1) Paul has just said that he would not eat meat at all if such eating would really scandalize any one of his brethren. In close connection of thought he now asks: **Am I not free?** He surely is, and not only objectively, but also subjectively, as far as his own conscience is concerned, free so that no man dare dictate to him. And yet, see the restriction he is ready to place on himself, 8:13.

The second question emphasizes the first: **Am I not an apostle?** Certainly, an apostle who is sent to proclaim the liberty in Christ Jesus is free and himself possesses this liberty most fully.

Paul's apostleship has no doubtful features about it: **Have I not seen Jesus, our Lord?** Paul is an apostle in the eminent sense of this term as it is applicable only to himself and to the Twelve and not to others like Barnabas, who are sometimes, but in a wider sense, also called apostles. The statement that he has seen the Lord Jesus (the perfect tense indicating the lasting effect of that vision) refers to the Lord's appearance to him on the road near Damascus when Paul was called to be an apostle, Acts 26:16-18.

Paul does not intend to indicate that he had seen Jesus before the latter's ascension, for such a view of his words is doubtful and not established by II Cor. 5:16. Nor would a mere seeing of Jesus during his earthly life have constituted Paul an apostle or been an important incident to establish his claim to this honor. After the vision on the road to Damascus Jesus appeared to Paul at various times, but then he was already an apostle. Paul writes "Jesus" because Jesus thus named himself in the vision, Acts 9:5, and Paul is also referring to the glorified person who at one time walked here on earth as "Jesus"; he adds "our Lord" because he saw Jesus in his divine lordship and with all believers has come to accept him as Lord and now serves him as his apostle.

Jesus made Paul an apostle. But Paul's work also proves him to be an apostle. **Are you not my work in connection with the Lord?** The phrase "in the Lord" modifies the entire sentence. The fact that you are my work is altogether "in connection with the Lord." Our versions read as though "my work in the Lord" is one phrase, but the noun and the prepositional phrase are at opposite ends of the sentence; this arrangement lends emphasis to both. When Paul calls the Corinthians his work, his effort is not to be placed on a level with the work of nonapostles who may also found congregations. For such nonapostles, as well as all their work, rest on the apostles, while these latter are directly connected with the Lord. Paul's great brevity in considering his apostolic office shows that no question had arisen in Corinth regarding this point.

2) Whatever standing may have been accorded Paul by others who had never met him and had

never known his work, in Corinth he was accepted as an apostle. **If to others I am not an apostle, yet at least I am to you, for my seal of apostleship are you in the Lord.** Paul mentions "others" only in passing since anything they may say in regard to his apostleship is of no moment. The condition is thus one of reality; οὐ negates only εἰμί, if the condition were to be negated, μή would be necessary. But this reference to others, whose opinion is of no consequence, helps to emphasize "you," the Corinthians, whose relation to Paul is very close: "yet at least I am to you," γε strengthens ἀλλά: "yet at least." An older idiom would be: "to you at least," R. 1148.

Paul at once explains why he can say so much in regard to the Corinthians when he is speaking about his apostleship by adding "for my seal of apostleship are you in the Lord." This repeats in different language what Paul meant by saying that the Corinthians are his work in the Lord. He uses the figure "my seal of apostleship." To the document which makes him an apostle, namely the Lord's appointment on the road to Damascus, the work which Paul did in Corinth is affixed like a seal that attests genuineness. This seal corroborates what the Lord did when he gave Paul his appointment. All other congregations founded by Paul would, of course, be similiar seals, each with its special value for the congregation concerned. It is best to regard "in the Lord" or "in connection with the Lord" as again modifying the entire sentence.

3) Paul thus says nothing more about the "others" with whom he has not come into touch and proceeds to direct his attention to the Corinthians. **My defense to those who examine me is this.** The terms are juridical. There may be some among the Corinthians who will wish to make a juridical examination of Paul's action as an apostle when he assumes

the possibility of various restrictions upon his liberty. Paul declares that he is entirely ready to submit to such an examination. In fact, he has already told the Corinthians in 4:3 that such an investigation is a very small thing to him. He does not admit that the Corinthians have the right to institute such an inquiry, he merely accepts the inquiry, even welcomes it. So he makes his ἀπολογία or "defense" before this tribunal somewhat as Socrates once made his defense at his trial before the 500 judges in Athens.

Does αὕτη, which stands at the end of the sentence, point backward or forward? The fact that the word is emphatic is, of course, unquestioned. The difference of opinion among commentators is acute. Some are certain that Paul's *apologia* has been made in the statement just written, namely "this" that the Corinthians are his seal of apostleship. Others declare that Paul's "defense" follows. Among these latter are our versions and R. 703. Stylistically considered, Paul's writings have no second instance in which a form of οὗτος, "this," when it is placed at the end of the sentence, refers to a preceding statement. But weightier than this strong linguistic proof is the thought which Paul presents. He is here not proving to doubters or questioners that he is truly an apostle. His letter is not to be sent to the address of the "others" who know nothing about him but to the Corinthians. Nor is the question at issue this, whether Paul is an apostle or not; the Corinthians raise no such question, for they themselves are Paul's seal of apostleship. The question on which Paul proposes to stand an examination is the one regarding Christian liberty, whether he has this liberty to the fullest degree and yet in practice can exercise all manner of restraint. In order to answer this question Paul is writing to the Corinthians; this he wants to clear up for them. And in this effort he uses himself as an example.

In v. 1, 2 Paul presents preliminary considerations: he shows that he is more than an ordinary Christian, that he is a true apostle of Christ, and that he is acknowledged as such by the Corinthians. In v. 3 he announces that he is ready to make his defense regarding the matter of self-restriction to any in Corinth who may want to question him. Then in v. 4 the questioning proceeds. So Paul's defense really begins with v. 1, and v. 4 begins the body of the defense.

The form of this *apologia* is exceedingly interesting. The Corinthians are far away, and Paul is in Ephesus. So Paul helps them. He himself conducts this judicial examination which he is pleased to undergo. The questions the Corinthians might put to him, and the doubts that may have prompted these questions with reference to the great principle itself or with reference to the way in which Paul applied this principle in his conduct, Paul formulates for the Corinthians and formulates in such a way that the answers themselves are clearly suggested. The entire method of presentation is masterly and masterful to the highest degree. May we add that Paul evades nothing in his presentation that the Corinthians themselves might ask, in fact, he probes more deeply and examines more truly than any court in Corinth could have done. We now see why v. 4 ushers in such a long array of questions.

4) The inquiry proceeds, and Paul makes it for the Corinthians. But it at once broadens — it must broaden. Paul cannot say "I" and refer only to himself, for the Corinthians might think that Paul is merely making an unwarranted exception of himself. They would ask: "What about the other apostles?" Paul eliminates all such questionings by at once saying "we"; and this "we" is not the majestic plural as is apparent from the use of the first person singular in

the verbs and the pronouns in v. 1-3, for no intelligent writer would turn from the latter to the former in the same connection. This point of contention is placed beyond doubt in v. 6 where Paul writes: "I alone and Barnabas."

Do you intend to say that we have not a right to eat and to drink? The signal that the expected answer is "no" is the interrogative particle μή; οὐκ merely negates ἔχομεν, R. 918, 1158, 1174. "You Corinthians," Paul says, "do not want to say anything like that." Observe the use of the key word found in 8:9 and its emphatic repetition in the following questions: ἐξουσία, "the right" to make this use of our Christian liberty.

"To eat and to drink" are aorists, hence they do not refer to the eating and the drinking that is necessary to support life, for it would be foolish to ask regarding that. Nor do these verbs refer to all kinds of food, including even idol meats, for the food and the drink are not mentioned at all. Paul is speaking about the right of the apostles to be supported with food and drink by the congregations they founded and served. Other pastors and preachers made use of this right; we know that Paul did not. But do the Corinthians wish to say that the apostles have no such right?

5) **Do you intend to say that we have not a right to lead about a sister as a wife even as also the rest of the apostles and the brethren of the Lord and Cephas?** This question is like the preceding one. "You Corinthians certainly do not intend to say anything like that." "A sister" is a believer, and "as a wife" is the common predicate accusative, a kind of apposition, R. 480. The apostles certainly had a right to marry and to take a wife along on their travels from place to place while they were engaged in their work. The idea that γυναῖκα means a *servians matrona*,

a woman assistant in missionary work, or merely a companion for the sake of company and to help with the cooking, etc., is even morally preposterous.

"Even as also (καί, pleonastic) the rest of the apostles" means that all of the apostles save Paul actually made use of this right and were married and took their wives along with them on their travels, or at least that the apostles as a class followed this course. What Paul says about this right includes the idea that the apostles themselves as well as their wives that accompanied them are entitled to support from the congregations whom their husbands serve.

As next in prominence to the apostles and certainly also in possession of the fullest rights of Christian liberty Paul names "the brethren of the Lord." We do not know to what extent these men engaged in the work of the church. Whether these brothers of the Lord (Matt. 13:55, 56 also names sisters) are natural children of Joseph and Mary who were born after Jesus, or are children of Joseph by a former marriage, or are only cousins of Jesus and children of Mary's sister and of her husband Alphaeus, is and probably must remain a mooted question. Each effort at a solution of the problem encounters serious objections. The fact of their special prominence suffices for the present connection. Some of them, perhaps all of them, availed themselves of the right concerning which Paul speaks.

"And Cephas" or "especially Cephas" distinguishes this leader of the Twelve from the classes mentioned and sets him forth as a most notable example. Mark 1:30 mentions his mother-in-law, and tradition gives either Concordia or Perpetua as the name of his wife. We have no definite details concerning her life. It is rather disconcerting to the papacy that Peter, who is regarded as the first pope, is represented as a married man in the Scriptures. The Corinthians certainly cannot think of singling out Paul as an exception and denying him the right which the other apostles and the most prominent persons in the church and even Peter himself were free to use.

6) **Or I alone and Barnabas, do you intend to say that we have not a right to forbear working?** The form of the question is still the same, and the implied answer is a decided "no." Here Paul's "we" becomes fully clear; it includes him and others. Barnabas had had no contact with the Corinthians but accompanied Paul on his first missionary journey and was decidedly prominent in the early days of the church's history. Paul and he, it seems, had agreed at the very outset not to accept support from their converts but to earn their own living, Paul by laboring as a tentmaker, and Barnabas by engaging in his trade — every Jew being obliged to learn some trade in his youth. We now see what Paul means in v. 4, 5 when he speaks about the right to eat and to drink and the right to take a Christian wife along with him on his journeys, namely to forbear working and earning his own support and to receive support from the fields of his apostolic labor.

7) The questions of this ἀνάκρισις or judicial examination continue but now deal with illustrations which show how self-evident the negative answers to the previous questions are. **Who goes soldiering at his own charges ever?** Why, the man for whom he fights furnishes him with provisions and even pays him for soldiering. The translation "at his own charges" gives the general sense of what, more literally translated, would be "with his own purchased (ὠνέομαι) provisions (ὄψον)." He does not buy his own food; the general commander buys that.

Again: **Who plants a vineyard and does not eat its fruit?** Again the reply, "Nobody." In fact, he will be the first to taste the grapes, and the entire harvest belongs to him. Compare Deut. 20:6, and Prov. 27:18 concerning the fig tree.

Again a third time: **Or who shepherds a flock and does not eat of the milk of that flock?** No one, of course. He who owns and tends the flock likewise owns all its product. Observe ποιμαίνει ποίμνην . . . τῆς ποίμνης, regarding which R. 478 says that "playing with paronymous terms" is perfectly good Greek.

These three illustrations are taken from entirely different experiences of everyday life and show not only that Paul is fully entitled to his rights but that it would be contrary to nature itself if any man denied him these rights. Yet logically such analogies are only illustrative; they are not proof or a fully convincing demonstration.

8) Therefore, in order that no one may reply that these are only analogies and thus evade the force of Paul's claims, he adds the double question: **Am I, do you think, saying these things only in man fashion? or does the law, too, fail to state these things?** Throughout and also here the only answers possible are "no." Paul is not saying these things (λαλῶ, "to utter," the opposite of to "be silent") only "in man fashion" so that the norm and the principle are only human, only "man." This silences the reply that Paul's human analogies refer only to ordinary human life and do not apply in the domain of the Christian or the apostolic life. Then Paul's deductions would, indeed, have but a slender support. In these matters the natural and the Christian life coincide; the analogies that are taken from the one apply fully to the other.

This truth is not only clinched by the second member of the question but is advanced to complete proof when Paul introduces "the law" itself, i. e., the Word of God. "Or does the law, too, fail to state these things" (λέγει, which always includes the substance of what is said)? No; the law, too, states them. In the first half of the question μή anticipates an expected negative reply; in the second half οὐ is not a corresponding anticipation of a positive reply, for it would then have to stand at the beginning of the sentence, οὐ λέγει = "not say" = "omit to say." The answer, too, is negative: No, it does not omit to say.

9) This is verified by γάρ. **For in the law of Moses it is written, Thou shalt not muzzle an ox when threshing.** The emphasis is on the phrase "in the law of Moses." Regarding the perfect γέγραπται see 1:19. The future "thou shalt not muzzle" is idiomatic in commands and in laws in general. The Gentiles had the practice of muzzling the oxen when they were driven around and around and perhaps drew rough sleds over grain that had been spread out in a circle in order to thresh it. Since it was more humane the law of Moses forbade such a practice and allowed the ox to eat his fill of grain while he was thus at work.

God's law is quite clear and simple regarding this point: he wants the ox to eat while he works at threshing. We read this law and generally find no more in it than a kindly regulation concerning brute beasts. It is that, too, and the Old Testament laws are emphatic in conserving the natural rights of even brute beasts. But Paul sees much more in it than a concern for such beasts. **You certainly do not think that it is only for the oxen that God cares?** The answer which Paul seeks to elicit is a strong "no." The verb μέλει is impersonal, literally, "Is it care of oxen to God?" — is that all? The genitive states what is cared for, and the dative the person who has the care. No; the care and the concern of God are not so limited, his care extends ever so much farther.

10) How far it extends and why it extends so far, the alternative question and its appended ex-

planation make plain. **Or does he say this altogether on our account?** Most certainly. **For it was written on our account that the man who plows ought to plow in hope, and the man who threshes—in hope of partaking.** Few men notice the real reason that God gave this law. They so generally overlook the fact that Paul points out by the repetition of the phrase "on our account" or "for our sakes." This law concerning oxen extends far beyond oxen. It really concerns them only incidentally; this law is chiefly a law concerning us, in fact, one that "altogether," πάντως, concerns us.

The ὅτι clause is explicative; it states in full what is implied in the emphatic phrase "on our account." The A. V. is correct; the R. V. regards ὅτι as causal: "because he that ploweth," etc. Moreover, this explication is in concrete and not in abstract form. Paul regards the plowman and the thresher as two of us on whose account this law was written into the sacred record. These two illustrate and show that this law concerning oxen applies to all of us. As these ought to work at plowing and at threshing in the hope of partaking of the fruits of their labors, so all of us should work in the same hope. This explicative clause is abbreviated in true Greek fashion while the English would be inclined to write it out in full: "that he who plows ought to plow in hope (of partaking), and he who threshes (ought to thresh) in hope of partaking." "In hope" is really "on hope," the labor rests on this basis; and the infinitive "of partaking" depends on both of the phrases that speak of hope. Thus, as Paul explains, this law concerning cattle was written into the Bible on our account.

There is much discussion in regard to the manner in which Paul applies this Old Testament law regarding threshing oxen. Paul is charged with treating this law in a way that is "altogether unhistorical" as though he claimed that God says oxen and yet does not mean oxen but us. Paul's treatment is therefore called "the completely developed allegorical method which dissolves all concrete historical and actual features and turns them into psychology and ethics." We are happy to say that this charge is untrue *in toto*.

Again, Paul is said to use allegory indeed but quite legitimately. He removes the historical sense and converts it into a type and an allegory by means of an application which amounts to a deduction *a minori ad majus*, i. e., applies what is said about animals to men. Yet such a statement attributes to Paul a procedure which, to say the least, has a questionable appearance.

Finally we are told that Paul is not using allegory at all, that he allows the full historical sense of the law regarding oxen to stand as it is, and that he merely applies this law also to us, i. e., to men in general, that from this law concerning oxen they may learn something concerning their relation to each other. This is the best of these three interpretations, and yet it, too, is unsatisfactory.

Luther has the key to the problem when in his striking way he makes the simple statement: "Oxen cannot read." The "thou shalt not" of the Scriptures is not addressed to cattle but to God's people. Moreover, "on account of us" means neither "on account of us men in general" nor "on account of us Christians"; Paul means "on account of us apostles and of all who work like us." Verse 11 employs "we" in this sense and even contrasts the apostles and their fellow workers with "you," the Corinthians; this is decisive also in regard to v. 10. This answers the charge that Paul is misapplying this law by emptying it of its historical meaning or by turning it into an allegory. Paul does not even make merely an application of this law by using it to illustrate what our relation to each other ought to be. What Paul does is something that is entirely different, something we find him doing throughout his writings: he goes back to the underlying basic principle.

Back of this simple law, back of a large number of simple divine statements, back of simple questions or complex questions asked, for instance, by the Corinthians, a basic principle will always be found. That principle is the only true key to the understanding of the law, the statement or the question and its answer. But we cannot understand a principle of this kind unless we see its range, notice that it extends far beyond an individual case to an entire series of cases. The moment we see that we begin to see clearly. For this reason Paul makes those digressions in his writings, which we meet so often, some of which are long. When we perceive the mastery of this method we also understand Paul.

Paul is far removed from changing the sense of God's law concerning the oxen that thresh. He needs that very sense because he gives an exposition of that very sense. What is the principle lying back of this law, what principle requires a law of this nature in the case of oxen? Paul names that principle: the worker shall participate in the fruit of his work. Or he shall work with the hope of participation. This applies to every worker, even to the oxen that thresh. Other examples are "he that plows" and "he that threshes," which means the actual plowman and the actual thresher. And this is true in the case of every worker, including, of course, the apostles and their work. The example of the plowman and the thresher are chosen with an eye to the work of the apostles and that of those who succeed them in the work of the church just as Jesus himself speaks of him that sows and him that reaps in John 4:36-38 and applies the very principle which Paul quotes from the law concerning oxen: the sower and the reaper are to rejoice together, namely in the blessed fruits of their labors. The oxen cannot understand this even when they feed while threshing. It is said "altogether on our account," and it is a pity if we fail to understand.

11) After the principle has been clearly set before his readers and has even been exemplified, Paul makes his application to the spiritual workers. **If we to you did sow spiritual things, is it a great matter if we your bodily things shall reap?** The natural answer is "no." The argument from the greater to the less is highly effective: "spiritual things — bodily things." The work of the apostles and of their successors produced for the church τὰ πνευματικά, the entire priceless wealth of spiritual blessings, but for their subsistence they could receive at best only a far less and cheaper return, τὰ σαρκικά (τὰ κατὰ σάρκα ὄντα, see 3:1-3), bodily things such as food, drink, lodging, etc. Here this latter term has no ethical meaning, hence we do not translate "fleshly" or "carnal" (our versions) but "bodily things," i. e., those that accord with the flesh of which our body is composed. Is it a great thing to produce such wondrous fruit and to receive so slight a return?

Paul writes "did sow," an aorist, because the sowing had already been done in Corinth, but "shall reap," a future, because this follows the sowing. Note the intentional juxtapositions of the pronouns, first ἡμεῖς ὑμῖν, "we to you," and next ἡμεῖς ὑμῶν, "we your." The sense of "we" is beyond question, which fact determines the meaning of this pronoun in v. 10. The plowing and the threshing spoken of in v. 10 are matched by the sowing and the reaping mentioned in v. 11. For plowing is undertaken in order to sow and reaping in order to thresh; and thus, too, the arrangement is naturally chiastic: the plowing precedes the seeding, while the reaping precedes the threshing.

Now we have the very expressions which Jesus used in John 4, namely sowing and reaping. The ordinary plowman and the thresher, the sower and the reaper get a part of the very grain they help to produce even as the ox eats of the very grain he helps to tread out; the apostles stand on a lower level, they can receive only what is on a level that is lower than the wealth which they help to produce.

12) It is not enough to make only this comparison in regard to things, Paul must add the other comparison in regard to persons. **If others share in this right over you, do not we yet more? Nevertheless, we did not make use of this right but we bear all things in order that we may furnish no hindrance to the gospel of Christ.**

The rightful claims of the apostles exceed in both directions: first when pay is spoken of, secondly when persons are thought of. Thus the two match. First: "is it a great thing" regarding this inferior pay? secondly: "do not we yet the more" deserve it than the others who keep taking it ($\mu\epsilon\tau\acute{\epsilon}\chi o v \sigma \iota v$, durative present)? "Others" in Corinth and elsewhere, others who preach and teach keep accepting support as a matter of course. They "share in this right over you," exercise their part of it without hesitation.

The verb governs the genitive, here $\tau\tilde{\eta}s$ $\dot{\epsilon}\xi o v \sigma \acute{\iota} a s$, which again introduces the key word, v. 4, etc. The genitive $\dot{v}\mu\tilde{\omega}v$ is objective: this right "over you," R. 500. If these others have and make full use of this right, the apostles surely have this right and could use it "yet more," for they are more entitled to take such support than all others could possibly be.

But what did the apostles do while they were in Corinth? "Nevertheless, we did not make use of this right." The historical aorist reports the fact. Here the closeness of the parallel with 8:9, etc., is apparent, **having a right and yet for love's sake refraining from** using that right; having the greatest right, more than others engaged in the same work, and foregoing it entirely. Paul is writing this to the Corinthians; so we may take it that "we" means Paul in particular and the two men who worked with him in Corinth, Silas and Timothy, and that none of them took support from the Corinthians. The other apostles very likely pursued a similar course elsewhere.

The second ἀλλά drives home the first; it adds the positive side to the negative. This is a favorite way of Paul's when he would especially impress a thought upon his readers. "But we bear all things," namely all privations involved in foregoing our right. The present tense says: "We do so right along, even now." The words are simple and brief and yet full of meaning. It is no easy burden this to preach and to teach and at the same time to earn enough to live and to travel from place to place. Paul's was a life of privation and of self-denials.

Yet however hard this made his lot and that of his assistants, he held to his purpose: "in order that we may furnish no hindrance to the gospel of Christ," δῶμεν, aorist, actually "give" such a hindrance, actually cause it by taking support. In what way the taking of such support would be such a hindrance is not stated; the Corinthians themselves will know, namely when they raise the suspicion that Paul is mercenary, that he preaches this gospel of Christ because he obtains his support from this work.

Paul's conduct is a fine example of a Christian who has the most perfect right to do a certain thing, and whom no one dare to deny this right, who, nevertheless, declines to use that right, yea, declines it completely. He has the fullest liberty according to nature and even according to law and yet voluntarily foregoes that liberty. He never does it arbitrarily; never to secure earthly advantage; and never because he weakly yields to the demands of arrogant men. The Christian foregoes his right for some truly Christian reason, namely for the sake of Christ and the gospel and the salvation of men. He voluntarily lays aside his right in order to help his brethren, especially the weak brethren. He will suffer much in order that they may not lose or be lost.

13) Yet Paul must say still more. Some subjects are of such a nature that they must be carried through to the end. To stop halfway is to leave a wrong impression. Every natural consideration gives Paul the right to take support, and so does every legal consideration which is supported by God himself. But finally also his right is upheld by every sacred consideration, both that embodied in the old Levitical arrangements and that embodied in the Lord's own regulations for the preachers of his gospel. So the judicial examination which Paul helps the Corinthians conduct in his case as to why he permitted love to rule him to the point of yielding his right and his Christian liberty goes a step farther. **Do you not know that they who are engaged in working with the Temple things eat of the things from the Temple; they who are engaged in waiting on the altar of sacrifice have their portion with the altar of sacrifice?**

Of course, the Corinthians know this. The priests and the Levites who do the work of the Temple receive their support from the Temple. Paul is certainly not thinking of pagan temples and heathen priests. The Corinthians have turned their backs on all pagan temples. Their priests do, indeed, also obtain their support from their temples, but all this paganism with its temples and its priests ought to be abolished and has no right to exist in the sight of God. An appeal to pagan practices would thus react on Paul himself and would destroy all that he is building up. God himself arranged the Temple and its services for the Jews. All of these arrangements had his sanction and were thus truly sacred. And this was God's arrangement, that they who are engaged in working with τὰ ἱερά should also eat τὰ ἐκ τοῦ ἱεροῦ, a beautiful paronomasia: Temple things or rituals and "things from the Temple," meat and money.

The parallel statement is added for the sake of emphasis and is effective because it has no connective: "they that wait on the altar," etc. The verb παρεδρεύειν = "to sit steadily beside," παρά of the verb calling for the dative. This sitting is one of readiness to offer the sacrifices. Paul quite properly refers to the great altar which stood in the court of the priests, on which certain portions of the sacrificed animal were burned; the remainder of the carcass was given to the priests. Being thus devoted to the altar, these priests of God have their share with the altar, συμμερίζονται, middle: receive their μέρος or portion for themselves. The Corinthians need not to be told that this was God's own arrangement. Christianity had superseded the old Temple ritual. Paul does not need to explain this change. The present tenses "eat" and "have their share with" are general and refer to the arrangement which God made concerning the priests.

14) Let no one say that this is Jewish and has no bearing on Christ and on the preachers of the gospel. **Thus also did the Lord ordain for those engaged in proclaiming the gospel to live by the gospel.** Paul does not again ask: "Do you not know this?" He himself solemnly states the fact. He does not quote the Lord's διαταγή or ordinance but only restates it from Matt. 10:10 and Luke 10:8. The aorist is historical and reports the undeniable fact as such. The present participle is qualitative: "for those

engaged in proclaiming," and describes his apostles and his preachers; it is like the two present participles occurring in v. 13: "engaged in working," "engaged in waiting on." The Old and the New Testaments combine in assuring full support to God's workers.

15) With his right to support so completely assured, what course did Paul pursue, what course does he still pursue? The nature of the case requires that Paul henceforth use the pronoun "I." Paul speaks only for himself and not for his associates. **Yet I have made use of not one of these things. And I did not write these things in order that it shall be thus in my case. For it is good for me rather to die; or no one shall make my glory void.**

The perfect tense "I have not used" includes the thought that Paul still pursues this course; and the pronoun "I" is emphatic, "I for my part," to say nothing about others whose case is not like Paul's. "To live by the gospel" includes many things: food, drink, clothing, etc. Paul says he made use "of not one of these things," he renounced all of them. He worked in Aquila's shop and supported himself *in toto*.

The addition introduced with δέ: "and I did not write these things in order that it shall be thus in my case," deals a deathblow to the suspicion which someone might be low enough to entertain, namely that Paul's secret purpose in writing these things is, after all, to get support from the people. The aorist "I wrote" refers to what Paul has thus far set down in proving his "right" in the matter of support. The phrase ἐν ἐμοί is a case of ἐν with persons: "in my case" or "in my person," R. 587. Nothing is farther from Paul's intention than the thought of changing his course. He at once states how far removed such a thought is and uses the explanatory γάρ: "For it is good for me rather to die" than that it should be so in my case, namely that I should accept support. Paul would prefer to die as a result of hunger or of privations rather than to accept support from his congregations. This seems at first glance to be an extravagant statement which carries the matter of foregoing one's Christian liberty and right absolutely to extremes. But let us pause a moment and wait until Paul has finished his writing.

Here a question arises as to the correct reading of the text. We accept the reading: ἢ τὸ καύχημά μου οὐδεὶς κενώσει, instead of the reading that has the purpose clause: ἵνα τις κενώσῃ (or κενώσει). We therefore translate: "or no one shall make my glory void," i. e., if, instead of dying, I continue to live by support from the church. Our versions follow the less accredited text: "for it were better (good) for me to die than that any man should make my glorying (should be: my glory) void. καύχημα is not the act of glorying, but that in which one glories, that which gives one the right to glory. The trouble with this reading is that all efforts to combine μᾶλλον ἤ in the sense of "rather than" are linguistically untenable; the two words do not belong together. Tischendorf assumes that this is an anacoluthon; R. 996 makes it "a broken sentence"; others find it to be an aposiopesis, an omission of a part of the sentence; ἤ, "or," is sometimes converted into ἦ, "verily," which the New Testament would then have only here. But the sentence is quite regular. Only two alternatives exist for Paul: either to die, say of nonsupport, if that should become necessary; "or" that his cause of glory remain intact.

16) But would Paul's glory not consist in his preaching of the gospel, in this alone whether it be with or without support? In this respect Paul's case is exceptional, for this reason he is now also speaking only about himself. **For if I preach the gospel I have no cause for glory, for a necessity lies upon me; for woe is unto me if I preach not the gospel.**

Others may find preaching a cause for glory; Paul's case is different. Why different? Because he *must* preach; a necessity, a compulsion rests upon him, which takes the matter entirely out of his hands. In fact, woe to him, if he does not preach! "Woe," οὐαί, is here used like a substantive, R. 270. Calamity, dire punishment from God would overtake Paul if he ceased to preach. This is surely astounding, and Paul intends that it shall be so. Such a statement is in need of an adequate explanation, and Paul now furnishes this explanation with γάρ.

17) **For if I do this of my own will I have pay, but if not of my own will I only have a stewardship entrusted to me.**

The two conditions contemplate two realities and are treated as such by Paul. First, if Paul's case is really this that he preaches "of his own will," by his own volition and consent, then he indeed has something in which to glory, something of which to be proud with a holy pride, then μισθόν, "pay," or "reward," would properly come to him, namely the future reward of glory and honor in heaven promised by the Lord, in which Paul could and would rejoice already now while he was doing his great work. But this is not at all Paul's case. He did not first become a follower of Christ and then, like the other apostles, of his own volition accept the Lord's call and commission to the apostleship.

Paul's case was the reverse. If I do this work of preaching "not of my own will," if this is my case — and it is — then my entire position is different. The two pivotal terms are ἑκών, "with my will and consent," and ἄκων, "without my will and consent." In Paul's case his heavenly Lord and Master himself decided the whole matter without in any way first preparing Paul, and without in any way first asking his consent. Thus Paul says: "I only have a stewardship entrusted to me," i. e., the Lord turned it over to me, and I still have it.

In order to understand Paul's statement we should remember that the οἰκονόμοι (4:1, 2) were slaves, whose masters simply gave certain goods or property into their hands to be administered in trust. The entire matter rested on the decision of the master to whom the slave in question belonged. The master did not ask: "Will you take this stewardship?" He only gave the order: "Take it!" The slave took it — woe to him if he was obstinate and refused! But when a slave, who had nothing to say in the matter, was put in charge of such a trust he had no claim to wages for administering this trust. Being only a slave and belonging bodily to his master, that master could and did use him as he saw fit. And that was the end of the matter. And such a slave was bound to be faithful, 4:1, 2. That was also taken as a matter of course.

All this throws light on the parable of The Talents and on that of The Pounds in which masters make their slaves stewards by simply issuing orders to that effect. We even have two examples of slaves who refused to act as stewards, and from the punishment meted out to them we may gather what Paul means when he says: "Woe to me, if I refuse to act!" The incident that in the parables the master rewards his faithful slaves when the accounting is finally made at the close of their stewardship is simply an astounding exception, an example of the magnificent generosity of *this* Master who far excels all other slave masters. The tremendous size of the reward shows that it cannot be conceived in the light of pay.

Here we meet one of the features that is frequently found in Christ's parables, which far transcends the human imagery because the latter is utterly inadequate to portray the divine reality but is able to portray that reality only by glaring contrast. As far as the claims of these slaves in the parables are concerned, even those of the most faithful, all of them are on a par with the claims of the slave mentioned in Luke 17:7-10, who, when he had done everything, had earned not even his master's thanks because he had done only what it was his obligation to do as a slave.

This is Paul's case exactly. When Jesus acquired him as a slave while he was on the road to Damascus, right then and there Jesus issued his order and told his slave for what work he had decided to use him. Paul received the order right there to act as an οἰκονόμος or "slave-steward" for his new Master: "Arise, and stand upon thy feet; for to this end have I appeared unto thee, to appoint thee a minister and a witness," etc., which uses the even still lower term ὑπηρέτης (see remarks on 4:1), a slave helper who just obeys orders without question, Acts 26:16. Placed into the apostleship and the work of preaching in this fashion, Paul has no credit due him, no pay of any kind, no reward. When then, as in II Tim. 4:8, he speaks of the crown that is laid up for him, which already now makes his eyes shine, this reward must, as in the parables, be referred to the astounding magnanimity of his divine Master.

18) Yet Paul is determined to have credit, pay, and cause to glory after all, slave though he is and therefore debarred from earning pay. He has not been in the company of his heavenly Master in vain, from his Master's magnanimity he has learned also to be magnanimous. **What, then, is my pay?** namely this pay that is due me after all, R. 759. Answer: **That when I preach the gospel I make the gospel without charge so as not to use at all my right in connection with the gospel.**

This subfinal ἵνα states the answer to the question and here has the indicative: "That I shall (actually) make," etc.; there is no thought of purpose: "that I may make," etc., our versions, which do not seem to be acquainted with this use of ἵνα. The point of Paul's answer to this question lies in ἀδάπανον, "without charge," free of expense to the congregations concerned.

The expression εἰς τό with the infinitive denotes result: making the gospel without charge results in this that Paul makes no use whatever of his right to receive support in connection with the gospel. Paul might invert this statement; it would be true either way. Yet the cause that impels Paul may logically well be said to be his concern for the people, and thus the effect or result is the non-use of his right.

Even as a slave-steward Paul has the right (here we again have this key word) to be fed, clothed, etc. while he is administering his Master's trust; the Master himself so ordained. Paul could exercise that right in the course of his work. It would not be wrong for him to do so. Then, he would, however, be like every other slave-steward with no claim on credit whatever. By foregoing his right as a steward, by making the gospel wholly without charge to the church Paul establishes a claim. He thereby imitates his great Master in a small way. Freely he dispenses his magnificent gifts to his servants, ten cities to one, five cities to another, so that his glory shines forth forever. Paul dispenses the gospel by his ministry, founds and builds up one congregation after another, asks absolutely no return so that his generosity stands forth to his credit and calls for recognition, if not on the part of men, then at least on the part of the Lord.

The verb καταχρήσασθαι does not mean "to misuse" or "to use unduly" but "to use fully or completely," and its negation denies all of it: "not to use at all." We correct the A. V.'s: "to abuse," and the R. V.'s: "not to use in full," i. e., yet to use in part. Paul makes no use whatever of this his right, hence also the constative or comprehensive aorist is employed; he is not establishing a partial but a total claim.

19) Paul adds an explanation which reveals to us the full extent of his surrender of the right that is his. He goes far beyond merely yielding his right to support. How much more he yields he now tells us. The arrangement of the sentences, the choice of words and of phrases are so perfect that we must marvel at the mastery here displayed. Paul's purpose goes far beyond securing "glory" or "due pay" for himself only. His deeper purpose in giving up so much in the interest of the gospel is to win as many souls as possible for salvation.

Though being free from all men, to all men I made myself a slave in order that I might gain the more men. Both πάντων and πᾶσιν are masculine as the context shows, and the two are juxtaposed for the purpose of emphasis: "from all, to all." The thought itself is highly paradoxical: on the one hand, to be free from all men; then, to be bound to all men. Luther had caught Paul's secret when he wrote regarding the liberty of a Christian man: "A Christian man is a free lord over all things and subject to nobody. A Christian man is a ministering servant in all things and subject to everybody." Yet Paul's paradox must be properly understood: when he made himself a slave to all men he did this of his own accord, he did it freely; it was the voluntary act of a free man: "Being free, I made myself a slave." Paul does *not* say: "I let all men (or any man) make a slave of me." To be made a slave thus is the very subversion of Christianity, 7:23: "Become not slaves of men."

"Being free from all men" means, first of all, to be free from an obligation that might result if Paul accepted support for preaching. If he accepted nothing whatever, no shadow of moral obligation could arise.

Paul does not need to specify other restrictions that might hamper his freedom in a similar way. A man who goes as far as Paul does in the matter of refusing support will not lag behind in other matters in order that he may be free.

"Free from all men" — what a weight these few words carry! Paul had broken with his entire past, with his own nation, and was not understood by many of his fellow believers. He had learned to endure envy and hate, to face danger and persecution, to look death in the face again and again — alone, depending only on his Lord. He had unlearned completely to bow to the opinions and the will of men. He is free, he enjoys the whole of Christian freedom, he is wholly sure of himself, he is dependent on no man, he is proud with a sacred pride, unyielding to the demands of any man.

But now the paradox: "to all men I will make myself a slave." This utterly outstrips any freedom which the Corinthian disciples and protagonists might vauntingly claim. The pagan Stoics, too, had much to say about inner freedom which enabled a man by philosophy and by training to rise far above either pain or joy. Paul would stagger these pagans when he declares: "I made mine own self a slave to all." No Stoic would understand that. Yet it only echoes the words of Jesus, Mark 10:43-45; Luke 22:26, 27. Even the Corinthians should by this time know far more about this freedom which makes men voluntary slaves.

Like a flood of light the purpose clause illumines Paul's paradox: "in order that I might gain more men." The verb κερδαίνειν is a technical missionary term which alternates with σώζειν in v. 22. "More men" = more than I should gain by pursuing a different course. Paul, too, is moved by the motive of Jesus who made himself lowly and poor in order to make as many as possible great and rich. The fact that this kind of slavery gives a man a place among the highest nobility in God's kingdom Paul does not add although Jesus did so.

20) Now there follow the striking details of Paul's self-imposed slavery. **And I became to the Jews as a Jew in order that I might gain Jews; to those under law as under law, yet not being myself under law, in order that I might gain those under law.**

The connective καί is epexegetical. Paul became, not a Jew, but "as a Jew" by living according to the Jewish fashion among the Jews and by using their forms of teaching when he sought to convert them. Having once been a Jew, he could do this perfectly. "In order to gain Jews" restates the great purpose of love.

While "Jews" and "those under law" are identical, "Jews" refers to nationality, and "under law" refers to religion. Paul has in mind the Mosaic law, but the absence of the article treats this law as one would regard law in general. The phrase ὑπὸ νόμον, with the accusative, takes the place of the locative with the genitive as indicating place and is found even with verbs of rest, R. 635. These people were scrupulous about legal prescriptions, and Paul accommodates himself to them when he is preaching the gospel by carefully avoiding anything that might arouse their antagonism. He thus observed their laws regarding food, drink, and similar matters.

But Paul at once safeguards himself: "yet not being myself under law." This explanation Paul must add for the sake of the Gentile Christians in Corinth lest they misunderstand; and he must add it also for the sake of the Jewish Christians lest they, in a different way, also misunderstand. For Paul and all Christians are completely free from all regulations of the ceremonial law. More will have to be said about being "under law" in connection with the next verse. Paul probably suffered not a little as a result of the course he thus pursued, for people who did not, and probably also would not, understand him added to his suffering. He again adds the refrain which tells of his motive and purpose: "in order that I might gain those under law."

21) To those without law as without law, yet not being without God's law but in Christ's law, in order that I might gain those without law.

The Gentiles were ἄνομοι because they had no legal code from God to regulate them. Paul accommodated himself to them by living as if he, too, were without law. He mingled freely with them and disregarded all Jewish observances which he followed at other times; he also, as for instance at Athens, formulated his teaching so that it might make the strongest appeal to the Gentile mind. Paul did not, of course, live in a lawless and in a godless fashion when he was among Gentiles. He did not act like a pagan or become a pagan, he was not utterly devoid of divine law. He was and he remained a Christian even among the Gentiles even as he was and remained a Christian among the Jews.

Just as Paul, when referring to his life among the Jews, inserts the safeguarding clause: "yet not being myself under law," so when he now speaks about his life among the Gentiles he carefully inserts even a double statement, a negative and a positive one: "yet not being without God's law but in Christ's law." As long as Paul speaks only about Jews and about Gentiles, the expressions "under law" and "without law" may be understood in a superficial sense and imply that the former have the law of Moses and live under it, and the latter have no such law and live without it. But the moment Paul refers to himself and says regarding himself that he is not under law yet not without law but in the law the entire subject is deepened.

In contrast with the Jews, Paul is in no sense a Gentile. The Jews, as long as they remain Jews, are under the law because they reject the gospel. The law binds, compels, curses, and damns them. The Gentiles know nothing about this law and because of this ignorance are not under it; yet because they, too, are devoid of the gospel, they, too, lie under the curse and condemnation of the law. From all this coercion and this damnation Paul, the Christian, is delivered by the gospel. In this sense he writes: "I am under law."

In contrast with the Gentiles, Paul is in no sense a Jew. The Jews are under the law outwardly and inwardly; Paul is not. The Gentiles are inwardly under the law, and only outwardly are they free from it; Paul is free both outwardly and inwardly. The gospel gave him this freedom. But through this very freedom from the law the gospel put Paul within the law. The law, once a relentless master and tyrant, is through the gospel now a beneficent friend and servant to Paul. Freely, of his own volition, Paul, the gospel Christian, delights to do the works of the law. As such a man he moves among both Jews and Gentiles. With perfect liberty he uses ceremonial regulations when he is among Jews, and with the same perfect liberty he discards all such regulations when he is among Gentiles; he follows both courses of conduct in order to win as many as possible for the gospel.

Under the law, Jew alone = under its outward regime.

Under the law, Jew and Gentile = under its power and its curse.

Without the law, Gentile alone = not under its outward regime.

First Corinthians 9:21, 22

Without the law, Christian alone = not under its outward regime nor under its power and its curse.

Not without the law, Christian alone = not deprived of its service.

In the law, Christian alone = using its service in doing its works through the free power of the gospel.

When Paul denies that he is an ἄνομος Θεοῦ and affirms that he is ἔννομος Χριστοῦ, the negation and the affirmation are only two sides of the same truth; and νόμος in the two adjectives (or are they predicate nouns?) is the same law, that of Moses. The two genitives differ only formally as to the sense, for an ἄνομος is such in relation to God, and an ἔννομος is such in relation to Christ. We venture the opinion that the two genitives are grammatically alike, both possessive and dependent on the noun νόμος which is embedded in each of the terms. Neither is a genitive because of the prefix used with the terms. R. 516 lists "God's" as a genitive ablative because of the prefix in ἄνομος while he is unclear in regard to "Christ's" and says only that this is "a bold use" of the genitive.

Now we again have the refrain: "in order that I might gain those without law," which states Paul's purpose and motive of love. The aorist subjunctive κερδάνω is derived from κερδαίνω, R. 1216, while the previous aorist subjunctive κερδήσω is derived from κερδάνω, R. 1217; the two verbs are only variant forms of the same root. The aorists denote actual winning for Christ.

22) I became weak to the weak in order that I might gain the weak.

"The weak" are Christians indeed, but because they are weak they are easily offended by the strong who act without regard to their weakness, 8:7; and thus the weak may perish. To them Paul condescends as if he, too, were "weak" by entering into their difficulties, avoiding offense, helping them to become strong. The term "weak" has a fixed meaning in connections such as this: weak and undeveloped in knowledge and in faith, compare 8:10. Paul does not need to add: "yet being not weak myself," for between the weak and the strong there is no such difference as between Jews and Christians or Gentiles and Christians. Once more we have the refrain: "in order that I might gain the weak." We now see why Paul selects the verb "gain" when he writes this refrain. It is wider in force than "save." The weak are saved, indeed, because they are Christians, but they can be gained for greater strength, for an advance in knowledge and in faith.

And now Paul summarizes: **To all men I became all things in order that by all means I might save some.**

All of the classes already mentioned are included in "all men"; and this expression would apply also to all other classes that one might wish to make. To all of them Paul has become "all things" according to the individual requirements of their particular cases. Now Paul uses the perfect "I have become," which again includes the previous historical aorists which referred to the mere past facts yet adds the idea that Paul continues thus even to the present moment.

This time the refrain is struck with variations: "in order that by all means I may save some." In the first place, note the beautiful paronomasia between πᾶσι — πάντα — πάντως — and πάντα in v. 23. Paul spreads out his arms and opens wide his heart of love by the use of these four terms, all of which mean "all — all." In contrast with these four "all" terms he writes save "some." Although he is not less than an apostle he knows that he will be able to save only "some." A note of humility creeps in here, one that is even today very comforting to us who are less than Paul when we, too, find that we can save only "some." And yet what joy and happiness it was to Paul and is to us that we are able to save at least "some," v. 19, "the more"! The verb σώζω is stronger than the verb "to gain" yet helps to define Paul's ultimate purpose also in regard to the weak and is more fitting in a conclusion.

It should not be necessary, yet it probably is, to point out the fact that in accommodating himself to the standpoint of his missionary subjects Paul never descended to a mere pleasing of men or to connivance with their false religious notions and their sinful practices. After only a few weeks of activity among them the Jews who were obdurate usually turned against Paul. In his practice Paul followed Jesus who could dine with Pharisees and with publicans and come into contact with harlots without receiving a stain or leaving a false impression. What Paul describes is the practical wisdom of a love that is truly strong and thus fully considerate. Let us admit at once that Paul's task was not an easy one. Nor is a true imitation of Paul an easy performance for us. The danger is always present that we may either yield too much to love, which then ceases to be love, or that we may forget something of wisdom, which then lands us in folly.

23) Up to this point all the purpose clauses reveal only Paul's desire to gain and to save others. Now we learn that this purpose extends also to Paul himself. **Now I do all things for the sake of the gospel in order that I might become a joint partaker thereof.**

Yes, Paul says, my motive is the saving interest of others, but this ultimately involves my own salvation. He means that his entire way of preaching the gospel with an eye to the love for others has its bearing on his own participation in the gospel. "For the sake of the gospel" is meant subjectively: for the saving success of the gospel among men generally, including also myself. If I do this work in any other way than the one I have indicated, if I omit this concern of love for others although many others may be saved through my work which is devoid of such love, I myself would not be saved. A great twofold interest thus holds me to my course. He has spoken about the interest for others and now speaks about the interest for himself, that he himself might be (the aorist: actually be) a συγκοινωνός of the gospel, a term that is used only here by Paul: one who shares with others in the saving fellowship of the gospel.

To some preachers this thought will certainly seem strange — that Paul would lose his own part in the gospel if he did not follow this one method of preaching the gospel. So many preachers think that they may choose their own method, do individualistically as they please in this regard, care more for the wool than for the sheep, for the crowd than for the souls, for their own personal, earthly interests than for the spiritual interests of men. They are sure that *they* will be saved no matter how they decide to preach the gospel. Paul explains that he might, indeed, preach the gospel and yet lose his own personal participation in that gospel. The point of his explanation is found in the last clause of v. 27.

24) **Do you not know that those who run in the stadium all run, yet only one receives the prize?** Of course, the Corinthians know all about this. Since the days of Alexander the Great athletic contests, held in public stadia, had become popular in the entire Hellenic world, and the people came in crowds to these athletic fields and watched the ἀγῶνες or contests much as the crowds now throng to the great college games and to baseball matches in the major and even in the minor leagues. Such a contest was well named ἀγών, for even the spectators agonized over it. Paul's illustration is taken from the major contests in which only a single prize was offered: "only one receives the prize."

The second and the third runners might obtain public mention, but they did not receive the coveted prize. In the smaller, local contests more than one prize was offered.

Paul at once makes the application: **So run that you may attain.** The *tertium comparationis* is not the entire contest so that the Christian race would have all the corresponding counterparts, many running with all their might, yet only a single victor emerging at the end. The *tertium* lies only in οὕτως. In all the races staged in the Isthmian games in Corinth, for instance, certain runners ran "so," others did not. "So do you run," Paul writes, like these prize winners, that you may capture the prize (aorist, actually capture).

25) A further and a somewhat different point (δέ) is added, that concerning the ἐγκράτεια and ἐγκρατεύεσθαι; these are technical terms that were borrowed from the training of ancient athletes, which extended over a period of ten months. **And every man engaged in a contest practices self-control in every respect,** does it as a matter of course. As it did in v. 24, the present tense states what takes place in all such cases; it is scarcely iterative as R. 880 states. While they are in training these athletes exercise complete self-control with reference to food, sleep, hours for practice, etc., and avoid everything that may hurt them and devote themselves to everything that may help them in their contests.

Now they, in order to receive a perishable crown while we one imperishable. The argument from the less to the greater is overwhelming: if those athletes practice such self-control merely to obtain a slight and fading earthly crown, shall we do less for a heavenly crown of glory that lasts forever? The two crowns are contrasted with each other by μέν and δέ, the οὖν only continues and means "now." The perishable crown consisted of wild olive, ivy, or parsley (Fausset); or of laurel, pine, or parsley, which was said to originate from the laurel wreath that was assumed by Apollo on conquering the Python (Smith). Our crown is imperishable, "an inheritance incorruptible, and undefiled, and that fadeth not away, reserved in heaven for you," I Pet. 1:4.

26) From the second person plural with which Paul bids the Corinthians run to win the prize he advances to the first person singular by telling what he for his part determines to do. And in his usual manner Paul now broadens the thought by adding the figure of boxing to that of the foot race. **I for my part so run as not uncertainly; I box as not flaying the air.**

In the New Testament we find τοι only in compounds; it is usually restrictive: "I for my part now" (not: "therefore," our versions). Paul begins with two negative statements which are followed in v. 27 by two corresponding positive statements. Note the two litotes in "not uncertainly" for "with complete certainty," "not flaying the air" for "striking home" or delivering a knockout. Οὐ with a participle makes the negative more decisive, R. 1137. Both expressions mean that Paul engages in the game so as to secure the victory and the prize beyond any doubt. It is pointless to dispute about subjective and objective certainty on Paul's part. True, a runner or a boxer may be very certain subjectively and yet be sadly beaten. Athletes love to crow in advance about their certain victory. Paul's case is altogether different. In the Christian profession and in the apostleship or the ministry we are to have and do have objective and subjective certainty combined. We do not merely hope to win, we — win.

The verb "to flay," δέρω, is very strong. But to flay or to knock the skin off the air is a ludicrous thought.

First Corinthians 9:27

To strike a terrific blow which lands on the air instead of on the opponent brings a laugh from the spectators. Yet this litotes conveys more than the idea that Paul merely lands his blows on his opponent's head or body; he knocks his opponent prostrate and wins the bout. Both figures depict the most strenuous effort and imply that only thus even a man like Paul can hope to win, only thus does he actually win.

27) The positive statement links into the negative by beginning with the figure of boxing. This is often done in Hebrew poetry so that even entire chains of thought are formed. A striking term that was used at the end of a statement is resumed in the following statement, and this is continued for a longer or a shorter line of interlocked thoughts. At the same time Paul weaves in new points and after the figure of boxing introduces the additional figure of making a slave. **I give my body a black eye, and I make it a slave lest in any way, after having preached to others, I myself should be rejected.**

We now learn who Paul's opponent is, namely his own body with its desires and its weak inclinations which are so ready to militate against his high calling. Paul says: "I hit it under the eye," ὑπωπιάζω (ὑπό = under, and ὤψ = eye). The A. V.'s translation is too delicate: "I keep under"; and the R. V.'s is too broad: "buffet," margin "bruise," which may apply to any part of the body. To hit a powerful blow under the eye is to knock the body out, which is precisely what Paul means. He does not maul his body, bruise it here and there or even all over, but lays it flat with the right blow in the right place.

To knock out is only a momentary victory gained in one bout. Now Paul's is a permanent victory. He must link in a new figure that will picture this permanency: "I make my body a slave" and keep it as a slave so that it is unable to assert itself again and to regain any mastery over me even as much as to dispute my control for one moment.

When we read all that Paul says about the body we should not catch the real point of his entire discussion if we failed to see just why he so prominently brings in this reference to his body. In many other connections he deals with the body and with its members plus the lusts that use these organs for their purpose. Thus in 6:12, etc.; Rom. 12:1. Here he refers to his body as an organism that requires food, drink, clothing, lodging, etc., in a word, support in order to live, support from the churches he served. This body of his would like to have abundant and rich support in order to live in a style that is befitting the body of an apostle, to say nothing about the greatest apostle of all. See the grand style in which prominent clerics live today! Now Paul says: "I knock this out of my body completely; lead my body around as a slave (this is the first meaning of δουλαγωγῶ); I never let it rob me of my glory, that I make the gospel completely 'without charge' to all those to whom I preach." Our versions are too refined also when they translate this degrading verb. It means complete slavery and not mere subjection or bondage, which may be much less.

Now there follows the final negative purpose clause, which explains the purpose clause used in v. 23, in which Paul states that he himself may be a joint partaker in the gospel. At the same time this purpose clause, which is found at the very end of the chapter, illumines the entire chapter, it reaches back to the desire to eat idol meats, continues on through the self-denials which Paul practiced, and culminates in Paul's determination to preserve his own share in the gospel: "lest in any way, after having preached to others, I myself should be rejected," the aorist denotes a final, decisive act: "should be a castaway," A. V.

This final purpose clause deals with the reality itself and drops the figures that have been used since v. 24. We should not, therefore, charge Paul with mixing his figures and with obscuring his meaning. Thus κηρύξας does *not* refer to the κῆρυξ who announced the various athletic events and the names of the athletes competing in the stadium. This gentleman himself never ran or boxed or entered any other event. Besides, Paul left the stadium when he brought in the new figure of leading about a slave. The same is true with regard to ἀδόκιμος, which has nothing to do with the games that were held in the stadium. This word is used in hundreds of combinations, and the effort to find in it a technical term that was applied to rejected or disqualified contestants is unrewarding.

A κῆρυξ is a herald; and κηρύσσειν, "to herald," to proclaim, to preach, is a standard term in the New Testament to designate this function. The verb, here the aorist participle κηρύξας, "after having preached" to others, is well chosen, for a herald may shout out an order or a piece of information without in the least letting his announcement affect his own heart and life. That is exactly what may happen in the case of a herald who is sent out to announce the gospel news to others. We fear that it happens more frequently than is ordinarily supposed. We even know heralds of Christ who have so little regard for the κήρυγμα they are to proclaim for the salvation of men that they modify, change, even pervert it, and yet announce: "Thus saith the Lord!"

Paul passes by this angle of the matter. He speaks about one who makes the correct announcement but fails to absorb a vital part of that announcement in his own life and actions. He has the γνῶσις or knowledge, he asserts his ἐξουσία or right, but he never appropriated the ἀγάπη or love which vitalizes and controls the use of both. This renders him ἀδόκιμος. This term implies that a test is made, and that whatever stands the test is accepted as δόκιμος, whatever fails to stand the test is rejected as ἀδόκιμος and is thrown out, cast away. The two adjectives and the cognate verb and the noun are frequently used with reference to ancient coins which were always weighed and otherwise carefully tested; the genuine and the full-weight coins were accepted as "proven," the others were rejected as "disproven." C.-K. 357.

What a calamity when a professing Christian finds himself "rejected" in the end! How much worse when one of the Lord's own heralds has this experience! Paul regards his work and even the way in which he does his work with extreme seriousness. The fact that he is an apostle is not yet proof to him that he will be saved. He knows the test that he must face. He applies that test to himself in this chapter and so attains both the subjective and the objective certainty that he will indeed not be a castaway.

CHAPTER X

Old Testament Examples and the Lord's Supper in Warning, 10:1-22

The fact that one may, indeed, partake of the abundance of divine grace and yet be lost in the end as Paul has feared in regard to himself in the last verse of the preceding chapter is now verified by notable examples from the Old Testament which exhibit the terrible experiences of the ancient Jews.

1) For I do not want you to be ignorant, brethren, that our fathers all were under the cloud, and all went through the sea, and all were baptized to Moses in the cloud and in the sea, and all ate of the same spiritual food, and all drank of the same spiritual drink; for they were drinking out of a spiritual rock that accompanied them, and the rock was Christ. But with the most of them God was not well pleased, for they were struck down in the wilderness.

"I do not want you to be ignorant" is a litotes for, "I want you to know," and is one of Paul's favorite turns of expression for introducing important communications and instructions; and γάρ offers the following as a substantiation of the preceding, namely Paul's concern lest he become a castaway — he who was so richly blessed. The address "brethren" appeals to the hearts of the Corinthians. What they must know and take to heart is sketched in detail. When Paul calls the ancient Jews "our fathers" he connects the Israelites with the New Testament Church, for both are God's people although some of each church are lost. Five times Paul repeats πάντες when he is describing the grace and the spiritual blessings which these fathers received. God included them "all"; if any of them were excluded and did not remain included, this was due wholly to their own action.

First they were all delivered from the bondage of Egypt by the miraculous hand of God. God was present in "the cloud," which is called a pillar of cloud in Exod. 13:20-22. All the Israelites were under this divine shelter when they came to the Red Sea. The imperfect ἦσαν in this list of verbs in the aorist does duty for the historical aorist since εἶναι has no aorist form. "All" likewise passed through the Red Sea and completed their deliverance from Pharaoh. Regarding the part played by the cloud in this passage through the sea compare Exod. 14:19, 20. Note also v. 22: "And the children of Israel went into the midst of the sea *upon dry land.*" What a wonderful deliverance the fathers experienced!

2) The readings vary between the aorist middle ἐβαπτίσαντο (which would be causative: "let themselves be baptized," R. 808; J. H. Moulton, *Einleitung in die Sprache des Neuen Testaments,* 256) and the aorist passive ἐβαπτίσθησαν, "were baptized," but the latter has the stronger textual authority although the middle appears in Acts 22:16. Being under the cloud and passing through the sea are here termed a baptism, they were analogous to Christian baptism. The preposition ἐν is usually termed instrumental, "by the cloud," etc. This might be conceived as an immersion in so far as the cloud would cast a shadow over the Israelites but scarcely in regard to the waters of the sea which in no way covered the Israelites who walked through "upon dry ground"; only the Egyptians were immersed, and that not figuratively but very literally. As for the cloud, this moved behind the Israelites, its function being to separate them from the Egyptians. No water from the cloud or from the sea was applied to the Israelites. It was likewise the function of the sea to separate.

What happened in the case of the Israelites is thus analogous to what happens through baptism in our case. In both instances there is water. In the type, the cloud and the sea separate the Israelites from the Egyptians. In baptism we are separated from the world. Secondly, the type shows a unification — Israel was henceforth a separate and sacred body, set apart for God alone. So baptism now unites all the baptized into one body that belongs wholly to God. Similarly the flood immersed the evil generation of Noah's day but bore aloft Noah's family high and dry; in this it, too, typifies Christian baptism, I Pet. 3:21. It separated Noah from that wicked generation and set him and his family apart unto God. This it, too, did by means of water.

The phrase εἰς τὸν Μωϋσῆν may be patterned after the similar New Testament phrase εἰς τὸν Χριστόν, but it can never be taken in the sense of *"into* Moses" or Christ. No baptism nor anything else could in any conceivable sense carry the Israelites "into" Moses. The idea expressed is one of union: "to," "unto," or "for Moses." This symbolical baptism united the Israelites to Moses as God's representative to them, the Old Testament mediator, in whom was foreshadowed Christ, the New Testament eternal Mediator, Deut. 18:18. The deliverance from the Egyptian bondage through Moses by this symbolical baptism through the cloud and the sea likewise typifies our deliverance from the bondage of sin and of death through Christ by means of Christian baptism.

3) As all the Israelites received the type of baptism, so all of them also received the analogous type of the Lord's Supper. The point of similarity lies in this that "they all" did eat, "they all" did drink "the same food" and "the same drink." *All* received and enjoyed the *identical* spiritual blessing. The manna given in the desert is called "spiritual food" because

it was in no wise a product of nature but "the corn of heaven" and "angels' food," Ps. 78:24, 25, a gift from the Spirit of God. Its origin was spiritual, and thus, although it nourished only the body, which Jesus points out so forcibly in John 6 in his discourse on the Bread of Life, this manna should have had an effect also upon the soul. Paul says no more regarding "the food."

4) Concerning the "spiritual drink" he says much more. The sentence introduced with γάρ explains, for this part of the subject is not as self-evident as is the other; moreover, a fanciful legend had grown up which calls for denial and correction. The two second aorists ἔφαγον and ἔπιον give the summary (constative) record of the historical fact: "they ate and they drank"; the imperfect ἔπινον presents an explanatory description: "they were drinking," drinking all along. No natural and ordinary rock can possibly furnish drinking water for anybody, whether he be in the desert or elsewhere. For this reason γάρ explains: "they were drinking out of a spiritual rock that accompanied them." Not once but, as the imperfect states, continually the Israelites were drinking, and from no mere natural rock although the water was twice made to gush out of such a rock, but out of a spiritual rock which was supernatural, divine, and not left behind in the desert as those two natural rocks were but accompanied the Israelites wherever they went in their wanderings. Moreover, Paul writes πέτρα, a rocky mass, a cliff of rock, and not πέτρος, a single, detached boulder; compare Matt. 16:18 regarding the same important distinction.

The old Jewish legend relates that after the first water-miracle recorded in Exod. 17:1-7 the rock which Moses struck rolled along on the journey of the Israelites until at the time of the death of Moses it disappeared in the Sea of Gennesaret. The second miracle, recorded in Num. 20:2-13, is connected with this same rolling rock. This rock had been lost on the journey when Miriam died, to whose merit the first miracle was ascribed. This rock did not return until the second miracle was to be wrought. Hence it was also called "Miriam's Well." Then also the well mentioned in Num. 21:16-18 is identified with the rock which gushed forth water as recorded in Num. 20:12, so that the *Targum Pseudo-Jonathan* says on Num. 20:19: "The well that had been given as a present to them climbed up with them on the high mountains and from the high mountains came down with them into the valleys, surrounded the entire camp of Israel, and refreshed them, each at the door of his tent."

Yes, Paul says, a modicum of the legend is true: a rock did accompany Israel throughout the desert wandering, a rock out of which they kept drinking all of the time. But this was not the rolling boulder of the legend although on two notable occasions a natural rocky cliff was used by Moses at God's command. This was a mass of rock that was far greater and far higher and entirely spiritual in its nature: "and that rock was Christ." This supernatural rock that never allowed Israel to perish of thirst in the desert — as any other similar expedition would quickly have perished — was Christ, the Son of God, who later became incarnate for our salvation. From him came the water when upon two occasions two natural rocks miraculously sent out streams of water, but he, and he alone, provided water for the Israelites day by day although he performed no miracle to accomplish this. Let no one imagine that the Israelites just happened to find water whenever it was needed, save upon those two occasions when none was to be had until the miracle furnished it. A wondrous provider accompanied them (not: "followed" as our versions translate). Just as he gave them manna daily, so daily he, too, provided water for them.

In fact, the God who led Israel out of bondage, who appeared to them in the pillar of cloud and of fire, who gave them the law and brought them to Canaan, was Christ, the same Christ who died for us on the cross and arose in glory. The people of the old and the people of the new covenants are one people, they are all under Christ. For this reason he gave them similar blessings: first a type of baptism, then the sacrament of baptism; first a type of spiritual eating and drinking, then the sacrament of divine food and drink in the Lord's Supper. Behind that manna and that water in the desert were the power and the presence of Christ just as he was in the pillar at the sea and in the dry road through the sea. Never once did he leave his people.

To Israel he could give only types, to us he gave the antitypes. Yet the types are as truly spiritual for the support and the nourishment of faith as are the richer antitypes. Each operates on its own plane, is suited to its own time. This is true with regard to all the types and the antitypes of the Scriptures. Paul is here not spinning fancies from his rabbinical mind; he is writing the deepest and the truest realities as they are paired in the two covenants.

Both "the food" and "the drink" given in the desert are called "spiritual." When in regard to the latter Paul adds that its source, too, was "spiritual," being even Christ himself, he does not thereby intend to deny that the source of the manna was "spiritual." While he feels constrained to say more regarding the drink because of the foolish Jewish legend that was connected with the rock, one can readily see that both the food and the drink came from the same source. Christ set the entire table for the Israelites in the desert during all those many years, and they should have recognized his presence and have worshipped his power and his goodness.

5) But in this very essential point they failed: "But with the most of them God was not well pleased," which is a litotes for "he was altogether displeased," he was angry. The negative οὐ, which is placed far forward, has the strongest emphasis, R. 418. There is a tragic contrast between the five repeated "all" and the Lord's blessing on the one side and "the most of them" and the Lord's curse on the other side. Every normal consideration and every right reasoning demanded that under this shower of divine grace, deliverance, and benefaction "all" should conduct themselves in such a manner that God would be well pleased with "all." But they so conducted themselves that he was well pleased with only a few and violently displeased with all the rest.

It is needless to furnish detailed explanations as, for instance, Stephen does. Instead of enumerating the logical reasons, which might allow room for argument, Paul at once introduces the summary evidential reason (γάρ) which at once excludes all argument and proves the Lord's displeasure beyond a peradventure: "for they were struck down in the wilderness." The two historical aorists, "was not well pleased" and "were struck down," simply state the facts; they are tragic enough as such. God is the agent behind the passive: the Israelites were struck down by him. Some died violent deaths, some natural deaths; but all of them save Joshua and Caleb died before Canaan was reached. Even Moses died before the Israelites crossed the Jordan because in one instance he gravely displeased and dishonored God. "They were struck down" does not mean that all those who died in the wilderness were also forever damned. Some were saved although they suffered this temporal judgment because of their sins.

6) After stating the sad facts regarding the Israelites during their desert journey Paul adds a

broad application. **Now these things became our examples to the intent that we may not be persons lusting after evil things even also as they lusted.**

"These things" is the subject, and "our examples" the predicate; the number of the verb is attracted to the predicate since it immediately precedes the verb. The margin of the R. V.: "in these things they became figures of us," makes "these things" an adverbial accusative, really, "as to these things"; but this reading is excluded by v. 11: "These things happened unto them by way of example," where "these things" is unquestionably the subject; the two verses are nearly exact parallels. The aorist passive form ἐγενήθησαν has the same sense as the middle, "became"; the Koine loved such passive forms and produced many of them and preferred them to the older middle forms. Paul tells the Corinthians that these happenings have come to be τύποι, "types" or "examples," for us in order that we may take warning from them.

The infinitive after εἰς τό is final: "to the intent that," etc., or: "in order that," etc. Instead of using the verb: "in order that we may not lust," Paul uses the copula with the noun: "that we may not be lustful persons," and thus uses the genitive κακῶν as the object of this lusting: "persons lusting after evil things," such things as are morally inferior and therefore ought to be shunned by us. "Even also as they lusted" adds the verb to the noun "lustful persons" and summarizes the entire lustful conduct of the Israelites by the use of the aorist tense. This emphasis on lust by means of the noun and the verb makes prominent the sin that so displeased God when he observed the conduct of the Israelites under the wondrous stream of blessings showered upon them during their desert journey. Instead of rejoicing in the spiritual blessings which God extended to them they constantly lusted after "evil things," those that were carnal in their very nature, and thus they aroused God's wrath.

7) The general application is now followed by the specifications which Paul has in mind. **Neither be ye idolaters as some of those, as it is written, The people sat down to eat and to drink and rose up to play. Neither let us commit fornication as some of those committed fornication and fell in one day twenty-three thousand. Neither let us tempt the Lord as some of those tempted and perished by the serpents. Neither murmur even as some of those murmured and perished by the destroyer.**

"Neither," μηδέ, is continuative as δέ often is, R. 1185. In all four instances the injunctions are given in the present tense and thus forbid a course of conduct. The first and the last are present imperatives, the other two are present subjunctives, which is a mere variation in style. The collective ὁ λαός is construed with a singular and then with a plural verb and thus touches the idea of unity and that of plurality contained in the term. While λαός is a general term for a large mass of people it is often used to designate the chosen people of God and here helps to indicate the serious nature of the wrong committed when a people of this kind practices idolatry. Regarding the perfect tense "it is written" compare 1:19.

The quotation is taken from the LXX of Exod. 32:6, which describes a case of indirect idolatry, namely the gay feast in connection with the golden calf. This image was idolatrous although it was intended for Jehovah; Paul, however, fixes attention on the feast which was entirely after the manner of idol worship. By doing this Paul strikes home directly at the Corinthians who thought that they, too, could preserve their relation to Jehovah while, pretending to make use of their liberty, they ate, drank, and amused themselves at idol celebrations. This very thing the Israelites of old attempted when they feasted upon the offerings brought to the golden calf and then rose up "to play," to dance and to have a gay time after the fashion they had learned from the idolatrous Egyptians. In this case Paul does not add that the Israelites were punished since this was well known.

8) The second specific case merely restates the facts as recorded in Num. 25:1, etc. Fornication was a regular practice in connection with idol celebrations. Paul thus adds the warning: "Neither let us commit fornication," etc., and intimates to the Corinthians to what their participation in idol festivities may lead.

The canonical Hebrew text, the LXX, Philo, Josephus, and the Rabbis, all have 24,000 whereas Paul writes 23,000. The explanation that Paul's memory is at fault is too easy since it exempts the commentator from all further research. The other explanation that Paul names only the number that perished "in one day," and that another 1,000 perished later, is not acceptable. Why should Paul not mention the entire number? Both figures appear to be round numbers, for few will contend that exactly 23,000 or 24,000 fell on that day. The number being so large, the figures intend only to approximate: more than 23,000 counted exactly, but not entirely 24,000. Taken in this sense, both figures are correct.

Moreover, we see why Paul takes the lower general estimate. We notice that he keeps writing that only "some" of the Israelites committed this sin and that sin. He is picturing these sinful outbreaks, not in the worst possible light, but only in as bad a light as consistency with truth compels. As he writes "some" where he could write "many," so he writes 23,000 where he could write 24,000. We often make our warnings too sharp and too strong, and our readers or hearers begin at once to discount our words and to evade the effect we seek to produce. Paul avoids this mistake.

First Corinthians 10:9, 10

He discounts wherever it is possible; hence his words strike the harder.

9) Paul again merely restates the Old Testament fact. The compound verb found in the injunction really means: "Let us not try out the Lord," and it is stronger than the simple form that follows: "as some of them tried (or tempted)" the Lord. When a compound verb is repeated, the simplex is regularly used; hence no difference is intended here. To try out the Lord is to go to the limit and to see whether he will show himself as God by punishing those who thus try him out.

The trial to which the Israelites put the Lord is recorded in Num. 21:4-6. This case is well chosen with a view to the conditions prevailing in Corinth. The Israelites were aggrieved because they had to forego the abundant supply of food which they once enjoyed in fertile Egypt. They loathed "this light bread," the manna. The situation was analogous in Corinth. The Christian profession demanded that the Corinthians should forego the old heathen enjoyments. But instead of rejoicing in their deliverance through Christ the Corinthians were dissatisfied and longed for the old pagan celebrations. It was not so much the participation in pagan sacrificial feasts which tried out the Lord but the dissatisfaction with the restrictions on their new faith. The imperfect ἀπώλλυντο, "they were perishing," pictures the scene which was enacted when this punishment "by the serpents" occurred, more and more of the Israelites died as the infliction continued.

10) The two instances of murmuring during the history of Israel are recorded in Num. 14 and Num. 16. Paul refers to the latter which also involved a rebellion against Moses and Aaron. Moreover, as a result of the latter only a part of the people perished, namely 14,700, whereas the former murmuring re-

sulted in a curse upon the entire people so that none of the adults who had left Egypt save Joshua and Caleb entered Canaan. "By the destroyer" also applies only to the violent destruction that occurred in the second instance; this expression cannot very well refer to the gradual dying in the desert. Paul's choice of just this case of murmuring as a warning for the Corinthians is again to the point, for the Corinthians also complained about Paul who voiced the Lord's will to them.

To murmur is to give audible expression to unwarranted dissatisfaction. Back of all murmuring against God and against his representatives is unbelief. God is no longer trusted, in fact, he is charged with leading us and treating us in a way that is wrong. Exactly that was the trouble with the Israelites, and for this reason God punished them so severely. Voices were beginning to be raised against Paul among the Corinthians; if they remained unchecked, the gravest danger might result. Hence Paul points to the Israelites as a warning. Some think that ὀλοθρευτής with the article signifies Satan, but the Biblical analogy points to an angel of God as being "the destroyer." The Hebrew account mentions no agent.

All of the four specific examples chosen by Paul apply quite directly to the Corinthians and are chosen for this very reason. The first two are closely related, likewise the second two. Idolatry and fornication appeared together in Corinth. Trying out God and because of dissatisfaction murmuring against God and against his apostle threatened to occur if the desire to commit the other sins should grow. The fourfold warning thus adequately meets the case of the Corinthians.

11) After having cited these examples in detail Paul returns to the general admonition begun in v. 6. He repeats that admonition and extends it. **Now these things continued to come to those by way of**

example, and they were written for an admonition to us upon whom the ends of the ages have come.

The first statement is only a variation of the main clause of v. 6. The verb is now an imperfect, συνέβαινον, "continued to come," and calls upon us to see "the things" one after the other as they are happening to the Israelites. For the noun "examples" or types, τύποι in v. 6, Paul now substitutes the adverb "by way of example," or typically, τυπικῶς. These accounts picture in types and in a typical manner what God's reaction must be in all similar cases. "These things . . . to those people," the two used in contrast (R. 703) imply: "similar things . . . to us." What happened to the Israelites is not exceptional by any means; it will in its way happen to God's people every time they turn away from him.

Beside these happenings as such Paul places the written record which God made of them. That is done because we know about "these things" only through this record. The aorist "was written" states only the fact, and the passive points to God as the agent through whom these things were put into writing. God had these things recorded for a purpose: "for an admonition to us" who would need to be reminded of these things in afteryears and would thus need a trustworthy record of them. This divine purpose God is carrying out now in the case of the Corinthians when, through Paul, he uses these things for their admonition, νουθεσία, which consists of words that remonstrate and reprove, compare Eph. 6:4; also I Sam. 3:13: οὐκ ἐνουθέτει αὐτούς, Eli did not even reprove his wicked sons with words. When Paul writes "us" he includes himself in God's admonitory purpose.

Paul's comprehensive world view is again in evidence in the relative clause: us "upon whom the ends of the ages have come." Instead of the abstract ουντέλεια, the "completion" of the eons, Paul writes more concretely τὰ τέλη, "the ends" of the eons. These "ages" or eons are all of the preceding eras since time began. All of them focus in the age of Paul and the Corinthians. The end of each preceding era points to the final or the Christian era. We Christians are the goal of all past history. All that the past ages have to tell us, as this is found in the divine written record, is to bear its fruit in us; all of these past events would have happened and would have been recorded in vain if at the apex of the ages their instruction, their admonition, and their warning were to go unheeded. A world fund is now at our disposal. We dare not let it lie idle, for only the Parousia is yet to follow. The perfect κατήντηκεν, "have arrived," "have come," implies that the goal of these ends of the ages has already been reached in the past, and that Paul and the Corinthians are now thus at that goal.

12) Standing, as we do, at the apex of the ages, with the entire Old Testament record spread out before us, a simple conclusion follows, one that summarizes the very "admonition" for which that record was made. **Wherefore let him that thinks he is standing take heed lest he fall.** He who thinks thus may or may not have a good reason for so thinking. The very possibility that he may not have is enough.

The second perfect ἑστάναι is always used in the sense of the present: "is standing." To stand means to be safe in the Christian faith and life. The Corinthians felt quite sure on this vital point and even prided themselves on what they deemed the fullest kind of evidence for their standing, namely their "knowledge" and their Christian "right." For their sakes, however, Paul writes this pithy warning: "take heed lest he fall," μή is clearly conjunctional, "lest," R. 430. The aorist points to an actual fall into sin. Some stress the tense so as to mean at once and completely to fall from grace into condemnation and judgment. This is, of course, included even as the Old Testament examples show that some fell and were lost. Yet an actual fall may not at once go that far even as in the Old Testament examples not all were lost. "Lest he fall" warns against all falling into sin and intends to keep us in entire safety, working out our salvation with fear and with trembling, aware of all the dangers and the pitfalls that threaten us. For this purpose, that we may walk guardedly, the Old Testament record was made. Let us use it accordingly.

13) In order the more to urge the Corinthians to heed this admonition Paul adds: **None save human temptation has overtaken you, but God is faithful, who will not permit you to be tempted above your ability but will make together with the temptation the way out, namely the ability to bear it.**

A temptation is any inducement to sin. The verb λαμβάνω, here the perfect εἴληφεν, is regularly used with reference to occurrences or conditions that "take" or "overtake" a person. Whatever temptation overtook you in the past, Paul tells the Corinthians, was only of the human kind, ἀνθρώπινος, such as comes to a human being, and such as a human being may endure. The translations: "such as is common to man," A. V., or, "such as man can bear," R. V., circumscribe the adjective by interpreting it. What Paul means by "human" temptation he himself states in the next sentence, a temptation which God keeps within our ability to endure. "Human" is, therefore, not in contrast to "devilish," nor does it denote only human origin in contrast with superhuman origin, for the devil is behind every temptation that assails a Christian.

The question has been raised as to whether Paul is still warning the Corinthians or is now encouraging them. Is he intimating that temptations may overtake them that are worse than the ones they have had to face thus far? Or does he point to their past temptations as samples of the kind which they will continue to face and be able to overcome also in the future? The exegetical answer lies in the following. God will not allow them to be tempted above what they are able to bear. Thus "human temptation" = a temptation that is not above human strength to withstand. If temptations past and future are also such, this means encouragement. But should Paul not rather frighten the presumptuous Corinthians instead of encouraging them? He has already given them a serious warning in v. 12. Besides, some Christians among the Corinthians are weak, aud Paul does not forget them. Especially they need encouragement. After the warning which points to the danger of their falling even the presumptuous need to be encouraged lest they now grow discouraged and become afraid.

With the adversative δέ Paul points the Corinthians to God and calls him πιστός, worthy of all reliance. On him the Corinthians are to depend and not on themselves for escape from the danger that always accompanies temptation. And God is, indeed, trustworthy as is demonstrated by the way in which he controls temptation. He does this in a twofold way. For, in the first place, he is the one "who will not permit you to be tempted above your ability." We can always rely on him for that. God reduces the tempting power so that it does not exceed our power to resist. God sets fixed bounds even to the devil, beyond which temptation dare not go as we see so clearly from the case of Job. We translate: "above what you are able," with the smoother phrase: "above your ability."

The agent behind the passive infinitive "to be tempted" cannot be God "who will not permit." Even by stressing the second verb so as to mean who "will make" the way out, God cannot be the tempter. "Neither tempteth he any man," James 1:13. Paul does not designate the tempting power in the present connection; "every man is tempted when he is drawn away of his own lust, and enticed," James 1:14. The fact that πειρασμός and the corresponding verb speak about "temptation" and not merely about "trial" the context indicates beyond a doubt.

In the second place, we can rely on God who "will make together with the temptation the way out, namely the ability to bear it." Paul does not say that God makes both the temptation and the way out. Paul does not at all say how the temptation is made, he indicates only that, when it is made, God provides "the way of escape" (R. V.) from its deadly embrace. The person tempted may not use "the way out," he may be caught and brought to fall, but this will be due wholly to his own perverse heart. Judas would not use the way out although Jesus opened it to him again and again. Peter used it and escaped.

We regard τοῦ δύνασθαι ὑπενεγκεῖν (second aorist from ὑποφέρω) as epexegetical, namely as stating what the way out is, R. 1067, 1087; we translate: "namely the ability to bear it." The way out is "to be able to bear the temptation," or as our versions translate: "that ye may be able to bear (endure) it." This may, however, be understood as indicating only God's purpose: the way out "in order that you may be able," etc. If purpose were intended by this expression, Paul would not be telling us just what the way out of temptation is; we should be obliged to guess it. Moreover, in order to make this an infinitive of purpose Paul ought to write out its accusative subject ὑμᾶς, for this is always and necessarily done when the subject of the infinitive, as in the case under consideration, differs from the subject of the preceding finite verb. The two statements: first, that God does not allow us to be tempted above our ability; secondly, that he makes a way out through this our ability, are only the negative and the positive sides of one and the same act of God. Both phases of God's act enter in our divinely wrought ability to endure the temptation and not to fall under its impact.

In chapters eight and nine the question regarding the eating of idol meats is considered from the viewpoint of the weak brethren who may be spiritually injured by such an action. In chapter ten this question is viewed from the angle of the persons themselves who thus eat and may thereby incur temptation and be brought to fall. Both views are naturally complementary. Yet the one has been pitted against the other. Paul is thought to contradict himself. At one time, we are told, he writes in a mild way and then in a severe way; at one time he does not prohibit this questionable eating and then reverses himself and absolutely prohibits it. Hence these chapters cannot have been written as a part of one and the same letter. Interpolations are evident to the critic's mind. So he posits various hypotheses, none of which are satisfactory.

14) Paul now draws his conclusion for the Corinthians from the entire preceding paragraph. To begin with, Paul's plea is summed up in one injunction. **Therefore, my beloved, continue to flee from idolatry!** The address "my beloved" is strongly affectionate and urgently pleading. It expresses Paul's love far more fully than the less intense "brethren" or "my brethren" would. The present imperative is durative: "continue to flee" — let that be the mark of your entire conduct. This injunction in no way implies that the Corinthians are already contaminated with idolatry, but it does imply that they are in danger of becoming contaminated with the gravest of all sins, which strikes directly against God. They must keep entirely at a distance from anything and everything of an idolatrous nature.

15) While the injunction to flee from idolatry is the only conclusion that Christians can draw from

the examples cited from Israel's history, the vital facts connected with the Christian profession that are evident to all eyes in our holy of holies, the Lord's Supper, lend ultimate authority to that injunction. These vital facts Paul does not merely emphasize on his own authority and then tell the Corinthians what he thinks their conduct in accordance with them should be. Paul never asks mere blind obedience; he always labors to secure obedience as a result of thorough conviction. So he writes: **As to sensible men I speak; do you yourselves judge what I claim.**

A man is "sensible" when he understands and thus judges in an intelligent manner. The aorist κρίνατε asks for a definite and a final decision, one that, once made, need not be made again; and ὑμεῖς is emphatic: "you yourselves" or "you for your part." We should also note the difference between λέγω and φημί when they are used side by side: "I speak" and "I claim." They, of course, perceive what Paul states and tells them; but they are to judge what Paul claims and asserts.

16) The questions which Paul now asks bring out the vital facts. All of them are plain, and all of them are undisputed. On the basis of these Paul wants the Corinthians to make a definite decision on their own account. Sensible Christian people will not only at once give the self-evident answers to these questions but will also perceive the force of these answers as far as conduct is concerned. **The cup of the blessing which we bless, is it not a communion of the blood of Christ? The bread which we break, is it not a communion of the body of Christ?**

Paul mentions the sacramental cup first because he intends to elaborate the statement regarding the sacramental bread. The construction is the same in both questions; "the cup" and "the bread," two nominatives, are placed forward, and each has the copula ἐστί at the end of the question; yet each of these two nominatives is attracted inversely and is made an accusative by the accusative relative that follows, R. 488, 718.

"The cup" is a natural grammatical (not rhetorical) figure which names the vessel when its contents are referred to, here the sacramental wine. To "the cup" the genitive "of the blessing which we bless" is attached, while to "the bread" just the relative clause "which we break" is added; but the force is the same: both the cup and the bread were blessed and received by the communicants. The expression: "the cup of the blessing" is an allusion to the third cup of the Passover, which originally bore that name: *kom habberakah*, because a blessing was pronounced over it. The sacramental cup was, however, not merely *called* "the cup of the blessing" like that third Passover cup, a consecratory blessing was and had to be pronounced over the sacramental cup. The present tense εὐλογοῦμεν denotes the action that necessarily took place, i. e., whenever the Sacrament was celebrated, R. 880.

Paul writes the cup "which we bless" and uses the plural and thereby indicates that the Sacrament belongs to the congregation; all that the pastor does when he is administering it is really done by the congregation through the instrumentality of the pastor. If the cup (and the bread) is not blessed by consecration, no sacrament is received. Paul does not say what words of blessing the apostolic church used. We are quite certain that they were not the words that were originally spoken by Christ when he consecrated the elements, for these words have not been preserved to us for the very reason, too, that we are not to repeat them. The power of Christ's words of blessing, once spoken when he instituted the Sacrament, extends to all time. Comparing Mark 14:12; Luke 22:17, etc.; and Matt. 26:26, 27, we conclude that Christ's original words contained both blessing and thanksgiving; beyond that we cannot go.

Our Sacrament complies with Christ's original words and has abiding power when we truly obey his sacramental command: "This do." In order to make sure of this essential point the church uses the so-called words of institution when she consecrates the elements and adds the Lord's Prayer instead of a prayer of her own. The words of institution plus this prayer are our εὐλογεῖν. The consecrated cup must, of course, also be received by the communicants in order that there may be a sacrament. But not merely a blessing of some kind suffices to make the cup thus received "a communion of the blood of Christ," it must be a specific sacramental blessing, i. e., one that certainly connects the cup with Christ and his original and efficacious institution of the Sacrament.

Paul cannot write *"the* communion" of the blood of Christ (A. V.), for such a statement might leave the impression that this is "the only" communion. John 6:53 shows that faith alone partakes spiritually of Christ's blood although this is not a sacramental communion. So Paul writes "a communion" when he is speaking of the blood and when he is speaking of the body, namely one that is sacramental. "Communion," κοινωνία, with the genitive of the object denotes actual and real participation, here an actual and a real participation in the blood of Christ, i. e., the blood shed on the cross for the remission of our sins. If either the wine of the cup or the blood of Christ is unreal, then a "communion" between them is also unreal, i. e., none exists. The cup, i. e., its contents, which is received by drinking, mediates this "communion" and not our faith or any other means or act.

As for ἐστί, this is the copula, and it can never mean "represents." The fact that a true and a real communion between the cup and the blood is predicated is evidenced also by the purpose for which Paul uses this statement, namely to warn the Corinthians against the table and the cup of devils because partaking of this table and of this cup would be a communion with devils, not a mere symbolical or figurative but a real communion with devils.

The statement regarding "the bread" is similar. Paul does not need to repeat the genitive and the relative: the bread "of the blessing which we bless," for this is understood. Whereas the relative clause: "which we bless," that is used with reference to the cup, mentions the consecration and omits the distribution, the clause used with reference to the bread: "which we break," does the reverse. Both the consecration and the distribution are necessary in order to have the Sacrament. Since the essential point in regard to both the cup and the bread is the "communion," Paul introduces no variation in this part of his statement. The blood and the body are each named separately and thus indicate the sacrifice on the cross.

The breaking refers to the thin, flat cakes of bread which were at first used in the Sacrament; these were probably used also in Corinth. The act of breaking this bread in no manner symbolizes the death of Christ. The Scriptures attest that the body of Christ was not broken. Nor is breaking of bread ever a symbol of a violent death or of death in any form (Krauth). In the Sacrament the breaking is done for the sake of distribution only. No counterpart such as spilling or pouring out occurs with regard to the cup.

17) Yes, the Corinthians must say that such a communion with the body and the blood of Christ takes place through the bread and the wine in the Sacrament. Paul could have attached what he now adds concerning this communion to his statement regarding the blood as well as to that regarding the

body; he prefers the latter. "Is this bread not the communion of the body of Christ?" Paul takes for granted that the answer will be: "It is indeed," and thus proceeds: **Because there is one bread, one body are we, the many.** This states the obvious result of the "communion" which the Corinthians would admit on the basis of Paul's question. The one sacramental bread, which mediates the sacramental communion with Christ's body, makes all who partake of that bread, no matter how numerous they may be, one body.

It is unfeasible to make "one bread" a predicate to "we are," to coordinate it with "one body" and thus to translate: "For we, being many, are one bread and one body," A. V.; or: "seeing that we, who are many, are one bread, one body," R. V. This is linguistically untenable and breaks the continuity of Paul's thought. It has Paul say that because we Christians are one bread and one body, therefore the sacramental bread is a communion of Christ's body. Our being one would make the sacramental communion. This is not true. *We* are made one *by* the one bread and its communion with Christ's body. In addition, to call us Christians "one bread" introduces an odd figure, one that is unnecessary since we are called "one body" in the very next statement. We supply ἐστί after εἶς ἄρτος, and all is clear, and Paul's statement is true.

Faulty as the translations offered in our versions are, the R. V. obscures the sense when in its margin it translates ἄρτος "loaf": "we are one loaf." This idea is rather fantastic. It is not clarified by the marginal translation: "seeing that there is one bread," i. e., loaf, for the bread is not "one" merely as bread. At each celebration in each congregation a different supply of bread was used. If loaves of bread were used in Corinth, a number of loaves would be required, and this number would be determined by the number of communicants. The matter becomes clear when we carefully consider Paul's statement. He is speaking about all of the bread that is used in all of the communion celebrations in all of Christendom, and all of this bread he calls εἷς ἄρτος. All of it is made "one" by the consecratory blessing which is followed by the distribution and the eating. More than this, all of it is made "one" by the one body of Christ of which it is the "communion" for all who partake.

This "one bread," thus made one sacramentally, makes all of the communicants in Christendom ἓν σῶμα, "one body." The argument is from the cause ("one bread" as the "communion of Christ's sacrificed body") to the effect ("the many" communicants made "one body"). If this bread were only a symbol of Christ's body it could make all of the communicants only a symbolic body and not a spiritual body.

The matter is so important for the point which Paul seeks to drive home to the Corinthians that he explains by a brief restatement: **for we all partake of the one bread.** First "the many," οἱ πολλοί, spreading out all of them in their great number, then, as Paul loves to do, "we all," gathering them into one mass, οἱ πάντες. How are the many made one spiritual body? We all partake of the one bread, τοῦ ἄρτου with the article of previous reference, of the consecrated bread just described.

The preposition ἐκ is merely pleonastic since this verb is also used with the genitive alone. The ἐκ phrase cannot be regarded as causal so that μετέχομεν would have its object understood: "for we all, *due to* the one bread, partake" (of the one body). If this were Paul's thought, the object "of one body" would have to be written out. What Paul tells the Corinthians is that all of us who partake of the one sacramental bread are thereby made one spiritual body. And we may add that Paul is not speaking in symbolism; as the cause of this oneness is objective and a reality, so also is the effect. We are actually and not merely symbolically one spiritual body. The fact that now and then unworthy communicants also partake of the sacrament is not taken into consideration.

18) The Corinthians certainly agree with Paul in their judgment (v. 15) that because the one sacramental cup and bread are the communion of the one sacrificial blood and body of Christ they make the entire multitude of communicants in Christendom "one body." This was true also with regard to the people of the old covenant as the Corinthians well know. **Behold Israel after the flesh. Are not they who eat the sacrifices communicants of the sacrificial altar?** You Corinthians certainly know that they are. The imperative that bids the Corinthians look at Israel lends a touch of vivacity. Paul is speaking about Israel "after the flesh," which as a nation gathers about the great altar of burnt sacrifice in the Temple at Jerusalem just as all Christendom now gathers about the sacramental altar of Christ. The question which Paul again asks invites the sensible judgment of the Corinthians.

This time Paul mentions the eating: "are not they who eat," etc.? From the consecration of the cup he advances to the distribution of the bread and now to the eating because the Christian Sacrament is not complete until the communicants eat and drink, and the consecration as well as the distribution have the eating and the drinking as their purpose. So the analogy is between the eating of the Israelites and the eating of the Christians, each at their altar. An Israelite who refused to eat of the sacrifices would thereby dissociate himself from the altar of Israel and from everything that was embodied in that altar. Every Israelite who did eat by that eating shared in everything for which the altar stood and which that altar intended to communicate to him.

Paul uses the significant adjective κοινωνοί in order to match the noun κοινωνία which was used with reference to the Christian sacrament in v. 16. Lacking the corresponding adjective in English, we are compelled to use the noun instead: are they not "communicants" of the sacrificial altar? They certainly are no less. To eat is to share in the communion of the altar. To eat is far more than ordinary eating that merely fills the stomach with meat. To eat is to have a part in all of the benefits of the altar and of the sacrifices laid upon it, i. e., to have the forgiveness which this altar mediates, the standing among God's people which it bestows, and thus the holiness with which it enfolds and surrounds. No, it was no small thing, no mere indifferent, meaningless act to eat of Israel's sacrifices that were brought on the altar of burnt offering.

19) Before making his application to the participation in pagan sacrifices and pagan altars Paul first cuts off a false deduction which someone might make from his analogy of the Israelite altar as though this analogy involves the idea that the pagan gods and the pagan altars are real gods and altars of real gods. **What, then, am I claiming? That an idol sacrifice is something? or that an idol is something?**

These questions again appeal to the good Christian sense of the Corinthians. When Paul asks what he is thus claiming he refers to the real communion which the Israelites had with their altar of the true God who exists. So he adds the double question regarding the idol sacrifice and regarding the idol itself. Has Paul forgotten what he has written in 8:4? Does he now in this statement regarding Israel imply that idols are after all real beings as the pagans suppose, and that idol sacrifices are sacrifices to real beings?

20) The very opposite is the truth. Paul's analogy is true, altogether true, although idols are not

real beings at all. **On the contrary, I am claiming that what the Gentiles sacrifice they sacrifice to devils and not to a god. And I do not want you to be communicants with devils.**

The strong adversative ἀλλά is elliptical: "On the contrary, what I claim is this that," etc. Thus Paul not only denies what the two preceding questions imply regarding a possible reality of pagan gods but most positively asserts what the real fact is regarding the sacrifices which the Gentiles offer. It is a great mistake to imagine that back of their idolatry and their idol sacrifices there is nothing but an empty vacuity. True enough, as 8:4 makes plain, the gods of the idols have no existence whatever; no being by the name of Jupiter exists, and this is true with respect to all other gods. But something does exist, something that is far more terrible than these pseudo-gods, namely an entire kingdom of darkness which is hostile to God, a host of demons or fallen angels who are ruled by the greatest of their number, namely Satan, Eph. 2:3; 6:12.

All altars, all sacrifices, and all worship that are not intended to serve the true God are thus actually though not necessarily consciously and intentionally devoted to these demons. As these wicked angels, under the leadership of Satan, rule the entire evil world, so in particular they are the originators of the spiritual darkness of which idolatry is the most terrible evidence. Hence all idol sacrifices, whatever the pagan ideas concerning them may be, are really sacrifices unto devils. Compare Deut. 32:17; Ps. 106:37; 95:5, which show that Paul is in a manner quoting Scripture in v. 20.

No wonder Paul adds: "And I do not want you to be communicants with devils." As he did in v. 18, he again uses the adjective κοινωνοί with the genitive for which we must again use the English noun. This time the genitive names the beings into whose communion or union one is brought by eating of idol sacrifices. The infinitive is durative: Paul does not want the Corinthians to become involved in such a union. For to be in any manner in communion with devils is to be cut off from communion with God, Christ, his body and his blood, and the blessings of Christ.

21) Paul states this in the most positive way and even repeats the statement in order to make it the more impressive. **You cannot drink the Lord's cup and the devils' cup; you cannot partake of the Lord's table and of the devils' table.**

Paul is speaking, not of the physical, but of the moral possibility. Both infinitives are durative: you cannot "be drinking . . . be partaking." A misguided Christian may attend an idol feast and not immediately lose his Christianity but he cannot continue this wicked practice without spiritual ruin to himself. "The Lord's cup" is the one received in the Lord's Supper, that conveys the Lord's sacrificial blood to the communicant. "The Lord's table" is the entire sacrament. Paul makes the cup prominent here whereas a moment previously in v. 17 he makes the bread prominent and thus keeps a fine balance.

He uses exact parallels when he writes "the devils' cup" and "the devils' table." The original question deals with idol meats only and says nothing about the wine served at idol feasts. But the entire idol feast with any and all food and drink is celebrated in honor of the idol. Hence it is impossible that a Christian communicant should drink of the wine thus served or partake of anything that is served on the banquet table. Compare the invitations to idol feasts noted in connection with 8:10. And thus Paul has answered fully the question of the Corinthians concerning things offered to idols.

22) Since this is the true situation regarding participation in idol feasts, a Christian who refuses to heed Paul's words has only one terrible alternative. **Or are we engaged in provoking the Lord to jealousy? Are we stronger than he?** The present indicative should not be read as though it were the deliberative subjunctive. The latter would be much weaker: "would we provoke," etc. The change from the second person to the first should also be noted. Is this, Paul asks, what "we" are doing? He quietly implies that what is right for the Corinthians is, of course, right also for Paul and thereby emphasizes the enormity of thus provoking the Lord who gave himself for us. Paul alludes to Deut. 32:21: "They have moved me to jealousy with that which is not God; they have provoked me to anger with their vanities," LXX, "with their idols" which are frequently termed "vanities."

It is safe to arouse only one who is weaker than we are. Hence the final question with its implied negative answer: "You certainly do not intend to say that we are stronger than he?" The very idea is preposterous and thus reduces this alternative to an absurdity. To say that God may be roused to jealousy, vindictive zeal, and wrath is to apply anthropopathic terms to him. The Scriptures constantly speak about God in this manner, yet without in the least attributing to him the imperfections and the faults that attach to human jealousy and human anger. Unbelief will always mock at these terms and misuse them for its own purposes until the day of reckoning comes. Since heaven's high language exceeds all human speech, God graciously condescends to speak to us in such human terms as we can understand. Yet we well know that they express the divine realities in an inadequate manner.

Conduct in Detail, 10:23-11:1

23) The main question about attending idol feasts has been fully answered with a peremptory negative. But this still leaves the question in regard to meats that were put on sale in the markets for the general public and the question about dining privately at some pagan's home where meat might be served which originally came from some idol sacrifice and was sold in the market. See the introductory remarks to chapter eight. Paul now answers these questions in detail.

He reverts to the principles already elucidated in 6:12, and 8:10, etc. **All things are lawful, but not all things benefit. All things are lawful, but not all things build up.** In 6:12 we have seen that the Corinthians set up the principle of complete liberty *in adiaphoris* and embodied it in the expression: "All things are lawful." Paul assented to the principle and now again does so. But he added and does so again the self-evident and normal limitations: first, "but not all things benefit," namely spiritually; secondly, "but not all things build up" spiritually. Regarding the details of conduct now to be discussed Paul thus says to the Corinthians: "The principle is right enough; let us now apply it, but, of course, only with its natural limitations. For it is folly to insist on doing things just because they are lawful when these things bring no benefit but rather hurt and harm either me or others. It is absurd to insist on doing things just because they are lawful when these things do not build up and further the Christian life but damage and destroy it for me or for others."

24) Paul therefore at once interprets the principle of Christian liberty of which the Corinthians seek to make so much and which they do not after all really understand. **Let no one seek his own** (interest) **but that of the other.** This interpretation itself may be called a principle, one that must always be

combined with the principle of liberty if the latter is to be applied successfully. This second is, of course, the principle of love about which Paul has already said so much. So he merely restates it in a simple way. This time he formulates it in a concrete way. He tells the Corinthians in the tersest manner what they are to do when they are following the promptings of love. He purposely states the principle in the broadest form so that it may answer all of the questions that now await solution. Not to seek one's own interest, τὸ ἑαυτοῦ, is, of course, not to be understood in an absolute way but must be considered in connection with the seeking of the interest of the other person. It excludes all selfish regard which cares nothing for the interest of other people. It demands that we have regard for the good of others also, for by doing this we shall serve also ourselves in the best possible manner.

25) After the principle has been adequately stated, Paul proceeds to make the specific applications. He begins with a consideration of the meat that is sold in the open markets. **Everything that is on sale in a butchershop eat, making no investigation because of the conscience.**

A μάκελλον, Latin *macellum*, is an ordinary butchershop where meat is on sale, "being sold" as the participle states. Paul tells the Corinthians to be altogether unconcerned about the nature of the meat that is sold in the ordinary butchershops; they are to buy and to eat and to be satisfied. This means that Christians are to make no investigations regarding the origin of any piece of meat; they are not to inquire whether it is a portion from an idol sacrifice or not. "Making no investigation because of the conscience," means that the conscience is to be left out of the matter entirely. "Do not trouble about your conscience — buy and eat." The phrase "because of the conscience" modifies only the participle. Paul does not say: "Do not make any inquiries because your conscience may be disturbed if you buy a piece from some idol sacrifice, or if you should not be certain that the butcher is telling you the truth, and the piece may after all be taken from an idol sacrifice." This would be poor ethics, merely closing the eyes so as not to see.

"Because of the conscience" refers, of course, only to the buyer's conscience and not to that of some other person who happens to see him buy or discovers that it is idol meat. If Paul had intended the latter he would have had to say as much. Paul's injunction applies especially to those who may be inclined to be weak and easily disturbed by unnecessary conscientious scruples. He urges them for their own sakes as well as for the sake of others to use their Christian liberty in the manner indicated. They are injuring no one by doing so. It is a mistake to inquire too carefully for reasons of conscience. Why?

26) **For the earth is the Lord's and the fulness thereof.** Without an introductory formula such as, "it is written," Paul quotes Ps. 24:1; he expects his readers to know that he is quoting. "Fulness," $\pi\lambda\acute{\eta}\rho\omega\mu\alpha$, is always to be understood in the passive sense: that by which something is filled. The earth and its fulness include all food; and this belongs to the Lord who created all of it; and no idol or demon can permanently appropriate it for himself. We are mistaken when we act as though this could be done. Buying food for our own table is an entirely different thing from dining at a feast that is given in honor of some idol. In this succinct manner Paul answers the first question. After the principle has been elucidated, the answer is quite simple.

27) Now the next question. **If one of the unbelievers invites you, and you desire to go, everything placed before you eat, making no investigation because of the conscience.**

The same rule of conduct applies in this case: eat everything and make no investigation of a conscientious nature. This unbeliever may or may not have bought idol meat for the meal, it makes no difference. Relatives and friends of Christians who are themselves still unbelievers may invite these Christians in friendly fashion. When Paul adds: "and you desire to go," i. e., to accept the invitation, he does not imply that, if he could, he would forbid the acceptance of such an invitation. All that he implies is that for some reason or other that is not connected with the question of idol meat the believer may not wish to go.

28) Yet, when he is dining out, a complication may arise; δέ marks the following statement as being something that is different from the general rule. **But if someone shall say to you, This is sacrifice meat, do not eat because of him that showed it and** (because of) **the conscience.**

When Paul spoke about the invitation to dine out he used a condition that expresses reality; when he now speaks about a weak conscience he uses a condition that expresses expectancy. Paul writes merely τίς: if "somebody" shall speak in this manner. Since no modifiers are attached, this "somebody" is often understood to refer to anybody save perhaps the host himself, to some pagan, perhaps, who offers friendly warning or is curious to see what the Christian will do, or to one with hostile intent who is eager to put the Christian into an embarrassing position. But Paul has not left τίς so undetermined. The entire discussion has been concerned with the exercise of our liberty with reference to offending weak Christians. The two preceding directions, v. 25-27, in particular are intended for just such weak Christians. "Someone" is, therefore, one of these. In this entire section Paul says nothing whatever about the exercise of our Christian liberty with respect to pagans.

The case is, then, that of a weak brother who may also be present as a guest and may have done what Paul has warned not to do, namely to inquire about the origin of the meat that is served at the meal, and may thus have discovered that some of it or all of it is "sacrifice meat." When he makes his discovery known at the table he would naturally use the term "sacrifice meat" and not "idol meat" in deference to the pagan host. The very fact that this weak brother feels such grave concern which will not let him rest until he has found out what he wishes to know about the meat, and the additional fact that he then feels constrained to communicate his finding to the other Christians, show that he is weak and needs the tender consideration of love.

Here the strong Christians must then use their Christian liberty in a truly intelligent and loving way: "Do not eat!" Their liberty lies in the fact that they may or may not eat, yet not in the sense that they may do as they please, eat or not eat without reason or for a wrong or a foolish reason. Their liberty lies in the ability to choose between eating and not eating with entire freedom as long as they are guided by both true knowledge and true love. To choose blindly where one can choose intelligently is to abuse liberty and not really to use it; and the same is true with regard to choosing inconsiderately where one can just as well choose considerately. Liberty is given to us, not in order to hurt ourselves and others, but in order to help ourselves and others. Why not eat in this case? "Because of the person that showed" whence the meat came. Why not on his account? The epexegetical καί answers: because of him "and of the (his) conscience."

29) Paul does not write: "and (because of) *his* (αὐτοῦ) conscience." He states it far more emphatically: **Conscience now I say, not at all thine own, on the contrary, that of the other, for why is my free-**

dom judged by some other conscience? Paul thus says: "As far as *thy* conscience is concerned, it would make no difference as to the nature of the meat, thou couldst eat; but for the sake of *this weak brother's* conscience and *his* timid and disturbing scruples refrain from eating."

This pronouncement requires explanation (γάρ) lest someone think that his conscience is bound and controlled by some other person's conscience. My own freedom of conscience is not subject to the ignorance and the weakness of some other individual's conscience. He cannot arrogate to himself the right to sit in judgment on my liberty and to order *me* to do what *his* conscience considers right and forbid *me* to do what *his* conscience considers wrong. In regard to this meat my conscience is wholly free to eat as I may desire. In fact, my conscience would not at all raise the question whether this is "sacrifice meat" or not. So it is not at all my own conscience but altogether that of the other person for which I have regard in this case. "Why is my freedom judged by some other conscience?" The question answers itself. No other conscience can and dare restrict my freedom.

We read ἱνατί and not ἵνα τί because we supply γένηται, R. 739. Note the difference: τὴν τοῦ ἑτέρου, "that of the other person," the particular one in this case; while ἄλλης = "any other" conscience no matter whose. By refraining from eating, Paul says, I wish only to shield the other person's weak conscience, and I do not for one moment make his or any other person's conscience a judge of my liberty, as to what I may or may not do, must or must not do.

30) This is amplified. **If I for my part partake with thankfulness, why am I slandered for what I on my part give thanks?**

The question again answers itself. Whoever would slander or speak evil of me would do so without a just reason. Such a slander would not at all apply to me. Why not? One reason has already been stated, namely "my liberty," my own conscience being wholly free in the matter. To this first reason another is added which is stated twice for the sake of emphasis and each time with an emphatic ἐγώ, "I for my part." How does Paul, who here and so often uses himself for the purpose of exemplification, eat of this meat? "I for my part partake with thankfulness," and again, "for what I on my part give thanks." He eats this meat as being a gift from God and in no other way. He eats it with thankfulness in his heart and with a prayer of thankfulness on his lips. What is wrong with that? Nothing. What right has any man, when he hears that Paul does this, to revile him for so doing? He has no right whatever.

The dative χάριτι does not mean "by grace" as our versions translate, i. e., "by God's grace"; for this emphatic dative is restated in the clause "for what I on my part give thanks." Whoever considers the meat in question idol meat could naturally not receive it with thankfulness and a prayer of thanksgiving. "I for my part" and its twice repeated emphasis contrast Paul and his thankfulness for God's gift with "the other" who beholds only idol meat and cannot give thanks.

The verb βλασφημεῖν means more than "to criticize"; it always refers to slanderous language used in connection with God, here to Paul's connection with God through the meat which is God's gift, and which no idol can appropriate to itself in distinction from God.

31) Paul now draws the final deduction with οὖν. This is again a broad Christian principle of conduct. In v. 23, 24 he began with the principle that centers in the spiritual benefit of our fellow men. He must go farther than that. Underlying this principle is another that is still more vital, in fact, the

ultimate principle of all Christian action. **Whether, therefore, you eat or drink or do anything, do all to God's glory!**

The connection alone suggests to Paul the two activities of eating and of drinking, but he now broadens both so as to indicate any and all eating and drinking apart from any particular food received at any particular time or place. Then Paul reaches out to any and to every deed a Christian may do: "or do anything," there is no emphasis whatever on the indefinite pronoun. "All" is just as broad and comprehensive.

"To God's glory" is to be taken objectively, so as really to glorify God, and not merely subjectively, so that we think we are glorifying him. This must be the sense, for the weak Christian might, indeed, think that he is glorifying God when in his ignorance and his false scrupulosity he shrinks from eating idol meat while he is reclining at a table of a friend and judges other men's consciences by his own faulty conscience; but God is not glorified thus. Again an unscrupulous Christian might think that he is glorifying God when he tramples on a weak brother's conscience and does him the gravest spiritual injury; but God is not glorified thus. Each truly glorifies God when each acts according to the full measure of his knowledge and his love, and when he seeks constantly to increase that knowledge and that love. We do all things for "God's glory" when the excellence of God's attributes is made to shine forth by our actions so that men may see it.

32) How we are to do all things to God's glory is stated by an appositional sentence which is joined to the previous one without a connective. **Be devoid of offense as well for Jews, as for Greeks, as for the church of God.** We make God's glory shine out to men when we are ἀπρόσκοποι to all of them, "devoid of offense," when in all things we act so that no one can take real offense, i. e., stumble in regard to God and

the gospel. Some may, indeed, *take* offense, namely wrongfully; we are not to *give* offense. The former no Christian can avoid; the latter all Christians are to avoid.

Paul broadens the principle of Christian conduct in two directions. Starting with idol meat, Paul lays down a principle which includes all eating and all drinking and all actions of a Christian. Starting with knowledge plus love to our brethren, Paul reaches up to God, to our supreme obligation to him. Again starting from our weak brethren, Paul finally includes all men. Here Paul at last touches the Christian's relation to the non-Christian world yet combines this relation with that to the church of God. All of it is summed up in the one word, ἀπρόσκοποι: Give no one just cause for offense. And here all three, Jews, Greeks, and the church, are on the same plane.

Paul does not enter into details. Offense to Jews may not be offense to Gentiles; offense to these may not be offense to Christians. Offense to any one and to all of these three classes will, however, center in this one point, that by some foolish or inconsiderate action we place a stumbling block in their path in regard to Christ and the gospel. No action of ours is to prevent a Jew or a Greek from coming to Christ, and no action of ours is to prevent a Christian from remaining with Christ and from ever drawing nearer to him. This is negative, but "devoid of offense" naturally includes its corresponding positive. All of our actions are to help the Jew and the Greek to come to Christ; they are also to help to hold and to strengthen our fellow Christians in their attachment to Christ.

"Jews" and "Greeks" are objective terms, for all men alike use these designations and not only each of these groups when they are speaking of themselves. "The church of God" is a subjective term, for men generally do not use it, we alone use it with reference to ourselves. When the world today speaks of "the church" it does not put into that term the sense which Paul had in mind when he wrote "the church of God." If the world would accept Paul's designation it would condemn itself as being outside of the assembly (church) that belongs to God; and this the world does not intend to do, at least not seriously. The term "Christian" as a parallel to "Jews" and "Greeks" was not yet in general use in Paul's time, so he writes ἡ ἐκκλησία τοῦ Θεοῦ, "the assembly of God."

33) Beside the negative "devoid of offense" Paul places the positive: **even as I also please all men in regard to all things, not seeking my own advantage but that of the many, that they be saved.**

From the second person plural which he has employed in v. 31, 32 Paul returns to the individualizing first person singular. How does Paul act so as to give no offense to any? He pleases all men in regard to all things. He has already described this in detail in 9:19-25, where he sums up: "I am become all things to all men." There is no fear that Paul will be misunderstood as though he seeks to curry favor with all men and yields to them in all things, even in those that are questionable. "I please" is written entirely from Paul's standpoint and not from that of "all men," many of whom he actually displeased when they discovered his true motive, namely that he intended to win them for Christ.

Thus he also at once adds: "not seeking my own advantage but that of the many." He forgot, in fact, entirely disregarded his own interest and sought only the interest of "the many," who are so named in contrast with himself as being only one individual. The idea expressed is that one man's interest is as nothing when it is compared with the interest of many men. Paul carries this thought to the highest point in Rom. 9:3, where he expresses himself much as Moses did in Exod. 32:32. Here he stops short with a reference to the earthly advantage which he might seek for himself in contradistinction to the heavenly advantage which he desires to secure for the many. The subfinal ἵνα clause mentions the apposition to "the advantage of the many," namely "that they be saved" (not final: "that they may be saved.") The aorist means "actually saved," and the passive indicates that God is the one who saves.

11:1) What Paul thus exemplifies by a reference to himself he urges upon all. **Be you imitators of me even as I also am of Christ!** Those who imitate Christ have a right to call upon others to imitate them. The point of comparison between Christ and Paul has already been clearly stated: Christ sought not his own advantage but that of others. He came to seek and to save. Let this mind that was in Christ and then in Paul be also in us.

CHAPTER XI

The Fifth Part of the Letter

Women Covering the Head, 11:2-16

2) It is unwarranted to say that Paul could not begin one of the main parts of his letter with a word of praise to the Corinthians. Certain interpreters conclude that this word of praise is the beginning of an independent letter which they surmise is Paul's lost letter. Some unknown redactor wove the two letters into one. Following this clue, they delete other parts of this composite letter and thus reconstruct both the lost letter (or a good part of it) and what they deem the canonical letter which is called the first to the Corinthians in the New Testament. Some go still farther and reconstruct three or even four distinct letters by applying this selective process. These different hypotheses, however, contradict and thus rather annihilate each other.

The question with reference to women covering their heads or leaving them uncovered was of recent origin in Corinth. It is safe to conclude that the subject was broached in the letter which the Corinthians had sent to Paul. The absence of a περί phrase at the beginning of Paul's reply on this matter may indicate that the Corinthians had made no formal inquiry. So Paul does not begin: "Concerning the covering of the head for women." As the tenor of Paul's instruction shows, this question regarding women had in all likelihood as yet not become so acute in Corinth as to prompt a direct inquiry to the apostle.

Those who think that a strong emancipation movement was in full progress among the Corinthian women draw rather strongly on their imagination. There is nothing in Paul's instructions which might justify this supposition. Quite the contrary. The Corinthians are in accord with Paul in regard to this question. What he has taught them regarding the position and the conduct of women is still in force among them. In their reference to the veiling of the women during worship the Corinthians seem to have said as much, perhaps in words that were similar to those which Paul uses, about their readiness to "hold fast the traditions even as I delivered them to you," v. 2.

Such an attitude pleases Paul. Ever ready to praise wherever he can, he praises the Corinthians in this connection. Then he sends them his instruction on the subject, which is couched altogether in an objective form. Only at the end, in v. 16, we note a subjective turn: "if any man seems contentious." A fair deduction from this admonition is the thought that a few contentious voices had been raised in Corinth which either merely questioned the necessity of the women covering their heads or advocated that they leave them uncovered. The congregation and the body of the women in it were not yet disturbed. As far as Paul's words reflect the situation, this appears to have been the state of affairs.

Now I praise you that in all things you are remembering me, and as I delivered to you the traditions are holding them fast.

The connective δέ merely turns to the new subject. The apparent paronomasia between μιμηταί in v. 1 and μέμνησθε in v. 2 is quite unintentional; the perfect tense of the latter verb is always used as a durative present. "In all things" is not the accusative object of "remember" since in the New Testament this verb is not construed with an object in this case; πάντα is the ordinary adverbial accusative: "as regards all matters," R. 479, 482. Nor is μου in the least emphatic as though Paul praises the Corinthians for following him in preference to other leaders. He praises the Corinthians because, in regard to every question that arises, they think of him and ask what he taught them on the subject.

The addition with καί intends to specify and to explain what Paul means by saying that the Corinthians thus remember him: "and as I delivered to you the traditions are holding them fast." Just to remember Paul is still indefinite, for they might remember him and his teaching and still not follow that teaching. Paul intends to say that the Corinthians remember him in a spirit of loyalty. They are not rebelling against the instructions which Paul had given them, not disregarding them and following contrary teachings. Had they not recently written a letter to Paul in which they asked him a number of important questions, which he is answering in his present letter? Disputes arose as to how much some of Paul's regulations really included, and differences of opinion on various points were voiced. New questions sprang up regarding which even the most loyal of Paul's friends were in doubt. They did not know just how to apply his principles. For this reason they wrote to Paul. Even the parties in Corinth should not be regarded as factions that repudiated Paul and his gospel; they only venerated other leaders higher than Paul. The congregation as such "is holding fast" (note the present tense) to Paul's traditions. Some of the members may question this or that point, may in their pride seek to improve on Paul, may be contentious because of their ignorance and inclined to be wayward; but the congregation as such is not disaffected.

Note the cognate terms παρέδωκα and παραδόσεις, "I delivered" and "deliverances" (traditions), the former helping to explain the latter. A "tradition" is any deliverance, any bit of instruction, any principle, and any rule of conduct which Paul handed over to the Corinthians when he was in their midst. The term is quite general and without technical ecclesiastical limitations. It includes points of doctrine as well as points of practice; moreover, these always go together, the latter growing out of the former. The connection decides whether the word in a special way, as in this instance, pertains to practice or to doctrine.

The question as to where Paul originally obtained what he thus handed on to the Corinthians can be answered only in one way: from the Lord, Gal. 1:12. Paul was a true apostle who was on a par with the Twelve. All were directed by the same Lord and the same Spirit. There were no clashes and no contradictions between them. The contention that Paul obtained these traditions or deliverances at secondhand from the other apostles or from other parts of the church is without warrant. If evidence is needed on this point, Gal. 2:9 more than suffices.

3) All indications point to an agreement between the Corinthians and Paul that women should cover their heads in public worship. We have no intimation to the effect that the women of the congregation are defying this custom. The only question is why this should be so; or more precisely why Christian women should adhere to this custom. Here we may remember that it is important not only to do certain things but to do them intelligently, for the right reason. So Paul's entire discussion intends to furnish the right reason and thus to confirm the Corinthians in their laudable practice.

Paul first lays down the great basic fact that must be noted and never be forgotten in this connection. **Now I want you to know that of every man the head is Christ while the woman's head is the man, and Christ's head God.**

We must take "of every man" as it stands. The fact that only Christian men accept Christ as their head while others do not does not change the truth "that of every man the head is Christ." This statement is placed forward because Christian women may forget that every man is under a head, and that it is therefore not at all strange that women, too, are under a head. It is entirely contrary to fact that women should seek to be like men on the supposition that men are independent. The men are not at all independent — their head is Christ. Yet "of every man the head is Christ" does not express the entire relation of Christ to a man but only the relation of subjection in his being and his life. Here one alone is head, "*the* head" (note the article); all men have one unit head. The figure suggested by "head" is the idea of superiority. In other words, the man is not independent, Christ is his head to whom he is subject.

In the next two statements the word "head" is without the article. R. 781 is right, this omission means that the man is not the head of the woman in the same sense as Christ is the head of the man. This is true also with reference to God as Christ's head. Each case is marked by a peculiar and a unique relation: 1) of God to our Mediator Christ; 2) of Christ to the man; 3) of the man to the woman. Specifically all three are different. No two correspond in all points. But in one respect they do most decidedly correspond. In all three cases we see a head and a subject to that head who acknowledges that head.

In all his mediatorial work Christ did not do his own will but that of his great Sender, ὁ πέμψας με (regularly used in John's Gospel). Thus God was "a head" for him. Because of creation the man was not independent but under his Creator. But Paul adds the fact of redemption to creation, for he speaks of the man, not as originally created, but as now also redeemed.

For this reason he does not say that the man's head is God but names the Redeemer, "Christ." Christ may in a general way be called the Redeemer of the woman as well as of the man. Paul calls him so in Gal. 3:28: "There can be no male and female, for ye all are one man in Christ Jesus," R. V. Yet the difference of sex remains as far as headship is concerned. The man has only Christ as his head, the woman has another head in addition to Christ, namely the man. She is not the man's head, nor is she under Christ only as her head.

Thus a number of questions are cleared up. Does Paul go back to the order of creation? He does, but in conjunction with redemption. Does Paul refer only to Christ's human nature when he is speaking of God as Christ's head? Paul refers to Christ in his redemptive work in which both natures of Christ were employed. In this work Christ carried out God's will with both natures. Yet this in no way subordinates the Son, who, in his essence as the Son, remains co-equal with the Father and the Spirit even as the Spirit, who is sent by the Father and the Son, remains co-equal with both. Is Paul using "head" as he does in Eph. 5:23, 32; 4:16? No; in Ephesians "head" is correlated with "body." Paul is not even, as some think, using the Old Testament figure of "head" in the sense of ruler over a body of people as is done in Judges 11:11; II Sam. 5:17; 22:44; II Chron. 19:11. Paul's *tertium comparationis* in the use of "head" is here restricted to the one feature of being over another according to an arrangement made by God.

4) Paul now applies the facts which he has stated concerning headship to the customs as they existed in Corinth and elsewhere.

Generally speaking, among the Greeks only slaves were covered, and the uncovered head was a sign of freedom. The Romans reversed this. The free man wore the pileus, the slave went bareheaded. When the latter was emancipated he was said *vocari ad pileum*. Yet the Romans, and we must add the Germans, were accustomed to pray while they were veiled. The Jews had the same custom, and we should not forget that Paul was originally a Jew. This veiling expressed reverence, the proper feeling of unworthiness to appear before God with an open face. Maimonides says: "Let not the Wise Men, nor the scholars of the Wise Men, pray unless they be covered." The Jewish covering was called the *tallith*.

All of this shows us that Paul is not laying down an absolute rule that is to be observed by Christians of all times in regard to covering the head or leaving it uncovered during worship. Not the custom as a custom is vital but *the significance* of a custom. If Paul were writing to Jews or to Romans or to Germans, all of whom covered the head during worship because of reverence and shame in God's presence, he would have to tell them that any man among them who violated this custom thereby showed lack of reverence and shame. But to write this to Greeks would be incomprehensible to them. They had an entirely different custom which had an entirely different significance. This significance is sound and good. Hence Paul explains it to the Corinthians at length and bids them to abide by their custom. For to abrogate it and to fly in the face of it means, in their case, not only to violate that significance but at the same time to disavow that significance. The fact that Paul sees this significance with a Christian's eye as pertaining to the true God and not with a pagan's eye as pertaining to idol gods should cause no confusion. The fact that he would use the Christian's eye if he were dealing with the opposite custom of other nationalities and not the pagan's eye is again beyond question. By so doing Paul is not introducing into these national customs something that is foreign and unjustifiable but is unveiling to Christians the full and the true significance of these customs which non-Christians grasped or felt only partially because the glory of the true God was hidden from them.

The Greek custom that was followed in Corinth brought to view the facts which all Christians should know, that Christ is the head of the man, and that the man is the head of the woman. Because it did this for Christian minds and Christian eyes the Greek custom was good and proper and should be preserved by those concerned. Violating it means to those who have this custom a clash with the divine facts reflected in this custom.

Paul first considers the man and then the woman: **Every man engaged in praying or prophesying;** and in v. 5: **and every woman engaged in praying and prophesying.** The man and the woman are described in exactly the same terms. The two activities naturally go together in the case of each. It is quite essential to note that no modifier is attached to the participles to denote a place where these activities were exercised. So we on our part should not introduce one, either the same one for both the man and the woman, for instance, "worshipping or prophesying *in church*," or different ones, for the man *"in church"* and for the woman *"at home."* By omitting reference to a place Paul says this: "Wherever and whenever it is proper and right for a man or for a woman to pray or to prophesy, the difference of sex should be marked as I indicate." Whether men are present or absent when a woman prays or prophesies makes no difference; also vice versa. Each remains what he is or what she is apart from the other.

An issue has been made of the point that Paul speaks of a woman as prophesying as though it were a matter of course that she should prophesy just as she also prays, and just as the man, too, prays and prophesies. Paul is said to contradict himself when he forbids the women to prophesy in 14:34-36. The matter becomes clear when we observe that from 11:17 onward until the end of chapter 14 Paul deals with the gatherings of the congregation for public worship and with regulations pertaining to public assemblies. The transition is decidedly marked: "that ye come together," i. e., for public worship, v. 17; "when ye come together in church" (ἐκκλησίᾳ, no article), v. 18; and again: "when ye assemble together," i. e., for public worship, v. 20. In these public assemblies Paul forbids the women, not only to prophesy, but to speak at all, 14:34-36 and assigns the reason for this prohibition just as he does in I Tim. 2:11, etc.

It is evident, then, that women, too, were granted the gift of prophecy even as some still have this gift, namely the ability to present and properly to apply the Word of God by teaching others. And they are to exercise this valuable gift in the ample opportunities that offer themselves. So Paul writes "praying and prophesying" with reference to the woman just as he does with reference to the man. The public assemblies of the congregation are, however, not among these opportunities — note ἐν ταῖς ἐκκλησίαις, "in the assemblies," 14:34. At other places and at other times women are free to exercise their gift of prophecy. In the present connection Paul has no occasion whatever to specify regarding this point. We may, however, think of Lois and Eunice who instructed Timothy, II Tim. 1:5; 3:15; of Priscilla, who was more able than her husband, who taught Apollos, Acts 18:24-26; and of other cases. The teaching ability of Christian women today has a wide range of opportunity without in the least intruding itself into the public congregational assemblies.

Every man who is engaged in praying or prophesying, **having his head covered, dishonors his**

head, i. e., "having something down from his head." Paul says this, not because some man in Corinth is liable to do such a thing, but in order to bring out the contrast with the woman. He shames or disgraces "his head," the Greek has the article of previous reference. We cannot refer "his head" to Christ and disregard the phrase "down from his head." Christ is not shamed by this man; the shame is on the man himself. By covering his head he makes a woman of himself. He acts as though he has a human head over him besides the divine head Christ, like the woman — which is not true. By thus discarding the honor that is his he puts shame on his own head. We may, of course, also say that this act of his reflects on Christ, but Paul does not follow out this thought.

5) **And every woman praying or prophesying with her head uncovered dishonors her head, for it is one and the same thing with her head shaven.**

Since the entire question concerns women, Paul speaks at length about them. The woman brings shame upon her head when she appears in public to pray or to prophesy "with her head uncovered," dative of manner, R. 530, 789. Here, too, it is her own head and not the man as her head. Paul might write regarding the man that he brings shame on "himself" and regarding the woman on "herself." Since it is the covered or uncovered head that brings shame, Paul very properly speaks about the shame resting on the head. The shame that results for the woman lies in her attempt to appear as a man, to arrogate to herself an honor that is not hers, which must be taken from her. This means disgrace for her. Every act on the part of a woman which denies her position as a woman under the headship of man is an arrogation that brings her dishonor. R. 530 reports that ὁ αὐτός (here the neuter τὸ αὐτό) is only here construed with the instrumental dative: one and "the same thing with her head shaven,"

i. e., with a razor. The perfect participle has the usual present implication. Paul at once states the drastic extreme which he proceeds to explain with γάρ.

6) For if a woman is not covered, let her also have herself shorn; but if it is a shame for a woman to have herself shorn or shaven, let her have herself covered.

"Not covered" is a case in which the negative practically coalesces with the verb: "not covered" = "uncovered," R. 1012, although in conditions of reality the protasis regularly has οὐ. We translate the two imperatives, which are probably hortatory, R. 948, with the permissive middle: "let her have herself shorn," "let her have herself covered," R. 809. The form ξυρᾶσθαι is the present infinitive and thus corresponds with κείρασθαι; both are again the permissive middle and are substantivized by the neuter article: "this thing of having herself shorn or shaven" is shameful. The form ξύρασθαι would be the first aorist middle infinitive, R. 1218.

As far as prostitutes are concerned, all the evidence that has been discovered proves that only a few of the very lowest type had shorn or shaven heads. As a class these women endeavored to make themselves as attractive as possible and did their utmost to beautify also their hair. We cannot, therefore, accept the idea that is advanced by not a few of our best commentators that in our passage Paul refers to the practice of prostitutes and intends to tell the Corinthian women that, if they pray or prophesy with uncovered heads, they act the part of lewd women.

Paul presents two alternatives regarding women to the Corinthians: either shorn or covered. Or, to carry it to its climax in both directions: either both covering and hair completely removed or a covering over the hair. The key to these alternatives is the conditional clause: "now if it is a shame for a woman to have herself shorn or shaven." This condition of reality, which implies that it would certainly be a shame, expresses a universal feeling and conviction regarding women (with a corresponding conviction regarding men, v. 14). We may express it in this way: It is the intent of nature that woman should wear long hair. Back of nature is the Creator. A beautiful head of hair is the natural crown which God has given to a woman. Made for man, she is to be attractive to him, and one of her great attractions is her beautiful hair. Hence to discard it is shameful for her. This explains the two alternatives. The first is negative, the other positive. The one extends in one direction and goes to the limit in that direction, the other extends in the opposite direction and also goes to the limit.

Thus the first: "If a woman is not covered, let her also have herself shorn." This matter of being merely uncovered is in reality only an inconsistency. She stops halfway. She only compromises. Halfway positions and compromises are untenable. Hence, let her carry out the idea to its legitimate and logical conclusion: "let her also have herself shorn." This will bring fully to view what she does only partially when she appears with an uncovered head for prayer or for prophesying.

Now the opposite deduction. If it cannot be denied that leaving the head uncovered is a grave step in the wrong direction, the outrageous nature of which appears fully when it is carried to its consistent limit by discarding also the hair, having it shorn, or by going to the absolute limit in this wrong direction, having all of it shaved off with a razor — then let the woman do the complete and the consistent thing in the right direction: "let her have herself covered." Then there will be no question in regard to shame or honor, in regard to her position as a woman having a man as her head according to the Creator's design.

This is a sample of Paul's consistent thinking. We have seen that he always goes to the bottom of a question, to the plain and decisive principle that is the key to that question and therefore to all others of the same kind. He never stops only on the surface, never goes only halfway, but always thinks a subject through. He does so in this case.

7) But why all these considerations about honoring and dishonoring the head? Why take the matter regarding the hair and the covering of the head so seriously? Paul has pointed to the answer already in v. 3, where he presented the relation of the man to Christ and the relation of the woman to the man. This he now restates and expands. Note the contrasting touches in μέν and δέ. **For a man ought not to have his head covered since he is God's image and glory while the woman is man's glory.** "Ought" expresses obligation, here the one growing out of the relation indicated. A man, as distinguished from a woman, is "God's image and glory." The term "image" is taken from Gen. 1:26, 27: "in our image, after our likeness."

These two phrases are usually regarded as a hendiadys, as expressing only one idea, that of likeness or resemblance; and it is said that there is no real distinction between *tselem,* εἰκών, "image," and *demuth,* ὁμοίωσις, "likeness." This identification of the two terms is, however, superficial. Trench shows that, while in some connections "image" and "likeness" may be used with the same general significance, this is not the case in the account of man's creation. "Image" is the German *Abbild* which invariably presupposes a *Vorbild;* this is not the case with "likeness." "Image" always implies derivation, "likeness" does not. The monarch's head on a coin is an image; likewise the sun's reflection in the water, a statue of stone or of other material, a child in relation to his parent. "Likeness" may be accidental; one egg is like another, one man may resemble another. Augustine points out that image always involves likeness, but that likeness does not always involve image. Trench follows this idea through the Arian and other controversies of the church and through the history of man from his creation to his restoration; his discussion deserves close study.

Thus Adam was "God's image," God's *Abbild,* who bore the impress and stamp of God as his *Vorbild.* Paul does not refer to the second term which is employed in Genesis, namely God's "likeness," when he here describes man. He passes by this lesser term. He substitutes a term of his own which brings out the full greatness that is contained in God's image: man is God's image "and glory."

Paul's use of δόξα has been faulted as being "highly exceptional" by calling one person the "glory" of another person, yet this is the very term that presents Paul's thought most clearly. When we ordinarily speak of God's glory we mean the shining forth of the radiance of his attributes. Paul has in mind the reflexion of God's attributes in his highest visible creature. Being, indeed, God's image, man is also God's glory, a mirror that reflects some of God's glorious attributes.

We now see why Paul is right when he denies that a man is obliged to cover his head when he serves God, when he, for instance, prays or prophesies. He may or may not cover his head for other reasons that have nothing to do with his relation to God and with a proper expression of that relation. He may even, like the Jews, cover his head in God's presence when he desires to express his humbleness and his reverence before God. But as God's image and glory his head should be uncovered — his head because it is the noblest part of his body and most expressive of his personality. When the act of covering his head appears in any way to be a denial of his being God's image and glory, it would certainly be improper, even wrong to cover his head.

In the case of a woman this is quite otherwise: "the woman is man's glory." Eve was not "God's image and glory" in the same sense as Adam was. Strictly speaking, according to her creation, which also redemption has not altered, she must be called "man's glory." Paul does not add the other term "man's image" although he could do so. The higher and the more elucidating term "glory" includes "image." Her entire creation places her in direct and immediate relation to man. She was made for man; she was to be his "helpmeet." The reverse cannot be said. Adam expressed the truth exactly: "This is now bone of my bones, and flesh of my flesh. She shall be called Woman, because she was taken out of man." Before Paul adds the obligation that rests upon her as far as expressing this relation to man is concerned he adds further explanations.

8) **For man is not out of woman, but woman out of man.** These are, of course, the facts. Adam was not in any way derived from ($ἐκ$) a woman; he was created directly by God. The opposite is the fact regarding woman. Eve was derived from ($ἐκ$) Adam: "bone of my bones, and flesh of my flesh." This involves another difference.

9) **For also man was not created on account of the woman, on the contrary, woman on account of the man.** "Man," without the article, any man whoever he may be; "on account of the woman," with the article, hence Eve. "Woman," without the article, some woman; "on account of the man," with the article, hence Adam. God made "a woman" for Adam, but not "a man" for Eve. God could, indeed, have created both man and woman, Adam and Eve, in one undivided act. Today many think and act as though God had really done so. But the fact is otherwise. Nor

should we think and say that at this late date God's creative act, which lies far back in time, makes no difference. The facts of creation abide forever. They can be ignored without resultant loss or harm as little as can other facts of nature.

10) Because these indisputable facts remain, all customs that truly symbolize these facts will meet approval on the part of all who bow fully to God, and all customs that contravene and deny this symbolism will meet with disapproval. **On this account the woman ought to have a power over her head on account of the angels.** In view of these unchangeable facts of creation a double obligation results when it comes to a custom like this and to the significance which it involves. One obligation rests upon the man, v. 7, and the other upon the woman. His head should be bare, hers covered.

Paul uses the same verb regarding both the man and the woman, ὀφείλει, "ought," which expresses obligation and no more. He is not laying down an unalterable law that shall be in effect for the church of all ages and of all nations. While the facts of creation to which Paul goes back are in their very nature unalterable, they cannot be made an equally unalterable law regarding customs for the simple reason that customs vary endlessly for reasons that are not at all concerned with these facts. Only under certain circumstances an obligation may arise in which these facts play a part as was the case here at Corinth and among the Greeks. Established customs that beautifully symbolize these facts "ought" not to be changed arbitrarily but intelligently retained until, without prejudice to these facts, in due course, customs change of their own accord.

Why does Paul call the covering on the woman's head an ἐξουσία? The apparent difficulty, which is sometimes unduly stressed, lies in the fact that "right," "authority," or "power" is ordinarily used in a subjective sense; here it would be the woman's *own* power or authority. This, however, clashes with the context which evidently speaks about the covering on the woman's head as being a symbol of *another's*, namely the man's power and authority over her. We should, then, take the term in that sense. Whether we construe "a power over her head," C.-K. 403, or "to have over her head," makes practically no difference. To call the head covering "a power" is figurative whether we call it a symbol of the power, C.-K., or specify the figure as a metonomy: "power" signifying "sign of power."

Paul adds the final phrase, "on account of the angels," as a matter that needs no elucidation whatever and as one that will be at once understood by the Corinthians. This fact is sufficient to dispose of a number of fanciful interpretations which have been given this simple phrase. The Analogy of Scripture decides the point that an unqualified mention of "the angels" refers to good angels. The simple manner in which this final phrase is added indicates that no new point is being introduced into the discussion. This brief mention of angels is thus involved in all that precedes.

"On account of the angels" implies that God's good angels are present when God's people come together to pray and to prophesy. Paul's view of God's creation in general and of God's people in particular always includes God's good angels. So the phrase simply means that, when we worship, we must not offend them by an impropriety. Such an offense would occur if women prayed and prophesied with uncovered heads and thereby displayed the fact that they had disregarded the station that has been assigned them by their creation. In regard to the nearness of the angels and their interest in us compare 4:9 where Paul speaks about the suffering apostles as being a spectacle also for the angels.

We thus reject the interpretation which refers this expression to evil angels who may be aroused to lasciviousness by seeing the uncovered hair of women at worship. Why should this arouse them any more than the uncovered hair of women when they are not at worship? Paul's phrase has no connection with Gen. 6:1-4; the interpretation of this passage which regards the sons of God as angels is unacceptable. With Meyer we exclaim: *Welche fleischerne Eindeutungen!* And some of these women were matrons and old women. C.-K.'s idea of angels as guardians over God's creative order is an invention to find an explanation for Paul's phrase.

11) With πλήν Paul draws attention to one vital point that should not be overlooked. This connective does not intend to point out the main thought with which Paul closes the discussion as B.-D. and R. 1187 assert. **Only, neither is woman without man, nor man without woman in the Lord.** "Only" means: let this not be overlooked. The predicate is "in the Lord." Whatever God arranged at creation when he made man the head, as far as being "in the Lord" is concerned, both are altogether equal. The man is not "in the Lord" in such a way that the woman is excluded, nor, of course, vice versa. Gal. 3:28 stands: "Ye are all one in Christ Jesus."

12) This equality of spiritual connection with Christ has even a natural background. Although God made man woman's head he also arranged an interdependence between the sexes. **For even as the woman is of the man, so also is the man by the woman; and this all is of God.**

"Even as . . . so also" makes plain this equality. Eve was taken out of (ἐκ) Adam. In this manner the sexes began. On the other hand, "the man is by the woman," διά, by or through the medium of natural birth. All men, just as all women, are γεννητοὶ γυναικῶν, "born of women," Matt. 11:11, not excepting even him who became incarnate by the virgin birth, Gal. 4:4. Both Adam and Eve are exceptional, for neither was born. Yet Eve and all of her descendants are classed together since they are all "of" (ἐκ) Adam; he alone came immediately from the hand of God. All other men have come through the medium (διά) of the woman, i. e., Eve and her daughters. In other words, the sexes are so interlocked that, when their connection with Christ is considered, neither sex is dependent on the other, neither sex has an advantage.

This is by divine arrangement. For τὰ πάντα is specific: "this all" regarding the two sexes; not general, "all things" (our versions), which would have to be πάντα without the article. And ἐκ is again the proper preposition since it denotes the direct source. It is not due to an arrangement that was inaugurated by men or women, nor to what we might call the nature of humanity alone.

13) One additional point must be considered in order to complete the discussion regarding the head covering for women during worship. The obligation which Paul points out in v. 7 and v. 10 rests, as he has shown, on the facts of creation. It amounts to this: customs that symbolize and reflect these facts are proper. The Corinthians may judge this as far as it applies to them. They need to do no more than to ask the question regarding the propriety of the custom in vogue in their midst and in regard to what nature teaches them in support of this their custom. This alone will suffice. **Decide in regard to your own selves: Is it proper for a woman to pray to God uncovered? Does not even nature itself teach you that, if a man wear long hair, it is a dishonor to him while, if a woman wear long hair, it is a glory for her? because her long hair is given her instead of a covering.**

Paul refers the matter to the good sense of the Corinthians themselves. The aorist imperative calls upon them to make a decision. The ἐν phrase is decidedly emphatic because of its position, and it does not mean that the Corinthians are to decide "in themselves," i. e., in their own minds, for nobody decides anything except in his own mind. Paul says: decide "in regard to your own selves," i. e., think of yourselves as you assemble for your public worship and as you engage in worship at home and then in a sensible manner decide what is proper for you. This is the ἐν with persons which Robertson translates "in your own case."

The question which Paul wants them to decide is this: "Is it proper for a woman to pray to God uncovered?" Paul adds no interrogative particle to indicate that he expects either a positive or a negative answer. The simple question is enough. He leaves out prophesying (v. 5), apparently only in order to shorten the question, for this is the original question with which this entire section deals.

The point of the question turns on πρέπον, whether it is "proper" for a woman to pray or to worship with her head uncovered. The verb πρέπω means "to shine forth," "to be distinguished"; hence the adjective = excellent, worthy, fitting, or "proper." We thus see that the obligation mentioned in v. 7 and v. 10 is one of propriety. This is general propriety since the next question turns on the teaching of nature; yet as far as the Christian is concerned, who does everything to the glory of God (10:31), even general propriety carries a Christian influence with it. Paul is quite certain what the answer will be, v. 2. When the Corinthians consider the custom they have they will certainly not call it improper.

14) The second question supports the first. This time Paul indicates by the form of the question that he expects it to be answered affirmatively: "Does not

even nature itself teach you?" etc. It certainly does. When Paul writes "nature itself," we understand, in view of what he has already said, that he has in mind nature as God has formed nature. Thus nature is here placed over against mere taste or transient fashion or faulty ideas. Certain things comport with nature and with the way in which God has made us; they are proper for that reason. Certain things are unnatural and for that reason lack propriety.

Thus, when a man wears long hair, this is really not in accord with the nature of a man. Some men may do that as Paul's condition of expectancy intimates, but that will be exceptional. In Corinth such long hair will make a man seem much like a woman and will thus bring a corresponding "dishonor" upon him. When Paul writes ἐὰν κομᾷ he has in mind long hair like that of a woman; we cannot say that he is thinking of men cutting their hair closely as the custom is now.

15) The case is quite the reverse and even more so in the case of a woman. If she wears long hair, this is not only an honor for her, but her long hair is "a glory for her." It gives her that womanly distinction: "because her long hair is given her instead of a covering." The preposition ἀντί has the idea of exchange, R. 574. The agent suggested by the passive perfect "has been and thus is still given" her is "nature itself." Paul's thought is this: if nature itself provides a covering for a woman, it is highly proper that she follow this hint of nature and cover her head during acts of public worship.

A περιβόλαιον is something that is thrown around one and "a covering" in that sense. One might argue that a woman's hair is covering enough since nature provides no other for her. But this is specious. The fact that woman's hair grows quite long by nature, much longer than a man's even if he never cuts it, and that thus there is bestowed on woman the gift of a περιβόλαιον, is nature's own indication that, when it comes to significant customs, she and not the man is to have her head covered in the presence of God during worship. "It is given her instead of a covering" means: in place of a covering, to take the place of a covering, and this establishes the decorum or propriety of wearing a covering over the head. For if long hair is an honor for a woman because it is given her in place of a covering, then any proper custom which accentuates this honor must be prized accordingly. This is the correct deduction which Paul has in mind.

What may we gather from Paul's discussion regarding the head covering of women at Corinth?

First, that the facts of creation and of nature stand unchanged. They should be recognized and accepted for what they are. To ignore them or to set them aside is always a mistake. In the end these facts as well as all the others are bound to assert themselves. One of the most fundamental natural facts is this that the sexes differ profoundly, far more so than is generally recognized. A basic feature of this fact is that God gave the headship to the man and not to the woman. All attempts to abolish this headship and to place the sexes on the same level must fail. Another, although a far lesser, feature of this difference is the fact that woman and not man has received a περιβόλαιον from God and from God's nature!

Secondly, many customs have sprung up that have no deeper basis than transient fashion. With these the Scriptures do not concern themselves. Some of them may be in what we are pleased to call good taste, others may by comparison be in bad taste. *De gustibus non disputandum.* Christians incline toward the former and away from the latter, but only for non-religious reasons.

Thirdly, some customs have a deeper basis. In their way they reflect creative or natural facts, lend a sort of expression to these facts, at least harmonize with them. These customs, not merely as customs, but as being significant in their character are seemly, proper, and worthy of retention. Hence the obligation to retain them with a mind that understands and appreciates why they are "proper." Yet obligation and propriety are not absolute and not necessary for all time and for all nations.

Fourthly, customs may be entirely different and even opposite among different people. Customs may also change more or less decidedly. Where these differences exist, or where these changes occur without a conscious intention to antagonize the facts of creation or of nature, no religious issue results regarding even the point of propriety. Only where changes are sought that are in contravention of the facts of creation and of nature must we proceed as Paul did when he was writing to the congregation at Corinth.

16) Paul breaks off the discussion with some abruptness. **But if anyone seems to be contentious, we for our part have no such custom, neither the churches of God.**

The condition of reality leads one to think that Paul expects some in Corinth "to be contentious," φιλόνεικος, "loving contention" as people who always insist that they are in the right, *rechthaberisch*. Paul refuses to be concerned with people of this kind. It is not his way to argue back and forth; ἡμεῖς is quite emphatic: "we for our part," Paul and his fellow workers. All of these were men so that the statement: "we for our part have no such custom," does not mean: "we Christians have no such custom as having women go bareheaded at worship." While συνήθεια is a mild term to apply to contentiousness, it is finely chosen by

Paul as being one who is himself wholly averse to contentions and to all forms of *Rechthaberei*. If he were contentious he would have chosen a harsh word; the choice of this mild term proves his own mildness.

In fact, this custom of mildness is characteristic of "the churches of God." Even regarding graver matters than those of Christian propriety they want no contentiousness, no love of strife, although they earnestly contend for the faith, Jude 3. The Augsburg Confession writes in the same spirit: "It is proper [the very term used by Paul in v. 13] that the churches should keep such ordinances for the sake of love and tranquillity, so far that one do not offend another, that all things be done in the churches in order, and without confusion, I Cor. 14:40; compare Phil. 2:14; but so that consciences be not burdened to think that they are necessary to salvation, or to judge that they sin when they break them without offense to others; as no one will say that a woman sins who goes out in public with her head uncovered, provided only that no offense be given." *C. Tr.*, 91.

The Sixth Part of the Letter

Disorders connected with the Lord's Supper, 11:17-34

17) Yet in transmitting this I am not praising that you come together, not for the better, but for the worse.

From a consideration of the covering of the head for women Paul turns to the disorders that are connected with the Lord's Supper. This manner of connecting a brief participial clause concerning a preceding subject with a main clause concerning a matter that follows has been called awkward and disjointed. But this criticism is unwarranted. When Paul begins to speak about the head covering for women in v. 2

he has a word of praise for the Corinthians, namely that in all respects they remember him and hold fast the directions which he originally gave them. He acknowledges their obedient attitude and then proceeds to instruct them in regard to the women by transmitting pertinent further directions to them. No women had as yet tried to dispense with a covering for the head while they were at worship; Paul is thus able to insert his word of praise.

When he comes to the new subject, the truth is quite different. Abuses had actually crept in, and nobody in Corinth had asked what Paul had originally told them concerning the Lord's Supper. Thus, while he transmits his directions regarding women with a word of praise, this praise must be omitted when he comes to speak about the assemblies for the purpose of celebrating the Sacrament. Instead of criticizing Paul for the manner in which he combines the references to the two subjects we have reason to admire the masterly way in which he links together the praise mentioned in v. 2 with the non-praise spoken of in v. 17.

Paul omits the pronoun; he does not write: "In transmitting this *to you* I am not praising *you*." Because of this omission of the pronouns Paul's words become more objective. The verb παραγγέλλω is frequently used with reference to military commands; hence the R. V.'s translation "in giving you this charge." This is a rather strong translation in the present connection since the matter regarding the covering of the head is not one that calls for such decisive commands. The original meaning of the verb is to pass along directions or orders from one person to another; hence we translate "in transmitting this," etc.

Paul is entirely frank when he tells the Corinthians that he is now not praising them. The litotes "I am not praising" is a mild way of expressing blame as if to say: "I should like to praise but I cannot, I am compelled to blame." The fault that excludes praise is promptly stated: "that you come together, not for the better, but for the worse." The negative phrase is reenforced by the appositional positive phrase. The case is deplorable in every way. The Corinthians should come together "for the better," so that their coming together results in spiritual improvement; instead of that their coming together results in spiritual detriment, and, as the present tense shows, this is a regular occurrence, it is not an exceptional thing. The comparatives contrast two results, one that should be and one that should not be. In addition to this contrast a relation is expressed: "better" when compared with "worse," and "worse" when compared with "better." *Gegensatz* (contrast) and *Steigerung* (comparison) are thus combined, R. 663.

We should note that Paul now writes: "you come together." This coming together or assembling for public worship is mentioned again in v. 18 and a third time in v. 20; in each instance the same verb is employed. It is repeated twice at the end of this section regarding the Lord's Supper in v. 33, 34; and again in 14:23, 26, near the close of the section regarding spiritual gifts. Paul thus marks with great plainness that the disorders of which he now speaks occur in the public assemblies of the congregation. In the section regarding the head covering for women no mention is made of public assemblies. This leads some to conclude that the women are also to cover their heads when they are praying in private at home whereas the correct deduction is only this, that as yet no woman had ventured to appear in public worship with a bare head, that some only raised the question whether it would be proper to do so. The point of private worship is quite minor; it is the appearance of women in public worship that is important.

18) Paul's preliminary charge that the Corinthians come together, not for the better, but for the worse, really extends from 11:17 to 14:40, for it pertains to the Lord's Supper and to the charismata or spiritual gifts. Grave improprieties had crept into the Corinthian assemblies in connection with the Sacrament and also in connection with the exercise of these gifts. Paul first takes up the disorders pertaining to the Sacrament; then in 12:1, etc., he deals with the charismata. **For when you come together in assembly, I am told that cliques exist among you; and in part I believe it.**

The term ἐκκλησία is here used in its original meaning of an assembly that is called together for a specific purpose. The Corinthians come together in an assembly for congregational purposes. The verb ἀκούω is used in the classic sense: "I am told," R. 803. The tense is an " 'effective' aoristic present, close akin to a perfect," R. 893. The action is durative only in the sense of indicating a state, it does not express a linear activity; hence does not mean: "I keep hearing," but: "I hear" and thus know, R. 881.

When Paul reports what has come to his ears he only summarizes the evil as it appears to his mind: "that cliques exist among you," σχίσματα, schisms or splits. We shall see presently just what Paul means. When he adds: "and in part I believe it," we see that he discounts even credible reports, he is loath to believe the worst even on testimony that is good. His is the true Christian attitude. Only too few follow it.

19) Paul is to some extent surprised and grieved because of what he is told, yet in the last analysis he is neither. This latter he explains with γάρ. **For there must even be divisions among you in order that those approved may become manifest among you.**

If we translate καί "also" and not "even" we, nevertheless, feel that αἱρέσεις is a graver term than σχίσματα. This would, of course, not prevent one from using the terms side by side and regarding them as mere synonyms. This has, in fact, been done quite frequently. A σχίσμα is a rent or a split. In the following verses Paul uses the term as denoting a clique, namely a division which does not as yet tear the congregation asunder. On the other hand, αἵρεσις, from αἱρέω, denotes something that one selects or chooses, thus a peculiar doctrine or opinion. In the New Testament it is used with reference to actual divisions, Acts 24:14; Gal. 5:20; II Pet. 2:1: "damnable heresies." The fathers applied it to heresy, the philosophers to philosophical tendencies, schools, or sects. Our versions translate "heresies"; the A. V. margin "sects"; the R. V. margin "factions." Both give the term a tinge of a rather grave meaning. Paul uses it here with reference to actual divisions which are disrupting the congregation.

With δεῖ Paul indicates the *necessitas consequentiae*, the necessary outcome of an evil course after it has been chosen. God lets the evil result of such a course become manifest but does so for purposes of his own. One of these purposes is to punish the wicked although Paul does not touch upon this. Another purpose is "that those approved may become manifest among you," i. e., that those approved of God as sound, true, and faithful may appear openly as such. When evil factions actually separate themselves from a congregation they help to show who the true members are.

The texts that read ἵνα καί connect the divine purpose closely with the idea of necessity. Paul thus tells the Corinthians that the cliques which have already been formed among them may grow more serious and result in actual divisions. Because so many practical, moral, and personal issues have already started in their midst, because they show so much disinclination and disability to eradicate these incipient differences, actual heretical views and teachings may develop and tear the congregation apart. That would be deplorable, but such results must appear in this sinful world; when they do come to pass they have one good feature: they reveal who the true members are.

The cliques of which Paul speaks cannot be identified with the parties described in 1:12; for these Paul calls "factions," ἔριδες, 1:11. As he describes the real nature of the latter, so he also reveals the true nature of the former. The "cliques" and the "divisions" are not identical. The former already exist in Corinth, the latter threaten to occur. The effort to establish the identity of the two terms by letting δεῖ εἶναι mean: "it is necessary that there *are*," is misdirected, for we should translate: "it is necessary that there *be*," i. e., if certain evil beginnings run their course as they may and will here and there.

20) With the resumptive οὖν Paul returns to the evils he touches upon briefly in v. 18. **When, therefore, you come together in one place, it is impossible to eat the Lord's Supper, for each in the eating consumes his own supper in advance, and one remains hungry, and the other is drunken.**

The genitive absolute states that this abuse occurs in connection with the gathering of the congregation; and the idiom ἐπὶ τὸ αὐτό adds the idea that all assemble "in the same place." Then, indeed, when all are gathered together in the same place they ought to show that they are also one body, but their disorderly actions make this impossible.

"It is impossible to eat the Lord's Supper" shows the gravity of the abuse that has crept in. It was the very purpose of these congregational gatherings to celebrate the Lord's Supper. But if anyone came to the meeting and expected this purpose to be carried out he found himself completely disappointed. The action of the members made a celebration of the Holy Supper impossible. The A. V.'s translation is incorrect: "this is not to eat the Lord's Supper"; for οὐκ ἔστι with the infinitive means "it is impossible" to eat, and "this" cannot be supplied since coming together and eating are not identical.

Κυριακὸν δεῖπνον refers to the Sacrament itself. The adjective Κυριακόν, from Κύριος or Lord, seems to have been used as early as the time of our epistle in conscious opposition to the pagan use of the title "Lord" as applied to heathen divinities and emperors, see Deissmann, *Light from the Ancient East*, 353, etc., where the subject is interestingly discussed at length. First came the Agape or Love Feast, a joint meal of which all the members partook. At the conclusion of this meal the Sacrament was celebrated. No evidence has been discovered to substantiate the view that the Sacrament was ever divided so that the Agape was placed between the eating of the sacramental bread and the drinking of the sacramental cup. Regarding the question itself consult Meusel, *Kirchliches Handlexikon*, "Abendmahl," concerning the words of the institution μετὰ τὸ δειπνῆσαι consult the author's interpretation of Luke 22:20.

Paul now explains why it is impossible to eat the Lord's Supper in the Corinthian assemblies: "for each one in the eating consumes his own supper in advance, and one remains hungry, and the other is drunken." The present tenses are iterative; this has come to be a regular practice in Corinth. The food for the Agape, from which some of the bread and the wine was reserved for the Sacrament, was brought by the members who came to the meeting. Some were poor and could bring little or nothing ("them that have not." v. 22). Now instead of taking all the food that was brought and apportioning it to all who were present so that each should receive a proper share, cliques were formed, and relatives, friends, those of one clique sat together, probably at private tables, the rich and prosperous separated from the poor, letting those who could bring little or nothing sit by themselves. Then each person consumed what he had brought irrespective of the poorer members, some of whom were slaves.

The expression προλαμβάνει ἐν τῷ φαγεῖν does not mean: "taketh before other," R. V., i. e., eats hastily what he has brought before all have gathered; but: "in the eating consumes in advance," paying no attention to the rest. In other words, the Agape ceased to be an Agape and degenerated into just ordinary eating, each clique eating by itself. This virtual abolition of the Agape made the celebration of the Holy Supper itself an impossibility. For at this time the two were still one celebration, the Agape leading up to the Sacrament. When the Agape ceased to be an Agape, the Sacrament was also virtually impossible. Perhaps an attempt was still made to celebrate the Sacrament, but the poor especially felt themselves excluded and ceased to commune.

The one sat there and hungered since he had brought nothing or had brought too little and received nothing from the rest who consumed their own. The other was drunken with wine, he consumed more of this than he should have done from the plenty which he and his friends had brought. And this "even at the Lord's table," R. 854. The last two clauses show drastically that under these circumstances the Sacrament quite naturally became an impossibility.

22) The pointed questions which now follow dramatically expose the gravity of this abuse. **What? do you mean you have not houses for eating and drinking? or do you despise the church of God and put to shame those that have nothing? What shall I say to you? shall I praise you? In this I praise you not.**

Here we have an instance of the conclusive γάρ used in a question as is the case in Matt. 27:23; John 9:30; Acts 19:30. The question thus has the nature of a justified conclusion which is drawn from the preceding, which may be a statement that someone has made, or, as here, a situation that someone has created. We render its force with "what?" Winer, *Grammatik des neutestamentlichen Sprachidioms, 6. Auflage,* 396; Robertson does not treat this subject.

By using μή Paul expects a negative answer; οὐκ merely denies ἔχετε. Paul intends to say: "You surely do not mean that you have no houses for eating and drinking? And yet this is what your actions imply." The outrageous character of the actions of the Corinthians is thus exposed. They *had* houses where they could eat and drink their fill, but by eating and drinking their fill during the meeting of the congregation and by disregarding the poor they acted as though they had no houses. The εἰς τό has the dative idea here, R. 1072.

In the question: "Why do you not use your houses?" there lies the graver one: "Why do you so use the church?" This is graver, for to use the church in this manner is to degrade it, hence to look down on it, to despise it, καταφρονεῖν used with the genitive, literally, "to think down." Here ἐκκλησία again has the original sense of assembly as it did in v. 18. The gravity of thus despising the church is strenghtened by the genitive the church "of God." Has the congregation forgotten so completely that this is "God's" gathering?

This genitive, too, lends force to the addition "and put to shame those that have nothing." For in "the church of God" God looks especially upon the poor. He does not put them to shame, nor will he have them put to shame by others, James 1:9, 10; 2:2-9. God is no respecter of persons.

Paul stands as a person who is nonplussed and shocked and asks himself: "What shall I say?" Then he remembers that in 11:2 he had praised the Corinthians; with grim irony he now asks: "Shall I praise you?" or, if we wish to include the next phrase in this question: "Shall I praise you in this?" The question itself cuts deeply. Its answer is decisive: "I praise you not," a strong litotes for: "I blame you." Both εἴπω, R. 928, and ἐπαινέσω are deliberative subjunctives although the latter might be regarded as a future indicative, R. 934. Both are aorists and denote one act of saying and of praising. In "I praise you not" the durative present refuses this praise continuously. Here in one of the most important matters of their faith that deals with the Sacred Supper itself the Corinthians, who in all things wanted to adhere to what they had received from Paul (v. 2), had allowed themselves to drift so far from his teaching. Paul restrains himself so as not to use strong terms of rebuke. He seems to ask himself: "Do these people really realize what they are doing?"

23) With calm patience Paul sets to work to repeat his original instruction to these disorderly Corinthians and thus to correct this flagrant abuse. **For I received from the Lord, what also I delivered to you, that the Lord Jesus in the night in which he was betrayed took bread and, after having given thanks, broke it and said: This is my body which is for you. This do in remembrance of me!**

With the emphatic ἐγώ: "*I* did receive . . . *I* did deliver to you," Paul contrasts himself with the Corinthians. What they had received from *him* is different from what they are now practicing in Corinth. Thus by a reference to Christ's own institution of the Holy Supper γάρ also substantiates why Paul can only reproach the Corinthians for the abuse which rendered its celebration impossible.

The first and the most important corrective, then, is that the Corinthians remember what Paul had delivered to them from the Lord concerning the Sacrament. The Agape is not a divine institution. Therefore Paul lays down no regulations concerning it. His concern is the Sacrament. What he has mentioned in regard to the improper conduct of the Agape has its point in the Sacrament because it makes its celebration impossible. The abuses current in the Agape would as such call for serious correction, but this correction is included in Paul's statement regarding the graver matter, regarding the Sacrament proper. If the proper celebration of the Sacrament is attended to, all else will be corrected.

Paul writes παρέλαβον ἀπὸ τοῦ Κυρίου and not παρά which only a few texts have. A verb that is compounded with παρά is generally followed by a phrase that begins with the same preposition. The conclusion is, therefore, drawn that Paul's use of ἀπό instead of παρά in the appended phrase means that he did not originally receive the words of the institution *immediately*, by a direct revelation from the Lord, but only *mediately*, through the Twelve or through some of the original members of the church. R. 579, however, warns us against such a radical distinction between the two prepositions save as etymology throws light on them. What he means we see on page 561: παρά calls attention to the fact that one is beside the person or place when he starts; ἀπό merely notes the point of departure; and ἐκ asserts that one has been within the place or circle before departing. So in Paul's phrase the preposition ἀπό conveys the idea that what he delivered to the Corinthians came "from" the Lord (point of departure). That is sufficient for his present purpose.

But while this explains the preposition found in the phrase, the force of παρά in the compound verb itself remains unchanged. Moreover, we frequently find ἀπό used where we know that the reception is immediate although the preposition itself does not stress this idea of immediacy as in Col. 1:7; I John 1:5; III John 7, and in other instances where some exclude the idea of immediacy as in Col. 3:24; Gal. 3:2. Therefore Paul's immediate reception of this revelation cannot be excluded on the basis of the preposition he uses. Paul himself tells us plainly how he received his gospel, which certainly includes the Lord's Supper as a vital part of it. It was "through a revelation of Jesus Christ," Gal. 1:11, 12, and not through an agency of men.

What Paul received, that he transmitted to the Corinthians. The two aorists "I received" and "I delivered" state the facts. Paul was not presumptuous enough to make a change in the transmission; the Corinthians were, however, making a change in retaining what was transmitted to them, a change that actually lost them the Sacrament. So Paul records the sacred words of the Lord's institution even as he originally delivered them to the Corinthians. Let them keep the Sacrament according to these words, and all will be well.

Because Paul's record of the words so clearly resembles the other three records which we possess, some conclude that Paul, who was not present at the institution itself, must have obtained them from the Twelve or at least through them although many years had passed before he came in touch with any of them. But if the Lord revealed the institution to Paul, the same exact agreement with the other three records follows as the only natural conclusion.

It was in the night in which Jesus was in the act of being betrayed, παρεδίδοτο, the imperfect to express an act in progress, that he instituted the Holy Supper. Paul may well have intended this preamble, which states the solemn hour of the institution, as a rebuke of the sort of assemblies at which the Corinthians were trying to celebrate the Sacrament. But in Paul's letter this preamble is necessary for the proper understanding of the entire institution of Christ, in particular also for the vital words "for you" and "in my blood" (v. 25). The three Evangelists need no such preamble because they record the actual history of the events as they occurred.

"He took bread" states the fact, hence Paul writes the aorist. This aorist is used throughout the record whenever the acts are mentioned. In general, in regard to the interpretation "we are certainly in duty bound not to interpret and explain these words of the eternal, true, and almighty Son of God, our Lord, Creator, and Redeemer, Jesus Christ, differently, as allegorical, figurative, tropical expressions, according as it seems agreeable to our reason, but with simple faith and due obedience to receive the words as they read, in their proper and plain sense, and allow ourselves to be diverted therefrom by no objectives or human contradictions spun from human reason, however charming they may appear to human reason." Abraham's example is mentioned in this connection when he received God's command to offer up Isaac, which seemed against both divine and human law and even in conflict with God's own promise concerning Isaac. "He understands and believes God's Word and command plainly and simply, as they read according to the letter, and commits the matter to God's omnipotence and wisdom, which, he knows, has many more modes and ways to fulfill the promise of the Seed from Isaac than he can comprehend with his blind reason." *C. Tr.* 987, etc.

24) "And after having given thanks broke it and said, This is my body which is for you." Some important texts add κλώμενον: "which is in the act of being broken for you," although the weight of evidence is

against this addition. Matthew and Mark read: "After having blessed," instead of: "After having given thanks." The thought is quite the same.

The disciples who were present at the institution could plainly see that Jesus was beginning a new act, one that was similar to the Passover, but one that was of far greater import. The words of thanks evidently referred to the bread in Jesus' hands and to the heavenly gift it was to convey. These words thus also prepared the disciples for the reception of the bread and the heavenly gift, for they were to receive both intelligently and not by way of surprise and in a state of wonder as to what Jesus was giving them. Christ's words of thanks, unknown to us though they are, remain efficacious for all time wherever the Sacrament is celebrated. Because of their nature they could not be efficaciously repeated. This same efficacious power resides, however, also in the words of Christ which are recorded. "Where his institution is observed and his words are spoken over the bread and cup, and the consecrated bread and cup are distributed, Christ himself, *through the spoken words*, is still efficacious *by virtue of the* first institution through his word, which he wishes there to be repeated," *C. Tr.* 999.

"He broke" the bread means that he did this for the purpose of distribution only. No parallel such as spilling or pouring occurs in the case of the wine. The breaking is incidental to the Sacrament. It has no symbolical significance, for the body of the Lord was not broken on the cross. "A bone of him shall not be broken," John 19:36. The R. V. is inaccurate when in the marginal translation to the four accounts it offers the rendering "loaf" instead of "bread." Loaves could not be baked from unleavened dough. Jesus had no "loaf," he had only a thin, flat cake of bread such as are still baked and eaten in the Holy Land quite generally; pieces of these were broken off when eating.

The author saw this baking and ate such bread during a visit to Syria and Palestine. "Bread is an inanimate thing: how can breaking it be like the putting of a human being to death? Breaking bread is the very symbol of quietness and peace, who would dream of it as an appropriate symbol of the most cruel and ignominious death? Bread is the representative food, and used in metaphor is the symbol of spiritual and supernatural food. The breaking of bread is the means of giving it as food, and as a symbol, the symbol of giving and taking a higher food. No one would dream of the breaking of bread as the symbol of killing a human body; and if so extraordinary a symbolic use of it were made, it would require the most explicit statement on the part of the person so using it that such was his intent; and when he had made it, the world would be amazed at so lame a figure." Krauth, *Conservative Reformation*, 723.

The Evangelists mention the giving to the disciples. Paul only implies this and proceeds with "and said" and follows with the words which the Lord then spoke: "This is my body which is for you." Matthew writes: "Take, eat; this is my body." Mark omits "eat." Luke omits both imperatives but adds to "my body" the modifier "being given for you," i. e., as a sacrifice on the cross. The essential point is that the consecrated bread be received and eaten.

The demonstrative τοῦτο means: what I now give you, *hoc quod vos sumere jubeo*. We should note that τοῦτο is neuter and hence cannot, grammatically or in thought, refer to ἄρτος which is masculine. The English "this" and "bread" obscure this distinction in gender, yet no student passes it by. "This" = the gift which Christ extends to his disciples. "It is no longer mere bread of the oven but bread of flesh or bread of body, that is, bread which is sacramentally one with Christ's body." Luther.

Much has been said regarding ἐστίν which is merely the copula that connects the subject and the predicate. Jesus spoke Aramaic and used no copula when he was speaking that language, for he needed none; but this fact does not remove or in the least alter the inspired ἐστίν that is found in the Greek records. It cannot mean "represents" as Zwingli contended. The characters $1.00 "represent" a dollar; no man would mistake them for a real dollar.

"My body" means exactly what the words say: in truth and reality my body. The addition "which is for you," τὸ ὑπὲρ ὑμῶν, "in your behalf," or according to Luke's fuller rendition: ὑπὲρ ὑμῶν διδόμενον, "in the act of being given for you" as a sacrifice on the cross, doubles the certainty as to the reality of the body, for Christ's own body and not the symbol of bread was being given for our redemption on the cross.

The rationalizing question: "*How* could the Lord by means of bread give his true and real body to his disciples?" has caused all the trouble that centers about these simple words. Some say that he does it by means of a transsubstantiation of the bread into the body so that he does not give the bread but only the body. Others say that he does not give his body, which is impossible, he gives only the bread, the symbol of his body.

We refuse to answer the question regarding the *how* because the Lord withholds the answer. We could probably not have understood the real answer if it had been given because the giving of his body in the Sacrament is a divine act of omnipotence and of grace which is beyond mortal comprehension. The Lord declares *the fact*: "This is my body," and we take him at his word. He knows the mystery of this giving, we do not. All rationalizing objection that this involves a gross, carnal, Capernaitic eating of raw flesh is unwarranted; the first disciples who had the body of Christ's humiliation before their very eyes when Christ's hand in a supernatural way gave them the gift of his sacrificial body never dreamed of such an eating. "My body" does not mean "a piece of my body."

Among the Evangelists only Luke also has the command: "This do in remembrance of me." Yet this command makes the first celebration an institution. The imperative is a durative present tense and denotes indefinite repetition: "This do again and again." The τοῦτο, "this," includes what Christ has just done, namely two essential acts which we usually term the consecration and the distribution. The phrase "in (or for) my remembrance" is an echo of the Passover rite: "And this day shall be unto you *for a memorial.*" A new and greater memorial is to take the place of the old. But this phrase does not mean that this Sacrament is only to remind us of Christ or of his death. "In remembrance of me" is to be the content of the entire sacramental act. And this remembrance is the oral reception of Christ's body that was sacrificed for us on the cross. When R. 595 says that εἰς does not mean "for" in the phrase "for my remembrance," which we usually translate "in my remembrance," he does not note the true force of the preposition, which points to a purpose and a result.

25) In the same manner also the cup after having eaten, saying: This cup is the new testament in my blood. This do, as often as you drink it, in remembrance of me!

Luke's record is much like Paul's. To the phrase "in my blood" he adds "which is in the act of being poured out for you" or "in your behalf," and omits the command: "This do," etc. The other two records mention the taking, the blessing, and the giving of the cup with the command that all are to drink. Matthew and Mark have: "For this is my blood," an exact parallel to the words regarding the bread. The latter adds to blood: "of the testament, which is being poured out for many"; to which the former adds: "for the forgiveness of sins." The remarkable fact is the perfect agreement of the four records in every essential point although the wording is diverse. Yet this very diversity is an aid in interpretation.

"In the same manner" includes everything that is now done with the cup: Christ took, blessed, gave it, and spoke words to parallel those regarding the bread. But nothing comparable to the breaking of the bread is recorded. Regarding μετὰ τό with the infinitive see R. 612; this is a common method for abbreviating a temporal clause: "after having eaten," i. e., the bread. Keil, however, regards the expression as a reference to the Passover meal; it thus indicates that this cup is not connected with the Passover cup; an entirely new act is now taking place.

"The cup," with its article, points to the one that was used during the Passover celebration. "The word 'cup' may mean, without metaphor: 1) the vessel meant to contain liquids, whether they be in it or not; 2) the liquid which is contained in such a vessel, or is imparted by it; 3) the vessel and liquid together. . . . In the words: 'He took the cup,' Luke 22:17, the word 'cup' is used in the third of these senses — he took the cup containing, and through it the contents. In the words: 'Divide it among yourselves,' the cup is conceived in the second sense — divide the contained cup by passing from one to another the containing cup, with its contents. In the words of the institution: 'This cup is the new testament,' the contained cup, in the second sense, is understood — the contained as mediated through the containing — that which this cup contains is the new testament in my blood. In such a use of the word 'cup' there is no metaphor, no rhetorical figure whatever. It is a grammatical form of speech; and if it be called a 'figure,' the word 'figure' is used in a sense different from that in which it is denied that there is a 'figure' in the first words of the Supper. We deny that there is a rhetorical figure in any part of the words of the institution." Krauth, *Conservative Reformation* 778, etc.

The cup contained wine diluted with water; on this all are agreed save some special pleaders. Matt. 26:29: "of *this* fruit of the vine," i. e., that which the Passover cup contained, excludes any and all other products of the vine such as unfermented grape juice, raisin tea, or grape syrup. The expression itself is derived from the Hebrew *pheri hagiphen*, a choice liturgical formula that denotes wine. Since a testament cannot be altered without invalidation, the use of any other liquid than actual wine made from grapes renders the Sacrament invalid so that it ceases to be a sacrament. Christ's testament stands only as he made it and not as we may change it.

Only Luke omits ἐστί in the Lord's word regarding the cup. Paul and the others have it in the same sense in which it was used with reference to the bread. "This cup" is not merely "this wine" but "this wine consecrated by the Lord to be the bearer of his sacrificial blood." The predicate is "the new testament in my blood," and the ἐν phrase modifies "testament" and not "this cup." The Lord's testament is forever linked with his sacrificial blood. Mark, therefore, writes "my blood of the testament"; and Matthew even makes the genitive attributive by placing the Greek article before the genitive. When the Lord gave "this cup" to the disciples, they received his blood as connected with "the new testament"; not the blood without the testament, nor the testament without the blood.

Monographs have been written on the term διαθήκη, "testament," and its connection with the Hebrew *b^erith*, "covenant." We see that the translators of our

First Corinthians 11:25

versions waver, the A. V. using "testament" in our passage, the R. V. "covenant" with "testament" in the margin. On this subject compare C.-K. 1062, etc. We here indicate the sum of the matter. The Old Testament dealt with the promises of God to his chosen people. Thus God placed himself in "covenant" relation to Israel. The heart of this relation, like the promises and the gifts of God to Israel, is always one-sided. It is always God's covenant and not Israel's, and it is not a mutual agreement. This covenant obligates Israel, and Israel assumes these obligations, but the covenant itself emanates entirely from God.

The LXX translated $b^e rith$, "covenant," $\delta\iota\alpha\theta\acute{\eta}\kappa\eta$, "testament," since this term has the same one-sided connotation; a will and testament emanates only from the testator. Christ, however, brought the fulfillment of the Old Testament promises. The result of his act is the fact that God's people now have the inheritance and are God's heirs: "If children, then heirs; heirs of God, and joint-heirs of Christ," Rom. 8:17. Thus we find the term $\delta\iota\alpha\theta\acute{\eta}\kappa\eta$ used in the New Testament in the sense of "will and testament" by which God bequeathes to us all the blessings that Christ has brought. Hence also, as here in Christ's institution of the Supper, this is called "the *new* testament," "new," however, not as a second testament, but as one that supersedes the old covenant, $\kappa\alpha\iota\nu\acute{\eta}$, in contradistinction to something old, not $\nu\acute{\epsilon}\alpha$, something that never existed before.

Both the old $b^e rith$ or covenant and "the new testament" were connected with blood. The former was sealed with the blood of animal sacrifice: "Behold the blood of the covenant, which the Lord hath made with you concerning all these words," Exod. 24:4-8. This blood typified and promised the blood of Christ, God's own Son, the seal of "the new testament" by which we inherit all that this blood has purchased and won for us. The old covenant could be written in animal blood because it consisted of promise; the new testament could be written only in the blood of the Son because it conveys the complete fulfillment of the promise, the actual purchase of our redemption. This is stressed by the strong possessive adjective which we may render: "in connection with my own (ἐμῷ) blood." This very blood together with the very body from which it flowed are now given us in the Sacrament to certify us as heirs of this "new testament" in Christ Jesus.

The word is "blood" and not merely "death" because a sacrifice and a specific death, namely a sacrificial death, are referred to. No other type of death could be connected with "the new testament," i. e., could establish it. While the Sacrament consists of two acts and two elements, "body" and "blood," these two are one and inseparable. There is no sacrificial body without sacrificial blood, and vice versa. If one should remark that the sacrifice had not as yet been made when the Lord instituted the Sacrament he is answered by the records which add the words which "is being shed for many," Mark; "being shed for many unto remission of sins," Matthew; "being given for you . . . even that which is being poured out for you," Luke, where the present participles are so significant. In that solemn night the Lord was in the act of making his sacrifice. To him it was present as though it had already been made. Nor do the Scriptures ever speak of the *glorified* body or the *glorified* blood when they mention the Sacrament; it is always the body *given*, the blood *shed or poured out*.

Paul records the institutional command in connection with the cup: "This do in remembrance of me," but he inserts the temporal clause of expectancy: "as often as you drink it." Every time the disciples drink the sacramental cup, this cup itself, just like the eating of the sacramental bread, is to constitute their remembrance of the Lord.

A still fuller exposition of the words of the institution is offered in the author's *Eisenach Gospel Selections* in connection with the text for Maundy Thursday, first and second edition (omitted in the third).

26) In v. 23 Paul introduces the account of the institution of the Sacrament with γάρ, "for," in order to substantiate his rebuke of the disorderly proceedings current among the Corinthians. Now he continues with a second γάρ and draws attention to the point in this account which especially calls attention to the gravity of the Corinthian disorders. **For as often as you eat this bread and drink this cup you are proclaiming the death of the Lord till he shall come.**

"For" intends to say: "This is what you must consider when you assemble for the Sacrament." Even if we did not have the other three accounts of the institution we see that Paul's account of the institution is completed in v. 25, for both γάρ and the reference to "the death of the Lord" show that Paul is now offering an explanation of his own, and that he does not continue reporting what the Lord said when he was instituting the Sacrament. Paul connects his explanation with the clause which Christ used: "as often as you drink it," but mentions both elements: "as often as you eat this bread and drink this cup," and indicates that he refers to the celebration of the entire sacrament.

Now what do we really do when we eat of the sacred bread and drink of the sacred cup and thus properly celebrate the Lord's sacrament? Paul answers with an iterative present tense, R. 880: "you are proclaiming the death of the Lord." No less a thing than that. "The death" is placed emphatically forward in the Greek, and Jesus is called "the Lord," and this title has the same grave significance it had in v. 23. Now, Paul would say, compare this proper way of eating and drinking the sacred bread and the cup with the way in which you Corinthians proceed when you conduct your preliminary Agape with the result that at times you cannot eat and drink the sacrament at all. Instead of proclaiming the Lord's death with all the solemnity this proclamation deserves you are proclaiming your own unworthiness.

There is no need to quibble about this proclaiming and to state that it means a special proclamation in words of our own. Every proper celebration of the Lord's Supper is a proclamation of the Lord's death. The words of the institution alone, when they are spoken over the bread and the cup, do not proclaim that Christ died for us; the entire action of the sacrament does that, especially our receiving his body and his blood given and shed for us. For the entire sacrament is based on the death of the Lord. Our reception of his body and his blood through the earthly elements is our remembrance of him and at the same time our proclamation of him, in particular of his death.

The fact that Paul is speaking generally about every proper celebration of the sacrament we see from the clause: "till he shall come," i. e., at the Parousia. With ἄχρις οὗ we may or may not have ἄν, R. 975, the sense being the same. From the night in which Jesus was betrayed onward until his return in glory at the last day this proclamation is to be made. The aorist subjunctive ἔλθῃ denotes a single future act and an actual coming. When Paul writes to the Corinthians that by properly celebrating the sacrament they proclaim Christ's death "till he shall come" he says nothing whatever about the time of Christ's coming. Paul does not know either the hour (period) or the day (date) of that coming; we know no more.

27) After thus explaining with two γάρ (v. 23 and 26) the major reason that Paul reproaches the Corinthians for their serious disorders he draws the grave conclusions that follow from the very explanations he has made. **Wherefore, whoever shall eat the bread or drink the cup of the Lord unworthily shall be guilty of the body and blood of the Lord.**

The stress is on the adverb "unworthily," and we should note the juxtaposition of "unworthily" and "guilty" in the Greek, the latter word also forms the pivot of the clause in which it appears: unworthily — guilty! As the first genitive "of the Lord" modifies both the bread and the cup and places them into sacramental connection with the Lord, so also the second genitive "of the Lord" includes both the body and the blood.

The little connective "or," which is placed between the bread and the cup, has quite a history. Some Protestants want this "or" changed into "and," as some codices also have it, because the Catholics justify their doctrine *sub una specie* by stressing the force of this "or." In order to escape the apparent correctness of the Catholic contention Winer, *Grammatik des neutestamentlichen Sprachidioms, 6. Auflage,* 391, and a number of commentators resort to the explanation that the first half of the Sacrament preceded the Agape, and the second half followed it, and that there was quite an interval between the two acts. Thus, it is thought, a person might receive the bread worthily and might actually have become unworthy by the time the cup was given. Even the reverse is supposed. R. 1188 writes that "or" "does not mean that some partook of one and some of the other, but that, whatever element was taken in this way (unworthily), there was guilt." We certainly know of no case in which only one element was received. If this is Paul's meaning, his remark is pointless. If both elements were received, then Robertson, too, leaves us with the thought that one element may be received worthily while the other is received unworthily — a matter that Paul is not discussing.

As to the Sacrament, the fact is that the two parts of it were never separated by an interval either originally when Christ made the institution or later when the Corinthians celebrated the Sacrament; compare the remarks on v. 20. The cup always promptly followed the bread.

Regarding the unworthy communicant Paul says that he is guilty of *both* the body and the blood of the Lord. Here Paul has καί, "and," which combines the body and the blood. Paul knows about no guilt that pertains only to the body or only to the blood.

In regard to "or" the grammatical answer is exceedingly simple. In some cases "or" connects alternatives, only one of which is taken by the writer, while the other is excluded. But "or" is used also in another sense, to present alternatives (two or more even), both or all of which the writer accepts. In Rom. 1:21 we read: men knew God but did not glorify him as God "or" give thanks. These are not alternatives, only one of which is correct; both are asserted as being true. As men did not glorify God, so also they did not give thanks. Again, Matt. 21:23 has "and who" gave you this authority, while Luke has "or who" gave it to you. In all instances where "and" can be put in the place of "or" without changing the sense — and our passage is a case in point — the force of "or" is *not disjunctive* but *conjunctive*. We are not to choose one of two, both are to be taken equally. "Or" simply makes us look carefully at each of the two as we consider them together. On this conjunctive "or" see also Rom. 2:4; 4:13; 9:25 as explained by the author.

The adverb "unworthily," ἀναξίως (positive adjective ἄξιος from ἄγω), refers to the drawing up of weights and thus signifies "of unequal weight," one side of the scales rising high, the other dropping low. In the present connection the communicant's heart, mind, and conduct do not accord with the sacred elements of the sacrament. The side of the scales which holds the sacrament drops down because of its weight while the side that holds the communicant's attitude rises upward because of its lack of weight. The nature of the unworthiness in the case of the Corinthians the context has already made plain and will continue to make still plainer. Paul's statement is general and applies to all forms and all types of unworthiness and therefore should not be restricted to the peculiar type of unworthiness found in Corinth.

He "shall be guilty" of the body and the blood of the Lord reads like the wording of a law, for legal codes employed the future tense in this manner. The term ἔνοχος = ἐνεχόμενος, being held fast in something and thus being "guilty." In the New Testament the violated object is placed in the genitive: "guilty of the body and of the blood." Each of the two nouns has its own article although the gender and the number are the same. The articles draw attention to each noun separately although "and" combines the two. The effect of these articles is similar to the effect of "or" in the first clause.

The question is constantly raised as to whether being guilty of the body and of the blood of Christ, as here charged by Paul, indicates the presence of this body and this blood in the Sacrament as one that is received also by the unworthy communicant. This presence is frequently denied. The classic method followed in this denial is to charge the opposite view with maintaining the following syllogism. Major premise: The object against which one sins must be present. Minor premise: In the Sacrament the object sinned against is the body and the blood of Christ. Ergo: These must be present. If those who do believe in the presence maintain such a faith on the ground of this syllogism, it would be child's play, indeed, to upset their faith, for the major premise is not invariably true. Take a royal seal or image as an instance. Its violation would certainly be a crime against the royal person, and this would be perpetrated without the royal person being present during the act of violation.

Those who accept the presence have themselves ever repudiated the syllogism imputed to them. Quenstedt is a favorite target for this charge of using a fallacious syllogism in support of the presence. But have those who make the charge read what he says? He subscribes to the observation: "Whoever violates a *diploma vel sigillum* thereby already insults the ruler himself." He applies this to the Sacrament: "The irreverent treatment of the symbols alone (meaning the bread and the wine) does not always involve guilt against the body and blood of Christ," i. e., as if these were present. The Sacrament is of a different type: "But the Eucharistic *signa* and *sigilla* do not merely signify but also certainly exhibit the substance itself of the body and of the blood of Christ. Therefore a violation of the Eucharistic *signa* does not act like a violation of a *diploma* or of a *sigillum* of a ruler." Such alleged analogies are spurious. They posit a *quid pro quo*, for they beg the question by silently assuming the absence of Christ's body and blood — that absence which they illustrate and thus prove.

The vital point in Paul's own words is omitted by those who seek to remove the presence from the Sacrament, especially in the case of those who commune unworthily. Like all other true defenders of the presence, Quenstedt writes: "But whoever in the Lord's Supper *eats this bread*, which is the κοινωνία (communion) of the body of Christ, or *drinks* the Lord's cup, which is the κοινωνία (communion) of the blood of Christ, unworthily, *eo ipso*, *by this very unworthy eating and drinking*, becomes guilty of the body itself and of the blood itself of Christ." *Theologia Didactico-Polemica*, IV, 251, etc. Luther emphasizes the same vital point: "St. Paul here joins together the bread and the body of Christ. . . . How is it that the sin against the body of Christ is connected with *the eating* if that body is not to be present in *the eating or bread?* He would have had to say: 'Whoever eats this bread unworthily sins against the Lord's Supper, or against God, or against the command, or against the Lord's order.' Now the nature and the manner of the words compel the conclusion that he *who eats* unworthily is guilty in regard to *what he eats.* . . . For the text mightily compels that the sin occurs *in the eating and the drinking* . . . and yet it says that the sin is committed against the body and the blood of the Lord." Walch, XX, 321; Erlangen, 29, 250, etc.

The sin of which Paul speaks is not some derogatory treatment of the bread and the wine as symbols (*diploma, sigilla*) of Christ's body and blood. This sin could be committed in various ways, for instance, by just *thinking* slightingly of the symbols. The sin named by Paul is committed only in one way, by unworthy eating and drinking. Paul is wholly true to his own report of Christ's words: *"This is my body"* which the Lord gives us *to eat*.

28) The fact laid down in v. 27, that the unworthy communicant makes himself guilty of the Lord's body and blood which he actually receives, leads to the admonition: **But let a man test himself, and so let him eat of the bread and drink of the cup!**

This is the proper deduction to be made from the danger of participating unworthily. A wrong deduction would be to remain away from the Sacrament and thus to avoid the danger. The present tenses are iterative to express customary action. The idea of ἐκ, when it is used with verbs of eating and drinking, is that of the ablative, to indicate taking a part of the bread and the wine, while the accusative would denote the mere consuming, R. 519. By δοκιμάζω the action of properly testing is referred to as coins are tested, those of genuine metal and full weight being accepted, the rest being rejected, 9:27. The communicant is to test himself as to his fitness for the Sacrament. He alone can do that. In the command there lies the supposition that the test will result favorably.

Paul does not state directly into what the communicant is to probe when he is testing himself. The context, however, indicates what is in Paul's mind. It will first be in regard to faith in Christ's words which are used in the very institution of the Sacrament, v. 23-25. Secondly, it will be in regard to the removal of anything from the heart that would clash with the reception of Christ's body and blood. This is done by true contrition and repentance.

On this injunction of Paul's is based the so-called preparatory or confessional service that precedes the Communion service proper. The demonstrative adverb "so" once more emphasizes the preparation which Paul has indicated. Note how the eating and the drinking are repeated throughout v. 27-30 as if the tremendous significance of these simple acts is to be deeply impressed. Luther has caught the full import of these repetitions.

29) "For" fortifies the preceding admonition, yet not by pointing out the benefit of such self-testing but by indicating the harm that results from its absence; "for" = "for otherwise." **For he who eats and drinks eats and drinks a judgment to himself because he does not discern the body.**

This is the situation against which to guard. Paul writes only: "He who eats and drinks" and omits renewed mention of the bread and the cup. This is done because these actions are the decisive feature and must thus be stressed as actions. "Unworthily," which certain texts insert, is not needed because of the added participial clause.

The entire statement deals with the unworthy communicant, namely concerning what he does by his eating and his drinking. He eats and drinks κρῖμα to himself, "judgment" in the sense of "a sentence of judgment"; not κρίσις, the act of judging or of pronouncing a verdict. The word used is not κατάκριμα, "condemnation," although, since the person is guilty, it would amount to this. Luther's *das Gericht* (especially with the article), which is adopted by the A. V.'s "condemnation," is too strong. Final damnation may result from communing unworthily, especially when it is continued indefinitely, but the "judgment" that is here mentioned by Paul may be removed by repentance. Verse 30 leads us to think that in its preliminary stages this "judgment" results in temporal penalties.

The final participle μὴ διακρίνων should not be construed with the subject: "he who eats and drinks not discerning," etc.; for if this were intended, the participle would be placed next to the subject. This participle modifies the verbs: he "eats and drinks not discerning." Greek participles of this kind are subject to a certain indefiniteness since the participial form fails to indicate the specific relation intended by the writer. This relation the reader must determine from the context. The R. V. has: "*if* he discern not," etc., with which Robertson agrees 1129, 1023. Yet if the sense is to be conditional, why should Paul reverse the protasis and the apodosis? To let the condition trail on behind seems to weaken its force whereas the condition would certainly be the vital point. We should note that the statement: "He eats and drinks a judgment to himself," is a categorical declaration and is complete in itself. We ask: "Why a judgment?" The participle answers: *"Because he does not discern the body."* This proves and substantiates the declaration and shows that no question about a judgment can be raised in such a case.

The extended paronomasia should be appreciated: κρίμα — διακρίνων — διεκρίνομεν — κρινόμενοι — κατακριθῶμεν (v. 29, 31, 32). Since διακρίνων and διεκρίνομεν in v. 31 are so near together they should be translated in the same way. The R. V. uses "discern" for both but has the less appropriate "discriminate" in the margin; Luther has *unterscheiden* and *richten,* which the A. V. follows by translating "discern" and "judge." The translations waver because in the case of the participle the object is "the body" (non-personal) and in that of the finite verb "ourselves" (personal). Even the verb "discern" does not fit "ourselves" very well. Yet the sense is plain: to discern the Lord's body means to perceive that in the Sacrament that body is really present and received. In v. 31: to discern ourselves means to perceive ourselves, when we commune, as partakers of the body and the blood of our Lord. Luther's idea in using *unterscheiden* to translate the participle is the following: "not distinguishing the body," i. e., treating it like ordinary food. He has some justification for this conception since in all probability this was the fault that existed in Corinth. Yet what Luther seeks to conserve is taken care of by the translation "discern." Whoever discerns the Lord's body in the Sacrament will, as a matter of course, "distinguish" this heavenly food from ordinary earthly food.

Paul writes very briefly "the body" and does not add "of the Lord" and does not mention "the blood." Both the genitive and the second object are, however, evidently to be supplied. The supposition that the sole mention of "the body" intends to indicate "the *breaking* of the bread" is a fanciful thought, for neither bread nor its breaking are mentioned but only "the body." Moreover, just preceding we have the twice repeated eating and drinking. To discern the body cannot mean to perceive and to judge aright that the bread symbolizes and represents the body, i. e., the body that is absent and far away in heaven. It must be the actual body that is present in the Sacrament itself and is given and eaten there.

30) Paul now states what eating and drinking a judgment really means; he does it by pointing to the judgment which has already begun among the Corinthians. **For this cause many among you are weak and sickly, and a considerable number are sleeping.** The Corinthians were perhaps wondering about these inflictions. Paul gives them an explanation. Let us not forget that these cases occurred in spite of the charisma of healing which had been granted to some of the members. The weak and the sickly remained as they were, and some died.

The adjectives ἀσθενεῖς and ἄρρωστοι are practical synonyms, both denote ailments. In the present connection these cannot be spiritual ailments, for κοιμῶνται must mean physical death. The use of this verb "are sleeping" is quite significant in this connection. In the language of the New Testament only those who are saved "are asleep," and this sleeping, of course, refers to their bodies and not to their souls. The "judgment" which Paul has in mind is at the worst an untimely physical death and not eternal damnation.

This raises the question regarding the physical effect which the Lord's Supper may have on the communicant. There is no Scriptural warrant that the Sacrament will produce a beneficial physical effect upon the sick, neither that the body and the blood will act as a charm (Adolph Wuttke, *Der deutsche Volksaberglaube*, 193, 318), or that they will serve as a natural medicine. The body and the blood do not act as a poison which makes an unworthy communicant sick or kills him. It is the sin of communing unworthily which, like other sins, entails the penalty of judgment. Paul does not say that the penalty of this unworthiness is invariably physical sickness or untimely death. The Lord alone decides what the penalty shall be. In Corinth the penalty is as Paul states it.

31) Paul shows how we may escape "judgment" when we are going to the Lord's Supper. **But if we would discern ourselves we would not be judged.** We must discern ourselves, form a right conclusion concerning ourselves. See the remarks on v. 28. A protasis with εἰ and the imperfect, and an apodosis with the imperfect and ἄν constitute a regular condition of present unreality, R. 1015.

When Paul says, "If we would discern ourselves we would not be judged," he implies that the Corinthians are not doing this and are hence receiving judgment. See the notes on v. 29 regarding the verb "discern." In v. 29 note the close correspondence between "a judgment" and "not discerning"; then the reverse in v. 31: "if we would discern we would not be judged." In both verses the point of emphasis is finely put, being pivoted on judgment and being judged.

Yet Paul does not emphasize the subject: if "we ourselves" would discern ourselves, for he does not intend to contrast ourselves and the Lord. The incorrect translation of the A. V. introduces this contrast by translating the two verbs in the same manner: "If we would judge ourselves we should not be judged," i. e., if we did it, the Lord would not need to do it. The contrast lies, not in the subjects, but in the verbs διακρίνειν and κρίνειν and in their voices, the first being active, the second passive. The first verb is compounded with διά, the second is without this preposition. Yet this fact does not make the first mean *unterscheiden*, "discriminate." Any right "discernment" which we may make regarding our fitness for the Sacrament is sufficient; we do not need to stress the idea of segregating this "discernment" from ideas that are wrong by a process of discrimination. We escape a penalizing judgment from the Lord simply by properly perceiving that in the Sacrament we eat and drink the Lord's own body and blood.

When Paul writes "we" he quietly includes himself and thus softens the tone of his words. Apostle though he is, he, too, does not escape judgment if he does not carefully discern his own spiritual condition. The way of safety which he points out is the one and the only way for all.

32) Just as in 10:13 Paul added a word of comfort to the serious warning there expressed, he does here. What about those who have hitherto failed in proper self-examination and self-discernment? Is no way of escape from the penalty which this has brought upon them open to them? In other words, what about the weak and the sickly? **Yet in being visited with judgment by the Lord we are being chastened in order that we may not be finally judged adversely together with the world.**

All present judging on the part of the Lord has the gracious purpose that we may not at last experience his adverse judgment and be condemned. Thus the Lord's judgments which he visits upon believers for the serious sins they commit are evidences of fatherly love and not of his damning wrath; in the case of unbelievers the judgments which he visits upon them in this life are advance indications of his final consuming wrath.

We should note the durative present tenses "being visited with judgment" and "are being chastened" in contrast with the punctiliar aorist "may not be finally judged adversely," i. e., "may not be condemned." The former two continue in hope of betterment in order that the latter may not set in and once for all destroy us. "To chastise" is to treat as a child, i. e., to correct, when necessary, with severity. Such treatment always evinces great concern for the one chastised. While chastisement is painful it still proves that we are children.

To think that Paul has the dead in Corinth especially in mind, and that he intimates that even after death they will receive benefit from the Lord's chastening, is to charge Paul with a bit of Romanism. Why not frankly say "Purgatory"? Paul commits the dead to God's gracious hands. He writes for those who are still living, who "are being visited with judgment," who "are being chastised." "The world" is the entire body of unbelievers. Luther says that Paul writes thus "because otherwise with our reason we could not well believe and grasp this. For after we learn, and this also is certain, that God punishes sin, our reason concludes nothing but that these punishments are without all mercy on God's part. Hence it falls from God and despairs of his grace."

33) The graver deduction is made with ὥστε in v. 27; with another ὥστε Paul now brings the minor regarding the outward conduct of the Corinthians at the Agape. First the heart, then the conduct. **Wherefore, my brethren, coming together to eat, wait for each other.**

The address brings a brotherly touch at the end but at the same time shows in what spirit Paul was writing throughout. Both the participle "coming together" and the verb used in v. 34, "may not come together," point back to the beginning of the discussion in v. 17, 18, 20 where this same coming together in a congregational assembly is prominently mentioned.

"To eat" refers to the Agape which was followed by the Sacrament.

"Wait for each other," i. e., until all are properly assembled, goes back to the unbrotherly procedure that was rebuked by "each one in the eating consumes his own supper in advance" in v. 21 because so many ate in cliques and disregarded the rest. This wretched conduct, which even made the Sacrament impossible, the Corinthians should by all means avoid.

34) Then the final point: **If anyone is hungry, let him eat at home in order that you may not come together unto judgment.**

Let no one make of the Agape and the Sacrament that followed an ordinary meal, a feast for satisfying hunger. Do this at home. The Agape is no dole even for the poor, and we should not deduce this from the reference to "those that have not" in v. 21. The arrangement seems to have been after this order: the wealthier members provided everything or nearly everything that was needed, the rest brought what they could, some, like the slaves, brought nothing at all. The Agape did not take the place of an ordinary meal as the modern church suppers do at which people eat to satisfy their hunger. Its purpose was to reveal the congregation as a loving, united body. Thus the fitting climax was the celebration of the Sacrament.

The purpose clause once more reminds the Corinthians of the one thing to be avoided, namely "judgment," v. 29. What a terrible coming together "unto judgment" instead of unto blessing! Κρίμα, with the suffix -μα, is a term that expresses result, thus a verdict and also its execution.

Now the rest, when I shall come, I will set in order. Still other points require attention, probably some of the details of the Agape. The supposition that Paul had heard about these other matters but was not sufficiently certain of them to give instructions is scarcely correct; they were matters that could be postponed.

Romanists use Paul's statement as a proof for their idea of apostolic tradition. We may well suppose that such unwritten traditions were circulated in the churches. But the Romanists are unable to state what these traditions were. For instance here in Corinth, what was it that Paul set in order when he arrived some months later? No one knows. In the New Testament ὡς is often temporal, and with ἄν and the subjunctive it denotes expectancy: "when I shall come" as I expect.

Great changes occurred in the early church. The Agape did not prove to be a permanent success. It was first transferred from the evening to the early morning "before it was light" (Pliny, *Epistles* 10, 42, 43, about 110 A. D.; *antelucanis coetibus*, Tertullian, *De Corona*, 3). Then the Agape was separated from the Sacrament; it was finally abolished altogether. Justin Martyr, about 150 A. D., describes the Holy Communion without mention of the Agape.

CHAPTER XII

The Seventh Part of the Letter

The Charismatic Gifts, chapters 12-14

We readily distinguish three sections in this extensive part of Paul's letter:
1) Charismatic gifts in general, chapter 12.
2) The better way: Love, chapter 13.
3) The gift of prophecy and the gift of tongues, chapter 14.

I. Charismatic Gifts in General. Chapter 12

1) The introductory περί phrase suggests that it is a caption to this entire part of the letter; it is like the similar phrases at the beginning of 7:1 and 8:1. These phrases indicate that Paul is answering inquiries which had been addressed to him in the letter which the Corinthians had sent to him. In all probability, however, Paul goes beyond the scope of the inquiry and writes all that he at the time deems necessary on so important a subject. The transitional δέ seems to correspond to πρῶτον μέν occurring in 11:18.

Now concerning spiritual gifts, brethren, I do not want you to be ignorant. In περὶ τῶν πνευματικῶν the genitive may be either masculine, like the nominative singular in 14:37, and denote persons, or neuter, like the accusative plural in 14:1, and denote gifts. Accordingly we might translate either: "Concerning persons with spiritual gifts," or: "Concerning spiritual gifts." Our versions, like Luther, decide for the latter and properly so. The plea that in the course of the elaboration Paul mentions persons is met by the fact that he also mentions gifts, and that, when gifts are discussed, the persons having them will also be indicated.

These "spiritual gifts" are clearly distinguished from faith, love, knowledge, and Christian virtues, the essential products of the Spirit found in every soul brought to Christ. In v. 4 they are called "the charismata" in the technical sense of this term, namely special gifts of the Spirit that were portioned out to different individuals. Some of these gifts have a natural basis in natural talents and abilities. The Spirit sanctifies and augments these talents for his high and blessed purpose, and thus they become charismatic. Others of these gifts have a supernatural basis and work in a miraculous manner. Both types of the charismata were richly evident in the apostolic church, but the latter type disappeared.

"I do not want you to be ignorant" is a characteristic formula of Paul's which he employs when he introduces important instruction. It is equivalent to: "I want you to know." Thus the object of this verse is to introduce the subject on which Paul desires to instruct the Corinthians.

2) He begins by briefly laying down the fundamental facts on which his instruction rests: at one time dumb idols, but now the Holy Spirit who enables us to confess that Jesus is the Lord. The textual question is permanently settled: Paul wrote ὅτι ὅτε. **You know that when you were Gentiles unto the dumb idols, even as you might be led, you were being led away.**

The majority of the Corinthians had been Gentiles. The first basic fact which these former Gentiles must bear in mind in connection with the subject of spiritual gifts and their proper use is that in their former life all spiritual manifestations were utterly unknown to them. All they knew were "the dumb idols." The fact that the adjective is appended with a second article gives to the adjective "dumb" as much emphasis as the noun "idols" has. This adjective is, then, not merely the current and thus the unemphatic description of the well-known idols.

Paul places "dumb" in contrast with the Holy Spirit, who not only himself speaks but makes us speak what no man could ever say on his own initiative. He makes it possible for us to confess Christ as Lord, yea, he enables us to speak "the word of wisdom" and "the word of knowledge," v. 8, and even divine "prophecy," 14:1. Paul may also be thinking about the gift of tongues, of which he knew the Corinthians were inordinately proud. What had "dumb" idols done in comparison with that gift? Paul merely says that the idols were dumb; this is an understatement, for they were actually lifeless.

The clause: "even as you might be led," contains the idea of repetition, R. 974, i. e., helplessly led at any time by those who had you in hand. The important verb is the participle at the end. Some regard this verse as an anacoluthon, like similar sentences in the classics. But this is unnecessary since ἦτε appears in the preceding subordinate clause and is thus automatically supplied with the participle at the end of the verse. This participle ἀπαγόμενοι is masculine although it is construed with the neuter ἔθνη in the ordinary Greek method of a *constructio ad sensum*. The simple verb "might be led" is placed beside the compound form "were led away," yet scarcely because of a similarity in sound only (R. 1033) but because of the thought. By leading the Corinthians to the dumb idols their religion led them away, i. e., misled them. Instead of receiving anything from these dumb and lifeless idols they were miserably cheated.

Both verbs are passive. The former is sometimes considered a middle: "as you might allow yourselves to be led"; but then the second should also be a middle:

"you allowed yourselves to be led away," for no difference is indicated between the two. The passives suit the thought exactly, the middles would add a complicating feature. The question is raised: "By whom were the Corinthians thus led and misled?" The answer then names either Satan and his evil spirits or the pagan priests. The better observation is that in this connection Paul lays no stress at all upon the agents; he intends that the Corinthians should think only of the dumb idols to which they were led.

3) On this first fact rests the second fact which Paul wants the Corinthians to bear in mind when they are considering the subject of spiritual gifts. **Wherefore I give you to understand that no one speaking in union with God's Spirit declares: Accursed is Jesus! and no one is able to declare: Lord is Jesus! except in a union with the Holy Spirit.**

"Wherefore" links the two facts together: "Because it is true that you were once misled and cheated by your old religion, for this very reason I want you to know that in the Christian religion everything is entirely different." In what way? In the church the Holy Spirit is active. The Spirit is twice mentioned with emphasis. Paul intends to make no sharp distinction by first calling him "God's Spirit" and then calling him "the Holy Spirit."

Paul twice writes "no man," which makes both effects of the Spirit seem to be negative. Yet the two modifiers show that the first effect is negative and the second is positive. This is evident also from what the Spirit does not make a man say and from what he does make a man say. These modifiers and these declarations are placed chiastically so as to attain a greater effect. Moreover, the two halves of the ὅτι clause are thus made of equal importance; what the Spirit never does is not to be merely a foil for what he always does.

Paul's statement is misunderstood when it is assumed that already in this verse he is speaking about spiritual gifts, in particular about the gift of tongues. This view states that Paul is here furnishing the Corinthians a criterion by which they may distinguish the genuine speakers with tongues from the spurious. The genuine have the Spirit and call Jesus "Lord," the spurious curse Jesus and have not the Spirit. But such a statement from the pen of Paul would be surprising. Were there members in the Corinthian congregation who cursed Jesus? And was it necessary for Paul to inform the Corinthians that such people were devoid of the Spirit? And where is there the least evidence that in Corinth or elsewhere pretending speakers with tongues had appeared who were deceiving the church?

In this preliminary, fundamental statement Paul is speaking about all believers. Whereas the Gentiles have only dumb idols and no divine personality to embrace or to repudiate, we Christians have the Holy Spirit. Paul is, however, not comparing two men, one who is without the Spirit, the other with the Spirit, one who is cursing Jesus, the other confessing Jesus. For every man who is without the Spirit does not curse Jesus; many do not even know about him. Paul is not taking in the whole world of non-Christians in contrast with all true Christians. He remains in a far narrower sphere. In both halves of his statement he is speaking only about one man, one who is animated by the Spirit, and points out what that man never does in contradistinction to what he always does. Thus both subjects are "no man." The first statement is expressed in the form of fact: "no man declares"; the second in the form of a possibility: "no man is able to declare" or "can declare." And the participial modifier: "speaking in union with God's Spirit," in the first statement, and the conditional clause: "except in union with the Holy

Spirit," in the second statement, are only formal variations which might also be reversed.

But why does Paul make the first statement so strong: "no man speaking in union with God's Spirit says, 'Accursed is Jesus' "? A milder statement would seem to suffice, for instance: "no man speaking in union with God's Spirit says anything against Jesus." The only answer that we can give is derived from the fact that when Jesus is strongly urged upon a man by the Spirit of God through the gospel, and that man scorns to accept him as Lord, he is very apt to voice his scorn in strong language. Thus to this day the Jews spit upon Jesus, and others who repudiate his divine Lordship and his blood atonement use vicious and even blasphemous language when doing so. Paul uses the personal name "Jesus" in this connection because the incarnate person is referred to.

The participle λαλῶν, "speaking" in contradistinction to keeping silence, differs from λέγει and its aorist infinitive εἰπεῖν, "declares" and "to declare," which always involve the thought that is spoken. "Accursed," ἀνάθεμα, a later form of ἀνάθημα, is the translation of the Hebrew *cherem,* something that is removed from the possession or the use of men and set aside for God as an object of his wrath and devoted to destruction or as a gift that is dedicated to God's acceptance. In Hellenistic Greek ἀνάθεμα is used to express the former idea and ἀνάθημα the latter idea. The later ecclesiastical anathema continues the former. Compare Rom. 9:3; Gal. 1:8. The title Κύριος designates Jesus as the divine "Lord" who is full of grace, truth, and salvation, and is embraced and confessed by faith. Paul and the early Christians seem to apply this title to Jesus in conscious opposition to the Gentile appellation "lord" which was bestowed upon pagan gods.

Whoever confesses Jesus as "Lord" has the Holy Spirit in his heart. This is true of all Christians irrespective of any other gifts which they may have received from the Spirit. Paul wants the Corinthians to understand this thoroughly when they consider the subject of spiritual gifts in detail. The fundamental gift is the Holy Spirit himself, through whom we confess Jesus as Lord. In truth, if we had no other gifts, this supreme gift would be blessedness and riches enough. The Corinthians need only to compare their former state as devotees to dumb idols with their present state as confessors of the Lord through the Spirit of God, then they will be happy and satisfied, indeed.

4-6) After this necessary introduction Paul proceeds with the transitional connective to show with what an abundance of gifts the Holy Spirit enriches the church. **Now there are distributions of charismata, yet the same Spirit; and there are distributions of ministrations, and the same Lord; and there are distributions of energies, yet the same God who energizes all things in all ways.**

The term διαιρέσεις appears only here in the New Testament and means, not "diversities" as our versions translate (for the fact that the gifts are diverse is too obvious to require statement), but "distributions." The gifts are parceled out so that one individual has this, another that gift. Yet these "distributions" are not so much the acts of parceling out as the result of such acts so that each one of us now has his own particular gift or gifts.

Paul considers all of the gifts together and designates them by three different names: first, "charismata" or gracious gifts; then, "ministrations," services freely rendered by us for the benefit of others; lastly, "energies," active forces, operations that result from the imparted spiritual energy. Viewed from one angle, they appear as charismata, from another as ministrations, and from a third as energies. Paul first bids us note their source as gracious gifts, secondly their purpose as benefiting others, thirdly their power as being full of spiritual energy.

Yet throughout, no matter how we may consider them, they are connected with God. When he is stating this connection Paul refers to the three persons of the Godhead but names the persons in inverse order since he has already mentioned the Spirit. He varies the connectives: δέ . . . καί . . . δέ but with no appreciable difference in sense. "The same Spirit" is the gracious Giver of all the charismata; "the same Lord" receives our ministrations for others; "the same God" is back of the spiritual energies we exercise through our gifts, he "who energizes all things in all ways."

Ἐν πᾶσιν is a phrase that occurs frequently in the New Testament; it is neuter like πάντα and characterizes God as "in every way" being the active source. Some, however, regard "in all" as a masculine and translate "in all believers." In v. 11 all of the gifts are said to be wrought by the Spirit, and in v. 27 all of the believers and their various gifts are said to constitute the body of Christ. Hence the connection of the Spirit with the charismata, of the Lord with the ministrations, of God with the energies is not intended to be exclusive but inclusive: all three of the persons are involved in all three of the relations. Formulated dogmatically, this reads: *Opera ad extra sunt indivisa aut communa.*

7) From the gifts and their connection with God Paul advances to the persons who are endowed with these gifts. First the comprehensive statement with the continuative connective; then in v. 8 the explanatory "for" to introduce the details. **Now to each one is given the manifestation of the Spirit for the purpose of the benefit.** The emphasis rests first on the dative "to each one" at the beginning of the sentence and secondly on the phrase "for the purpose

of the benefit" at the end of the sentence. Two things are thus made prominent: each believer has his gift, and every bestowal of a gift is for the common good.

"To each one" cannot apply only to each individual in the class of those who are favored with gifts as distinct from another class which has no gifts. This is placed beyond dispute by the lengthy elaboration beginning with v. 12. Nor is the πρός phrase deprived of emphasis, although it has the emphatic position at the end, because Paul does not at once elaborate this common benefit. Paul often holds an important point in reserve and in due time dwells on it more fully. He does that here, for in the detailed comparison beginning with v. 12 he shows how each member of the church benefits the entire body by rightly employing his particular gift.

Whereas in the preceding verses Paul has used the plurals charismata, etc., he now uses the singular "the manifestation of the Spirit." This expanding of an idea by means of plurals and then concentrating it into a singular is characteristic of Paul's mind and shows the mastery of his thinking. There is considerable dispute as to whether "of the Spirit" is an objective or a subjective genitive. The reference to II Cor. 4:2: "the manifestation of the truth," the only place besides this verse where we meet φανέρωσις, is not decisive because "of the Spirit" is a person, and "of the truth" is not. We may manifest the truth (objective genitive) while the Spirit may manifest his presence in the gifts which he bestows (subjective genitive).

When the question is properly put it practically answers itself. What is it that is given to each of us? Is the gift this that *we* make manifest the Spirit for the common good, or this that *the Spirit* manifest himself in us by his gift for the common good? Certainly the latter. This answer is supported also by the analogy of Scripture which never speaks of our using the

Spirit but always of his using us. One may, indeed, wonder why Paul does not write: "In each person the Spirit manifests himself for the common good" instead of saying: "To each one is given the manifestation of the Spirit," etc. The sense is practically the same and thus helps to show that the genitive in question is subjective: the Spirit does the manifesting and not we.

Yet Paul's formulation has the advantage of introducing the significant verb "is given": to each of us *is given* whatever *gift* we have — a point that was very necessary for the instruction of the Corinthians who liked to boast about their gifts and forgot that they were *given*. The question is also asked whether ἡ φανέρωσις is general and includes all the charismata, etc., or only individual and refers to whatever gift an individual may have. The term combines both ideas, it is individual as well as general. For "to each one" singles out each person as an individual, and yet "to each one" also includes everyone, omitting none.

Luther translates the final phrase *zum gemeinen Nutzen,* which our versions adopt by translating "to profit withal," literally, "for the benefit," i. e., the well-known benefit for which all gifts are intended. Not we, not God, but our fellow Christians and others are to share in this benefit. The preposition πρός indicates purpose or intent. Paul employs the substantivized neuter participle τὸ συμφέρον, "that which profits," whereas in 7:35 and 10:33 he has the substantivized adjective τὸ σύμφορον although some texts have the participle in the latter passage. Because each gift is intended to benefit others Paul calls all gifts "ministrations" in v. 5. The gifts make us stewards and call for their administration; they convert us into altruists. This obligation is only too often forgotten.

8) Each person has his gift, and he has it for the benefit of others. Paul now lets the gifts pass before us in beautiful array and ushers them in with

First Corinthians 12:8

γάρ as explaining that each person does have his gift. **For to one through the Spirit is given expression of wisdom while to another expression of knowledge according to the same Spirit; to someone else faith in the same Spirit while to another charismata of healings in the one Spirit, and to another energies of miracles, and to another prophecy, and to another discernings of spirits; to someone else varieties of tongues while to another interpretation of tongues.**

Paul himself indicates three groups: 1) ᾧ μέν . . . ἄλλῳ; 2) ἑτέρῳ followed by four ἄλλῳ; 3) again ἑτέρῳ . . . ἄλλῳ. The first two gifts are a pair; so also the last two. In the middle group "faith" stands alone, and the other four gifts are two pairs that are related to "faith." So much regarding the arrangement of the list. It does not intend to be exhaustive, for Paul presently mentions still other gifts, v. 28; see also Rom. 12:6, etc. Paul lists these gifts:

Two involving *the intellect*:
    Expression of wisdom
    Expression of knowledge.

Five involving *faith*:
    Faith itself
    Healing } Deeds
    Miracles }
    Prophecy } Speech
    Discerning of spirits }

Two involving *the tongue*:
    Tongues
    Interpretation of tongues.

Paul varies the prepositions: διά to denote the mediation of the Spirit with regard to the first gift; κατά to indicate the norm or the determination of the Spirit with regard to the second gift; ἐν to mark the sphere of the Spirit with regard to the next two gifts. Since "in" (in union with) is used with the third and fourth, and the rest are without an introductory preposition, it seems best to suppose that "in" is to be supplied with all that follow. The three relations indicated by the three prepositions are by no means identical. They express the idea that in the act of giving (δίδοται) the Spirit acts as a mediating, a normating, and a containing agency.

Paul writes λόγος in connection with both "wisdom" and "knowledge" and thus indicates the "expression" of both in words or discourse for the benefit of others. "Wisdom" and "knowledge" are synonymous. The line that divides them is not at once apparent. This moves some to conclude that there is little or no difference between them. Yet Paul clearly intends to name two gifts. However they may be related, they are certainly distinct. It is unnecessary to search outside of the Scriptures in an effort to determine the difference. Those who have done so, even with a demonstration of great learning, have produced only rather questionable results. The Scriptures themselves say very much regarding wisdom and knowledge.

In 1:30 we have defined σοφία as consisting of all the gracious, heavenly, and efficacious thoughts of God embodied in Christ Jesus for the enlightenment of our souls. Paul clearly differentiates this divine wisdom from fleshly, worldly, and mere human wisdom, 1:20; 2:5, 6, 13; 3:19; II Cor. 1:12; James 3:15; etc. As this wisdom is embodied in Christ Jesus, so it likewise consists in the gospel. The ability to state this wisdom to others is the best and the highest spiritual gift.

The "expression of wisdom" is thus always mediated "through the Spirit." Through him we are enabled, not only to apprehend this wisdom in our own hearts for our own salvation, but also to convey what we have apprehended to others for their salvation. In the gift we must include also the ability to apply the divine wisdom in a practical way to our own and to other men's lives, Rom. 16:19; Eph. 5:15, 17; James 3:13; I Cor. 3:18.

The distinctive feature of γνῶσις is the personal apprehension of the details of the gospel. It, too, deals with the gospel, but there is nothing in the term that includes speculation or speculative and philosophic ideas. "Knowledge" deals with the explanation, the unfolding, and the correlation of gospel facts, or we may call them doctrines. The "expression" or λόγος of knowledge is the ability to impart this personal knowledge to others. This gift is of great value to teachers, to apologists, and to many others in the church. Paul pairs it with the highest gift.

9) When it is listed as a charismatic gift "faith" or πίστις cannot be the *fides salvifica* but must be the *fides miraculosa* as described in Matt. 17:20 and its context; 21:21; the Gospel parallels, and I Cor. 13:2. In Matt. 7:22 it appears that this wonder-working faith may be found also in nominal Christians who are devoid of saving faith. By means of this charisma things that are otherwise impossible are actually accomplished when they become our tasks in the course of our calling. In Matt. 17:14, etc., the Lord's disciples who had this charisma failed to get results because of their secret unbelief for which the Lord chided them. He there also tells them how to strengthen this gift so that it may be made operative when it is needed. In 13:2 Paul appropriates the Lord's own description: "faith so that I could remove mountains," μεθιστάνειν, transfer them to a new location when they are in the way. This description seems to be couched in proverbial language and is equal to saying: perform what seem to be not mere impossibilities but the greatest of impossibilities.

The next two gifts are designated by plurals: "charismata of healings" and "energies of miracles";

both of the genitives are appositional. Previously Paul had called all gifts both "charismata" and "energies"; he now uses both terms in a specific, we may even say a technical sense, the one with reference to healings and the other with reference to miracles. The plural of the governing noun as well as the plural of its genitive are significant and indicate that all healings and all miracles are in each separate case gifts. We should not think that healings and miracles were wrought at will by the person concerned. In each instance a specific intimation came to them from the Spirit that the act should be performed, and not until that moment did it occur, but then it always took place without fail.

It was thus when Peter and John healed the lame man at the Gate Beautiful, Acts 3:1, etc. How many times had they walked past this lame man as he sat daily begging at the gate! But on that morning the Holy Spirit conveyed the information to the apostles that they should heal him. For this reason Peter and John looked so earnestly upon the beggar and then spoke the words that healed him with such assurance.

The case of the damsel that cried after Paul in Philippi is equally plain, Acts 16:16, etc. On many days she cried, and Paul did nothing. Then Paul suddenly turned and healed her. He must have received the intimation to do so from the Spirit.

A third plain case is that of Peter at Joppa, Acts 9:36. This we may place among the energies of miracles. When the friends of Dorcas brought Peter into the death chamber, he prayed in order to learn the Lord's intention, which in this case was to bring Dorcas back to life. We may conclude that every case of healing from sickness or of working a miracle was similar to these although the Biblical narratives do not always supply us with the details that show the Spirit's intimation. In each instance the gift or the energy is bestowed by a communication from above for that case alone. Lacking such communication, even the apostles made no attempt to perform a miracle.

10) Note how well "energies" matches its appositional genitive "miracles" or "powers" since a work always requires the corresponding power. We may, of course, say that healing also requires power since it, too, appears as a miracle, but Paul calls healing a charisma or gracious gift and reserves δύναμις to designate acts of another type. For this is one of the outstanding Biblical terms to designate miracles, "being, as they are, outcomings of that great power of God, which was inherent in Christ, who was himself that 'great Power of God' which Simon blasphemously allowed himself to be named, Acts 8:9, 10; and was by him lent to those who were his witnesses and ambassadors," Trench.

"Prophecy" is used to designate the gift or the office of a prophet. In Rom. 12:6 it is mentioned together with two other gifts. This term is used in a double sense: broadly to indicate any and all ability to communicate the saving will of God to others so that every true teacher and preacher may be called a prophet; and more narrowly to designate the receiving and the communicating of direct and specific messages from God. The apostles were prophets in both senses of the term. Their regular assistants were prophets in the former sense. Agabus, Acts 11:28; 21:10, and Philip's daughters, Acts 21:9, were prophets in the latter sense.

Allied with this gift are "discernings of spirits." I John 4:1 speaks of proving or testing the spirits and offers a simple criterion by which the test can be made. "Discernings of spirits" is again plural and denotes abilities that are developed in one or in more directions for the purpose of penetrating into what lies back of certain utterances or works in order to determine whether they truly emanate from the Holy Spirit or whether they represent pretenses of the human spirit or contain the deceptions of some spirit of evil. All Christians are to "prove the spirits, whether they are of God"; but certain difficult cases occur, for which more than common Christian discernment is necessary. False prophets love to use deceptive language. For the purpose of unmasking these prophets the Lord provides this gift and thus enables his church to turn from lying spirits to the one Spirit of truth.

So much has been written about the gift of tongues that the result is a confusion. This is in good part due to the extraneous material that is introduced. The subject is one that concerns exegesis alone. We ask: "What do the Scriptures say about this gift?" We rule out all reference to pagan manifestations, to later phenomena in the church, to the cries and shouts uttered at revivals, etc., no matter of what character any or all of these may be. And especially do we not construct in advance a theory about these tongues and then interpret the Scriptures according to this theory.

Since the promise regarding "tongues" or regarding "new tongues" (the better reading) mentioned in Mark 16:18 was first fulfilled at Pentecost in Jerusalem and shortly thereafter at Cæsarea, Acts 10:44, etc.; 15:8, and since this phenomenon did not appear in Corinth for a number of years after these first occurrences, we must ask whether a difference exists between the "tongues" spoken in Jerusalem and in Cæsarea and those spoken in Corinth. The answer is that they are the same. As the promise is one, so the fulfillment is one regardless of the place where the fulfillment occurs.

The next step is to recognize the fact that Luke's description as given in the Acts is decisive for what Paul writes in Corinthians. This is reversed by some. They seek to determine what happened in Corinth and then either square Luke's account with what they think occurred at Corinth or posit two different gifts of tongues. Aside from the time when Luke and when Paul wrote this method of approach is unsatisfactory. For Luke is the one who fully describes what the tongues are while Paul takes for granted that his readers know what they are and therefore offers no description. Luke writes for a reader (Theophilus) who may never have heard of this gift, at least may never have seen this gift in operation. Paul writes for readers who have often heard members of their own congregation speak in tongues. This is decisive as to the Scriptural starting point.

Regarding the multitude at the time of Pentecost Luke reports Acts 2:6: "Every single man was hearing them speaking in his own language" (exact translation). Still more clearly Luke reports that the multitude asked in astonishment: "And how are we hearing, every man in our own language in which we were born?" Then there follows the list of nationalities who said that they heard the disciples speak the languages in which they were born. These nationalities even state the contents of what they heard: "We are hearing them speaking with our own tongues the great things of God." Here we have the significant dative ταῖς ἡμετέραις γλώσσαις which uses the specific term γλῶσσαι (which is used in the promise recorded in Mark and regularly by Paul) and the strong possessive adjective ἡμετέραι, "our own tongues" or languages. Can we be in doubt that the γλῶσσαι had never been learned by the disciples? And this fact is decisive for the gift of tongues, also for that found in Corinth.

We therefore do not accept the view of Cremer and of his latest editor, Julius Koegel, in *Biblisch-theologisches Woerterbuch der Neutestamentlichen Graezitaet* that the gift of tongues that occurred at Jerusalem and elsewhere consisted in speaking *die Sprache der neuen Welt, der Erloesten und Seligen* (the language of the new world, of the redeemed and the blessed). This view contradicts the term "tongues" which is used throughout to designate this gift, for this term is plural and not singular: *die Sprache* (the language). Or are we to think that different languages are spoken by the redeemed in heaven, and that these different languages constitute "the language (singular) of heaven"? What answers Cremer and Koegel answers also all others who refer to the languages of heaven in an effort to explain the phenomena that occurred at Corinth or at Corinth and at Jerusalem and at Cæsarea. Neither Luke nor Paul refer to the language or the languages of heaven.

To explain the plural γλῶσσαι the statement is made that "tongues" denotes only the substance of what is spoken, namely in one case prayers, in another psalms, in a third blessings, etc., I Cor. 14:15. But in Luke's record the contents, "the mighty works of God," are clearly distinguished from the languages, "our own languages"; the two, contents and languages, cannot be combined into one. Moreover, a psalm may contain also a prayer or a blessing or both combined.

The expression ἕτεραι γλῶσσαι found in Acts 2:4 has been stressed and contrasted with ἄλλαι which does not occur. The point is made that Luke should have written ἄλλαι if he has in mind "other" human languages, and that his use of ἕτεραι compels us to think that he refers to non-human languages. But ἄλλος and ἕτερος are regularly used interchangeably with no difference in meaning, and they never indicate a difference as great as the one here made (human——non-human). This interchangeable use is illustrated in the very section now under consideration, v. 8-10. Only in certain pointed contrasts (and these are infrequent) is a difference indicated as in Gal. 1:6, 7. In addition λαλεῖν ἑτέραις γλώσσαις which occurs in Acts 2:4 is elucidated by 14:21. "In the law it is written, By men of strange tongues, ἐν ἑτερογλώσσοις, and by lips of strangers will I speak unto this people"; to which Paul adds: "wherefore tongues, αἱ γλῶσσαι, are for signs," etc. Here the very adjective ἕτερος in the compound ἑτερογλώσσοις, which is to prove the point of non-human languages, proves the reverse.

In Mark 16:18 καιναὶ γλῶσσαι is used, "new" tongues or languages. This adjective is said to mean *unerhoert*, "unheard of." C.-K. regard καιναί as equivalent to ἕτεραι (correctly) but take it in the sense of a heavenly language (incorrectly). But this adjective never means "new" in the sense of *unerhoert*. This is the sense of νέος, an adjective which is never applied to the gift of tongues. Καινός is always "new" compared with what is "old," as differing from the "old." The Corinthians have their own language, which is old to them; and when they hear some of their own members speak "in new languages," these are "new" to them because they are foreign languages, "other" than the one to which they are accustomed. Instead of proving that Paul has in mind "the language of heaven" when he uses καιναί, the term proves the opposite.

Paul writes: to someone else "varieties of tongues," γένη γλωσσῶν. Because of this word "varieties" we are told that one person could not speak several of these tongues if they denote human languages. But why not? Could one person at one time not be gifted to speak in one language and at another time in another language? Where is the intimation that one person could be gifted to speak only and always in but *one* language?

Much labor has been spent on letting γλῶσσαι mean *Sprechweisen, Ausdrucksweisen* (variety of exprespression), and the like, and this is done in order to explain the use of the plural. It has been said that the translation "language" and "languages" is inadequate throughout chapter 14 whereas the opposite is true. But the object back of regarding γλῶσσαι as "manners of speaking," "ways of expressing," is to maintain the view of *one* language which has different ways and manners of expression, i. e., the language of heaven. But "manners of speaking" and "ways of expression" do not suggest "the language of heaven." If Paul had in mind "the language of heaven," why does he not write γλῶσσα οὐρανοῦ just as he writes "the tongues of the angels" when he refers to the language of angels in 13:1?

Some say that the tongues were whisperings and mutterings; that they were a mixture of elements and rudiments that were taken from many languages; that they were angel languages or angel-like languages; that they consisted of archaic, extremely poetic, and odd provincialisms that were put together in a confusing fashion; that they were inarticulate cries. Those who hold such views say that, not the ego of the person spoke, but only his tongue, and that his speech consisted of incomprehensible sounds, partly sighings, partly cries, disjointed words, strange combinations, that were uttered in a highly excited state, and that for this reason the hearers thought that they heard a medley of languages. Another theory regarding the separation of the mind and the tongue has the latter speak "a language corresponding to the ecstatic vision of the mysteries of God," which statement is not very clear.

The "tongues" are sometimes regarded as a miracle of hearing — the speakers spoke their own native language, but at the time of Pentecost the Spirit made this sound to the ears of the listeners as though they were hearing all the other languages that are enumerated by Luke. Was this the case also at Corinth? Smith, *Bible Dictionary,* article "Tongues," makes the miracle of Pentecost a miracle of memory although he leaves us in the lurch regarding the phenomenon that was observed at Corinth. We are told: "It must be remembered that in all likelihood such words as they then uttered had been heard by the disciples before. At every feast which they had ever attended from their youth up they must have been brought into contact with a crowd as varied as that which was present on the day of Pentecost, the pilgrims of each nation uttering their praises and doxologies. The difference was, that, before, the Galilean peasants had stood in that crowd, neither heeding, nor understanding, nor remembering what they heard; now they had the power of speaking it clearly and fully. The divine work would in this case take the form of *supernatural exaltation of memory*, not of imparting a miraculous knowledge of words never heard before. We have the authority of John 14:26 for seeing in such an exaltation one of the special works of the Divine Comforter." But John 14:26 promises remembrance of "whatsoever I have said to you," a matter that is far different from the miracle of tongues that occurred at Jerusalem, to say nothing about Corinth. This effort of making the miracle one of memory would still leave it a miracle and would involve the understanding as well as the memory.

The gift of tongues which the Corinthians rated as being probably the highest and most desirable Paul places next to the last and combines with "interpretation of tongues." The understanding of this last gift is of necessity governed by the conception of the gift of tongues. The interpreter understood the language that was spoken and translated the sense of what was said so that all understood. This view does not conflict with 14:2: "no one understands." For if "no one" is made absolute, all possibility of interpretation is excluded no matter what conception we may have of "tongues." The only explanation possible would be that in every instance a special divine revelation was granted to some person present which enabled him to interpret and to translate. Nowhere do we, however, find a hint to that effect.

If speaking with tongues means speaking the language of heaven, then the only interpretation possible would be the result of a direct revelation. The gift of tongues was, moreover, in some cases combined with the gift of interpretation, 14:5, 11. Several gifts were sometimes granted to a single person, for instance, to Paul himself, 14:6, 19. From this combination of the gift of tongues with that of interpretation we may, perhaps, gather that the interpretation was not always a translation. The person who was moved by the Spirit to utter something in a foreign language which he had never learned might at times know and feel the general sense of what his tongue was moved to speak. Thus he could relate in the vernacular what he had uttered in the unknown tongue. In fact, Paul urges that such of the Corinthians who had the gift of tongues should pray for this additional gift.

This leaves the question as to how one who naturally knew a foreign language that was used by those who spoke with tongues and who then used his natural knowledge in giving the interpretation to the congregation can be said to possess a gift of the Spirit. We must remember that we are here on the very lowest level of the gifts, for Paul is at pains to instruct the Corinthians to this very effect. Interpretation is the last and thus the lowest of all the gifts. It utilizes a natural ability by sanctifying it and employing it for spiritual ends.

We have analogous cases even today. The man who has a thorough knowledge of Greek and of Hebrew is greatly admired by the church and is, perhaps, even elected to a professorship in some seminary. Yet his gift is of a low order; it is only linguistic after all. Its value lies in the fact that it may serve as a medium for far higher ends. In other words, its true value lies in its sanctification for these ends. Unsanctified, its use may result to the detriment of the church. See what rationalistic and skeptical exegesis has done to the church in spite of the fact that it has been advocated by scholarly linguists.

11) After having enlarged upon the details in v. 8-10 Paul binds them all together in v. 11. **Now all these the one and same Spirit produces, apportioning to each one severally even as he wills.** The neuter plural πάντα ταῦτα includes all of the gifts mentioned irrespective of their Greek grammatical order. The idea expressed is not that as gifts all of them are given by the Spirit but that as abilities and powers all of them are produced and operated by the energy of the Spirit. Although the gifts are many and various in their form, the energy back of them and in them is the same: "the one and same Spirit," he "energizes" all of them. This is one of the vital points regarding the gifts which Paul would have the Corinthians know. It will act as a strong corrective against false valuation of one gift in comparison with another — all of them flow from one and the same divine energy. What is said in v. 4-7 is thus restated pointedly and emphasized.

Yet the thought of gifts and of giving is by no means dropped (note the verb in v. 7). It is in a compact way added by the neuter participle that modifies Πνεῦμα: "apportioning to each one," etc. The idea contained in the verb διαιρεῖν is that the Spirit separates and portions out the gifts, cf., R. 580 on the force of διά. The combination ἰδίᾳ ἑκάστῳ is classic, B.-D., 286, 1: "to each one severally." We may regard ἰδίᾳ as an adverb (Liddell and Scott) or as a dative of manner (R. 530) by supplying ὁδῷ (R. 653). But we should read them together: "to each person in particular," i. e., in a way that is suitable to that person. In his distribution the Spirit never ignores the make-up, characteristics, age, position, and other particular features of a person. The gift fits the man.

"Even as he wills" places the distribution within the discretion of the Spirit. While this shows that the Spirit is sovereign in the bestowal of his gifts it leaves no room for the thought that this sovereignty is exercised with arbitrariness or partiality after the manner of self-willed earthly sovereigns. "Even as he wills" should remove all complaint on our part and thus all envy, on the one hand, and all boasting, on the other. What a blessing it is for all of us that the distribution lies in the Spirit's hands, and that he allots the gifts as he does!

12) The connective γάρ introduces the entire elucidation that follows in this paragraph. It consists of an illustrative analogy that is to elucidate all that is contained in v. 4-11, in particular the summary of all of it. Verse 12 introduces the illustration that is to be used and at once indicates the points on which the comparison turns. **For even as the body is one and has many members, yet all the members of the body, being many, are one body, so also Christ.**

"Even as ... so also" presents the comparison. On the one hand the human body, on the other hand Christ. The points of this comparison to be noted are predicated only regarding the human body yet apply equally to Christ. Read thus, the statement is complete. Verse 13 does not apply to Christ the points that are predicated regarding the human body in v. 12; v. 13 does something quite different.

Look at the human body. What do we see? Oneness in multiplicity. This is also true regarding Christ. This is the *tertium comparationis*. Paul then expands this most beautifully in order to bring it fully to view. In doing this he first goes forward from the oneness to the multiplicity even as he says: "the body is *one* and has *many* members"; he then goes backward from the multiplicity to the oneness even as he says: "and *all* the members of the body, being *many*, are *one* body." This procedure is chiastic in form. Its effect is to produce emphasis: each of the two points (oneness and multiplicity) is strengthened in the reader's mind by the repetition. Regarding the human body Paul needs only to state the facts. Everybody knows them. Yet we note that in the second half of the chiasm he repeats the idea of multiplicity: "all" and "being many," because he intends to stress the fact that MANY are one and not the reverse that ONE is many. This should be kept in mind as we read on.

We might have expected Paul to write: "so also *the church*." He writes instead: "so also *Christ*." We should miss Paul's meaning if we supposed that he is here speaking of Christ as the head of the church. The idea of headship is foreign to the illustration. Christ and the church are combined as constituting a unit just as the human body is a unit. This is another and a bolder way of expressing what he writes in Gal. 3:28: "Ye all are one man in Christ Jesus." But this combining (we may even say identifying) of Christ with the church is by no means a dissolving of Christ, making him "impersonal in a pantheistic manner" as is stated by some. The mystical union of Christ with the church, he in us, and we in him, as little dissolves his personality as it dissolves our personalities. It conserves both because it is not pantheistic (which abolishes both the personality of God and that of men) but truly spiritual, a soteriological union that is mediated by the Word and the sacraments.

13) The simple statement "so also Christ" obviously needs elucidation. **For also in union with one Spirit were we all baptized unto one body, whether Jews or Greeks, whether slaves or free; and we all were made to drink one Spirit.** The two connectives are distinct and not a unit like the Latin

etenim. When Christ is compared to the human body, καί bids us add what baptism does to all of us in this regard, and γάρ indicates that this helps to explain the comparison, B.-D. 452, 3. By baptism all of us were made "one body," and Christ is in all of us. When we see what the Spirit has done with all of us by means of our baptism, namely converted all of us into one spiritual body, we see how Christ can be compared with the human body and its many members. Christ and we are one.

This makes baptism much more than an *opus operatum*, the outward performance of a sacramental ceremony. Much more, too, than a symbolic sacramental rite which only pictures union with Christ, a union that is effected by some other means and not by baptism itself. For we were baptized "in" one Spirit, in union with him, in vital connection with him. This Spirit operates in baptism, works a spiritual change, produces a new spiritual life, establishes a new spiritual relation, Gal. 3:27-29. Because of its position the phrase has the fullest emphasis. Its best commentary is John 3:5: "born of water and the Spirit." The act of baptism is, of course, necessary as an act, but the vital feature of the act is the union with the one Spirit who gives us the new birth in Christ through the act.

We ought, therefore, not speak about "being immersed in the one Spirit," or about the one Spirit "flooding about us," or about "the flooding wave of the Spirit," which convert the Spirit into a fluid. Paul does not speak of a flood, wave, flooding, or immersion even with regard to the water of baptism. The New Testament does not indicate the mode that was used in administering baptism, but it does indicate in a surprising number of instances and with great clearness that one mode was not used, namely immersion. The preposition ἐν is not instrumental, for the Spirit is not something "with" which we could be baptized. He is a person and not a fluid substance.

"We all" indicates a large number in which Paul includes also himself. The specifications: Jews and Greeks, slaves and free, combine number with great variety. Paul stops with nationality and social status since these are sufficient for his purpose. Yet the greatness of the phenomenon thus briefly sketched should not escape us. Think what the Jew was and then picture the pagan Greek. Then see how these extremes of humanity were drawn into Christ and thus melted and fused together. What was lower than a slave, a human chattel with practically no rights? Picture the free citizens, many of them lordly and high and owning slaves. And now Christ is in them, and they are one. What numbers, what individual varieties in these great classes! Since Christ is in all of them, behold, all of them are "one body" just like the many members and organs of the human body — one unit, only one that is far grander and far more wonderful than a mere physical human body.

The phrase εἰς ἓν σῶμα, "unto one body" (not "into," our versions), states the result. The aorist ἐβαπτίσθημεν states the past fact. Paul says that we were all baptized; that this was done in connection with the Spirit; and that this resulted in making us one spiritual body. But these facts pivot on the numerals: in *one* Spirit — we *all* (Jews, Greeks, etc.) — unto *one* body. The *one* Spirit takes *all* of us and makes us *one* by baptism. To be baptized in connection with the Spirit means, not that the Spirit is only in some outward way connected with this application of water, but that he is inwardly and efficaciously connected with the application. His very nature and the regular method of his working lead to this conclusion. So also does the effect of baptism: through baptism the Spirit makes us "one body," which means one living, spiritual organism.

Outward agencies are sufficient to produce various outward organizations (not living organisms) to which men *belong*. Only the one Holy Spirit is by the spiritual means of baptism able to bind together our souls in the body that we *are*.

Paul adds the second statement: "and we all were made to drink one Spirit." As is the case in so many instances, "and" introduces a new statement which is intended to help us to understand what the preceding statement conveys. The new verb "were made to drink" is figurative. Jesus uses this figure in John 7:37-39; also in 4:14. When we are baptized in union with the Spirit we are made to drink the Spirit; and the latter tells us what the former means. John 7 shows that this drinking is the reception of the Spirit; he himself is the drink. John 4 adds that this drink is the water of life, i. e., the reception of true spiritual life. All who are thus baptized and are thus made to drink have spiritual life, have received the Spirit himself, so that in this manner they form one body, one living spiritual organism. For this reason both verbs, "were baptized" and "were made to drink," are aorists that denote past acts which took place once in the case of each person concerned. John 7:38 makes plain that the Spirit, once received thus, remains a permanent possession; compare Rom. 8:9-11. The life that was once given lives on; we continue alive and need not to be made alive again daily. That, too, is why both verbs are passive. Baptism, the Spirit, and life are bestowed upon us as gifts by God. All synergism is excluded when we are made one body with Christ. The accusative object with a passive verb is entirely regular, R. 485.

Here we again have the pivotal terms "all" and "one." And again the two numerals are abutted for the sake of greater emphasis: first, "we *all* unto *one* body"; then, we *"all one* Spirit" are made to drink. "All" — not one baptized member is excluded from the body; "one" body, "one" Spirit — one unity even as the Spirit is one and makes all of us truly one. In both statements "we all" includes the baptized children, which is the reason that being "made to drink one Spirit" refers to baptism alone and not to the Lord's Supper which is not administered to children; nor is there a reference to the three means of grace in general, Word and sacraments. Babes are able to receive the Spirit only by baptism. They, too, are members of the "one body" which is Christ and dare never be left out. And we may add that they, too, by natural birth may be either Jews or Greeks, slaves or free.

If the point be raised that this discussion deals with spiritual gifts and therefore refers only to adults and not to babes, we should remember that in the case of some gifts the Spirit utilizes inborn, natural abilities. John the Baptist leaped in his mother's womb, Luke 1:41; Paul himself was chosen equally early in his existence for his gifted work in the church, Gal. 1:15. Moreover, the fundamental gift, which constitutes the basis for all charismatic gifts, is the one Spirit who is received by baptism.

14) In v. 12 "for" introduces the human body as an elucidation of the statement made in v. 11 that the Spirit produces all of the gifts and distributes them as he wills. In v. 13 "for also" adds a further elucidation that shows how there comes to be a body of Christ. Now in v. 14 Paul adds at some length the detailed elucidation in regard to the human body with its many and its various members which is so analogous to Christ's body with its many and its various baptized members. The connection is so clear that we need to supply nothing. Paul himself makes the application to the body of Christ in v. 27-30.

A careful reading of v. 14-30 reveals that Paul is offering objective instruction. The Corinthians are to bear in mind (v. 1) what Paul here tells them. The effort to discover in this paragraph, for instance in the speeches of the different members of the body, special references to faulty conditions in Corinth has proved unsatisfactory. The fact is evident that throughout chapters 12 and 13 Paul presents general instruction on the subject of spiritual gifts. Not until we reach chapter 14 is the situation obtaining in Corinth considered. Even in this chapter the first 25 verses continue in the form of instruction and compare at some length the gift of prophecy and that of tongues. The situation obtaining in Corinth, however, furnishes the background for these 25 verses. Not until we come to v. 26 does Paul attend to the special needs of the Corinthian congregation.

The effort has been made to show that in the use he makes of this comparison with the human body Paul is borrowing an idea from the Stoics. Both the general idea and not a few of the details are then taken from pagan sources. We are told that the state had been likened to the human body and its members; also the complex of men and of gods. A special point is made of the συμπάθεια in v. 26. The old fable with which, according to Livy and others, the orator Menenius Agrippa quieted the quarreling Roman citizens does duty in this connection. The other members of the body charged the stomach with being lazy and with allowing itself to be nourished. Thereupon the hands refused to raise food to the mouth, the mouth to accept food, the teeth to chew it. They would bring the stomach to time. The result was that the entire body became emaciated and enfeebled. Then these members at last saw their mistake. Thus one commentator concludes: "I do not doubt that Paul borrowed from Stoic popular philosophy." All that he grants is that in his characteristic way Paul modified what he borrowed.

A glance at the pagans and at Paul's discourse reveals that there is a gulf between them. The fact that both used the human body and its members for the purpose of illustration is a mere coincidence. This illustrative material is about as old as the world. Priority of use establishes no ownership unless some direct quotation follows. Jesus freely used such material in his parables. Yet neither he nor Paul quote when doing so. When Paul refers to the human body he shows an insight into the relation of its different members to which no pagan mind ever attained.

But the decisive point lies in the use to which this common material is put. Here we meet the gulf. Take the earthly seed that is sown, sprouts, and produces a harvest. Anyone could use it in drawing an illustration. But who ever saw heavenly realities reflected in these qualities of earthly seed? It is Jesus and after him Paul in I Cor. 15 who thus glorify this earthly illustrative material. How simple the parables of Jesus appear, and yet no human mind has ever produced comparisons that equal the parables of the Lord in any way. Paul has been in the Master's school. He does not need to borrow from pagan philosophers — they have nothing to lend him. In his *Parables,* p. 12, etc., Trench points out *the essential difference* that underlies this exalted use of earthly illustrative material. He quotes Milton:

> "What if earth
> Be but the shadow of heaven, and things therein
> Each to other like, more than on earth is thought?"

The earthly does not resemble the heavenly, but the heavenly is reflected in the earthly. Unless a man knows the heavenly he cannot use the earthly as Jesus and Paul use it. A conception such as that of the body of Christ never entered a pagan mind. How, then, can such a mind use the illustration of the human body as the apostle uses it? On the other hand, how can a king like Paul borrow from the beggarly mind of a Stoic?

So Paul writes καί (in order to proceed) γάρ (and to elucidate still further): **For also the body is not one member but many.** How obvious, yet how important in this connection! The proposition is self-evident and needs no proof. It forms the theme of all that follows. It contains the two basic facts that must be understood when spiritual gifts are considered. One of these facts deals with the body, the other with the members.

1) *The Body* — its constitution — just how it comes to be what it is — v. 18: "Now hath God," etc.

2) *The Members* — their relation — just how this comes to be what it is — v. 24: "God tempered," etc.

The first fact settles all envious complaint, the second all prideful disdain.

Paul thinks of the spiritual body of Christ throughout. But throughout he views this spiritual body in the mirror of the human body. This is, however, not allegorizing, for Paul nowhere identifies any one member of the spiritual body with a member of the human body. Allegory would demand this. The impossibility of meeting the requirements of an allegory appear when we come to "our uncomely parts." Commentators who follow practical interests find an allegory in Paul's statements. They succeed in the case of a few members and faculties, but "the smelling" upsets their scheme, to say nothing about "the feeble," "the less honorable," and finally "the uncomely parts." When Paul makes his own application of his illustrative analogy in v. 27, etc., he gives no hint of allegory.

15) Paul proceeds without a connective. **Suppose the foot shall say: Because I am not a hand (therefore) I am not part of the body; not for this reason is it not part of the body.** Paul supposes such

First Corinthians 12:15, 16   521

a foolish case, hence the condition with ἐάν: "If the foot shall say." The preposition ἐκ is to be taken in the sense of the partitive genitive: "not of the body," i. e., not part of it. The negative with παρὰ τοῦτο negatives only this phrase: "not for this reason," because the foot is dissatisfied with not being a hand, is it excluded from the body. The foot may grumble and talk foolishly all it pleases, it nevertheless remains a member of the body. The A. V. translates as though this were a question; it does likewise in v. 16. But there is no indication of a question. Paul states a self-evident fact: the foot remains a member. Regarding παρά with the accusative in the sense of *propter* see R. 616; B.-D. 236, 5.

16) And suppose the ear shall say: Because I am not an eye (therefore) I am not part of the body; not for this reason is it not part of the body.

This duplication, like all repetitions, emphasizes the point. To be sure, we shall say that what is true regarding the complaining foot is equally true regarding the complaining ear. All of their complaining changes nothing. It is not only useless, it is foolish. For the body simply cannot be one member, it is of necessity many, v. 14. And many members have different functions. How foolish for the foot to grasp something or to shake hands with somebody when it is needed for walking and for moving the body from place to place. Likewise the ear when the body needs it for hearing. These are wrong comparisons when the foot prefers being a hand, or the ear being an eye. These self-disparagements indicate a spurious humility, perhaps even envy, which should be eradicated. These complaints militate against the very idea of the divinely created body, which is not one member but many. All such wrong ideas are certainly futile, for the body just naturally remains a body, the foot being a part of it, and the ear likewise.

Although Paul states the proposition only in the negative form, the positive counterpart is implied. The foot should be happy that as a member of the body it is able to serve as a foot in carrying the body from place to place; the ear and all the other members should do likewise. For this makes the body: many members functioning together in a great complex of service, each attending to its part. Instead of complaining all should voice satisfaction; instead of self-disparagement there should be self-appreciation — both should be combined with gratitude. This is true also with regard to all the members of the church. Suppose a member were actually what these complainers say: not a part of the body — what would it be? In terms of another comparison, it would be a dead branch, fit only to be burned. Thank God, then, for the place he has assigned to you and joyfully perform your part!

The foot and the hand are bodily extremities, the ear and the eye are two of the bodily senses. There is a certain relation between the two in each pair and thus a certain fitness in placing together the two in each pair. Moreover, πούς and οὖς are similar even in sound and may thus be paired.

17) Suppose, however, that the wish of the ear were granted, and, since it esteems the eye so highly, suppose that it should actually become an eye. Other members may then have the same opinion about the eye and the same privilege of becoming the eye. What would be the result? The whole body would be an eye. **If the whole body is an eye, where is the hearing?** If the wish of the ear were fulfilled, the hearing would be gone. The condition is one of reality, one that considers the wish of the ear as actually being carried out. And the "if" clause of reality tacitly implies that all the other members may also have their wish to become an eye granted.

Or the ear and its hearing might be so admired that the nose and the other members might desire to be an ear. **If the whole body is hearing, where is the smelling?** Our versions translate both conditional sentences as though they expressed present unreality. But this would necessitate the inserting of the imperfect tense of the verbs and ἄν in the apodosis. Paul omits all verbs; because he disregards them, the sentence becomes a condition of reality.

When Paul asks in the first question: "Where is the hearing?" and in the second: "Where is the smelling?" he really employs an understatement. For if the whole body is converted into an eye or into an ear, one may ask: "Where are all the other members and the functions that a body requires in order to be a body?" But in many instances understatements are psychologically more effective than complete statements. They allow the reader or the hearer to supply what is left unsaid. And when he does this, the effect made on his mind is the greater. When Paul speaks of the smelling without mention of the nose, our minds are led to think of all the other functions of the body, any one or all of which could be mentioned in this connection.

18) The cure for all such wrong and really absurd desires is a return to the great divine fact: **But now God did set the members, each one of them, in the body even as he did will.** The two aorists are decisive, they state the fact. This is what God did, did by his creative act when he formed the human body. He made the body to consist of many members. Each one he set into its place in the body. The plural "members" has the distributive singular "each one of them" as an apposition. Do any of us presume to find fault with what God did? Does envy, false humility, self-disparagement, or whatever else may blind us lead us to think that we can improve on God's act? Well, the fact stands: God made the human body as it is.

19) The full implication of the absurd improvements suggested by dissatisfied members is now made evident. **And if they all were one member, where were the body?** If one member would become another, and if this privilege were granted to all, and if all should select what they deemed the most illustrious member, and if all became that one member (for this is the logic of the situation), where would the body be? There would be no body, and, although Paul does not add this, there would not be a single member either. This is the absurdity that results: dissatisfaction would end in self-abolishment. "Where is the hearing, where the smelling?" Verse 17 properly ends with the question: "Where is the body?" Because of the imperfect ἦν in the protasis, this is a condition of present unreality, the imperfect with ἄν in the apodosis being omitted because it is worded in the form of a question.

20) So the divine fact is once more stated, and now in its tersest form. **But now there are many members but one body.** This fact will ever assert itself, and we should do well to allow it to correct and to remove all false and absurd notions that may enter our minds. The first δέ is adversative, the second is a balance to μέν. The statement repeats what is contained in v. 14 as well as in v. 18.

Paul's statements can without difficulty be applied to the spiritual body of Christ. Each member of the church has his gifts and his functions. The Spirit has assigned him to the place which he occupies in the great organism. Blessed is he who joyfully accepts what the Spirit has done and therefore rids himself of all dissatisfaction. Note that "even as he did will" in v. 18 is the counterpart to "even as he wills" in v. 11. The verbs are equivalent in meaning; the only difference is in the tenses. The creative act of producing the human body is one and lies in the historic past, hence the aorist; the work of the Spirit who forms the spiritual body of Christ still continues, hence the durative present tense.

21) Paul's theme is: The Body — not one member but many. We who constitute the church and are individually gifted by the Spirit must ever keep this great fact in mind. A living illustration of it is ever before us in our own human body. This helps us to avoid all dissatisfaction with ourselves. The medicine to correct this fault, to which many of us are prone, is found in the first part of the great fact: the body is *not one member* but many. Another fault needs treatment, namely disregard of other members. The remedy for its cure lies in the second part of the great fact: The body is not one member but *many*. So Paul proceeds: **And the eye cannot say to the hand: Need of thee I have not! or again the head to the feet: Need of you I have not.**

Again the members speak as was the case in v. 15 where the first fault was presented. This time the eye and the head voice their wrong sentiments, the one disparaging the hand, the other the feet. We see that the head is named only as being one of the members and therefore cannot by way of allegory denote Christ. It is characteristic of Paul to write the singular "hand" and then the plural "feet"; he is master in combining the two numbers. There is a difference between the hands. Although both are hands, the right is supreme. No such difference appears regarding the feet. Moreover, one hand may act independently of the other, but the feet operate together. This may seem to be a slight feature, yet it does not escape Paul. Two plurals would wipe out all distinction while the plural "hands" and the singular "foot" would be absurd.

In v. 15, 16 the foot speaks about the hand, and the ear about the eye. We are accustomed to class together the hand and the foot, the eye and the ear, and think of them as performing similar tasks although in these combinations we always name the foot and the ear last. Paul therefore very properly has the foot and the ear complain and not the hand and the eye. Again we class together the eye and the hand, the head and the feet and always use this order in each pair. There is a dissimilarity in each pair, yet there is also a sort of correspondence. The eye reaches out to the far horizon, the hand only to objects that are close by; the head is the highest, the feet are the lowest. Paul therefore very properly has the eye disdain the hand, and the head scorn the feet.

While all this indicates a wonderful understanding of the relation existing between the members of the human body, Paul, who is thinking chiefly of the spiritual body of Christ with its variously gifted members, really sees in the human body only a reflection of the relation that exists between the members of this higher body. Where is envy, and where is proud disdain most apt to occur in the body of the church? Envy, where we see corresponding similarity; disdain, where we see corresponding dissimilarity. I am inclined to envy one who is in my own class and one who, nevertheless, seems to be favored more than I am. I am inclined to disdain those who are not in my class, whose gifts and whose position seem to be much below mine. When he is speaking about this disdain Paul lets the eye and the head speak. Because the eye is able to reach out to great distances it is the member which may scorn the hand which is able to grasp only nearby objects. Because the head is placed so high it is the member that may look down with disdain on the feet plodding away down in the dust. Those who are endowed with greater and higher gifts (ministrations, operations, v. 4, 5) may thus foolishly think that they do not need those who have lesser gifts.

First Corinthians 12:21

In v. 15, 16 the words of the foot and of the ear come first; then follows Paul's flat contradiction: It, nevertheless, belongs to the body! In v. 21 the contradiction comes first: The eye "cannot say"; then follow the words of the eye and of the head. The arrangement is chiastic. But in both cases the wrong thought and utterance are contradicted by means of a fact. In the first case Paul says: "It is, nevertheless, a fact that the foot and the ear belong to the body, let them think and say what they will." In the second case Paul says: "The fact is that the eye and the head cannot say what they foolishly do think and say, i. e., they cannot truly say what they do." "If they shall say" in v. 15, 16 is thus elucidated by "they cannot (truly) say" in v. 21. For actually to say what one cannot truly say is wrong. He *ought not* to say what Paul supposes him to say (first pair) and what he actually says (second pair).

In v. 15, 16 Paul first contradicts, and in v. 17-20 he then explains. Similarly he contradicts in v. 21 and then explains in v. 22-25. Both explanations present the same great fact, namely God's creative act. Paul does not philosophize. He is a theologian of fact to his very finger tips. The foot and the ear suffer under a false conception of the body, and this raises the question: "The body — just how is it constituted?" The eye and the head suffer under a false conception of the members, and this raises the question: "The members — just how are they related?" Paul explains by simply stating the two facts: 1) ὁ Θεὸς ἔθετο; 2) ὁ Θεὸς συνεκέρασε. 1) The Creator set the members, each one in his proper place — this is the fact in regard to the constitution of the body. It corrects all perverted and all absurd notions regarding the body. 2) The Creator intermingled the body, mixed the members together in complete interdependence — this is the fact regarding the relation of the members. It corrects all perverted and all harmful notions regarding the members.

22) When one member declares regarding another: "Need of thee I have not!" Paul answers ἀλλά, "On the contrary!" or we may translate, "Nay!" The very opposite is the fact. **On the contrary, the members of the body seeming to be more feeble are much more necessary,** or "much rather necessary."

Paul groups the members that may be despised as being unnecessary under three classes: 1) such as are "more feeble"; 2) such as are "less honorable"; 3) such as are "uncomely." He answers each derogation in turn. But he differentiates between the three groups of members. The seemingly weaker members seem so only to the prideful; hence δοκοῦντα in v. 22: they "seem" so but are really not so. Those less honorable are considered so by all of us, and we have a reason for considering them so; hence ἃ δοκοῦμεν, v. 23: we all consider them so and rightly. The uncomely parts are uncomely apart from anybody's opinion: hence in v. 24 we have no modifier at all but just the designation as such.

23) Against the first type of derogation Paul enters a flat denial: "On the contrary!" These members are wrongfully looked down upon as being "more feeble"; they are not so in fact and thus are actually decidedly necessary to the rest. The second group Paul treats differently. **And those members of the body which we think are less honorable, on these we bestow more abundant honor.** For the neuter plurals found in this verse and in the next we may supply μέλη from v. 22 as the A. V. does or leave them as they are and translate "parts" as the R. V. prefers. The matter of more or less honor is determined by general opinion. We ourselves bestow or withhold honor for certain justifiable reasons. Paul finds no fault with us on this score, so he writes: "those members which we think are less honorable," and he includes himself in "we."

But what do we do with these members? Despise them? Say that we do not need them? Wish we were rid of them? Nothing of the sort: "upon these we bestow more abundant honor." This is the fact — rather astonishing but a fact, nevertheless. We, with whom the entire question of honor rests in the first place, we, including Paul, first regard these members as "less honorable" and then reverse ourselves and heap the more honor upon them. And the undeniable fact that all of us do this once more contradicts and thus ought also to correct the arrogance of any prideful member of the body which dares to say: "Need of this or of that less honorable member I have not."

Paul does not intimate how we make good the deficiency of honor. We shall scarcely go amiss when we think of the clothing which we put upon them. Even in society the meanest trades are those with which we can least dispense. A nation may exist without astronomers and philosophers as has been well said, but the day laborer is essential to the existence of a people. You may look down on the cook and on the washerwoman, but you do not dispense with them. Yet in society day laborers, etc., are not given honor; so this illustration illustrates only the point of their necessity.

The final type of derogation deals with the private parts, *pudenda*, τὰ αἰδοῖα, which all decent people actually hide completely, namely the seat and the sexual organs. Paul adds no modifier to this group, for these "uncomely members" are just what they are apart from anybody's opinion. If despising any parts of the body can be justified, these are the parts which, one might think, would most deserve such treatment. All of us have them, yet all of us are ashamed of them. The more striking is Paul's paradoxical assertion of the actual fact concerning these parts of the body: **and our uncomely members have more abundant comeliness.** The Greek is even stronger, for the α privativum in ἀσχήμονα declares that these members have *no* decency at all and then the εὐ in εὐσχημοσύνην reverses this statement and declares that these very members have *excellent* decency, a truth which the adjective "more abundant" even emphasizes.

How can these members be despised on the score of indecency when they abound in decency? Paul states only the fact of the case, that they so abound. That fact is enough; he does not need to add anything. The decency is usually supposed to consist in the clothing with which these parts are covered. But this would only combine groups two and three, the lack in both being made good by the same means, namely clothing. This also overlooks the verbs "we put upon" and "they have." We ourselves supply the deficiency in natural honor of the second group by means of clothing; but the natural lack of decency of the third group is not made good by us at all — these indecent parts have their own abundant decency. This consists in the natural feeling of shame, in the natural modesty, which they inspire. Hence these parts are not really clothed like other parts of the body; they are hidden from sight, are covered. The aprons of fig leaves mentioned in Gen. 3:7 are quite distinct from the "coats of skins" with which God "clothed" Adam and Eve, Gen. 3:21.

24) **Whereas our comely members have no need** refers to such a need as the uncomely ones have. We are certainly not ashamed but proud of them, and we love to display them. It seems strange that anyone, after translating "our uncomely members" in v. 23, can refuse to translate "our comely members" in v. 24 and insists that the genitive ἡμῶν be drawn to the predicate: "have no need *of us*."

A derogation that is based 1) on the lack of needfulness, 2) on the lack of honor, 3) on the lack of decency is thus refuted by the corresponding fact in each case. But lack of these separate facts is the fundamental unit of God's own creative act. Paul arrives at this all-decisive fact from one angle of approach when he makes final settlement with the complaining foot and the ear in v. 18; he now arrives at the same all-decisive fact from another angle when he makes final settlement with the supercilious eye and the head. These prideful members operate with a false conception of the relation of the members of the body to each other. The only way in which they can be finally corrected is to set forth the true relation which the Creator himself established between the members of the body.

But God did mix the body together by making a gift of more abundant honor to the member that falls short in order that there may be no schism in the body, but that the members may be anxious for each other in the same way. This God did; the aorist "mixed together" (our versions: "tempered together") states the creative fact, the aorist participle "by making a gift" does likewise. And the strong adversative ἀλλά places this fact in contrast with all wrong notions regarding the relation here discussed.

When God made this mixture of the body, all of the different members could not be placed on the same level. When they are compared with others, some fall short, literally, "come behind." Paul uses a comprehensive term to describe such a member: "the one that falls short." We have seen how some come behind others: one group only apparently so, another in our general estimation, a third actually so. God was fully aware of this lack when he made the body as he did, for he himself made good the lack by granting "more abundant honor" to each of these members.

The comparative adjective "more abundant" which is repeated for the third time and made prominent by these repetitions, cannot refer to the other members: "more abundant" honor than theirs. For this, too, would destroy the balance among the members, and only reverse their order by now making the feebler, the less honorable, and the dishonorable the most honorable of all. "More abundant" refers to the lack of the member itself, which is deficient in one or the other of the three ways. "The one that falls short" and "more abundant" are significantly juxtaposed in the Greek. Thus by granting this gift a general equality is secured.

The aorist participle δούς expresses action that is simultaneous with that of the main verb, which is also an aorist συνεκέρασε (συνκεράννυμι). This is often the case when the aorist participle follows the verb although the nature of the two actions really decides this point. God grants the "honor" to all of the deficient members, i. e., by the creative act itself, by the manner in which he there intermingles the members by making some especially needful, by arranging that some should be clothed, and that some are shielded by shame.

25) The purpose which God had in mind in all of this was to forestall what some foolish members would now, after all, precipitate upon the body: "in order that there may be no schism in the body," no disunion and disruption. To this negative side of the purpose the positive is at once added: "but that the members may be anxious for each other in the same way." If τὰ μέλη were intended to be a totality like πάντα τὰ μέλη in v. 26, the verb would necessarily be singular; it is plural because the sense is distributive: each member is to be concerned about the other. The positive side of God's purpose is not the mere counterpart to the negative; it goes much farther. The opposite of schism is only unity and peace. But it is God's purpose that the members may all have the same deep concern for each other. The verb μεριμνᾶν is more than "to have care" (our versions); it is "to be anxious"; and τὸ αὐτό is emphatic — one and the same interest is to be the anxiety which all have "in behalf of," ὑπέρ, each other.

The present subjunctives in the two purpose clauses really leave the question open as to whether the divine purpose is actually realized or not. Aorist subjunctives would imply that it is. The sense of the latter is: "that there shall be no schism . . . that the members shall be anxious," etc.; of the former: "that there may be no schism . . . that the members may be anxious," etc. Paul writes present subjunctives because he is thinking also of the members of the church. God's purpose is, indeed, fulfilled in the human body, but in the church much is yet to be desired.

26) To the fact of God's intermingling the body with the intent just stated Paul adds the fact of the result. **Moreover, whether one member suffers, all the members suffer with it; whether one member is glorified, all the members rejoice with it.** Our daily experience attests these two facts. All the members suffer with the suffering member, not disjointly but as a whole, πάντα τὰ μέλη, since God intermingled them and made them an organism. So also when one member receives δόξα or glory which gives it joy, the whole intermingled organism rejoices. Luther expounds: "See what the whole body does when a foot is trodden on, or a finger is pinched: how the eye looks dour, the nose draws up, the mouth cries out, and all the members are ready to rescue and to help, and none can leave the other, so that it means, not the foot or a finger is trodden on and is pinched, but the entire body. Again, when good is done to one member, that suits all the others, and the entire body rejoices therein. This is how it ought to be also in Christendom since it, too, is composed of many members in one body and has one mind and heart, for such unity naturally has the effect that one is concerned in the good and the hurt of the other as in his own." Walch, XII, 978; compare Erlangen edition, 8, 18 and 20.

Paul says that it is a fact that when one suffers, all suffer, etc. We readily see that this is true with respect to the human body. But what about this fact in regard to the spiritual body where so many members are faulty? The very purpose of Paul's illustrative analogy is by means of the facts concerning the human body to show, not what *is true* with regard to the spiritual body, but what *ought to be true*. He also shows how unnatural and how wrong it is when it is not thus. The foot and the ear of the human body never speak as they are represented in v. 15, 16; but members of Christ's body both speak and act in such a way. The eye and the head never speak as they are represented in v. 21; but members of Christ's body both speak and act in such a way. So also all of our bodily members suffer when one member is hurt or rejoice when one member is crowned with glory and distinction; but with regard to the spiritual members of Christ this is often not the case. But this spiritual body *ought to be* as the human body *is*. Paul's analogy vividly illustrates how unnatural, abnormal, unreasonable, outrageous it is for the members of the spiritual body of Christ to act in contravention of the very constitution of their own body.

27) The picture is complete. As Paul drew each line of the illustration, we felt and saw what he meant in regard to ourselves as members of the church — how natural and right is the proper use of our gifts in harmony with the other members of the body, and, by contrast, how unnatural and wrong are all thoughts and actions that are in conflict with that harmony. It is accordingly an easy matter for Paul to make the application, which, therefore, also needs to be but brief. **Now you are Christ's body and members each in his part.** This is the fundamental fact of the great reality which Paul has illustrated.

Paul is writing to the Corinthians and therefore cannot use the article: you are *"the"* body of Christ, for this might make the impression that they are Christ's entire body. Yet the absence of the article does not mean that the Corinthians are "a body" of Christ, for no plurality of bodies of Christ exists. As in so many instances, the omission of the article stresses the quality of the noun, R. 794 j. Just what Christ's body is as to nature and to quality, that you Corinthians are. We now also see what Paul means when he writes in v. 12: "so also is Christ"; he means "Christ's body," which is composed of all of us in whom Christ dwells. The genitive "of Christ" has been called subjective and objective, both of which are untenable, for these two genitives are possible only when the governing noun contains a verbal idea. There is no verbal idea in "body" with which a genitive in the sense of either a subject or an object could be combined. This genitive is plainly possessive: Christ's own body, which is made his own by his indwelling.

Being a body, it has members, all of whom are, of course, true believers. They are "members" (again there is no article because their quality as such is referred to) ἐκ μέρους, "severally" or "each in part," *ein jeglicher nach seinem Teil*, Luther. This adverbial phrase, R. 550, 597, indicates how the Corinthians individually belong to the body. In 13:9-12 this idiomatic phrase is used to show a contrast with perfection while here there is a contrast with completeness. No one member is the complete body, each is only a part.

We may here settle the question as to whether Paul would assign certain corresponding spiritual members to the individual bodily members. Paul nowhere identifies eye, ear, smelling, hand, foot, head, even by implication, with definite members of the church. In other words, Paul is not in any sense writing an allegory. No hint appears that when Paul speaks about three groups of bodily members he has in mind definite members of the church who are analogously grouped. Who are the "feebler" members of the human body? Most commentators reply, "The eye and the ear as compared with the hand and the foot." But in Paul's illustration the eye spurns the hand as being utterly feeble, unable to reach as far as the eye. This is true also regarding the ear when it is compared with the foot. Such a view regarding the members of the first group is serious enough. It becomes more serious when the eyes and the ears are referred to the preachers and the hearers of the church, for this changes the entire body of the church into mere eyes and ears, and this would be an unheard-of monstrosity.

Next comes the thought that the "less honorable" members of the human body are the arms, legs, shoulders, and hips, because they are clothed although in southern localities like Corinth arms, shoulders, and legs are often entirely bare. Others think that these bodily members denote all of the church members who have no church office. Paul has not spoken one word about arms, legs, etc. And why should the arm and the shoulder have no office in the church when the hand has such an office, for in every movement shoulder, arm, and hand act together? Hip, leg, and foot do the same.

The "uncomely" parts are taken to be the seat and the organs of elimination. Hofmann would have us think of the genital organs as "enjoying the distinction that they reproduce the race." What distinction the seat "enjoys" he does not say. Fortunately, no commentator, not even Hofmann, has allegorized these parts and the "distinction they enjoy." This collapse of the allegorizing view should be convincing. Paul presents nothing beyond an extended illustration, and for each feature of his illustration he carefully states the *tertium comparationis*. It is a law that no illustration should be stressed beyond this *tertium* (the point of comparison). Together with Paul we abide by that law.

28) Paul first mentions the great fact regarding the Corinthians themselves: they are Christ's body, each is a member of it. We sense two implications: 1) each member will have some function to perform and will thus have some gift; 2) the body of Christ includes all others who, like the Corinthians, are believers. To this first great fact and its evident implications Paul now adds (καί) the second fact. **And God did set some in the church: first apostles, secondly prophets, thirdly teachers, then miracles, then charismata of healings, helps, managements, varieties of tongues.**

Paul twice mentions the Creator's act regarding the human body: in v. 18, "God did set," etc., and in v. 24, "God did mix," etc. So Paul now writes regarding the spiritual body: "God did set," etc. While this seems to be a parallel only to v. 18 it in reality includes also v. 24, for the mixture in the church appears in the variety of offices and of services which God "did set in the church." The verb is placed before the subject and is thus made emphatic: it is God's *act* — see what he *did*. This act extends far beyond the Corinthians who are only one congregation among many, and to whom, as a congregation, many members are yet to be added. Hence Paul writes: God did set "in the church" and takes in the entire church of all places and all ages.

Some interpreters refer to the psychology of Paul to account for his writing οὓς μέν without following it with οὓς δέ, but the former is simply the demonstrative "some," R. 696; and aside from his rapidity of thinking Paul or any other writer is always free to proceed as he desires when he introduces classes. Grammatically Paul is guilty of no irregularity that is due to his swift mind; in fact, because of this very swiftness he would know in advance what he is saying. In Eph. 4:11 he exercises the same freedom and writes τοὺς μέν and follows this with τοὺς δέ. Moreover, in our passage "some" is divided by the following specifications. Paul intends to mention only certain prominent persons and gifts in the church from the apostles downward to tongues and to omit the lesser gifts which were distributed so that each member had his gift.

Much is also made of the fact that Paul names three sets of persons and follows these with functions and abilities and no further mention of persons. In Eph. 4:11 the entire list contains persons while in Rom. 12:6, etc., two functions lead the list which are followed by individuals who exercise some gift. This shows that Paul's lists are not stereotyped. The conclusion is, therefore, unwarranted that "apostles, prophets, and teachers" possessed permanent gifts and thus held recognized and fixed offices in the church while in the case of the other gifts such permanency does not appear and that at this time there were no regularly established offices of this type. The apostles worked as the result of a definite and even an immediate call into an office that was fixed and permanent from the beginning. But prophecy was a gift that was not dependent upon such a fixed office, it was much like healing, miracles, etc., and in its simple form was open to an indefinite number of Christians. It is Paul's evident intention not to distinguish fixed offices from occasional functions that were exercised in the church but to call attention to the great variety of notable gifts and functions that were distributed in the church.

In connections such as this the term "apostles" is distinctive; it refers to those who were immediately called by Christ, the Twelve and Paul and Matthias, the substitute for Judas. While it is true that the term is used also in a wider sense so as to include men like Barnabas and other personal helpers of the Twelve and of Paul, yet to insist on the wider meaning in connections like the present makes the term indefinite. The one distinction of the Thirteen remains: their immediate call. So also does their supreme function in harmony with this call: the apostles constitute the foundation of the church for all time, Eph. 2:20, not, indeed, in their persons, but through the Word which they conveyed to the church. The Word in its written form governs the church until the end of time.

Regarding "prophets" see v. 10, the gift of "prophecy." This gift is at times taken in a broad sense as in 14:1 and then refers to every ability to communicate the saving will and truth to others; again the expression is taken in a narrow sense and then refers to the fact of receiving direct communications from God and transmitting them to the persons for whom they are intended. When "prophets" are mentioned in a prominent manner in the New Testament they are ranked next to the apostles as is done in the present instance. In Eph. 2:20 they are even put in the same class with the apostles because but one Greek article is employed. The apostles themselves were the most notable New Testament prophets. All the other New Testament prophets were of a lower rank. Most of them are not named in the New Testament. None of them had a call such as the apostles had received. Mark and Luke are two who were inspired by the Spirit and composed three of the books of the New Testament.

The third class consists of "teachers" who have the gift of conveying instruction. In Eph. 4:11 "shepherds and teachers" form one class, namely pastors of local congregations who lead or govern and instruct. Yet these two functions were often separated. In the present list "managements" appear separately; and in I Tim. 5:17 two classes of elders are indicated: those that rule well and those that at the same time also labor in the Word and in teaching.

Regarding δυνάμεις and "charismata of healings" see v. 10. In the Scriptures ἀντιλήψεις is used only in the sense of *Hilfeleistungen,* "helps," abilities for rendering helpful services such as assisting the destitute, the sick, the persecuted, the troubled, etc. The term reminds us of διακονίαι which was used in v. 4, "ministrations" or services for the sake of the service. We at once see that an indefinite number of members may possess this valuable gift in some form because the range of service is rather wide. And we may note that Paul is not dividing the members into two great classes, one that has gifts, the other that is without them. Although he offers no complete catalog of gifts here as he does not in v. 4, etc., he, nevertheless, thinks of at least some gift that was bestowed upon each member.

A κυβερνήτης is a helmsman who steers a vessel, and thus this gift consists in managing and directing others whether officially as presbyters, pastors, or bishops or in unofficial ways. Some men and some women of the church, including even young people, have this gift to a marked degree and profit the church not a little by rightly putting it to use. "Helps" and "managements" are a significant pair. Regarding "varieties of tongues" see v. 10.

29). After this brief survey of the various gifts Paul returns to the main point of his instruction, namely to the wide and varied way in which the gifts are distributed among the many members. Some have this, some that gift as God has made apportionment to each. All cannot have the same gift. Some gifts are denied, must be denied to some of us. **Are all apostles? are all prophets? are all teachers? are all gifted with miracles?** The evident and expected answer, as is indicated by the interrogative particle μή, is: "No, all are not, only some are."

Our versions translate the last question: "Are all workers of miracles?" Something must be supplied since δυνάμεις does not mean persons but "miracles" or miracle-working powers. We might supply "have": "Have all miracles?" The supposition that Paul would here curb the ambition that would possess all of the gifts is unwarranted.

30) The rhetorical questions continue: **have all charismata of healings? do all speak with tongues? do all interpret?** Paul omits two of the gifts that are listed in v. 28 and adds one that is not in this list but is found in v. 10. His intention is evident: so numerous are the gifts that it makes no difference in regard to the point here stressed whether some that are mentioned in one list are omitted or others that are found in some other list or in no list are added.

31) It is plain that all cannot have the same gift. That might, however, imply that each member is simply to accept whatever gift has fallen to his lot and therewith remain content. This is true in part, but only in part. One may also seek and obtain certain other gifts. **But strive zealously for the greater charismata.** Compare 14:1. The injunction is general, which explains both the plural imperative and its natural counterpart, the plural object. To regard this plural object as implying that each and every member is to strive for any and for all of the greater gifts is to misunderstand Paul's thought.

The greatest of all gifts is the apostleship with its immediate call and its wonderful work. Yet no striving on our part will bring us this gift; it was reserved for only a very few who were living at the time of the founding of the church. One of the great gifts is to be a pastor. Yet because of their sex women as a class are debarred from this gift. Thus Paul's injunction to strive zealously for the greater gifts has its evident and its natural limitations. These limitations extend even farther. Some of even the lesser gifts call for a natural aptitude and a qualification which are markedly denied to many of us. All our striving will not bring us the gift. Paul knows all this very well; he assumes a like intelligence on the part of his readers.

"The greater gifts" are those that benefit the general body of the church more than some other gifts do. Paul himself gives us an illustration in chapter 14 when he ranks the general ability to edify the church through prophecy far above the ability to speak with tongues. This is our cue for understanding what he means by bidding us to strive for the greater gifts. To strive zealously means more than to pray; it includes effort toward cultivating and toward producing a receptivity and a fitness on our part. The Spirit bestows the gifts, but he bestows them only on those who are fit to receive them. He, too, works the fitness but does so only in those who allow him full sway in their hearts. Many of us could have gifts that we now lack, and we could have them to a greater degree than we now have them. This is especially true with reference to some of the greater gifts such as wisdom, knowledge, acquaintance with the Word, ability to explain it to others, ability to win others for the gospel, etc.

The first point is the type of the gift desired; we are to admire, value, and seek the higher types. A second point must be taken into consideration when Paul is speaking of the acquirement and the use of any gift. This is the motive for having and for employing the gift, namely the motive of love. In this regard the Corinthians are gravely deficient as we have already seen in other connections in earlier chapters. Just what this motive of Christian love is Paul intends to tell the Corinthians at some length. He introduces this part of his instruction by saying: **And besides I point out to you an exceedingly excellent way,** namely for this zealous striving to which I urge you.

Blass and others would change the reading because the wording is somewhat unusual. Although the phrase καθ' ὑπερβολήν modifies a noun, it is quite plain. Paul tells the Corinthians to seek the *superior* gifts and adds (ἔτι) that he will now show them a *superior* way for seeking them. The emphatic adjective: the "greater" gifts is thus balanced by the emphatic phrase: a way "in excess," one that exceeds, i. e., in excellence for its purpose. The sense is, however, not that this exceedingly excellent way is to be sought in place of the gifts, as a substitute for them. The idea expressed is not that "love" is more excellent than gifts. This introduces a false contrast and would call for an adversative connective, namely δέ or ἀλλά in place of Paul's καί and ἔτι. Nor does Paul elaborate the thesis that love is preferable to gifts. In 14:1 he urges us to seek both. Love is to be the all-dominating motive in seeking and in using spiritual gifts.

CHAPTER XIII

II. The Better Way — Love. Chapter 13

Gregory Nazianzen, one of the three celebrated Cappadocians of the fourth century, a defender of the Nicene faith, and one of the most celebrated orators of the early church, writes in regard to this chapter on love that here we may read what Paul said about Paul. It is true: only a man in whose heart the Spirit of God has kindled a faith like Paul's could evidence a love like Paul's and on the basis of his own experience of that love record its glories in what may be called the Psalm of Love. Paul's own heart lies open before us in this chapter. Here is the motive power, faith working through love, that sent him over land and sea to preach to others the unsearchable riches of Christ. Here is the inner power that sustained him amid all his labors, burdens, trials, sufferings, persecutions. Here is what made him rise superior to hunger and hardship, false friends and bitter foes, bodily infirmity and dangers of death. We cannot understand this man save as we understand his faith and its fruit of Christian love. All of his great joys and abilities, his high and holy office, his exalted position in the church, his stupendous task and his astounding success — all of them are what they are and what they came to be because of his love. This we must realize when he tells the Corinthians that besides his instruction on the spiritual gifts themselves he now shows them the inner, spiritual power that must energize all of these gifts if they are to be of real benefit to the church.

1) If I speak with the tongues of men and of angels yet have not love I have become sounding

brass or a clanging cymbal. When a man who has his own heart full of love writes about love he is apt to use a personal touch; so in these opening verses Paul uses the first person "I." "He passes the judgment by way of example upon himself: that if he were such a person, in order the more to startle others." Luther. Paul has the condition of expectancy in the first three verses, ἐάν with the subjunctive, not because he expected this condition sometime to be fulfilled in himself, but in order to present this supposition in a vivid and realistic form for strong rhetorical effect.

To "speak with the tongues of men" is to use other tongues, languages, or dialects which the speaker has never learned. So the apostles and others spoke at the time of Pentecost. See the exposition on "tongues" in 12:10. These manifestations, like miracles, etc., were signs and were not intended to be exhibited in the ordinary work of preaching and teaching. Because the Corinthians placed too high a value on "tongues," Paul, who lists this gift at the end in 12:10, 30, here considers it first.

The addition tongues "of angels" outbids what the Corinthians know in this line. When angels speak to men they use human language, but Daniel, John in Revelation, and Paul himself when he was caught up to Paradise heard unutterable things. Perhaps we may say that they actually heard the tongues of angels as they speak in heaven. Paul puts the thought into the superlative, beyond which it is impossible for a creature to go: Suppose that I as the Lord's apostle have the highest possible gift of tongues, those that men use, and those even that angels use — how you Corinthians would admire, even envy me and desire to have an equal gift!

We cannot assume that Paul is writing only hypothetically when he refers to "tongues of angels," for this would conflict with his evident purpose, namely to show that love must animate all, even the highest gifts. All else that Paul writes about angels shows them to be real, and so their language is real. There is no difficulty in the plural γλῶσσαι as it is here used with reference to men and with reference to angels, for the singular (14:2, 4, 13, 14, 18, 19) is used interchangeably with the plural (14:5, 39) when this kind of speaking is designated. Whoever spoke thus used some *one* tongue or language and not a number of them at the same time. Paul's supposition is this: if the entire range of languages, including even the language of the angels, were given me so that on one occasion I could speak in this, on another occasion in that language. The plural "tongues" as here used in no way compels us to think that the angels in heaven speak a number of languages.

The unreality of Paul's supposition lies in the general assumption as such. Paul did have this gift to a high degree, 14:18, but he could speak only in some foreign human languages and not by any means in all of them and not at all in the language of the angels. What he here supposes is the ability to use any and every language including that of heaven. He extends the gift to its utmost height, beyond what it ever was or could be. "Yet if I have not love," even this supreme gift would be all in vain as far as God's purpose in the bestowal is concerned.

Here we have the theme of the entire chapter: ἀγάπη, "love." The following description shows that love to men is meant, but this in its widest range. And ἀγάπη is much deeper than φιλία or the love of mere affection and personal liking or attachment. While the term is not unknown among pagan writers, the sense which we have given it is native only to the Scriptures, chiefly the New Testament. It points to a love that patterns after God's love. It always implies that love is directed by spiritual intelligence and that it aims at accomplishing a corresponding spiritual purpose. Only where there is faith in the heart is this love ever found, for it springs from this root alone. No pagan writer could possibly use the word in this spiritual sense.

God loved the world. It was a vile world reeking with sin. He could not draw it to his bosom and kiss it (this would be φιλία) because all of this foulness permeated its very nature. When God turned his love (ἀγάπη) upon the world he realized all of the world's vileness (intelligence) and in love, by sending his Son and the gospel, determined to save, cleanse, and purify the world (purpose). Thus did God love.

We are to love even our enemies. Yet they are full of the vileness of hate. Can we put our arms about them and kiss them? They would repulse us and revile us. But our love can see their awful condition (intelligence) and can seek to overcome and to remove it by showing them only kindness and patience (purpose). Like the world, they may or may not allow this purpose of love to be attained. Yet this is what love to our enemies means. Where this love does attain this its purpose, for instance, where God wins men from their sins, or where our enemies become our brethren, this love goes right on with its intelligence and changes the latter to accord with the new and happy relation.

When love is wholly absent, we know that its root, namely faith, is also dead. Yet μὴ ἔχω, "have not love," includes also all cases when believers speak because they are prompted by the pride of the flesh or by some other sinful motive and thus "have not love." Even though it be the highest type of miraculous speaking, yet when love is dead or dormant or inactive, "I have become sounding brass or a clanging cymbal." The verb γέγονα is placed forward for the sake of emphasis. Here the perfect tense implies more than the usual present condition; it indicates that despite all of the past advantages and all of my wonderful gift, I am after all nothing more than a strident, empty sound. Even miraculous speech is nothing, as far as the speaker is concerned, without love.

"Brass" is used in manufacturing trumpets and horns, and this produces powerful, penetrating sounds, which are indicated by ἠχῶν, "sounding" or resounding. Cymbals clash or clang when they are struck together. Their sound is even imitated in the neuter participle ἀλαλάζον, which is derived from the verb denoting a battle cry and more generally any loud cry of joy or pain. The terms themselves and also the repetition of the figures denote sound to the superlative degree and thus correspond well with the superlative idea expressed in tongues of men and of angels. Although all such superlative speaking was ranked by the Corinthians as the very highest kind of a gift, it would be nothing but an empty, tremendous noise — if it remained without love.

While the gift would still remain as a sign (14:22), and the interpretation of the prayer or the praise spoken would still benefit the hearers, the person himself who speaks without love would be no better than a lifeless brass instrument which someone else causes to sound or to ring. The idea that another is the real speaker when the gift of tongues is exercised underlies the comparison with brass musical instruments. The idea is also prominent that the gift itself is really only an instrument that is intended to be used with love, for a higher purpose, and not merely for the gratification of pride or for ostentation. We may apply this thought to the gift of eloquence and oratory and to that of a beautiful voice in song.

2) In a cumulative way, with increasing and finally overwhelming effect, Paul heaps up these καὶ ἐάν clauses, using two in this verse, and another two in the next. **And if I have prophecy and know all**

mysteries and all knowledge, and if I have all faith so as to transfer mountains, yet have not love, I am nothing. Two gifts are now placed side by side, and both are made superlative. Moreover, both exceed what has been said in the first verse. Paul's material is so abundant that he dispenses it with both hands.

We have discussed "prophecy" in connection with 12:10, 28. This is a higher gift than speaking with tongues although it is well to recall that God is able to use some very unworthy persons for the purpose of prophesying: Balaam, King Saul, and Caiaphas (John 11:51). Paul seeks the superlative in prophecy and secures it by adding "all mysteries and all knowledge," for which the appropriate verb is inserted, εἰδῶ (R. 1215, εἰδέω and εἴδω): "and see, perceive, and thus know." The words that designate the two objects are so placed in the Greek that the two adjectives "all" appear side by side and thus become more emphatic. The statement is cumulative: 1) prophecy; 2) plus all mysteries; 3) plus all knowledge. For one may be a prophet and yet know very few mysteries; and yet again, even if one knew all mysteries he might yet lack volumes of other knowledge that is not included in mysteries. The three concepts, however, belong to one general class, the mark of which is really to know in contrast with mere utterance as it appears in the gift of tongues.

In order to catch the full force of the superlative which Paul uses for knowledge in this conditional sentence we must ask: "What prophet ever knew all of the mysteries that are involved in God's plans of grace and of providence, to say nothing about countless lesser mysteries? And then the territory that lies outside of mysteries, that of 'knowledge' in its widest sweep, millions of facts and their correlation — what prophet ever covered all of this territory?" Paul intends to carry the supposition beyond the bounds of human possibility, and more so in this verse than in v. 1 (tongues of angels), for only by placing the gift so high can he make us understand to the full what the absence of love really means. There is little difference in force whether the article is used: πᾶσαν τὴν γνῶσιν, "all knowledge," or whether it is omitted: πάσῃ γνώσει, "every knowledge," as in 1:5. "There is an element of freedom in the matter" for the writer, R. 772, so that in both instances we may translate "all knowledge."

First only the tongue; then the head and knowledge and this combined with faith. "All faith" includes everything that can be termed faith, but, as we see at once from the addition, not "faith" in the sense of saving trust in Christ, for he who has that has the true root of all love and could never be οὐθέν, "nothing." The faith referred to is mentioned by Jesus in Matt. 7:22: "Lord, Lord, have we not . . . in thy name cast out devils? and in thy name done many wonderful works?" Yet the Lord rejects these people. However strange it may seem to us that men should speak with tongues, should actually prophesy, should even have miracle-working faith without saving faith and its product love, the fact stands nevertheless. It was possible for nominal members of the church to possess and to use certain spiritual gifts. This anomaly is the basis of our entire chapter. Love, which is more precious and wonderful than all gifts, alone makes the gifts precious possessions to those who have them.

Paul again supposes the superlative *"all* faith" and combines this with the supreme specimens of its work: "so as to transfer mountains," μεθιστάνειν, compare Matt. 17:20; 21:21. This proverbial expression is plainly figurative and describes "faith" as being able to perform seeming impossibilities, to remove mountains of obstacles, win astounding victories such as Gideon's, accomplish wonderful tasks. But however great this "faith" and its mighty works may be, without love it not only amounts to nothing for me, even I myself "am nothing," οὐδέ plus ἕν, "not one thing." Men may admire, honor, elevate me, the inner essential of personal value is gone, its place is a vacuum. Whatever good I may do for the church with this astounding gift is no mark of my own value and no credit to my own person. The Lord's verdict has already been pronounced: "I never knew you," Matt. 7:23. Here there is light on much of the learning, philosophy, science, and great achievements of today as they are found outside of Christ, saving faith, and Christian love although they are the accomplishments of nominal church members.

3) A third comparison rounds out the entire thought. Paul has thus far spoken about gifts without dwelling on a particular exercise of them. Now he adds voluntary deeds of apparent unselfishness, yea, of self-sacrifice. **And if I feed all my possessions away, and if I deliver my body over in order that I be burned, yet have not love, I profit nothing.**

The verb ψωμίζω means to feed by placing morsels of food into the mouth and then in general to divide and parcel out. The personal object is usually mentioned; our versions supply "the poor," yet Paul omits the object. We may think of an Ananias and a Sapphira who actually give their all but have not love. Luther writes: "To give is, indeed, a fruit of love though not yet love itself. Love is a spiritual gift which moves the heart and not only the hands. Love is the name, not for what the hand does, but for what the heart feels." The works of love are thus often imitated by those who have no love and yet desire to enjoy the praise of love.

Here again a companion piece is introduced, and once more a superlative, namely an extreme case of self-sacrifice: "if I deliver my body over in order that I be burned." The idea usually connected with this burning is that of martyrdom by fire. The difficulty connected with this interpretation is the fact that we have no record of an instance of this kind of martyrdom occurring during Paul's time. Various conjectures are offered to aid us, namely that Paul may be thinking of Dan. 3:19, etc., or of II Macc. 7, or of the torturing of witnesses by means of glowing tin, which Seneca calls *ignis*. But Paul speaks about himself, and he was a Roman citizen, and these were not tortured at all. This statement applies also to him as a possible martyr — as a Roman he could not be executed by burning.

Other cases of voluntary burning such as that of the Indian sophist who accompanied Alexander, of another Indian at Athens, and of Proteus at Olympia are sporadic and conflict with Paul's thought because these men merely despised life and threw it away with stoic indifference; they merely committed spectacular suicide. Paul pictures an act of supreme self-sacrifice that is made with a pretense of love for others, it is a companion piece to the giving away of all possessions. Since Paul speaks hypothetically in both instances, and since we know about no actual cases of either kind, it seems best to abide by the hypotheses and to go no farther. Both are suppositions of an extreme action and no more. These acts are apparently prompted by love yet in reality are not the result of love.

The form καυθήσωμαι is extensively discussed by the grammarians. The variant καυχήσωμαι: "in order that I may glory," does not deserve enough attention to earn a place in the margin of the R. V. It ruins the thought, for self-glory is a decided evidence of the lack of love for others. Although it is found in three important texts (Aleph, A, and B) and in some of lesser importance, it ought to be discarded. This leaves καυθήσωμαι and καυθήσομαι, both of which are merely future indicatives. The long and the short *o* were used interchangeably in a few indicative forms, R. 200, etc.;

also 324. We agree with B.-D. 28 in rejecting the Byzantine future subjunctive for this passage, which R. 876, 1216 willingly accepts on the strength of the use of the long vowel.

For the third time, like a refrain, comes the addition: "yet have not love." This is the one constant amid the variants of gifts, abilities, and deeds. This constant is decisive, all else is not. Let what I do be ever so sublime, without love "I profit nothing." Here there is another step in the gradation: first, the gift itself is likened to the sound of brass; next, the man who has the gifts is said to be nothing; finally, any credit or profit that might come to him from God for his deeds is declared nothing. "O how many marks of immortal human fame are mortal before God and do not follow their doers because they have not been made alive by immortal love!" Besser. The inside of many a deed is different from the outside, and God always lifts the cover, yea, for his eyes no cover exists.

In this first part of Paul's chapter on love he establishes *Love's Supreme Value* by showing how nothing avails without it. The greatest gifts and the grandest deeds together with all their greatness and their grandness are nothing, make us nothing, and bring us nothing if love be absent. Solemn and deep the dull refrain runs through these verses: "yet have not love," and not a syllable is changed. A narrowing downward also appears as we proceed: one might easily speak with tongues and yet lack love; he might less easily know all mysteries, etc., and be without love; and least of all do we expect kind acts and self-sacrifice without at least some love. When it comes to writing so as to put the richest thought into every word and clause, inspiration forever exceeds what human genius can do. While these three verses are negative in form they, nevertheless, imply a corresponding affirmative thought, namely that with love present in the heart all gifts and all works become the treasures which God intends them to be for their possessor.

4) First, love absent; now, love present; hence also we three times have the subject ἡ ἀγάπη. The Greek idiom, like the German, can use the article with abstract nouns. If, as Paul shows, love has such immense value, what really is love? Instead of attempting a definition Paul gives us a rich description. By being placed before our eyes in what it does and does not do this mother of all virtues is made known to us. When we see love thus, its value appears anew, but from a different angle, namely that of its own characteristic features. Paul personifies love. Olshausen says that he does this because love is never perfectly represented in any one individual Christian. So this photograph of love is given us in order that we may hold it alongside of our love to see whether the two are as exactly alike as they ought to be.

Love suffers long, is benignant; love envies not; love vaunts not itself, is not puffed up, acts not unseemly, seeks not its own, is not provoked; takes no account of the bad; rejoices not over unrighteousness but rejoices with the truth; suffers all things, believes all things, hopes all things, endures all things.

The love which Paul describes goes out to our brethren and to our fellow men. "Love suffers long." This first stroke of the brush shows that we are to be given a portrait of Christian love as it finds itself amid the sins, evils, and trials of a fallen world. Trench distinguishes μακροθυμία as referring to persons from ὑπομονή as referring to things. In the Scriptures "longsuffering" has to do with injurious persons and does not let their ignorant, mean, or malicious actions arouse the resentment and the anger which they deserve.

"Endurance," ὑπομονή (see ὑπομένει in v. 7) deals with trials under which it bears up with noble courage. Only "longsuffering," μακροθυμία, and never ὑπομονή is naturally ascribed also to God. Men may resist and antagonize God and thus arouse him to anger. When he withholds his anger he "suffers long." Mere things cannot arouse God; trials, tribulations, persecutions do not apply to God, hence he cannot manifest ὑπομονή, literally, "remaining under." When Paul thus names the ability to suffer long as the first feature of love, we should note that this is a Godlike feature. The world is full of evil men, and even in our brethren much evil meets us. When this evil strikes us, and our natural reaction would be resentment, indignation, anger, bitter words, blows perhaps, then love steps in, "suffers long," keeps calm, endures, and does this continually no matter how long the offense may persist.

Paired with this more passive side of love is a corresponding active side: love "is benignant," χρηστεύεται, shows its possessor to be χρηστός, useful, helpful, friendly. Trench remarks that this *benignitas* was predominantly the character of Christ's ministry, which dispensed deeds of gentle kindness among all the lowly and the needy with whom he came in contact. Thus to Godlike "longsuffering" there is added Christlike "benignity."

Paul does not describe love to us in the role of performing great, wonderful, and astounding deeds; he prefers to show us how the inner heart of love looks when it is placed among sinful men and weak and needy brethren. He does not picture love in ideal surroundings of friendship and affection where each individual embraces and kisses the other but in the hard surroundings of a bad world and a faulty church where distressing influences bring out the positive power and value of love.

There now follows a list of negatives, the last of which is paired with its opposite "rejoices not . . . but rejoices." "Love envies not," οὐ ζηλοῖ (from ζέω, to seethe), is without selfish zeal, the passion of jealousy and envy. The term is used also in a noble sense with reference to honorable emulation, but in the New Testament it is used only in the ignoble sense. When love sees another prosperous, rich, high, gifted it is pleased and glad of his advantages. Love never detracts from the praise that is due another nor tries to make him seem less and self seem more by comparison. The practice of the world is the opposite. The negatives used in Paul's description suggest corresponding positives. Instead of being envious love is satisfied with its own portion and glad of another's greater portion.

A natural companion to lack of envy is lack of boasting: "love vaunts not itself," οὐ περπερεύεται, it never becomes a πέρπερος, a braggard. The very idea is foreign to its humble nature.

Behind boastful bragging there lies conceit, an overestimation of one's own importance, abilities, or achievements. Hence the next step: "is not puffed up." From envy to boasting, from boasting to puffing oneself up is a natural sequence in the psychology of lovelessness. He that exalteth himself shall be abased; he that humbleth himself shall be exalted. Thus in this case the positive virtue is Christian humility and lowliness of mind.

Paul has mentioned being puffed up repeatedly in 4:6, 18, 19; 5:2; 8:1. Yet the conclusion which some draw, that Paul's description of love, especially its negative side, is derived from manifestations which he found among the Corinthians, is too narrow. Paul describes love as it really is with all of its main characteristic features. Even if Corinth had not existed, every line of this description would be true. In regard to some points, where we know the loveless tendencies of the Corinthians, we see these very tendencies contradicted by Paul's picture of love. These applications are, however, only incidental and may in a similar way be made to any other congregation and do not as such dominate the picture here sketched.

5) The next link in the chain is that love "acts not unseemly," οὐ ἀσχημονεῖ, contrary to the σχῆμα, form, fashion, or manner that is proper. When pride puffs up the heart, unseemly bearing and conduct naturally follow. Tactlessness forgets its own place and fails to accord to others their proper dues of respect, honor, or consideration. Love is forgetful of self and thoughtful toward others. Paul himself is a good example. No matter where he might find himself, among friends or foes, before people or before rulers and kings, he always knew how to act as became his station and the position into which he was placed. "Who taught this tentmaker such noble and beautiful manners, such perfect tact in all his bearing, that even the great in this world were compelled to respect him?" Besser thus points to the positive feature suggested by Paul's negative statement, the propriety of bearing and conduct. See Trench regarding σχῆμα.

The proper bearing of love is due to its genuine unselfishness, for love "seeks not its own," the things that belong to oneself, one's own pleasure, profit, honor, etc. True love is always unselfish. How easily said, how hard to attain! Selfishness lies at the root of a thousand evils and sins in the world and in the church: between rich and poor, capital and labor, nation and nation, man and man, church member and church member. Cure selfishness, and you plant a Garden of Eden. As when one draws a beautiful face and makes one feature after another stand out until the eyes at last light up the whole and give it complete expression, so in this portrait of love the inspired artist paints the eyes full of unselfishness, seeking in every glance not their own but that which is another's. Yes, this is love: no envy, no boasting, no pride, no unseemliness because it is altogether unselfish. Not for self (negative) = for others (positive).

If we bear in mind this trait of unselfishness we shall the better understand the next feature: "is not provoked," οὐ παροξύνεται (our word "paroxysm"), is not embittered or enraged by abuse, wrong, insult, injury. While love treats others with kindness, consideration, unselfishness it, in turn, receives much of the opposite. Paul's life was full of such experience especially from his brethren in the flesh who ought to have especially loved him. He did not accuse them, Acts 28:19; he did the opposite: "Bless them which persecute you," Rom. 12:14. Instead of vicious outbursts (negative) he entertained good wishes and gave blessings (positive).

Closely connected with this attitude is the following: "love takes no account of the evil," οὐ λογίζεται τὸ κακόν. "Thinketh no bad" in the A. V. misses the sense of the verb and overlooks the article: *"the* evil," *the* baseness or meanness which is inflicted upon us; not "evil" as it inheres in our own minds and hearts. This pairs with the preceding characteristic. This also explains the verb. Love keeps no account book for the entry of wrongs on the debit side which are eventually to be balanced on the credit side with payments received when satisfaction is obtained for these wrongs. Love forgets to charge any wrong done to itself. It is neither enraged at the moment, nor does it hold a grudge in vindictiveness afterward. Chrysostom has well said: "As a spark falls into the sea and does not harm the sea, so harm may be done to a loving soul and is soon quenched without disturbing the soul." We ought to note that οὐ λογίζεσθαι is the very verb used to describe the pardoning act of God: he does not impute to us our guilt, Ps. 32:2; Rom. 4:8; II Cor. 5:19; but imputes to us righteousness for Christ's sake, Rom. 4;6-11; 22-25; James 2:23.

6) In fact, love has no pleasure in wrong at all: it "rejoices not over unrighteousness." In τὸ κακόν the quality of meanness in the act itself is exposed; in ἡ ἀδικία the quality that runs counter to the norm of divine right, God's δίκη. Thus God's verdict stands against the act; he pronounces it unrighteous. Anything that is wrong in God's sight grieves a heart that is full of love, not merely because the wrong hurts the one to whom it is done, but especially because God is displeased with the wrong and must punish the wrongdoer. Instead of rejoicing over the wrong (negative) love grieves over the wrong (positive).

For this last link in the negative statements Paul himself supplies the positive counterpart: love "rejoices with the truth," not "in the truth," A. V. It is evident that the verbs are opposites: "rejoice not" — "rejoice with"; but it is not so evident that "unrighteousness" and "truth" are also opposites. Paul has more of these surprising opposites; this is due to the penetration of his thinking. Compare Rom. 2:8: they that disobey the truth but obey unrighteousness. "Truth" is the gospel verity, the divine, saving reality. Where unrighteousness prevails truth is of necessity absent. Unrighteousness prevails where the heart has pleasure in it, loves it, and thus rejoices in it. There the love that Paul describes is absent. But where the heart "rejoices with the truth," embraces it gladly, finds pleasure in possessing it, there unrighteousness is driven out.

Paul's theme, ἡ ἀγάπη, deals with the ethical side of gospel truth, i. e., with the conduct that rests on the saving reality of Christ and the gospel. This love finds pleasure in every progress which truth makes in the hearts of men, namely in every bit of their conduct which shows that they love and obey this truth. Thus we see how love grieves over unrighteousness but rejoices with the truth. Yet σύν in the verb does not personify the truth as if truth itself rejoices and love associated itself with truth in this rejoicing. The preposition indicates sympathetic inclination, and the dative "with the truth" is the object toward which this sympathetic joy inclines.

7) After the negative Paul now makes some positive statements. Yet these negatives and these positives are not merely grammatical. They are more. The former declare: "Nothing of this — nothing of this, etc."; then the latter exclaim: "All of this — all of this, etc." Thus Paul completes "the golden chain" of his praise of love, each jewel matches the next until the characterization is complete.

Love "suffers all things," πάντα στέγει. In the classics this verb usually means "to cover," "to fend off," from which the meaning "to endure," "to suffer" is derived as in 9:12 and in the present connection. The English "beareth all things" should not lead us to think of a load that is placed upon and held up by the arms of love. The figure has reference to enduring and quietly suffering inflictions. Love never complains that it is made to endure and to suffer too much; its capacity for suffering is very great. Remember all that the Lord's love suffered.

Love "believes all things" and refuses to yield to suspicions of doubt. The flesh is ready to believe all things about a brother and a fellow man in an evil sense. Love does the opposite, it is confident to the last. Here and in the next statement πάντα is to be understood in the good sense: "all that is best," while in the first and in the final statement "all" is to be taken in the bad sense: "all that is worst." Thus the four "all" are placed chiastically. Luther writes in explanation of the Eighth Commandment: "Excuse him, speak well of him, and put the best construction on everything."

Love "hopes all things." This is, however, not the hope which is directed to God in expectation of all good gifts from him but the hope that is directed toward our brethren and our fellow men, which expects what is best from them. Paul hoped in the case of the obdurate Jews and ceased not his prayers and his labors. Hope knows no pessimism. Yet the basis for this hope of love is not mere natural optimism but the effective grace of Jesus Christ. Love always expects that grace to conquer and to win its way.

Finally, love "endures all things" in the sense of brave perseverance. "The man ὑπομένει, 'endures,' who under a great siege of trials bears up and does not lose heart and courage," Trench. Etymologically this verb means "to remain under," hence it is the opposite of φεύγειν, fleeing away and giving up in defeat. When we defined "longsuffering" we already saw that ὑπομονή refers to things and not to persons. We hold out under pain, injury, and the like.

In these four statements the inner power of love is revealed: her head is held high, her eye is bright and shining, her hand steady and true, her heart strong with strength from above. This love has rightly been called "the greatest thing in the world." Paul does not describe love in its greatest works, sacrifices, martyrdoms, triumphs; he goes into the ordinary circumstances of life as we meet them day by day and shows us the picture of love as it must be under these. We find ready excuses when great things are made the goal of our attainment; Paul cuts off all such excuses. Be a true, everyday Christian in the exercise of love, then all great triumphs of love will take care of themselves. He who fails in the ordinary works of love will not even have an opportunity when the supreme moment for the performance of the extraordinary arrives.

8) First, it is love that lends *value to gifts and to works*; secondly, it is love that has *its value in itself;* and now thirdly, it is love that *in value outranks all else.* Or we may say that Paul shows the value of love 1) by its *absence,* 2) by its *presence,* 3) by *comparison.* Love is permanent, all else passes away. Thus love is the greatest.

Love never falls; but whether prophecies, they shall be done away; whether tongues, they shall cease; whether knowledge, it shall be done away. The verb used is πίπτει (some texts have ἐκπίπτει, "falls away"), "falls" so as to disappear and to be gone. Luther translates *hoeret nimmer auf.* "Without change of its inner essence love passes over into eternal joy because it is eternal life already in time," Besser. And as love never ceases, so also "its operations, its life and blessings, its beauty and power," Osiander.

The connective δέ is adversative and prevents us from translating: "Love never falls even if prophecies shall be done away," etc. The verbs are omitted in the three protases. We may leave them out when we translate into English: "whether prophecies . . . whether tongues," etc.; or we may insert them: "whether there are (not: be) prophecies," etc. The "prophecies" are either the charismatic gifts themselves or the exercise of these gifts, actual acts of prophesying but not the facts or the truths prophesied, for they, too, endure. Even the conditional form: "whether there are prophecies," etc., points to the temporary character of these gifts; for even now these gifts are at certain times withheld by the Spirit. But aside from temporary cessation the point will at last be reached when all of the instructive and the admonitory features of "prophecy" will no longer be needed, and when all of its revelatory phases will be fulfilled and will thus be superseded. Then all prophecies "shall be done away," literally, shall be put out of commission by being rendered useless.

The gift of prophecy is certainly wonderful, highly to be prized, altogether necessary for the church — think of the highest exponents of prophecy in the Old Testament and also of those in the New. Yet eventually there shall be no more prophets even of the lower type, those who only teach and admonish. The line of prophets will cease, and the work and the results of prophets will no longer be needed.

This is also true regarding "tongues," this remarkable gift to the early church. Paul writes: "they shall cease," stop, and they have, indeed, stopped long ago. The verb παύσονται is exactly suited to the subject. A speaker "pauses" and speaks no more; so tongues shall lapse into complete silence.

"Knowledge," too, shall disappear, namely the intellectual gift of formulating, coordinating, and setting forth with clearness the divine truth so that men's minds may grasp its contents, 12:8. This, too, is a gift which is intended to serve us only in our present imperfect state. With reference to this gift Paul uses the same verb which he had employed when he was speaking about prophecies: "shall be done away," put out of commission because they are no longer serviceable. The least importance is attached to tongues, they shall just naturally turn into silence. Prophecies and knowledge are far more important and, as the same verb that is employed with reference to both shows, belong to the same class. God shall finally put them aside; he is the agent back of the two passive verbs.

Paul is speaking regarding the consummation when Christ shall return in glory, and when the kingdom of grace shall merge into the kingdom of glory. Then all need of prophets will cease and also all need of the revelations which they have made to us here below and of the instructions and the admonition which they gave us, for heaven itself will reveal all of its mysteries to us directly. Tongues and languages such as we know at present shall no longer be needed, for all of us shall understand and speak the perfect language of heaven. Study, reasoning, and learning will no longer be needed, for instead of this gift which was granted to only a few and on which the many depend the new earth shall be filled with the heavenly knowledge of the glory of the Lord as the waters cover the sea, Hab. 2:14. But love? — love shall not pass away with these, for it is not a possession that serves only earthly and temporal purposes.

9) **For we know in part, and we prophesy in part; but when the complete shall come, that in part shall be done away.** Here there is stated the reason that two of these gifts shall not and cannot endure. Other reasons might be added, but this one is all-sufficient for the apostle's purpose. The tongues are not again mentioned, which is an indication that they are on a far lower plane although the Corinthians would rank them as being on a level with the other two and most certainly would value them higher than love. Tongues and languages in general as we know them here are evidently not to endure eternally. The penalty inflicted at Babel is not to be carried over into the other world. As the mention of tongues is omitted, so in v. 8 Paul does not speak about the "faith" that he mentioned in v. 2. He would probably regard it as necessary to add a lengthy explanation in order to differentiate this "faith" from the one which he intends to mention at the end of his discussion. The phrase ἐκ μέρους is placed forward for the sake of emphasis; it is the opposite of ἐκ τοῦ παντός.

Our knowing is "in part," partial, and thus inadequate. We never know with full comprehension, full penetration, complete mastery. In all our knowing there is something left that we do not know, a beyond to which our little brain and our intellectual ability do not reach. Knowledge attains a depth of miles, and our mind is a line that is only a few fathoms long; how can we hope to sound it?

This is also true with regard to prophesying. We constantly come to impassable barriers. Speculation tries to leap over them but fails to reach anything save uncertainties. Therefore, too, it is a prime theological and a Christian virtue to be satisfied with the limits which the Word sets for us, and never to try to go beyond them. Such a limitation seems humiliating to many, but their efforts to go beyond the limits set lead them only into bogs and swamps of error. Even many of the truths which the Scriptures present to us — how inadequately do we apprehend them intellectually: the Trinity, the Incarnation, the workings of providence, etc.! Ever we arrive where Paul arrived in Rom. 11:33. This is true in regard to even the far lower domain of nature: we know only in part. What are matter, life, light, electricity, and a thousand other things? We know not what they are; we know only this or that about them. In the words of a noted scientist: *Ignoramus, ignorabimus;* we do not know, we shall not know. The pride of so many scientists is pricked and deflated by this little phrase "in part."

Yet this discounting of knowledge and of prophecy is not to destroy the value of what we do know and what has been revealed to us. For to know God and Christ in faith is life eternal for us, John 17:3. But all of the forms of our earthly knowing and our prophesying of spiritual things serve only an earthly and a temporal purpose. Both shall eventually be vastly surpassed.

10) This shall occur "when the complete shall come." That is τέλειον which has reached the τέλος or goal in comparison with what is still undeveloped or on the way. Here the incomplete state in which we

now live forms the contrast. We are able to know and to prophesy only in a partial and an incomplete way. A complete state will eventually come, τὸ τέλειον, when we shall attain the goal for which we are now striving. In other connections τέλειος denotes the state of mature manhood in contradistinction from a νήπιος or παῖς. See Trench.

The aorist subjunctive ἔλθῃ marks the great future moment when the goal shall be reached, namely the Parousia of Christ. Then this entire state of imperfection which is now evident upon the earth will be abolished, for it will have served its purpose. An entirely new way of apprehending, of seeing, and of knowing shall take its place. Even then we shall not know all things — omniscience belongs to God alone, and even the angels do not know the deep things of God, which only the Spirit of God searches. In heaven we shall know in a heavenly manner.

The phrase ἐκ μέρους does not mean "fragmentary." This view introduces the idea that we have only a fragment of knowledge here and there, and that from these fragments we are unable to construct anything that is complete until our knowledge shall finally see things as a whole. A misleading application is then sometimes made. We are to consider each fragment by itself, are not to combine them in any way, we are especially not to draw conclusions from one fragment to another when we construct the Analogy of Faith, nor to harmonize one statement of Scripture with another when a contradiction seems to appear. Yet the fact of the matter is that the Scriptures place an entire system of spiritual knowledge before us, articles of faith that are well articulated and joined together. Yet this entire body of coordinated knowledge is ἐκ μέρους, partial, able to convey to us only a part of the full reality which we shall at last come to know. Melanchthon stimulated his love for dying by thinking about the joy of knowing the mysteries of the Holy Trinity no longer merely "in part" but in the complete heavenly manner.

11) A beautiful analogy illustrates Paul's meaning. **When I was a child I spoke as a child, I had the interests of a child, I reasoned as a child; now that I have become a man I have put away the things of the child.**

Paul compares his childhood with our present state and his manhood, which is so different from childhood and such an advance upon it, with our future state of glory. With the reference to his childhood he illustrates ἐκ μέρους, and with the reference to attaining his manhood he pictures τὸ τέλειον. Also this point of comparison is true: the child is in the man when he is fully developed; so we who are now in lowliness will be the individuals who are eventually glorified. Yet the child cannot expect more than to speak and to act as a child; so we must now expect to know and to prophesy only "in part." When the goal of manhood is reached, "the things of the child" (so the Greek and not "childish things," as in our versions) are put away. So when we reach τὸ τέλειον, the heavenly completeness, we shall put away what was formerly "in part."

The verb ἐφρόνουν points to the thoughts, the interests, and the strivings of a child while ἐλογιζόμην refers to the reasoning. The imperfect tenses picture habitual actions of the past. Paul's analogy is general and should not be stressed so as to make the child's speaking analogous to speaking with tongues in the church, and the child's thinking analogous with prophesying in the church.

The two perfect tenses have their usual present implication. Yet the force of γέγονα may be questioned. It may be regarded as having aoristic force, R. 898, etc.: "when I became," and stress the *point* of becoming. But it may be regarded as having a strong present force as is done in the R. V. which even adds "now" to make this evident: "now that I am become." It is a fine point of distinction which the grammarians may discuss. The other verb is simpler: "I have put away" the things of a child, and they remain thus put away.

12) In v. 11 Paul uses the typical singular "I" when he is speaking about that which is true with respect to all of us. He individualizes and makes concrete the truth which he expounds. He might have continued to use "I" in v. 12. But with a masterly touch he inserts one clause which has the plural "we" in the verb and thereby shows that every "I" refers to all of us. **For we now see by means of a mirror in a dark saying but then face to face; now I know in part, but then I shall know fully even as also I have been known fully.**

Paul is explaining the point of his illustration used in v. 11 and hence has the connective "for." "We see" needs no object, for the seeing itself is stressed no matter what the object may be. This seeing is done "by means of a mirror," which makes it imperfect. The ancients used metal mirrors, yet we should not suppose that these mirrors were dull and offered only a dim reflection; they were bright enough. The *tertium comparationis* is found in the fact that as we see only the reflection and not the person or the object itself in a mirror, so we, who are children and know only in part, now see the divine realities only as they are reflected in the mirror of the Word and not directly as they are in fact.

The preposition διά indicates a medium or a means which intervenes between us and the object of our sight. The fact of the matter is that God himself produced this medium. He descends to us in the Word and speaks about heavenly realities in a human way, for the Word is couched in human expressions. Only in this way can we become cognizant of the heavenly truth. To speak in a heavenly way would defeat his purpose; and to show us heavenly realities directly without the mirror of the Word would simply blind and destroy us.

The phrase ἐν αἰνίγματι is well rendered by Luther: *in einem dunklen Wort* and should not be separated from its context by a comma, for αἴνιγμα is a dark saying; and even in Num. 12:8, οὐ δι' αἰνιγμάτων, whence Paul may have borrowed this term, the idea of "sayings" should be retained. Yet the phrase does not introduce a new figure, and Paul is thus not guilty of mixing figures. The phrase is to be understood literally. Paul himself interprets his figure of seeing by means of a mirror. This adding of literal expressions to figurative terms by way of interpretation is often misunderstood. In his *Parables* Trench calls it Biblical allegory, a weaving together of figures and reality. It is extensively used in the Scriptures. The most perfect example is the allegory of the Vine and the Branches in John 15 where the figure and the meaning are intertwined almost throughout.

The translation "darkly" makes the phrase adverbial and loses the idea of "saying." An "enigma" is always a saying, one that does not as yet offer full clearness but leaves much for future solution. It must thus be received by faith and will eventually be followed by sight, II Cor. 5:7. The Scriptures regularly employ earthly terms when they are speaking about divine and supernatural realities. Think of the parables, the types, thousands of comparisons, Paul's use of human illustrations in this very connection. All of these are riddles more or less. The statement that Paul cannot call the Word of God an enigma is answered by the consideration that he is speaking relatively, by way of comparison with the future perfect revelation. Melanchthon writes: *Verbum enim est velut involucrum illius arcanae et mirandae rei, quam in vita coelesti coram aspiciemus.*

There is no need to introduce the rabbinical tradition regarding Num. 12:8, concerning Moses and the prophets, in which it is stated that Moses saw God through a window of single glass while the prophets saw him through one of nine thicknesses. Nor will it aid us to learn that a certain kind of window was known in these early times, which was made of *lapis specularis* (isinglass), called *specularia*; yet these were not called ἔσοπτρα but δίοπτρα.

"Now" we see imperfectly, "then," when we reach heaven, "face to face," which we may regard as an adverbial expression modifying "we shall see" understood. The preposition πρός is quite often used to indicate "living relationship and intimate converse," R. 625. In this manner God sees us now; we shall also arrive at this directness and no longer need the medium of the Word. Thus we shall see Jesus as he is, I John 3:2; yea, even God himself, Matt. 5:8; whereas we are now able to see both only in the Word and more dimly in their works in nature. This direct seeing will be the height of joy and blessedness.

Paul repeats: "Now I know in part," again with concrete personal individualization in order to place over against this the glorious heavenly opposite: "but then," etc. As a translation of ἐπιγνώσομαι καθὼς καὶ ἐπεγνώσθην the American Committee of the R. V. offers: "then I shall know fully even as also I have been known fully," and differentiates the compound verb from the simple form. The addition of the preposition to the simple verb makes the sense intensive and perfective, a knowing which penetrates completely, R. 827; C.-K.; Trench. Even the simple γινώσκω denotes the knowing of loving appropriation, knowing as one's own. Compare Matt. 7:23: "I never knew you," i. e., as my own; John 10:14: "I know mine own, and mine own know me." The dogmaticians very properly call this *noscere cum affectu et effectu*.

The aorist "have been known fully" is constative and includes all of God's knowledge regarding Paul and sums all of it up in one point. Commentators mention especially Paul's election and his conversion as being included in this knowing. Yet we should be careful not to restrict the force of this verb in any way. As God's direct and all-penetrating knowledge takes into account every one of his children already in eternity and, of course, through all of life, so we, too, shall at last know God directly and completely to the highest degree in which this is possible for his children.

13) The conclusion of Paul's description is as perfect in every way as are all of the other lines of the picture. **And now remains faith, hope, love, these three; yet the greatest of these love.** The simplicity of the words united with the loftiest meaning is the height of beauty. The last word is ἡ ἀγάπη — yes, that should be the final note.

"Now" is not temporal but logical. Paul is not saying that faith, hope, and love remain only now, for this life; he says the very opposite: all three remain forever. "But now" = considering all of the gifts that shall be put away completely and the abilities that shall be transformed such as knowledge — how about love? We have already learned that love never falls, v. 8. But more must be said, something that lifts love to its highest pinnacle so that, when this final excellence is mentioned, nothing remains to be added regarding love. This is, however, not the idea that, while all else is put away or changed, love remains and outlasts all of them. This is not the fact. Paul says that no less than three remain: faith, hope, and love. The verb is quite emphatic because of its position and refers to all three of the subjects equally. The fact that it is a singular makes no difference. This is often the case when a number of subjects in the singular follow the verb, and it implies that each of these subjects is to be referred to the verb; besides, τὰ τρία ταῦτα, a neuter plural, calls for a singular verb, R. 405. "These three," Paul says, "remain," and not merely one of the three.

In a certain way faith will cease and be turned into sight (II Cor. 5:7), namely inasmuch as the Word, the present medium for faith, will be taken away when we at last see Christ as he is. In another way faith remains eternally, for our trust in the Triune God shall never cease. To all eternity faith connects us with God and with salvation. For this reason Paul writes: "And now remains faith."

This is equally true with regard to hope. In Rom. 8:24, etc., hope as a sure expectation that is based on solid realities is compared with its coming consummation, the final possession and enjoyment of all for which we now hope. That is quite different from what Paul says here about hope. Hope remains as the expectation of the ever-new unfolding of glory in the future state. Heaven is not one everlasting monotony which, once attained, leaves nothing further to expect. The angels sing ever-new praises to God. So we, too, shall pass from one to another of the joys which God has prepared for us.

It is naturally difficult for us to speak on this subject because of our present inferior knowledge. For one thing, eternity is not time, not even an endless stretch of time, but timelessness, the opposite of time, Rev. 10:6. Yet we are fettered to conceptions of time even when we try to think in terms of eternity. So we can speak about heaven only in a poor, human way. But the glories of heaven are inexhaustible, and we shall never get through exploring them. Thus Paul writes: "And now remains hope."

His sentence is so constructed that if faith and hope remained only until we enter heaven, love, too, would remain only that long. It is impossible to drop faith and hope at the golden portal and to take only love with us. Such a construction is made impossible in still another way, namely when Paul adds with strong emphasis: "these three." He ties a band about these three as if, after naming them, he asks us to stop a moment and to contemplate these three which constitute one great unit, the supreme class of spiritual possessions, the class that endures eternally in contrast with the other class which endures only for time.

And now there comes the final surprise. Paul has combined faith, hope, and love into one great unit possession that is marked by endless endurance and is distinguished from all other possessions. After all, love must then share its throne with two others. After all, we must then discount what was said about its high position. This is the very effect which Paul wishes to create. With one stroke all such thoughts are changed: "yet the greatest of these love." There is no reason for translating the comparative μείζων with the English comparative "greater" as is done in the margin of the R. V. In the Greek of the New Testament period the distinction between the comparative and the superlative began to be erased, R. 668. This is not the case in English. Hence, when in the Greek three are concerned, we may have "greater," but in English this would be incorrect, we must say "greatest."

Paul simply makes the assertion and leaves us with the question as to how love is the greatest of the trio. One thing is, of course, clear: love is not greatest because it *outlasts* faith and hope but because it *outranks* these two. But how does it outrank them? The best answer is that of Bengel: *Ac Deus non dicitur fides aut spes absolute, amor dicitur.* Love alone makes us like God. "For love is of God; and everyone that loveth is born of God, and knoweth God," I John 4:7. Also v. 12: "If we love one another, God dwelleth in us, and his love is perfected in us." Especially v. 16: "God is love; and he that dwelleth in love dwelleth in God, and God in him."

What John says regarding our love while we are in this earthly state may surely be used to cast a light upon our state above where it will be love that brings us into the fullest union and communion with God. It is faith's nature to receive, but love gives; and giving is greater than receiving. God's fullest purpose is attained in us when we are filled with love. Hope also looks forward to receiving, but love is full possession and completed joy. And for every new joy which hope receives in heaven love will be the response on our part. When we come to rest on the bosom of God, it will be by love.

CHAPTER XIV

III. Prophecy and Tongues. Chapter 14

The preparation has been made. Paul has instructed the Corinthians concerning spiritual gifts in general, chapter 12; he has in addition impressed upon them the value of love and its supreme necessity in the exercise of all spiritual gifts. With all this clearly before his readers, Paul now takes up the gift of tongues. The Corinthians overestimated this gift and thus became unbalanced. Paul now proceeds to correct this mistake. He does it by showing at some length that prophecy is the most needful and the most fruitful gift for the church. He makes an extended comparison between prophecy and tongues and thereby brings to view the inferiority of the latter. A few needful regulations are appended at the end, v. 26-40.

1) Pursue love, yet strive zealously for the spiritual gifts, but rather that you prophesy. The transition is simple and perfect. After what has been said about the value of love only one admonition is in place: "Pursue love!" While in both the Greek and the English this verb has lost most of its figurative meaning, it has lost none of its strength. In the classics we have διώκειν with objects such as "honors," "pleasure," "the good," etc., Liddell and Scott. Paul thus very properly bids the Corinthians "pursue love" in order to obtain it and through it to enrich their hearts. We pursue love when we set our hearts earnestly to practice love.

"Yet," δέ, adds something, but something that is different. Here it is zealous striving for the spiritual gifts. Paul has already said: "Strive zealously for the greater charismata," 12:31. He repeats that admonition by using the same verb (see the remarks on 12:31) but a different noun. For "charismata" are both "gracious gifts" and "spiritual possessions" that come from the Holy Spirit. The plural form of the verb and the plural object are explained in connection with 12:31. While Paul emphasizes the fact that love is the supreme need for the proper use of all gifts he wants love to have gifts that are of effective use in the church. Gifts are the hands through which love serves.

All such gifts are to be desired. But some are "greater," 12:31, and thus to be preferred. Paul accordingly writes that the Corinthians are to strive zealously for the most useful of all gifts: "but rather that you prophesy." The comparison in "rather," which is strengthened by δέ, lies between the other gifts and this important one, prophecy. The ἵνα clause is subfinal and is here an object clause, the object of the verb "strive zealously." In English it is translated "that you prophesy" (not "*may* prophesy"). On this subfinal ἵνα consult R. 991, etc. All of the older commentators and translators find a purpose in these ἵνα clauses, which is incorrect.

2) The transition has been made, and now the new subject is at once taken up: "What value is to be attached to the gift of tongues?" Very little in comparison with prophecy. The reason is advanced by γάρ. It consists in a comparison between prophecy and tongues. **For he that speaks in a tongue speaks not unto men but unto God, for no one understands, but in spirit he speaks mysteries. But he that prophesies speaks unto men edification and admonition and consolation.** This states the difference with full clearness. It rests on love and thus on the benefit wrought for the church by the gift. On this score prophecy outranks tongues in a decided way.

The man who speaks in a foreign language in reality speaks not unto men but only unto God. "For no one understands" makes this plain. The people hear the speaking, but they do not comprehend the meaning of what is said. Since an individual speaks at a definite moment, the singular "in a tongue" is in place. Regarding the subject of tongues see the remarks on 12:10. "No one understands" does not mean absolutely no one, for one who has the gift of interpretation, i. e., who is conversant with the particular foreign language used, would understand. Paul himself speaks about the possible presence of an interpreter, v. 27, 28; in fact, the speaker himself may be able to act as an interpreter, v. 5, 13. But in this opening statement these ramifications of the subject are not touched. The audience in general does not understand the strange language. Such a speaker, therefore, speaks only unto God, for God alone understands him. The trend of Paul's thought is left when the speaker's intention is introduced as though he intends to address only God. Paul states only the fact: he speaks unto God as indicated.

After the negative statement that no one understands a corresponding positive statement is attached: "but in spirit he speaks mysteries," i. e., "things mysterious" that are not understood by the audience. And these things are uttered πνεύματι, referring to the speaker's own spirit (v. 14) and not to the Holy Spirit. When one is speaking with tongues, no discursive thinking takes place as is the case in ordinary speaking. The usual mental powers are not operative so as to govern the speaking. The human spirit is directly influenced by the Holy Spirit and finds words placed upon the tongue and is impelled to utter them aloud. The speaker may or may not understand the words which he thus utters. In either case they come to his lips without previous reflection and are due to an immediate impulse that affects his spirit.

3) As Paul thus gives us a fair impression of the gift of tongues, so, by way of contrast, he tells us quite

clearly just what prophecy of the ordinary type is. The person prophesying, i. e., exercising this gift, "speaks unto men," namely in their own language so that they can easily understand. He is fully conscious of what he speaks, and when he is speaking he uses all of his mental faculties. The substance of what he speaks is "edification, admonition, and consolation." While these nouns designate the contents of the prophetic utterance they at the same time indicate the purpose for which the contents are intended.

"Edification" in the Biblical sense of the term is every presentation of divine truth which increases and strengthens faith and spiritual life. It thus includes all true Christian instruction which is often called indoctrination. Edification is accomplished by enlightenment, by enabling the hearers to know and inwardly to grasp the divine truth, to assimilate and to make it their own. Examples of this feature of prophecy are found in the doctrinal part of all Paul's letters, notably in Rom. chapters 1-11; Eph. chapters 1-3; etc.

The term παράκλησις should not be translated "comfort," for this is included in παραμυθία, but "admonition" of all kinds. This feature is well illustrated in the admonitory part of Paul's letters, Rom. 12, etc.; Eph. 4, etc. Yet doctrinal and ethical content is often interwoven, and the former supports the latter. We cannot, however, say that edification is the genus, and admonition and consolation are the species. The three are coordinate.

"Consolation" or παραμυθία deals with the Christian's condition in this hostile and evil world where he must endure persecution and affliction of every kind. Consolation intends to lead him to understand the nature of what he must endure and to enable him to hold out cheerfully and valiantly to the end. Examples of consolation are found in many places in the Scriptures, for instance in I Pet. 4:12-19; Heb. 12:1-13.

Paul's brief description of the gift of prophecy shows that it does not deal only with special, direct revelations from God to certain chosen instruments (prophecy in the narrow sense as revelatory) but that it extends much farther and includes all of the uses that are to be made of all of the divine truth that has been revealed to us. Thus all true preachers and teachers of the gospel are prophets in the general or broader sense because they offer edification, admonition, and consolation to their hearers. All true Christians who are able to impart the gospel truth privately in a similar manner exercise the gift of prophecy to this extent. Here, too, we see how one may use zeal and more and more acquire this precious gift for fuller and more effective use in the church.

4) Speaking with tongues is restricted and offers no admonition or consolation whatever. Also when it is used independently and without interpretation, its ability to edify is restricted to the speaker himself. Paul adds this point to what he has just said. **He that speaks in a tongue edifies himself while he that prophesies edifies a church.** The one benefits only himself, the other benefits a church, ἐκκλησίαν, "an assembly," no article. The value of these gifts is according. While Paul says that both "edify," and while he makes no distinction as to the substance of this edification, we shall see presently that in regard to the gift of tongues the range of edification is far narrower than it is with regard to prophecy. Speaking with tongues is restricted to prayer, singing, blessing, and giving thanks, v. 14, etc., and does not include the wide field of instruction, admonition, and consolation, which prophecy covers.

5) Yet this comparison between the two gifts is not to be stressed unduly so that the gift of tongues is entirely disregarded because of its inferiority when it is compared with prophecy. **For I would**

have you all speak in tongues, yet rather that you prophesy; and greater is he that prophesies than he that speaks with tongues unless he interpret in order that the church may receive edification.

Paul writes this in explanation of the comparison which he has just made. The Corinthians might draw the conclusion that Paul does not want them to use tongues at all. "No," Paul says, "for I want you all to speak tongues" as far as that is concerned. He wants it understood that he recognizes quite fully what real value tongues have, and by no means does he desire to rob the Corinthians of this gift. The point at issue is not that tongues are best discarded altogether but that they be not overrated and prophecy underrated. Tongues stand on a lower level than prophecy — that is the point to be remembered. So Paul's wish is that all might speak with tongues, yet he would rather have all of them prophesy. The subfinal ἵνα clause is an exact repetition of the one employed in v. 1. It parallels the accusative and the infinitive clause which precedes it, it is a second object clause that is dependent on the verb θέλω and thus does not express purpose.

A simple δέ adds the fact that he who prophesies is "greater" than he who speaks with tongues. The Corinthians were ambitious to attain greatness; they sought it partly in a mistaken, partly in a false way. Paul shows them what true greatness is. Why it lies in the direction of prophecy rather than of tongues has already been indicated, and Paul indicates it again: the profit to the church is greater, and love always seeks that kind of profit. When Paul writes about an individual who speaks on this or on that occasion he uses the singular: he that speaks "in a tongue"; but when he speaks about an individual in general who is endowed with this gift he properly uses the plural: he that speaks "in tongues," for at one time one language and at another time a different language may be used by the same individual. Moreover, the gift as such seems to have been generally designated by the plural "tongues."

"Unless he interpret" notes the exception when one and the same person has two gifts, that of tongues and that of interpretation. The other possibility that a second person might act as an interpreter is not mentioned here since Paul is comparing only the person who is prophesying with the person who is speaking with tongues.

The combination of ἐκτός with εἰ μή is a pleonastic idiom, R. 640, 548. The point of this exception lies in the purpose clause: "in order that the church (ἡ ἐκκλησία, the local assembly) may receive edification," i. e., at least some edification. The aorist of this clause points to actual reception in the specific instance where interpretation occurs. In a way, by adding the interpretation and thus securing the end that some edification results for the local church, the speaker with tongues rises somewhat to the level of a prophet; of course, only in a way since instruction, etc., is not conveyed by tongues but only prayer, etc.

What Paul thus says about the person who has the gift of tongues and also produces edification is really an understatement. Although he may edify he can do this only in a small way and not to the same extent that a prophet could. Yet Paul's understatement is psychologically more effective than if he were to write down the full limitation of tongues, for the Corinthians cannot but feel that Paul could say more, and thus a tendency to contradict Paul and to defend tongues against Paul's statement is excluded from the outset.

We often defeat our own end when we are too earnest in opposing a mistaken view or a fault and make our words a little too strong. The hearer notes this and automatically discounts all that we say and generally even more than he really should because he is induced to do this by our overstatement even though this may be ever so slight. Paul is an excellent example of how to win people away from wrong views in a psychological manner.

6) Paul speaks concretely already in v. 2-5 when instead of comparing the abstract gifts he compares the persons using the gifts. In v. 6 he speaks still more concretely by introducing his own person as speaking now with the one, now with the other gift. This explains both the introductory νῦν δέ and the personal address "brethren." With both Paul draws as near as possible to his readers. **And now, brethren, if I shall come to you speaking with tongues, what shall I profit you unless I shall speak to you either by way of revelation, or by way of knowledge, or by way of prophecy, or by way of teaching?**

It is too narrow a view when "and now" is regarded only as a logical transition, either as introducing a positive thought after a negative one, or as introducing the reality after a statement that expresses unreality. This is an instance of the emotional use of this adverb, which is indicated by both the personal address "brethren" and the introduction of Paul's own person: "if I shall come to you," etc. Compare R. 1147; the true force of the Greek often appears only when the original is read aloud with the proper inflection. Paul intends to say: "And now, brethren, let me bring this matter still more closely home to you. You know that I intend to come to you. Very well; suppose I came speaking only in tongues, what would I profit you? Evidently very little." In order to see Paul's point the Corinthians need only to think of his coming visit and of his speaking to them only with tongues throughout that visit. What profit would they have from that visit?

The question really ends with "what shall I profit you?" For the answer regarding Paul's coming and his speaking to the Corinthians only with tongues must be made at this point, and that answer must be chiefly negative. In the clause "if I shall come speaking" the participle is the chief word, the action of the main verb being merely incidental to the thought. The coming to Corinth is the subordinate act, the speaking with tongues is the main act, and Paul could write simply: "If I shall speak to you with tongues." This stress on an accompanying participle is quite usual in the Greek.

But Paul's question is really made a double one by the next clause: "unless," etc.; for he certainly will profit the Corinthians very much if he speaks to them in any one of these four other ways on the occasion of his coming visit. This "unless" clause parallels the "except" clause used in v. 5. As the latter shows that only by interpretation profit results for the Corinthians, so the former points out that the real profit to be derived from Paul's visit will be only by his speaking as much as possible by way of revelation, knowledge, prophecy, and teaching. Yet Paul does not mean that these four or any one of them would furnish the interpretation or translation of such tongues as he might use. These other four are distinct gifts whether they appear in conjunction with tongues (and their interpretation) or separately from tongues. The point that is stressed is that, on the one hand, interpretation and, on the other hand, revelation, etc., use the vernacular, the language which all of the Corinthians understand. Thus it is not really the speaker with tongues as such who profits the local church but the interpreter and still more the speaker of revelation, etc. No revelation, knowledge, prophecy, or teaching were ever couched in the strange idiom of tongues. At the time of Pentecost, after the speaking with tongues was concluded, Peter preached in the vernacular. Tongues were used only for prayers or for blessings, and they always called for interpretation.

Paul simply coordinates the four gifts: "either by way of revelation, or by way of knowledge, or by way of prophecy, or by way of teaching." Revelation and knowledge go together since they are possessions, prophecy and teaching go together as activities. Yet again, revelation and prophecy go together since a prophet needs revelation in order to prophesy; and knowledge and teaching go together since a teacher must have knowledge in order to teach. Paul merely coordinates the four with "or," as if to say: "Take which you will of these four." The reason for this is the fact that, when Paul comes to Corinth and brings profit to the congregation, it will be by way of one or more of these four.

What elevates these four gifts above tongues is not so much the conscious activity which was exercised in using them, for the conscious spirit ($\pi\nu\epsilon\acute{\upsilon}\mu\alpha\tau\iota$, v. 2) was also deeply stirred when tongues were used. It is going too far to make the speaker with a tongue only "a physical tool" (think of Pentecost). The difference lies chiefly in the medium of language employed and thus in the resulting profit for the church. Paul is not thinking about what the respective speakers experience personally when they are speaking but about what the congregation receives, on the one hand, from him who uses an unintelligible language, on the other, from him who uses intelligible language.

"Revelation" is any portion of divine truth that is made known directly by God. Its formula of presentation is: "Thus saith the Lord." It remains revelation whether it is uttered by him who personally receives it from God or by others who obtain it at secondhand. Revelation is fundamental, for all knowledge, prophecy, and teaching are based on revelation even to this day. "Knowledge" is the understanding of any portion of divine truth, a clear insight into what that truth contains, see 12:8. "Prophecy" in the narrow sense is the first reception of some revelation from God and its utterance unto others. In the wider sense all who use any portion of revelation for "edification, admonition, and consolation," v. 3, are prophets. In the present connection Paul seems to be using the word in this wider sense. "Teaching" instructs in any portion of divine truth. These four gifts interlock and overlap and merge into each other.

7) In the illustrations which Paul now introduces the *tertium comparationis* lies in the intelligibility of the sounds produced and in the "profit" (v. 6) for those who hear the sounds. **Though soulless instruments furnish a sound, be it pipe or harp, unless they furnish a distinction in the notes, how shall what is piped or what is harped be known?**

Ὅμως, here and in Gal. 3:15 = "although" and is concessive. True, this is not ὁμῶς, "likewise" (R. 233). But when R. 1154 makes it adversative, its position in the sentence an instance of hyperbaton (423), and in addition to this makes it modify participles (1155, 1188), we dissent. Our versions are correct; B.-P. 903, and B.-D. 450, 2 leave us uncertain; the classics do not help us. In both passages the concessive adverb is to be construed with the very next word: "though soulless things"; Gal. 3:15: "though (only) a man's." This is concession although we may continue with "yet." Examine the passages and all that is offered regarding them.

A flute or a lyre may, indeed, furnish a sound, but unless this includes a distinction in tones, how will one know what is being played? The distinction of tones refers to some melody that is played.

8) Another illustration is added with καί, and γάρ makes it an explanation of the preceding one. **For, moreover, if the trumpet gives an uncertain**

sound, who shall prepare himself for battle? A trumpet of war that merely sounds, although its sound be ever so loud, means nothing to the soldier. The emphasis is on "uncertain." The proper notes of the signal must be blown, or the blowing is useless. "It is rather gratuitous to doubt the direct middle παρασκευάσεται, 'prepare himself,'" R. 807.

9) The point of these illustrations is now stated. **Thus also you, unless by the tongue you furnish speech easily understood, how shall what is spoken be known? for you will be speaking into the air.**

"Thus also you" makes a comparison with the point in mind. The phrase "by the tongue" is placed before the conjunction ἐάν for the sake of emphasis. As the musical instruments referred to in the illustrations are made for the purpose of producing sounds, so the tongue is to produce speech in the assembly of the church or anywhere for that matter. Unless the tongue furnish speech that is "easily understood," how shall we know what is spoken? The parallel is closely drawn by using δῶτε with reference to the speaking, the same verb that was used in v. 7, 8. But now instead of the negative ἄδηλον, "uncertain," we have the positive εὔσημον, "easily understood." We at once see what Paul means: tongues merely make a sound in the hearer's ears, but revelation, etc., convey a meaning that is easy to understand.

"For" is elliptical: "for, unless you do so," etc. And now the corresponding negative is expressed: "you will be speaking into the air," speaking quite uselessly and not into the minds and the hearts of your hearers. The periphrastic future ἔσεσθε λαλοῦντες (R. 353, 889) expresses linear or durative future action, for which the simple Greek future would not suffice. In these forms the present participle is timeless, R. 1115.

10) In v. 9 Paul makes the application to the Corinthians by a statement that is closely parallel to the two that were used with regard to musical instruments. One must use "speech easily understood" or he will be speaking "into the air." But more should be said. So Paul begins again as he did in v. 7, 8, but now advances from musical instruments to human voices, φωναί, v. 10, 11. As he did in v. 9, he once more follows this with "thus also you" in v. 12. We therefore have a parallel between v. 7-9, on the one hand, and v. 10-13, on the other, and the second half of the parallel is an advance on the first.

There are, it may be, so many kinds of voices in the world, and none voiceless. This merely states the well-known fact on which the observation (οὖν) about to be made in v. 12 rests. The world is certainly full of all kinds of human voices, and every kind has voice quality: it sounds aloud and can be heard. "So many kinds," τοσαῦτα, is modified by εἰ τύχοι (which is much like τυχόν), "it may be," one of the few remnants of the optative still found in the Koine; 15:37 has another. Paul is certain that the kinds of voices are so many, yet with "it may be" he indicates that the number may be more or less — many either way.

While it is true that in the classics φωναί at times means "languages," and some interpreters think that this word has that meaning here, even they pause before γένη φωνῶν, "kinds of languages." We might be inclined to accept "languages" as the meaning in the present connection because this rendering would support the fact that "tongues" signify all kinds of foreign languages. But ἄφωνον which occurs in the next clause does not suit the idea of "languages." This is true also regarding τὴν δύναμιν τῆς φωνῆς occurring in v. 11. We are obliged to translate: **"There are so many kinds of voices,"** sounds made by the throat and the mouth. And not a single kind is "voiceless" or soundless so that it cannot be heard. This proposition is self-evident.

11) There now follows the observation which Paul attaches (οὖν) to this obvious fact. **If, then, I do not know the meaning of the voice I shall be to him that speaks a barbarian, and he that speaks a barbarian to me.**

Plato often uses δύναμις in the sense of "significance" or "meaning." "The voice" with its article points to the particular voice that is used in any one instance. Paul mentions but one speaker and only himself as the listener. To be sure, he hears the man's "voice," "language" would be out of place. But unless Paul comprehends the meaning of what this voice communicates he will be a barbarian (a foreigner) to the man who is speaking with that voice. Paul, too, on his part will consider the man a barbarian (foreigner). The verb "I shall be" simply states the fact. And ἐν ἐμοί is probably forensic: in my opinion or judgment. The Greeks classified all men as Greeks or barbarians. So Paul would quite naturally call the man who utters these strange sounds with his voice (not Greek, of course, which Paul would understand) a barbarian; and this man, finding himself unable to make Paul understand, would from his standpoint as a non-Greek reciprocate and call Paul a barbarian.

We at once see how this applies to using the voice when one is speaking with tongues. We also see that what Paul describes here refers to foreign languages. The speaker uses his "voice" when he is speaking the language that is incomprehensible to Paul. The very term "barbarian" settles the point regarding the "voice" that is used in speaking a foreign language and thus also in the analogous case when a member of the church similarly uses his voice in speaking with tongues (foreign human languages).

12) As he did in v. 9, so Paul here once more makes the application to the Corinthians by using the identical formula: "Thus also you." But now the application reaches the final stage and therefore takes the form of admonition. **Thus also you, since you are zealots for spirits, with a view to the edification of the church seek that you abound.**

Paul admits in this admonition that the Corinthians are "zealots for spirits." In their way the Corinthians obey the injunction: "Strive zealously for the spiritual gifts," v. 1. But the chapter on love has pointed to more than the mere possession of gifts. The chief aim of these zealots must be the use of their gifts "with a view to the edification of the church." This important phrase is therefore placed forward: "with a view to the edification of the church seek that you abound." The ἵνα clause is subfinal, the object of the verb. The phrase, too, modifies "seek" and not "abound."

The genitive πνευμάτων is objective because of the verbal idea contained in the noun zealots. To be "zealots for spirits" = to strive zealously for spirits. The use of "spirits" in this connection has puzzled many. The English versions escape the difficulty by the translation "spiritual gifts"; others by translating "spirit powers," neither of which = πνεύματα. The idea that certain heavenly spirits are connected with the charismata just as evil spirits operate in the possessed is foreign to the Scriptures. The view that Paul is accommodating himself to a form of expression that was used by the Corinthians is unacceptable. Nor does Paul now contradict what he writes in 12:11, etc., that "the one and the same Spirit" is the source of all gifts. First John 4:1, 2 aids in the solution: "Believe not *every spirit*, but prove *the spirits* . . . Hereby know ye *the Spirit of God: every spirit*," etc. John speaks about "the Spirit of God" and yet uses "every spirit" and the plural "the spirits" when he speaks about the individual church members and about the Holy Spirit's activity in them. In 12:7 Paul writes similarly about "the manifestation of the Spirit" as it is given to each one as though the Spirit individualizes himself in each person. Compare "the seven Spirits of God" in Rev. 1:4; 5:5; 5:6 where the symbolical plural "seven" is used. So Paul writes "spirits" in our passage and again "the spirits of the prophets" in v. 32. This term "spirits" designates the different manifestations of the one Holy Spirit in the individual Christians. C.-K. 950.

13) Paul makes his admonition more specific. **Wherefore let him that speaks with a tongue pray that he interpret.** The ἵνα clause is not final. Paul does not say that the speaker with tongues is to pray with the purpose or intention of interpreting. This ἵνα states the object of "pray," i. e., the contents of the prayer. The point is immaterial whether this prayer is: "Lord, enable me to interpret," namely what I now speak with a tongue, or: "Lord, grant me *the gift* of interpretation" for all my speaking with a tongue. Paul mentions two actions: one with the substantivized participle "he that speaketh with a tongue," the other with the imperative "let him pray" (whether before or after speaking with a tongue). What Paul urges upon those who are zealous for gifts is that, if they have the gift of tongues, they also pray for the gift of interpreting whatever they may be given to speak with a tongue. The reason for this has already been stated, namely that the church may receive edification, v. 12.

The more important question is how one who speaks with a tongue and prays for the ability to interpret his utterance may attain that for which he prays. If speaking with a tongue or tongues means speaking the language of heaven or some non-human language, then the prayer for interpretation could of necessity be answered only by God's granting a special divine revelation for each separate case of speaking with a tongue. But if tongues are foreign human languages, then one may hope to have the earnest desire (ζηλωταί and ζητεῖτε, v. 12) and the prayer answered to be able to interpret without such a constantly repeated special revelation.

As has been pointed out in connection with the general subject of gifts, the Spirit uses also the natural endowments of Christians in developing and producing gifts for the service of the church. This applies to the gift of interpreting some tongue (language). Contact with those who are speaking such a tongue and the efforts to acquire it produce the ability to interpret what may be spoken in that tongue under the influence of the Spirit. Thus, in one way or another under providential leading the prayer can, indeed, be answered. Compare the remarks on 12:10, "the interpretation of tongues."

14) Paul has a justification (γάρ) for his injunction regarding interpretation. **For if I pray with a tongue, my spirit prays, but my understanding is barren.** This is always the case when the ability to interpret is lacking. Paul exemplifies by speaking about himself, his spirit, his mind. And he exemplifies by naming one form of utterance with tongues, that of praying, other forms will be mentioned presently. This "praying with a tongue" is different from the praying for ability to interpret mentioned in v. 13. The prayer mentioned in v. 13 is spoken in ordinary language, here in v. 14 the prayer is made in a tongue or a foreign language.

Paul differentiates between πνεῦμα and νοῦς. The possessives "*my* spirit" and "*my* understanding" are identical. "My spirit" is my own spirit, the immaterial part of my being in which my ego centers, which is able to receive impressions from God. This πνεῦμα is distinguished from the ψυχή which is the same immaterial part of my being but as being connected with the σῶμα or body and animating this body so that it lives. The νοῦς is the power that exists in the immaterial part of my being, which performs all mental operations up to and including discursive thinking. Regarding the psychological features of the distinctions compare Delitzsch, *Biblische Psychologie*, 184.

When I pray in a tongue, and thus my "spirit" prays, this is by no means an unconscious act. I know that I speak, and I know also and feel that the Holy Spirit moves my "spirit," and that I am uttering spiritual words and thoughts. But this activity of my "spirit," although it is conscious enough, extends no farther; my νοῦς or "understanding" is inactive and thus ἄκαρπος, "barren," "unfruitful," producing no distinct thoughts (which is its ordinary function) and thus producing no reception of thoughts in others who hear my utterance, v. 2. As far as spiritual benefit is concerned, my spirit alone receives that. And even this benefit is small, for my understanding is inactive. My spirit receives only dim impressions. But all of the gifts are to profit the church, that is their real purpose. To achieve this there must be interpretation of what "my spirit prays." Hence the previous injunction to pray for interpretation.

15) Now there follows the deduction, which is introduced by the question: Τί οὖν ἐστι; literally, "What, then, is there?" **What, then, follows? I will pray with the spirit, and I will pray with the understanding also, I will sing with the spirit, and I will sing with the understanding also.** The future tenses are volitive; they state a determination on Paul's part, R. 874. His understanding as well as his spirit shall pray and sing. He adds a second form of speaking

with tongues. This means that, as far as Paul is concerned, he will not speak with tongues unless he can also interpret, for when he is interpreting, the understanding is used.

16) In v. 14, 15 the first person exemplified, and in v. 16, 17 the second person does the same. The change from the one to the other puts the exemplification beyond question and at the same time lends vivacity as if Paul would say: "Take me, for instance!" and then: "Take thyself, for instance!" After the strong affirmation which is even repeated for the sake of emphasis in v. 15 Paul considers the negative possibility. The Greek ἐπεὶ ἐάν is equivalent to "otherwise," A. V. "else," R. 965, literally, "since if." **Else if thou bless in spirit, how shall he that occupies the place of the unlearned say the amen to thy thanksgiving since he does not know what thou sayest? For thou, indeed, givest thanks well, but the other is not edified.**

This is undoubtedly what the listener would experience. Here a third form of utterance with tongues is introduced, εὐλογία, "blessing," which is also called εὐχαριστία, "thanksgiving"; the former emphasizes the form of speaking ("speaking well," i. e., good words to God for his grace, etc.), the latter emphasizes the contents (the gratitude toward God). The dative πνεύματι states that only the speaker's "spirit" is employed in his utterance since this is made in a tongue and not in his "understanding."

What will the result be? Why, the hearer will not know what thou art saying and thus will not be able to respond to thy unintelligible words with the amen of assent. Paul puts this truth into the form of a question: "How shall he say the amen," etc.? He thus lets the person addressed himself furnish the answer. The subject of ἐρεῖ is placed before πῶς in order to make it emphatic: "he that occupies the place of the unlearned, how shall he," etc.? This prolepsis of the subject is entirely natural, R. 460.

There is much discussion in regard to the term ἰδιώτης and the noun τὸν τόπον, "filling or occupying the place of the ἰδιώτης." We have the plural in v. 23 together with ἄπιστοι. We may at once say that we decline to accept the view that these were "guests" who occupied special places that were reserved for them in the meetings; or that they were catechumens who had not yet been baptized, and that Paul mentions one of these because he is concerned about missionary interests. The definite article with "he that occupies the place," etc., does not carry such a connotation; nor does the participle "filling or occupying the place." If a guest or a catechumen are unable to understand, would those who are not guests or not catechumens understand?

The term ἰδιώτης is quite common and describes a person who occupies a private position in contradistinction from an official of some kind, or one who lacks technical or expert knowledge in contradistinction from an expert in some special line; hence in a broad sense he is "a layman." In the present connection this word refers to a Christian who is inexpert in the matter of tongues, "unlearned" (our versions) in this respect. Instead of merely using the term "the unlearned," "the layman," Paul very properly describes the man: "he that occupies the place of the unlearned." Paul intimates to the person whom he addresses as "thou": "Just imagine thyself in his place." "The place" of the man who is unlearned is his general position in the assembly by virtue of his inexpertness. Many others will be in the same position. We have no evidence that there were reserved seats in the church buildings of this day. Paul has the singulars "thou" and "he" in order to make the matter more pointed.

In v. 23 he has two plurals: the whole church and men unlearned, and varies this in v. 24: all (plural), and someone unlearned (singular). This is typical of Paul who constantly varies numbers, combines positives and negatives, and turns the thought now in one, now in another direction until his purpose is completely attained. Let us recognize and admire this flexibility and this versatility.

"Amen" is the transliterated Hebrew word for "truth" or "verity" and used in the Greek as now in many languages in order to express full and decided assent. "The amen" indicates the particular assent in the case about which Paul writes. It is set like a seal of approval "upon," ἐπί, thy giving of thanks.

In order to make perfectly plain the reason that this inexpert hearer is unable to add intelligent approval to what he hears Paul adds: "Since he does not know what thou sayest." Here Paul himself defines what he means by "the unlearned." This is the disadvantage connected with all speaking with tongues before unlearned people; unless intelligent interpretation is added, no one knows what is being said, no one can approve.

17) With "for" Paul adds the explanation regarding the two persons to whom he refers, the speaker and the hearer. Instead of using the contrasting particles μέν and δέ he uses the stronger μέν and ἀλλά: "For thou, indeed, givest thanks well, but the other is not edified," receives no spiritual benefit. Thus Paul again arrives at the cardinal point of his discussion regarding gifts, namely the edification of the church members.

18) The conclusion of the entire matter is now presented in the form of a personal resolution that was made by Paul himself (θέλω, v. 19). **I thank God, I speak with tongues more than you all; nevertheless in church I am resolved to speak five words with my understanding in order that I may actually**

instruct others rather than ten thousand words in a tongue.

While Paul greatly reduces the value of speaking with tongues he by no means despises this gift. He himself possesses this ability in a high degree and thanks God for it. If the Corinthians are proud of having this gift in their midst, Paul can tell them that he is able to speak with tongues more than all of them. The verb λαλῶ and its tense do not intend to indicate that Paul constantly does this kind of speaking in following his work. This verb resembles our English "I speak this or that language," i. e., I have this ability. Nor does the plural "in tongues" mean that, whereas the Corinthians speak only a few foreign languages, Paul speaks many. The number of the languages spoken is not stressed at any point in the discussion. "More than you all" refers to a higher degree of endowment by the Spirit. The entire spiritual equipment of the apostle, which he has received for his great office, also in regard to this gift exceeds anything that appears among the Corinthian church members, all of whom are of the ordinary class.

19) If the Corinthians were to possess this gift to such a high degree, how they would glory in it and use it excessively! Paul thinks quite otherwise: "five words," enough to construct one pithy sentence, uttered with the understanding "at church" before the people "in order to instruct others" are preferable to "ten thousand words in a tongue" because in spite of the excessive number they convey nothing to the hearers. The emphasis is on the phrase "at church" (no article), R. 792. Paul says nothing here or elsewhere about using tongues in private devotion, and it is best not to draw a conclusion regarding this point. Regarding θέλω ἤ without μᾶλλον see R. 661. The verb expresses determination. The aorist subjunctive κατηχήσω refers

to instruction that is actually imparted by means of the five words.

20) Thus far Paul has shown the uselessness of tongues as far as the congregation is concerned, since without an interpretation tongues cannot address the understanding and, like prophecy, tend toward edification. With a brief preamble he now draws attention to a feature that is connected with tongues, of which the Corinthians, it seems, have not thought at all. In the case of unbelievers speaking with tongues tends only to confirm them in their unbelief.

The preamble to this part of the exposition is put into the form of a kindly admonition. **Brethren, be not children in mind, on the contrary, in baseness be babes but in mind be mature.** The address as well as the substance of the following indicate the beginning of a new paragraph. To be children in mind is to act as though the mind is still in the undeveloped stage of childhood. The plural of φρήν (φρένες, here the locative dative ταῖς φρεσίν), the diaphragm enclosing the nobler viscera, heart and lungs, is used by the Greeks to designate the ability of the mind to think and to judge. The apostle intimates that despite all their pride in knowledge and wisdom the Corinthians are still "children" as far as judging aright concerning the effect of tongues is concerned. Like children they delight in the gift as such and yet fail to see all that is involved in the inconsiderate use and display which they make of this gift.

With a quick turn of thought that is suggested by the idea of being children in a certain respect Paul is reminded of a field in which it would be creditable to the Corinthians to be children, yea, babes: "on the contrary, in baseness be babes," νήπιοι, so young and inexperienced as not to know how to practice anything in the nature of κακία. This is, however, not "malice" (our versions), ill will against someone. It is good-for-nothingness (5:8), moral inferiority, for the adjective κακός describes a person or a thing as not being what he or it should be according to nature, idea, or purpose. We have no reason in the present connection to think of the superlative sense of the word *Bosheit* or "wickedness," for the Greek word for this idea is πονηρία.

To be a babe is to be even less than a child; a babe can do nothing at all. Why Paul should add this remark about being babes in baseness is a puzzle to some. They think that it is a remark that just occurs to the writer when he wants to balance a previous expression. Yet this is never Paul's way, to say no more. The puzzle is solved when we catch Paul's meaning. It is κακόν to use a gift (here that of tongues) so that it does not serve its true purpose. To use it with a display of vanity is childish; to ignore its purpose by disregarding edification is wrong. Add to this what Paul is now about to show, a foolish use that helps to rebuff the unbelievers who might be won to faith, and we have exactly what κακία implies; and this is what Paul urges the Corinthians to avoid.

Instead of being children in mind the Corinthians are to be τέλειοι, "mature," having reached the goal; compare the remarks on 13:10. In the present connection Paul refers to people who are fully able to use their powers of thought and of judgment. In this verse the three locative datives are used with a noun (παιδία), with a verb (νηπιάζετε), and then with an adjective (τέλειοι), R. 524, which is an interesting variation.

21) The chief trouble connected with the thoughtless and the childish use of tongues is made plain by means of a quotation from Isa. 28:11, 12. **In the Law it is written: In strange tongues and by lips of strangers will I speak to this people, and not**

even thus will they listen to me, says the Lord. This is not quoted from the LXX but is a direct translation from the Hebrew which omits a part of v. 12 and adds "says the Lord." The version of Aquila agrees with Paul's translation as far as the word τούτῳ. Regarding the perfect tense "it has been written" see 1:19. The term ὁ νόμος designates the Old Testament. By using the first person "I will speak" whereas the Hebrew has the third, Paul himself indicates that he is quoting in a free manner. For his purpose the "stammering lips" of the Hebrew are of no importance, but the foreign language employed in this case is exactly the feature which he intends to stress: "In strange (foreign) tongues and by lips of strangers (foreigners) will I speak to this people." By this paraphrase Paul thus brings out the vital thought of Isaiah's prophetic utterance.

Jehovah threatens to send barbarians upon the kingdom of Judah, namely the Assyrians with their barbarous speech, which would sound like stammering to the Jews and be wholly foreign to their ears. They would not heed the pleading of the Lord's prophets, he will now speak to them through the lips of these cruel, barbarous conquerors. Will God's obdurate people listen at last? No; even this measure will be in vain: "and not even thus will they listen to me." Isaiah's prophecy was duly fulfilled at the time of the Assyrian invasion.

Not a few happenings of this nature, whether they are predicted or not, are in one way or in another typical of future occurrences. In some important feature a striking resemblance can be noted. That is the case here. The point in which the Old Testament type referred to by Paul agrees in a striking manner with the antitype now appearing in Corinth is the foreign, unintelligible tongue which leaves unbelieving hearts unchanged and even increases their hardness.

In both instances unbelievers are involved: the unbelieving people of Judah, and in Corinth pagans who may attend the services of the church. In both instances an unintelligible language is spoken: in the case of Judah, Assyrian, and in Corinth, tongues. In both instances the effect is negative: the men of Judah remain unbelieving, the Corinthian unbelievers scoff.

22) Paul draws a conclusion from Isaiah's prophecy, especially from the statement that the Judeans would not listen to the Lord. **Wherefore tongues are for a sign, not for the believing, but for the unbelievers, while prophecy, not for the unbelievers, but for the believing.**

The point to be noted in regard to both the tongues and the prophecy lies in the phrase "for a sign"; and εἶναι (here εἰσί) combined with εἰς: "to be for," etc., expresses, not the nature of tongues and of prophecy, but the effect. In the present connection Paul does not, of course, refer to the interpretation of tongues since that would be out of place. From the Old Testament prophecy he concludes that unintelligible tongues, like the unintelligible language of the Assyrians in Judea, have a certain effect upon unbelievers. The effect is that of an unintelligible sign which naturally arouses hostility. Unintelligible tongues have no such effect upon believers, could not have in the nature of the case, and hence they are not *such* a "sign" to them.

Regarding signs for unbelievers with this negative effect compare Luke 2:34: this child Jesus . . . "for a sign which is spoken against." John 2:18-22, the Temple destroyed, and "in three days I will raise it up." Matt. 12:39, "the sign of Jonah, the prophet," also 16:4. The parables of Jesus had a similar effect upon unbelievers; they, too, were unintelligible to them, were even intended to be so, Matt. 13:10, etc.

"Prophecy" is the reverse. Since the two statements are exact parallels, we must supply "is for a sign" and not merely "is." But in this case the term "sign," because it is intended for believers and not for unbelievers, is understood as a sign of grace and not of displeasure and of judgment. Prophecy is a gracious gift of the Spirit for all believers, a precious means of salvation, its prominent feature as compared with unintelligible tongues since it is easily understood in regard to what it conveys. In the nature of the case God has no such gracious gift for unbelievers. He can do and does only one thing: he opposes their wicked unbelief. The datives are throughout regular indirect objects. So we see God using two signs: one of judgment for unbelievers and one of grace for believers.

Yet it is God who speaks objectively, on the one hand, in the Assyrian tongue and in the Corinthian tongues and, on the other hand, in all prophecy. Although God speaks objectively, subjectively the unbelievers do not hear him and thus remain what they are; only believers hear what he says and receive the blessed effect of his words. In this connection we may note that Paul's parallel between the foreign language of the Assyrians and the tongues spoken in Corinth rests on the fact that the latter were likewise foreign human languages.

23) With οὖν Paul draws out the fuller meaning concerning what he says in regard to tongues and to prophecy and to their effect as signs. **Accordingly, if the whole church come together in one place, and all speak with tongues, and men unlearned and unbelieving come in, will they not say that you are mad?** This will assuredly be the effect.

Paul's description is concrete and vivid. Suppose (ἐάν) that the entire church comes together in one place where it usually meets for worship. Suppose that all of the members thus assembled speak in tongues, not, of course, in a simultaneous babel but, let us say, in due order, one after the other. It is easy to see why Paul puts his supposition in this strong way: "the *whole* church" and *"all"* members speaking with tongues. It is because all of the Corinthians loved and admired tongues above all other gifts. So in his supposition Paul grants them their wish, he pictures a service in which all are assembled, and all speak with tongues. Interpretation is, of course, disregarded.

The supposition goes on. Suppose further that a number of pagans, who have in some way been attracted by the church, enter into this assembly, people who are unlearned in tongues and unbelievers. They sit down and listen to all of these church members as they are talking in tongues, an unintelligible torrent of sounds. What will, what must be the effect upon them? "Will they not say that you are mad?" Why, even in Jerusalem where tongues first appeared this was the effect upon the unbelievers: "But others mocking said: 'They are filled with new wine,'" Acts 2:13. Is this the effect which the Corinthians desire to produce? While it is God who speaks through tongues in Corinth even as he did in Judea through the Assyrians, the Corinthians must now see that the more this unintelligible speaking is increased, the effect produced upon unbelievers must of necessity be the reverse of what they would desire.

Paul again writes ἰδιῶται. The meaning of this term is the same as it was in v. 16, laymen in regard to tongues, persons who are unable to understand them. In v. 16 the context implies that the layman spoken of there is a believer and belongs to the church while in v. 23, 24 Paul explicitly states that unbelievers and nonmembers are referred to. The combination ἰδιῶται ἢ ἄπιστοι, "unlearned or unbelieving," denotes one and the same class, "or" adds only an alternative designation. "Or" is usually, however, made disjunctive so that we have two classes: 1) the unlearned (thought to be Christians or near-Christians); 2) unbelievers.

These unlearned are thought to be visitors from some other congregation who are unacquainted with tongues; proselytes or catechumens who have not yet been baptized; people who are merely unacquainted with Christianity and not hostile unbelievers. "Or" is not disjunctive but conjunctive and definitive as it is in v. 24 and in Luke 20:2.

24) Paul now introduces prophecy into his supposition. Behold the difference as to the effect! **But if all prophesy, and one unbelieving or unlearned comes in, he is convicted by all, he is put through examination by all, the secrets of his heart are made manifest; and thus, having fallen on his face, he will worship God, declaring that truly God is among you.**

There is no need again to mention the assembling of the whole church. As all of the Corinthians desire tongues, so Paul desires that all may prophesy, v. 5, instead. Now suppose that all of them do; of course, in proper order. The present subjunctive προφητεύωσιν, like λαλῶσι in v. 23, pictures the action in progress: "suppose all are engaged in prophesying." Again the supposition proceeds: "and suppose one unbelieving or unlearned comes in" and listens to all of this prophesying, which is, of course, entirely intelligible to him. The aorist εἰσέλθῃ, like εἰσέλθωσι in v. 23, merely marks the fact of the entrance. Paul very properly now has the singular "one unbelieving or unlearned" and not the plural as he did in v. 23. Conversion is a personal and an individual matter.

The indefinite τις, "one," is to be construed with both ἄπιστος and ἰδιώτης, for it designates one person only and not two, which latter would call for the wording "*one* unbelieving or *one* unlearned." In the combination "one unbelieving or unlearned" "or" adds only an alternative term. As was the case in v. 16 and v. 23, ἰδιώτης receives its connotation from the context. In verses 16 and 23 it means one who is minus ability regarding tongues; here in v. 24, one who is minus ability in regard to prophecy. For this reason, it seems, Paul now places "unbelieving" first and "unlearned" second.

What happens in this case Paul puts into the form of facts. Since this supposition climaxes what he, Paul, desires for the Corinthians (that they *all* prophesy), he states what *he* knows will happen. In v. 23, where the supposition climaxes what the Corinthians desire (that they *all* might speak with tongues), Paul lets the Corinthians say what *they* think will happen ("will they not say?" etc.). When Paul speaks about the effect of tongues as a sign he uses only one brief statement, namely the assertion of the unbelievers: "You are mad." When he describes the effect of prophecy he dwells on it at length and reaches a climax in the declaration of the new convert: "Truly, God is among you," v. 25.

The effect produced on this unbelieving visitor who was hitherto unacquainted with prophecy is first sketched in three statements: he is convicted — put through examination — his heart's secrets are made manifest. These three may be combined in the thought: he is brought to repentance. Conviction works the consciousness of guilt in the unbeliever's soul. This is the effect of prophecy in the wider sense (see v. 2), for Paul adds convicted "by all." The conscience is touched and aroused from its sleep. The law is brought home to the sinner. "He is put through examination by all," not κρίνειν ("judged," our versions), nor κατακρίνειν ("condemned"), but ἀνακρίνεσθαι, put through a course of questioning as when one is questioned and examined by a judge in a court. This describes the detailed effect produced on the sinner's heart by all of this prophesying. Question after question strikes home and reveals his sin and his guilt to him.

The statement that Paul has a *hysteron proteron* by placing conviction before examination is due to a misunderstanding of the second verb or of the situation. The result of this stirring of the conscience, which is intensified by the self-examination produced by this prophesying, is that "the secrets of his heart are made manifest," i. e., to his own consciousness. These "secrets" are the motives, the impulses, and the tendencies that lie veiled and covered under the sinner's words and his deeds such as the utter lack of fear and love to God and the absence of love to his fellow men and, coupled with these negatives, the positive enmity against God and hatred and malice against men, etc. He thus begins to see himself as he actually is. The light of prophecy which pours in upon him and uses first the law and then the gospel thus reveals to the sinner the entire inwardness of his ungodly and unrighteous life. He is brought to repentance.

25) After this description of what takes place inwardly in the sinner's heart as a result of the prophecy which reaches the conscience through the law Paul adds the outward, visible, and audible effects of the prophecy which reaches the heart through the gospel. In prophecy law and gospel are always used conjointly, and it is always the law which penetrates first, and this is followed by the blessed effect of the gospel. The sinner is brought to faith and to the confession of faith: "and thus, having fallen on his face, he will worship God," etc. This prostration is a confession of sin and a confession of faith combined. The act is even more significant than words alone would be. Among Orientals acts are always more demonstrative than among us Occidentals. Today the head bows in crushed humility, or the knees sink to the floor when sins are confessed.

In the Greek the participle "having fallen on his face" is the accompanying action, and "he will worship

God" is the main act. The verb προσκύνειν = "do obeisance," *anbeten*, "worship" in the sense of submission to God, confessing, praising, and exalting him as the true God. This entails a full and an adequate confession of faith.

Thus the "unbeliever" who came in departs as a "believer," and all of this has been accomplished through the gift of prophecy. This is an effect that all the tongues in the world could not produce. Paul adds the final touch: "declaring that truly God is among you." Whereas tongues produce the scoffing reply: "You are mad!" prophecy produces the reply: "God is among you!" Whereas tongues are a sign to unbelievers and confirm their unbelief, prophecy is a sign to the believers which works faith by its power and, by turning the unbeliever into a believer, becomes a sign of grace also to him.

Thus the discussion ends. Tongues are of little use to believers, of no use to unbelievers. Even that little use depends on a second gift, interpretation. Prophecy is of the highest value. It edifies all believers and converts unbelievers. Tongues thus meet the great saving purpose of the church only slightly, through the medium of another gift. An excess of tongues is of no profit, it is rather a detriment. If it consumes the entire time of worship it is decidedly the latter. Prophecy meets the saving purpose of the church in the very highest degree. We can have no excess of prophecy.

26) The careful and the detailed instruction given in v. 1-25 is followed by careful and detailed directions regarding procedure by telling the Corinthians just what to do in their church services so as to employ the charismata in the most beneficial way. The kindly address "brethren" asks the Corinthians to receive these directions in a brotherly spirit. The opening question is like that occurring in v. 15. **What,**

then, follows? i. e., in regard to the way in which you should proceed with these charismata in your meetings. **When you come together, each has a psalm, has a teaching, has a revelation, has a tongue, has an interpretation. Let all things be done unto edifying.**

We need not stress "each" unduly, for in a large assembly, where old and young and even children are present, many come only to hear. In a perfectly natural way "each" refers to those who have some gift to exercise in that special service. Paul mentions a number of gifts without employing connective particles; he simply places them side by side as they may readily occur in such a meeting. Yet we see that it is Paul's purpose to compare especially two gifts, prophecy in general and tongues. For each one "has a psalm, has a teaching, has a revelation" details the functions of the gift of prophecy in the wider sense.

A "psalm" was one that was uttered in the vernacular, cf., Eph. 5:19; the utterances in tongues follow separately. "Teaching" is any piece of instruction on some appropriate point of doctrine or ethics. "Revelation" is not a direct communication from God to the speaker but some portion of the Word of God which the speaker deems it necessary to bring to the attention of the brethren.

The ordinary functions of prophecy are thus placed first for reasons already indicated. Now there follows "a tongue," an utterance in a foreign language but with the complement "an interpretation" that translates the tongue. Bengel comments on the repetition of ἔχει, "has": *Eleganter exprimit divisam donorum copiam*. The indicative merely states the fact: each one *has* this or that charismatic offering for the benefit of the assembly.

After thus sketching the situation that obtains when the congregation assembles for worship Paul states the principle that is to govern the proceedings: "Let all things be done unto edifying," πρός, toward this end. First, the gifts must be of a kind to edify; secondly, what is done with them when the assembly is come together must likewise serve this great end.

27) After he has placed the situation and the principle before his readers Paul tells them in detail how to proceed. Yet he reverses the order and speaks about tongues first and about prophecy second and thus produces a chiasm between v. 26 and v. 27. This has the advantage of placing the practical instructions in regard to the most important gift, that of prophecy, in the important place at the end. **And if one speaks with a tongue, let it be two or at the most three and in turn, and let one person interpret. Yet if there be not an interpreter, let him be silent in church and let him speak to himself and to God.**

"And if," εἴτε, might have a second εἴτε following in v. 29, but Paul uses δέ in order to contrast prophecy with tongues. "If one speaks with a tongue" does not refer to one individual only but is a general expression: this or that person. The Greek needs no verb, but in English we add "let it be" in order to obtain a smoothness of translation. No more than two, at the most three, are to use tongues in any one gathering; κατά is used in the distributive sense: *je zwei*, etc. "At the most," τὸ πλεῖστον, is an adverbial accusative, R. 487, 550, and a true superlative, R. 670. Speakers with tongues are not to take up the entire time of the meeting and thus leave little or no opportunity for prophecy. Moreover, they are to speak ἀνὰ μέρος, "in turn," R. 571. This sounds as though in Corinth these speakers at times failed to restrain themselves and spoke simultaneously and created unseemly confusion.

"And let one person interpret" is to be understood *ad sensum*. There is no reason to stress εἷς to mean one person only for the two or the three speakers with tongues. What Paul requires is that no one speak with a tongue unless a prompt interpretation follows. Just as only one person at a time shall speak with a tongue, so one person shall follow the tongue with the interpretation. This may be the person who speaks with a tongue, for he himself may have also the ability to translate, v. 13; it may also, of course, be another person. Whether one person interprets for two or for three speakers with tongues will depend on whether the two or the three use the same foreign language, or, if they use different languages, whether the interpreter is linguist enough to translate two or three.

28) However, no interpreter may be present at the meeting. In this event no one is to speak with a tongue. This implies that the speaker with a tongue can ascertain in advance whether an interpreter is present or not. How can he do this? He could not do it if tongues are the language of heaven or a mystical non-human language. Then interpretation would have to come as a special revelation for each case, for who is ready to assume that interpretation consists in the actual knowledge of the language of heaven or of the non-human language? Yet no speaker with a tongue could possibly ascertain in advance whether the Spirit were ready to grant someone the required revelation at the time. Thus he could never determine whether he should proceed to speak or not. This again shows that tongues are not the language of heaven or non-human utterances.

Tongues are foreign human languages. Any speaker with a tongue may easily know in advance whether someone is present in the assembly who understands the particular language which the Spirit communicates to him. Previous tests and experiences place this beyond question. This applies to each of the two or the three speakers who are allowed by Paul at any one service. Each may speak a different foreign human language. Each will know the name of the particular language which the Spirit grants him to speak. A glance tells him whether an interpreter is present or not. If none is at hand, he remains silent. Such interpreters will have interpreted before and will thus be known for their ability by all.

This applies only to such speaking ἐν ἐκκλησίᾳ, "in church," in the public assembly. Outside of the assembly anyone may speak in a tongue all he desires: "and let him speak to himself and to God," literally, "and to himself (emphasis) let him speak and to God (again emphasis)." "Let him speak to himself" does not mean silently, in his own heart, because the word "speak," which is so regularly used with reference to tongues, means audible utterance. Paul tells this speaker "to speak" *ad libitum* in any private way. Yet the sense is not that he and God are to listen to this private speaking. The sense is that this speaking is between himself and God and thus for the speaker's own edification, v. 4, in that his feelings and his desires, finding outlet in his speaking, rise unto God. So much concerning the practical regulations in regard to the use of tongues.

29) Now there follow the regulations in regard to prophecy. **And let prophets speak two or three, and let the others discern.** Paul does not need to repeat "when you come together," v. 26; that is understood. Who the prophets are we know from v. 26: those who have a psalm, a teaching, or a revelation, namely a gift of the Spirit that enabled them to make such an offering for edification of the church.

We again have the restriction as to number: only "two or three." Paul is not in favor of prolonging the public service. More may desire to speak, but an opportunity shall be given to only two or three. Paul does not repeat "at most" in connection with "three," yet he does not do this in order to grant greater liberty to prophecy than to tongues. The omission is made for the sake of brevity. The Corinthians will understand that the limit is to be three. On the other hand, "two or three" does not say that "as a rule or under all circumstances" so many must speak. Paul merely indicates that the rule that applies to tongues and that which applies to prophets are to be the same. By granting as many speakers to tongues as to prophets Paul desires to intimate that he is not unduly restricting tongues and quenching the spirit, I Thess. 5:19. Nothing is said about making a selection, say by the elders, as to who the two or the three are to be. Yet we may assume that such a practice was followed.

"And let the others discern" refers to the other prophets who are present and not to all the others in the assembly. "Discerning of spirits" is a special gift, one which naturally accompanies the gift of prophecy although certain other members may also have it to some degree. The article in the expression οἱ ἄλλοι refers to προφῆται and shows that "the others" are also "prophets." Discerning protects the church against error, whether this is innocently and ignorantly offered to the church, as is often the case, or with conscious opposition to the truth. Luther writes: "What is meant here by 'the others'? Is it the mob? By no means. This means the other prophets who help to preach in the church and to improve the congregation; they are to judge and to help see that preaching is rightly done." Discernment always deals with "spirits" since these are the source from which every prophetic utterance flows; see the remarks on 12:10. The effect is, however, always to reveal the true doctrine as being true and divine, the false as being false and devilish. When we are speaking of the latter we need not think about demonism since all lies and all deceptions emanate from Satan.

30) As the number of speakers is to be limited, so also is the length of the addresses. **And if to another sitting by a revelation is made, let the first be silent.** The speaker, it seems, would stand. If, however, another, while he was seated and thus not speaking by the Spirit's help (note the passive ἀποκαλυφθῇ, the Spirit being the agent back of the verb) thinks of some pertinent word of revelation and rises to utter it to the congregation, either to corroborate or to correct what has just been spoken, the speaker having the floor at the moment is to yield it. It seems that the custom which obtained in the old Jewish synagogues was thus introduced into the churches, namely an edifying discussion by two or three speakers in turn.

31) Paul cuts off every objection that this regulation would quench the spirit of prophecy. **For you can all prophesy one by one that all may learn, and all may be admonished.** Paul addresses the prophets directly, hence he employs the second person. The emphasis is not on "all" but on the verb: You *can* prophesy under this arrangement, do not fear that you cannot. If not at one service, you *can* speak at another, of course, "one by one," and so "all" in turn. After the verb the emphasis is on the κατά phrase (the distributive use of the preposition, R. 606, 608). Paul will have no confusion.

The double ἵνα clause again emphasizes the purpose that is to be served. Paul has employed but one word and has called it edification; here he divides this concept into two parts: "that all may learn," instruction, "and that all may be admonished," application. The verb παρακαλεῖν means to address by urging, admonishing, encouraging, and comforting, all of these interwoven, or one of these features being especially prominent. One of the functions of prophecy is παράκλησις.

32) When Paul directs that speakers with tongues are to be silent in the event that no interpreter is present he intimates that these speakers are able to control themselves. What he only intimates in their case he now states directly in the case of the prophets. **And spirits of prophets are subject to prophets.** These are not spirits which possess the prophets; they are not distinct from the prophets and able to control the prophets as mere instruments. In other words, these are not spirits that compel the prophets to speak at their pleasure so that the prophets cannot help themselves. We have no evidence that such views were prevalent at this time.

In English we should call these spirits of the prophets their souls, the immaterial part of their being which receives impressions from the divine Spirit and from his Word. These spirits are thus subject to their owners, they speak when these will it. Hence a prophet may desire to speak and may have something important to convey which has been given him by the divine Spirit and the Word and yet for good reasons may refrain from speaking. Proper self-control is a virtue that any prophet may well cultivate even today.

33) The fact that the spirits of the prophets are subject to the prophets rests on another and an ultimate fact. **For God is not a God of confusion but of peace.** The two genitives are possessive genitives in the predicate in place of an attribute after the copula, R. 497. Confusion, topsy-turvy doings, do not belong to God. Quite otherwise. But Paul does not add the direct opposite of confusion: God is a God "of good order." Instead of mentioning the direct opposite he mentions the motive or purpose which underlies this opposite: he is a God "of peace," connected with "peace" in the sense of well-being and quiet satisfaction. Confusion is full of sinful zeal ($\zeta\tilde{\eta}\lambda$ος) and contentions ($\check{\epsilon}\rho\iota\delta\epsilon\varsigma$). God does not want the church to

be disturbed and upset by the manner in which his gifts are used; he wants it to grow and to prosper in peace.

The clause: **As in all the churches of the saints,** is by most of the ancients, by Luther, and by our versions connected with the preceding sentence, but nearly all modern exegetes connect it with the following sentence. The statement that God is not a God of confusion but of peace is certainly complete in itself. Why should Paul, in corroboration of this fact, desire to point the Corinthians to all the other churches, i. e., to what takes place in them? If any other church tolerates confusion that church, too, is in disharmony with God just as well as the Corinthians. But regarding the public speaking of women in Corinth, Paul may well refer the Corinthians to the established custom that obtains in all the other congregations. So we construe: "As (the practice is) in all the assemblies of the saints, let the women keep silence in the assemblies," those in which you come together for your public worship. The spirit of individualism which prompts one congregation to do what it prefers although it thereby contradicts its sister congregations and perhaps offends them is foreign to Paul. He ever conserves true fellowship, loving regard for others, inward and outward harmony. In this spirit he points the Corinthians to all the other churches in connection with this question.

34) Paul's prohibition of all public speaking of women in the churches is in the nature of an appendix to his directions about the public use of tongues and of prophecy. All that he says in v. 26-32 applies only to men. **As in all the other assemblies of the saints, let the women keep silence in the assemblies, for it is not permitted to them to speak; on the contrary, let them be in subjection even as also the Law declares.**

Whether they have the gift of tongues or of prophecy makes no difference, in fact, Paul's prohibition is intended for just such. And this prohibition is general and complete. From the little that Paul says we cannot properly infer that this question was acute in Corinth, and that women attempted to speak in the assemblies. The question may have been broached, but no more than this had occurred. Paul only rounds out his instructions and thus anticipates any movement in this direction.

He adds an explanatory γάρ. This order in regard to women does not emanate from Paul personally: "for it is not permitted to them to speak." This right is not "turned over to them," ἐπιτρέπεται αὐταῖς, i. e., it is withheld from them, turned over only to the men. The *Textus Receptus* has the perfect tense: "has not been turned over" and thus is not now (the usual sense of this tense as including also the present), R. 1220. We are told in a moment who withholds this permission. Here the fact alone is stated.

"On the contrary," ἀλλά, "let them be in subjection." The A. V. translates: "They are commanded to be under obedience." This is Paul's own positive conclusion, but it is one which he only repeats and thus makes his own. It has a much older source. On the meaning of the verb here used, ὑποτάσσεσθαι, as well as on the corresponding noun, ὑποταγή, compare Eph. 5:21, 22; I Pet. 3:1, 5; Col. 3:18; I Tim. 2:11, and many other passages: "to be put in array under" (passive), "to put oneself under" (middle).

Paul is referring to sex and does not restrict himself to the relation of marriage; note γυνή and ἀνήρ in I Tim 2:11, etc. This is placed beyond question by the clause: "even as also the Law declares." This is the original authority which refuses to turn over to women the right of speaking in public in Christian assemblies, the authority whose dictum Paul appropriates and reports. "The Law" = the Old Testament as the will and the Word of God. The best answer to the question where and how "the Law" does what Paul says is I Tim. 2:13, 14: "For Adam was first formed, then Eve (the creation of man and of woman, the sexes); and Adam was not beguiled (by the serpent), but the woman, being beguiled, hath fallen into transgression" (by emancipating herself from her concreated subjection and acting with unwarranted independence). Thus the Law, the Old Testament, subjects woman to man by the very act of creation before the fall and again because of the fall, when woman first ignored this subjection.

Paul informs the Corinthians that what is recorded concerning woman in Genesis is not a temporary arrangement but a permanent one that endures as such for the Christian Church. Any act on the part of woman which sets aside her subjection to man is in violation of "the Law," the will of God expressed in creation and stated in his Word. An act of such a nature would be the speaking of women in the public services either in a tongue or in prophecy. Ergo, "let the women be silent in the assemblies." Just how far this prohibition extends is shown by I Tim 2:12: "But I permit not a woman to teach, not to have dominion over a man, but to be in quietness." In many places woman may speak and teach even publicy, but in no place where she will exercise "dominion over a man" by her teaching.

It is unfair to charge Paul with an inferior view regarding woman because he himself was unmarried and to assert that he voices only his own personal opinion when he gives such direction to the Corinthians. Back of Paul is the divine νόμος or Word. And that binds him as well as us. Nor can one say that what Paul wrote was well enough for his time and age which assigned a different position to woman than does ours. If woman is now assigned a different position, this is done, not by God, but by man, and by man in contradiction to God. The claim that the sexes are equal collides with the simple fact that God did not make them equal, and no amount of human claiming can remove or alter the divine fact.

The various questions which are today raised in regard to the place of women in the church find their solution just where Paul found his when the question was touched regarding woman's prophesying or speaking with tongues in public worship in Corinth, namely in the divine principle of the Law. Whatever sphere we may assign to woman in our church practice today dare not contravene her divinely ordained subjection and obedience, for this would conflict with God's own order.*

Some texts place v. 34, 35 after v. 40. One text advances v. 36-40 ahead of v. 34. Some critics even cancel some of these verses. All such questions we

---

* "How the granting of voice and vote to women in all congregational meetings can do anything but place women completely on a level with men in all such meetings and thus gravely interfere with their divinely ordered subjection and obedience, we are unable to see. In all cases where women now have such voice and vote they certainly are on an equality with men in these meetings.—But the matter of voice and vote is one entirely apart from the natural rights of women in the church. Thus in questions of doctrine and conscience sex cannot count in any way, and any woman concerned must be heard. Again, in undertaking important work ordinary wisdom will be enough to go and consult those women whose support should be enlisted. Even in minor matters such as providing a desired service or arranging details concerning which women may well have proper wishes of their own, good sense will meet these wishes on their part. All these things have been done for many a year in the churches without going to the length of placing women on a par with the men in giving them voice and vote in all congregational meetings, and without depriving them in the least of their favored position in the church."—From an Opinion of the Theological Faculty of Capital University, Columbus, Ohio.

leave in the hands of the textual critics who have the proper textual apparatus at their disposal.

35) Women are not even to ask questions in the public assemblies and thus start discussions and in this way secure opportunity to speak publicly. **And if they desire to learn anything, let them ask their own men at home.** The emphasis is on "at home." The translation of our versions: "their own husbands," tends to confuse the English reader, for it leaves the impression that Paul is speaking about the relation of husbands and wives as married people whereas he is speaking about the two sexes as such whether they are married or not.

Paul conceives the congregation as being composed of families in which the women have their family connections, husbands, brothers, fathers, etc. The exceptional case of a lone woman without male connections of any nature in the church is not considered in the formulation of a general directive. There is no need to add in order to meet such exceptions: "Let such inquire of the elders or of friends." It seems that in the early church the custom prevailed to ask questions at the public services, very probably on subjects that were brought up by the prophets. It would thus be natural for the more forward women to claim the privilege of at least asking questions.

The fact that the asking of questions in the open assembly is practically equivalent to speaking publicly before the congregation and is barred for this reason we see from the reason with which Paul supports the order that women should ask at home. **For it is shameful for a woman to speak in church.** The point of this statement is broken off when it is taken to mean: "shameful in the general estimation of people." Paul has no modifier with αἰσχρόν, "shameful." The term does imply that the act mentioned is "shameful," highly improper, in someone's judgment. The only judge to whom Paul has appealed in this entire connection is "the Law," the divine Word, and thus to God himself. So Paul does not mean or imply: "in my judgment, or in that of the churches, or in that of the general public." All these could be discounted; the latter two are also variable. The Corinthians might reply to Paul: "*You* think so, but *we* do not." And the opinions of the general public in matters of this kind, even when they are correct, are decidedly secondary as proof for the church.

36) The two final questions on this subject contain a touch of irony that is intended to sting the haughty Corinthians. **Or was it from you the Word of God went out? or came it to you alone?** Both the "or" are alike, and there is no reason for making the first exceptional and translating it as an exclamatory "What?" as our versions do. In both questions "or" is elliptical: "Or" if this is not your idea, is it this that *from you* the Word of God went out? "Or" if not this, then that *to you alone* it came? The emphasis is as indicated. Both questions are preposterous in a way and even absurd. No congregation is expected to entertain them.

Paul once more reveals what is implied by the term ὁ νόμος in v. 34, namely that God himself is the sender of his Word. The force of the first question lies in the suggestion that the Corinthians perhaps desire to take the place of God and to claim that they formed and sent out the Word. This question is not wide of the mark; people and churches do act in this way. Their actions imply that they know better than God and his Word, for they make God and his Word mean what *they* think they should mean.

The second question is an alternative but has the same force. Yet it does not mean that the Corinthians act as though they were "the mother congregation of Christendom" as some understand this question, and that the Corinthians may thus presume to say what is right or what is wrong conduct for women. Although Paul refers to the practice of other congregations in v. 33 he does not base his directions on the mere custom established in the mother congregation in Jerusalem and on the approval of the daughter congregations that followed. His authority is God and the Word. And his question evidently means: "Are you the only ones in the world who have God's Word and are thus able to tell all others what it contains?" It is ridiculous that any man or any congregation should act in this way. Yet not a few act in this very way. Although throughout all ages of the past God's people have had the Word, these innovators presume to ignore all of them as though they had never existed and now arise to tell us what God's Word contains. They conduct themselves as though they had just received the very first communication that God ever granted to men.

On the strength of Paul's decided imperatives it is usually assumed that the Corinthian women were already speaking in the public assemblies. But Paul nowhere says: "I hear that your women are doing this." Compare 1:11; 5:1; 6:7; 11:18, where Paul states what actually took place in Corinth. This section regarding women resembles 7:12-20, where Paul is warding off a danger instead of correcting an abuse that is already established. As long as Paul does not charge the Corinthian women with speaking in public, Christian ethics compels us to assume that this question had as yet only been discussed, and that no more than this had occurred.

37) The discussion regarding spiritual gifts, which extends through chapters 12-14, is now concluded. All that remains is that Paul affix the seal of authority to what he has written. **If anyone thinks he is a prophet or spiritually gifted, let him make acknowledgment in regard to what I write that it**

is of the Lord. But if anyone does not acknowledge, he himself is not acknowledged. What Paul writes to the Corinthians in chapters 12-14 is "of the Lord." On that score there is no question in Paul's mind. He knows that he has recorded not merely the results of his own reflections and decisions, but that he has written as the *interpres Christi*. "Of the Lord" means under the Lord's direction, that which was promised specifically to the apostles.

Therefore a judgment that the Corinthians may pronounce on what Paul writes is really a judgment, not on Paul, and not on his writing, but on themselves. "If anyone thinks he is a prophet," etc., let him prove that he is not mistaken in regard to himself, "let him make acknowledgment in regard to what I write, that it is of the Lord." If he fails to see the divine character of Paul's words, the proof is conclusive (evidential proof) that this man is no prophet, that he really has no spiritual gift.

Paul proceeds exactly as Jesus did when he spoke with the Jews in John 8:47: "He that is of God heareth the words of God," acknowledges and receives them as such and thus proves his claim to be of God; "for this cause ye hear them not, because ye are not of God," you yourselves furnish the evidence for this conclusion. The word ἐντολή, "commandment" of the Lord (some texts have the plural), should be cancelled because it is an addition to the text. The term πνευματικός is general: one who is possessed of any spiritual gift, who would thus be competent to judge what Paul writes.

38) The reading ἀγνοεῖται, "he himself is not acknowledged," is preferable to ἀγνοείτω, "let him not be acknowledged," i. e., as a prophet and as a man who is spiritually gifted. There is little difference in substance. Between ἐπιγινωσκέτω and ἀγνοεῖται we have the same sharp contrast as in II Cor. 6:9. He who does

not acknowledge that what Paul writes is of the Lord is himself not acknowledged as the prophet and the gifted man he pretends to be. The passive "is himself not acknowledged" should be understood according to the context. Hence it does not mean that the Lord does not acknowledge him, but that Paul and the church do not recognize him as what he claims to be.

The translation: "But if any man is ignorant, let him be ignorant," loses too much of the force of the original. Paul would merely be setting him aside. Men in and out of the church still delude themselves by thinking that they are able to pronounce on the Lord's Word whereas by every such pronouncement they pronounce only on themselves alone, either that they apprehend the Word (for which they deserve acknowledgment) or that they fail to apprehend it (for which they themselves forfeit acknowledgment).

39) The entire matter is now briefly summed up. **Wherefore, my brethren, strive zealously to prophesy and forbid not to speak with tongues.** The first injunction is positive: "Get as much as possible!" The second negative: "Get some of it!" The arrangement is chiastic: verb — object; object — verb. In a masterly way the precise valuation to be placed on each of the two gifts is made plain in the fewest possible words. And these injunctions come with a brotherly appeal and ask to be heeded accordingly.

40) As far as the practical directions are concerned, these are summed up in the same perfect way. **But let all things be done in a seemly way and in due order.** The adverb = in becoming form, *in wohlgesitteter Weise*, which is the opposite of egotistic disorder. The adverbial phrase = according to order, i. e., one speaking at a time, the opposite of confusion.

CHAPTER XV

The Eighth Part of the Letter

The Resurrection of the Dead. Chapter 15

The manner in which Paul introduces this subject indicates that no inquiry in regard to it had been addressed to him. It may be possible that the congregation as such had not as yet become disturbed by doubt regarding the doctrine of the resurrection. While the chapter in its entirety is addressed to all the "brethren" (v. 1, 50), we see that the two central parts, which establish the fact and the manner of the resurrection in answer to wrong views, ascribe these views only to certain indefinitely designated persons, "some among you," v. 12, and "someone" whom Paul calls a "fool," v. 35, 36. Who these indefinitely designated persons were we have no means of knowing.

We need not ask to which of the four parties (1:12) in Corinth these persons belonged; and we cannot conclude that they belonged to the party of Apollos. The view that they belonged to this party has been arrived at by a process of elimination: since Peter, Paul, and Christ taught the resurrection in so decided a manner, the doubters would not belong to those parties; ergo, they must have belonged to the party of Apollos. But this assumes, on the strength of our ignorance concerning the details of Apollos' teaching, that he did not teach the resurrection as emphatically as the others who were made heads of parties. This assumption does not agree with Acts 18:27, 28 and with I Cor. 16:12. We have no right to think that Apollos was less emphatic in teaching the resurrection than any other Corinthian teacher was. We do not know to what party these doubters belonged, or whether they belonged to any party. Paul does not designate them more definitely.

Nor is it likely that the doubters of the resurrection are identical with the moral liberalists whose ideas Paul refutes in 6:12, etc., and against whom he urges the resurrection in 6:14. For if they doubted the resurrection, how could Paul hope to gain anything by pointing them to the resurrection when he was correcting their loose moral views?

Nor can Paul's doctrine of the resurrection be traced to certain mediating views of the ancient Jews. We are, on the one hand, pointed to the rationalism of the pagan Greeks, which simply refused to accept the resurrection of the body but held that the body is only an evil ($κακόν$), or a fetter ($δεσμός$), or a dungeon, yea, a grave for the soul ($σῶμα$-$σῆμα$, "body-tomb"), from which death frees the soul (Orphic teaching and Platonic philosophy). When these Greeks became Christians they readily believed, we are told, the immortality of the soul but balked at the resurrection of the body. We are, on the other hand, informed (very briefly) that according to the popular view the bodies of the dead were thought to arise in their material grossness. Between these two extremes Paul is to steer his course. Yet not independently. We are told that he belonged to "certain Jewish circles" and adopted their teaching concerning a spiritual or ethereal resurrection body which was eventually received by the soul. Paul is thus thought to be fighting against two errors, the Greek spiritualizing, skeptic view and the gross popular, materialistic view. Into this framework the entire chapter is placed. Such is the origin of Paul's teaching.

But those "certain Jewish circles" to which Paul is said to belong probably never existed. Paul's doctrine cannot be traced to any merely human sources. Paul is in agreement with all the other Biblical writers who in one grand chorus proclaim the actual resurrection of the physical body that is deposited in the grave. The bringing forth of this body is the incomprehensible miracle wrought by Almighty God. "I believe in the resurrection of the body" and in no substitute doctrine whether it emanates from "certain Jewish circles" or from another circle.

The structure of this chapter is simple. Verses 1-11 restate the facts of the Christian faith regarding the resurrection of Christ. Verses 12-34 establish the resurrection of the dead. Verses 35-54 answer the question regarding the resurrection body. Verses 55-58 close with a word of triumph and cheer. One fact was in Paul's favor: those who questioned the resurrection of the dead still believed firmly in the resurrection of Christ. If they had denied that they would have departed so completely from the historic foundation of faith that Paul would have treated them as apostates. As it is, Paul makes Christ's resurrection the fulcrum for his presentation of the doctrine that we, too, shall be raised from the dead. Thus the first eleven verses are thetical in form, a restatement of undisputed facts.

I. *Christ's Resurrection, 1-11*

1) The first sentence is masterly in every respect. It fits the situation exactly. Paul does not begin by naming the subject which he intends to treat and by stating why he comes to do so. He starts with a reminder of the pertinent gospel facts on which the faith of the Corinthians rests. Not until he reaches v. 12 do the Corinthians hear that some men in their midst make this entire discussion necessary. This form of presentation is highly effective for securing the fullest and the most unbiased attention.

Now I remind you, brethren, of the gospel which I preached unto you, which also you received, in which also you stand, through which also you are saved: with what statement I preached the gospel to you if you hold it fast, unless you believed in vain.

Since the gospel itself and those parts of it which are here named by Paul are well known to the Corinthians, the verb γνωρίζω, which ordinarily means, "I make known" to you, has the force: "I remind you of." The entire sentence is dominated by the term "gospel." We have the noun "gospel" and the repeated verb εὐαγγελισάμην which means "preached the gospel," and four relative pronouns which have "gospel" as their antecedent. Now the gospel is the mediate source of salvation. Therefore a sentence such as this, every member of which hinges on the gospel, ought to sound exceedingly sweet to the Corinthians. To be so thoroughly reminded of these gospel facts ought to stimulate their faith although they as yet do not know just why Paul makes the "gospel" ring in their ears. This "gospel" is no indefinite good news but the great news of salvation through the mediation of Christ.

The first two relative clauses have verbs in the aorist which state historical facts. They recall the fact that Paul preached this gospel to the Corinthians when he first came to them, and that the Corinthians received this gospel when he brought it to them. The entire story of Paul's first visit to Corinth is thus recalled to the minds of Paul's readers. The last two relative clauses deal with the present, and the tenses of the verbs used are durative: "in which also you continue to stand — through which also you are in course of being saved." The perfect ἑστήκατε is always used with a present meaning. Standing means established and continuing firm in faith as a tree stands when it is well rooted.

The verb σώζειν signifies to deliver or rescue and to place into a position of security, soundness, and joy. The three καί, "also," in the last three relative clauses are cumulative. Upon the first past fact a second is laid, and upon these two past facts two additional present facts are laid, the entire four are great and delightful. Thus a few strokes sketch the entire blessed story of the Corinthians until the moment of Paul's writing.

2) However, neither the gospel in general as gospel, nor the connection of the Corinthians with this gospel, is the point of this reminder which Paul is stating for the Corinthians. All of this is only the preamble to Paul's reminder. Its real point appears in the indirect question: "with what statement I preached the gospel to you." Paul wants to remind the Corinthians of the λόγος, the particular "statement," which he used when he brought the gospel to them. The emphasis is on τίνι λόγῳ and not on εὐαγγελισάμην, which is a mere repetition of this verb. What Paul wants the Corinthians to consider is the particular λόγος or statement in which he embodied the vital substance of the gospel for the Corinthians.

We do not accept those explanations which have λόγος mean intention or manner: "with what intention I preached the gospel to you"; or "in what manner." Nor does λόγος mean "formulation," for in the following verses Paul does not present a formulation but only the facts which he originally preached to the Corinthians as the heart of the gospel. These facts are Christ's death for our sins, his burial, and his resurrection on the third day, v. 3, 4. These facts constitute the "statement" which Paul used in preaching the gospel. The dative τίνι λόγῳ is one of means: "by means of what statement" I preached, etc. Whether Paul used some fixed formula in presenting this "statement" of the facts indicated or used no formula, is unimportant in this connection. All that Paul preached in Corinth, no matter concerning what part of the gospel, centered in his "statement" of the facts of the death, the burial, and the resurrection of Christ. Without this "statement" all else would have been empty and without saving power.

This helps us to establish the construction of the indirect question. Both R. 425 and B.-D 478 point out the fact that it is impossible to draw the indirect question into the conditional εἰ κατέχετε as the A. V. translates: "If ye keep in memory what I preached unto you." To amend the text itself by cancelling the εἰ of the conditional clause and thus securing a new sentence in which κατέχετε governs the indirect question (B.-D.), is too radical to merit attention. The idea of R. 738 that τίνι is an equivalent of the ordinary relative because if an indirect question were to be introduced at this place it would come with a jolt, overlooks the fact that Paul needs this very indirect question — it is the climax of his entire sentence. The construction is simply: γνωρίζω . . . τίνι λόγῳ κτλ., "I remind you . . . by means of what statement I preached the gospel to you." The R. V. has the correct construction although it translates "in what words," plural, which is not accurate enough.

"If you hold it fast," namely this statement of the gospel, merely raises the question, not as a doubt on Paul's part, but as an intimation to the Corinthians to examine themselves on this point. With this condition of reality Paul on his part assumes, and for the entire purpose of his presentation must assume, that the Corinthians do continue to hold fast (of course, not in their memories merely but also in their hearts by faith) what he once preached to them, i. e., the gospel and in particular the statement which embodied the heart of that gospel. Paul thus says: "I take it that you do hold this fast."

Paul sees but one possibility in keeping with which he could assume that the Corinthians no longer hold fast what he preached to them: "unless you believed in vain," ἐπιστεύσατε, an ingressive aorist, pointing to the time when the Corinthians first "came to believe." The adverb εἰκῇ, "in vain," means "at random," i. e., so that your believing led you nowhere, brought you nothing. In the case of a real believer such an assumption is an impossible idea. True faith always brings salvation and a thousand blessed effects connected with this salvation. Regarding the pleonastic ἐκτὸς εἰ μή see 14:5.

This opening sentence is so masterly because its positive half, up to and including the indirect question, is so formulated as to elicit from the Corinthians a decided and an enthusiastic "yea," while its negative half, the condition and the exception, are so formulated as to elicit an equally determined "nay" in regard to even the possibility suggested. This "yea" and this "nay" mutually support each other and coalesce in the unit idea of full certainty. The interpretation that Paul strikes a balance between the two and leaves the issue in doubt as far as the Corinthians are concerned, whether they still abide by the "yea" or after all now tend toward the "nay," is unacceptable. The very opposite is the fact. Doubly supported, once by a "yea" on the part of the Corinthians, and again by a "nay," Paul proceeds.

3) He now restates to the Corinthians the λόγος which embodies the very heart of the gospel which he had preached to them, which they unquestionably hold fast to this day, knowing that their faith is not in vain. "For" is to be taken in this sense. **For I delivered to you in the first place what also I received, that Christ died for our sins according to the Scriptures, and that he was entombed, and that he has**

been raised on the third day according to the Scriptures.

Paul goes back to the time when he first preached in Corinth. At that time "I delivered to you" this λόγος. The phrase ἐν πρώτοις is practically an adverb, "firstly," "in the first place," since it was most important in all his preaching. From the verb παρέδωκα we see what apostolic "tradition," παράδοσις, means, and why it was so termed; it was the teaching given or handed over to the hearers.

The relative clause: "what also I received," is usually stressed to mean that Paul received this λόγος from men, in the same way in which he in turn passed it on to men. It is stated that Paul would otherwise have added "from the Lord" although a reason for this view is not apparent unless the context should demand it, which it does not. The other reasons advanced are less convincing, namely that the verbs "I delivered" and "I received" are parallel, and that v. 3 and v. 11 are parallel, and that Paul mentions only Christ's one appearance to him, that on the road to Damascus. But in Gal. 1:11-2:2 Paul is at pains to prove historically that he did *not* receive his gospel from men in any manner whatsoever, not from the apostles who were the first authorities (for years passed before he even met any of them), and certainly not from ordinary Christians. He declares in Gal. 1:12 that it was "through revelation of Christ." He uses the identical verb παρέλαβον and even adds that he was not taught. In the present passage Paul speaks about the very heart of the gospel: that Christ died for our sins, etc., — this is what he received and not merely the bare historical information that Christ died, was buried, and arose. Compare the notations on 11:23.

Paul is not in this connection committing to writing the entire contents of the gospel or even only a brief summary of it; he is recording "the statement" to which he refers in v. 2 which consisted of the three great facts that follow. The first fact is "that Christ died for our sins according to the Scriptures." "Christ" is not an appellative but a personal name. This Christ did not sink into a state of coma from which he afterward recovered; he actually and truly died, ἀπέθανεν, the aorist to express the historical fact. He died because he was killed. He died because his soul was separated from his body just as men still die today.

His dying, his burial, and his resurrection belong together; the latter of necessity presupposes the other two. But Paul's "statement" is not mere history, it is gospel, therefore he adds "for our sins," ὑπέρ, in behalf of them. Only one thought fits the ὑπέρ phrase, namely that of atonement for sins. Since Paul is writing to Corinthian believers, "our" sins is sufficient in the present connection. Yet this phrase is vital, for without this phrase the Corinthians would not have understood on the occasion of Paul's first preaching, nor would they understand at this present writing, that Christ's resurrection is also meant in a soteriological sense, Rom. 4:3 and other passages. Only because he died as the atoning sacrifice for our sins can the resurrection of Christ redound to our salvation.

The second addition, "according to the Scriptures," namely the Old Testament prophecies concerning his atoning death, removes all thought that Christ died as men ordinarily die. His death is a part of God's wonderful plan for our salvation, Isa. 53, etc. For this reason it was foretold and then occurred as it had been foretold. But "according to the Scriptures" includes everything that was foretold concerning the significance and the efficacy of Christ's death; when Christ died, all of this, too, became everlasting reality.

4) "And that he was entombed" or buried is added without a modifier. Even the Apostles' Creed reads: was crucified, dead, "and buried." This addi-

tion is necessary; first, because it attests the reality of Christ's death, and secondly, because it shows that his death was like ours, for we, too, are buried after death. The latter is important because, like Christ, we who die shall have our bodies raised again. Paul intends to write at length regarding this resurrection of our bodies. Since the entombment is really a part of Christ's death, no modifiers are needed when this statement is added.

The third item of Paul's λόγος again has modifiers: "and that he has been raised on the third day according to the Scriptures." Here the perfect tense after the two aorists is prominent. It draws a sharp distinction, R. 844, "Paul wishes to emphasize the idea that Jesus is still risen," R. 896. The perfect tense normally records a past fact together with its present effect or result. Christ is now and continues to be in the condition of one who was raised from the dead. The addition "on the third day" is positive in regard to the historic reality of the resurrection. It fixes the exact time after the death and thus forms a natural transition to the appearances of the risen Savior. Paul again adds "according to the Scriptures," and this addition has the same force it had with reference to the death; both are equally mentioned in prophecy as cardinal acts in the divine plan of salvation. There is no indication that in v. 3, 4 Paul is reciting a fixed formula such as is found in the Apostles' Creed. We know of no other case in which the wording used is like that which is here employed by Paul.

The question is raised as to whether the phrase "according to the Scriptures" includes only "he has been raised" or also the time, "on the third day." The answer that only Hosea 6:2 and possibly II Kings 20:5, neither of which is quoted to this effect in the New Testament, could be used as proof, is unsatisfactory, for neither of these passages refers to Christ's resurrection. One asks why the miracle wrought for the Prophet Jonah is omitted when Christ himself refers to it in Matt. 12:39, 40 as indicating the length of time which he would remain in the grave.

The mythical notion current among Persians and Jews that for three days the soul remains near the body and does not go to its place until the fourth day, and the supposition that this explains Martha's cry recorded in John 11:34 and the assertions made in Acts 2:27, 31 and 13:35-37 that the body of Jesus saw no corruption during the three days in the tomb, are perhaps referred to in this connection in order to have the account of Christ's resurrection "on the third day" take on the coloring of a myth. Why did the women hurry to Christ's tomb on Easter morning in order to complete the embalming of his body? Because in that climate corruption sets in almost immediately after death, and the women feared that it might have already advanced so far as to render their task impossible. Martha was sure that the body of Lazarus already stank. The body of Christ suffered no decay because, as the passages in Acts inform us, God did not suffer this as he had foretold this through David.

5) Beginning with the very day of Christ's resurrection, Paul records in chronological order a number of appearances of the risen Savior in attestation of the momentous fact of his resurrection. He gives no complete catalog of these appearances, not because he does not know about those which he omits, but because he follows a selective principle. Paul presents those witnesses that are most important to the Corinthians and to the church in general for attesting the historical reality of Christ's bodily resurrection. This he did when he first came to Corinth, and he therefore does the same now.

The suggestion that Paul omits the appearances to the women because the women were witnesses only to the apostles and not to the world, may be correct. But the other suggestion that Paul omits the appearances which had a pastoral import (Luke 24:13, for instance) is contradicted by the very first appearance which Paul records, for this appearance to Peter alone was undoubtedly intended to assure him personally of the Savior's pardon for the sin of threefold denial. This pardon was later (John 21:15, etc.) also pronounced publicly, and Peter was formally reinstated into his office.

And that he appeared to Cephas; then to the Twelve. Then he appeared to above five hundred brethren at once, of whom the most remain until today although some fell asleep. Then he appeared to James; then to all the apostles. And last of all, as to the dead foetus, he appeared also to me.

The verb ὤφθη (ὁράω) is a passive: "he was seen," and is idiomatically construed with the dative as a few of these passives are. It is used also in Luke 24:34, and Paul employs it throughout this catalog of the appearances. Although there is a pastoral purpose connected with the appearance to Peter, namely the assurance that the risen Lord had pardoned his fallen apostle, the event has a much greater importance. The other apostles, with the exception of John (John 20:8), still doubted (Luke 24:22-24); but when Peter reported that he had seen the Lord, they joyfully believed: "The Lord is risen indeed, and hath appeared to Simon." The appearance to Peter is so important because he was one of the apostles, their leader we may say; because he was the first apostle to see the Lord; and because he saw the risen Lord on the very day of his resurrection. Peter is thus the first decisive witness named by Paul.

In connection with this passage a number of unsatisfactory remarks are found in modern commentaries such as that "the flesh" of Christ perhaps remained in the tomb; that Paul fails to use as evidence "the open tomb"; that Acts 10:41 has a materialistic view concerning the risen body; that Christ could not appear in his heavenly δόξα or glory. Paul's and Luke's ὤφθη is also clouded with doubt. It is said to denote "subjective vision" in "the modern psychological sense," a seeing ἐν πνεύματι, "in the spirit" only "like all the heavenly viewings," whereas the verb denotes seeing with the natural eye as any person or any object is seen. Christ also called the other natural senses into activity: "Handle me, and see . . . he showed them his hands and his feet (to touch and to feel) . . . they gave him a piece of broiled fish, and he took it and did eat before them," Luke 24:39-43. Christ asked Thomas to put his fingers into the print of the nails and his hand into the open side, John 20:27. There can be no doubt that Peter saw the very body that was laid in the tomb, that body the identity of which he placed beyond question. Paul will presently describe its new condition which enabled it to pass through the rock of the tomb and through the walls or the locked door of a room.

"Then to the Twelve" is attested also by John 20:19, etc.; Luke 24:36, etc.; Mark 16:14. This occurred late in the evening of the day of the resurrection, immediately after the two disciples from Emmaus had returned and had made their report, Nebe, *Auferstehungsgeschichte* 180, etc. "The Twelve" is used as a standard term, although the defection of Judas had left only eleven, and has no reference to Matthias who later took Judas' place. There is no reason to believe that Paul wishes to include also other appearances of Christ to the Twelve or to a part of their number such as are recorded in John 20:26, etc., and 21:1, etc.

6) Paul next lists the appearance "to above five hundred brethren at once." He does not specify the time or the place of this grand event. He writes only

"then" and begins a new sentence; there is no ὅτι to continue the preceding dependent clauses. It is the great number of the witnesses which is in this instance so important to Paul, more than 500 brethren, and all of these were together at one time and in one place.

None of the evangelists records that so many believers saw the risen Savior at the same time. Yet we have cogent reason for combining Paul's statement with Matt. 28:16, etc. Before his death Jesus tells his disciples in a significant way: "Howbeit, after I am raised up I will go before you into Galilee," Mark 14:28. After the resurrection the angel bids the women to remind the disciples: "And lo, he goeth before you into Galilee," Matt. 28:7. Then Jesus himself meets these women and repeats the direction to the disciples: "Go tell my brethren that they depart into Galilee, and there shall I see them," Matt. 28:10. So we are finally told: "The eleven disciples went into Galilee unto the mountain where Jesus had appointed them," and there he appeared to them and gave them the Great Commission to evangelize the world.

There is no reason for this repeated and emphatic summons to distant Galilee and even to a specific mountain there if only the eleven are concerned, whom Jesus had met twice in Jerusalem, namely on the day of his resurrection and eight days later, Luke 24:36; John 20:26. All is clear when we think that the eleven together with all of the other disciples of Jesus assembled in Galilee for this especially appointed meeting with Jesus. A meeting of this nature could not be held in or near Jerusalem, for in this city there were at most only 120 disciples. It was easier for these to travel to Galilee than for the more than 380 who lived in Galilee to come to Jerusalem, to say nothing of other difficulties.

The occasion fits the number assembled. It was for the purpose of the majestic announcement of the

Great Commission. It was proper that this should be a public meeting which included the entire body of the Lord's brethren. Here, on a mountaintop, this host came together at the appointed time. Word had been circulated among them. Removed from observation by outsiders, all of them assembled. The exact day is unknown. It must have been after the appearance at the Sea of Galilee, John 21:1, etc.; it probably occurred toward the end of the forty-day period.

The gathering on a mountain marks a noteworthy event. On a mountain Jesus preached his great sermon, Matt. 5-7; on a mountain he chose the Twelve; on a mountain he showed himself in the glory of the transfiguration. On mountain heights heaven and earth, as it were, meet, and the risen Savior speaks about his power over heaven and earth. With the vast expanse of the sky above him, and the vast panorama of earth spread beneath him, Christ stands in his exaltation and his glory — a glorious vision, indeed!

An important point in regard to this great number of witnesses who beheld the risen Lord at one time is the fact that, when Paul writes, most of them still "remain," i. e., are alive and continue to repeat their testimony with their own lips. "Though some fell asleep," with its aorist, merely records the fact. Death converted into a sleep is the effect of Christ's resurrection; they died as "children of the resurrection," Bengel.

7) Paul continues: "Then he appeared unto James," who must be one of "the brethren of the Lord" (cousins, as we may take it, of the Lord, sons of Clopas and the Virgin's sister), 9:5, the later permanent head of the congregation at Jerusalem. We have no other record of Christ's appearance to him. His prominence in the church accounts for the fact that Paul mentions him in this list of witnesses. He ranks next to the apostles themselves, Gal. 1:19. We

must conclude that Peter, although he is at first mentioned alone, was among the Twelve, and we must also conclude that the Twelve were among the 500. The Twelve had received Christ's orders to meet him in Galilee, and John 21 shows that they were there. James must have been there also although, like Peter, he is now named alone.

"Then" he appeared "to all the apostles." The term "apostles" is used in a wider sense since it follows the more specific designation "the Twelve." In this wider sense it came into use after the events here recorded when certain assistants of the apostles, like Barnabas, Acts 14:4, 14, like Timothy and Sylvanus, I Thess. 2:6, were at times called "apostles." Just who is included in the present instance we are unable to say although we may well include James. Paul's record suffices for the appearance here listed; no other record of it has been left us unless it be, as Nebe 382 surmises, that more than the eleven were present at the appearance when Christ ascended to heaven.

8) "And last of all, as to the dead foetus, he appeared also to me." This concludes the list of witnesses who were to attest Christ's resurrection to the world. Other appearances such as that to Stephen, Acts 7:55, to Paul, Acts 18:9, etc., had an entirely different purpose. A tone of deep humility accompanies the words "also to me"; it is expressive of Paul's feeling that as a non-believer he had no right whatever to be thus distinguished by the Lord.

This feeling is completely evident in the addition "as to the dead foetus," which our versions misunderstand with their translation "as unto one born out of due time." This strong designation does not intend to repeat the thought that Paul was called to the apostleship rather late, for this is implied in "last of all." An ἔκτρωμα is an abortion, a dead foetus, and not a child born to parents in late life when a birth is no longer expected, nor a child born before the full period of gestation although it is able to survive. The dead foetus is naturally expelled from the womb because it is dead. When Christ appeared to Paul on the road to Damascus, Paul was utterly devoid of spiritual life, a violent persecutor of Christ and of Christ's followers. This is an answer to those interpretations which insert into the figure the *tertium comparationis* of suddenness, of violence, or of absence of means in connection with Paul's spiritual birth. The true *tertium* Paul himself indicates in a moment.

The article has been unduly stressed: "*the* dead foetus," in order to find in this figure a vile name that was applied to Paul by his enemies. Paul is thought to take up this ugly term, in a manner to admit its truth as applying to himself, yet also in part to offer a correction. This is a heavy burden to place on an article. But Paul is not thinking of his enemies in this entire record. We never have difficulty in knowing when Paul deals with his slanderers. In such cases he uses more than an article. Paul himself applies this term to himself and at once tells us in what sense it is to be understood. He uses the article because he intends to say that he alone among the apostles is *the* unworthy one who came to be placed among their number.

9) This is the force of Paul's own explanation. **For I am the last of the apostles, that am not fit to be called an apostle because I persecuted the church of God.** For this reason Paul likens himself to an abortion, to whom the risen Lord nevertheless appeared. "Last," ἐλάχιστος, is a true superlative, R. 279; yet it does not here refer to a point of time as though he was made an apostle long after the Twelve but to the thought of character, as having at one time been a persecutor of the church. He is "not fit to be called an apostle," οὐκ εἰμί, even now as he pens these words; Paul does not write ἦν, "was." What he

once did still haunts him, not as an aspersion cast upon him by others who resurrect his past in order to besmirch him, but as a depressing memory that is still active in his own heart. Others may or may not recall, he himself ever will. The crime is too great: "because I persecuted the church of God." That final genitive "of God" weighs so heavily upon his soul.

Bengel has the correct interpretation: *Ut abortus non est dignus humano nomine, sic apostolus negat se dignum apostoli appellatione.* The *tertium* in τῷ ἐκτρώματι lies in the utter worthlessness, the total unfitness to be called an apostle for the terrible reason assigned. Paul does not say that he is an abortion as far as believers in general are concerned — he is not thinking of this great class of Christians — but as far as the apostles are concerned. They were apostles who had been duly selected and appointed by the Lord after a course of training and preparation. And to them the Lord appeared. Paul was a persecutor of the church, a vile, dead thing spiritually, fit only to be carried out and buried from sight. Yet to *him*, to him while being *such*, the risen Lord also appeared. He, the abortion, placed at the side of these living men, treated, honored, dignified like them by the Lord!

10) But much more must be said. God took this dead, vile thing, the most rabid persecutor of his church, and by his wondrous grace made not only a Christian of him but also an apostle, and not only one who was fit and worthy to be placed at the side of the other apostles but one who outranks the rest in his work, one who labors more abundantly than they all. **But by God's grace I am what I am; and his grace toward me did not prove empty; on the contrary, I did labor more abundantly than they all, yet not I; on the contrary, the grace of God with me.**

The emphasis is on χάριτι Θεοῦ, *Gottesgnade*, without the articles, which absence stresses the quality of each of the nouns. Thus this is "grace" in the fullest sense, the *favor Dei* toward the unworthy and damnable sinner, which by its blessed means of grace removes all the deadly guilt, implants the new life from God, and in the case of Paul elevates him to the apostolate and enables him to do the great work which he did. Only "God's grace" could accomplish such a deed. The abject lowness of the sinner Paul is thus put in overwhelming contrast with the supreme greatness wrought by God. The relative clause: *"what* I am," is not the same as *"who* I am," and not quite οἷος, *qualis,* "of what kind," but "a more abstract idea," R. 713. We prefer to say a more concrete idea, namely all that Paul is as an apostle.

While καί coordinates the next clause grammatically, it really explains what God's grace did with Paul: "and his grace (ἡ χάρις with the article of previous reference) toward me (who originally was such a dead, vile thing) did not prove empty." The verb ἐγενήθη is weightier than the English "was"; the R. V. would reproduce its force by "was not found." The aorist sums up all that this grace proved to be in Paul's case. It demonstrated that it was not κενή, empty, hollow, or without inner substance. This adjective points to the quality of the grace itself. "Not empty" is a litotes for the positive idea "genuine," being in the fullest sense exactly what the term "grace" expresses. The synonymous adjective μάταιος points to the effect, and its negative would mean "useless," not attaining its purpose. The attributive phrase εἰς ἐμέ is made too important in our versions: "which was bestowed upon me." It is only a phrase that is attached to "grace" like an adjective: "his grace toward me." When it came in contact with Paul it proved itself grace indeed.

Over against the negative "not empty" Paul places the strong opposite: "on the contrary," ἀλλά. But he takes only one half of the step in the first clause and reserves the other half for a later clause. After he has said that this grace was not empty, we expect Paul at once to say what this grace actually did to show that it was not empty. This Paul does, but not at once. He first makes a statement that does not directly concern this grace at all but concerns himself: "on the contrary, I did labor more abundantly than they all," namely as an apostle compared with all the other apostles. The verb κοπιάω refers to labor that requires strenuous exertion that tires. Yet this exertion on Paul's part is not the chief point as though Paul put more sensational effort into his work than the other apostles put into theirs. We should combine "labored" with "more abundantly" in the sense that, while Paul put much exertion into his work, he produced greater results than the other apostles, no matter what exertion they put forth.

Only when the fruits of this labor are made the chief point can Paul in the next clause turn about and ascribe everything he has done to the grace of God. To be sure, it was grace that prompted him to work so strenuously, but one may often work with tireless zeal and yet bring forth only meager results. We are not able to say just how much effort the other apostles put forth; it must have been a great deal. No one is able to make a comparison with Paul on this point. For Paul to do so would not be seemly; it would sound too much like self-praise, which is far from Paul's mind. It would also convey the criticism that the other apostles should have worked harder than they did and thus have been equal to Paul. All this disappears when the point of Paul's statement is perceived, namely that he is thinking about the result of his labor. As a matter of mere fact these results are outstanding; witness the record of the Acts and the evidence in Paul's epistles.

Paul intends to say a great deal when he compares results he has achieved with those of the other apostles. Exactly how much? Does he intend to say that he accomplished more than any one of the other apostles or more than *all* of them together? The words as they stand express the latter thought. If Paul desired to say the former he should have added a limiting term: more than "*any one* of them all." In v. 7 πᾶσιν means "all" in the sense of one body, and it is natural to regard αὐτῶν πάντων in the same way. This accords, too, with Paul's intention of praising God's grace in the highest degree and with the facts recorded in the Acts and in the epistles.

Although Paul must truthfully say what he does regarding the results attained by him he does not dream of taking any credit to himself. For there now follows the main statement: "yet not I; on the contrary, the grace of God with me." This contrast of "I" with "the grace of God" is conclusive evidence that Paul thinks chiefly of the results of his labor. It is literally true: grace alone achieved all these results. Paul is not merely ascribing them to grace with a sort of humble generosity on his part. When he thinks of what he originally was and then looks at these results he finds only one explanation: "not I — but God's grace."

Yet the addition σὺν ἐμοί, "with me," is necessary. Compare Mark 16:20; I Cor. 3:9, where this σύν appears in connection with the apostles. It in a way restates what Paul has in mind when he uses the verb "I did labor." In the first part of v. 10 we have ἡ εἰς ἐμέ, the article before the phrase while in the latter part of this verse we have σὺν ἐμοί minus the article. A fine point is involved. The former phrase shows that grace alone is active; the latter that Paul, too, is by no means inactive. Grace and Paul are in association. While the laborer must say, "Thy pound hath gained ten pounds!" this laborer is not the slothful servant who folded his hands and did nothing. If the article were placed before the phrase, we should have: grace alone and not I in any sense did labor. Our versions translate as though Paul has used the article; they may not intend to convey the sense we have indicated but may have translated thus only to attain a smoothness of diction. It would, however, be a mistake to picture God's grace and Paul's effort as two horses together drawing a wagon, *C. Tr.* 907, 66, for the two are not coordinate. Paul's effort is, in the last analysis, due to God's grace, and it is put forth only as long as the Holy Spirit rules, guides, and leads him.

Verses 9 and 10 are a digression. But it is not Paul's purpose to defend himself and his office against opponents in Corinth. To attach such a defense to a statement concerning Christ's appearance to him on the way to Damascus would be strange indeed. Moreover, these two verses do not constitute a defense. Paul is moved to add this disgression as an expression of his inmost feeling in response to the greatness of the grace vouchsafed to him. When he thinks back to that great moment near Damascus and to all for which God has since used him he is overwhelmed with humble, shamefaced gratitude and joy; he must worship and magnify the grace that wrought it all by using him.

11) After this digression οὖν returns to the main thought. **Whether, then, I or they, so we are preaching, and so you did believe.** This brings the presentation of the grand testimony regarding the resurrection of Christ to its conclusion. Paul's thought runs to one point: no matter which of these competent witnesses the Corinthians examine, no matter to which of these notable heralds they listen, they will always hear the identical testimony and proclamation: "The Lord is risen; he is risen indeed!" We

have no reason to find in the juxtaposition of "I" and "they" more than a natural emphasis on each pronoun; it is certainly not an effort on Paul's part, by a pointed contrast between himself and others, to squelch derogations on the part of personal opponents.

The two adverbs "so" indicate manner. "So" = by announcing these facts we do our preaching; and the second "so" = by relying on these facts you did your believing until this time.

The difference in the tense of the two verbs is marked. The present tense is simple: "we are preaching," i. e., continue to do so right along. More must be said regarding the aorist ἐπιστεύσατε. It is usually regarded as being ingressive: "so you came to believe" when this λόγος (v. 2) was first preached to you. The reason assigned is that in v. 2 this same aorist is regarded as being ingressive, and v. 11 is taken to be a repetition. Yet when Paul repeats he nearly always varies the thought in some way. We may accept the ingressive idea in regard to v. 2, although the aorist may well summarize the entire course of believing until the present moment (constative). In the case of v. 11, however, we have a definite reason for thinking of the more extensive constative sense.

The aorist ἐπιστεύσατε follows the durative present κηρύσσομεν, and the two verbs are correlative: preaching is intended to engender believing, believing is the normal response to preaching. If the preaching is durative, we may well expect that the correlative believing will match this continuous preaching. Paul could have used the present tense to express this thought: "so you are believing" right along. But the constative aorist does more. "We are preaching" means: as long as we preach at all. No matter whether men refuse to believe or are willing to believe, we do not stop preaching "so." The constative aorist puts the matter of believing differently. It sums up the believing of the Corinthians from its inception to the present moment and stops with that moment. What about continuing? The present tense would include the continuation; it would go on indefinitely. By pointing the Corinthians to the present moment the constative aorist bids them ask: "What shall we do from now on?" And that is exactly the question at issue in this chapter. Voices in Corinth are questioning the resurrection in general. If they are right, then Christ is *not* risen, and all of this testimony adduced by Paul is false. Then the Corinthians must change what they have believed until this moment. We thus conclude that the aorist used in v. 11 is plainly constative.

The introduction to the grand subject has been concluded, the foundation for what follows has been laid. The very center of the Christian faith has been emphasized. Throughout this presentation the question must have come into the minds of the Corinthian readers: "Why?" This ample introduction is bound to arouse their attention to a high degree. Paul has purposely withheld all intimation as to what his purpose and aim may be. Psychologically this is perfect. It enables the Corinthians, even the doubters among them, to give their undisturbed attention to the central fact on which their faith rests and in their inmost hearts to reaffirm the faith they have held to the present moment. No deflecting thought has had an opportunity to disturb this reaffirmation. No one could say regarding what Paul has thus far written: "Yes — but!" This is what so many minds are inclined to do (because of the flesh) when they see in advance whither some great truth would lead them — they begin to hesitate about fully accepting that truth even though they have held it thus far. Paul successfully checks such foolish proceeding on the part of the Corinthians. Now, with their faith in Christ's resurrection again rising full and strong in their hearts, he flashes on the screen with one vivid sentence the startling, utterly unfounded denials at which this entire introduction has aimed from the very beginning. The effect produced must have been very strong when Paul's words were first read in Corinth.

II. *Our Resurrection, 12-34*

12) First, the question of surprise which is followed by all the negative deductions that it contains, v. 12-19. Then the affirmation of triumph with all the glorious truth it involves, v. 20-28. Finally, the application with its questions, protestation, and admonition, v. 29-34.

The connective is only the mild transitional δέ. **Now if Christ is preached that he has been raised from the dead, how are some among you saying that there is no resurrection of (the) dead?** The condition is one of reality, for Paul assumes beyond fear of contradiction that Christ is so preached, namely by all of the apostles, in fact, by all Christian preachers and prophets. He is being so preached even in Corinth at this very time. "Christ" is used here as it was in v. 3, the person is named according to his office. The passive "is preached" is broad and general and very appropriately omits all reference to the persons engaged in this work since the preaching and its substance are now the only issue. The Greek loves the personal construction, R. 658: "Christ is preached," and as an apposition to "Christ" the clause which states what is preached is added.

Paul puts this into compact form: "that he has been raised from the dead." The perfect tense is explained in v. 4. The passive voice implies that God is the agent who raised Christ. The Scriptures make both statements: that God raised Christ, Rom. 6:4; 8:11; Matt. 16:21; 17:23; 26:32; and that Christ himself arose, Mark 9:21; Luke 18:33. In both expressions the act is due to the divine power which is Christ's equally with the Father. Jesus has power to lay down his life and to take it back again, John 10:18. The apostle properly uses the passive here and makes God the agent because of the parallel which he has in mind regarding our resurrection, which is the work of God.

In the phrase ἐκ νεκρῶν note the absence of the article, which absence stresses the quality of the noun: dead people, being dead, so that the sense is "from death." The idea contained in ἐκ is that of separation, R. 598. This phrase occurs 35 times with reference to Christ, a few times with reference to other individuals; it is also used in a figurative sense. Two passages refer to the resurrection of many, and in these this standard phrase can have no other meaning than the one indicated.

Certain chiliasts speak of two resurrections: one at the beginning and one at the end of the millennium. To support this teaching they take ἐκ νεκρῶν to mean: "from among," "out from among the dead." In their literature on this subject they print the Greek and point to the Greek preposition, which aims to impress those who know little or no Greek. This gives the appearance of reproducing only the literal meaning of Scripture but in reality misses the literal meaning. There is no article: "from *the* dead" in the Greek. The idea contained in this phrase is not that, when Christ arose, he left all the other dead behind; a student of Greek does not think of the other dead when he reads this phrase, nor has he a right to do so on the basis of this phrase. Christ came out of death and re-entered life; that is what the phrase literally and actually conveys.

No wonder, then, that this phrase is never used with reference to the ungodly; such a use, to say the least, would be misleading. When the ungodly are called forth from their graves, this summons is not an escape from death on the part of their bodies but an entrance of their bodies upon a state that is far worse than the decay in the grave. Yet some chiliasts make much of the absence of this phrase with reference to the ungodly.

It is easy to feel the surprise expressed in Paul's question: "How say some among you," etc.? Who these who are designated by the indefinite pronoun "some" are we have no means of knowing; see the introductory remarks to this chapter. Since the Corinthians were Greeks they would be inclined to philosophic ideas and reasonings. It seems safest to assume that these deniers of the resurrection were a few educated members of the congregation who revived some of the views that were advocated by Greek pagan philosophers. What such philosophers thought on the subject is shown by Acts 17:32. These doubters in Corinth were Christians, for, like the entire congregation, they, too, believed the resurrection of Christ. For this reason, when he aproaches the subject, Paul makes sure that this essential point remains unshaken. If Christ arose, then the resurrection is established, for then it has already begun.

These doubters set up the proposition "that there is no resurrection of the dead," that such a thing could not be, namely a rising up to life of bodies that are dead and buried. The verb λέγουσιν means that they were making this assertion. No articles are used with ἀνάστασις νεκρῶν, *Totenauferstehung*, which gives this proposition an academic sound. Of course, if it were allowed to persist it would soon become much more. Paul is nipping this error in the bud. How this wrong theoretical proposition became established in the minds of these men Paul does not indicate, he deals only with the claim as such.

Human reason always finds objection to this wonderful doctrine and in one way or another attempts to show that it cannot be true. Paul sees at once what others at first apparently failed to see: the resurrection in general cannot be denied without ultimately advancing to a denial also of Christ's resurrection. Both stand and fall together. What the denial of the latter implies is no less than destruction of the entire faith of the congregation, i. e., the abolition of the gospel in all its parts. This terrible result is the weapon which Paul uses to crush the incipient error in Corinth and to establish and to safeguard the truth.

13) The logical basis of Paul's reply is absolutely unassailable: a universal negative cannot be established if one fact to the contrary exists. Thus the single fact of Christ's bodily resurrection once for all invalidates the assumption that denies the bodily resurrection in general. But instead of applying this incontestable proof at once, Paul first analyzes the negative proposition and points out all that it necessarily involves. It is far more than an academic or abstract idea. It is a deadly fountain from which a poisonous stream flows. By establishing Christ's resurrection the fountain as well as the stream are swept out of existence.

But if there is no resurrection of (the) **dead, neither has Christ been raised.** Paul restates the Corinthian denial in the words already used and then adds the first terrible deduction. This plain and self-evident deduction must have come to the first readers with a shock. The condition is one of reality in which the negative is normally οὐ, R. 1011, etc.; and the perfect tense in the apodosis makes no difference, R. 1008; regarding the tense see v. 4. The resurrection deals with the body. Christ's body was given into death on the cross and then, like any dead human body, was placed into the tomb. He was flesh of our flesh, bone of our bone, and in this respect altogether one with us although in person he was the Son of God. So it cannot be argued that he was a different and a higher being and therefore exempt from the rule that the dead are not raised. The apostle also disregards such an evasion of the point.

14) The second deduction is linked up with the first. **But if Christ has not been raised, then our proclamation is empty, your faith also is empty.** This is again a condition of reality with οὐ, and the perfect tense is now used in the protasis, and ἄρα occurs in the apodosis to indicate the evident nature of the conclusion. This conclusion naturally extends in two directions, that of the apostolic proclamation, and that of the Corinthian faith. The noun τὸ κήρυγμα corresponds with the verb κηρύσσειν used in v. 11, 12 and denotes the contents of the announcement. The proclamation and the faith are correlative, for the proclamation is intended to engender faith, and faith rests on the proclamation. If Christ were not raised, if Christ were dead forever, both the proclamation and the faith would be "empty," hollow, like a nut without a kernel. All gospel preaching, every assertion and every promise which are a part of the gospel, would be a mere sound of words without reality back of them. The same would be true regarding faith or confidence that is made to rest upon such preaching. In plain language, the preaching would be a lie, and the believing would be trusting in a lie. The preachers would be like those who sell fake stocks, and the believers like those who buy fake stocks. The Greek makes the two predicate adjectives κενόν and κενή strongly emphatic by their position: "*empty* then our proclamation, *empty* also your faith."

15) A third deduction is linked up with the second. **Moreover, we also are found false witnesses concerning God because we bore witness against God, that he did raise Christ whom he did not raise, if so be that the dead are not raised.**

"Moreover," δέ, adds a new and different point, and καί adds the idea that this means nothing less than false witnesses. The entire proclamation rests on testimony, that of chosen witnesses concerning the reality of Christ's resurrection, v. 5-8. If this proclamation and the faith resting on it are false, then these witnesses are "pseudo-witnesses," liars, and all of their testimony is nothing but a lie. That is reprehensible when the witnesses and their testimony deal with ordinary matters of this life; but it is infinitely worse when they deal with God himself and with the acts of God. The genitive in the expression "pseudo-witnesses of God" is not subjective, for God never testifies through false witnesses — a monstrous thought. This genitive is objective: "false witnesses concerning God," who testify falsely about him.

This is fully corroborated by the next clause: "because we bore witness against God, that he did raise Christ whom he did not raise." "We are found" means: we are now (present tense) exposed, discovered to be, just plain lying witnesses. This is the plain proposition which all of those must accept who today deny the reality of the bodily resurrection of Christ. They can maintain their denial only by making all of the witnesses who beheld the risen Savior (from Peter downward to Paul) liars. Besides, they make also the ancient prophets liars, who bore a witness that God himself had told them, namely, that he would raise up the Messiah whom he never intended to raise up. Yet this blasphemous denial is today made from many pulpits which claim the Christian name. They may tone down their statement by saying that the prophets were subjective liars who did not know that they were lying; but a well-intentioned liar is often much worse than a conscious liar.

Paul states more than the simple reason that these witnesses could be exposed as liars. He recapitulates and in typical Pauline fashion reverts to his original proposition, namely that some say there is no resurrection of the dead. Thus the entire presentation of v. 12-15 is combined into a compact unit. "Because we bore witness" has the aorist which states the past fact as such. This may be simply the historical aorist, yet even as such it is constative, for Paul has just repeated this testimony in v. 5-8 *in extenso* and has included his personal testimony. So this aorist sums up into one point all of the testimony which the chosen witnesses uttered concerning the Lord's bodily resurrection.

All of this testimony would be κατὰ τοῦ Θεοῦ, which is to be rendered "against God" and not "of God" as is done in our versions. The preposition does not mean "against" but "down upon." It is used with the genitive after verbs of swearing, this is perhaps done because the hand was placed down upon the thing on which the oath was taken. So when the oath was taken on God himself instead of on some object, the preposition was retained, R. 607. Paul makes no mention of an oath on the part of the witnesses whom he indicates. Their witness itself, dealing, as it does, with God and with Christ, is sacred testimony of the highest degree. There is no need to swear by God that God raised up Christ.

The direct contradiction between the testimony and the fact (if the contention of the Corinthian deniers is, indeed, true) is sharply put: "that he did raise Christ whom he did not raise, if," etc. The verbs and their objects are arranged chiastically: verb — object; object — verb. This places all the emphasis on the verbs: "*did* raise — *did not* raise"; an absolute yea against an absolute nay. Of course, this clash of the yea-testimony with the nay-facts exists only on the condition "if so be that the dead are not raised." In the compound εἴπερ, πέρ has the note of urgency by stressing the "if": "if so be," "if indeed," R. 1154. Paul, as it were, lays his finger on this evil "if" as if to say: "Yes — if!" The moment this "if" disappears, the clash between the testimony and the fact vanishes like a painful mirage, and the testimony is seen to reflect the fact and nothing but the fact. The addition of ἄρα emphasizes the close connection between the "if" clause and the main clause, "because," etc.

Three points have been noted that deserve attention: 1) the identity of the category into which Paul places Christ's bodily resurrection and our own bodily resurrection; 2) the sacredness of the apostolic testimony regarding the former; 3) Paul's fanatical self-delusion if the appearance of Christ to him is, indeed, a psychological hallucination which makes his own spiritual transformation and his entire gospel rest on this delusion and on the pitiful mental weakness that made such a delusion possible.

16) One series of deductions has been concluded. A second series must be unfolded in order to display still more fully the fateful consequences that lie hidden in the Corinthian error. This second series corroborates (γάρ) the first. Paul again begins as he did in v. 13 and correlates Christ's resurrection with that of the dead generally. **For if the dead are not raised, neither has Christ been raised.** This is the key to the preceding and again the key to the following. Both verbs are true passives as are those occurring in v. 12-14 and at the end of v. 15, all stress the agency of God. The present tense ἐγείρονται resumes the same tense that occurred at the end of v. 15: if the dead "are not raised," it is a gnomic present (R. 866) that is always timeless and is often used in doctrinal statements as in the present instance. Its best commentary is the noun found in v. 12: there is "no resurrection of the dead." The perfect tense of the verb used in the apodosis is explained in v. 4.

17) From the first deduction, which is now made for the second time, Paul hastens to the second. **But if Christ has not been raised, your faith is useless, you are yet in your sins.** This deduction has been made already in part in connection with the preaching mentioned in v. 14, where both the preaching and the faith are said to be "empty." But more must be said. So Paul takes up this deduction independently and expands it and also follows it with two further deductions along the same line, v. 18, 19.

In v. 14 Paul says: your faith is κενή, "empty," hollow, without a reality on which to rest. Here he says: your faith is ματαία, "useless," idle, it gets you nothing. Our versions use "vain" to translate both synonyms, which obscures the important difference. Bengel: κενή, *sine vera re*; ματαία, *sine usu*. Only because faith is regarded as "useless" can Paul add the next clause: "you are yet in your sins." For faith is to benefit us, bring us something, namely the greatest of all treasures, the forgiveness of sins. If it brings us nothing it is "useless." On the other hand, faith is "empty" when the Word to which it clings is untrue, unreal. Though it cling ever so firmly it grasps only an empty shadow, a delusive lie. The two ideas are clearly distinct, yet they are also closely related, for a faith that is empty and rests on empty air is for that very reason also of no use whatever.

This uselessness is made evident by the statement: "you are yet in your sins," in your guilt and condemnation; compare John 8:21. To be in our sins = in their deadly sphere where all of our sins surround us and accuse us before God as so many deadly wolves about to tear us to pieces. Make the Savior what you please, if he failed to rise from the dead he is useless, for he cannot free us from our sin, the one thing for which we need a Savior. If there is no resurrection, there is also no redemption, no reconciliation with God, no justification, no life and salvation. If Christ is still dead, then every believer is still dead in trespasses and sins. As long as Christ, our surety, is not released, it is certain that our debt is not paid, we are still liable, no matter how much we may trust in some supposed payment or in some release without payment. Christ's resurrection is the positive proof that his sacrifice was, indeed, sufficient and fully accepted by God. Therefore, Christ was raised for our justification, Rom. 4:25. To reject his resurrection is to reject the efficacy of his sacrifice, and the death which he died is just as useless as our faith in such a dead Christ.

18) The second deduction already includes a third: **and accordingly they that fell asleep in Christ did perish.** In the New Testament Greek ἄρα is not always postpositive. It denotes a correspondence with the preceding: "accordingly," and καί adds this corresponding point to the one that precedes. When Paul wrote this letter near Easter of the year 57, some of the Corinthians had already died, believing and trusting in Christ to the end.

Paul uses the significant designation: "they that fell asleep in Christ" (11:30). The substantivized participle is qualitative and describes these persons by stating this one past act of theirs, hence it is an aorist; the passive form is to be taken in the sense of the middle. But note well, "in Christ," in union with him by true faith. To fall asleep in Christ is the beautiful Scriptural expression to designate the Christian's death; his body sinks into peaceful slumber presently to be awakened by the risen Lord to a new and a glorious life in his presence. This very designation is already a denial of the Corinthian error, a clear testimony to the heavenly hope of the resurrection of the dead at the last day according to Christ's promise.

One word reveals the tragedy like a blow: ἀπώλοντο, second aorist middle, "did perish." When these believers closed their eyes in death, at that moment they perished completely and forever with body and with soul. We also say that they are lost or damned. The sense is the same. In this crushing way Paul brings home to his readers what the denial of the resurrection really involves. He who persists in this denial writes over every believer's tomb: "Lost!" or, what amounts to the same: "Damned!" Nothing more heart-rending could be said. The entire hereafter is shrouded in the blackest night. This blackness has swallowed up those who have passed beyond and waits to swallow up those whose life is now swiftly passing away. And this some foolish Corinthians, whether they realize it or not, were putting in place of the light and the hope that shine beyond the grave for every believer.

The verb "to perish" has been stressed to mean "to be annihilated," to be deprived of existence. This has then been taken to mean that no hell or no hell-fire exist for the wicked. But in sacred language ἀπολλύμενος means perishing by losing salvation in contradistinction to σωζόμενος, being saved by obtaining salvation. He who perishes is forever separated from God, heaven, eternal life. His body and his soul share the fate of Satan in the eternal torment of hell. For an examination of all the pertinent passages see C.-K. 787, etc.

19) As he did in the case of the first series of deductions in v. 13-15, so in the case of this second series Paul draws a summary. This second summary reaches back and includes all that precedes in regard to faith in Christ. **If we are such people only as have hoped in Christ in this life we are of all men most pitiable.** The condition contemplates reality. We should note the position of μόνον which is placed emphatically at the end of the εἰ clause. This implies that it is not to be construed with the ἐν phrase as is done in our versions: "in this life only." The adverb

modifies the entire clause or, what amounts to the same thing, the predicate ἠλπικότες. This participle with the following ἐσμέν is not a circumscribed perfect tense but a simple predicate with the copula.

Paul describes the Christian believers from the standpoint of death, i. e., the death which causes them to perish. They are people who had hope throughout their earthly life from the moment they came to faith and to the hope embodied in faith; but their death reveals that this their hope was an illusion. That is the type of people they are. The perfect participle conveys the idea that they at one time embraced this hope and then clung to it until they died. "In Christ" connects the activity of hoping with Christ and with all for which he stands. The fulfillment of the hope rests in him.

If this is all that we are, people who have cherished an illusion until the hour of their death, then "we are of all men most pitiable." This, of course, implies that all who are without faith and hope in Christ, all non-Christians, are certainly also pitiable. They live and die without God and hope in this world. But it is still more pitiful, because it is far more tragic, to have a great hope in the heart throughout life, to shape the whole life according to that hope, to crucify the flesh, to war against temptation, to bear the cross, to suffer reproach and many other ills for the sake of this hope, and then in the end to have that hope turn out to be an iridescent bubble, a vacuous dream. This is Paul's commentary on a Christianity that exists for this life only without regard to what is to come thereafter. Yet this is the type of Christianity that not a few seek to popularize at the present time. A Christianity without a risen Christ and the sure and certain hope of our resurrection from the grave, whatever men may say in laudation of its moral influence and its good works, is worse than none.

First Corinthians 15:19

The logic which Paul employs in this paragraph has been challenged as being merely an argument *ad hominem* or as being a mere appeal to the emotions, which is effective only for certain people in a subjective way. Preachers are also cautioned in regard to their Easter message; they are told that they must remember that Paul's logic is unsound. Let us examine this challenge. Logical deduction starts with an admitted proposition. Here it is the proposition: "There is no resurrection at all." This the Corinthian doubters believe and assert. They are thus bound to accept every necessary deduction that is involved in that proposition. That is the logic of this case. Unless these doubters are ready to accept these necessary deductions they are forced to drop their proposition or to alter it so that those deductions do not follow.

Now what does Paul do? Make emotional appeals? Not for one moment. In his entire presentation not one emotional term is found. Argue *ad hominem?* That means to single out some admission that is made only by these doubters and by this admission to assail their proposition. In his entire presentation Paul singles out nothing incidental; he adheres absolutely to the original proposition in its true and genuine sense as maintained by these doubters. The deductions which he draws are simple, clear, inescapable. In fact as well as in logical thinking they *must* ever be drawn. Beyond the shadow of a doubt every deduction lies in the original proposition. This is true logic, unassailable and deadly. It could not be truer or stronger. This has been recognized throughout all the centuries. Unless he wishes to discredit himself, no commentator can at his late date call Paul's deductions unsound.

The logicians (Taylor's *Logic;* Reiser's *Humanistic Logic*) define the *argumentum ad hominem* as an attack on the character of the opponent instead of on the contention of the opponent. We submit that this would be no *argumentum* at all even as such attack on character is used only when men have no real argument. When the wicked Jews had no argument whatever they shouted that Jesus was a Samaritan, that he had a devil, and finally picked up stones to stone him. Vilification and personal attack should not be called *argumentum ad hominem*. Needless to say that Paul is here using nothing of this kind. He is using sound deduction. He is using not even *argumentum ad hominem* in the true sense of the term, namely an argument based on some admission of his opponents.

Paul's argument is called a *reductio ad absurdum* by some. But this is a misconception. The end of Paul's logical chain is not in any sense an absurdity. It is the height of tragedy. It evokes no laughter; it leaves us shocked and dismayed because of what the Corinthian doubters maintain in their original proposition. All of Paul's deductions are negative. Each deduction is a negation in form as well as in fact. The deductions must of necessity be negative because the original proposition is a universal negative: "There is *no* resurrection of the dead." Paul's logic is as sound and as inevitable as are the negative syllogisms of Jesus in John 8:39, 40, 47.

20) By means of his deductions Paul has pitilessly pursued the Corinthian error to its last, desperate conclusion. He has welded about that error a chain so ponderous and unbreakable that it lies fettered forever, never again to free itself and to harass believers. Logic, the genuine logic of reality, however, requires one additional thing: the demolition of the universal negative that there is *no* resurrection by means of the tremendous, undeniable, and admitted fact that Jesus Christ did rise from the dead. Even the Corinthian doubters knew and admitted this fact. Something had blinded their eyes so that they failed to see that this

one fact destroyed their entire proposition regarding the resurrection.

With a sudden dramatic turn, which is as effective as all of the reasoning by deduction which Paul employs, he hurls the great Easter fact at the Corinthian error. It has throughout trembled for expression in his own heart and no doubt also in the hearts of the Corinthians when they heard these inexorable lines read in their assembly. But Paul does far more than merely to introduce the fact of Christ's resurrection as it took place on Easter morning. That fact, which is merged with our coming resurrection, transports Paul's mind to the end of time, to the final triumphant consummation when "God shall be all in all." Only when Christ's resurrection is thus seen in its glorious connection with the final consummation is its full significance apprehended.

But now Christ has been raised from the dead, first fruits of them that are asleep. Paul simply announces the great fact. He has already recorded the full historical evidence for it in the first paragraph of the chapter, and that evidence forever attests the fact. "But now" — thank God what a relief! Compare Rom. 3:21 for an exact parallel; "now" refers, not to time, but to the thought. "Christ has been raised," the tense is the same as that used in v. 4. "From the dead" is explained in v. 12. Like a climber in the Alps, who trembles on the brink of some bottomless gulf with the rock already crumbling beneath his feet suddenly finds himself at a turn where the path stretches safe and wide before him, so we feel when, after the journey through verse 19, we step across into verse 20.

All of the deductions which Paul has knit so tightly he now unravels with one motion. All of them are false because the original proposition is false. They collapse like a house of cards when the breath of truth is blown upon them. The exact opposite of all these dreadful deductions is true. And more, infinitely more, is true — because Christ has been raised from the dead. He was raised, not like Jairus' daughter, the widow's son at Nain, or Lazarus at Bethany, to walk again in this life and to pass through death a second time, but he was raised by the glory of God, lifted up into the glory which he had in the beginning with the Father (John 17:5), with a name that is above every name (Phil. 2:9).

Highly significant to all who believe in him is the apposition added to "Christ": "first fruits of them that are asleep." The figure of "the first fruits" suggests the image of a great harvest which is ushered in by the first sheaf that is presented as an offering to God, Lev. 23:10. The noun is singular in the Greek, but the English idiom prefers a plural. "First fruits" has no article since the term is general. The figure occurs regularly in the New Testament, I Cor. 16:15; Rom. 11:16; 16:5; James 1:18; Rev. 14:4. Its connotation is that of certainty: as certainly as Christ was raised, so certainly shall we be raised. For as the first sheaf cannot be harvested and offered unless the entire harvest is ripe and ready, so Christ cannot be raised unless all of us believers are ready to be raised also. God sees us as being thus ready. The interval of time does not count with him. The dead believers are called "they that are asleep," the perfect participle is somewhat different from the aorist used in v. 18: they that have gone to sleep and now slumber. Compare also v. 6. Paul, of course, writes only concerning Christians.

The three persons whom Christ raised to life during his earthly ministry cannot be referred to as constituting a part of the great resurrection since they had to undergo death a second time and are now among those that sleep. Enoch and Elijah were translated bodily to heaven and did not die at all. Paul makes no reference to the saints that arose after Christ's resurrection and appeared unto many in the holy city, Matt. 27:52. Christ alone is the "first fruits"; and with him the great and final resurrection has actually begun.

21) By way of explanation (γάρ) Paul unfolds what lies in the significant apposition: "first fruits of them that are asleep." **For since by man death, by man also resurrection from death.** All of the nouns are without articles, and no verbs are employed. This means that each noun is stressed as to its quality, and that the weight of meaning lies wholly on the nouns. We have difficulty only in rendering the last genitive νεκρῶν into English, for we cannot say "resurrection of dead" like the German *Totenauferstehung* but must use the article: resurrection "of the dead," or reproduce the sense: resurrection "from death." We have no right to insert verbs, either "came" in both statements as our versions do, or "came" in the first and "shall come" in the second as R. 395 and others do. Paul does no more than to fix this exact parallel: man the death medium — man also the resurrection medium. There is a reason for this parallel to which Paul points with "since"; but what this reason is he withholds for the moment.

We are told that Paul draws this parallel on the basis of an ancient apocalyptic principle which is basic to all ancient apocalyptic thought, namely that the start of time and the end of time must correspond. We are told that Paul adopted this thought and so drew the parallel: Death through man at the start — resurrection through man at the end. The answer is that, if Paul had drawn from such turbid sources as Jewish apocalyptic fancies, he could never have penned this divine chapter.

22) A second γάρ explains still further. **For even as in Adam all go on dying, thus also in Christ**

all shall be made alive. Now we know whom Paul has in mind when he twice writes in v. 21: "through man." The one man is Adam, the other man is Christ. He even places the article before each name (which the Greek allows but not the English) in order to mark each of these two persons as being well known.

But Paul now changes the prepositions. From διά which he used in v. 21, which makes each person only a medium, he advances to ἐν, which makes each person a sphere, one circle being drawn by Adam, the other circle being drawn by Christ. R. 587 scarcely does justice to this preposition when he renders it "in the person of" the Adam (whom we all know) and "in the person of" the Christ (whom we all know). For this rendering does not agree with the verbs which Paul now uses and with the force of their tenses.

Paul states a fact that is connected with each of the two notable persons whom he has named. Just as in v. 21 he bids us not to look for verbs, so he now fixes our attention upon two verbs which he himself writes. Paul does not say that "in the person of Adam" all died, i. e., when death struck him, and likewise that "in the person of Christ" all came to life, i. e., when he arose and came to life. R. 827 himself calls the tense of the first verb, ἀποθνῄσκουσιν, a frequentative present: "they go on dying." This is correct, for Paul states the fact: a continuous process of dying. This tense is, therefore, not a timeless gnomic present. In Rom. 5:12 Paul makes an entirely different statement, namely that in the one sin by which Adam fell all men sinned, and that thus by that one sin death came upon all men. In other words, Adam's one sin was the death of all of us. In Romans, Paul therefore uses aorists; but here in Corinthians he has the iterative present. In Romans he stresses the historic fact that occurred in the tragedy of Eden, in Corinthians the continuous fact that progresses from Eden to the last day.

In the statement regarding Christ, Paul cannot use another present tense and say: "thus also in Christ all go on being made alive," i. e., in the person of Christ who arose on the third day. For this is not the fact. Paul is speaking about those who die, whose bodies are laid in the grave as a result of the process of dying which he has just mentioned. These bodies remain dead — Paul himself says they are asleep. Whenever this sleeping is mentioned it, of course, refers to the bodies of believers and never to their souls, for these do not sleep. Paul uses a future tense, ζωοποιηθήσονται, which R. 872 rightly calls punctiliar: "they shall be made alive" in one grand act at the last day. This is again the fact. Thus beside the continuous *process* of dying Paul places the final *single act* of bringing the dead bodies back to life.

The two prepositions ἐν are, therefore, in no way mystic but, like all of the other words used in these two clauses, expressive of plain facts: "in Adam," "in Christ" = in connection with Adam, in connection with Christ. And the connection is according to each of the two persons — how else could it be? The one is a natural, the other is a spiritual connection. The one is by natural descent from a sinful progenitor who brought death and dying upon us all by his sin; the other by a spiritual regeneration through faith in the Redeemer who conquered sin and death and brought life and immortality to light by his resurrection. Yet we should not extend Paul's words so as to include more than he himself puts into them. He discusses the bodily resurrection of believers only — of these alone; he states that all of us believers die now, and that at last all of us shall be raised. This process of dying is due to our connection with Adam; the coming event of our resurrection is due to our connection with Christ.

This helps us to explain the two πάντες, "all," concerning the force of which there is considerable confusion. The two words appear without modifiers because none are needed. "All" are dying; "all" shall be made alive. The same persons are referred to. "All" = all believers. Yes, it is true, unbelievers as well as believers die so that we must say, "All men die." But Paul is not instructing the Corinthians in regard to all men, he is speaking only about believers and throughout his discussion does not mention unbelievers. This is very plain when we consider the second "all": "all in Christ." None are in connection with Christ save by true faith alone.

In an effort to determine who is referred to by the two "all" we decline to have recourse to Plato and to Plato's metaphysical thought that in the author of a series all the successors are included just as in an idea all the individual phenomena of that idea are included. By thus finding Platonic influence behind Paul's words the first "all" is found to mean "all men" because that would be in keeping with Plato's thought. The second "all" seems to have a limitation because Paul writes "all in Christ," but this cannot be Paul's intention, for according to Plato's conception of "the idea" "all men" ought again to be the sense. But Paul and not Plato wrote v. 22; and Paul is not a philosopher-theologian but a fact-theologian to the very core. So true is this regarding Paul that he is governed, not even by abstract ideas or abstract forms of thinking, but by the simple actualities and realities.

In order that the Corinthians might understand the resurrection of believers at the last day it is vital that Paul should combine the continuous dying as being still in progress due to Adam's fall with the final act of Christ when he shall call back to life the dead bodies of his saints at the end of days. Did some of the Corinthians think that their dead should be rising now even as Christ died and then quickly arose on the third day? They have their answer in this statement of Paul's. Let us observe also the voices of the verbs: "go on dying" is active, for we die of ourselves; but "shall be made alive" is passive, for only by the power of Christ shall our bodies be made gloriously alive at the last day.

"How does Paul know all of this?" has been asked. This question introduces the supposition that what Paul writes is a "theory" at which he has arrived, and that, while he presents this theory with a great certainty, his theory really rests on old apocalyptic sources. But nobody has as yet been able to produce the actual apocalyptic Jewish writings from which Paul drew his "theory." In due time, however, these writings will no doubt be found. But we ask: "Is some apocalyptic document necessary in order that Paul may learn that 'in Adam all (the saints) die'?" That is a Catechism truth. So also is the next clause that "in Christ all (the saints) shall be made alive." How often did Jesus say concerning every believer: "I give unto him eternal life and will raise him up at the last day"? Paul had the Old Testament and knew how to use it. To cap all, Paul spoke as an apostle and a prophet by revelation from Christ, Gal. 1:12. Thus also Paul does not advance a "theory" but presents the realities themselves; no wonder he speaks with unhesitating certainty.

23) Paul proceeds by adding another point (δέ) to his explanation. **Yet each in his own order; as first fruits Christ, then they that are Christ's at his Parousia.** This new point must be added (δέ) to what Paul says concerning all believers, namely that they shall be made alive.

But this new point is misunderstood when the idea of "order" is stressed so that Paul is thought to answer the question: "In what *order* (or succession) does the resurrection take place?" Paul does not have groups in mind, the one rising now, the other later, each being like a τάγμα, literally, "a military troop," that appears when it is called. Then the lone person of Christ would also be designated as a "troop," which is not true. The question is one in regard to the believers only, concerning whom Paul says that they shall be made alive: "*When* shall their bodies be raised from the grave?" The answer appears in the final phrase which for this very reason is in the emphatic position at the end: These believers shall be made alive "at his (Christ's) Parousia."

The connection of thought with v. 22 is quite free and yet altogether clear. After stating that "in Christ all shall be made alive" Paul adds: "Yet each in his own order" and then states the order. The connection is thus *ad sensum* and not formally with the subject "all" or with the verb "shall be made alive." For when Paul continues: "as first fruits Christ," we see that Christ is not included in "all," nor does the verb "shall be made alive" refer to Christ, for he is already raised from the dead. Yet the statement of v. 22, "that in Christ all shall be made alive," of necessity involves also the resurrection of Christ, for without it no believer will ever be raised. For this reason Paul mentions Christ's resurrection first, and then adds that of the believers together with a reference to the time when they shall arise. A proper and exact instruction concerning our resurrection must state just what Paul writes to the Corinthians.

What is said concerning Christ is thus preliminary. The fact that he has already been raised Paul has stated in v. 20 by significantly calling him "first fruits" of them that sleep. It is in connection with the idea of "first fruits" that the question arises as to *when* the harvest proper shall follow. This will be "at the Parousia." Thus the statement: "each in his own order," receives its appropriate explanation: "as first fruits Christ, then they that are Christ's at his Parousia." The great resurrection harvest will not occur until that time.

The word ἕκαστος, "each," should, therefore, not be stressed, either by itself or in connection with τάγμα, so as to imply 1) Christ 2) those that are Christ's 3) all the rest. Nor should τάγμα be stressed to mean "a military troop": first troop, Christ; second troop, believers; third troop, unbelievers. Again the decisive term ἀπαρχή, "first fruits," should not be lightly regarded as though it were only incidentally attached to Christ. This is the very term which shows how many Paul has in mind, and in what "order" they are to come. For this reason "first fruits" is repeated from v. 20 and is even placed emphatically before Christ: *"as first fruits Christ."* "Each in his own order" means exactly two and not three. First fruits are followed by the harvest, and that is all; never also by a second "harvest," if this second could by any stretch of the imagination be called a "harvest." Christ is "first fruits" only with respect to believers, "those that are his." He stands in no connection with unbelievers; he is absolutely not their "first fruits." By so emphatically calling Christ "first fruits" Paul excludes all unbelievers.

In v. 22 Paul writes "all," and we now learn from him who these are: "they that are Christ's." The Greek is satisfied with the genitive of possession, and we need not supply: they that are "disciples" of Christ as R. 767 does. Those do not identify "all" in v. 22 with "they that are Christ's" who feel that Paul *must* mention also unbelievers.

The word παρουσία (παρά plus εἶναι) is the standard New Testament term for the second coming of Christ at the last day. Deissmann, *Light from the Ancient East* 372, etc., finds the term used extensively in Hellenistic Greek to designate the arrival of kings and emperors. Coins were struck, and at times a new era was dated from such a coming. Yet the conclusion is not warranted that this pagan use of the term gave rise to the Christian use. This is shown conclusively from the use of this term on the part of the disciples when they in Judea asked Jesus about his Parousia, Matt. 24:3. No pagan influence was evident in the case of these disciples.

Moreover, Christ's Parousia is never called "the Parousia of the King" but that "of the Son of man." The term seems to be of Jewish origin. The Jews expected the Messiah's coming or Parousia, and the Christians, from Christ's time onward, used the word to designate Christ's coming at the last day. A synonymous expression is ἡ ἡμέρα αὐτοῦ, "his day," 1:8; II Cor. 1:14; II Thess. 2:1, etc.; and other passages. Not until the day of the great Parousia will the believers' bodies be raised from their graves. See C.-K. 406, etc.

24) The proper instruction concerning the resurrection must go back as far as Adam, v. 21, and forward as far as God who shall finally be "all in all." Only in this its true setting can the resurrection be understood. It is not merely a theoretical or academic question but a vital link in the great chain of facts, which begins with the fact of Adam's fall and our dying and ends with Christ's redemption and his kingdom's consummation. Here again Paul displays his comprehensive and all-embracing view of the realities and facts involved.

Some of his commentators do not keep pace with him — which is one reason for the vagaries which they present. Paul does not stop with the announcement made in v. 23 that the believers shall arise at the time of Christ's Parousia. We must know more. But the idea is not that these are entirely different matters or matters that are only loosely connected with our resurrection. They are matters that are vital to our resurrection as being the necessary complement of Christ's resurrection as the first fruits. Therefore Paul is not leaving the subject in v. 24. So little as Paul leaves the subject when he goes back to Adam, so little does he now leave it.

Then the end, when he shall deliver the kingdom to the God and Father, when he shall have abolished all rule and all authority and power. The observation is correct that v. 24 begins a new sentence.

But ἀπαρχή . . . ἔπειτα (v. 23) . . . and now εἶτα (v. 24) do not mark three stages in the sense of three periods of time. Some are of the opinion that Paul teaches two different resurrections, first a general resurrection of the saints, secondly (after an interval presumably of a thousand years) a general resurrection of the damned. The fact remains that "as first fruits" is a predicate *noun* that is attached to "Christ": "as first fruits Christ," and it is thus different from the two *adverbs* that follow. Again, the fact is that "first fruits" has and can have only *one* correlative, namely the general harvest which consists of "those that are Christ's." Thus "Christ" and "those of Christ" constitute a complete whole.

In the face of these facts some still think that Paul has in mind a third group, and that he refers to this third group. We are told outright: "Paul teaches the double resurrection." He derives it from Jewish apocalyptic sources. John 5:29 is quoted as proof that Jesus himself taught the double resurrection whereas the words: "The hour cometh, in which all that are in the tombs shall hear his voice, and shall come forth," prove the opposite.

Because of the long interval that obtains between the resurrection of Christ and that of the Christians a similar long interval is assumed between the resurrection of the Christians and that of the non-Christians. Thus one assumption is added to another: 1) a double resurrection is taught; 2) a long interval (a thousand years) intervenes. This long interval is found in εἶτα, "then," which is made parallel with ἔπειτα, "then" or "thereupon," in v. 23. But "then" in v. 23 is not the word that tells us about the interval between Christ's resurrection and that of the Christians. "Then," ἔπειτα, may mean immediately after or at any time after. It is the final phrase "at his Parousia" which informs us about the interval that will occur in this case. Paul adds no corresponding phrase or corresponding expression when he writes: "Then the end." What right have we to insert or to assume such a phrase: "Then the end — after a thousand years"; or: "Then the end — after an indefinitely long interval"? In John 5:29 "the hour" is a unit and not a duality that is divided by a long interval. "The hour" is the day of the Lord, the last day. And "all ... shall come forth" presents "all" as another unit, all the dead (Christians and non-Christians), and not again a duality that is divided by a millennial interval.

In v. 23 "then" or "thereupon," ἔπειτα = "at his Parousia." Paul himself defines the adverb by means of the phrase. He does the same in v. 24 with regard to "then," εἶτα; this he defines by two "when" clauses: "Then ... when (ὅταν)." And "then ... when" go together even more closely than "then ... at" (ἐν) in v. 23.

Paul writes simply: "Then the end," and omits the verb as not being necessary. Our versions translate quite correctly: "Then cometh the end," and use the present tense. Those who think of a double resurrection supply a future tense: ἔσται, "then *will be* or *will come* the end." This permits the interval which they find, for they may extend this future tense into a thousand years or as far as they please. The only difficulty is that Paul sets down no verb and no tense; and a doctrine which is based on a verb or a tense that are inserted rests on what does not exist. "Then the end," with neither a verb nor a tense or any kind, means: then at the Parousia. No known rule of language allows us to supply a future tense, to say nothing about the long interval.

What is τὸ τέλος, "the end"? This term that indicates time Paul himself defines at once by means of the two "when" clauses: "the end when" the events now stated occur. The occurrence of these events constitutes the end. The thought is quite the same when we regard τὸ τέλος as "the goal"; it is reached "when" these acts are performed. The proposal to regard "the end" as "the end of being made alive" in the sense that then, after the long interval, also the wicked shall finally be made alive and as the last τάγμα or "troop" come out of their graves, is untenable, for it finds in the simple noun "the end" what it cannot convey.

Some give τὸ τελός the meaning "then the rest," namely the wicked, i. e., then they, too, shall be made alive, of course, after the long interval. But this meaning is unknown even to the dictionaries. Finally, some take "the end" in the sense: "Then the resurrection end," i. e., then "the last act of the resurrection which, as is self-evident from the preceding, pertains to the non-Christians." The interval is, of course, again assumed. While this attempts to interpret only "the end" and after a fashion retains the true meaning "the end" or "the conclusion," this interpretation is not derived from the words of Paul but from the interpreter's subjective views.

According to Paul the "end" is "when he shall deliver the kingdom to the God and Father, when he shall have abolished all rule," etc. As "the end" is a designation of time it is naturally defined by two temporal clauses: "the end . . . when . . . when," etc. (ὅταν . . . ὅταν, really indefinite: "whenever . . . whenever"). The two tremendous acts here recorded constitute "the end." The end is not something by itself, nor is it merely accompanied by these two great acts; still less does an interval lie between the end and these acts. Two objections are raised to this interpretation. First, a parallelism between ἔπειτα and εἶτα, which has already been answered above. Secondly, that no mention is made of the wicked. The latter is not true, for as we shall see, they are in a way mentioned. What Paul says is that the Parousia and the resurrection usher in the end, namely the abolition of all hostile powers (here, indeed, including the wicked) and the transfer of the kingdom to God.

The better reading is παραδιδῷ and not παραδιδοῖ although both forms are present subjunctive, R. 312, 1214, and other authorities; the latter is not an optative. The present tense is punctiliar because of the nature of the act, namely the deliverance of the kingdom to God. Regarding "the kingdom" compare 4:20. This kingdom denotes, not the church or the persons of the saints, but the rule of Christ, the King. His kingdom here on earth is found wherever he rules with his grace and his gifts. He rules with his grace in Word and Sacrament throughout his church. This rule he received from the Father, and when the end comes, when all the work of grace has been completed according to the Father's will, then Christ will return this rule and authority with all that it has accomplished to the Father's hands, Phil. 2:9, etc.; Eph. 1:21; Acts 2:33, etc.; Heb. 1:3, 13. The one Greek article: "the God and Father" combines the two nouns as designations for one and the same person: God who is also Father, the first person of the Godhead.

Shall Christ then cease to rule? The angel said to Mary: "Of his kingdom there shall be no end," Luke

1:33. As little as the Father fails to rule now when Christ exercises the rule, so little will Christ cease to rule when he delivers the rule to the Father. Although nothing is said about the Holy Spirit, we may be sure that this is true also with regard to him both now and when the transfer is made. This is well expressed dogmatically: *Opera ad extra sunt indivisa aut communa.*

Some stress the fact that the rule of Christ is now invisible and spiritual, and that the rule of the Father will be visible and infinitely glorious. Luther does this in the comparison: "Now one sees the light but not the sun itself; but when the clouds are taken away, one sees the light and the sun together all in one." This, however, attempts to describe the effect of the transfer upon us instead of the transfer itself and what it may mean for Christ and for the Father. Christ and the Father are one. There is no difference in their majesty and glory. This transfer indicates no subordination of the Son to the Father as little as the transfer of the rule to Christ originally involved a subordination of the Father to the Son. All three persons rule now and forever because of the oneness of their being, yet *per eminentiam* Christ rules now, the Father eventually. This is as close as we can get to the ineffable mystery in the light of the revelation that is now granted us. Instead of speculating or rationalizing let us believe and worship.

In the second "when" clause the verb καταργήσῃ is the aorist subjunctive. The addition of κατά lends the verb a perfective force, R. 851: "shall have put down utterly." The aorist tense has similar force: "shall have completed" this act. At the same time in this second clause this tense conveys the thought that the putting down of all opposition precedes the action of transferring the kingdom which was mentioned in the first clause and which is expressed by the present subjunctive: Christ shall transfer the kingdom when he shall have utterly abolished all opposition.

Chiliasts say that it will take a thousand years after the Parousia to accomplish this victory. But the Parousia itself completes this victory, for its climax is the final judgment at the last day. According to Matt. 24:29, etc., the loosing of Satan and the last great battle occur before and at the time of the Parousia, with which also Rev. 20 agrees. Paul uses κατεργεῖν in 1:28 and 2:6 and often elsewhere in many combinations where this verb suits his thought. One is, therefore, quite astonished to find this verb called "a technical dogmatic-apocalyptic term"; yet when we again look at the way in which Paul uses the word, we are rather astonished that it should have been called by such a name.

The fullest designation of the hostile powers that shall be utterly put down at the time of the Parousia is found in Eph. 1:21. In our passage Paul uses only three of the terms that are found in Ephesians and combines the second and the third: "all rule and all authority and power." The multiplicity of these enemies of the kingdom is expressed by "all" and not by "rule, authority, and power." The idea is not that some have ἀρχή, others ἐξουσία, and still others δύναμις, but that each enemy, demon or human, has a certain rule and with it a certain authority and power. In Ephesians Paul adds the thought that each has also a certain lordship and a certain name or title. The world is full of these enemies, for instance, worldly or atheistic scientists. They have a sphere in which they exercise rule and domination, in which they claim authority and refuse to let anybody contradict or correct them, and combined with this authority they exercise power, the power to mislead their followers and to cast out their opponents.

The same thing is true regarding pseudo-churches, heretics, and all ungodly, antichristian combinations in the world. Back of them is the kingdom of darkness in which Satan is supreme with his rule, authority, and evil power, and the evil spirits in their various evil capacities, some operating in one line, some in another, each thus with his rule and with his authority and power. Until the Parousia all of them remain active, being restricted only by the power and the providence of Christ, Matt. 28:18: "All authority hath been given unto me in heaven and earth." But when "the end" comes at the time of the Parousia, the final and complete overthrow of all these enemies shall take place, and the kingdom of Christ shall rise in triumph forever. Paul does not merely heap up terms for rhetorical effect (i. e., without definite meanings) when he writes "rule, authority, and power."

25) With γάρ Paul explains why Christ does not transfer the kingdom until he has put down all hostile "rule," etc. **For he must reign until he shall have put all his enemies under his feet.** Paul is not quoting Ps. 110:1 but is restating its contents, in particular the clause: "until he shall have put," etc. No difficulty whatever is caused by transferring what God said: "Until *I* make thine enemies thy footstool," to what Paul here says that Christ does: "Until *he* (Christ) shall have put all his enemies under his feet." The psalm does not imply that Christ shall sit idly at God's right hand until God lays all these enemies prostrate under Christ's feet. God puts these enemies under Christ's feet by making Christ the omnipotent Ruler and King. We have the same truth when the Scriptures tell us that God raised Christ and that Christ himself arose. The charge that Paul's use of the passage from the psalm changes its sense to the very opposite is unwarranted.

All types of necessity are expressed by the impersonal δεῖ, literally, "it is necessary"; it is often translated "must." Here the necessity is that of the divine arrangement by which Christ rules and continues to rule as King, βασιλεύειν, durative present. Paul has already said that Christ shall transfer the kingdom to his Father and has also added the time when this shall take place, namely at the Parousia, the end. Moreover, he has added that at that great day Christ will have put down all hostile forces forever. We now learn that a divine necessity lies back of all this: Christ's rule as King (βασιλεύειν) *must* extend that far. He would not be truly a King and rule as a King if at the end, when he transfers the kingdom, any enemies remained active. If even a single enemy were left who might use any measure of power at the time of the Parousia and the end, Christ would not be the King that God intended him to be as witness Ps. 110:1 and other prophetic passages such as Ps. 2:6, etc.

With ἄχρι οὗ (the LXX's translation of the psalm has ἕως οὗ, which is a mere variation) we may or may not have ἄν. The aorist subjunctive θῇ denotes completeness: "shall have put." "All his enemies" defines who is meant by "all rule," etc., in v. 24. "Under his feet" brings out the full force of "shall have abolished," v. 24. Their power shall be broken utterly and forever so that they shall not rise from the ground or stir a finger against the King. After this reigning as King is thus absolutely complete, Christ shall return his commission to the Father who gave it to him.

26) As being especially pertinent to this entire instruction concerning the resurrection Paul adds: **As a last enemy the death is abolished.** This personifies "death," which some find "surprising," but which is not at all so for one who knows his Old Testament as Paul does. Death is here regarded as an independent enemy, as one that is singled out from among the many enemies of Christ and the kingdom. When Satan's work through sin is done, death stands out as the result, a dreadful foe, indeed. And this

death now lays low the bodies even of believers and holds them until Christ's Parousia.

In a sense death is already swallowed up in victory because by the gospel its sting is broken for all believers. In another sense death still reigns over us, namely for the time being. The victory over death which is now ours through the gospel shall not be fully revealed until death itself is forever abolished. This abolition is not a separate act of Christ's, one that follows our resurrection. *Destructio mortis resuscitatio mortuorum.* Ambrose. When the bodies of the godly are raised to eternal life, death itself shall disappear. This means, not merely that no more bodies shall die, but that what is called death shall no longer exist. Death is dependent upon Satan, sin, etc. All of these shall be abolished, and so death as the last enemy shall also disappear. The philosophic view of death as a "principle" is foreign to Paul, who deals only with realities and not with abstractions and philosophical conceptions.

The verb καταργεῖται (compare the aorist in v. 24 and the remarks on its meaning) is the dramatic or prophetic present, a counterpart to the historic present and frequently found in New Testament predictions. This tense startles and arrests. It affirms and does not merely predict. It conveys a sense of certainty. R. 869, etc. The main emphasis is, however, on the predicative designation "as a last enemy" and then on the subject "the death" as the position of these terms in the sentence shows although the tense of the verb is also striking. In v. 24 the verb καταργήσῃ has the emphatic position so that in v. 26 it is not necessary to repeat this emphasis since that would overemphasize and thus produce a wrong impression. From among "all his (Christ's) enemies" mentioned in v. 25 "the last enemy" is singled out. Death is naturally last since it constitutes the climax of the destructive work of all the other hostile powers. The abolition of this enemy shall thus also be last and shall mark the final part of the abolition which leaves no enemy on the scene.

27) The fact that "death" must also be abolished is now substantiated. **For, all things he did put under his feet.** Paul has no formula of quotation; yet the words following "for" are found in Ps. 8:6. It may seem remarkable to us, but in the New Testament this psalm is repeatedly interpreted in a Messianic sense, Matt. 21:16; our passage; and Heb. 2:6, etc. We may accept the general assumption that Paul does not use a formula of quotation because this psalm is so well known. In Matt. 28:18, without reference to this psalm, Jesus attributes to himself just was this line which Paul quotes declares, namely that all power has been given to him in heaven and on earth.

A careful reading of Heb. 2:6-18 shows us just how this psalm has a Messianic sense, i. e., how what this psalm says about man in general at the time of his creation, about his dominion over all things, involves Christ and the subjection of all things to him, including also and especially death. Through sin man lost his dominion over the creatures and the powers of earth so that only vestiges of that dominion remain. In the end every man succumbs, and his body yields to death. Then Christ joined himself to us, made us his brethren (Heb. 2:11-14), even died (v. 9 and 14: "through death") in order by his "propitiation" (v. 17) to "bring many sons unto glory" (v. 10). It is thus that Christ, our Brother, has all things placed under his feet, namely for our sakes, in order to restore us to our original high and glorious position. And this of necessity includes among "all things" that are made subject to Christ as our Redeemer that terrible enemy "death" in order that he "might deliver all them who through the fear of death were all their lifetime subject to bondage" (v. 15).

Nothing exhibits sinful man's loss of dominion as does "death." A thousand tiny and great forces in nature are busy killing our race. Already while Christ was on earth, death had to obey him and to yield up its prey at his command (Jairus' daughter, etc.). Death received its own deathblow when Christ arose from the tomb. And at the end death shall be abolished forever. It is thus that Ps. 8 becomes truly Messianic, and that the line which Paul quotes, which refers to man in Eden, directly involves also Christ: for our sakes "all things," including death, "God did put in subjection under his feet."

In order to correct a possible misunderstanding Paul adds the remark: **But when he said that all things have been put in subjection, it is evident that this is with the exception of him who did subject unto him all things.** This may well be called an exegetical statement, one that explains just how far "all things" in the quotation from the psalm extend: they do not include God himself. Yet this is more than a mere grammatical deduction, i. e., that the verb "to subject" must except the person who did so subject. For what the grammatical terms express is itself true. God cannot subject himself to another. This statement is quite necessary at this place because at the end (v. 28) Christ will subject himself to God.

In the line quoted from the psalm the subject is God: *God* put all things under Christ's feet. No change of subjects is indicated when Paul continues: "But when he saith," etc. It is *God* who speaks. The words of the psalm which God speaks are even restated: "But when he saith that all things have been put in subjection." But now the perfect is used whereas Paul before used the aorist. This perfect is entirely proper in the restatement: in the line quoted from the psalm the aorist ὑπέταξεν, "did subject," states the past fact, which is enough; in the restatement the perfect ὑποτέτακται, "have been subjected," conveys the idea that this, once done, continues in effect indefinitely. The tenses are thus exactly used.

An entirely different sense is secured by assuming a parenthesis and by continuing the sentence on through v. 28: "But when he (Christ) shall have said (to God at the last day): 'All things are put in subjection!' (evidently excepting him that did subject all things unto him); when I say all things have been subjected unto him, then shall the Son also himself," etc.; see the R. V. margin. This reading pictures the scene at the end when Christ makes, as it were, his final report to the Father and states that the work of subjecting all things, even death, is completed. This reading seeks to satisfy the aorist tense εἴπῃ and the perfect tense ὑποτέτακται by means of the parenthesis indicated and by letting the second ὅταν clause resume the first ὅταν.

The objections to this reading are the following. The subject at the beginning is changed from God to Christ without the least warning. No reader could guess this change. Paul writes an involved and broken sentence whereas he has throughout constructed only simple sentences. And in this cumbersome sentence the fact that all things are subjected to Christ is repeated three times — why so often? Emphasis requires only one repetition. The aorist ὅταν εἴπῃ, "when he said," which is a mere variant for the present ὅταν λέγῃ, "when he says" (either of which could be used), is without linguistic necessity stressed to mean: "When he shall have said." The perfect ὑποτέτακται is now taken in the less usual sense of a line of action reaching a point of termination: ————> |, instead of the far more usual sense of a point of beginning extending in a line of effect: | ————>. Finally, δῆλον ὅτι is given the unusual meaning "evidently." We, therefore, decline to aecept this reading.

28) After explaining that, when God placed all things under Christ's feet, he naturally excepted himself, Paul is ready for the final statement. **Now when all things have been subjected to him, then also the Son himself shall subject himself to him that did subject all things to him in order that God may be all in all.** This is the supreme climax involved in the resurrection of the dead.

The second aorist subjunctive ὑποταγῇ points to the great moment when "all things shall be subjected" or "shall have been subjected" (the English may use either) to Christ. When that grand moment arrives, the Son shall do what Paul now says. As in v. 27 God is the subjecting agent, so in v. 28 God is again the agent back of the aorist passive. But Paul now changes the subject of the main clause and leaves no doubt about it, for he continues: "Then also the Son himself shall subject himself," etc. This clinches the point that, if in v. 27 Christ is intended to be the subject of εἴπῃ and ὑποτέτακται directly after ὑπέταξεν has God as the subject, Paul would certainly make it plain by simply inserting "Christ."

Our versions regard ὑποταγήσεται as a future passive: "shall be subjected" by God. But this form is also a future middle, R. 809, and here the thought calls for the middle sense. When all things are subjected to Christ, force is brought to bear upon them; they are conquered and thus subjected. After such a thought Paul would not write a passive and say that the Son, too, shall be subjected, for the implication would be that force is brought to bear also upon him in order to coerce his subjection. The opposite is the fact. By a free act, in harmony with the whole divine plan that made him supreme over all things, Christ subjects himself to the Father, regarding whom we once more read that it is he who "did subject all things to him," namely to Christ.

Commentators debate concerning the final clause as to whether it depends on the preceding participle: "who did subject all things unto him (Christ) in order that God may be all in all"; or whether this final clause modifies the entire preceding sentence or the action of Christ in subjecting himself. A decision is not difficult to reach. We have twice before heard that God subjected all things to Christ. When this act is now mentioned for the third time, it would be strange, indeed, to have the remark concerning its purpose appended as a kind of afterthought. Moreover, the tremendousness of this divine purpose "that God may be all in all" is the climax of the entire paragraph with all that it contains about Christ's resurrection, about our resurrection, and about the end. The ultimate purpose of all of these acts is that finally "God may be all in all." This final clause, therefore, modifies the entire last sentence.

We have had πάντα so often as a neuter that we cannot now regard "all in all" as meaning "all things in all men" although this masculine is said to mean "in all godly men." There is no restriction in the expression "all in all." Why should there be a restriction? But the fact that God shall be all in all is not the doctrine of the *apokatastasis* or restoration of all things, i. e., that even the ungodly and the devils shall at last be restored and brought into communion with God. The Scriptures know only the opposite of this doctrine, which opposite Paul also declares in the paragraph before us. Such an unbiblical view cannot be substantiated by a simple predicate like "all in all."

In 12:6 we read concerning God: "who works τὰ πάντα ἐν πᾶσιν, all the things in all ways," i. e., all spiritual gifts, abilities, and good works in all possible ways. The τὰ πάντα is definite here and the object of "who works." Paul now writes πάντα (no article), makes "all" the predicate, and adds ἐν πᾶσιν. The sense is "that God may be all-supreme." Ἐν πᾶσιν is a frequently occurring adverbial phrase: "in all ways," or in English, "in every way." Here, after the copula, "all in all" is best regarded as one predicate expression. The words are not to be separated: "that God may be all things — in all things." God is not "things" in any sense of the word.

When "all in all" is said to mean "the life ground" common to all things, "the citadel of salvation filling the needs of all," these words obscure a tangible meaning for the reader. What Paul says is plain: after all things are at last subjected to Christ, and he himself subjects himself to God, then God shall be supreme, "all in all," in one perfect harmony with not a hand or a voice in the whole universe raised against him.

Christ has disposed of the wicked and the devils. Their rule, authority, and power are abolished so that no trace of them is left. All of these enemies are under Christ's feet so that none of them can ever show themselves or do anything. They are judged, undone, in hell. The new heavens and the new earth shall know them not. This is the absolute opposite of an *apokatastasis*.

On the one hand, Paul's statement that "the Son himself" shall subject himself to God is used in proof of the subordination to the Father, which thus destroys the equality of the three persons of the Godhead. On the other hand, we are told that it is not the business of exegesis to investigate whether Paul's statement agrees or disagrees with the Bible doctrine regarding the Holy Trinity. If this is not the business of exegesis, then exegesis has no business at all. If it cannot give a correct answer to this question of subordinationism, which involves the very doctrine regarding

God himself, then all else it may attempt to give is valueless. Paul either does or does not teach the equality of the divine persons when he says that the Son will subject himself to the Father. Which is it? The answer must be exegetical and not dogmatical, for all true dogmatics rests wholly on true exegesis; it is wholly dependent and never independent.

The answer is simple. He who subjected all things to Christ is the Father, the first person of the Godhead. It is also Christ, the Son ἔνσαρκος, incarnate, not the Son ἄσαρκος, apart from his incarnation, who has all things put under his feet, all things made subject to him. This incarnate Son delivers the kingdom to his Father at the end, lays the work assigned to him, complete and perfect, into the Father's hands and by this act subjects himself to the Father. Thus ὁ Θεός, "God," not one person merely but the Triune God, Father, Son, and Holy Ghost, shall be "all in all," supreme in eternity.

Up to the moment of this glorious consummation an economic division of functions exists between the three persons of the Godhead in regard to this sinful world and its salvation. In this very paragraph the Father does certain things, and the Son does other things. While nothing is said about the Holy Spirit, other passages tell us about his part of the work. In this economic division the incarnate Son rules as King and Lord. He thus stands in the foreground for his church. When the consummation is reached, this position shall cease, in the very nature of the case it must then cease, for its final object is then attained. From that moment onward ὁ Θεός, the Triune God in all three persons conjointly, one God, shall stand supreme amid glorified humanity in the new heaven and the new earth. "And I heard a great voice out of the throne saying, Behold, the tabernacle of God (the Triune), is with men, and he shall dwell with them, and they shall be his peoples, and God himself (the Triune) shall be with them, and be their God," Rev. 21:3.

This also answers the question: "Does Paul intend to say that the Son shall then rule no longer?" What about Gabriel's word to Mary: "He shall reign over the house of Jacob forever; and of his kingdom there shall be no end"? Luke 1:33. As Christ now rules in his kingdom of grace he shall, indeed, cease to rule when the work of grace is completed. But this kingdom of grace shall merge completely into the kingdom of glory. "Grace" and "glory" only mark the two stages of the kingdom, for this kingdom is one. It will forever be and remain *his* kingdom, founded, built, brought to consummation by him. When Christ turns this kingdom over to the Father, this does not mean that the Son will then be deprived of this kingdom and his rule, the Father taking his place. Then the Triune God will rule in the unity of the three persons with all his glory fully revealed. In that unity the God-man has his place. Luke 1:33 is true as is also the Nicene Creed which declares regarding the glorified God-man: "Of his kingdom there shall be no end." Read Rev. 22:3: "the throne of God and of the Lamb."

29) Paul groups his material perfectly. In the preceding paragraph he presents our resurrection as resting on that of Christ and as thus being an integral part of all the tremendous facts that center in Christ. In the new paragraph, which begins with this verse, Paul presents our resurrection as being vital to the entire Christian life from the moment of its beginning in baptism onward to the immanent moment of its close in temporal death. We may put it into simple words: 1) Our resurrection is vital to the restoration that centers in Christ; 2) Our resurrection is vital to the restoration that centers in our own selves.

If there is, indeed, no resurrection, then the entire Christian life, as it faces temporal death, is vacuous.

To call this part of Paul's presentation an *argumentatio ad hominem* that is based only on the admissions of Paul's readers and thus hoisting them on their own petard is unwarranted. See the remarks on v. 19. The facts back of baptism and back of the Christian life are facts whether the Corinthians admit them as such or not. If they do admit and believe them, so much the better for the Corinthians. But these facts are not mere subjective opinions held by the Corinthians, they are not in the least dependent upon anyone's admission.

It is also a misunderstanding to regard this new paragraph as a reversion to v. 17 and 19 as if Paul inappropriately inserts at this place what should have been inserted after v. 19. Paul never writes in a loose and scattered fashion. All of the preceding instruction hinges on Christ directly, i. e., on his resurrection and on all that goes with it. The new instruction rests on the resurrection in general, both Christ's and our own: "if the dead are not raised at all," ὅλως. The resurrection of Christ and of ourselves underlies the entire Christian life as this faces death, eventual death or imminent death. Paul presents this basic fact, which has its own convincing power as a fact.

Else what shall they do who are baptized with a view to the dead? If the dead are not raised at all, why at all are they baptized with a view to them? The condition is abbreviated to the mere conjunction ἐπεί, R. 1025. "Else" = if all that is stated in the preceding is not fact. The interrogative form is dramatic and strikes home, for when the reader himself faces and answers this question he will be the more convinced. Whereas the former paragraph addresses no one (except v. 12), this paragraph is entirely personal and ends in direct admonition. The future tense: "What shall they do," etc., is not the logical future, which refers only to a sequence of thought and not to actual future time. This is a deliberative future used rhetorically, R. 876, for Paul asks the Corinthians in regard to what certain people shall do at an actual future time.

He calls them οἱ βαπτιζόμενοι ὑπὲρ τῶν νεκρῶν, which we render, "They are baptized with a view to the dead." The tense of the participle lays no stress on the element of time, which is true also with regard to the following verb βαπτίζονται. It is, therefore, not in contrast to the aorist and the past. The present timeless participle describes those who receive baptism at any time, whether in the past, present, or future. We, therefore, do not accept the meaning they that are now being baptized in distinction from others who were baptized before this time or are to be baptized in the distant future. An aorist participle would be out of place since it would restrict the thought to those who were baptized in the past and disregard all others.

All of the Corinthians are, of course, among the baptized, and so this designation includes all of them. But it also includes all others at other places who are baptized plus all others who receive baptism anywhere and at any time. The one mark that is characteristic of all of them is baptism, the sacrament which makes us Christians. It includes all who are or ever will be Christians, infants as well as adults. Paul will in a moment speak about ἡμεῖς, "we," namely the apostles and their assistants, concerning whom he has something especial to say in addition to baptism; and then he also exemplifies by speaking about himself alone. He starts with the reception of baptism because this begins the spiritual life of all Christians, and because this very beginning already connects us with death and with the resurrection. Rom. 6:3-5 tells us that baptism joins us to Christ's death, burial, and resurrection. Gal. 3:27, 29 makes it plain that by baptism we become "heirs according to promise," and we know of no heavenly inheritance without both Christ's resurrection and our own.

This connection is made plain by the phrase ὑπὲρ τῶν νεκρῶν, "with a view to the dead." All efforts to disconnect this phrase from the participle, to which every reader naturally joins it, and to attach it to the main verb: "what shall they do, for the dead?" have proved futile. Nor would anything be gained by such a construction, for the same operation would have to be performed with ὑπὲρ αὐτῶν in the next question, which cannot be done since βαπτίζονται is the only other word left. In both instances the preposition indicates *the motive* for the reception of baptism, a duty which ὑπέρ frequently performs in classical as well as in New Testament Greek, for instance, in Rom. 15:8.

The phrase does not mean that the baptism of certain living persons conveys benefit to other persons who are already dead. This would necessitate the absence of the article; Paul would have to write ὑπὲρ νεκρῶν. "*The* dead" of whom Paul speaks are not any persons who are dead but the baptized Christians who died as such Christians in the sure hope of a blessed resurrection. Their example, i. e., their baptism and their godly life and final death in this sure hope, furnishes *the motive* that prompts the living also to desire and to receive baptism for the same blessed purpose. Paul's question, therefore, has this sense: that all who are thus moved to receive baptism have no hope, and their baptism is wholly in vain if there is no resurrection (for Christ and for Christians). This is the force of: "Else what shall they do?" etc.

This is likewise true with regard to the second question: "If the dead are not raised at all (if neither Christ nor Christians are raised), why at all are they baptized in view of them" (i. e., the dead)? In this second question the condition, which is compressed

First Corinthians 15:29

into "else" in the first question, is fully written out: "If the dead are not raised at all"; and ὅλως, "at all," includes the entire resurrection, that of Christ as well as that of Christians. Regarding the gnomic present tense ἐγείρονται, "are raised," see the remarks on v. 16. The present tense βαπτίζονται has the same meaning as the present tense of the participle in the first question: it includes all receptions of baptism at any time. The καί after the interrogative has the classic meaning: why "at all" are they baptized because of this motive? The translation of ὑπέρ: "for the dead," i. e., for their benefit, is untenable.

This little preposition has been the cause of such a volume of varied views that it is useless to make a list and to show wherein each of them is unsatisfactory. We mention only two of these views. The phrase is translated "for the benefit of the dead," i. e., of such who died without baptism. A Christian who has been baptized, we are told, allows himself to be baptized a second time, as a substitute for some person who died without baptism, on the supposition that this baptism would be credited to the dead person. A specific name was invented for this sort of baptism, it was called "Vicarious Baptism." In support of this supposition we are referred to reports of Tertullian, Epiphanius, and Chrysostom regarding such perversions of baptism among the followers of Cerinth and of Marcion. What happened among these heretics is carried back across the years to Corinth in order to explain a preposition which complicates the efforts of these interpreters. It is needless to say that the New Testament knows nothing about "Vicarious Baptism"; and that if Paul had discovered the beginnings of such a perversion in Corinth he would have opposed it in no uncertain terms. Nor would such a man as Paul was stoop to make use of this "superstition" for "tactical" reasons, i. e., in order to win a point in an argument.

The other view identifies "the dead" with "those that receive baptism" so that these persons consider their own death when they are baptized and ask themselves: "What would our death be if there is no resurrection?" But the phrase at the end of the second question cannot be understood in the sense suggested.

30) Just as the baptism of all Christians in view of the dead, whom they must sooner or later join, would be devoid of all meaning if there is no such hope as the resurrection from the dead, so also the risks incurred by men like Paul would be senseless and foolish. **Why do we ourselves also face danger all the time?** The connective καί adds this question to the one that precedes as being a question of the same kind. Yet τί καί may also be regarded in the classic fashion: "Why at all," as in v. 29. The emphatic ἡμεῖς, "we," cannot include all of the Corinthians or all of the baptized, for they are not always in danger as this is true regarding Paul and his fellow workers. These men devote all their energies to preaching the resurrection and joyfully go from one danger into another. What would be the sense of such a course of conduct if no resurrection awaited them at the end? The noun ὥρα is used in the sense of "time" (not "hour") and in v. 31 is followed by the more specific phrase "from day to day"; and the accusative πᾶσαν ὥραν denotes extent: "all the time."

31) The last of the three questions introduced by "why" is clinched by the strongest kind of an assertion on Paul's part. **From day to day I die — I protest by that glorying in you, brethren, which I have in Christ Jesus, our Lord!** Paul faces deadly dangers so constantly that he is able to write: "From day to day I die," κατά being used in the distributive sense. The present tense "I die" is iterative, R. 827. Death is his daily companion. Paul uses himself as an example of the entire group that is included in

"we." He points the Corinthians to his own concrete case. He never knows at what moment some blow of persecution may strike him down. It is strong language and yet not too strong. While it is hyperbolic in a sense, this hyperbole is the natural expression of the apostle's deep feeling and is therefore justifiable.

This is the only time νή is found in the New Testament although it is a common Attic exclamation in solemn asseverations and oaths, literally, "yea" or "truly," and it is well rendered by our versions in its true force: "I protest," R. 1150. It is always used with the accusative. The possessive pronoun ὑμετέραν may be either subjective or objective: "your glorying in me" or "my glorying in you," as the context must determine. Here it is the latter (R. 685), for the Corinthians do not glory in Paul as they well might; many of them glory in other leaders, 1:12, etc.

The relative clause: that glorying "which I have," etc., is decisive as to Paul's meaning. Paul is proud of his successful work among the Corinthians. He glories in it; καύχησις is the act of glorying. Yet Paul would never take undue credit to himself. He is only the Lord's instrument while he is doing his work, and when that work shows marked success as it did at Corinth, Paul returns all the credit to Christ. He has the right to glory only "in connection with (ἐν) Christ Jesus, our Lord," whom he designates with his full soteriological title. This very name and title is full of the idea of the resurrection. Without the resurrection we should have no "Christ Jesus, our Lord," to commission Paul, to accomplish great things through Paul, to make the Corinthians Paul's glory, pride, and joy. The word "glorying" is, indeed, subjective, something that Paul does; but this subjective act rests on objective fact, namely on the Corinthian church with all of its spiritual realities. And this fact rests on one that is still greater: "Christ Jesus, our Lord," in and by whose living power all that exists in Corinth is wrought.

Paul is quite able to present the great facts of our faith in calm, deliberate, objective fashion, and he does this on many occasions. But he is also able to present these facts so that his heart with all its throbbing feeling wells up in these facts. He never forsakes the facts no matter how deep his emotion may be when he utters them. He uses even νή, coupled with the personal appeal "brethren," in this instance. The resurrection is absolutely vital no matter in what manner one presents its reality. Therefore it is so vital, too, when this apostle thinks of his past work and success and of his daily experience in facing death. Take away the resurrection, and everything related to Paul, all his work and all his trying ordeals, would be nothing but monumental folly.

32) From the general danger that stalks Paul "all the time" he advances to the threats of death that come one after another "day after day" and then closes with a particular instance that must have occurred at a specific moment in Ephesus where he is writing this letter. The same climax is found in the verbs: "we face danger" — "I die" — "I fought with beasts." **If after the manner of men I fought with beasts at Ephesus, what does it profit me?** Did Paul actually fight with wild beasts in the arena, or is ἐθηριομάχησα figurative to designate a battle with vicious, bloodthirsty human enemies? As might be expected, the commentators are divided into two camps. For us the question resolves itself into another: "What exegetical reasons decide one way or the other?" Lacking sufficient exegetical grounds, the best course to pursue is to leave the question unanswered.

The question is not answered by the proposal to read the sentence as a condition of unreality: "If I had fought, etc., what would it have profited me?" with ἄν omitted in the apodosis, which, we are told, is permissible with τί τὸ ὄφελος. The phrase κατὰ ἄνθρωπον is taken to mean: "according to man's will," i. e., if things had gone as men desired them to go. Acts 19:23, which records the riot caused by Demetrius, is regarded as a reference to the occasion when this supposed eventuality nearly overtook the apostle.

This answer to the question is unsatisfactory. The omission of ἄν would not suggest to a Greek reader that a condition of unreality is intended. This alone is decisive. The phrase "according to man" always denotes manner and not will and cannot be taken to mean: "according to man's will." With regard to Acts 19:23, etc., we should not forget that Paul was a Roman citizen and thus could not be cast to the lions or to wild beasts. Moreover, he left Ephesus immediately after that tumult. He undoubtedly wrote this letter in Ephesus before that disturbance occurred. So this letter could not contain a reference to that happening.

When Paul assures the Corinthians by his own pride in them in Christ Jesus that he "dies" daily, it is clear that he uses the verb figuratively, for he is still alive, and no one can die more than once, he cannot actually die "day after day." When Paul now adds an exemplification of this general statement that he dies day after day, the reader has no difficulty in understanding the new dramatic term: "I fought with beasts at Ephesus" in the same figurative manner as meaning: "Right here in Ephesus I faced death as one who fights with wild beasts." The close relation existing between "I die daily" and its exemplification "I fought with beasts" furnishes the exegetical reason for regarding the latter verb figuratively as we do the former. This, too, is the reason that Paul does not need a modifier to show that the second verb is also used figuratively.

Its aorist tense states a past fact in a condition of reality. This aorist is usually regarded as a reference to some individual instance when Paul's bloodthirsty enemies endangered his very life. Yet we are not sure that only one event is referred to. If this were the case, it cannot be the one mentioned in Acts 19:23, etc., for the reason already assigned. Paul writes without adding a modifier such as "in Ephesus." This would indicate that the Corinthians caught his reference and needed no further hint. The aorist may, however, be constative and sum up into a unit a number of dangerous happenings such as he mentions to the Ephesian elders in Acts 20:19: "trials which befell me by the plots of the Jews." We are not certain whether only a single event or a group of events is referred to, and even less certain which events these would be.

The position of κατὰ ἄνθρωπον makes it decidedly emphatic so that the sense of the entire question hinges on this phrase: "after the manner of men," i. e., if I did incur this mortal danger only in the manner of ordinary men who are moved merely by temporal considerations such as gain, honor, ease, and the like. "What does it profit me?" literally, "As to what is there profit for me?" Evidently as to nothing. From the standpoint of ordinary men what possible gain is secured by the work of an apostle who has to face these mortal encounters as Paul did face them right there in Ephesus? Only on the supposition that Christ arose, and on the supposition that we shall arise, and on the supposition that all is true that depends on this assurance, only then is Paul no fool in facing death in the pursuit of his great calling.

In the so-called *Acts of Paul* there appears the legendary story that Paul was first thrown before a lion, then before other beasts, but that, like Daniel in the lions' den, he was not touched by them. Apart from this legend it has often been thought that Paul was actually thrown to wild beasts in Ephesus. Since Paul was a Roman citizen and as a consequence was exempt from anything of this sort, and since he was ever ready to assert his Roman rights, a situation must be supposed in which he would have no opportunity to assert these rights. This puts a strain on the imagination and has the appearance of inventing a set of circumstances in order to gain an explanation. When Paul in II Cor. 11:24 makes a long and detailed list of all notable sufferings which he endured he says nothing about being thrown to the beasts in Ephesus.

But does Paul not overlook the thought that the souls of the dead might live on in glory with Christ even if their bodies are not raised from the grave? Cannot the Corinthians answer all of Paul's deductions and inductions by this simple reply? They cannot. If there is no resurrection, then Christ is not risen, and then all salvation for soul as well as for body disappears.

"What does it profit me?" Nothing! Very well, Paul continues: **If the dead are not raised, we will eat and drink, for tomorrow we die.** Then we will make the best of it, and this is what it is. The conditional clause: "If the dead are not raised," should not be construed with the preceding question, for this already has its condition and cannot well have two; besides, the phrase "after the manner of men" is the correlative of the clause "if the dead are not raised." The present tense has the sense found in v. 12: "there is no resurrection of the dead" and is explained as a gnomic present in v. 16.

The subjunctives φάγωμεν καὶ πίνωμεν are usually regarded as hortatives: "let us eat and drink," as is done in our versions; but R. 931 is correct when he lists them as volitives: "we will eat and drink," as expressing a volition in regard to the future. The reason for this resolve is sound: "for tomorrow we die," so we will enjoy ourselves while we can. Paul adopts the LXX translation of Isa. 22:13 as being adequate to express his own thought in this case. Compare this same philosophy as found in the apocryphal Book of Wisdom, 2:2-9; Seneca: *Bibamus, moriendum est*; an inscription on the entry to a merchant's house in Pompeii: *Lucrum, gaudium*, Gain and a good time. The attempts to tone down Paul's words as though he really does not mean what he writes contradict the very injunctions which now follow. If death ends all, life has really little more to offer than eating and drinking, creature comforts like those of the brute.

33) Paul closes the instruction on the reality of the resurrection with pointed admonition and rebuke. **Be not deceived!** as the tense shows, means: "Do not go on being deceived! Deception runs its course; do not be persuaded to enter on or to continue in this course." As the passive shows, deception is communicated by deceivers.

Paul makes this plain by means of a quotation: **Bad company corrupts good manners.** Paul may have known this saying only as a proverb and so appropriated it here. Menander, the Attic comic poet, has it in *Thais*. He may have originated this line, or he, too, may have found it already coined. Menander has many apt maxims and for this reason was much read in the schools. Not much can be deduced from Paul's use of this proverbial saying concerning his acquaintance with the Greek poets. He quotes from two others, namely Aratus (Acts 17:28) and Epimenedes (Titus 1:12).

While ὁμιλίαι means "communications" and "conversations," the term is here used to designate "associations" or "company" with a definite influence. If these associations are κακαί, "good for nothing" and thus "bad," they are bound to corrupt and to ruin manners that are χρήσθα, "serviceable" and thus "good."

First Corinthians 15:33, 34   699

The adjectives are contrasts; the one means worthless, the other serviceable and thus full of worth. Paul intends to say in the present connection that association with deceivers who are full of skeptical ideas is bound to react hurtfully on the good ways of life (ἤθη) of Christians. Instead of letting the divine truth mold their manner of living they let the false and insidious ideas of their associates mislead them. Even one bad apple spreads rot among many others. He who rejects the resurrection cannot live and act like one who truly believes this divine reality; compare v. 58. This is, of course, a sharp edge which is turned against "some among you," namely the doubters mentioned in v. 12; and it warns them, too, against the pagan authors of their skeptical ideas.

34) The negative admonition: "Be not deceived," is followed by the positive: **Sober up in the right way!** to which is appended the explanation: **and sin not!** The aorist is both peremptory and indicative of one decided action, that of coming out of a dazed or drunken state. "Awake up," R. V., suggests a condition of sleep, while ἐκνήψατε suggests a condition of drunkenness. The appended adverb δικαίως, "in the right way," i. e., the way that is right in God's sight, intimates that the doubters in Corinth imagined that they were thinking soberly and that they assailed the believers as people who are being carried away by foolish and fanatical notions because they actually believe such an impossible doctrine as the resurrection.

It is the way of all rationalists and all skeptics to pose as clear-headed, sound, and sober thinkers and to charge true believers with blind acceptance of "dogmas" that are nothing but narcotics. Our present-day scientists are often arrogant in their superiority. They alone know the facts, they alone do straight and sober thinking, they alone are right, and woe to him who dares to challenge their claims! Against this pseudo-soberness and pseudo-saneness Paul launches his little adverb δικαίως. Here, too, this derivative of δικαιοῦν retains its forensic meaning, for "rightly" means rightly in the judgment of God and not merely in my own judgment. The Pharisees claimed: "We see!" John 9:41, and proceeded with mighty assurance "to justify themselves," Luke 16:15; but the judgment of God declared them wickedly and wilfully blind and cast them out. So Paul commands the Corinthians to be sober in the true way that God approves. He is rightly sober who sees and believes the divine realities as God reveals them, and who does all his thinking so that every thought accords with these realities. And this man does not need to wait for the divine verdict that he is rightly sober; that verdict is recorded in a thousand places in Holy Writ.

"And sin not" with its present tense means literally: "and do not go on missing the mark." There is, then, a kind of thinking and of reasoning that seems to be sanely sober and is yet wholly wrong because it goes on missing the mark, namely the true mark set by God for all our thinking, the realities about God, his will, his work, etc. This is the worst kind of sinning, for it affects not only our conduct but corrupts the very heart, the source of all conduct. "Sober up rightly!" Paul calls to the Corinthians, and go on hitting instead of missing the mark.

Do the Corinthians wish to know why Paul speaks to them on this subject in such peremptory fashion? Paul answers with a γάρ: **for some are afflicted with ignorance of God; to move you to shame I tell you this.** That is the trouble with "some" (see v. 12). Paul says more than that "some *are* ignorant"; he says that "some *have* ignorance" like a disease that is afflicting them spiritually. Thinking that by denying the resurrection they are displaying great γνῶσις or "knowledge," they actually display ἀγνωσία, "ignorance," the opposite of knowledge. Their coin is counterfeit, Rev. 3:17, 18.

They are to blame for this ignorance which they carry around with them and which they try to sell to others as knowledge. For this reason Paul adds with great plainness: "to move you to shame I tell you this." The preposition πρός indicates aim or purpose, R. 626. When we render this expression into English we are compelled to translate the Greek noun with a verb: "for shame" = "for filling you with or moving you to shame." The idea is not that Paul sees something shameful in the Corinthians as the A. V. translates it: "I speak this to your shame"; but that by means of this rebuke Paul intends to make the Corinthians feel ashamed of themselves, namely for having anybody in their midst who denies the resurrection. The presence of these skeptics brings disgrace to the entire congregation, and the congregation ought to realize this and to purge itself.

Paul is not theorizing when he writes: "We will eat and drink," etc., v. 23. He, of course, presupposes that the Corinthian believers will recognize this unchristian language for what it is, but we may well conclude that the deniers of the resurrection carried out their convictions by loose living, for which reason Paul warns against their company which corrupts morally. False doctrine never aids true moral conduct but works to corrupt that conduct. Whatever eats at the root (doctrine and faith) damages or destroys the fruit (love and Christian virtues). Matt. 7:16, 17.

We are often told that errorists are just as "good" (morally) as those who believe and confess God's truth, perhaps even "better"; but Paul does not agree, for this is contrary to nature. Doctrine is never an indifferent thing even though it be decried as "dogma"; it always works itself out in life. Doctrine may be held merely by the intellect, but this is decidedly abnormal and thus quite exceptional. The rule is more important than the exception. Let us, too, sober up in the right way and never condone or excuse erroneous teaching by telling ourselves that it has little or no effect on right living. Nor let us cling to the fallacy that only aberrations so great as the denial of the resurrection produce moral decline, for every falsehood works evil according to its falsity, and often a little leaven leavens an entire lump out of all proportion to its seeming littleness. A small germ may carry destruction to the entire body. The process is often hidden from observation so that we cannot meet the challenge for a full diagnosis and proof in each individual case; nevertheless, like causes produce like results.

III. *The Resurrection Body, 35-58*

From the mighty *fact* of the resurrection Paul now advances to the wonderful *manner* of the resurrection. Yet in the discussion of the change which our bodies will undergo in the resurrection the basic question is still the reality of the resurrection itself. This elucidation concerning the change is intended to remove the main objection of the skeptics in regard to the possibility and the actuality of the resurrection. These skeptics ask the very question which Paul now puts forward. They can conceive of the human body only in its mundane form as we see it in this life. Bodies of this kind, even if they are by the power of God brought back to life from the dust and the decay of the grave, are unfit for heavenly existence. So the skeptics conclude: There is no resurrection. Perhaps they only ask the question and leave it to the believers to give what answer they can and then scoff at the answer by presenting the view that bodies which are brought back to life would have to be just like our bodies are at present and have the same gross substance and the same functions.

35) Paul meets this question regarding the constitution and the character of the resurrected bodies squarely and fully. **But someone will say: How are the dead raised?** Just what πῶς, "how," refers to is at once made clear by putting the question in a little different way (δέ) : **and with what manner of body do they come?** The two present tenses are gnomic presents, both are timeless as they are customarily used in doctrinal propositions, see v. 16.

36) When he answers this question Paul first removes the ignorant assumption that influences the questioner, namely that the living human body can have only one mode or manner of existence, that which we see in this life. A simple analogy suffices. **Fool! What thou thyself sowest is not quickened unless it die.** The adjective ἄφρων is a nominative used as a vocative, which is a frequent use of this case. The term is not an address but an exclamation: "Fool!" i. e., "Fool thou art!" Does this man try to make a joke of the resurrection and to turn the laugh upon simple believers by stating that the dead body will be patched together again from the dust, once more to begin its round of life in eating and drinking, digesting and eliminating, sleeping and working, begetting and keeping house? What a fool to think of the resurrection in so pitiful a way! This is a caricature and not the reality.

"What thou thyself (σύ is emphatic) sowest is not quickened unless it dies." This fool refutes himself every time he sows seed. He then reckons with a dying which results in a quickening to a new and wonderful life; in truth, this strange quickening, he knows, cannot occur unless the dying precedes. Compare Christ's similar analogy in John 12:24: dying grain and resulting fruit, the first being necessary for the second, and the second wholly dependent on the first.

In our effort to apply an analogy or a comparison we should not go beyond the point of the comparison. Here it is decomposition and yet new life. The first is necessary for the second, the second dependent on the first. The analogy is not between the germ in the seed and something similar to it in our dead and buried bodies, for nothing similar to this germ is found in our dead and buried bodies. The analogy is not between the bulk of the seed and the bulk of the dead body so that both bulks act alike. For the bulk of the former decomposes and remains decomposed, and only the germ shoots up into a plant, while our very dead and buried bodies rise from their graves and leave nothing behind. The germ of the plant develops, produces new kernels as fruit, and these repeat the process indefinitely. Not so our bodies when they rise. By finding new and strange features in Paul's comparison we miss Paul's meaning and perhaps find new doctrines that are based only on our own analogies from nature and not on Paul and the Scriptures. The fact concerning the resurrection is not that a germ which is hidden in our dead bodies comes forth while our dead bodies themselves remain dust and ashes. The view, moreover, that the Lord's Supper is intended to preserve in our bodies during this life such a resurrection germ, which then slumbers in the grave until the resurrection morn, is therefore unwarranted.

37) There is, then, a dying which results in a quickening and a new life. But this should not be misunderstood. **And what thou sowest, thou sowest not the body that shall be but a bare grain, it may chance of wheat or of some other kind.** The καί is explicative; some call it epexegetical. The sentence which it introduces is an explication of the one that precedes. It, therefore, offers no second or new point

of the analogy; it aids us only to understand the true point which has already been stated in regard to a decomposition which ends in a quickening and a new life. It is a bare, little kernel of grain that one sows, nothing more; yet everybody sees and knows that not this bare, little kernel comes forth from the ground. The little kernel rots, and the quickening of it does not mean that it again becomes what it was originally.

All conceptions of the resurrection to the effect that the bodies of the dead shall return to their former coarse existence are thus eliminated by Paul's analogy. All skeptical objections that seek to ridicule the doctrine on this score evidence an ignorance of what the doctrine is. The future participle γενησόμενον, "that shall be," is ingressive punctiliar, R. 892. In εἰ τύχοι, "it may be," literally, "if it should happen," a remnant of the optative is found, it is a stereotyped phrase, R. 1021.

Much has been said about the adjective γυμνόν, "bare," "naked," which Paul applies to the kernel of grain. It is called a technical term in this connection and also a new figure which complicates the analogy. The matter is quite simple, for Paul himself places "a bare grain" in contrast with the plant that grows out of it so that we understand exactly what he means. The complication results when Paul's commentators have this little adjective mean "bare of clothing," and when this idea is transferred from the kernel to the dead body of the believer in the grave. The next step is to introduce a misinterpretation of II Cor. 5:2, etc., where the word γυμνοί also occurs. In this latter passage "naked" is not used with reference to our bodies but with reference to souls that are without the heavenly home. Finally, Plato and the Greeks are introduced with their views of naked or bodiless souls. The conclusion of these various views regarding the word "bare" or "naked" is the teaching that, when our souls leave their bodies behind in the grave, they are clothed with what are called "resurrection bodies" and are thus not left "naked." It seems that these novel "resurrection bodies" are now in heaven awaiting the time when our souls shall arrive in order that they may then be properly dressed.

Second Corinthians 5 does not speak of the resurrection. The fact remains that we sow only a bare, little kernel in the soil, and it is not this same bare, little kernel that presently rises out of the soil.

38) In the same, simple fashion Paul completes his thought. **But God gives it a body even as he did will, and to each of the seeds a body of its own.** Note the contrast between "thou" and "God." We merely do the sowing, that is all; nor can we do more. God does the rest.

Paul is not delivering a biological lecture. He is constructing a simple analogy which all of his readers are able to understand whether they are scientific biologists or not. A dying results in a quickening and a new life — we see it in the seed which we plant. God's creative act is back of what we see and not a will or an arrangement of ours. What goes into the ground is a bare seed, what comes out is a beautiful plant. God is responsible for this marvel: "God gives it a body." Paul does not stop with the so-called "laws of nature" or at a halfway station. He goes back to God who created all the processes of nature. This he does in beautiful harmony with the purpose of his analogy, for the resurrection of our dead bodies is also altogether an act of God's.

More than this: God does what we see him doing with the kernel of grain "even as he did will" ($\dot{\eta}\theta\acute{\epsilon}\lambda\eta\sigma\epsilon$, an aorist) when, at creation, he ordained that each plant should yield seed "after his kind," Gen. 1:11. "And it was so," and due to that original divine volition it has been so ever since. Each kind of seed grows its own body; each is true to its nature. We now speak of it in learned botanical terms, Paul is content to draw attention to the great creative fact as such. Because our botanists often study only the botany of the case they lose sight of God and the law which he ordained at creation. They eliminate God and creation and substitute their speculative "evolution." The words: "and to each of the seeds a body of its own," thwart every speculation of this kind. A seed of wheat produces a plant of wheat and no other species of plant; and so does every other kind of seed. In the resultant plant every seed gets "a body of its own," always the one God originally designed for it, the one God now gives it. The vast world of nature demonstrates this in endless succession. "Great oaks from little acorns grow" and not great elms or beeches, nor little currant or raspberry bushes.

The simple analogy is thus made secure against misunderstanding: seed and body go into the ground — new living forms result; but in both cases with a marvelous change that is due entirely to God's almighty will and power. To be sure, what is said concerning the seed is fitted closely to what is meant regarding the body. Why find fault with Paul for that? Whoever drew a correct analogy in any other way? It is a fault in us that we so seldom go back far enough.

39) As far as bodies are concerned, God commands the most wonderful possibilities. Astonishing examples are before our eyes at every turn. The supposition that in the resurrection our bodies must have the appearance which they had in this earthly life is invalid; God is able to renew our dead bodies in a form of existence that is utterly different from that in which we now see them. **Not every kind of flesh is the same flesh; but there is one of men, and another of beasts, and another of birds, and another of fishes.**

Instead of "all flesh" (our versions) we translate "every kind of flesh," R. 1163; and "the same flesh" means the same in identity. There are great differences in structure, quality, functions, etc. We are unable to render into English the gentle touches of the particles μέν and δέ; the repeated δέ marks contrast, which our "and" fails to indicate. Since ἄλλος has the meaning "different," R. 747, we may translate: "One of men, and a different one of beasts," etc.

In this enumeration Paul seems to have in mind Gen. 1:10, etc., but he reverses the order and omits reptiles. He thus secures four different kinds of flesh, the usual rhetorical number for indicating that all of the kinds are referred to. The word κτῆνος means a domestic animal. In creation God was not restricted to one kind of flesh; how can he then be restricted in the resurrection? The human body which we bury shall rise again, but, although it remains the very same body, it will appear wonderfully different in the resurrection. We see this in the case of Christ: the identical body, now dead, now risen; now laid limp and lifeless into the tomb, now come forth glorified.

40) Paul at once reaches farther, to the very limits of creation. This is Paul's way — he never stops halfway. **Also bodies celestial and bodies terrestrial; yet one the glory of the celestial while a different one the glory of the terrestrial.**

We need not supply the verbs even in the English since all is clear without them. Whereas in v. 39 Paul writes "flesh" he now employs the broader term "bodies." Some conclude that these are organic, living bodies because, as it is used in the preceding verse, "flesh" refers to living creatures. So they state that the celestial bodies are angels and the terrestrial all living creatures on earth. But the assumption that angels have some sort of ethereal bodies is speculative and usually leads to the extravagant conclusion that even God has some sort of a tenuous body. Moreover, we should look back, not only to v. 39, but to v. 36, and also forward to v. 42. Then we see Paul's gradation: 1) just a kernel of grain; 2) different kinds of flesh; 3) celestial and terrestrial bodies in general. We should also apprehend the point of difference which Paul wants us to note with reference to the latter kinds of bodies, namely the different δόξα or glory of each. Paul is not speaking about bodies, one class of which we cannot see, whose "glory" is hidden from our view, which we cannot even imagine; but about bodies, all of which we ourselves can see, and both kinds of which we can compare as to their "glory."

These celestial bodies are sun, moon, and stars. We see how they shine with a light and a radiance that are far above every kind of body that is visible to us here on earth. Paul is not addressing a group of chemists regarding the molecular or atomic structure of heavenly and earthly bodies. He is writing to plain, ordinary people regarding a matter that all of them constantly see. The fact that the material of which all of these bodies in our universe are composed is quite the same really helps Paul's thought; it certainly causes no interference with it. Although their structure is the same, their appearance is vastly different. Although the substance of our human bodies is the same whether they are lying in the grave or are glorified in the resurrection, their appearance in these two states is vastly different.

The term σῶμα, "body," is in place. Paul is not speaking about a difference between organic and inorganic structure. Even secular writers often use "body" to denote material substance. There is a contrast in ἑτέρα μέν . . . ἑτέρα δέ, R. 749, and not merely one of degree as is the case in v. 41. The celestial bodies have a radiance of light which is entirely lacking in the terrestrial. The latter have only a beauty of color and an attractive form.

41) A difference of glory is evident among the celestial bodies themselves. Since this is a difference only in the degree of brightness, Paul uses ἄλλη and ἑτέρα. **One glory of the sun, and another glory of the moon, and another glory of the stars; for star differs from star in glory.**

The absence of a connective seems to make v. 41 a continuation of v. 40. Paul dwells only on the difference existing between the heavenly bodies and leaves the recognition of the difference existing between the earthly to his readers. "Sun" and "moon" need no article in the Greek since each is the only one of its kind. We, too, say "sun, moon, and stars" and use no article even with reference to the latter. For the genitive with διαφέρει see R. 455. This verb means only "differs" and not "excels." The point in which the difference appears is expressed by a prepositional phrase: "in (point of) glory," although an accusative: "as to glory," or a dative: "in regard to glory" would also be in place. Paul simply draws attention to the many differences that appear in bodily forms. God never finds himself restricted when variety in forms is concerned. So he knows what he will do with our bodies when he calls them forth from the grave, how beautiful and how glorious he will make them appear in the resurrection. Paul is not writing about the differences that will appear between the saints and the fact that some will shine in greater glory than others. This difference is referred to in other passages of Holy Writ, it is not mentioned in this verse.

42) We who see all of this variety in the creatures which God called into being and placed before our eyes ought to have no difficulty as to the form and the character of the bodies which God will bring forth from the graves at the resurrection. The application which Paul now introduces by the brief statement: **So also the resurrection of the dead,** is lovely and striking in every respect and must always call forth our highest admiration.

43) **It is sown in corruption; it is raised in incorruption. It is sown in dishonor; it is raised in glory. It is sown in weakness; it is raised in power. It is sown a natural body; it is raised a spiritual body.** As was the case in v. 39, four statements are made, and this number covers the whole matter. Yet the climax is found in the last statement; it is like the keystone in an arch and makes the answer to the questions as to how the dead are raised, and with what kind of body they come, complete.

Paul returns to v. 36 when he writes "it is sown," i. e., into the ground. In v. 36 the seed is placed into the soil; here it is the dead human body that is so placed. Thus σπείρεται, "it is sown," is to be understood figuratively: the dead body is buried in the grave. Paul does not need to add "the body," for nothing else can be supplied. The present tense of the verbs is gnomic as is explained in v. 16. There is even a rhyme in σπείρεται and ἐγείρεται. The subject of the latter is identical with that of the former. The identical body that is first buried is afterward raised. To think of two bodies, one that is buried and remains buried, and a second that is raised out of the grave, is unwarranted. Whence would this second body come? and how could it have entered the grave?

In three of the contrasts Paul uses ἐν phrases, in the fourth he employs adjectives. Each phrase describes the condition of the body: first, when it is buried; secondly, when it is raised. In each case ἐν states what is connected with the body. The idea is that of sphere, enclosing the entire body. In each of the three pairs of phrases we have direct opposites.

We are buried "in corruption," we are raised "in incorruption." The corruption is very evident when we bury a dead body. The body decays: "Dust thou art, to dust returnest." Perhaps it is necessary to recall Martha's exclamation before her brother's tomb: "Lord, by this time he stinketh!" John 11:39. Incorruption is the opposite of corruption or decay. It is easy to say this, but it is impossible really to understand it as long as we are in this world where only decay is constantly before us. Incorruption is a timeless state, perfect, constant, changeless.

The dead body is buried "in dishonor," it is raised "in glory." We, indeed, try to honor the dead whom we bury by clothing them in their best, giving them a fine casket, flowers, our attending presence, etc. All of this is well; it means much if we have the sure hope of a blessed resurrection with reference to the dead. What it means when this hope is absent we need not say. Yet the body itself is enveloped "in dishonor" — we soon hurry it from sight. In a little while its decomposition would cause us to shrink from it in horror. In the resurrection this identical body appears in glory. This does not mean that honor and glory are merely heaped upon it from the outside, but the body itself is made glorious, it is like that of Christ at the time of the transfiguration, radiant and shining. We have never seen this heavenly condition and are powerless to describe it adequately.

The dead body is buried "in weakness," all of its ἰσχύς or strength is gone. Not enough strength is left to draw one breath. To say that only the strength to resist decay is gone is too narrow a view. Helpless lies the dead body, wholly a prey to nature's elements. At the time of the resurrection this identical body appears "in power," filled with the ability to do all that its new state requires. This is not power as we know it now in our living bodies but transcendent power, beyond all that our minds can now conceive. Luther writes: "As weak as it is now, without all power and ability when it lies in the grave, so strong will it eventually become when the time arrives, so that not a thing will be impossible for it if it has a mind for it, and it will be so light and agile that in an instant it can float both here below on earth and above in heaven."

44) All that Paul expresses in these six phrases he now sums up, yea, transcends. Paul uses the word σῶμα, "body," the same body which is at one time in a condition that is properly described as being merely "natural" and again in a condition that is quite the opposite, namely "spiritual."

Man is composed of two parts; the one is material, the other immaterial. The latter is in the Greek designated by two terms, ψυχή and πνεῦμα. The ψυχή is the immaterial part as it animates the material part or body and makes it alive. The πνεῦμα is the same immaterial part, but as it is open to impressions from the supreme πνεῦμα, the Spirit of God. Death separates the immaterial from the material part, but ψυχή and πνεῦμα cannot be separated, being one entity; these two can be distinguished only as two sides of a unit. At the moment of death both are withdrawn, and the body lies lifeless.

In English we use the two terms "soul" and "spirit" to designate man's immaterial part, but "soul" is not a true equivalent for the Greek ψυχή. In English usage "soul" and "spirit" are nearly alike in force and in meaning. In the Greek ψυχή often means only "life," that which animates the body (not, however, ζωή, the spiritual life principle); it often also designates "person." The fact that the Greek ψυχή lies on a far lower level than the English word "soul" appears from the lack of an English adjective form which is derived from "soul" to match ψυχικός which is derived from ψυχή.

Hence in translation we can only approximate this Greek adjective by substituting "natural" or in some connections "carnal."

The "natural body" that is placed into the grave is the body that is in this life animated by the ψυχή, which causes all the organs to function in their processes. When the ψυχή is withdrawn, and the lifeless body is laid into the grave, it is merely this sort of a body, ψυχικόν, "natural." Paul intends to describe only the present natural state of the body and not the spiritual condition of the person to whom the body belongs. The adjective may, of course, be used also for the latter purpose as is done in 2:14; here, however, the person is a true believer and hence spiritual. In the resurrection this "natural body" comes forth completely changed into a "spiritual body." This does not mean that the body is now constituted of spirit or πνεῦμα just as σῶμα ψυχικόν does not mean that the body is composed of soul or ψυχή. The new condition of the body is such that it is now in all respects a proper organ for the spirit and is thus called "spiritual." This does not mean that in the resurrection the πνεῦμα instead of the ψυχή animates the body. What takes place is something far higher and grander than a mere reanimation; it is a complete transformation and glorification of the very substance of the old body.

At one time the entire body was dominated by the ψυχή; the body was really its organ. Regeneration and sanctification changed this only in part; they moved the body and its members to many spiritual functions of worship, prayer, service, etc., yet not perfectly. In the resurrection the πνεῦμα, which is the inner seat of the reborn spiritual life, will dominate the body completely so that all of its substance is controlled by the "spirit," and it itself is so changed and exalted as perfectly to respond to this control. This does not refer to a substitute body which is composed of a new substance such as the ether of which some have thought. Nor does the ψυχή perish so that of the immaterial part of man only the πνεῦμα is left. Just as the material part will be identical and entire, so also the immaterial part. But the latter will assume a far higher type of control than that which was possible in this life, one that is spiritually perfect in every respect. Christ speaks of this new condition: "In the resurrection they neither marry, nor are given in marriage, but are as the angels of heaven," Matt. 20:30; Luke 20:36; compare I Cor. 15:48, 49.

When Paul uses these terms does he draw on pagan, Hellenistic sources? Some who propound this question and search the literature of pagan philosophy and of the pagan mystery cults give an affirmative answer. The fact that the two words ψυχικός and πνευματικός were in existence before Paul wrote is not convincing, for this is true regarding a large number of specific terms which are used in the New Testament. The hypothesis that Paul found these terms in use among the Corinthians and that he employed them in his letter in order to give his readers their correct import by using them in the true gospel sense, is untenable. If Paul intends to recoin these terms he fails to indicate his purpose by a single hint. It has not been established that the Corinthian Christians knew and used these terms in a pagan sense. Philosophic and cult terms that are occasionally found in a few writings never become the common property of a group of people such as compose an ordinary Christian congregation. Paul never puts the terms "natural" and "spiritual" into the mouth of the skeptics whom he corrects. They appear only in Paul's own elucidations just as do all the other words which he uses to express his thought. He uses them also in other connections, especially the term "spiritual." In every instance we need not go outside of the Old and the New Testaments to understand what Paul means by these terms and to see why he uses them.

Since the point of Paul's answer to the question, "With what kind of bodies are the dead raised?" lies in the clause "it is raised a spiritual body," Paul centers his further instruction on this clause. For the fact that we shall rise with a "spiritual body" is a thought that is so important and so high in every respect that its mere enunciation is not sufficient. So Paul proceeds: **If there exists a body natural, there exists also one spiritual.**

45) We might expect Paul to pass by the existence of "the natural body" as being a truth that is quite self-evident to his readers. It is after a fashion self-evident; but Paul is concerned that his readers should know just what he means by "the natural body," for unless they do they will not understand what he means by "the spiritual body," and they may doubt its existence and be inclined to reject the resurrection in spite of what he has stated thus far. Therefore Paul points his readers to Gen. 2:7: **Thus also it has been written** (the perfect tense: has been written and is still on record) in regard to the natural body: **The first man Adam became a living soul.**

The point of emphasis lies in the predicate phrase εἰς ψυχὴν ζῶσαν, which is used instead of a predicate nominative, R. 458, "a living soul," for this explains the previous expression "a natural body," one that is animated by the ψυχή or soul and is thus ψυχικόν. Paul wants his readers to understand that God himself so made man that his body is now animated by the soul. When God breathed his breath into the body of inert earth which he had formed, the first man became a living soul. All of Adam's descendants are like him in this vital feature: in the body of every one of us there is a living soul or ψυχή. From Adam onward every human being has an animated body of this kind, σῶμα ψυχικόν.

Both the Hebrew and the LXX read: "Man became a living soul." Paul is taken to task for reproducing this in the fuller form: *"The first man Adam became a living soul."* Paul is charged with a rabbinical and targumistic practice which adds all manner of remarks to a Scripture text as though they belonged to the original. The specific charge is that Paul put into the quotation the very thought which he intended to draw out of it and thus deliberately altered the Scripture quotation in his own interest. But when Paul adds the word "first" and the name "Adam" he in no wise changes the sense of the original. These additions are intended only to aid Paul's readers in understanding the original sense of the passage. In the quotation "man" means "Adam" and not man in general. The addition of "Adam" emphasizes the true sense of the original. And "first" refers to Adam as the progenitor of all other men. It would be of no consequence whatever if only in his own person Adam became a living soul, and if all of us were not likewise living souls.

We now also see why Paul introduces the quotation with οὕτως καί, "thus also" it is written. He intends to say that, when he speaks about a natural body, this is the very way in which the Scriptures themselves speak in Gen. 2:7 when they say that Adam became a living soul. The quotation concludes with this sentence regarding Adam. And Paul does not intend to make the next sentence, the one about the second Adam, a part of the quotation. This charges Paul with manufacturing half of the quotation, the chief half, which he needs for his purpose. Paul would then assume the ignorance or inadvertence of his readers, and do that in the matter of a Scripture passage which was so well known. He would then defeat his own purpose; for the moment his fraud is discovered, all who see what he has done will call him a liar.

Others suppose that this statement about the second Adam is a quotation in summary which is based on different Old Testament passages such as Isa. 42:1; 48:16; Joel 3:1, etc.; Ezek. 39:29 which are interpreted messianically. The difficulty is that in none of these or in any other passages is Christ called "the last Adam." This summary is evidently an effort to meet what seems to be a difficulty.

Finally, Paul is thought to find a hidden meaning in Gen. 2:7, a kind of implication which he then puts into the words: **The last Adam a life-giving spirit.** Or instead of finding an implication Paul draws a logical deduction that is based on the idea of contrasting counterparts: if it is true that the first Adam is a living soul, then it must be equally true that the last Adam is the opposite, a life-giving spirit. This deduction Paul is thought to record as a part of the quotation itself.

In the first place, Paul is too honest not to differentiate between the original quotation and his own deduction — if he makes a deduction. In the second place, this supposed deduction is nothing of the kind. For the creation of Adam in no way implies a second Adam. If Adam had not sinned, Christ would never have come; the living soul of Adam would never have needed rescue by the life-giving spirit of Christ.

Paul's quotation from Gen. 2:7 ends with the statement concerning Adam and adds nothing about Christ. It is Paul himself who in words of his own choosing sets down beside the passage from Genesis the statement: "The last Adam a life-giving spirit." These commentators evidently assume that Paul is in v. 45 trying to prove the double assertion which he made in v. 44, that if a natural body exists, a spiritual body must also exist. But οὕτως καί, "thus also," does not introduce a proof. It shows only how the Old Testament speaks about Adam. It does *not* speak about Christ in a corresponding way. It is Paul who calls Christ the last Adam and as such a life-giving spirit. As little as Paul *proves* anything from Gen. 2:7 regarding "the natural body," so little does he attempt *to prove* anything from this or from any other passage regarding "the spiritual body." Paul actually states two great facts: one concerning Adam, the other concerning Christ. The fact that Christ is, indeed, the last Adam and a life-giving spirit Paul *proves* at the very beginning of this chapter when he repeats at length the evidence for his resurrection from the dead (v. 3-11), and when he records at length all that this resurrection involves (v. 20-28). If that does not show that Christ is the last Adam, a life-giving spirit, then nothing that the Old Testament says anywhere can prove it.

Now we see, too, why in the quotation from Genesis Paul inserts the two words "first" and "Adam." They do, indeed, bring out the true sense of the passage most clearly. These two words at the same time match the designation which Paul wishes to apply to Christ when he now calls him "the last Adam." Yet let us note that "the first Adam" does not receive his name from "the last Adam," but vice versa. This answers the view that Paul inserts these two words into Gen. 2:7 for the reason that he wants to read something about Christ into Gen. 2:7.

Adam is the "first" man, and he bears the name "Adam" whether there is a Christ or not and apart from any title that Christ may bear; and Adam became "a living soul" at his very creation whether Christ should ever appear as "a life-giving spirit" or not. Christ and his work and his titles are based on Adam and on Adam's sin and not the reverse. Paul does not give a dogmatical turn to Gen. 2:7. He simply states the undisputed facts that Adam is the first man, that his name is Adam, and that in his creation God made him a body that was animated by a soul. Paul then describes Christ and again states only the facts regarding him and now uses terms that match those which he employed when he was speaking about the progenitor of our race. These terms are well chosen to designate the great facts which Paul has already recorded concerning Christ. Christ may, indeed, be called "the last Adam, a life-giving spirit."

The parallel between the two is close, and there is yet a great difference between them. Both Adams are progenitors, yet the one is a progenitor of only a natural, the other of a spiritual race. From the one we have received only "a natural body" (σῶμα ψυχικόν) because at his creation he came to be only "a living soul" (εἰς ψυχὴν ζῶσαν); from the other we shall receive "a spiritual body" (σῶμα πνευματικόν) because he came to be for us "a life-giving spirit" (εἰς πνεῦμα ζωοποιοῦν). The first Adam left us on this low level and necessitated the coming of the last Adam because sin and death entered the world. This tragic fact underlies the entire chapter. In the term "life-giving" there lies the concept "life," ζωή, the heavenly life principle which never dies but ascends to glory and blessedness. Paul fitly calls Christ the "last" Adam, there can and will be no other who has the function of an Adam. Since Christ followed Adam he may also be called "the second Adam."

In the statement concerning Christ we supply ἐγένετο, "became," an historical aorist, which raises the question as to when Christ became a life-giving spirit. Some assert: at the creation or even before the creation. Then we are told that God created both Adams, the one with a natural, the other with a spiritual body, the one only living, the other life-giving. Where Paul obtained this idea we are not told, but a search to discover the source is being made. It seems that the Midrash and the Talmud contain no clue, and even Philo taught that God first created only the idea of man and then formed Adam, and Philo never connects this idea of man with the Messiah. In accord with this view "life-giving" is regarded as a creative power or δύναμις by which all creatures were called into being. This view is thus only a modern revival of ancient Gnosticism.

"Became" is also referred to the incarnation. The life-giving power is then attributed to Christ's divine nature, which necessitates an appeal to the communication of attributes in order to help to explain. But the statement is valid that after the incarnation, when the Son "became" man, he possessed throughout his earthly life a σῶμα ψυχικόν, a natural body of flesh and blood that was animated by a human soul; he ate, drank, labored, slept, suffered, died, just like other men, he was in the form of a servant, in the likeness of men (Phil. 2:7), although, even when he was tempted he remained without sin (Heb. 4:15). It is even true that before the incarnation, throughout the Old Testament, Christ was the Mediator of spiritual life. But he was this just as he is now our Mediator, not because of the act (incarnation) by which he *began* his work, but because, having begun, he gloriously *finished* this work as Paul has fully set forth in v. 3-11.

In his resurrection and his glorification Christ literally and historically "became the last Adam, a life-giving spirit." We should consider the resurrection and the enthronement at God's right hand together: "Wherefore also God highly exalted him, and gave him the name which is above every name," Phil. 2:9. One form of that supreme name is "the last Adam, a life-giving spirit." He still has his human body and will have it forever, which is now "the body of his glory," Phil. 3:21. When Paul writes that he became "a life-giving spirit" he does not mean that Christ discarded his body and that he now exists in heaven only as a spirit. We should not separate the two words πνεῦμα ζωοποιοῦν. "Life-giving spirit" designates Christ in relation to us: he is the fountain of spiritual life for us. That spiritual life flows, not from his body, although it has become a spiritual body and the body of his glory, to our body; but from the spirit that dwells in his glorious body to our spirit that dwells in our body and thus quickens us spiritually and gives us life (ζωή). In the Holy Supper Christ's life-giving spirit employs even his body and his blood given and shed for us so that we may eat and drink for the nourishment of our spiritual life.

In all of this it is the human πνεῦμα of Christ that gives us life. In that human spirit of his the ego or person is the eternal Son of God (in humiliation as well as in exaltation). Yet not the mere union of the person of the Son with the human spirit, soul, and body makes him for us the fountain of life, but the expiating work which he accomplished for us does. As the one who died for us and rose again he now brings back life and immortality to us.

This giving of life to us begins in regeneration, when we receive the ζωή which passes right through temporal death into a blessed eternity. This begins in us the work of the last Adam who is a life-giving spirit. The consummation of this work is the resurrection and the glorification of our bodies which shall then again be joined to our souls and our spirits and be made spiritual bodies, v. 22. "Who shall fashion anew the body of our humiliation, conformed to the body of his glory, according to the working whereby he is able even to subject all things to himself." Phil. 3: 21; Col. 3:4; I Thess. 4:16, 17.

In this life the ordinary animation of our body continues even though we are spiritually reborn, but in the resurrection the spirit takes complete control of the body which has been gloriously refashioned so as to respond fully to that control. Here our spirit rules the animated body only partially, as a refractory subject; there it shall rule the body perfectly as itself being a truly spiritual subject. Here we still distinguish between ψυχή and πνεῦμα, there this distinction will have faded away. It is thus that we lay into the grave a natural body, σῶμα ψυχικόν, and in the resurrection receive a spiritual body, σῶμα πνευματικόν.

46) **Nevertheless, the spiritual is not first but the natural; then the spiritual.** Neither the context nor the sense requires that we supply "body." Paul states simply the historical fact and no more. He speaks of only two and states the order in which they occur. The first in this order is τὸ ψυχικόν, "the natural," which belongs to the ψυχή; the second is "the spiritual," which belongs to the πνεῦμα. What is briefly and pointedly summarized here is more fully developed in the following verses: first Adam, then Christ; first those who belong to Adam, then those who belong to Christ. Paul has no philosophy of the matter, he records simply the historical facts.

Because Paul places the negative first by saying that the spiritual is *not* first, that seems to be an indication that some of his readers were inclined to philosophize instead of adhering simply to the facts. They seemed to think of these matters abstractly and thus concluded that the spiritual ought to precede the natural. They may then take the next step and argue that the spiritual, being the original, ought alone to remain. Thus they repudiate the natural and arrive at the rejection of the bodily resurrection. Paul eliminates all such deductions by this simple statement of fact and by its elucidation in the following verses.

Paul is not speaking abstractly as though he is stating a law, one that is bound to work itself out.

This has been called the law of creation which proceeds from the lower to the higher in a kind of evolution. A misleading philosophy is then built up on this law. The fall is regarded as a necessary consequence of a state of mere natural life. It is regarded as a step upward although it at first proceeded downward. A moral natural life according to the light of natural religion is said to lead upward to the spiritual life in Christ. This law is then extended so as to include the history of nations who rise from barbarism to civilization; it also includes the development of individuals, whose natural feelings and affections become sources of their spiritual devotions; it finally includes nature itself, in that lower forms produce higher forms, and imperfect forms bring forth perfect forms. Paul speaks about two and about no more. Paul gives us the order in which these two appear. He would subvert his entire gospel if he made the natural bring forth or produce the spiritual. Paul is not recording a law or "a principle of universal application."

Nor was the last Adam created at the beginning, before the first Adam, so that we should normally expect the last Adam to become operative before the first; yet we are told that the activity of the last Adam is held in abeyance until the period of the last Adam has run its full course. Thus that which is natural comes first, that which is spiritual follows. This is so contrary to truth that it should not be advocated in a Christian commentary.

47) The summary of the fact mentioned in v. 46 is followed by the detailed specifications of that fact. **The first man is out of the earth, earthy; the second man is out of heaven.** Paul refers to the two Adams of whom he has just spoken. He now calls Christ the "second" man instead of the "last" in order to match v. 46 where he writes "then" the spiritual. Paul characterizes the first man with respect

to his body and the second man with respect to his person. "Out of the earth" and "out of heaven" denote origin (ἐκ); the one is derived from the earth, the other is derived from heaven. The origin is twice mentioned, but these origins are opposites. Therefore he who is "out of heaven" cannot be derived from him who is "out of the earth," nor can the latter be the source of the former.

Being "out of the earth," Adam is "earthy," χοϊκός (Gen. 2:7: χοῦν ἀπὸ τῆς γῆς, LXX). The constitutional feature about him which corresponds with his origin is his earthy body that is formed from the dust. This is not the case with regard to Christ. It is a textual question whether Paul wrote a term to match "earthy" in the statement regarding Christ. Some texts read: "the second man is Lord (or the Lord) out of heaven." The preponderance of evidence is against this addition. "Lord" also does not match "earthy." Paul leaves the place for a correlative term blank; he evidently does this because human language affords no term which may describe the substance of Christ's glorified body without the fear of misunderstanding.

But are the soul and the spirit of Adam not also of heavenly origin, breathed into his body by the Creator himself? And is the human body of Christ, born of the Virgin Mary not a descendant of Adam, "out of the earth," just as much as Adam's body? Both observations are quite true. The first man has a heavenly side, the second man an earthly side. And we must add that Christ retained his earthly body, transformed it, and elevated it into the glory of the Trinity, that body that came from his human mother. Nevertheless, Paul's antithesis stands: there is an absolute difference in origin as well as in being between Adam and Christ. Adam began with the dust of earth. God formed that dust into a body that was composed of earth. Then, without knowledge, consent, or activity of this body,

God breathed his breath into it. Thus Adam became a living being. The complete opposite is true regarding Christ. The person of the Son of God existed from all eternity. By that person's own volition and power a human body was conceived in the womb of the Virgin, in which this person became incarnate, not for the purpose of his own existence, but for the purpose of redeeming our fallen race. Thus Adam is "out of the earth, earthy"; Christ "out of heaven."

We must add more. Formed as Adam was, with a soul and a spirit breathed into him before a volition of his own existed, it became his task to make his spirit the master of his entire being, we may say to spiritualize his soul and his body. God gave him the necessary ability to achieve this great purpose of his being. By a volition that was in harmony with his own spirit and with the help of God who bestowed that spirit upon him Adam could and should have risen to the intended height and have obtained the state of glory that was awaiting him. Adam failed. His spirit abdicated its mastery. His ψυχή usurped the high function of his πνεῦμα. In him and in his descendants the spirit no longer rules; the control has gone to his animated body. Man is now "earthy" even in his thinking and his willing. His spirit is enslaved, reduced to the low level of only the consciousness of his personal being, with only conscience left as "the spirit-remnant in psychial man" (Zezschwitz). Man has become materialized.

But from the very beginning of his earthly being, by his human spirit in which his divine person ruled, Christ controlled perfectly his body as well as his soul (ψυχή). He is lord of himself. By his own free will he humbled himself in order to work out our salvation. Thus while he was on earth he did not appear in glory. Paul is not concerned about this phase here; he looks at "the second man" in the exaltation of his resurrection and his ascension, when he who is "out of heaven" is fully revealed as such by his return to heaven. Compare Delitzsch, *Biblische Psychologie*, 334, etc. While it is impossible to exclude the incarnation from ἐξ οὐρανοῦ, "out of heaven," since this underlies all that appears in the glorified risen body of Christ, Paul here compares and contrasts Adam as the one who began in Eden with Christ after he reached heaven.

48) After the two great heads of our race, Adam, the earthly, and Christ, the heavenly, have been placed before our minds in due order and in contrast to each other, Paul connects those who share their nature with each of these heads. **As the earthy one, such also the earthy ones; and as the heavenly one, such also the heavenly ones.** Paul uses no verbs with their relation of time to disturb our thoughts. We shall understand him best if we omit even the usual "is" and "are" which are used in translation only because the English is mechanical in this respect. The English also lacks inflections to indicate number and gender in adjectives; so we add "one" and "ones" to aid us in understanding the sense.

Paul's two statements are precise parallels and exact opposites. The first statement is obvious: Adam is earthy, and all others who are earthy are like him. All of us are by nature the children of Adam. As such our distinguishing mark is the fact that we are earthy. Ours is a body of earth that is controlled by the ψυχή, and the πνεῦμα is thrust out of control. It is the body and its present condition to which Paul points with the term "earthy." All of Adam's children — psychic bodies; no more.

On the other side is Christ, "the second man." He is "the heavenly one," and all others who are "the heavenly ones" are like him. It is not stated how they obtain their heavenly quality; we know that it is by grace through regeneration. Paul does not employ prolepsis when he is speaking about "the heavenly ones," for all ideas of verb and tense are omitted. The terms "the heavenly one" and "the heavenly ones" are taken from the phrase "out of heaven" which occurs in v. 47. Yet Paul is careful not to say that, as Christ is "out of heaven," so those who are like him are also "out of heaven," for that would make these the equals of Christ, which is a palpable falsehood. Paul is speaking only about bodies and about their characteristic quality, bodies in which the πνεῦμα rules as it should, pneumatic bodies, "heavenly" in this sense. Paul is thus thinking, not of the beginning of this condition as we experience it here on earth, but of the completion and consummation in the resurrection. Grace and regeneration begin the change; the resurrection consummates it. Phil. 3:21.

49) Paul answers the question, "With what kind of bodies are the blessed dead raised?" He gives the direct answer in v. 44 and the culmination of that answer in v. 49. When he presents his answer *in extenso* he begins with a duality in v. 36 (seed, plant). He lets this expand into a multiplicity (all kinds of flesh, of bodies, of glories). He then returns to dualities in v. 43 (corruption, incorruption, etc.). And finally, as his answer comes to a close, he reaches a unity (the image of the earthy is gone, the image of the heavenly alone is left). This is a part of the mastery with which Paul presents his thought, and it is worthy of more than passing attention, for he exhibits this mastery everywhere.

We now have the verbs for which we have been waiting, and both have the inflectional subject "we." Both verbs are decidedly emphatic by position, and, although they were at first withheld, satisfy fully now. **And even as we did bear the image of the earthy one, we shall also bear the image of the heavenly one.** First an aorist, ἐφορέσαμεν, "we did bear," from φορέω, the stronger form of the common φέρω, to designate usual and continuous bearing (garments and the like). In contrast with this aorist Paul places the same verb in the future, φορέσομεν, "we shall bear." Both tenses are viewed from the moment of the resurrection at the last day. When that great event takes place, both the aorist and the future are true. Then we can and will say: "We *did* bear" the image of the earthy one, and that is now done with forever as far as our bodies are concerned; now "we *shall* bear" the image of the heavenly one forever and ever.

A textual question arises in regard to the future tense, as to whether we should read the future φορέσομεν, "shall bear," or the aorist subjunctive φορέσωμεν, the hortative, "let us bear." The textual evidence is preponderantly in favor of the subjunctive as a glance at the codices shows. But this is a case where the textual evidence, which is otherwise so decisive, cannot be accepted. It would be exceedingly strange that a paragraph which is so entirely didactic as this one is should reach its close with a final contrast that begins again in simple didactic fashion and then suddenly continues with hortation. It would be strange, indeed, that by means of the aorist Paul should place us at the resurrection moment at the last great day and then with a hortative subjunctive should force us back to the present moment in which the Corinthians and Paul are living as he writes these words. This is so inconceivable that we find general agreement in accepting the future tense as the correct reading: Luther, our versions, a long line of commentators. Moreover, the textual difficulty is easy of solution as R. 200 himself shows: the long ω and the short ο were often confused when writing Greek words.

The term εἰκών, "image," merits close attention. It "always supposes a prototype, that which it not merely resembles, but from which it is drawn, an *Abbild* corresponding to a *Vorbild*, as the monarch's head on a coin, the sun's reflection in the water, a statue in stone or metal, a child in relation to its parents. The companion term ὁμοίωμα, 'likeness,' may mean only superficial resemblance, as an egg is like another, one man appears like another though they are not akin." Trench. The image we now bear in our bodies is, indeed, one that is derived from the earthy one, namely Adam; and the image we shall bear is also truly derived from the Heavenly One, namely Christ. What our bodies will look like and with what heavenly powers and functions they will be endowed when they come forth at the resurrection like unto Christ's glorious body, we may dream about but cannot now describe.

50) In the final clause of v. 49 the thought of the entire paragraph comes to a close. The effort to attach v. 50 to that paragraph produces an odd appendix. A new subject is now introduced which is marked as such also by the fraternal address. No proper question which the Corinthians may ask is to be left unanswered by Paul. **Now this I say, brethren, that flesh and blood are unable to inherit God's kingdom, neither does corruption inherit incorruption.** The preamble: "This I say," as well as the address, make the statement that follows emphatic; and "I say" together with "brethren" lend a personal touch.

"Flesh and blood" is one concept, and the quality of the nouns is stressed by the absence of the Greek articles: "flesh and blood as such"; the verb, too, is necessarily the singular (Souter's text, for some unaccountable reason, has the plural). "Flesh and blood" describes the human body as it exists in this life; previously Paul called it a "natural or psychic body." We should observe the distinction between the body as such and the condition or form in which the body may appear. Jerome says well: *Alia carnis, alia corporis definitio est; omnis caro est corpus, non omne corpus est caro*. Now our body is like that of the brute beasts, flesh like theirs, blood like theirs. In this animal like state the body cannot enter heaven.

Yet the truth of the resurrection of the body is lost when we speculate about the material particles of the body and conclude that they do not endure forever; when we introduce the physiologists who tell us that during the course of seven years every material particle of the body changes; and when we thus take Paul's words to mean that only the spiritual principle of life abides, and that this principle attracts to itself such material particles as shall serve it for a suitable eventual habitation. In other words, the body that we bury remains buried; whatever it is that arises is something else. There is a tendency to read into this chapter, the very purpose of which is to establish the doctrine of the resurrection of the body (the identical body which we bury), the reverse of that doctrine.

The body of Jesus grew and developed just as our bodies do, it had the same metabolism and the same cellular change. That body died, and that identical body rose gloriously transformed, no longer subject to what we call the laws of nature, to the physical changes and the renewals of organic flesh and blood, and to the limitations of matter because of time and space. Rocky walls did not hem in his body, nor did locked doors bar it out. Thus our bodies will be "conformed to the body of his glory," Phil. 3:21. The fact that after death our physical substance disintegrates and scatters creates no difficulties for God so that he could not bring those bodies back gloriously transformed. The only difficulties are those which are made by men's minds when they cling to the observations which physiologists make regarding "flesh and blood," and when they associate these with Christ's miraculous "working whereby he is able to subject all things unto himself." Christ knows what he will do and how he will proceed in restoring this "flesh and blood" after it has become dust; we do not know and can never know.

We do not reduce the significant verb "to inherit" to the meaning "to have." We likewise do not make it a figure of speech for some other idea. To be sure, the inheritance is given to us, and we also have it (Col. 3:24; Acts 20:32; Gal. 3:18), but it is given to us by the testator as heirs according to his testament (the promise), and we receive and have it only as heirs, only according to the provisions of that testament. There is no reason for modifying the meaning of the verb in the present connection. "Flesh and blood cannot inherit God's kingdom" for the simple and sufficient reason that God's testament nowhere contains a clause which names flesh and blood as the heir. All men are by nature flesh and blood, and only believers are named as heirs in the testament. What makes believers heirs according to the testament is not their natural flesh and blood but their regeneration, their adoption as children and as sons of God. This includes the bodies of God's heirs, which already in this life become temples of God that are sanctified by his indwelling, which shall be changed entirely from mere natural flesh and blood and become glorified in the resurrection of the dead.

"God's kingdom" is, of course, identical with Christ's kingdom, for we do not know of two kingdoms, one God's and another Christ's. Christ reigns in this kingdom until he at last delivers it up to God; see the remarks on v. 24. To inherit God's kingdom means much more than merely to receive a place in that kingdom as one of its subjects. Already in this life we ourselves are royal, I Pet. 2:9, actual kings who reign, Rev. 1:6; 5:10; 20:6; and in the life to come crowns await us, II Tim. 4:8; James 1:12; I Pet. 5:4;

Rev. 2:10; 3:11, and a great coronation day when we, the sons of the King, shall have authority over five cities, yea, over ten, and shall sit with the King in his throne, Rev. 3:21, and shall reign with him forever, II Tim. 2:12.

When Paul speaks of inheriting the kingdom he places us in the midst of these realities. See the author's *Kings and Priests*, especially the first three chapters. Now it is impossible for "flesh and blood," for our bodies as they exist in this life, to receive this royal inheritance. Our present physical nature is totally unfit to exercise the supreme prerogatives that are here implied. A tremendous transformation must take place before our inheritance can be completely turned over to us. The fact that this change shall, indeed, take place is the positive implication that lies back of Paul's negative statement regarding the impossibility of ordinary flesh and blood inheriting the kingdom.

The two clauses of v. 50 constitute a *parallelismus membrorum,* in which the second clause restates the thought of the first in such a way as to make it fully clear: "neither does corruption inherit incorruption." For the concrete terms "flesh and blood" and "God's kingdom" Paul substitutes the abstract terms "corruption" and "incorruption." The opposite is often done, namely when categories are to be elucidated by exemplifications. The thought process is the reverse here: when we see the real nature of "flesh and blood," i. e., that it is "corruption," and the real nature of "God's kingdom," i. e., that it is "incorruption," we perceive that the two are direct opposites and exclude each other because of their very nature. Corruption contradicts incorruption, and vice versa.

Paul records the fact: "corruption does not inherit incorruption" — it never does. Whereas he first asserts the impossibility: "cannot," he now seals this impossibility by stating the fact: "does not." We usually do the reverse: we first say that a thing *is* not so and then clinch this by adding that it *can* not so. But in this case the reason that the thing *can* not be so is not at once apparent. That reason is then presented by the use of terms which show that the thing *is* never so. In other words, because corruption *does* not inherit incorruption, never does, therefore flesh and blood *cannot* inherit God's kingdom. The logic, even as logic only, is incontrovertible: on the fact "does not" it rests the conclusion "cannot." The present tenses are in order because the statements are doctrinal.

Both $\phi\theta o\rho\acute{a}$ and $\grave{a}\phi\theta a\rho\sigma\acute{\iota}a$ are derived from the same root and are thus opposites even etymologically: the corruption, ruination, in plain words in this connection, decay, rot. Flesh and blood do not remain flesh and blood but break up. Their organic existence is destroyed; the organism disintegrates; only dust and ashes are left, which disappear among the elements. How can a body of such a nature, as long as it remains thus, inherit incorruption? The latter denotes indestructibility and changelessness of nature and of form as well as of substance. Incorruption = immortality. God's kingdom above remains just as it is, in timeless existence, in eternal immutability, in changeless perfection like God himself. Corruption is found in our flesh and blood because of sin; God's kingdom is incorrupt because sin is excluded from its very nature. This kingdom cannot break down or disintegrate. Only when sin together with its effects are completely removed from our bodies, which takes place in the resurrection, do our bodies attain incorruption and thus inherit God's kingdom.

51) The negative propositions stated in v. 50 raise the question regarding those who shall be alive at the Parousia. Paul gives the answer at once. **Be-**

hold, a mystery I declare to you: We shall not all fall asleep, but we shall all be changed, in a moment, in the twinkling of an eye, at the last trumpet; for it shall trumpet, and the dead shall be raised incorruptible, and we shall be changed.

The exclamation "behold" draws special attention to the following. This Paul declares to be "a mystery," something that no man can know except by direct revelation from God. Yet a widely known commentary says that Paul is assuming a mysterious air; that what he states never came into his mind until this moment of writing, and that others had expressed the same truth long before Paul thought of it. Paul wrote twice on this subject, here and in I Thess. 4:16, 17. No one before him ever knew or recorded what Paul here reveals. We do not know when and how he received this revelation.

The grammarians and the exegetes are confused with regard to the force of οὐ, "not," which is found in the clause: "we shall not all fall asleep." The negative, of course, belongs to the subject or to the verb. Some prefer the one construction, others the other. One finds no example of πάντες οὐ, the negative placed after the numeral; B.-D. 433 finds a very plain example. One finds an exception which permits the negative to be separated from the verb; the other states that exceptions are impossible. Robertson contradicts himself: on page 423 he states not to read: "none of us shall fall asleep," and on page 753 advises to do this very thing.

A number of variant readings are also introduced and the question is asked, what views of Paul's thought these readings reflect, but these readings are altogether negligible. Finally, the assertion is made that "we all" refers only to Paul himself and to the Corinthians; that Paul asserts that neither *he* himself nor any of the Corinthians shall die (fall asleep), yet *both he and they* died, which makes Paul a false prophet; or he asserts that "we all" shall not die, and yet they *did die*, which again makes him a false prophet. Truly a snarl!

The fact is that it makes no difference whether we join "not" to the subject or to the verb. "Not all," they say, means "none." Very well. If none die, then all remain alive; and if all fail to die, then all remain alive. The mistake made by these learned commentators lies in the sense which they attribute to the adverb "not": they make "not" *absolute* so that "not all" = none; and "not fall asleep" means none fall asleep. The difficulty disappears when we perceive that "not" is a *partial* denial and no more. "Not all" shall fall asleep = some shall, but not all, some shall still be found in their flesh and blood at the end. Or, combining "not" with the verb, all "shall not fall asleep" = only some shall, the rest shall be alive at the end. Luther and our versions join "not" to the subject, which is quite in order although it is immaterial.

We at once see that the persons to whom Paul refers cannot include only the Corinthians and Paul. Many other believers were living at that time. How can Paul then write such a restrictive "we" and place it only into the inflectional ending of the verb? This quiet "we" is general and includes all believers who are such when Paul is writing or who shall be such at any future time. Paul has no revelation to the effect that neither he nor any of the Corinthians will die, that all will be alive at the Parousia, see 11:30. The address "brethren" at the beginning of this paragraph in no way compels us to understand "we all" in this verse with reference only to Paul and the Corinthians. To be sure, this paragraph is addressed to the Corinthians. They are to know about this "mystery," but surely not they alone. This mystery reaches far beyond the brethren at Corinth.

The error that is evident in this connection is the general assumption that Paul expected to be alive at the Parousia. So his words are said to mean: "I myself shall not die before Christ returns, nor shall you Corinthians, for Christ shall come back in a very short time." This did not, of course, prove to be the truth. We are told that Paul was simply mistaken (like the old Millerites and other "time-setters"). The simple fact is that Paul did not know when Christ would return. He was in the exact position in which we are. All that he knew, and all that we know, is that Christ may come at any time. So Paul spoke in his time exactly as we still speak in ours, namely in two ways: Christ may come immediately; or he may delay a long while. We know neither the hour (ὥρα in the sense of period) nor the day (date). In the passage before us Paul says nothing at all regarding the time.

"We shall all be changed," refers to all believers whether they are dead or alive when the end comes; Paul is speaking about our bodies. These bodies, he says, "shall be made other," ἀλλαγησόμεθα, which is translated "shall be changed" or altered. Just what shall be done with them Paul in a moment tells us in detail. Back of the passive verb stands the divine almighty agent who shall work this miraculous change. The entire chapter thus far certainly shows that the dead bodies in the grave must undergo a great change before they, too, are able to enter heaven. The same is true regarding the bodies of all believers who are still alive at the end as "flesh and blood." Those who refer Paul's statement that we shall "all" be changed only to the believers who are living at the end get themselves into difficulties.

52) This change shall be wrought upon the bodies of all believers, dead or alive, "in a moment, in the twinkling of an eye." The repetition of the phrase emphasizes the instantaneousness. An ἄτομον is some-

thing that cannot be cut or divided (compare the word "atom"). The very instant will be indivisible. "The twinkling of an eye" = "the cast, glance, or glimpse" of an eye, *Augenblick*. As the creative acts recorded in Genesis, including the animation of Adam's body, were instantaneously timeless, so the final change at the end will be.

"At the last trumpet" recalls Matt. 24:31 and I Thess. 4:16, although "last" does not occur in these passages. This adjective leads some to refer to the seven trumpets mentioned by the rabbis and Revelation, at least two of them, one in connection with the so-called first and the other in connection with the so-called second resurrection. But Paul has the *last* trumpet sound to summon the believers whereas the theory requires that he should have the *last* sound to call the wicked. "Last" is absolute and marks the last moment of time. We may take it that an angel will blow that trumpet at the Lord's command, see Matt. 24:31. As miraculous as the end itself is with its stupendous events, so also is this trumpet and its sound. The whole earth shall hear it just as, when Christ descends from heaven, all eyes shall see him. No human mind can truly imagine or describe, not to say explain, these events. Why a trumpet blast will be used — who can say?

Paul adds further explanations and attaches them with two γάρ. The first presents the facts of the change, the second (v. 53) a description of the change itself. It is difficult to reproduce the terse σαλπίσει in English. The verb is either impersonal as the German commentators think because they can translate: *es wird posaunt;* or the subject is implied in the verb: "the trumpet shall trumpet," R. 392. The more important point is the repetition: "at the last *trumpet* — it shall *trumpet*," which makes this feature emphatic. God gives the signal, and God determines the moment.

By means even of the passive form of the two vital verbs, "shall be raised," "shall be changed," we are pointed to God. Paul does not write "then" shall the dead be raised; or "when" the trumpet sounds. His clauses are paratactic, coordinate: "it shall trumpet, and the dead, etc., and we," etc. Each of these three acts is to receive our full attention.

At the sound of the trumpet "the dead shall be raised incorruptible." The fact that they shall be raised we know from the preceding although this is now stated in so many words. The future tense has the effect of a glorious promise: they shall be raised, there is no doubt about the coming fact. The emphasis is, however, on the adjective "incorruptible." We have had full preparation for it in v. 50. "The dead" are the dead bodies in the grave; souls do not arise and are not raised. Bodies are corruptible, v. 50. Not in their old form as "flesh and blood" shall they be brought forth out of the earth but without even a trace of the corruption and the decay that held them for so long a time. At the instant of the resurrection they shall be without corruption — the same bodies but in a new state.

"And we shall be changed" repeats "all we shall be changed" which was stated in v. 51. Paul does not need to add "all." But the pronoun "we," $\dot{\eta}\mu\epsilon\hat{\iota}\varsigma$, is now written out in full whereas it was before contained only in the inflectional ending of the verb. "We" = all believers, those who died and are now raised and those who are living at the end. The latter do not drop dead at the sound of the trumpet, at once to be raised again with the other dead. Living as they are, the miraculous change which comes over the dead will come over them, too, in the same instant. The fact that the emphatic pronoun "we" cannot denote the living as distinct from "the dead" we have seen already in connection with the unemphatic "we" which was used in v. 51.

53) The second γάρ elucidates still further by describing the change that shall take place with regard to all of us, dead or alive, at the last day. **For this corruptible must put on incorruption, and this mortal must put on immortality.** In the Greek δεῖ denotes all forms of necessity as well as of propriety, and the context reveals which form is intended. In the present instance there is a temptation to take "must" in the absolute sense as though Paul is referring to an abstract law or principle which is operative in the entire world as such. This has been defined as the triumph of the eternal-divine over all things perishable, earthly, that are dominated by sin and death. If Paul intended "must" to be understood in this sense he himself would be a philosopher like these his commentators. He plays no such role; he merely reports what the Lord has revealed to him. This "must" is neither abstract nor absolute. It states what God has ordered and arranged in his plan for our restoration. In other words, "must" is soteriological.

In v. 50 Paul states what cannot and, in fact, does not take place: "Corruption does not inherit incorruption." Now, with the same form of parallelism, he states what must and will take place. But he could not say: "Corruption must put on incorruption; mortality must put on immortality." Instead of the abstract nouns "corruption" and "mortality" he feels constrained to use concrete terms: "this corruptible," "this mortal." The abstract word "corruption" may, indeed, be used as a designation for the corrupt human body, but in itself it means the corruptive power, and when it is used concretely with reference to the body it refers to that body which has this corruptive power dominating it. As such it can neither inherit nor put on incorruption. For that would be the same as to say that "flesh and blood" inherit or put on incorruption. As long as it is "flesh and blood," a body dominated by corruption, this is impossible. So Paul writes "this corruptible," and then, specifying more closely, "this mortal."

These are concrete terms and denote the body itself which has been wrecked or is in the process of being wrecked by the power of corruption and of death. That body, although it is now in so sad a condition, can both inherit and put on the new form and the quality of incorruption and immortality. In other words, corruption and mortality can be and according to God's arrangement will be driven out by incorruption and immortality. "This" is deictic as though Paul were pointing to his own body.

"Corruptible" is the wider term; "mortal" is the narrower which implies the particular agency of death. The one helps to define the other. But both terms apply to the dead bodies in the grave and to the bodies of believers who are living at the end. Paul has twice said: "we shall be changed." We now see what he means: our bodies shall be clothed with incorruption and immortality. "Incorruption" (see v. 50) is the new heavenly condition and form which ever remain perfect. Every trace of sin and of its effects is gone, and in their place there are the glory, beauty, and power of an imperishable life, "an inheritance incorruptible and undefiled, and that fadeth not away, reserved in heaven for you," I Pet. 1:4. Its other name is "immortality," a condition and a corresponding form that are free from the power of death and from any deterioration or change which death works, they are fadeless because of the unchanging powers of eternal life.

It is worth observing that both terms that are here used by Paul are negative. They deny what is now in our bodies, corruption and death. They are unable to state the heavenly opposite that will surge through our bodies when the great change is wrought. The nearest Paul comes to positive statements regarding this matter is in v. 43, 44, 49. Yet even there the terms that sound positive are positive only in contrast with the negative, they deny the negatives: spiritual — not psychial; heavenly — not earthy. This is ever true with regard to conditions in heaven and in the life to come; the Scriptures use negatives to a great extent, Rev. 21:4; or figures, viz., Matt. 8:11. The realities are too ineffable for mundane minds and language.

Paul uses the figurative verb, ἐνδύσασθαι, "put on" (accusative with infinitive after δεῖ), an aorist to express the instantaneous act, it is repeated for the sake of emphasis. This does not, of course, mean that corruption and mortality shall merely be covered up and hidden from view by having a mantle of incorruptibility and immortality cast over them in order merely to hide what is underneath. These two are opposites that exclude each other to such an extent that whoever puts on the new garment must first lay off the old. It is like being clothed with the garment of Christ's righteousness, which means laying off the garment of sin and guilt and the filthy rags of our own righteousness. In this life sin and guilt keep appearing again and again and must again and again be removed by daily contrition and repentance whereas when we put on incorruption and immortality, corruption and death are gone forever.

This figure, like all others that are employed in connection with this subject, can convey only a part of the great reality. All of them understate even when they are made as strong as possible. The figure of putting on a garment may not seem to be as strong as it might be, for it stresses appearance, the visible exterior that meets the eye of others. Yet this seems to be the very reason that Paul employs this figure. He leaves it to the two mighty nouns incorruptibility and immortality to take care of the total inward change that transforms our bodies and uses the verb to intimate how we shall then appear to all who behold us in our bodies. Thus the figure of the garment points to our δόξα, the heavenly radiance which shines forth from our bodies and thus appears as a garment of glory.

54) The description continues. **Now when this corruptible shall put on incorruption, and this mortal shall put on immortality, then shall come to pass the saying that has been written: The death was swallowed up in victory.**

There is something grand and solemn about the way in which Paul repeats the words he used in v. 53. Like the chords of a triumphal song, he makes them ring in our ears. Let them sink in deeply! Some codices omit "this corruptible shall put on incorruption," but the evidence of the best texts proves that the words are genuine, and they certainly heighten the effect. By extending the conditional part of the sentence the apostle keys up our expectation the more as to what the conclusion will bring. The construction is regular in a condition of expectancy, ὅταν with the subjunctive followed by the future indicative. The aorist subjunctive is like the aorist infinitive that was used in v. 53 to indicate the instantaneous act of putting on. "Then" points emphatically to the great moment described in the "when" clause. All of us are waiting for the great consummation marked by this "when" and "then."

The λόγος or "saying" which Paul quotes is found in Isa. 25:8, "having been written" there and standing thus to this very day, it is an imperishable, infallible Word of God (this the force of the perfect participle).

It is now only a written word, but the reality which it states will presently appear when what this word declares "shall come to pass" and actually occur.

Isaiah wrote: "He (Jehovah) swallows up death forever," which the LXX translated: "Death, having prevailed, swallowed up men." Paul rejects the translation of the LXX and retranslates the Hebrew. Although he changes the active verb into the passive, let us note that this leaves Jehovah as the agent and is thus only a formal change, one that more adequately agrees with the present connection. The Hebrew *lazenach*, which Delitzsch and Eduard Koenig render "forever," is probably derived from *nezach*, to shine or be victorious (Aramaic, Syriac, etc.), and thus *lazenach* came to be rendered εἰς νῖκος, "in victory" or "victoriously." This rendering is found frequently, and Paul makes use of it (νῖκος is a later form for νίκη, "victory").

The verb is placed forward for the sake of emphasis: "Swallowed up was the death"; and the aorist of the completed act fits the moment pointed to by "then," i. e., when this "word" shall have come to pass. The figure in "swallow up" is drastic and expresses complete destruction. Luther: "The Scriptures announce how one death (Christ's) devoured the other (ours)." "And death shall be no more," Rev. 21:4. "The death" = the bodily death, the destructive power that is in us at birth and finally lays our bodies into the grave. "In victory" is decidedly important for bringing out the true sense of the original Hebrew.

Read Isaiah's triumphant song. Death is not merely destroyed so that it cannot do further harm while all of the harm which it has wrought on God's children remains. The tornado is not merely checked so that no additional homes are wrecked while those that were wrecked still lie in ruin. The destruction of death is far more intense: death and all of its apparent victories are undone for God's children. What looks like a victory for death and like a defeat for us when our bodies die and decay shall be utterly reversed so that death dies in absolute defeat, and our bodies live again in absolute victory. Yea, more! for these bodies will be restored, not merely again to be "flesh and blood," but henceforth to be incorruptible, immortal, "spiritual" (v. 44), "heavenly" (v. 49).

55) The exalted feeling which throbs through the preceding verses with their balanced terms and paralleled lines now bursts forth in dramatic paralleled questions that apostrophize death itself. **Where, death, thy victory? where, death, thy sting?** The two questions are an allusion to Hos. 13:14. This mode of using the thoughts and the words of another because of their special force and beauty is a regular procedure on the part of all good writers, and so it is also followed by Paul. No quotation is intended but only an adaptation of another's thought and language to those of the writer. Sometimes the setting is entirely new and different although it is not in the present case. We naturally expect the New Testament writers to appropriate freely from the Old Testament because their minds are full of the thoughts and the expressions of the old prophets. The A. V. serves as such a storehouse for us when we live in its thought and its language.

Paul retains Hosea's apostrophe to death. The Hebrew has an exclamation which the LXX changes into questions. Paul prefers the latter. The effect is not changed, for the questions, too, are highly dramatic. The best codices address "death" in both questions although the Hebrew has *sheol* in the second, which the LXX has translated *hades*. Since Paul speaks only of death he goes no farther when he now borrows from Hosea. The Hebrew reads: "O death,

I will be thy plagues; O *sheol,* I will be thy destruction."
The LXX: "O death, where is thy punishment? where
thy sting, O *hades?"* Paul appropriates "sting" (the
A. V., following the *textus receptus,* places "sting"
into the first question; the R. V. follows the better
texts). Hosea has Jehovah announce nothing less than
the utter abolition of death so that Paul can do no
better than to appropriate Hosea's words when he
himself points to the destruction of death in the resurrection at the last day.

Paul sees death forever conquered and sings a song
of triumph over the vanquished foe. It is important
to preserve the emphasis in both questions. This rests
on the interrogative "where." The vocative "death"
(or if we prefer: "O death!") is placed in the middle
of the question where it has little emphasis. *"Where?!"*
interrogative and exclamatory in one, implies the
answer *"Nowhere!"* just as emphatically. The possessive σοῦ is separated from its noun by the intervening
vocative. Now the Greek likes to place pronouns forward in this fashion; yet in this case the separation
places an emphasis on "thy": *"Thy* victory is crushed
by *another's."* Death's victory seems assured, so assured that the world is full of skeptics regarding even
the possibility of a bodily resurrection. Among these
skeptics there are found even "Christian" preachers
and theologians. Look at these dead bones in countless
graves, all of this dying from which even God's people
are not exempt. Is death not supreme in victory?
The reality is otherwise. Death is only an instrument
in God's hands and, having done its temporary work,
is thrown aside; resurrection steps in and by its
supreme victory reverses all of that which seemed a
victory for death.

The instrument which death uses in its apparent
victory is called death's "sting." The figure in κέντρον
is scarcely that of the ancient goad for driving oxen,

for the oxgoad does not kill while death's "sting" kills. It must be either a sharp, deadly weapon or a poisonous sting; it is likely the latter. Death thus pierces all of us, and no protection against its murderous "sting" has ever been found.

Hosea has written *sheol* in the second exclamation: "O *sheol*, I will be thy destruction!" The Hebrew *sheol* refers to the place where death's power is displayed. This term is broad and thus is used in various connections in the Old Testament. But there is considerable confusion in regard to this term. In the Old Testament all men are said to pass into *sheol* since all must give up life and enter into death. This type of statement disregards the difference that separates men in death. Then the Old Testament uses *sheol* in an intensified sense with reference to the wicked, with the implication that *sheol* is their proper punishment.

When the LXX translated the Old Testament they had only the Greek term *hades* (the unseen place) to use for the Hebrew term *sheol*. The fact that *hades* is only a translation of *sheol* in the Greek Old Testament and thus in the Greek quotations from the Old Testament has sometimes been overlooked. When we interpret such passages we should go back to the Hebrew and see in what sense *sheol* is used, whether in the broad or in the narrow sense. The New Testament Greek, apart from Old Testament quotations, uses *hades* in the specific sense of "hell," the place of torment for the damned. This appears with the greatest clearness from the description which the New Testament appends to *hades*.

Thus the use of *sheol* and of *hades* in the Scriptures becomes clear. The bodies of all of the dead enter the grave. The souls of the righteous pass at once into the hands of the Father and of Christ (Acts 7:59; Phil. 1:23; etc.); those of the wicked are cast into *hades* or hell. The godly souls never enter *hades*, never enter *sheol* in the sense of hell. Only their bodies enter *sheol* in the sense of the state of death and the grave. It is, therefore, unwarranted to deny the existence of hell on the strength of those Old Testament passages that employ *sheol* in the broad sense. Wherever the New Testament uses *hades* without quoting this word it never means "grave" but always means "hell."

Nor is *hades* an intermediate place between heaven and hell, neither does this intermediate place receive the souls of all the dead, godly as well as wicked. This intermediate place is said to contain two compartments: an upper one for the souls of the blessed, a kind of anteroom to heaven; and a lower one for the souls of the damned, an anteroom to hell. There are thus four places in the hereafter: heaven — the upper hades — the lower hades — hell. These four approach the Catholic five. The souls in the two chambers of this intermediate place are retained there until Christ's return and then enter either heaven or hell. But those in the lower chamber may escape by a probation after death, before Christ returns. In fact, some state that an extensive mission work is in progress in this lower half of *hades*. Some think that the saints in the upper part of *hades* were released by Christ at the time of his descent into hell. The place is now apparently vacant.

56) Paul does not leave us with the figure of the sting. He tells us exactly what this figure means and by so doing places all that he says regarding death on the strongest kind of foundation. **The sting of the death — sin; the power of the sin — the law.** No verbs are used, not even the copula, for the full impact of the thought is delivered by the nouns. Sin is the murderous weapon of death. Take sin away, and death is harmless. Paul uses the abstract term

First Corinthians 15:56

ἡ ἁμαρτία for "sin" and refers to all that is properly included in this concept. The term itself means "missing the mark," i. e., which is set by the divine law. We thus see that Paul associates the sin and the law as correlatives. Even the smallest sin has in it the power to kill. Men try to play with "the sting of the death" and hope to avoid its fatal stroke. That game is impossible; the thing cannot be done.

Sin is always connected with God's law, for the law sets the mark, and by missing the mark the sin obtains its fatal reaction. The law never submits or consents to be violated; it always reacts against the violator. For the law is not merely so many words of a code, it is the divine will itself. To challenge that will is to declare war against God. In this way the law is the power of the sin. Take away God's will and law, and all right and all wrong, all sin and all righteousness disappear. But this means to take away God himself — and us also. In fact, sin does try to thrust the law and God aside as if they do not exist and could thus be treated with impunity. In this way the law becomes the death power of the sin. It reacts instantly, makes itself and the God back of it felt, with invincible power it strikes and kills.

In this way the death comes to be (Rom. 5:12), and in this way it slays and slays: the sin and the law are behind it. Even when Christians now come to die they are not spared all of the bitterness of physical death since their dying, too, results from sin, for we still need a last repentance in death. Old Matthias Claudius said on his deathbed: "I have studied all my life to be ready for this hour, yet I did not think it would be as serious and severe as this." And Vinet writes: "On the countenance of death, however blessed it may appear, there still rests a reflection of the wrath of the Highest." Men may despise life, but that does not mean that they have really made ready to die; and they may despise death, but that does not say that they have really conquered death.

It is worth while to note that ὁ θάνατος — ἡ ἁμαρτία — ὁ νόμος have the Greek article and are thus definite, almost personified, "the death" is even apostrophized. This is also the case in Romans beginning with 5:12, with the distinction that "the death" = the death power, "the sin" = the sin power, while ἁμαρτία = only sin in general or what is sin. So also ὁ σκότος is the darkness power. In Revelation we have as companions "the death and the hades," both are personified. By disregarding the articles, which are not used in this way in English, some lose the thought which these articles convey in the Greek.

57) With two strokes Paul has displayed the real inwardness of the death; with one stroke he now displays the real inwardness of the abolition of the death. The two strokes are didactic, this last is exultant. **But to God thanks, to him that gives to us the victory through our Lord Jesus Christ.** The emphasis is on "God," who is, therefore, placed first and is also in contrast to the forces of sin and death because of δέ. In v. 56 Paul looks down, in v. 57 he looks up. The author of the miraculous change which Paul describes is the Triune God; hence all our thanks belong to him.

The cause for Paul's gratitude is expressed by an attributive participle that is attached to "God," and this participle is the present tense. This tense is sometimes taken to mean that our future victory over death is as certain as though we had it now. It is sometimes taken to define the very nature of God: it is his nature to give the victory to us. The fact is that the participle does duty for a relative clause. The tense is simply durative: "he that keeps giving." While it does describe God it does so by telling us about his continuous giving by a grand act of grace. The participle does not speak only about what God will do at a future time but about what he does now and does continually. The victory is bestowed upon us now, hour by hour. We obtain it from God in ever-increasing measure. Compare I John 3:2 for the thought. This wonderful giving deserves the deepest thanks on our part. "Thanks" and "to him that gives" are intimate correlatives.

Paul repeats τὸ νῖκος, "the victory," and the article points back to what Paul has said about this victory. It is just one word, but one that sums up all that Paul has written in this chapter, one that brings all of it to one focal point. The consummation of this victory is attained in the great change that is wrought upon the quick and the dead at the last day. "Victory" connotes enemies and battle, but it is not for us, for we should never win. This stupendous victory is being given to us. The last phrase therefore names the Victor, names him as the medium through whom the victory gift becomes ours. "Our Lord Jesus Christ" is his full personal and official name in which "our Lord" voices faith, confession, and adoration on the believer's part. It is fitting that this glorious resurrection chapter should end with the name of him who is the Resurrection and the Life for all of us.

58) The instruction concerning the resurrection has been concluded. As at the close of the first half of the chapter a word of admonition is appended in v. 33, 34, so one is added at the close of the second half. That former admonition is negative: not to be deceived, not to be drunken with non-knowledge; this final admonition is quite positive. **Therefore, my brethren beloved, be steadfast, unmovable, abounding in the work of the Lord alway, having realized that your labor is not empty in the Lord.** So the entire chapter ends with the title "Lord."

Much can be said regarding ὥστε, "therefore," which reaches back over the entire chapter. Even if we connect this conjunction with v. 57 only, in particular with God's giving us the victory, the result is practically the same, for the entire chapter comes to a climax in this victory gift. This "therefore" bases the practical on the doctrinal. It shows how true doctrine results in godly life. Doctrine is a statement of the divine facts. When these facts are apprehended they automatically shape the life. Take away the doctrine with its substance of divine facts, and the life drifts and is blown about by every wind of (false) doctrine, Eph. 4:14, which ignores or denies the facts. The true doctrine is in its very nature one, ever will be one and the same; false doctrine is always manifold, its very nature is division, non-unity. With the facts in our possession, we have something to live for; when these facts are absent from our hearts, what have we to live for?

When Paul calls the Corinthians "my brethren beloved" he voices his own tender love for them, his ἀγάπη, the love of full understanding and of highest spiritual purpose, which is deeper than the φιλία of liking and affection. At the same time Paul appeals to the Corinthians to show themselves worthy of being addressed by such a title. As brethren Paul and the Corinthians must be truly one in the hope of the resurrection, truly one in receiving the gift of victory through Jesus Christ.

The imperative γίνεσθε, as its tense shows, means: "continue to be." The observation is correct that in the Greek of this period the idea of becoming has disappeared from this verb in such connections as we have here. Hence we cannot translate it "become steadfast," and there is no thought of growth or process. "From now until death be and remain steadfast!" is Paul's admonition. He presupposes that the Corin-

First Corinthians 15:58 753

thians are steadfast; by no means that they are unsteady and are to achieve steadfastness.

The adjective ἑδραῖοι means "sitting," established in a seat, and thus fixed, settled, firm, solid. It thus refers to our own inner faith and conviction. Having a victory so great and vital, our first obligation is to be firmly and fully settled in it and thus to realize for ourselves its greatness and its glory, its preciousness and its power, and to abide in it with happy and thankful souls. So many are inwardly unstable, are like water or sand, never settle down solidly in the gospel and its glorious faith. They allow their hearts to be fixed elsewhere; and as empty as these other ideas are, so empty is their attachment to them.

The companion word is ἀμετακίνητοι, from κινεῖν, to set in motion, to shift; the Germans thus call their motion picture shows *Kinos*, and we say cinema. "Be not shifted from your position!" is Paul's admonition. This refers to outward solicitation and attack. Foes are always ready to assail our faith. Some strike at it with open denial, some with subtle error that leads us to compromise our faith and our confession, and some come with immoral temptation. They seek to turn us, who are victors in Christ, into slaves of men. Paul bids us to stand "unmovable against all of them." The verbal is passive and thus points to the evil agents that would move us. The English "unmovable" is somewhat stronger than the Greek which means "unmoved." "Be not carried away by divers and strange teachings: for it is good that the heart be stablished by grace," Heb. 13:9.

Solid personal conviction that is settled and firm against every assault is and must ever be our first response to the heavenly truth revealed to us. Then there follows a second response which may be summarized as tireless diligence. The present participle περισσεύοντες is ranged alongside of the preceding adjectives, and the tense makes it durative: "being more than enough," being rich to superfluity, "abounding." What a word for the thousands who work, pray, give, suffer as little as possible! Because of our wealth of heavenly spoils and our eternal victory in Christ we can afford to "abound." We are not called to idleness and mere enjoyment but to diligent effort "in the work of the Lord." If Christ is not risen, and if no transformation awaits us, then we should have no real work in life. Creature enjoyments would be our all, v. 32b. But now a thousand voices call upon us to be busy and tireless. Paul is an excellent example in following his own admonition.

Paul significantly calls this the work "of the Lord." He has instituted this work, and all of it belongs to him personally. This is the work of the gospel, the work of filling our own hearts and our lives with the truth, the power, and the light of the gospel and the hearts and the lives of as many others as possible. This is the work of the church which has places and tasks for every one of us. Its nature is spiritual throughout. This significant genitive "of the Lord" should correct the so-called "church work" of many who busy themselves with worldly tasks in the churches, with mere humanitarian "social service" and a hundred other things with which the Lord and the gospel are not concerned.

"Alway" adds another point: in youth and in age; in pleasant as well as in somber days; when many work with us, and the work is a joy, and when we plod on alone with heavy hearts; when we have already done much, and when others have done scarcely anything — "alway," πάντοτε.

The next participle εἰδότες is a perfect and thus modifies περισσεύοντες. We are to abound in the Lord's work since we "have realized" that it is not empty. The word κόπος means toil, exertion that is hard and tires. It matches "abounding." Strenuous effort in abounding work needs something adequate to produce and to sustain it. This is the certainty of success. When the labor is ended, the laborer will not stand there with empty hands. That is the case with all who work for money, honor, and mere temporalities; when they are through working, their hands are empty.

"Not empty" is a litotes, a negative form to express a positive idea, namely "wonderfully productive" of everlasting results. But note that "not empty in the Lord" belongs together. Because our labor is in connection with the Lord, therefore it is highly productive. All of the harvest and all of the reward come from him, Matt. 28:20; 20:8; Luke 19:17. Without him all of love's labor is lost. What an inspiration this assurance of success produces! How it freshens the tired laborers! Paul is an illustration of observing his own words.

The Lord's work is spiritual, and its results are therefore for the greater part invisible to our eyes. We cannot measure the faith, the love, the virtues in the hearts of God's people. In the case of the most of our earthly work the result is easily measured. A bricklayer lays so many bricks in so many hours and receives so much pay. A merchant sells so much in his store and makes so much profit. But it is not so in this work of the Lord. We cannot count or take inventory. The results are too intangible. The Lord alone sees and knows. We often feel as though our efforts are in vain and are therefore liable to become discouraged, to cease the strong exertion, or to stop altogether. Hence this apostolic assurance: "having realized that our labor is not empty in the Lord." This deep conviction sustains our spirit to continue to the end with joyful confidence, John 4:36.

CHAPTER XVI

The Ninth Part of the Letter

Business and Personal Matters, Chapter 16

1) The new subject is introduced by a περί phrase exactly as the subjects were in 7:1; 7:21; 8:1; 12:1: "Concerning the collection for the saints." This phrase heads the paragraph as a sort of caption and is only loosely attached to the sentence. Here, too, the phrase leaves the impression that the Corinthians had asked Paul about the matter of the collection in the letter which they had written to him, and that Paul now makes his reply. **Now concerning the collection for the saints, as I gave order to the churches of Galatia, so also do you.**

Since the Corinthians know about this collection and ask for further instructions from Paul, the question arises as to when and how they had been told. Paul hopes to raise a large sum by calling into action all of the congregations which he had founded. We read here about the orders which he had given to the churches in Galatia, and in II Cor. 8:1, etc., we read about the churches in Macedonia. The time for gathering funds is to extend over a period of about a year, II Cor. 8:10. There are three ways in which this important matter may have been brought to the attention of the Corinthian congregation: 1) in the letter which he had sent them (5:9), a letter that is now lost, Paul may have asked the Corinthians to cooperate, and they had replied in the letter which they sent to Paul; 2) Paul may have presented the matter of the collection to the Corinthians when he made his second brief visit to them, cf., II Cor. 13:2 where he refers to this visit; 3) one of Paul's messengers may have been commissioned to present the matter to the Corinthians. We have not data on which to base a preference.

The same question arises in regard to the churches in Galatia. Paul writes that he gave them orders as to how to proceed. That is all we know. Had he sent them a circular letter or a messenger? We have no answer. In v. 3, 4 Paul states how he proposes to have the funds, which are to be gathered in Macedonia and in Greece, carried safely to Jerusalem; as to how the money collected in Galatia is to reach its destination we have no knowledge.

The object of the collection is to bring relief to the Christians in Jerusalem and in Palestine. The distress must have been widespread in order to call out such extensive relief measures. The supposition that this distress is a result of having all things in common is unwarranted. In the first place, this practice in Jerusalem meant only that, as the need arose, the richer members disposed of some of their property and gave the proceeds to feed the poor. The congregation at Jerusalem was never a communistic colony.

In the second place, when the congregation at Jerusalem grew to rather amazing proportions, beyond 5,000 men, and then recruited itself from the ranks of even the priests (Acts 4:4; 6:7), the first persecution broke out and scattered many far and wide (Acts 8:3, 4). Years had passed since the ardor of that love in Jerusalem was manifested. Although it was ethically beautiful, its impracticability must have appeared the longer it was tried. The present poverty among the saints at Jerusalem was the result of a general depression that was due to periods of famine. Already in the year 44 Paul and Barnabas brought alms from Antioch, Acts 12:1. At that time the famine in Palestine continued for about four years. Under the emperor Claudius other parts of the realm were likewise affected by famine conditions.

The manner in which Paul writes to the Romans, when he finally reaches Corinth again (Rom. 15:25-28), indicates that the depressed conditions at Jerusalem were not acute but chronic at this time. This explains why Paul's relief measures are not rushed through with utmost speed but are allowed to consume some time. We gather that his object was to collect such sums as would put the poor at Jerusalem permanently on their feet. Paul's motive for this undertaking was not merely charity but the payment of a great debt of gratitude: "For if the Gentiles have been made partakers of their (Jews') spiritual things, they owe it to them also to minister unto them in carnal things," Rom. 15:27. As the spiritual blessing was permanent, so also this carnal blessing is to afford permanent relief.

The term λογία (or λογεία), "collection," from λογεύω, "I collect," is used only here in the New Testament, but it was discovered in the ostraca and the inscriptions found in Egypt and elsewhere and is there used in the sense of religious collections for the temple of a pagan god, etc. These payments on the part of pagans were made even on a specific day of the month, Sebaste day (probably "emperor's day"). Yet we cannot say that Paul copies his idea of having the Christians give Sunday by Sunday from the custom of the pagans, for the contributions of the latter were paid from month to month while the Christians were to retain their gifts at home until such a time as they should be called for.

The historical aorist διέταξα conveys the idea that, as far as the Galatians are concerned, the question as to how to proceed in collecting the funds is settled. The aorist imperative οὕτως καὶ ὑμεῖς ποιήσατε, "so also do you," settles the matter for the Corinthians. A simple evangelical method is thus put into operation in all of the churches under Paul's leadership. One good method, and that for all. This is a good example for the churches of today.

2) That method is now stated. **On the first day of the week let each of you lay by him in store as he may prosper, in order that no collections be made when I come.** The first day of the week is Sunday, and κατά is distributive so that we may translate: "Sunday by Sunday let each of you lay by," etc. It is a fair inference that Sunday was the day which was set aside for the public worship of the Corinthian congregation, and that this custom was also followed in Galatia and in the other churches that had been founded by Paul. After the manner of the Hebrew, the LXX uses the cardinal μία (ἡμέρα), "one" (day), with "Sabbath" (σαββάτου or σαββάτων) in place of the original πρώτη, "first," and this usage persists after its origin has been forgotten. Thus Sunday is called "(day) one of the Sabbath," i. e., with reference to the Sabbath. This means also that Paul counts the days according to the Jewish week of seven days when he is writing to Corinth with its many Gentile members. The Jewish week was known far beyond the groups of Jews who were scattered over the Roman Empire at this time, and it continued to spread still farther.

Each member is to deposit with himself each Sunday the amount of his gift for that week and preserve it as a store or treasure, θησαυρίζων. The participle completes the idea of the main verb: "let him lay by by treasuring up"; the future participle of purpose is usually used thus, B.-D. 351, but because of the repetition involved Paul here has the present. Each member is to keep the growing amount "by him," παρ' ἑαυτῷ, in his own home, and is not to deposit it with the church at once. The probable reason for this advice is the fact that at this early date the churches supervised by Paul were not yet organized to the extent of having official treasurers who were duly appointed to take charge of congregational funds.

How much each member is to give each Sunday is left to his own decision, "as he may prosper," literally, "as to what," as to the amount he may prosper. On one Sunday he may be able to lay by more, on another Sunday less. Luther seems to have had a text that read εὐδοκῇ, *was ihm gut duenkt*, instead of εὐοδῶται, "as he may be fortunate," "as he may prosper." Paul makes the measure of God's blessing to us the measure of our return to him.

Although Paul comes from Judaism, and the Corinthian church has its contingent of Jews, at no time does he propose the old Jewish system of tithing to the churches under his care. The only references to tithes found in the New Testament take us back into the Old Testament, Heb. 5:7-9, or criticize the Pharisees at Christ's time, Matt. 23:23; Luke 11:42; 18:12. This is quite decisive for us.

Other considerations support this adverse decision. Poor people cannot tithe; they may actually need help. A laborer who has small wages and a large family also cannot tithe; those who have a surplus of income and the rich could tithe, but giving a tenth would not place even these on an equality with others in the matter of giving, the disproportion would still be great. The New Testament knows only the spirit of voluntary giving, and its only directive as to the amount is Paul's evangelical rule which is devoid of even the appearance of legalism: "as he may prosper."

Paul's purpose in ordering contributions from Sunday to Sunday is that, when he finally arrives in Corinth, the work may be entirely done. The plural λογίαι, "collections," refers to the accumulations made by the individuals; each would have his *logia* made. The present tense γίνωνται accords with this: the collections are not to proceed after Paul arrives. Then it will be necessary that each individual simply bring in his accumulation.

3) Paul adds a word regarding the transmission of this gift from Corinth to Jerusalem. **And when I arrive, whomsoever you shall approve, with letters accompanying, I will send to carry your bounty to Jerusalem.**
The aorist indicates the moment of Paul's arrival, and the subjunctive the future time when this shall come to pass. The Corinthians themselves are to select and to approve the persons who are to take the money to Jerusalem. This is, however, scarcely done because Paul does not wish to carry the money lest someone later charge him with stealing some of it. Paul may never have entertained such a thought.

In the first place, it is fitting that those who give shall also send their gift. This is an example of Paul's perfect tact in such matters. In the second place, by means of such a committee Paul properly desires to bring the Corinthians into personal contact with their brethren in Jerusalem. The men selected by the Corinthians would return and would report in detail regarding Jerusalem and the conditions that were prevalent in the old mother congregation. Paul is concerned about such contacts and their effect in strengthening the feeling of fraternal oneness.

It is grammatically possible to construe the διά phrase with the preceding verb: "whomsoever you shall approve by letters" (our versions), but this cannot be done when we note the sense of what Paul writes. The approving of the men who are to transfer the money is done by a vote of the congregation, and only after that vote has been taken do they receive credentials. Paul says distinctly: "them I will send." If these men bear letters from the congregation, the congregation is their sender and not Paul. Only by offering letters from Paul himself are they able to show that Paul sends them.

It is usually supposed that these letters are to be addressed to persons in Jerusalem, the ultimate destination of the committee. But in all probability Paul intends to add letters to friends of his in other congregations which lie on the route to Jerusalem; and these would be written in order that the committee may secure safe lodging and be assisted on its way. If it travels by land through Macedonia, Ephesus, etc., this is rather important; if by sea, letters to Cæsarea are valuable.

Moreover, we see that this entire project goes far beyond being a grand piece of charity to the needy. It is connected with Paul personally as an apostle to the Gentiles and with all his successful work among the Gentiles. Through all of these churches that had been founded by him Paul is now reaching out to the mother church in order to cement all of them together the more. This is Paul's collection in an eminent sense, and it is thus that he writes: "I will send them with letters."

The preposition διά is not instrumental in this phrase, for the sending is not done "through" or "by means of" letters. The preposition διά has its original sense "between," so that the letters appear as companions on both sides, somewhat as our English "with letters" may be understood. We may incidentally note how readily letters are written by Paul, and doubtless also by others at this time. How many letters of this kind Paul penned during his apostleship and sent with different representatives of his no one knows, but he evidently sent not a few.

Paul uses the beautiful term ἡ χάρις ὑμῶν to designate the gift that is to be sent. In the broader sense χάρις means anything that delights, any kindly favor. When it is used in connection with sin and guilt the word always means unmerited grace and favor. Here the money gift for Jerusalem is termed a kindly and gracious favor which is bestowed upon the recipients with a kind and gracious spirit.

4) In any case, Paul intends to give the committee which transports the funds from Corinth letters as indicated. He may do more: **and if it shall be worth while for me to go also, they shall go together with me.** He means that, if the collection is of sufficient size, he, too, will go to Jerusalem, and the committee may accompany him. His own going thus depends on the outcome of the collection. He is not thinking of the safety of the funds while they are in transit when he speaks about his own going; or of his presence in Jerusalem to control the distribution; or to secure a favorable reception for himself in Jerusalem. The term ἄξιον, "fit" or "worthy," points to apostolic decorum. It would not be dignified for Paul to go if the offering turns out to be comparatively small. In any case, not Paul himself but others are to carry the funds. If the sum is small, it is more fitting that the committee go alone; but if it is large, Paul, the apostle, will also go. Bengel writes: *Justa aestimatio sui non est superbia.* The infinitive with τοῦ is often construed as a genitive after ἄξιον, but it seems to be the subject: "If for me to go is fitting, they shall go with me." R. 1061, 1066.

5) Paul twice refers to his coming to Corinth (v. 2, 3; compare also 4:19). He now reveals his plans in detail and adds the reason. **Now I shall come to you when I have gone through Macedonia, for I am only going through Macedonia, but with you, it may be, I shall remain or even winter, that you may send me forward whithersoever I may go.**

According to II Cor. 1:16 Paul originally planned to go directly by sea from Ephesus to Corinth, then to visit Macedonia and to return to Corinth, and then to proceed to Jerusalem, Acts 19:21. In the letter now lost Paul probably so informed the Corinthians. For the reason stated in II Cor. 1:23, etc., Paul changed his plan and now informs the Corinthians regarding that change. He now plans to go by land from Ephesus, passing through Macedonia and then through Greece to Corinth. This new plan he eventually carried out as we see from II Cor. 2:15 and from Acts 20:1, 2. Paul was later severely censured for altering his plans, and in Second Corinthians he makes an extended reply to the charge of fickleness.

The force of the explanatory (γάρ) repetition: "for I am (only) going through Macedonia," lies in the contrast with the following statement: "but with you, it may be, I shall remain or even winter." It is not Paul's intention to linger in Macedonia but to pass through it as rapidly as may be possible and to stop at each of the churches only a short while.

6) But he proposes to make a longer stay among the Corinthians, παραμενῶ, "I shall remain" for some time as the addition of παρά to the verb indicates. It is spring when Paul writes this letter at Ephesus. He hopes to reach Corinth at the beginning of the coming winter and to spend the entire winter in Corinth. He actually spent three months there, Acts 20:2. Yet he adds τυχόν, a neuter participle that is used like an adverb, "it may be," "perhaps." Some necessity may arise that will compel Paul to cut short his visit in Corinth. Unable to foresee possible contingencies, he refrains from making his promise absolute.

The purpose clause introduced by ἵνα is only loosely attached to the sentence: "that you may send me forward (on my further journey) whithersoever I may go," i. e., that you may render me this service. This, of course, means more than merely to send along a few friends to see Paul safely aboard ship or to travel a short distance with him on the journey by land.

It includes the advance preparations for the journey, recommendations, perhaps letters, planning the route and the ship connections, perhaps also some travel equipment, a store of food, some clothes, etc.

Here there is a touch of the friendly spirit of Paul that reaches out to the Corinthians. He intends to favor them with a stay of notable length and with an acceptance of their kindly service when he at last proceeds on his journey. In Acts 19:21 Luke informs us that Paul eventually decided on going to Jerusalem. When Paul writes this verse he has not fully decided and thus leaves his destination "whithersoever I may go" to future decision. The journey as it was afterward made by Paul and his several companions is described at length by Luke in Acts 20:3, etc.

7) Two consecutive γάρ clauses bring explanation. **For I do not wish to see you now by the way, for I hope to remain with you some time if the Lord shall permit.** This is Paul's wish and his hope; but he is not certain whether they shall be realized. While abundant work awaits him in the Macedonian churches, Paul intends to do this as rapidly as possible and thus to be free to remain in Corinth for some time. His more important work is to be done in the latter place, and he intends to allow ample time for it.

What τυχόν which was used in v. 6 means we now see from the clause: "if the Lord shall permit," ἐπιτρέψῃ, "shall turn over to me" and thus permit. In all of his movements and his work Paul waits on the Lord's directions and permission, for all his work is in the Lord's service. The little adverb ἄρτι, "now," has been much discussed. If it were πάλιν, "again," or ἄρτι πάλιν, "now again," we should have support for the fact of a prior brief visit in Corinth on the part of Paul. But the mere adverb "now" furnishes no evidence for such a second visit.

766 *Interpretation of First Corinthians*

8) After telling the Corinthians about his plans for spending some time with them Paul informs them regarding the time when he expects to leave Ephesus. **But I will remain at Ephesus until Pentecost.** Paul is writing a short time before the Jewish Passover festival and intends to leave after a period of about two months, after the Jewish Pentecost festival. This mention of "Pentecost" is not evidence that a Christian festival by this name was celebrated at this early date at Ephesus or at Corinth. If this were the case, other evidence would be needed to establish the fact. In the present connection "Pentecost" is used merely to indicate a date.

9) The reason that prompts Paul to wait so long in Ephesus before starting on his journey is explained by γάρ. He is certainly not waiting in order to join in the Jewish celebration of Pentecost before he starts, Gal. 4:10. No Christian Pentecost celebration is known at this early date. Paul delays for an entirely different reason. **For a door, great and effectual, is open unto me, and there are many adversaries.**

"Door" is figurative for opportunity to advance the work of the gospel. "A great door" is a great opportunity. It is often stated that Paul weakened his figure when he added the second adjective "effectual" or "energetic," but this view is the result of misunderstanding. Paul's idea is not merely that of a great door standing ajar but of a great door into which one enters in order to accomplish a task. Paul's figure is much deeper and more intensive than some of his commentators think. "An effectual door" is one that is not merely looked at but is made use of effectually. Acts 19:19, 20 describes the great opportunity to which Paul refers, and Acts 20:1 reports when he left Ephesus.

But here, as in so many places, Paul also met strong opposition: "opponents many." Compare I Cor. 15:32

and Acts 19:23, etc. Paul uses only two words with reference to his present work, but they are quite eloquent. He is one against "opponents many," but his victory is assured.

10) In 4:17 Paul tells the Corinthians that Timothy is on his way to Corinth. From Acts 19:22 we learn that Timothy was accompanied by Erastus, "the treasurer of the city" of Corinth (Rom. 16:23), a person of importance. It is Timothy "who shall put you in remembrance of my ways which are in Christ, even as I teach everywhere in every church," 4:17. Just what news Paul had received from Corinth when he gave Timothy his commission we do not know. The duty assigned to Timothy shows that the Corinthians were to be reminded of Paul's teaching regarding the true wisdom of Christ as opposed to all spurious wisdom.

Since Timothy's mission is mentioned by Paul in connection with the first part of his letter, it is fair to conclude that Paul had already heard from "those of Chloe" (1:12) the news regarding factional contentions in Corinth, when he sent Timothy, and that it was Timothy's task to endeavor to correct these disturbances. Then, it seems, the letter from the Corinthians to Paul arrived together with all the additional news which we see reflected in Paul's letter of reply. Timothy was already on his way, but via Macedonia, so that he would stop at the various churches along his route, which would delay his arrival at Corinth for some time. The letter which Paul is writing will be taken to Corinth by the direct sea route, and Paul expects it to reach Corinth before Timothy's arrival. All that Paul has heard about Corinth after he had sent Timothy away makes him anxious regarding the reception which his messenger will receive. So he here tells the Corinthians what treatment they are to accord Timothy upon his arrival. **Now if Timothy comes, see to it that he be with you without fear, for he is engaged in the Lord's work even as I also am. Let no one then despise him.**

Paul uses a condition of expectancy, for he thinks that Timothy will arrive a short time after this letter reaches Corinth. Timothy was still a comparatively young man. His mission in Corinth, as the development of events now reveals, will be harder to execute than Paul had supposed when he first dispatched Timothy. Some of the more haughty and puffed-up members may imagine that this young man from Lystra, whom they all know well, need not be treated with much respect because of his youth. They may show arrogance and thus try to intimidate Timothy. For this reason Paul writes pointedly: "See to it that he be with you without fear," i. e., let no one intimidate him and make him afraid. Afterward, when Timothy was the pastor at Ephesus, Paul wrote to him: "Let no man despise thy youth," I Tim. 4:12. That Timothy was by nature a timid person is an unfounded supposition. He must have been both brave and competent in order to carry out missions such as the present one and afterward to be placed in charge of the entire work in the province of Asia.

The fact that it is Timothy's youth of which some may seek to take advantage appears from the way in which Paul supports his order not to intimidate him: "for he is engaged in the Lord's work even as I also am." The Corinthians are to respect the person for the sake of his divine work. And Timothy's work is identical with Paul's. The apostle puts the two on the same level and insists that the Corinthians do likewise. We cannot, then, accept the conjecture that Paul fears that opposition against himself may threaten also Timothy's standing in Corinth. If Paul has fears in this regard he does not betray them in this letter.

11) What Paul says about Timothy, the fact that he is to be ἀφόβως, without intimidation, is now turned about: "Let no one depise him!" We see that Paul does not cherish fear in regard to the congregation as such but in regard to only one or the other individual in the congregation. Someone may assume an arrogant attitude and try to disconcert Timothy during the meetings. The verb ἐξουθενέω means to treat as οὐδέν, as nothing, as not worth considering; and the aorist subjunctive with μή is the regular construction in negative commands that need the aorist. This aorist is probably ingressive: "Let no one begin to despise him," R. 851, etc. When someone is not to start an action, the aorist is proper; but when someone is to cease an action that he has alreay begun, the present is the proper tense.

This prohibition deals with only one individual or another who may become overbearing; the next imperative addresses the entire congregation. **But send him on in peace that he may come to me, for I expect him together with the brethren.** After having treated Timothy with all due respect, when his work is now done, the Corinthians are to send him forward on his journey back to Ephesus and to Paul. What this sending forward implies is stated in connection with v. 6. The expression "to send forward in peace" is not derived from the formula: "Go in peace!" For the context implies that "in peace" is meant in contrast to the preceding injunctions not to intimidate and not to despise Timothy. Paul wants Timothy's mission to proceed and to end in a peaceful way so that, when he leaves, no trouble or strife are to be left behind. And Timothy is to come from Corinth directly to Ephesus and to Paul.

770   *Interpretation of First Corinthians*

The apostle writes that he is expecting him, i. e., is anxious to receive his report, especially that part of it which deals with Corinth. While Paul does not say that he wishes that Timothy might hurry back as soon as possible, the fact that he is expecting Timothy implies that the Corinthians are not to detain him unduly in Corinth. As soon as his mission is ended, he is to be sent forward to Paul.

The meaning of the final phrase is debated. Does "together with the brethren" modify "him" (Timothy) so that Paul is expecting Timothy together with Erastus and other travelling companions; or does the phrase modify "I expect" so that Paul and other brethren in Ephesus are awaiting Timothy's arrival? Some decide in one way, some in another, and some are undecided. The same question arises in connection with v. 12 where the same phrase also appears at the end of the sentence. It is most natural in each of the two verses to take the phrase exactly as it stands: "him together with the brethren." More than one person was usually sent on important missions such as this one of Timothy's.

12) **Now concerning Apollos, the brother,** reads exactly like the other περί phrases that occur in 7:1; 8:11; etc., with which, like captions, Paul introduces the topics concerning which the Corinthians had asked him in their letter. In the present case, too, the phrase is loosely attached at the beginning of the sentence. In their letter the Corinthians had asked Paul to send Apollos to them since they were anxious to have him come. Apollos had labored in Corinth for quite a while and had done so very successfully. We do not know just when he left the city. We have no more evidence that Apollos had taken an active part in the party strife at Corinth than we have for Paul's connection with that strife. From Paul's man-

ner of writing we gather that Apollos was not in Ephesus at this time.

So Paul replies to the request of the Corinthians: **I urged him much to come unto you together with the brethren; and it was not at all his will to come now, but he will come when opportunity offers.** The aorist "I urged him" makes the impression that Paul did this at once after receiving the letter from Corinth, and also that at the moment of Paul's writing Apollos is temporarily absent from Ephesus. This also explains why at the conclusion of this letter Paul has no greetings from Apollos to the Corinthians. We cannot translate πολλά "many times," which is improbable. As in v. 19, this adverbial accusative is used in an intensive sense and means "much." In other words, when Paul spoke to Apollos he made a strong plea that he go to Corinth with the brethren who were to deliver Paul's letter. Apollos, however, had good reason for declining. Here, too, the phrase "together with the brethren" should be taken just as it stands; "to go to you together with the brethren"; it should not be construed with the main verb: "I urged him together with the brethren."

We have no intimation that Paul and Apollos are not on the most friendly of terms, for Paul could then not have urged Apollos as he did. Nor do the circumstances prevailing in Corinth, in particular the party wranglings, play a part in the decision of Apollos not to go to Corinth at this time; the intimation conveyed by Paul's words points in the opposite direction. Apollos cannot spare the time to go now. For this reason he wills not to go at present. Paul states this in an impersonal way: οὐκ ἦν θέλημα. The imperfect ἦν does duty for the aorist since the verb εἶναι has no aorist.

The word θέλημα, "will," is without modifiers, and for this reason some suppose that God's will is referred to, i. e., that it was not God's will that Apollos should go now (R. V. margin). But the context restricts us to the will of Apollos. Apollos promises to come when a good opportunity offers itself. So it is a matter of finding the proper "season," καιρός, or time. We thus assume that Apollos is busily engaged and cannot leave but that he agrees to make the desired visit just as soon as his present work permits. When Paul writes this, Apollos is already absent from Ephesus in order to do this other work.

13) With a few pithy, admonitory words Paul concludes what we may call the substance or the body of his letter. **Be watchful; be firm in the faith; be manly; be strong! All of your affairs, let them be done in love!**

These five imperatives are frequently grouped together as a chain. It is not characteristic of Paul to put five units together in this fashion, and not at all his manner to end even a paragraph, to say nothing of the contents of an entire letter, with such a number of diverse and merely coordinate thoughts. At the conclusion Paul always reaches a unit focal thought. This is the case here. He writes four brief, coordinate admonitions and then ties the four together into a final unit. Not five but four are used by Paul when he desires to state the whole substance of any subject matter rhetorically.

He writes two sentences. The first has four imperatives in the second person plural; the second has only one imperative in the third person singular. Even this change from the plurals to the singular is characteristic of Paul. He might easily have phrased the final verb ποιεῖτε instead of γινέσθω: "All your affairs, do them," etc.; but this is not his manner of writing.

The five tenses are present to express durative and continuous actions. The first four verbs belong closely together as constituting a compact group. Only the second of these four verbs has a modifier, the phrase "in the faith." We may say that this phrase is needed to complete the meaning of the verb στήκετε, literally, "stand in the faith," since the verb itself would not be definite enough, whereas the other three verbs need no such addition. Yet by lending completeness to the one verb this phrase, by introducing the word "faith," gives to the four closely related verbs the vital point about which they turn. It is "the faith" regarding which we are also to be watchful, manly, and strong. "In the faith" is then to be matched by the corresponding phrase "in love" which is found in the final admonition. Faith is and must be first, love is and must be second. Faith produces love, always; the very nature of the two does not permit a reversal.

Each of the four imperatives is directed against an opposite condition and course of conduct. "Be watchful!" means: "Be not careless, indifferent, or easily deceived!" "Watch!" means: "Keep your eyes open!" We are watchful against enemies or hostile influences. The watcher raises an alarm against danger. See Isa. 56:10. While in this connection the watchful eye guards "the faith," this is never done with a disregard of immoral conduct, for faith is always endangered when the eye is sleepy or dulled against wrong conduct.

"Be firm in the faith!" recalls 15:1: "in which also ye stand" or "are firm." The admonition to stand and to be firm is directed against wavering, uncertainty, or doubt, the result of which is so often that the faith is lost. We stand in the faith, not like a dead post that has been driven into the ground, but as a living tree that fixes its roots ever deeper into the ground. The connotation is growth and increasing firmness. Its opposite is to depart from or to fall away from the faith, I Tim. 4:1, "forsaking the right way," I Pet. 2:15; compare Demas, II Tim. 4:10. The phrase "in the faith" is compact and includes both the faith which we believe (objective, doctrine, *fides quae creditur*) and the faith by which we believe (subjective, confidence, *fides qua creditur*). The subjective idea becomes plain in the verb "stand."

The next two imperatives recall the LXX's translation of Ps. 31:24: ἀνδρίζεσθε καὶ κραταιούσθω ἡ καρδία ὑμῶν. The verb ἀνδρίζεσθαι is found only here in the New Testament but occurs frequently in the LXX and in the classics. The translation: "Quit you like men!" is attractive and striking but does not reflect the tense. The Greek means: "Be men constantly!" or: "Show yourselves men always!" Paul refers to the virtue of Christian manliness with its strong connotation of bravery and unflinching courage, but it is used here in connection with maintaining the faith. The opposite is to be cowardly, fainthearted like women, timid like children, Eph. 4:13, 14.

Christian manliness is one of the great virtues. In this admonition the men as men are to be examples for the entire church. The Greek has no similar verb or other derivative from "woman" that designates a virtue that corresponds to manliness that is derived from "man." To play the woman or to be womanish conveys no virtue in the Greek. Even in the English "womanly" and "womanliness," while they express virtues, restrict themselves to one sex. But all of the Corinthians, men, women, and children, are to show manliness. This explains the fact that we find so many texts which apply specifically to women in the church and none which restrict themselves to men.

The final imperative of the group: "Be strong!" or: "Show strength!" namely κράτος, "strength" in action (as distinguished from ἰσχύς, "strength" merely in possession), is closely related to the display of courageous manliness. The connotation is that we are to be invincible and victorious in the faith. Its opposite is to be weak and easily defeated. The durative tense does not, however, imply that we are to become strong as though we are weak to begin with, but that, being strong, we constantly show our strength in every situation that may call for this quality. This will, of course, like all true exercise of strength, also develop the strength in us although the verb and the tense which Paul uses do not themselves contain this thought.

14) When Paul writes πάντα ὑμῶν, "all your affairs," he includes the entire work of the Corinthian congregation, different features of which he has discussed in his letter. All of this work centers in faith and thus requires watchfulness, firmness, manliness, and strength. But it also requires love, this supreme fruit of faith. Paul's letter has already shown the vital need of love; he has also described this love at length; the Corinthians have also been made to feel their deficiency of love. So Paul makes the last admonition the indispensableness of love. We may translate: "All your affairs, let them be connected with love!" The preposition ἐν marks the sphere. Everything in the Corinthian congregation is to be and is to move in that sphere; nothing is to be outside of it. This "love" is ἀγάπη, the love of full comprehension and of spiritual purpose; see 13:1. Thus love is the final word. The durative present tense, like the four preceding duratives, means that this love is to continue and is never to be absent. It, too, will grow the more it is practiced.

15) The arrival in Ephesus of Stephanas and his two companions from Corinth induces Paul to say a few words in regard to them before he adds the greetings and brings his letter to a close. **Now I urge you, brethren, (you know the family of Stephanas, that it is Achaia's first fruits, and that they**

set themselves for service to the saints) that you also submit yourselves to such persons, even to everyone that cooperates and toils.

The sense of what Paul writes is quite assured, but the grammar affords a problem. If οἴδατε is indicative, we must insert a parenthesis as our versions do, and ἵνα in v. 16 is subfinal and states what Paul beseeches the Corinthians to do. If, however, οἴδατε can be made an imperative, then it is this verb that states what Paul urges upon the Corinthians, and the ἵνα clause denotes purpose. We should thus translate: "Now I urge you, brethren, recognize the family of Stephanas . . . in order that you may look up to such," etc. The fact that οἴδατε is never used as an imperative in other passages is rather decisive. The grammars pass by our passage.

In kindly fashion Paul requests the Corinthians to honor Stephanas and his family (the Greeks always say "house" for family) because of their eminent service to the church. Paul himself baptized this family, 1:16. This must have occurred at Athens before Paul came to Corinth, for Stephanas is called "Achaia's first fruits" and not the first fruits of Corinth. In all of Greece the family of Stephanas was the first to come to faith as a consequence of Paul's preaching. That explains, too, why Paul does not at once think about this family when he tries to remember whom he had baptized in Corinth (1:14). He had, indeed, baptized this family, but this had taken place at Athens.

One distinction of this family is that it is Paul's "first fruits of Achaia" — an abiding honor. A second distinction is that this family has rendered much service to the saints. Paul says that they actually "put themselves in line," ἔταξαν ἑαυτούς, for such service; they made a regular business of it. Paul uses the beautiful term διακονία, service for service's sake, service rendered of one's own accord with an eye only to the benefit resulting for others.

"For service," εἰς διακονίαν, without the article, permits us to include any and all kinds of service. This says a great deal with regard to the family. Their home had evidently been transferred to Corinth, and that occurred a sufficiently long time previously to permit them to perform the service which Paul now recalls to the minds of his readers. That Paul himself and his companions are to be included among "the saints" who benefited by this service is doubtful. If Paul had benefited he would surely give an intimation of that fact, for he is always anxious to acknowledge personal favors.

We may conclude that the family of Stephanas had means and some prominence (see v. 17) which enabled them to do much for "the saints." Yet down to the present day experience proves that families of slender means often distinguish themselves in this manner above many others who are financially much more able. What service was rendered we can only surmise, for Paul offers no intimation. Some think of hospitality, help to the sick and needy, offering their home for meetings, and the like. Others think that Stephanas helped in the matter of the collection for the saints at Jerusalem, and they add even that he had not been supported in this matter as he should have been by others in Corinth. Yet this is not probable, for the collection had not begun that early.

Another surmise finds in the service rendered by men like Stephanas the beginnings of the various offices in the church, these voluntary services eventually leading to definite appointments through elections by the church. While it is true that willing and competent persons are still chosen for congregational offices, we are without evidence that such voluntary services crystallized into permanent offices in the case of Stephanas or of others. The first seven deacons of the congregation at Jerusalem were appointed because of the need that made itself felt and not because of service which the appointees had rendered before that time, Acts 6:1-6. The view that Stephanas was a deacon at the time when he came to Paul is unwarranted.

16) Paul's request of the Corinthians is: "that you also submit yourselves to such persons, even to everyone that cooperates and toils." This ἵνα clause is subfinal and states the contents of Paul's request. When Paul writes "you also," this "also" is reciprocal: they (the family of Stephanas) have done their part, now you also do yours. This matches the correspondence between ἔταξαν ἑαυτούς and καὶ ὑμεῖς ὑποτάσσησθε τοῖς τοιούτοις. The first verb means to range oneself in line for something, and the other to range oneself under someone. This correspondence between the verbs is lost in the English translations although it is vital for the sense. "Be in subjection unto such" (R. V.) says too much; and "obey such" is beside the point. When Paul writes "range yourselves under such persons" he wants the Corinthians to look up to people of this kind, i. e., to respect them, to heed their counsel, advice, and admonition.

But Paul at once broadens his request of the Corinthians so as to include all other families and all other individuals of this kind. The plural "to such persons" designates the class which is described in the parenthesis; and the singular "even to everyone that cooperates and toils" points to each individual in this class and describes each one anew. There is fine tact in this generalization in that the attention of the Corinthians is centered on the real reason for Paul's request. No one can say or feel that Paul wants the Corinthians to look up to the family of Stephanas because Paul likes them so well and may thus be partial to them. Combined with this tact is the wide range of Paul's mind which at once sees also all of the others in the church who joyfully line themselves up in her service. They constitute a class of which all the Corinthians should be proud, an upper class into which all should aspire to enter (Matt. 20:26-28), an upper class under which it should be a pleasure for the rest to work.

When Paul describes the individuals he uses two qualitative participles and combines them with one article: "everyone that cooperates and toils." The first participle brings out the point that such a person "works together" with others in this voluntary diaconate or service; and the second adds the thought that in this cooperation he does not seek the easier part but voluntarily takes the hard work, *laesst sich's sauer werden*. Paul does not imply that the Corinthians are reluctant to pay proper deference to Stephanas and to the others in the congregation who are like him. He is here, at the end of his letter, not voicing a covert criticism. That would be neither tactful nor wise. What moves Paul to add this request of the Corinthians regarding the family of Stephanas is the love which he has preached so strongly to them in this letter. This family deserves such intelligent and purposeful love (ἀγάπη), and Paul points out how it should show itself.

17) Two others had accompanied Stephanas from Corinth. **And I rejoice over the coming of Stephanas and Fortunatus and Achaicus because the lack of you these filled up. For they eased my own spirit as well as yours. Therefore acknowledge such men!**

The Latin names of these two companions of Stephanas' are the basis on which rests the supposition that they were either slaves or freedmen, and that the one or the other belonged to the household of Stephanas. The surmise that they belonged to the household of Chloe (1:11) would change what Paul says about them in conjunction with Stephanas into cutting irony — the last thing that Paul would put into a valediction. When forty years later Clement of Rome writes to the church at Corinth he mentions a certain Fortunatus. This man was a presbyter in the Corinthian church and was installed as such by the apostles, Zahn, *Introduction*, I, 269. He may be the same Fortunatus that is mentioned in this letter, but he would necessarily have been rather young when Paul wrote. Concerning Achaicus we know nothing further.

What pleases Paul in regard to the coming of these three from Corinth is the fact that they made good for him a certain ὑστέρημα, lack or deficiency. The objective genitive ὑμῶν states this lack; it is "the lack of you," i. e., the Corinthians themselves. Paul would like to have the Corinthians where he can talk to them instead of being obliged to write to them from a distance. This objective genitive answers the supposition that what Paul lacks or misses is a more friendly and deferential tone in the letter which the Corinthians had sent to him or a sufficient show of love on their part in that letter. But the object lacked is ὑμῶν, "you," the persons of the Corinthians. This lack the three messengers from Corinth "filled" for Paul, ἀνεπλήρωσαν, literally, "filled up" like a vessel that is otherwise not full enough. Paul can talk with them, ask them many things about the Corinthians, and hear all that they had to communicate. That is what rejoices Paul. Here we again meet a kindly touch on the part of Paul. The very way in which he writes "the lack of you" must please his readers in Corinth. The genitive is not subjective, stating that these three messengers provided something in which the Corinthians are remiss, either gifts or love or deference to Paul. The apostle makes no such charge at the end of his letter.

18) Paul himself explains (γάρ) what he means by this lack and how it is being made good. "They eased my own spirit and yours." If Paul and the Corinthians could have met, both his mind and theirs would have been put at ease regarding all of the questions that had arisen. Through the presence of these three representatives this was actually accomplished in a way. By their presence these three furnished easement to Paul's spirit and at the same time, by enabling the congregation to confer with Paul through them, furnished a like easement to their spirit. It must be a great satisfaction to the Corinthians to feel that they once more enter into fraternal contact with Paul by means of this delegation, especially since this contact has actually been made.

This is again a tender touch. Paul thinks not only of himself but also of the Corinthians. He credits them with solicitous feelings that are just like his own. He suggests that, as he is concerned that all things should be well with them, they, too, are concerned about him, that he may know just how things stand with them. By sending these men the Corinthians have done a double favor, one to Paul and one to themselves. The aorists ἀνεπλήρωσαν and ἀνέπαυσαν convey the idea that these good offices are now actually accomplished. The Corinthian representatives have done their part well in every respect. "Therefore acknowledge such men," recognize them for what they are and for what they have done. These three are happily not exceptions. Paul can write "such men," for there are others like them, and Paul is the last to forget or to leave such a delightful fact unnoted. Here again Paul's view is broad. He overlooks no one, and yet those immediately concerned receive their full due.

After reading what Paul himself says regarding these three men we may look at the questions that are asked regarding their presence with Paul while he was writing his letter. Did they come to Ephesus merely on private business? Is it a mere coincidence that they are with Paul at this time? Did other messengers from Corinth bring the letter from the Corinthians to Paul, messengers to whom he makes no reference when he is writing his reply? Does Paul write so significantly about what these three did for him and also for the Corinthians and say not one word about the real messengers who had been sent from Corinth with the Corinthian letter?

These questions answer themselves. Only on the supposition that these three men are sent to Paul as accredited representatives of the Corinthian church are Paul's words concerning these men in place. If they are sent as such representatives they must be the bearers of the Corinthian letter to Paul, for no other reason can be assigned that would prompt the Corinthians to send three representatives such as these to Paul just at this time. The moment we say that somebody else brought the letter, perhaps those of the household of Chloe (1:11) or other persons unknown to us, we are confronted with a questionable situation: 1) that Paul says nothing whatever about the bearers of the letter when concluding his reply; 2) that he writes as he does about these three visitors. These three may or may not have had other business in Ephesus in addition to bringing the letter; we are constrained to assume that they brought the letter. Then also they are the ones who will return to Corinth with Paul's reply; and they are the ones to whom Paul refers in v. 12, they are the ones with whom Apollos might have returned to Corinth if he could have found the time just then.

19) Now there follow the fraternal greetings. **The churches of Asia salute you. Aquila and Prisca salute you much in the Lord with the church in their house.**

The verb ἀσπάζομαι means literally "to embrace" and is used regularly for *salutare*, "to salute," to greet, on arrival and on departure and also in letters. "The churches of Asia" are those of the coastland, Asia Minor, where Ephesus is located. We need not assume that Paul has just recently visited these churches and told them about Corinth, or that representatives of these churches are present with Paul while this letter is being written. Paul himself writes these greetings as the spokesman of these churches. They are all under his care, and their feelings and sentiments are fully known to him. The supposition that any one of these churches would refuse to salute the Corinthian church is not to be entertained.

From the largest group Paul proceeds to the smallest, Aquila and Prisca (the diminutive is Priscilla) and the church or assembly in their house. Regarding the phrase κατ' οἶκον αὐτῶν, which is here used attributively and thus appears between the article τῇ and its noun ἐκκλησίᾳ, see R. 608. It is more than a mere genitive: the church "of their house"; it is rather the church "pertaining to their house." We meet expressions like this repeatedly in Paul's letters.

As to the thought we have only what these expressions themselves convey. It is assumed that a larger or a smaller part of the congregation of any city was accustomed to assemble in the house of some family who freely granted this privilege when other suitable places for meetings were not readily found. Aquila and Priscilla were well known to the Corinthians, for Paul had lodged with them when they lived at Corinth and when Paul came to found the Corinthian congregation and worked together with Aquila at his trade of tent-making, Acts 18:2-4. Some codices add: "with whom also I lodge," which may, indeed, be true to fact although the best texts omit this clause. Aquila and Priscilla moved from Corinth to Ephesus when Paul left Corinth, Acts 18:18, 26. They later moved back to their original place of residence, namely Rome, Rom. 16:3. The adverbial accusative πολλά is added in order to mark the close relation of this couple to the Corinthians: they greet you "much"; compare the same word used in the same sense in v. 12.

20) The third group is again a large group. **All the brethren salute you.** This refers to the brethren at Ephesus. Although they are included in the first group, it is natural for the Ephesian brethren to send their special greetings. While "all the brethren" seems indefinite, this very feature prevents us from thinking only of the friends who are present with Paul while he is writing or of any other small group.

Concluding these greetings, Paul adds: **Salute one another with a holy kiss.** The salutations of the churches and the friends from afar signify that all of these brethren are in fraternal accord with the Corinthians, one with them in faith and in love. Then the Corinthians, too, must be in the same fraternal accord with each other. Their own mutual salutation is to express this accord and to serve as a response to the salutations from afar. The medium for this is "the holy kiss," Rom. 16:16; II Cor. 13:12; I Thess. 5:26; I Pet. 5:14. Each person turned to his neighbor in the assembly and bestowed or received a kiss, and this bestowal and this receiving expressed the fact that all were in one true, spiritual accord. This kiss of fellowship was of the nature of a public ceremony and bore a public significance. The word "holy" guards this kiss against misconceptions.

Bestowing a kiss upon the brow or the cheek as a sign of friendly accord, affection, and honor, dates back very far among Oriental people. This meaning of the public kiss makes the act of Judas, when he betrayed Christ with such a kiss, so unutterably base. In certain European countries men still offer and receive the public kiss of honor. In the church the fraternal public kiss continued in use for centuries. It came to mean also reconciliation when penitents were received back into fellowship; it likewise expressed mutual forgiveness when it was practiced between the members of a family just before the Lord's Supper was received. It is still retained in the East where the men and the women sit apart and thus use the salutation. In the Roman ritual the *pax*, a small piece of metal or wood which the priest kissed and then sent around so the congregation might kiss it, was substituted for this ancient custom.

21) Paul has dictated his letter up to this point, and some capable amanuensis did the writing. Now Paul himself takes the pen and, as we may say, himself signs the letter. **The salutation with my own hand, Paul's.** Nothing is to be supplied. The dative "with my own hand" modifies the preceding noun "the salutation." The writing of this noun is itself Paul's salutation to the Corinthians. The genitive Παύλου is appositional to the genitive idea in the possessive pronoun ἐμῇ although this is in the dative. We must translate: "With my own hand, that of Paul"; and not as our versions: "The salutation of me, Paul," etc. The genitive does not modify "the salutation," R. 416. Yet by means of this genitive Paul signs the letter and makes it his own. Compare II Thess. 3:17; Col. 4:18.

22) Paul's heart still throbs with emotion which refuses to be suppressed. Before he adds the customary benediction as the last word (Gal. 6:18; Phil.

4:23; I Thess. 5:28; II Thess. 3:18; Philem. 25), his spirit and his hand almost involuntarily react to all the perversions and all the abuses which he is attempting to correct in Corinth by means of this letter, and he records his apostolic verdict regarding all those who may dare to remain obdurate and to continue in their evil course. **If anyone loves not the Lord, let him be anathema!** The words are a curse like the thunders of the ancient prophets. Not merely Paul and his indignation are behind them but the Lord himself as Jehovah is behind the thunders of the prophets. Therefore Paul adds: **Maran atha,** "Our Lord cometh."

This is the only passage in which Paul uses φιλεῖν with regard to our love to Christ, which recalls the significant change from ἀγαπᾶν to φιλεῖν in Christ's transaction with Peter recorded in John 21:15-17. Φιλεῖν means liking, affection, personal attachment while ἀγαπᾶν is much deeper, the love full of intelligence and true comprehension which is thus also directed by true and lofty purpose. We are not told to like our enemies but to love them; and God does not like the foul world, yet he loves it. We catch the force of Paul's words when we reproduce their force: "If anyone does not even like the Lord," etc. Whoever lacks even this lowest, cheapest type of love is, of course, hopeless. Mere affection prompts us to do many worthy things. It is motive enough to impel us to desist from what displeases the person who is cherished by such affection. If we lack even this affection toward Christ, our hearts are cold and dead indeed. To be sure, all of us are to rise to the higher motive, the love that fully understands the Lord, his Word, and his ways, that thus embraces him and all that is his with clear and conscious comprehension, and that then harmonizes all its purposes in thought, word, and deed with this blessed, glorious Lord.

In the New Testament ἤτω is the form for the third person singular imperative "let him be!" The term ἀνάθεμα is a later form of ἀνάθημα, a translation of the Hebrew *cherem*, something that is removed from the possession or the use of men and set aside for God as an object upon which God's wrath rests and which is thus devoted to destruction or as something that is dedicated to God as a gift that is acceptable to him. In Hellenistic Greek the former is used in the meaning "accursed," and the latter to designate an offering or a sacred gift. The later ecclesiastical anathema is derived from the former use. Paul turns all those who have not even affection for the Lord and are not willing to show this lowest form of love for him in their thought and their action over to the judgment, not of a human, but of the divine tribunal. Paul has not been writing about slight matters. They ultimately involve the divine judgment.

Like a seal Paul stamps the Aramaic exclamation: "Maranatha!" upon the curse he has just recorded. The two Aramaic words are written with Greek letters and are often one word. That poses the problem of separating the Aramaic words. We may read either: "Maran atha," "Our Lord is come"; or: "Marana tha," "Our Lord, come!" The pronoun "our" has no stress so that we may also translate: "Lord, come!" Rev. 22:20. The A. V. is mistaken in combining "Anathema Maranatha!" as though both together mean a curse. "Maranatha!" is a sentence by itself. Zahn, *Introduction*, I, 303, etc., deals exhaustively with the linguistic features involved.

The substance of what Paul writes is identical whether we divide in one way or in the other, whether we read the words as an assertion or as a prayer. For the declaration: "Our Lord is come," refers, not to his coming into the flesh, but to his coming to judgment. The past tense is here the prophetic past and speaks of a future event as already having taken place. "Our Lord is come" means: is come to judgment. He is come to execute the curse upon all who do not love him. This, of course, fits the context perfectly. The other rendering: "Lord, come!" means in Zahn's words: "Lord, come and put an end to all strife and to all activity of hostile forces in the church!" This cry or prayer also fits the context. It appeals to the Lord to come and to visit the anathema upon all whose hearts turn away from him.

The question is naturally asked as to why Paul put this short sentence into Aramaic instead of translating it into Greek. The former Jews in the congregation could, of course, at once translate this bit of Aramaic for the Greek members. One might be tempted to connect this Aramaic exclamation with the Petrine party (1:12) in Corinth and surmise that Paul intended it as a special warning to them. But this is unwarranted. Paul mentions this party only incidentally. Why he should now in closing his letter throw a bomb at these people is incomprehensible. This is about the most improper place to deliver a blow at one small group. Paul is speaking broadly to all his Corinthian readers. The context is decisive, and this holds us to the preceding anathema.

Strange to say, on the basis of the Peter party a Judaistic movement is postulated for Corinth, and this letter of Paul's is supposed to be in good part Paul's defense against and attack upon this movement. Yet the most careful reading and critical examination of the entire letter show not even the slightest Judaistic machinations and no trace of a reaction on Paul's part against men and doctrines of this type. "Maranatha" cannot be explained on a basis of this kind. Other fanciful reasons as to why Paul writes in Aramaic in this connection merit no consideration.

The gospel began in Aramaic in Jerusalem and then reached out into the Greek world. Certain Aramaic terms like amen, hosanna, Abba-Father were transported across the line of language. "Maranatha" appears in the Eucharistic prayer in the *Didache*, 10, 6. We need not surmise that this expression was formally established in a liturgy in Asia Minor or in Europe. Paul speaks Aramaic as his native tongue — that is enough. The two words are a set expression and thus readily come to his mind. A deep solemnity attaches to them, which exactly reflects the deep emotions that are filling Paul's heart at this moment. Thus these words flow into his pen.

23) Paul's emotion has had its expression. He now adds the words of blessing in his customary way. **The grace of the Lord Jesus Christ be with you.** The χάρις is the unmerited favor of the Lord and all the gifts that flow from that favor. To the sinner this grace extends unmerited pardon, and all of us still sin daily. We ask for this pardoning grace every time we pray the Lord's Prayer. But every other gift that we receive from the Lord likewise flows from this grace "without any merit or worthiness on our part," Luther. The source of this grace is "the Lord Jesus Christ," who is named according to his person (Jesus), his work (Christ), and his saving relation to us (Lord).

24) This letter is peculiar because Paul adds another word after the formal benediction which assures the Corinthians of his love to them. **My love with you all in Christ Jesus!** The statement utters a fact; if we supply anything, it must be "is." Throughout this letter there runs the note of "love," ἀγάπη, which the Corinthians were in danger of forgetting. The immortal thirteenth chapter, which actually pictures this love, is part of this letter. This

description of love belongs here if anywhere in the apostolic letters. Now Paul does not merely write about love, he exercises it to the full. Hence this final assurance.

The apostle's great heart swells once more. Whatever other emotions he has shown in writing this letter, love is the deepest, richest of them all. And it embraces all the Corinthians, those who distress his heart as well as those who delight his heart. Back of every one of his admonitions to them stands his heart of love. The last word is and must be "Christ Jesus." He and he alone is the sphere in which Paul's love lives, moves, and has its being. Into that sphere of love Paul, like a magnet, draws all who come into contact with him. The "amen" has been added by a later hand.

Blessed are they who by faith possess the grace of the Lord Jesus Christ and are one with Paul in the love that binds him and them together in Christ Jesus.

Soli Deo Gloria

www.ingramcontent.com/pod-product-compliance
Lightning Source LLC
Chambersburg PA
CBHW071849290426
44110CB00013B/1076